Miguel A. Roig-Francolí
College-Conservatory of Music
University of Cincinnati

Harmony in Context

harmony

Second Edition

McGraw Hill
Connect Learn Succeed™

The McGraw-Hill Companies

Published by McGraw-Hill, an imprint of The McGraw-Hill Companies, Inc., 1221 Avenue of the Americas, New York, NY 10020.

This book is printed on acid-free paper.

1 2 3 4 5 6 7 8 9 0 DOC/DOC 0

ISBN: 978-0-07-313794-0

MHID: 0-07-313794-4

Vice President, Editorial: *Michael Ryan*
Publisher: *Christopher Freitag*
Managing Editor: *Marley Magaziner*
Developmental Editor: *Nadia Bidwell, Barking Dog Editorial*
Editorial Coordinator: *Sarah Remington*
Marketing Manager: *Pamela S. Cooper*
Senior Production Editor: *Carey Eisner*
Design Manager and Cover Designer: *Allister Fein*
Interior Design: *Jamie O'Neil*
Manager, Photo Research: *Brian J. Pecko*
Production Supervisor: *Louis Swaim*
Composition: *10/12 Times by MPS Limited, A Macmillan Company*
Printing: *45# Pub Thin Plus, R.R. Donnelley & Sons*

Cover: Vicente Pascual. *Aquatio I*, mixed media on canvas. 2005. © Artists Rights Society, New York/VEGAP, Madrid.

Library of Congress Cataloging-in-Publication Data

Roig-Francolí, Miguel A., 1953–
Harmony in context / Miguel A. Roig-Francolí.—2nd ed.
p. cm.
ISBN-13: 978-0-07-313794-0 (hardcover : alk. paper)
ISBN-10: 0-07-313794-4 (hardcover : alk. paper) 1. Harmony—Textbooks. 2. Music theory—Textbooks.
I. Title.
MT50.R689 2011
781.2'5—dc22

2009050028

www.mhhe.com

Dedication

To my wife, Jennifer, and my sons,
Gabriel and Rafael.
And to the memory of my father.

"Tell me, and I may forget.
Show me, and I may remember.
Involve me, and I will learn."

Anonymous Pedagogue

About the Author

A native of Spain, Miguel A. Roig-Francolí holds graduate degrees in composition from the Madrid Royal Superior Conservatory and Indiana University, and a Ph.D. in music theory from Indiana University. He is currently a Professor of Music Theory at the College-Conservatory of Music, University of Cincinnati, and has also taught at Ithaca College, Northern Illinois University, Indiana University, and the Eastman School of Music. His research interests include Renaissance compositional theory and practice, the music of Ligeti, large-scale coherence in post-tonal music, and the pedagogy of music theory. Roig-Francolí is the author of *Understanding Post-Tonal Music* and *Anthology of Post-Tonal Music* (McGraw-Hill, 2008), and his articles and reviews have appeared in numerous journals and encyclopedias in the United States and Europe. Roig-Francolí's compositions have been widely performed in Spain (including performances by nine major symphony orchestras and by the National Ballet of Spain), England, Germany, Mexico, and the United States. He has received commissions from the National Orchestra of Spain and the Orchestra of Spanish Radio-TV. Among his many honors are first prize at the National Composition Competition of the Spanish *Jeunesses Musicales* (1981), second prize at the UNESCO International Rostrum of Composers (Paris, 1982), the Medal of Honor from the Superior Conservatory of Music of the Balearic Islands (2004), and the University of Cincinnati's A.B. "Dolly" Cohen Award for Excellence in Teaching (2007) and George Rieveschl Award for Creative and/or Scholarly Works (2009).

Contents

Preface *x*
A Message to the Student: *Why Do We Study Music Theory?* *xv*
Acknowledgments *xvi*

Introduction: *The Fundamentals of Music* *1*

Chapter A Pitch: Notation and Intervals 2

The Notation of Pitch 2
Intervals 4
Consonant and Dissonant Intervals 14

Chapter B Rhythm and Meter 19

Durational Symbols 19
Pulse, Beat, and Meter 21
Tempo 22
Simple and Compound Meters 22
The Notation of Meter 23
Metric Accent 25
Choosing a Meter to Notate a Melody 26
Asymmetrical Meters 27
Irregular Divisions of the Beat 28
Irregular Rhythmic and Metric Relationships 29
Some Notes on the Correct Notation of Rhythm 32

Chapter C Tonality: Scales and Keys 38

Modes and Scales 39
Key Signatures 42
Other Modes and Scales 46

Chapter D The Rudiments of Harmony I: Triads and Seventh Chords 55

Chords 55
Triads 57
Seventh Chords 60

Chapter E The Rudiments of Harmony II: Labeling Chords; Musical Texture 68

Harmonic Function, Roman Numerals 68
Figured Bass 70
Musical Texture 73

Chapter F Introduction to Species Counterpoint 84

The Melodic Line in Species Counterpoint 85
General Guidelines for Two-Part Counterpoint 88
First Species (1:1) 88
Second Species (2:1) 91
Third Species (4:1) 93
Fourth Species (Syncopated) 95

Part 1 *Diatonic Harmony* *105*

Chapter 1 The Connection of Chords 106

Harmonic Progression 106
Notating, Voicing, and Spacing Chords 110
Chord Connection: The Principles of Part Writing 112
Voice-Leading Guidelines for the Three Basic Types of Progression 118
Melodic Style 120
Voice Independence 121
Why All These Rules? 123

Chapter 2 The Tonic and Dominant Triads in Root Position 129

The Tonic Triad 131
The Dominant Triad 131
The I–V–I Progression 131
Characteristic Soprano-Bass Patterns 134
The I–V–I Progression as a Form-Generating Structure 135
Pitch Patterns 140

Chapter 3 Harmonic Function; The Subdominant Triad in Root Position 145

The Basic Harmonic Functions 145
The Subdominant Triad 146
Characteristic Soprano-Bass Patterns 149
A Model to Elaborate the Fundamental Progression 151
Pitch Patterns 154

Chapter 4 Triads in First Inversion 159

The Triad in First Inversion: Uses and Function 159
The Neighbor V_6 162
Characteristic Soprano-Bass Patterns 165
Elaborating the I–V–I Progression 166
Pitch Patterns 168

Chapter 5 The Supertonic; Melody Harmonization 174

The Supertonic in Root Position 174
The Supertonic in First Inversion 176
Characteristic Soprano-Bass Patterns 178
Elaborating the I–V–I Progression 179
Harmonizing a Melody 179
Pitch Patterns 184

Chapter 6 Nonchord Tones 188

The Passing Tone 189
The Neighbor Note 192
The Anticipation 193
Incomplete Neighbors 193
Suspensions 197
Pedal Point 203

Chapter 7 $^6_4$ Chords 210

Consonant $^6_4$ Chords: The Arpeggiated $^6_4$ 210
Dissonant $^6_4$ Chords 212
The Neighbor $^6_4$ 212
The Passing $^6_4$ 214
The Cadential $^6_4$ 215
Characteristic Soprano-Bass Patterns 220
Elaborating the I–V–I Progression 221
Pitch Patterns 222

Chapter 8 The Dominant Seventh and Its Inversions 227

V_7 in Root Position 227
Inversions of the Dominant Seventh 232
Characteristic Soprano-Bass Patterns 236
Elaborating the I–V–I Progression 237
Pitch Patterns 241

Chapter 9 The Leading-Tone Triad 248

Doubling and Voice Leading 248
The Passing vii°_6 249
vii°_6 as a Dominant Substitute 251
The Leading-Tone Cadence 252
Characteristic Soprano-Bass Patterns 254
Elaborating the I–V–I Progression 254
Pitch Patterns 255

Chapter 10 Cadences 260

Authentic Cadences 260
The Half Cadence 263
The Plagal Cadence 264
The Deceptive Cadence 265
Pitch Patterns 268

Chapter 11 Melodic Organization I: Phrase Structure 274

Motive 274
Phrase 275
Period Structure 277
Form Diagrams 279
More on Period Structure 280
Phrase Group 283

Chapter 12 Melodic Organization II: Thematic Development; Phrase Extension 290

Melodic Developmental Techniques 290
Phrase Extension 298

Chapter 13 Harmonic Rhythm; Metric Reduction 308

Harmonic Rhythm 308
Metric Reduction 314
Compound Melody 318
Writing Your Own Progressions 320

Chapter 14 The Mediant, Submediant, and Subtonic Triads 330

The Mediant and Submediant Triads as Prolongations of the Tonic 330
Other Uses of the Mediant and Submediant 334
The Subtonic 338
Characteristic Soprano-Bass Patterns 340
Elaborating the I–V–I Progression 342
Harmonizing a Melody with Keyboard Figuration 342
Pitch Patterns 348

Chapter 15 Other Diatonic Seventh Chords 354

General Doubling and Voice-Leading Guidelines 354
The Leading-Tone Sevenths 355
The Half-Diminished Seventh 356
The Fully-Diminished Seventh 357
The Supertonic Seventh 362
The Subdominant Seventh 367
Characteristic Soprano-Bass Patterns 370
Elaborating the I–V–I Progression 370
Pitch Patterns 372

Chapter 16 Harmonic Sequences 378

The Descending Circle-of-5ths Sequence 380
The Ascending Circle-of-5ths Sequence 385
Sequences by Descending 3rds 386
Sequences by Descending and Ascending Steps 388
A Summary of Harmonic Sequences: Elaborating the I–V–I Progression 392
Pitch Patterns 393

Part 2
Chromatic Harmony and Form 399

Chapter 17 Secondary Dominants I 400

Chromatic Harmony 400
Tonicization: Secondary Dominants 402
V_7 of V 403
V_7 of IV (iv) 407
Characteristic Soprano-Bass Patterns 410
Elaborating the I–V–I Progression 410
Pitch Patterns 412

Chapter 18 Secondary Dominants II 420

V_7 of ii 420
V_7 of vi (VI) 422
V_7 of iii (III) 425
V_7 of VII 426
Characteristic Soprano-Bass Patterns 428
Elaborating the I–V–I Progression 428
Deceptive Resolutions of Secondary Dominants 429
Sequences with Secondary Dominants 429
Secondary Key Areas 435
Pitch Patterns 437

Chapter 19 Secondary Leading-Tone Chords 445

Secondary Leading-Tone Seventh Chords 446
Secondary vii°_7 Chords in Inversion 451
The vii°_7 Over a Pedal Point 454
Elaborating the I–V–I Progression 455
A Chromatic Harmonization of a Diatonic Tune: Bach, Chorale 21 456
Pitch Patterns 458

Chapter 20 Modulation to Closely Related Keys 465

Key Relationships: Closely Related Keys 465
Diatonic Pivot Chord Modulation 467
Modulation to V 470
Modulation to the Relative Major and Minor Keys 473
Writing Pivot Chord Modulations 477
Chromatic Modulation: Chromatic Pivot Chords 478
Writing Chromatic Modulations 479
Modulation and Phrase Structure: Sequential and Phrase Modulation; Modulating Periods 481
Harmonizing Modulating Melodies 485
Pitch Patterns 488

Chapter 21 Small Forms: Binary and Ternary; Variation Forms 498

The Binary Principle 498
Binary Tonal Types 499
Binary Formal Designs 501
The Ternary Principle 507
Variation Forms 511

Continuous Variations 512
Sectional Variations 516

Chapter 22 Contrapuntal Genres 525

The Two-Voice Invention 525
Bach: Invention no. 3, in DM 526
The Fugue 529
Bach: Fugue no. 2 in Cm from *The Well-Tempered Clavier,* I 532
Some Additional Fugal Techniques 534
The Fugato 534

Chapter 23 Modal Mixture 541

Borrowing Chords from the Minor Mode in a Major Key 542
Borrowing Chords from the Major Mode in a Minor Key 549
Change of Mode 550
Characteristic Soprano-Bass Patterns and Elaborations of the I–V–I Progression 552
Pitch Patterns 553

Chapter 24 The Neapolitan Chord 560

The Neapolitan Sixth 560
Tonicization of the Neapolitan 565
The Neapolitan in Root Position 565
Tritone Substitution: The Neapolitan as a Substitute for V_7 567
Pitch Patterns 569

Chapter 25 Augmented Sixth Chords 574

General Features and Types of +6 Chords 575
The Italian +6 577
The German +6 579
The French +6 584
Other Types of +6 Chords 585
Summary 588
Tonal Relationship between the Neapolitan and the +6 Chords 589
Pitch Patterns 590

Chapter 26 Chromatic Modulatory Techniques: Modulation to Distantly Related Keys I 597

Chromatic Pivot Chords 597
Writing Chromatic Pivot Chord Modulations 604
Modulation by Enharmonic Reinterpretation of the Gr +6 605
Writing Modulations with +6 Chords 610
Modulation by Enharmonic Reinterpretation of vii°_7 611
Writing Modulations with vii°_7 Chords 614
Pitch Patterns 615

Chapter 27 Modulation to Distantly Related Keys II; Linear Chromaticism I 627

Chromatic Third Relationships 627
Triads Related by Chromatic Third 628
Keys Related by Chromatic Third: Common-Tone Modulation 630
Linear Chromaticism I: Linear Chromatic Chords 634
Altered Triads 634
Augmented Sixth Chords with Dominant and Embellishing Functions 636
The Common-Tone Diminished Seventh Chord 641
Pitch Patterns 644

Chapter 28 Introduction to Large Forms 651

Sonata Form 651
Mozart, Piano Sonata in CM, K. 309, I (Anthology, no. 25) 654
The Rondo 659
A Five-Part Rondo: Haydn, Piano Sonata in DM, Hob. XVI:37, III (Anthology, no. 21) 660

Chapter 29 Expanding Functional Tonality: Extended Tertian Chords; Linear Chromaticism II 667

Expanding Chordal Sonorities: Extended Tertian Chords 667
Linear Chromaticism II: Linear Expansions of Tonality 675
Appoggiatura Chords 675
Chromatic Sequences Revisited 677
The Descending Circle-of-5ths Sequence 677
Nonsequential Linear Processes 685
Pitch Patterns 689

Chapter 30 The German Romantic *Lied*: Chromatic Harmony in Context 698

The German Romantic *Lied* 698
Analysis 1: Schubert, *Erlkönig* 699
Analysis 2: Schumann, "Widmung" 705
Modulation by Enharmonic Reinterpretation of V^+ 707
Analysis 3: Wolf, "Das Verlassene Mägdlein" 708
Pitch Patterns 712

Chapter 31 Toward (and Beyond) the Limits of Functional Tonality 717

Tonal Ambiguity and Implied Tonality 717
Equal Divisions of the Octave 724
Parsimonious Voice Leading: The PLR Model 729
Beyond the Confines of Functional Tonality 737
Pitch Patterns 740

Appendix
Transposing Instruments 746

Musical Example Index 751
Subject Index 761

Preface

This textbook strives to strike a balance between a variety of pedagogical and theoretical approaches to teaching music theory. Moreover, the author has sought to provide the richest possible musical context for the study of harmony. The following are the basic principles that govern this book's style:

1. ***Purpose and Intended Audience.*** This is an essentially complete harmony and analysis textbook. It is meant to be used by undergraduate music majors, and it covers all the common-practice tonal harmony usually studied in undergraduate theory core curricula over a period of three or four semesters in the freshman and sophomore years. Music fundamentals are summarized and reviewed in the introductory chapters. Because harmony exists only in the context of musical form, form and formal processes are studied throughout the book, both in discussions of specific pieces within chapters dealing with harmonic topics, and in chapters devoted to the main formal types and genres in part 2.
2. ***Music Theory in Context.*** The "context" to which the title refers is not only the formal context of harmony. The book also includes frequent references to the metric and rhythmic contexts of harmony, as well as to its historical and stylistic contexts, and to the relationships between drama, text, and harmony in vocal music. Also taken into consideration is the *professional context of the music student.* Students are encouraged and guided throughout the book to understand the relevance of what they are studying here (harmony, musical processes, form) to the better understanding of the music they listen to and perform daily. And they are constantly encouraged to translate this better understanding of processes, tonal direction, harmonic and formal function, and so on, into *better performances and better listening,* thus providing a true context for "theoretical" work.
3. ***Organization and Style.*** Good, logical organization, clarity of exposition, and easy-to-use format are primary considerations. The style of presentation is concise and efficient, although in general the outline format has been avoided: Explanations are necessary and pedagogically desirable, and so are analytical discussions of pieces. A clear and visually attractive layout, as well as the use of section and subsection headings and lists where appropriate, are essential aspects that contribute to the effective organization of this book.

   Teaching the student how to think analytically about music and how to make connections between analytical thought and performance decisions has been a major concern in this book. A "Socratic" pedagogical approach has often been used for this purpose. By first asking questions on examples, rather than providing immediate answers, I have tried to involve the reader in an active process of inquiry and discovery as a learning tool.
4. ***Coverage.*** The contents are thorough, with equal attention devoted to all significant areas and concepts of tonal harmony, including a detailed coverage of late-Romantic chromatic harmony. The book is aimed at providing both craft in written harmony and the techniques of voice leading, and good understanding of harmonic

processes as found in actual music. Chords throughout the book are not presented as isolated vertical units, but rather as *functional* components within larger musical segments, which at the same time also result from horizontal or *linear* processes. These functional and linear processes are themselves studied in their role as form-generating structures within the context of long-range tonal designs. This book's pedagogy is thus based on a synthesis between the functional and linear approaches to hearing and understanding harmony.

5. ***Musical Examples.*** Each chapter includes numerous examples from the literature, illustrating virtually every concept that is introduced and discussed throughout the book. Besides chapter examples, a musical anthology is also provided in the second part of the accompanying workbook, and anthology items are often referred to in the text. Women and minority composers are broadly represented in both the book's musical examples and the anthology. The jazz, musical theater, pop, and rock repertoires are also amply represented. Recordings for all the musical examples from the literature included in both the book and the anthology are provided as MP_3 files. For additional information, consult the text's Web site at www.mhhe.com/roigfrancoli2e.

CONTENTS AND PEDAGOGY

The introductory chapters provide a review of fundamentals, and introductions to both musical style and species counterpoint (acknowledging the fact that many instructors like to teach pedagogical counterpoint either during or at the beginning of harmony curricula). After that, the book is structured in two parts: part 1, "Diatonic Harmony," and part 2, "Chromatic Harmony and Form." Part 1 begins with elementary definitions and voice-leading guidelines, and covers each of the diatonic triads and seventh chords separately and progressively. Other major topics studied in this first part are harmonic function, texture, cadences, nonchord tones, phrase structure and melodic organization, harmonic rhythm, metric reduction, and diatonic sequences.

Part 2 includes secondary dominants, modulation to closely related keys, modal mixture, the Neapolitan sixth, augmented sixth chords, altered triads, extended tertian chords, chromatic sequences, and a thorough study of modulation to distant keys. Binary and ternary forms are fully discussed in the context of modulation to closely related keys, with emphasis on long-range harmonic design. Two more chapters on contrapuntal genres and larger formal types cover the study of inventions, fugues, sonata form, and rondo. In chapter 30, the essential concepts of chromatic harmony are summarized and reviewed, now in the context of the German Romantic *Lied.* Chapter 31 is devoted to the study of late-nineteenth-century nonfunctional chromatic harmony.

Basic formal concepts such as phrase and period structure are central to the study of harmony. The study of small forms in association with modulation (chapter 21) is also highly recommended. Chapters 22 and 28, on the other hand, are mostly meant for programs that integrate the study of large forms within the study of harmony. In some theory programs, however, large forms and contrapuntal genres are studied in a separate course toward the end of the theory sequence (perhaps using one of the available textbooks focusing exclusively on form). Instructors who follow the latter type of curriculum may simply prefer to skip chapters 22 and 28, fully or partially. Doing so will cause no detriment to the study of harmony as found in adjacent chapters.

Individual chapters include clear expositions of harmonic function, voice-leading guidelines, and study of standard progressions for the specific chord or technique discussed. A section titled "Elaborating the I–V–I Progression" unifies the harmonic chapters, showing the role of each new chord or group of chords in elaborating the basic harmonic progression, I–V–I. The pedagogical stress regarding chord progressions is on standard, normative *harmonic and voice-leading patterns.* To emphasize this approach further, chapters include a section on characteristic soprano-bass patterns. Also stressing the concept of harmonic pattern, the *melodic pitch patterns* at the end of each harmonic chapter present linearized harmonies and chord connections, and should be used for singing or as aural exercises. Workbook chapters include a section of *keyboard harmony* that allows practice of various harmonic concepts at the keyboard. Students are encouraged to discover and discuss the practical application of the harmonic concepts studied in each chapter in sections titled "Practical Application and Discussion." The importance of these sections, which will help students make the connection between what they study in theory class and their performance experience, cannot be sufficiently emphasized. A list of "Terms for Review" at the end of each chapter provides a taxonomical summary of the chapter's contents.

EXERCISES AND MATERIALS FOR FURTHER STUDY

Exercises and musical examples for analysis are included in a worksheet following each chapter, which instructors may want to use for in-class practice. The accompanying workbook provides a second set of exercises to be used as assignments, plus the anthology. Students are required to realize a variety of tasks, including analysis, chord spelling, realization of short progressions, four-voice chorale-style exercises, melody harmonization (beginning in chapter 5), writing their own progressions (beginning in chapter 13), and writing keyboard harmonizations (beginning in chapter 14). The types of exercise found in the corresponding worksheet and workbook sets will not necessarily be exactly parallel. This allows for greater exercise variety (if a type of exercise appears in a particular worksheet, a different type is occasionally requested in the corresponding workbook set, rather than repeating all the same types already featured in the worksheet). Answers to the analytical questions in both the worksheets and workbook, as well as sample realizations for most of the harmony exercises, can be found in a separate instructor's manual.

Additional materials for further study and analysis are provided for many chapters in the form of PDF files in the *Harmony in Context* Web page at www.mhhe.com/roigfrancoli2e. Instructors can print and use these materials in class if they want to do so, particularly in advanced and honors sections.

Post-Tonal Chapters. A five-chapter unit titled "Introduction to Post-Tonal Music" is available online in PDF format for *Harmony in Context* instructors (see the

Harmony in Context Web site at www.mhhe.com/roigfrancoli2e). These five chapters explore the compositional and musical processes of twentieth-century post-tonal music, leading students to greater understanding and appreciation of this challenging and important repertoire. This unit is intended for schools and departments that teach post-tonal music at the end of the sophomore year as part of the harmony and analysis sequence, as opposed to devoting a complete course to it. The chapter titles are as follows: "Introduction to Pitch-Class Set Theory and Analysis"; "Pitch Centricity"; "Twelve-Tone Music"; "Rhythm and Meter in Post-Tonal Music"; and "Compositional Developments after 1945."

NEW TO THE SECOND EDITION

The main purpose of the revision for the second edition of *Harmony in Context* has been to clarify the book's text and pedagogy and to reorganize some of the materials to further contribute to this clarification. Chapter contents have been streamlined where possible, unessential detail and unnecessary material have been cut off, and new section headings and lists have been provided to break existing text into shorter and more clearly understandable (as well as visually appealing) units.

Chapter Reorganization. The following points summarize the most salient aspects of chapter reorganization for the second edition.

1. In the introductory chapters, the chapter on species counterpoint now follows the chapters on the rudiments of harmony. Third species is now also included in the counterpoint chapter. The former chapter G, on musical styles, has been deleted from the book (and moved to the Web page).
2. The supertonic is now introduced in an earlier chapter (chapter 5), immediately following the chapters on the subdominant and on triads in first inversion.
3. Chapters on nonchord tones, $^6_4$ chords, and the dominant seventh are now also presented earlier. Chapters 10 though 13, on the other hand, constitute a module devoted to formal and rhythmic concepts, including cadences, phrase structure, melodic organization, and harmonic rhythm.
4. Harmonic sequences are now contained in their own chapter, which closes part 1 as chapter 16. Chromatic sequences are covered in chapters 18 and 29.
5. The section on variation forms has now been integrated into the chapter on small forms (chapter 22).
6. The former chapter 23, which covered both the Neapolitan and augmented sixth chords, has now been split into chapters 24 (the Neapolitan) and 25 (augmented sixth chords).
7. The new chapter 31 brings together material previously contained in chapters 29 and 30.

Additions and Other Changes. Given that my intention was to shorten the book as much as possible without compromising the quality of the pedagogy or the contents,

I have been careful with the addition of new material. The main additions to the second edition (other than numerous minor additions in specific chapters) are as follows:

1. Two new sections are included in most harmonic chapters, titled "Characteristic Soprano-Bass Patterns" and "Elaborating the I–V–I Progression." The former shows the most characteristic two-voice frames that can be harmonized with the chord or chords being studied in a particular chapter. The latter illustrates the use of particular chords in the elaboration of the basic I–V–I progression. These two sections provide a thread of continuity through the harmonic chapters in the book, as well as a unifying pedagogical paradigm that focuses the student's understanding of harmonic structure.
2. New sections outlining step-by-step spelling procedures for some particular chords (particularly secondary dominants, secondary diminished seventh chords, and augmented sixth chords) have been added to the corresponding chapters.
3. Extended keyboard harmony sections are located at the end of each harmonic chapter in the workbook. The added keyboard exercises are tied to both the two new sections discussed in point 1 above, and to some of the written exercises (on Roman numeral and figured bass realization and melody harmonization) in both the worksheet and the workbook.
4. The *Harmony in Context* Web page has absorbed much of the material deleted from the printed text, particularly the sections formerly titled "Further Analysis" and other more advanced sections. These and other materials are now available to instructors as online PDFs.
5. Although the linear orientation of the book's harmonic pedagogy has not been altered, reductive graphs (other than metric reductions) have been replaced by other pedagogical graphs that illustrate similar concepts without using Schenkerian-style graphic notation. Different levels of harmonic activity, for instance, are now indicated by different levels of Roman numerals under a conventionally notated progression or score. Simpler formal line diagrams have replaced the more-complex looking formal bass reductions used in the first edition.
6. Complete recordings for all examples in the text and the anthology are now available as MP_3 files (consult the text's Web site at www.mhhe.com/roigfrancoli2e).

Miguel A. Roig-Francolí

College-Conservatory of Music
University of Cincinnati

A Message to the Student

WHY DO WE STUDY MUSIC THEORY?

When we perform or listen to music, we are dealing with an artistic expression that unquestionably reaches us emotionally. Musical composition and performance (as well as listening), however, are not only emotional—no more than we, as humans, are made up *only* of emotions. There is also an intellectual, rational aspect to music. Music is a means of expression, a language (albeit an abstract one), that functions according to a system and a set of principles and conventions. We can immediately tell a Mozart sonata from an Indian rāga or a piece for Japanese shakuhachi because the languages they use are different.

We all would agree that when actors recite, say, Shakespeare, their knowledge of English vocabulary, grammar, and syntax is a great asset to their understanding and rendition of the structure, rhythm, and form of what they are reciting. Similarly, our knowledge of normative English allows us to enjoy the beauty and idiosyncrasies of Shakespeare's expression.

Musical performance is made up of at least three essential components. The technical component is achieved by hours of practice. The instinctive, emotional aspect (which we usually call "musicality") is part of what we know as "talent," and is partially innate and partially acquired by listening to good music, having a good teacher, or playing with good musicians. Finally, many musical decisions are intellectual or rational. Such decisions require information and understanding. Our study of the musical language provides this understanding, as well as many criteria to evaluate or appreciate more fully the beauty of specific works. The better we understand the normative, conventional syntax of musical discourse, the better we can enjoy, both as performers or listeners, the styles of specific composers or the richness of their particular musical idioms.

This understanding of the musical system is provided by the study of music theory in its many branches (such as harmony, counterpoint, form, and analytical techniques). Many of the things we will learn in the book have a direct bearing on both performance and listening. We will learn that a chord or set of chords creates a tension, and why it does so; that this tension may or may not be resolved, that the resolution may be delayed, avoided, prolonged; that some chords do not have a structural entity, but rather act as "harmonic ornaments," or simply prolong other chords that do have a structural role; and that these, and many other harmonic forces, generate larger expressive units such as phrases, periods, sections, and whole compositions.

A good composer knows the musical language, and composition is as rational as it is emotional; besides following their instinct and "inspiration," composers plan and realize the shape and structure of their musical works by means of intellectual processes. All of it is directly relevant to performance and to listening, at least if their full potential is to be achieved. The beauty of understanding, provided by music theory, is a rewarding complement to the emotional experiences afforded by music making.

Acknowledgments

Among the many individuals whose direct or indirect contributions have been instrumental to the completion of this book, I would first like to acknowledge two groups of persons: my teachers and my students. Some of my teachers who deserve special recognition are Miguel A. Coria (with whom I first studied harmony and counterpoint in my native Spain); my counterpoint teachers at Indiana University, Lewis Rowell and the late Douglass Green (to whom I am especially indebted for many of the ideas behind the design of chapter F); and Mary Wennerstrom, with whom I studied (and from whom I learned a great deal about) music theory pedagogy. A special token of recognition goes to David Neumeyer and Marianne Kielian-Gilbert, under whose supervision I first taught written theory, as a graduate assistant, at Indiana University. Many of their ideas, methodologies, and musical examples are still reflected in my own teaching, and certainly in this book.

The book grew out of years of teaching undergraduate theory at Indiana, Ithaca College, Northern Illinois University, the Eastman School of Music, and the College-Conservatory of Music (CCM) at the University of Cincinnati. I am grateful to my students at these institutions, as well as to my counterpoint and music theory pedagogy students at Eastman and CCM. My teaching assistants at CCM have provided expert feedback on various aspects of the book over the years. I have learned a lot from all of them, and without them this book would never have been written.

The musical examples were originally copied on Finale by Patrick Long. Joseph Hupchick was in charge of examples for the second edition. I am grateful to both of them, and also to the three institutions that provided generous grants to defray copying costs: Northern Illinois University, the Eastman School of Music, and the College-Conservatory of Music at the University of Cincinnati.

Many of the example and anthology recordings from the first-edition CDs appear in the second edition's MP$_3$s. I am grateful to the following individuals for their valuable contributions to the recordings: Nathan Hess (producer of the first-edition recordings), Darijus Spakauskas (first-edition recording engineer), Javier Clavere (general producer of the new second-edition recordings), Kim Pensyl (producer of the jazz, pop, and musical theater examples), and Michael Hughes (second-edition recording engineer). I am particularly indebted to all the CCM students and faculty who performed for the recordings, and whose names are acknowledged on the MP$_3$ files. I have been moved and inspired by their artistry. I also want to thank Naxos for allowing us to use many of their recordings for both the textbook and the anthology audio files.

Walter Everett made a substantial contribution to the book by providing all the musical examples from the jazz, musical theater, popular song, and rock repertoires. Many good ideas and suggestions offered by reviewers were incorporated into the text. Reviewers for the first edition included Claire Boge, Miami University; Richard Brooks, Nassau Community College; Walter Everett, University of Michigan; Joseph Kraus, then at The University of Nebraska; Eric McKee, Pennsylvania State University; Paul Paccione, Western Illinois University; Edward Pearsall, The University of Texas at Austin; Penelope Peters, then at Oberlin Conservatory; Gary Potter, Indiana

University; Elizabeth Sayrs, then at Kenyon College; and Judith Solomon, Texas Christian University. Second-edition reviewers have included John Brackett, University of Utah; David R. Castro, University of Texas at Arlington; Margaret Grant, Northern Kentucky University; Helen Hudgens, North Park University; Mark McFarland, Georgia State University; Kurt Sander, Northern Kentucky University; Bruce Atwell, University of Wisconsin, Oshkosh; Steven Block, University of New Mexico, Albuquerque; Gregory D. Carroll, University of North Carolina, Greensboro; Thomas Cody, Penn State University; Dan Duncan; Kurt Ellenberger, Grand Valley State University; M. Rusty Jones, Butler University; Jeff Junkinsmith, Shoreline Community College; Christopher Kenney, University of Rio Grande; Heidi Von Gunden, University of Illinois, Champaign; Jeff Perry, Louisiana State University, Baton Rouge; Steven Roens, University of Utah; Jonathan Schwabe, University of Northern Iowa; and Naomi Sofer.

I am grateful to my CCM colleagues, David Carson Berry, Steven Cahn, Catherine Losada, Samuel Ng, and Robert Zierolf, for their support and feedback; to the McGraw-Hill team, my publisher Chris Freitag, editor Nadia Bidwell, copyeditor Barbara Hacha, designer Allister Fein, production supervisor Louis Swaim, and production editor Carey Eisner, for their continued trust and support and for their numerous ideas and suggestions. Encouragement, support, and patience are also gifts I have received in abundance from my wife, Jennifer. I thank her not only for these intangible gifts, but also for the many hours she invested word processing and editing large parts of the first-edition manuscript. Moreover, many ideas she offered, as an experienced performer, on ways to make connections between theory and performance were incorporated into the book.

To all of them go my acknowledgments and sincere gratitude.

INTRODUCTION

The Fundamentals of Music

Chapter A

Pitch: Notation and Intervals

Unlike music in other cultures, the Western tonal music tradition has been built largely on notated sound, at least before the advent of such twentieth-century styles as jazz and rock. The notational system we use, developed throughout the Middle Ages and the Renaissance, is based on a variety of symbols and conventions that regulate the notation of pitch and rhythm. These symbols allow us to write on paper, and then to read, any musical sounds or combinations of sounds, as well as their relative durations and the groupings that result from these durations. In this chapter we will review the basic principles for the notation of pitch in Western music.

THE NOTATION OF PITCH

The Notes

The fundamental, standard Western collection of notes is made up of seven pitches. When ordered from lowest to highest or highest to lowest, such a collection is called a **scale.** If a scale contains only the seven basic, unaltered pitches, we call it a **diatonic scale.** In English, we use seven letters (**letter names**) to refer to the seven pitches of a diatonic scale: C–D–E–F–G–A–B–C. Notice that after the seventh pitch, B, the first pitch, C, appears again. Because this C is eight notes away from the original C, we say that it is (or it sounds) an *octave higher*. The same seven notes recur in the form of different octaves, as you can easily see in example A.1.

The upper part of this example shows the location of the notes on a keyboard. Note that the same seven notes appear in several octaves. Although the letters used in each octave are the same, we also use numbers to indicate which octave a pitch belongs to. In this system, the pitch we usually call **middle C** is C4. All the pitches in this octave, from C to B, may carry the suffix 4, as in F4, A4, or B4. The octaves above this **middle octave** are indicated by the **numerical suffixes** 5 to 8, whereas the octaves below it carry the suffixes 3, 2, and 1, respectively.

Example A.1

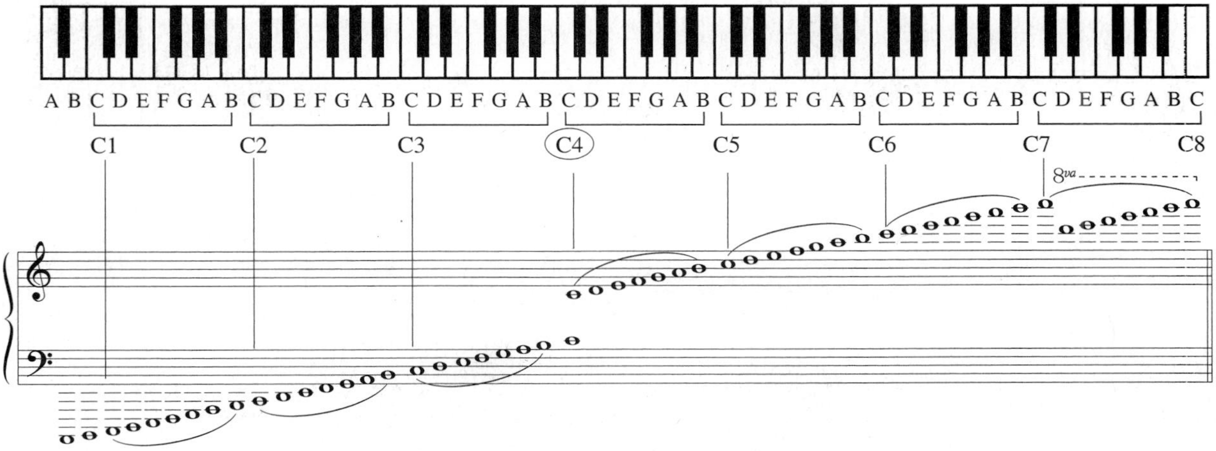

The Staff

We notate pitches by means of note heads on a **staff.** A staff consists of five **lines.** For the time being, our note heads will be white notes. We can write a note on each of the five lines, or in each of the four **spaces** between the lines. We can also extend the staff by adding additional lines, which we call **ledger lines.** Example A.2 shows pitches notated on lines, in spaces, and with ledger lines.

Clefs are used to indicate which letter names correspond with each of the lines and spaces in the staff. Although there are many possible clefs, we will illustrate here only the four clefs most commonly found in modern scores: the **treble, bass, alto**, and **tenor clefs.** The treble clef is a **G clef**; that is, it shows where the pitch G is notated. The bass clef is an **F clef,** and both the alto and tenor clefs are **C clefs.** Example A.3a shows each of these clefs and the pitch each of them indicates. Example A.3b shows the notation of middle C with each of these clefs. By using clefs, we can avoid writing too many ledger lines (which make for cumbersome notation). This is illustrated in example A.3c, where

Example A.2

Example A.3

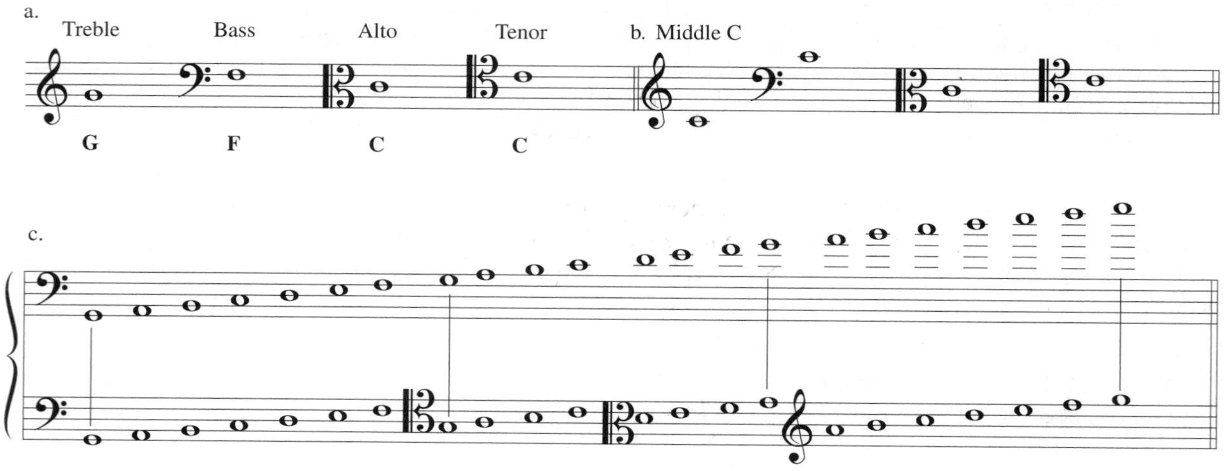

the same scale is notated first with a single clef and then with several clefs. In modern scores, the viola is mostly written in alto clef, and the cello, bassoon, and trombone use mostly bass and tenor clefs.

In the lower part of example A.1 you can see what we call a **grand staff,** in which two staves are connected by a brace. The bass clef is used in the lower staff, and the treble clef is used in the upper staff. The grand staff allows us to notate the complete range of the keyboard, with the help, of course, of ledger lines above and below it.

EXERCISE

To practice identifying and notating pitches in various clefs, refer to exercise 1 in worksheet A at the end of this chapter.

INTERVALS

Half Steps, Whole Steps, and Accidentals

Look at the keyboard in example A.1 and observe the following points:

1. Although the diatonic scale contains only seven different notes (the white keys of the keyboard), there are twelve different keys if you also count black keys.
2. The modern Western tuning system (**equal temperament**) divides the octave into twelve equal parts. The resulting twelve-note scale is called the **chromatic scale.**

3. The distance between two adjacent pitches in the chromatic scale is called a **half step** or **semitone.** The half step is the smallest distance between two different pitches in the standard Western tuning system.
4. Going back to the diatonic scale (the white keys), you can see that some adjacent pitches are related by half step (E–F and B–C), while the rest of them are at the distance of two half steps (C–D, D–E, F–G, G–A, and A–B). Each of the latter has a black key between each of the dyads (a **dyad** is a pair of pitches). The distance of two half steps between two pitches is called a **whole step** or a **whole tone.**

Although the chromatic scale has twelve different pitches, we use only seven different letters to designate notes. To notate the remaining five pitches (the black keys) we use symbols known as **accidentals.** Accidentals (which always *precede* the affected note) raise or lower a note in the following ways:

1. A **sharp** symbol (♯) raises a note by a half step.
2. A **flat** symbol (♭) lowers a note by a half step.
3. A **natural** symbol (♮) cancels out any previous accidental.
4. A **double sharp** symbol (𝄪) raises a note by a whole step.
5. A **double flat** symbol (♭♭) lowers a note by a whole step.

We can easily observe that any of the twelve pitches can be notated in different ways using accidentals. To begin with the most obvious, each of the notes represented by black keys can be spelled as a sharp or as a flat note. The pitch between C and D, for instance, is both C♯ and D♭. White-key notes, however, can also be notated by means of accidentals: D is the same pitch as C𝄪, C is the same as D♭♭, F is the same as E♯, and so forth. Notes that are spelled differently but sound the same, such as C♯ and D♭, are said to be *enharmonic*. Example A.4a shows the two possible spellings (the **enharmonic spellings**) for each of the black-key notes in the chromatic scale. In practice, however, we use only one of the spellings at a time. Which one we use is determined by the harmonic and musical context, as we will study throughout this

Example A.4

a.

b.

c.

book. As a general melodic principle, however, sharps are often (but not always) used in ascending passages and flats in descending passages. Examples A.4b and c illustrate an ascending chromatic scale using sharps and a descending chromatic scale using flats.

A result of enharmonic spellings is that we can notate a half step in different ways. A half step spelled using different letter names, as in C–D♭, is called a **diatonic half step,** whereas the same half step, spelled using the same letter name, C–C♯, is a **chromatic half step.**

Types of Intervals

An **interval** is the distance between two pitches. If the two pitches sound simultaneously, the interval is **harmonic.** If the pitches sound successively, the interval is **melodic.** The right hand (upper staff) in measures (mm.) 5–7 of example A.5 is eminently melodic, and its intervals are heard horizontally, or melodically. The left hand (lower staff), on the other hand, presents a succession of vertical, or harmonic, intervals. Are the intervals in each hand in mm. 8–10 harmonic or melodic?

To label intervals we use two terms. The second term denotes the **size of the interval:** second, third, fourth, and so on. (2nd, 3rd, 4th, etc., will be used to indicate the interval size.) The first term describes the **quality of the interval** (perfect, major or minor, and augmented or diminished). Thus, we speak of a minor 2nd, a perfect 4th, a major 6th, and so forth.

Intervals can be **ascending** or **descending.** The same note names, C and F for example, may be used to denote two different intervals: the ascending distance between C and F (C–D–E–F) is not the same as the descending distance between C and F (C–B–A–G–F).

To determine the size of an interval, count the number of notes between the two pitches, including both pitches in your count. Thus, an ascending C–F is a 4th (four notes, C–D–E–F); an ascending E–C is a 6th (E–F–G–A–B–C); a descending C–F is a 5th (C–B–A–G–F); and a descending A–G is a 2nd (A–G).

Example A.5 Paul Hindemith, Interlude, from *Ludas Tonalis,* mm. 5–10

Example A.6

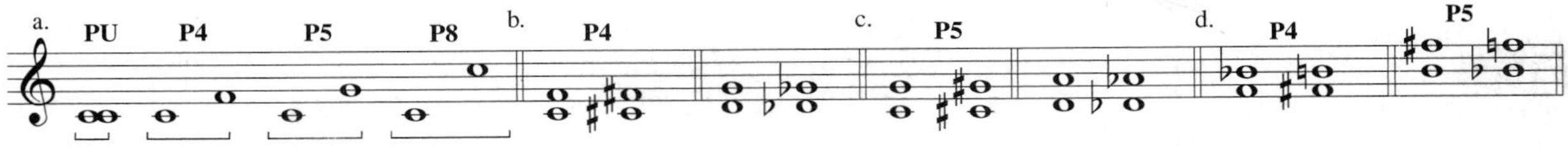

Perfect Intervals

The modifier **perfect,** used to indicate the quality of certain intervals, refers to the pure and essential sound of these intervals. The only perfect intervals are the perfect unison (abbreviated PU), the perfect 4th (P4), the perfect 5th (P5), and the perfect 8ve (P8). Examples of each of these intervals, starting from C, appear in example A.6.

1. The perfect unison or perfect prime (PU) is the interval formed by any pitch and itself (C–C, D–D, E♭–E♭, F♯–F♯, etc.). The P8, on the other hand, is formed between a pitch and its octave projection, as in C4–C5, D2–D3, and so forth.
2. The P4 is made up of five half steps. You should learn by memory all the possible P4s built from diatonic (white-key) pitches. In ascending form, these are C–F, D–G, E–A, F–B♭, G–C, A–D, B–E. You can see that the only "glitch" in the system is the P4 from F, which requires an accidental (B♭). The interval F–B♮ is not a P4, because it contains six, and not five, half steps. If we want a P4 with B♮ as the upper pitch, then we need an F♯: F♯–B♮.
3. The P5 is made up of seven half steps. The ascending P5s from white keys are C–G, D–A, E–B, F–C, G–D, A–E, and B–F♯. Here again, the only "glitch" also involves the notes B and F. Seven half steps up from B take us to F♯. If we want a P5 with F♮ as the upper pitch, we need a B♭: B♭–F♮.
4. How about spelling P4s and P5s from pitches other than white keys? Leaving aside the P4s and P5s involving the notes B and F, an accidental applied to any of the pitches in the P4s and P5s listed above automatically requires the same accidental for the other pitch. For instance, in the P4 category, you will have C♯–F♯, D♭–G♭, E♭–A♭, and so on. And in the P5s, you will end up with C♯–G♯, D♯–A♯, E♭–B♭, and so on. Examples A.6b and c illustrate the application of accidentals to P4s and P5s; example A.6d shows the P4s and P5s involving the notes B and F.

Measures 1–6 of example A.7 are exclusively made up of perfect intervals. Identify and label all of them. Then identify and label the perfect intervals in mm. 7–12.

EXERCISE

To practice writing perfect intervals, refer to Exercise 2 in worksheet A at the end of this chapter.

Example A.7 Fritz Kreisler, "Praeludium and Allegro," for Violin and Piano, mm. 1–12

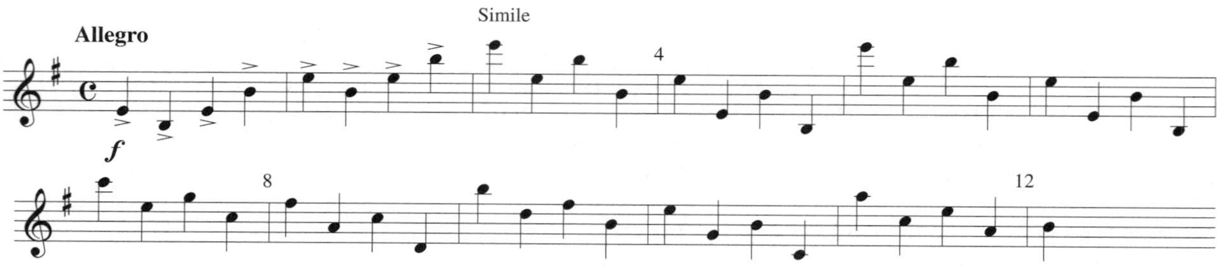

Major and Minor Intervals

Refer to the chromatic scale in example A.4a. If you try to build a 3rd up from C, you will probably think first of the pitches C–E. That is indeed a 3rd. The pitches C–E♭, however, also form a 3rd. Several intervals allow for two possible standard forms, one smaller and one larger in size. These intervals are the 2nd, 3rd, 6th, and 7th. In each of these cases, the larger interval is called **major** (abbreviated M), and the smaller interval is called **minor** (abbreviated m). In all cases, the difference between major and minor is a half step (major is a half step larger than minor). Examples of each of these intervals presented in ascending form from C appear in example A.8.

1. *M and m 2nds.* We have already discussed these intervals as the whole tone and the semitone (whole step and half step). The M2 contains two semitones, and the m2, the smallest possible interval in our system other than the unison, is made up of a single semitone.
2. *M and m 3rds.* The m3 contains three semitones, and the M3 four. As we will study in chapter E, these intervals are the basic building blocks for triads (three-note chords). The lower interval in a major triad (C–E–G) is a M3 (C–E), whereas the lower interval in a minor triad (C–E♭–G) is a m3 (C–E♭).

Example A.8

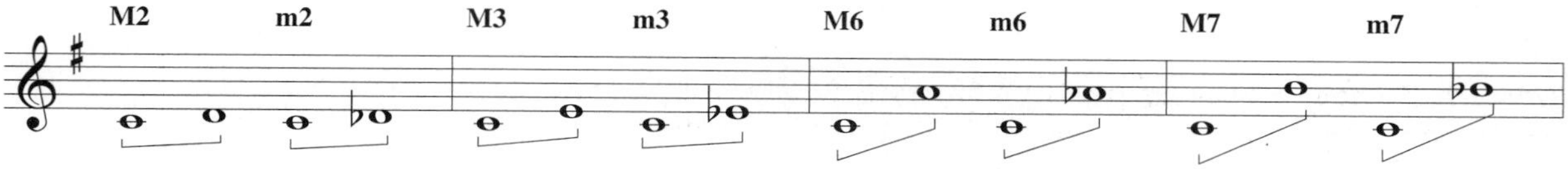

3. *M and m 6ths.* The easiest way to figure out these intervals is by referring them to a P5. A M6 (C–A) is a whole step larger than a P5 (C–G), and a m6 (C–A♭) is only a half step larger than a P5.
4. *M and m 7ths.* Here again, it is easier to figure out these intervals with reference to the P8. The M7 (C–B) is only a half step smaller than the P8 (C–C), whereas the m7 (C–B♭) is a whole step smaller than the P8.

The following passages will allow you to practice the recognition and labeling of 3rds (example A.9a), 3rds and 6ths (example A.9b), and 2nds and 7ths (example A.9c). For further practice, identify and label all the nonperfect intervals in example A.7.

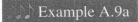

Example A.9a Johann Sebastian Bach, Prelude no. 6 in Dm, from *The Well-Tempered Clavier,* I, mm. 1–6

Example A.9b Frédéric Chopin, Étude in CM, op. 10, no. 7, mm. 2–5

Example A.9c Richard Wagner, Prelude to *Tristan und Isolde,* mm. 18–28

EXERCISE

To practice writing M and m intervals, refer to exercise 3 in worksheet A at the end of this chapter.

Augmented and Diminished Intervals

In example A.9b you may have noticed some intervals that do not fit our perfect/major/minor definitions. In measure 4, for instance, the fifth dyad in the right hand, E♭–A, is a 4th (from E to A there are four notes), but it contains six half steps. It is one half step larger than the P4. The ninth dyad, E♭–F♯, is a 2nd (two notes from E to F), but its three half steps make it one half step larger than the M2. In measure 2, on the other hand, the eleventh dyad (D–A♭) is a 5th, but its size is

Example A.10

a.

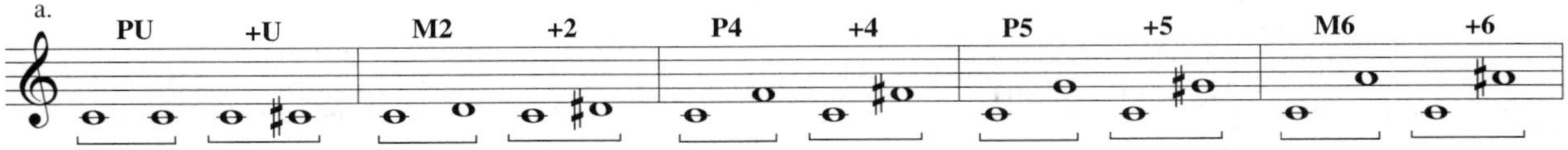

b.

only six half steps, one half step smaller than the P5. These are all **augmented** or **diminished** intervals.

1. An augmented interval (abbreviated +) is a half step larger than the corresponding P or M interval. Although any interval can be augmented, the most frequent among these intervals are the +2 (three half steps) and the +4 (six half steps). The +6 is also a prominent interval in chromatic harmony, and so is the +5. Example A.10a shows some augmented intervals, along with the P or M intervals from which each of them is derived.
2. A diminished interval (abbreviated °) is a half step smaller than the corresponding P or m interval. The diminished intervals most frequently found in music are the °5 and the °7. Some diminished intervals, along with the P or m intervals they are derived from, appear in example A.10b.

Because the +4 consists of three whole tones (C–D–E–F♯), it is often called a **tritone** (a term which is sometimes also used, inaccurately, to refer to the °5). The tritone appears in the diatonic scale between F and B (see example A.9b, m. 3, third dyad). We have already discussed that to spell a P4 or a P5 involving the pitches F and B we need some accidental. The reason is that, with no accidental, F–B is an +4, and B–F a °5.

Notice also that, although sometimes augmented or diminished intervals can be spelled enharmonically as perfect, major, or minor intervals, the two groups of intervals have very different musical functions. In isolation, for instance, an +2 (A♭–B) may sound like a m3 (G♯–B), but in a musical context these are two very different intervals. Sing or play, as an example, the two interesting non-Western scales in example A.11, both of which feature +2s, and you will appreciate the characteristic melodic color of the +2 in contrast to the m3. In Western music, however, the +2 is considered awkward melodically, an interval usually to be avoided.

Example A.11

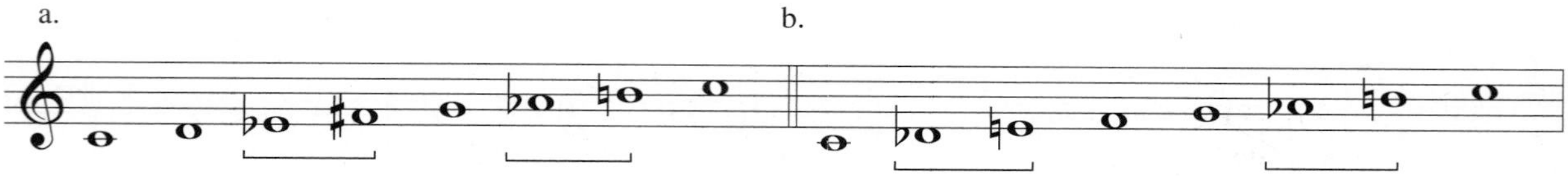

EXERCISES

To practice writing augmented and diminished intervals, refer to exercise 4 in worksheet A at the end of this chapter. To practice enharmonic spellings of intervals, refer to exercise 7 in worksheet A at the end of this chapter. To practice writing and identifying all intervals, refer to exercises 5, 6, and 11 in worksheet A at the end of this chapter.

Compound Intervals

All the intervals we have seen so far are no larger than an octave **(simple intervals).** Intervals larger than an octave are called **compound intervals.** Musically, a compound interval results from the addition of a simple interval plus an octave. Numerically, however, the size of a compound interval results from the formula: simple interval $+ 8 - 1$ (or simple interval $+ 7$). In other words, a compound second will be a 9th ($2 + 8 - 1 = 9$), a compound third will be a 10th ($3 + 8 - 1 = 10$). Very often we reduce compound intervals to their simple equivalents mentally, and we speak of "a minor 3rd" when what is written is really "a minor 10th." Jazz musicians, however, are very familiar with a type of chord that uses compound interval terminology, and which we will study later in this book (see chapter 29): ninth, eleventh, and thirteenth chords. The simple/compound equivalences are as follows:

2nd → 9th

3rd → 10th

4th → 11th

5th → 12th

6th → 13th

7th → 14th

8ve → 15th

EXERCISE

To practice identifying compound intervals, refer to exercise 8 in worksheet A at the end of this chapter.

Interval Inversion

You may already have observed that two different intervals are possible with any two pitches: C–F is a 4th and F–C is a 5th (both ascending). A 4th plus a 5th equals an octave (C–F–C, ascending). These intervals are the **inversion** of each other.

1. To invert an interval, place the lower pitch an octave above, over the higher pitch. Or place the higher pitch an octave below, under the lower pitch.
2. Two intervals related by inversion add up to an octave. Numerically, they add up to nine. All the intervallic inversions by size are presented in the following table:

U → 8ve (8 + 1 = 9)	8ve → U
2nd → 7th (2 + 7 = 9)	7th → 2nd
3rd → 6th (3 + 6 = 9)	6th → 3rd
4th → 5th (4 + 5 = 9)	5th → 4th

3. When you invert an interval, the intervallic quality also inverts in the following way:

P inverts into P

M inverts into m

m inverts into M

\+ inverts into °

° inverts into +

Example A.12 presents a summary of intervallic inversions as explained above.

Example A.12

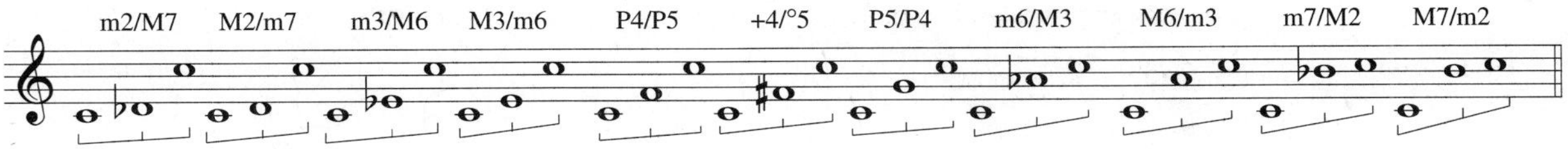

NOTE

Intervallic inversion provides a quick and accurate means of spelling large, more difficult intervals. To spell a large interval, we need to think of its intervallic inversion in the opposite direction. For instance, an ascending m7 from G♯ can be derived by thinking of a descending M2 from G♯, that is, F♯; and a descending M6 from B♭ can be calculated by thinking of an ascending m3 from B♭, that is, D♭.

EXERCISE

To practice writing intervallic inversions, refer to exercise 9 in worksheet A at the end of this chapter.

CONSONANT AND DISSONANT INTERVALS

The concepts of intervallic consonance and dissonance are largely determined by cultural and historical contexts and will vary depending not only on the world culture under consideration, but also within Western music on such factors as geographic location or historical period. Our present discussion of these intervallic categories will be based on criteria that apply, at least in a general way, to Western music roughly from the fifteenth century to the late nineteenth century.

Intervals are **consonant** if they produce a sense of stability. **Dissonant** intervals, on the other hand, create a sense of tension or instability, which we normally perceive as a clash that requires resolution to a consonance. The consonant intervals are the unison, the 8ve, and all the intervals found in major and minor triads, along with their inversions: P5, M3, m3, m6, M6, and P4 (see example A.13). All other intervals are dissonant: m2, M2, m7, M7, and all augmented and diminished intervals.

The most stable consonances are the U, 8ve, and P5. These are called **perfect consonances.** 3rds and 6ths are called **imperfect consonances.** The **P4** (perfect 4th) is sometimes consonant and sometimes dissonant, depending on its context, as we will discuss in chapters D, F, and 7.

Example A.13

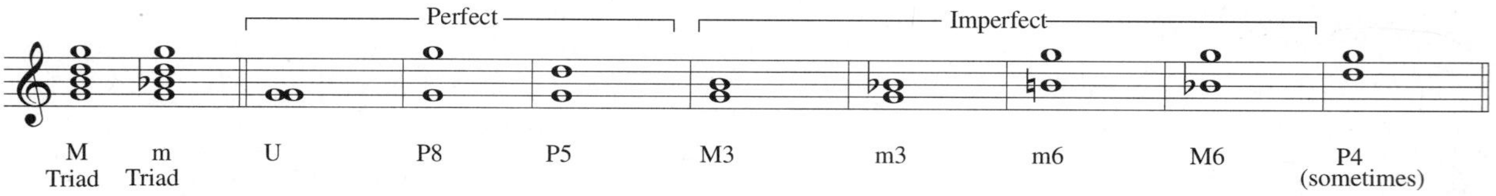

FOR FURTHER STUDY

For additional chapter A materials, refer to the *Harmony in Context* Web page at www.mhhe.com/roigfrancoli2e.

ASSIGNMENT

For an assignment based on the materials learned in this chapter, refer to chapter A in the workbook.

Terms for Review

Scale
Diatonic scale
Letter names
Middle C
Middle octave
Numerical suffixes for octaves
The staff
Lines, spaces, ledger lines
The clefs
Treble, bass, alto, tenor clefs
G, F, C clefs
Grand staff
Equal temperament
Chromatic scale
Half step, semitone
Dyad
Whole step, whole tone
Accidentals
Sharp, flat, natural, double sharp, double flat
Enharmonic spellings
Diatonic half step
Chromatic half step
Interval
Melodic and harmonic intervals
Interval size, interval quality
Ascending and descending intervals
Perfect intervals
Major and minor intervals
Augmented and diminished intervals
The tritone
Simple and compound intervals
Interval inversion
Consonant and dissonant intervals
Perfect consonances
Imperfect consonances
The perfect 4th (P4)

Worksheet A

Knowing the intervals and their relationships is an essential component of musicianship. The following exercises will help you verify your knowledge and will show you possible ways to learn and practice intervals. You should, however, work on your own at memorizing as much as possible all the intervals from any given pitch. Knowing and memorizing the keyboard will help you in this task. For instance, you should know, without having to think about it, all M and m 3rds up and down from any pitch. Having a clear picture of the keyboard in your mind can facilitate your memorization of intervals.

EXERCISE 1

1. Name the notes in exercise 1a, and provide the octave suffix for each of them.
2. Notate the notes in exercise 1b in the correct octave.

EXERCISE 2

1. In exercise 2a write the perfect intervals above the given notes.
2. In exercise 2b write the perfect intervals below the given notes.

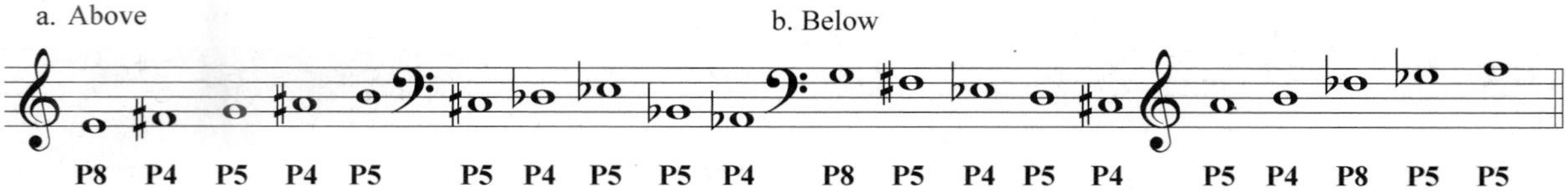

NOTE

In this exercise and the ones that follow, do not write enharmonic equivalents unless specifically requested to do so. In other words, F–B♭ (a P4) is not the same as F–A♯ (What interval is this?), although the two intervals sound the same.

EXERCISE 3

1. In exercise 3a write the following M or m intervals above the given notes.
2. In exercise 3b write the M or m intervals below the given notes.

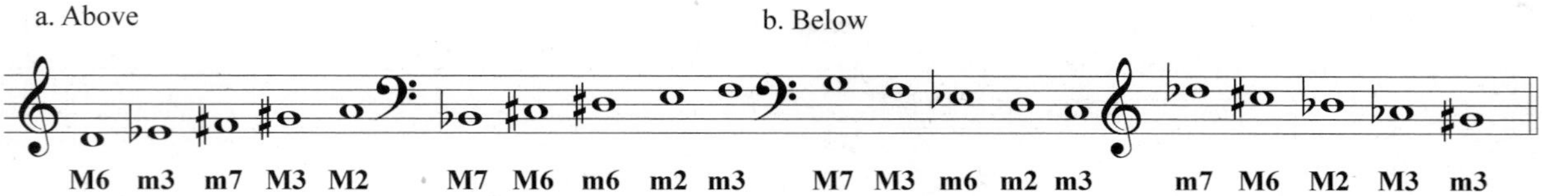

EXERCISE 4

1. In exercise 4a write the + or ° intervals above the given notes.
2. In exercise 4b write the + or ° intervals below the given notes.

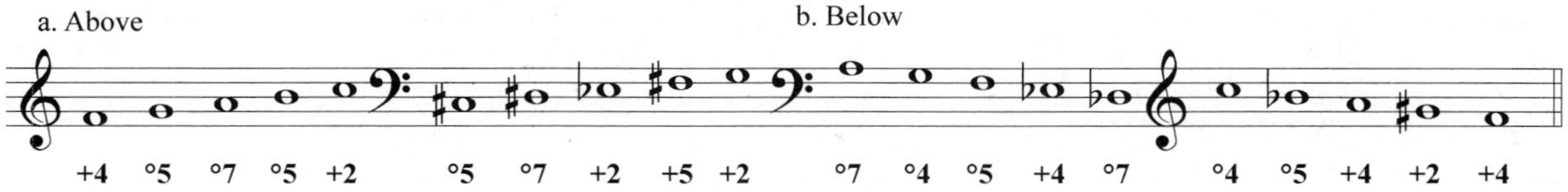

EXERCISE 5 Write the intervals above and below the given notes as requested.

EXERCISE 6 Identify the intervals by size and quality.

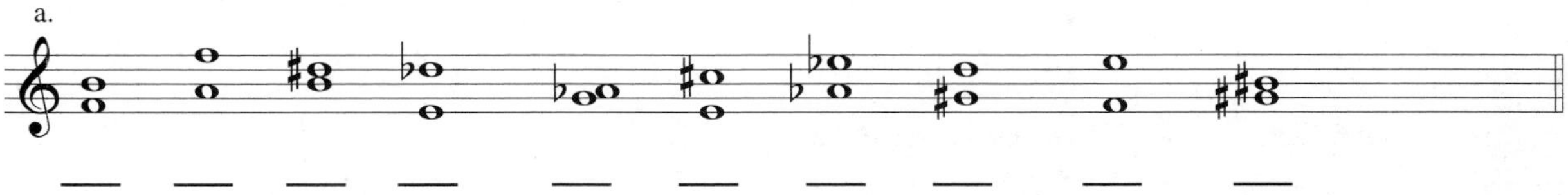

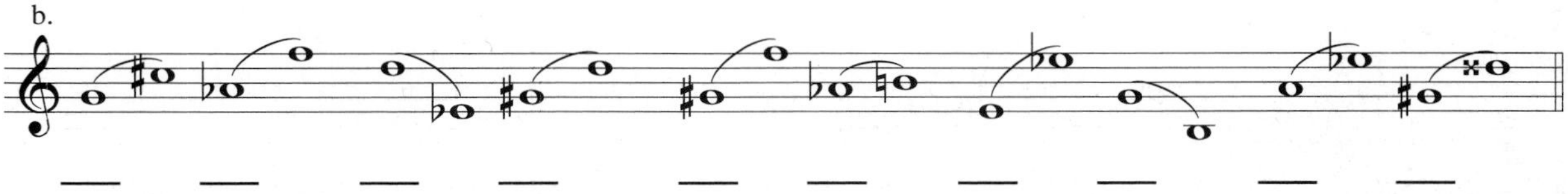

EXERCISE 7 Identify the intervals by size and quality. Then, renotate the lower note enharmonically and identify the resulting interval.

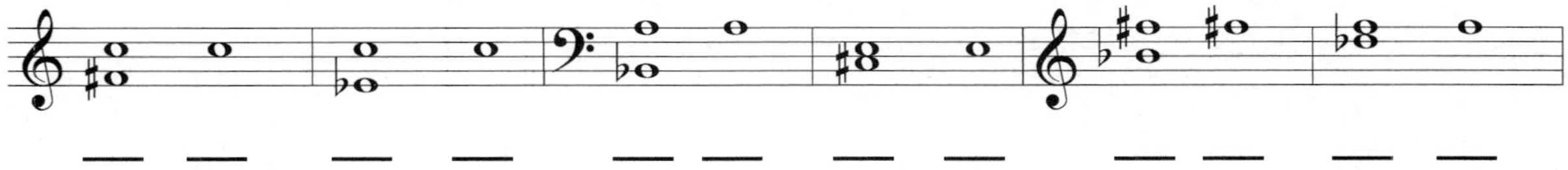

EXERCISE 8 Identify the compound intervals by size and quality. For each of them, provide labels for both the actual compound interval and its simple equivalent (e.g., M10–M3).

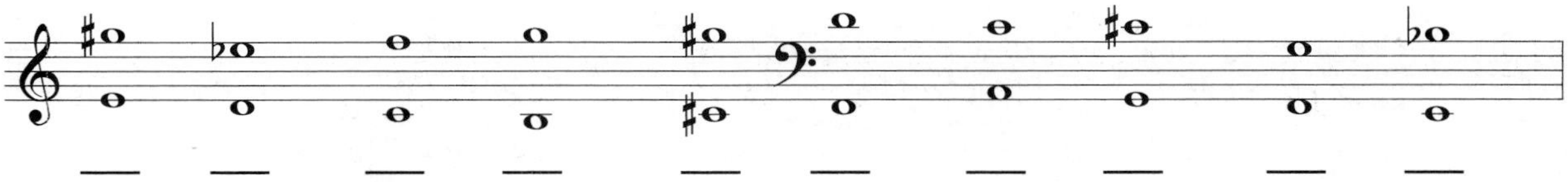

EXERCISE 9 Write the intervallic inversion for each of the following intervals. Identify both the given interval and its inversion.

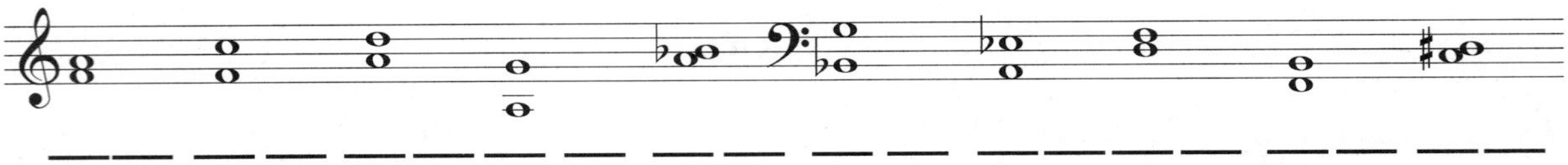

EXERCISE 10 Refer back to exercises 6a and b. Under each of the intervals in these exercises, write a C or D depending on whether the interval is consonant (C) or dissonant (D).

EXERCISE 11 In the melodic examples from the literature in example A.14, identify each of the numbered intervals by size and quality.

Example A.14a B. Bartók, *Music for String Instruments, Percussion, and Celesta,* I, mm. 69–71

Example A.14b J. S. Bach, Fugue 24 in Bm, from *The Well-Tempered Clavier,* I, mm. 1–4

Example A.14c J. S. Bach, "Kyrie," from Mass in Bm, mm. 10–15

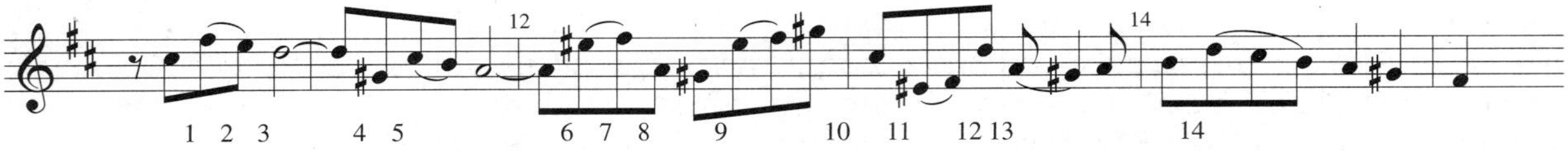

Chapter B

Rhythm and Meter

Sing or play the tune "London Bridge." The following observations will be immediately clear to you:

1. Not all notes have the same *duration.*
2. Notes are *grouped* in various ways. The melody can be *partitioned* into these groups, and some of the groups form durational *patterns* that are repeated (such as, for instance, the pattern to the words "falling down" in our tune).
3. Regardless of the note durations or patterns, you can easily tap what we usually call the "beat," that is, you can "keep time" to the music by establishing a regular "pulse." Your pulses, however, will not all be equally stressed. Some of them will naturally come out more *accented* than others. If we notate pulses (accented or not) as syllables in italics, and accented beats as syllables in boldface, we will come up with the following interpretation of the "London Bridge" words:

   London *bridge* is ***fall***ing *down,* ***fall***ing *down,* ***fall***ing *down,*

   London *bridge* is ***fall***ing *down,* ***my*** *fair* ***la***dy:

These are temporal aspects of the "London Bridge" tune, having to do specifically with rhythm and meter. This chapter will focus on the rudiments and notation of rhythm and meter. The term **rhythm** refers to the *grouping, patterning, and partitioning of musical events* (such as notes), whereas **meter** refers to the *measurement of the number of pulses between regularly recurring accents.* In most Western music, meter provides the framework and context against which we hear rhythm. We will now study the notation of these two temporal aspects of music separately.

DURATIONAL SYMBOLS

To notate rhythm, we need **durational symbols,** that is, symbols that express the relative duration of notes. The elements of rhythmic notation needed to express duration are represented in example B.1a. Durational symbols are made up of **note heads, stems,**

Example B.1a The Elements of Rhythmic Notation

Example B.1b Basic Durational Symbols

VALUE	NOTE	REST
Breve (double whole)	𝅜 = 𝅝 + 𝅝	𝄺 = 𝄻 + 𝄻
Whole	𝅝 = 𝅗𝅥 + 𝅗𝅥	𝄻 = 𝄼 + 𝄼
Half	𝅗𝅥 = 𝅘𝅥 + 𝅘𝅥	𝄼 = 𝄽 + 𝄽
Quarter	𝅘𝅥 = 𝅘𝅥𝅮 + 𝅘𝅥𝅮	𝄽 = 𝄾 + 𝄾
Eighth	𝅘𝅥𝅮 = 𝅘𝅥𝅯 + 𝅘𝅥𝅯	𝄾 = 𝄿 + 𝄿
Sixteenth	𝅘𝅥𝅯 = 𝅘𝅥𝅰 + 𝅘𝅥𝅰	𝄿 = 𝅀 𝅀
Thirty-second	𝅘𝅥𝅰 = 𝅘𝅥𝅱 + 𝅘𝅥𝅱	𝅀 = 𝅁 𝅁
Sixty-fourth	𝅘𝅥𝅱	𝅁

and **flags** or **beams.** The chart in example B.1b presents all the basic durational symbols, their equivalence in terms of the next shorter duration, and the notation of the **rest** equivalent to each of the durations.

EXERCISE

To practice equivalences among various durational symbols, refer to exercise 1 in worksheet B at the end of this chapter.

Example B.2

a.

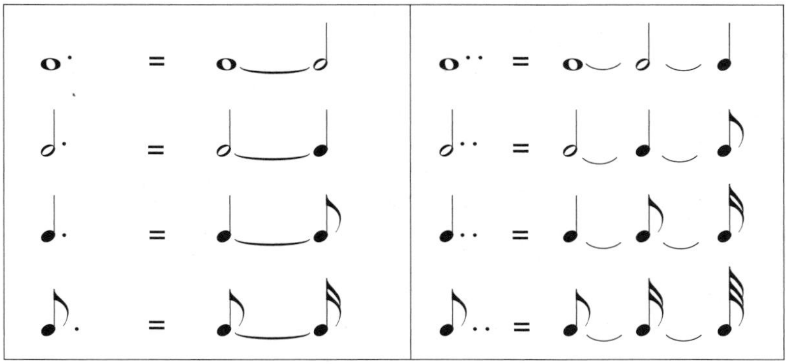

b.

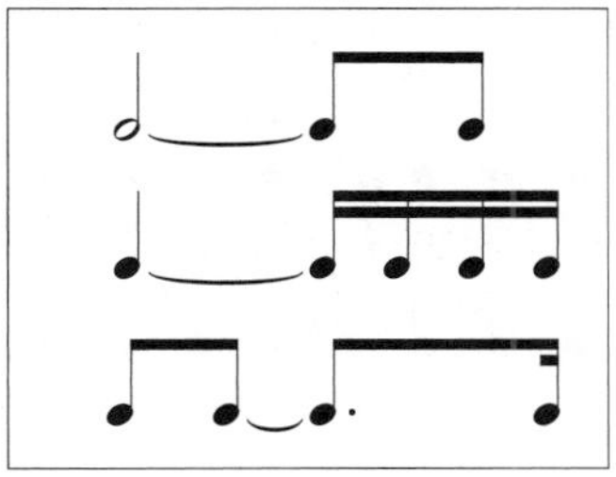

The possible durations that can be notated increase enormously when we use dots and ties. A **dot** added *after* a note or rest increases the duration of that note or rest by half its value. A **double dot** increases the duration of a note or rest by three-quarters its original value (half the original duration, plus half the first dot). **Ties** are used to connect two values of any kind. Of course, we can express dotted notes by means of ties (this is how they have to be notated over a bar line) but, on the other hand, we can write many durations by means of ties that cannot be expressed with dots. Example B.2a shows some dotted notes and their equivalent notation with ties; example B.2b presents some tied values that cannot be expressed in any other way.

EXERCISE

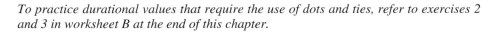

To practice durational values that require the use of dots and ties, refer to exercises 2 and 3 in worksheet B at the end of this chapter.

PULSE, BEAT, AND METER

Consider the undifferentiated stream of time points that appears in example B.3a. These are regularly recurring time points, which we call **pulses.** Now tap or say (on "tah") the line in example B.3b. We have added an accent every other pulse. Accents are points of emphasis, and through them we create groupings in the stream of pulses. The grouping in example B.3b is "in two." In example B.3c, the accents appear every three pulses, and they create a grouping "in three." Similarly, the grouping in example B.3d is "in four." These examples illustrate meter, as defined on page 19. For a musical context to be metric we need pulses and recurring accents. We will refer to pulses in a metric context as **beats.** In other words, the time points in example B.3a are pulses, whereas in the other three examples the same time points become beats because the regularly recurring accents provide a metric frame.

Example B.3

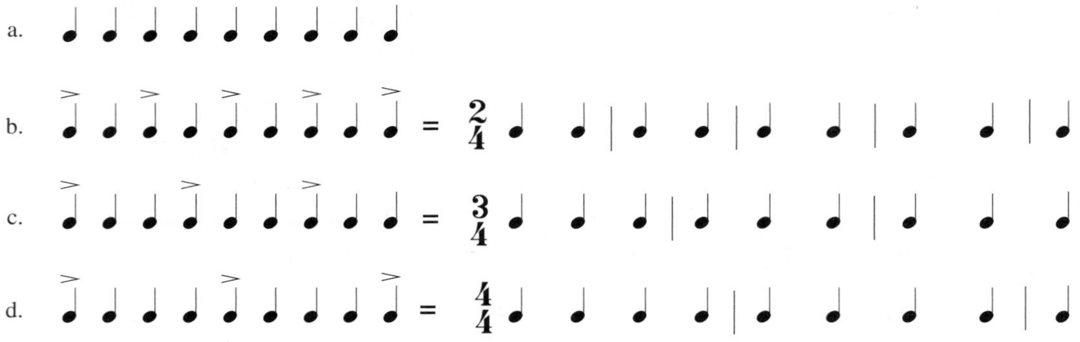

TEMPO

Because the exact meaning of some meter signatures depends on how fast the music moves, we need to review the concept of **tempo** at this point. The term *tempo* (Italian for "time") refers to the speed of the beat. Most frequently, Italian terms (**tempo markings**) are also used to describe the tempo of a movement or composition. These terms are relative and have meant different things in different historical periods. In general, tempos (or tempi) were faster in the Baroque and Classical periods than in the Romantic period. A Baroque *adagio,* for instance, would be performed faster than a late-Romantic *adagio.* Having said this, however, the slow tempos (listed from slower to faster) are *grave, largo, lento,* and *adagio*; the moderate tempos are *andante, moderato,* and *allegretto*; and the fast tempos are *allegro, vivace,* and *presto.*

A more "objective" measurement of tempo is provided by metronome markings. In scores from the last two centuries one often finds a metronome marking accompanying, or replacing, the tempo marking. The letters M.M., which stand for "Maelzel's metronome," often precede the metronome marking. The metronome setting (a number) indicates fractions of a minute. Thus, M.M. "♩ = 60" means a quarter note per second (60 quarter notes per minute, or fairly *adagio*); "♩ = 80" means 80 quarter notes per minute (*moderato*), and "♩ = 120" means a quarter note every half second, or 120 quarter notes per minute (a fast tempo).

SIMPLE AND COMPOUND METERS

Sing the tunes "Camptown Races" and "Greensleeves," while you tap or conduct the beat in each case. (If you don't know these tunes, you can also try "Mary Had a Little Lamb" and "Row, Row, Row Your Boat.") Then sing them again, and now *divide* the beat. That is, tap more than once per beat, following the beat division appropriate to each song. If you are doing this right, you will have come up with two divisions per beat in "Camptown Races" and "Mary Had a Little Lamb," and three divisions per beat in "Greensleeves" and "Row, Row, Row Your Boat." Meters with a duple division of the beat are called **simple meters,** whereas meters with a triple division are **compound meters.** Now sing "Pop Goes the Weasel," "Star Spangled Banner" ("O Say Can You See"), "Old MacDonald," and "My Bonnie," and determine whether each is in simple or compound meter.

THE NOTATION OF METER

A complete metric unit is called a **measure**, and measures are indicated by **bar lines.** Meters are indicated by means of **meter signatures** or **time signatures.** A meter signature consists of two numbers written one over the other. The exact meaning of meter signatures changes between simple and compound meters, as we will discuss next.

Meter Signatures in Simple Meters

The most common simple meters are $\frac{2}{4}$, $\frac{3}{4}$, and $\frac{4}{4}$. The upper number in meter signatures for simple meters is 2, 3, or 4. In simple meter, the upper number indicates the *number of beats per measure.* Thus, in $\frac{2}{4}$ there are two beats per measure, in $\frac{3}{4}$ there are three, and in $\frac{4}{4}$ there are four. The lower number indicates the **value of the beat.** By convention, "4" means "quarter note." The beat value in each of the three meters we have just mentioned ($\frac{2}{4}$, $\frac{3}{4}$, and $\frac{4}{4}$) is, then, a quarter note. The lower number 2 means a half note per beat, and 1 means a whole note. Similarly, 8 means an eighth note, and 16 means sixteenth note. Examples B.3b, c, and d show how each of the metric phrases, which we first notated by means of accents, can be notated using a meter signature and bar lines.

Any meter with two beats (such as $\frac{2}{4}$, $\frac{2}{2}$, or $\frac{2}{8}$) is called a **duple meter.** Meters with three beats (such as $\frac{3}{4}$, $\frac{3}{2}$ or $\frac{3}{8}$) are **triple meters,** and meters with four beats ($\frac{4}{4}$, $\frac{4}{2}$, or $\frac{4}{8}$) are **quadruple meters.** Notice that $\frac{4}{4}$ can also be referred to as **common time** (symbol 𝄴), and $\frac{2}{2}$ as **cut time** (symbol 𝄵).

Meter Signatures in Compound Meters

The most common compound meters are $\frac{6}{8}$, $\frac{9}{8}$, and $\frac{12}{8}$. The upper number in meter signatures for compound meters is 6, 9, or 12. **Compound meter signatures,** however, lend themselves to some confusion if we think of them in the same terms we defined above for simple meters. The beat in such compound meters as $\frac{6}{8}$, $\frac{9}{8}$, and $\frac{12}{8}$ *is the dotted quarter,* not the eighth note. The eighth note is the beat *division.* In other words, the top number in these signatures does not indicate the number of beats per measure, but rather the number of divisions. And the bottom number does not indicate the value of the beat, but rather the value of the division. $\frac{6}{8}$ will normally be conducted *in two* because it has two beats (compound duple); $\frac{9}{8}$ is normally conducted *in three* because it has three beats (compound triple), and $\frac{12}{8}$ *in four* because it has four beats (compound quadruple). The beat note in each of these compound meters is the dotted quarter note. Each of these meters, however, is often subdivided in slower tempos. Thus, a $\frac{6}{8}$ with a *largo* indication

Example B.4 Simple Meters

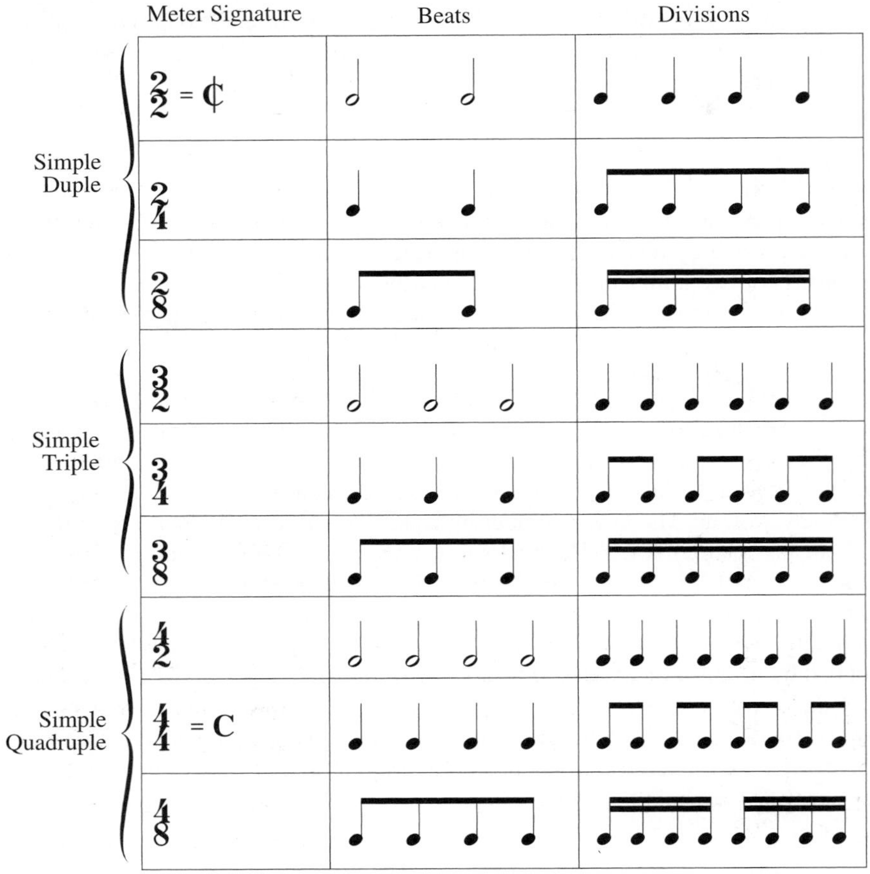

will be conducted or felt *in six*. Examples B.4 and B.5 present a summary of the most common simple and compound meters and their characteristics.

EXERCISES

To practice identifying simple and compound meter signatures and counting beats in a variety of simple and compound meters, refer to exercise 4 in worksheet B at the end of this chapter. To practice providing meter signatures for given rhythmic passages, and identifying rhythmic errors in given meters, refer to exercises 5 and 6 in worksheet B at the end of this chapter.

♪♪ Example B.5 Compound Meters

	Meter Signature	Beats	Divisions
Compound Duple	$\frac{6}{4}$	𝅗𝅥. 𝅗𝅥.	♩ ♩ ♩ ♩ ♩ ♩
	$\frac{6}{8}$	♩. ♩.	♫♫♫ ♫♫♫
	$\frac{6}{16}$	♪. ♪.	
Compound Triple	$\frac{9}{4}$	𝅗𝅥. 𝅗𝅥. 𝅗𝅥.	♩ ♩ ♩ ♩ ♩ ♩ ♩ ♩ ♩
	$\frac{9}{8}$	♩. ♩. ♩.	
	$\frac{9}{16}$	♪. ♪. ♪.	
Compound Quadruple	$\frac{12}{4}$	𝅗𝅥. 𝅗𝅥. 𝅗𝅥. 𝅗𝅥.	
	$\frac{12}{8}$	♩. ♩. ♩. ♩.	
	$\frac{12}{16}$	♪. ♪. ♪. ♪.	

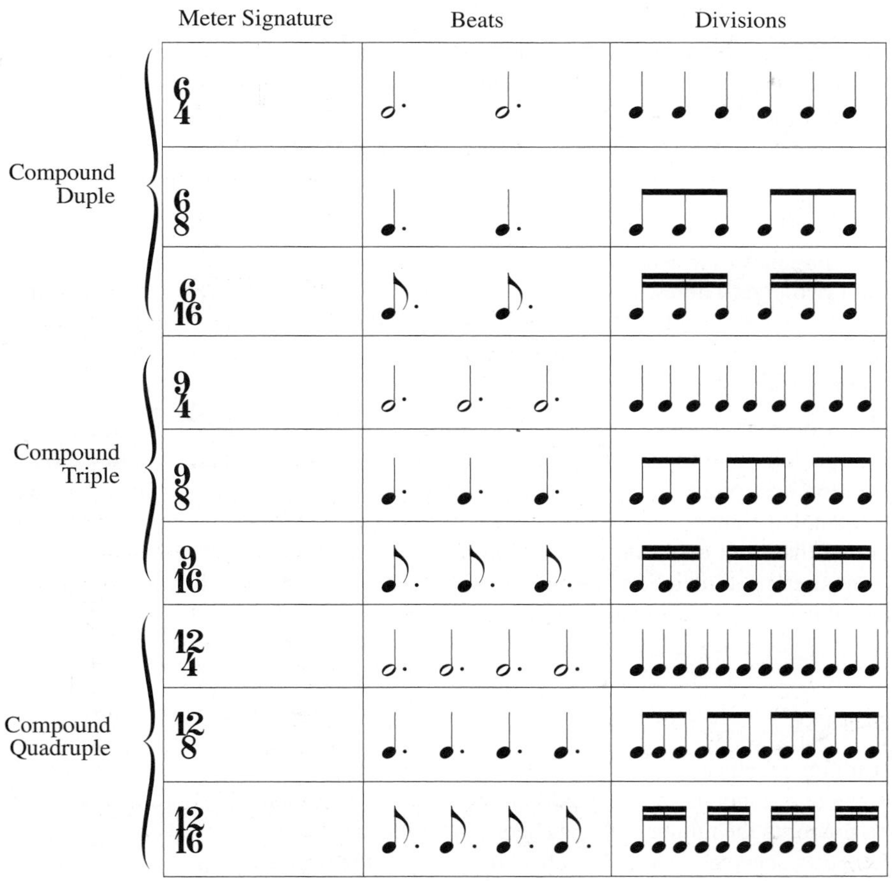

METRIC ACCENT

We have already seen that beats in a metric context are not all equally stressed. That is, some beats are naturally more accented than others as a result of the grouping of pulses into regularly recurring patterns. We call these accents, which result from metric organization, **metric accents. Strong and weak beats in all meters** are illustrated below.

1. In duple meter beat 1 is strong and beat 2 is weak. We will use the symbols – for strong and ⌣ for weak.

$$\frac{2}{4} \quad \overset{-}{1} \ \overset{\smile}{2} \ | \ \overset{-}{1} \ \overset{\smile}{2} \ \|$$

2. In quadruple meter the odd-numbered beats are strong (1 and 3), whereas even-numbered beats are weak (2 and 4). Beat 3, however, is weaker than beat 1.

   – ◡ – ◡   – ◡ – ◡

   $\frac{4}{4}$ 1 2 3 4 | 1 2 3 4 ||

3. In triple meters, only beat 1 is strong. In principle, beats 2 and 3 are weak. Beat 2, however, is often stressed by a variety of means, one of which is illustrated in example B.11a. Thus, although beat 2 is metrically weak, we may indeed perceive it as either weak or strong depending on the musical context.

   – ◡ ◡   – ◡ ◡

   $\frac{3}{4}$ 1 2 3 | 1 2 3 ||

4. These same strong-weak relationships also apply to beat divisions. In a beat divided into two eighth notes, the first one is strong, the second one weak. If the division is into four sixteenth notes, notes 1 and 3 are strong, and notes 2 and 4 are weak. In beats divided into 3 notes (in triplets or compound meters), note 1 is strong, and notes 2 and 3 are weak.

The first beat in a measure is called a **downbeat**; the last beat is an **upbeat.** Weak beats, especially upbeats, create a metric tension that usually calls for continuation to a resolution, a strong beat or downbeat. Sing the beginnings of "Happy Birthday" and "Star Spangled Banner" ("O Say Can You See"). You will find that both are in triple meter and that both begin on upbeats (on beat 3). An **anacrusis** is a note or group of notes that begins a melodic phrase on an upbeat. The type of melody which begins on an upbeat is called an **anacrusic melody.**

CHOOSING A METER TO NOTATE A MELODY

Determining whether a melody is in duple or triple meter and determining whether it is in simple or compound meter should not be much of a problem. This process basically entails counting the number of beats between downbeats (which we will easily perceive as metrically accented beats), and checking whether the beat division is in two or three. Once we have decided on these points, however, several possibilities arise. Take, for instance, the tune "Oh! Susanna." There seems to be no question that its meter is simple quadruple, as notated in example B.6a. It is difficult, however, to distinguish between quadruple ($\frac{4}{4}$ or **C**) and duple ($\frac{2}{4}$ or $\frac{2}{2}$) meters and, as a matter of fact, that is often an arbitrary decision of the composer. Examples B.6b and c show two alternative notations for "Oh! Susanna," each of which is perfectly plausible. What is at issue in each of these versions is what value gets the beat and how long the measure is. Notice that we could also assign example B.6c a $\frac{4}{8}$ meter signature without changing the notation in any other way.

The same notational ambiguities apply to compound meters. In example B.7a we have chosen to notate "Pop Goes the Weasel" in $\frac{6}{8}$, that is, with a dotted quarter beat. The notation in example B.7b, in $\frac{6}{4}$ (we have doubled the value of the beat, which now is a dotted half note), is also perfectly correct. These examples show the relativity of

Example B.6 Stephen Foster, "Oh! Susanna"

Example B.7 "Pop Goes the Weasel"

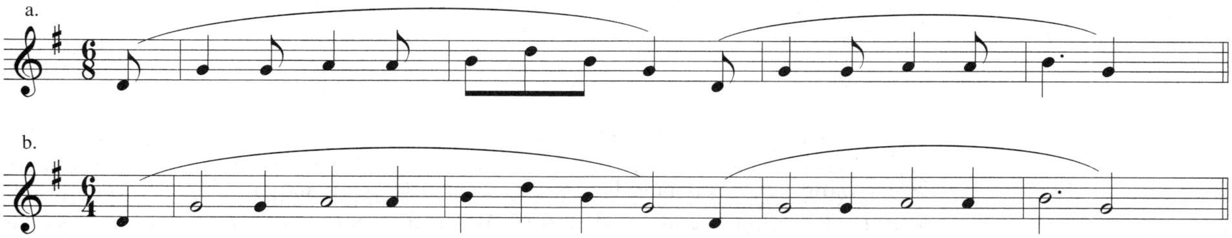

exact meter signatures. What matters mostly is to identify and represent correctly the fundamental metric parameters (duple or triple, simple or compound).

EXERCISE

To practice various possible metric notations for a melody, refer to exercise 7 in worksheet B at the end of this chapter.

ASYMMETRICAL METERS

All the meters we have discussed so far are **symmetrical** or **divisive.** We think of them in terms of their divisions, and the divisions form symmetrical patterns. A different type of meter, however, is **asymmetrical** or **additive.** When we think of $\frac{5}{8}$, for instance, we

Example B.8

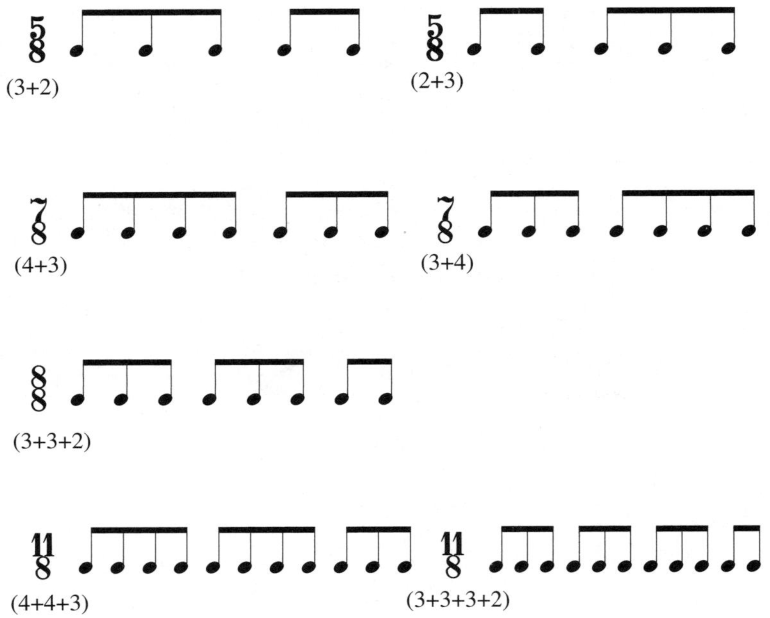

usually think of two combined metric units (3 + 2 or 2 + 3) that form an asymmetrical metric structure. Similarly, $\frac{7}{8}$ and $\frac{11}{8}$ are asymmetrical meters. All of these meters are conducted in unequal beats. $\frac{5}{8}$ is usually conducted in two (subdivided as 3 + 2 or 2 + 3). How would you conduct $\frac{7}{8}$ and $\frac{11}{8}$? Notice that $\frac{8}{8}$ (very much unlike $\frac{4}{4}$) is often an asymmetrical meter to be conducted in three: 3 + 3 + 2. Example B.8 shows some possible patterns with asymmetrical meters.

IRREGULAR DIVISIONS OF THE BEAT

Although the normal division of the beat in simple meters is into two or four parts, and the normal division of compound beats is into three or six parts, beats (or any note values) can also be divided irregularly. Thus, beats or notes that would normally be divided in multiples of two can also be divided into three parts **(triplets),** five parts **(quintuplets),** six parts **(sextuplets),** seven parts **(septuplets),** and so forth. Beats or notes that would normally be divided in multiples of three can also be divided into two parts **(duplets),** four parts **(quadruplets),** and so on. The notation of the most frequent irregular divisions of notes is shown in example B.9.

Example B.9

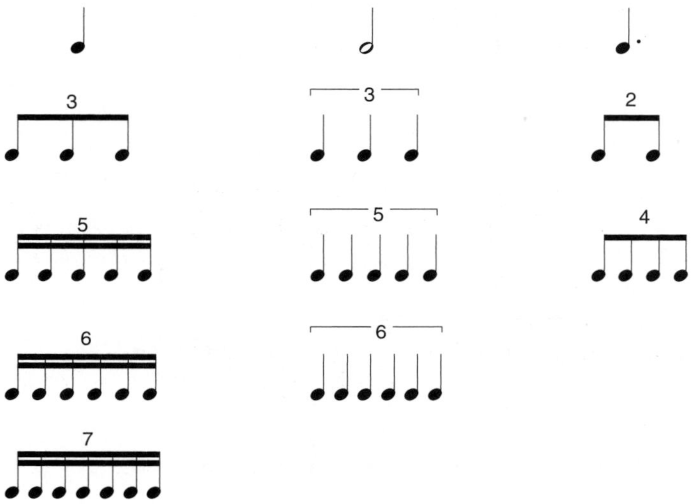

IRREGULAR RHYTHMIC AND METRIC RELATIONSHIPS

Meter and rhythm allow for numerous irregular relationships, which have often been used by composers to break the regularity of notated meter, metric divisions, and metric accents. We will now mention some of these possible irregularities.

1. **Syncopation** is the rhythmic contradiction of a metrical pattern of strong and weak beats. This occurs when a metrically weak beat or beat division is emphasized by a rhythmic and/or dynamic accent (example B.10a).
2. **Hemiola** consists in the juxtaposition of, or interplay between, three and two beats at the metric level. A usual hemiola pattern is based on the alternation of $\substack{6\\8}$ and $\substack{3\\4}$ (that is, alternating two and three beats, as in Leonard Bernstein's song "America," from *West Side Story*). In another type of hemiola, a sense of three $\substack{2\\4}$ measures (or of one $\substack{3\\2}$ measure) is created in the place of two $\substack{3\\4}$ measures. Both of these types of hemiola are illustrated in examples B.10b and B.10c. In the Robert Schumann example, the notated meter suggests beats grouped in three, whereas the beat grouping we actually hear is in two.
3. Whereas metric accents create a recurring pattern of strong-weak beats, other types of accent may generate patterns that conflict with the underlying metric patterns. Accents that result from grouping, note length, a sense of harmonic or tonal arrival,

Example B.10a

Example B.10b

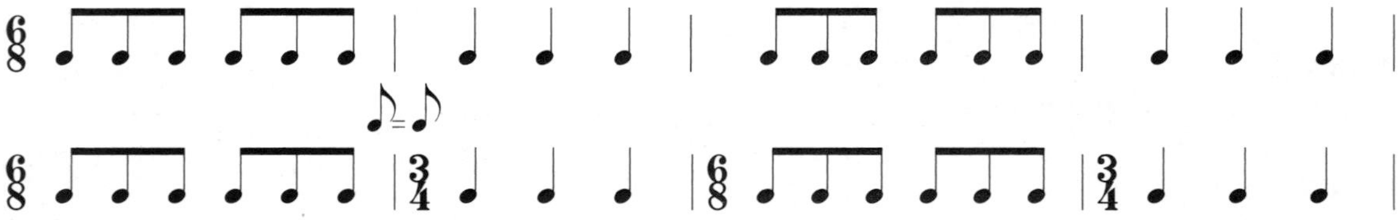

Example B.10c Robert Schumann, Symphony no. 3 in E♭M, I, mm. 1–7

and other nonmetrical factors, are **rhythmic accents.** In the phrase from Bach's "Chaconne" reproduced in example B.11a, we hear a rhythmic accent on beat 2 of a $\frac{3}{4}$ meter, produced by the longer note and the dotted rhythm pattern, both of which begin on beat 2. A rhythmic accent produced by the duration of a note (that is, by a note of longer duration) is called an **agogic accent.** As we saw on page 26, beat

Example B.11a J. S. Bach, "Chaconne," from Partita no. 2 in Dm for Violin Solo, mm. 1–5

Example B.11b Johannes Brahms, Intermezzo in CM, op. 119, no. 3, mm. 23–25

2 in triple meter may be weak or strong, depending on the context. This example illustrates a case of a strong beat 2 in a $\frac{3}{4}$ meter, and the stress is produced by agogic accent.

4. In example B.11b, on the other hand, Johannes Brahms explicitly requires an accent on the last eighth note of every beat by writing a *sforzando* mark (*sf*). An accent created by a dynamic mark is called a **dynamic accent.** Notice that syncopations are usually heard as accented notes. What kind of grouping does this syncopation/dynamic accent generate in the right hand, and how does it conflict with the metric grouping?

EXERCISE

To practice identifying syncopations and hemiolas, refer to exercise 8 in worksheet B at the end of this chapter.

SOME NOTES ON THE CORRECT NOTATION OF RHYTHM

The following are some points that should be observed when copying rhythmic notation by hand.

1. If you are writing a single melodic line, stems should go up if the note is below the middle line and down if the note is above the middle line. If the note is on the middle line, the stem may go up or down, depending on the stems of adjacent notes (example B.12a). All stems should be of equal length (spanning a length of three staff spaces, or four consecutive staff lines).
2. If you are writing two voices on the same staff, the stems for the upper voice will go up, and the stems for the lower voice will go down (example B.12b).

Example B.12

a. Right / Wrong

b.

c. Right / Wrong

3. Beams that connect groups of notes should reflect the standard metric grouping (the beats) for the meter of the passage, rather than obscuring it (example B.12c).
4. In dotted notes that are on a line, dots are usually placed above the line (not *on* the line).
5. Meter signatures are written only at the beginning of a piece (unless there are meter changes). They should not be written again at the beginning of each staff.
6. The whole-note rest can be used to indicate a full measure of rest in any meter, even if the measure does not add up to four beats (for instance, in a $\frac{3}{4}$ measure).

EXERCISE

To practice renotating rhythms providing appropriate beamings, refer to exercise 9 in worksheet B at the end of this chapter.

ASSIGNMENT

For an assignment based on the materials learned in this chapter, refer to chapter B in the workbook.

Terms for Review

Rhythm
Meter
Durational symbols: breve, whole, half, quarter, eighth, sixteenth, thirty-second, sixty-fourth notes
Note head, stem, flag, beam
Rest
Dot
Double dot
Tie
Pulse
Beat
Tempo
Tempo markings
Simple meters
Compound meters
Measure
Bar line
Meter signatures (Time signatures)
Beat values
Duple meter
Triple meter
Quadruple meter
Common time
Cut time
Beats in compound meters
Metric accents
Strong and weak beats in all meters
Downbeat
Upbeat
Anacrusis
Anacrusic melodies
Symmetrical (divisive) meters
Asymmetrical (additive) meters
Irregular divisions of the beat
Irregular groups in simple meters: triplet, quintuplet, etc.
Irregular groups in compound meters: duplet, quadruplet, etc.
Syncopation
Hemiola
Rhythmic accent
Agogic accent
Dynamic accent

Worksheet B

EXERCISE 1 Supply the information required in the blanks.

A 𝅝 note = ________ ♩ notes

A 𝅗𝅥 note = ________ ♪ notes

A ♩ note = ________ 𝅘𝅥𝅰 notes

A ♪ note = ________ 𝅘𝅥𝅱 notes

_____ 𝄾 rests = 1 ▬ rest

_____ ▬ rests = 4 𝄽 rests

_____ 𝄿 rests = 1 ▬ rest

_____ 𝅀 rests = 2 𝄿 rests

EXERCISE 2 For each of the following patterns, write the equivalent duration with only one note value. (You will need dots in some cases.)

♫ =

♪ 𝅘𝅥𝅯 𝅘𝅥𝅯 (beamed) =

𝅘𝅥𝅯 𝅘𝅥𝅯 𝅘𝅥𝅯 (beamed) =

𝅗𝅥 ♩ ♩ =

♪ ♪ ♪ ♪ ♪ ♪ (beamed) =

𝅘𝅥𝅯 𝅘𝅥𝅯 𝅘𝅥𝅯 𝅘𝅥𝅯 ♪ (beamed) =

♪ ♪ ♪ (beamed) =

♩. ♪ =

EXERCISE 3 Show, by means of tied notes (as few as possible in each case), the value of each dotted or doubly dotted note.

♪. =

𝅗𝅥.. =

♩.. =

𝅘𝅥𝅯. =

EXERCISE 4 Using the fewest possible notes, along with ties where needed, write a single duration lasting the number of beats specified in each of the following cases. Include bar lines if more than one measure is needed. In a parenthesis after the required number of beats, write whether this meter is simple or compound, and what the beat value is (see the provided example).

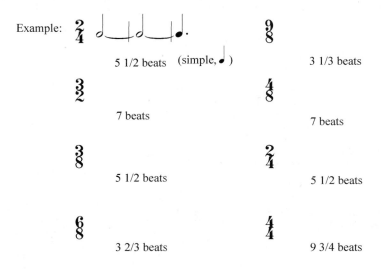

Example: 2/4 

5 1/2 beats (simple, ♩)

9/8

3 1/3 beats

3/2

7 beats

4/8

7 beats

3/8

5 1/2 beats

2/4

5 1/2 beats

6/8

3 2/3 beats

4/4

9 3/4 beats

EXERCISE 5 Write an appropriate meter signature for each of the following examples.

EXERCISE 6 Locate and correct a total of eight mistakes in the following examples.

EXERCISE 7 Transcribe the following melody from $\frac{6}{8}$ to $\frac{6}{16}$ and $\frac{6}{4}$.

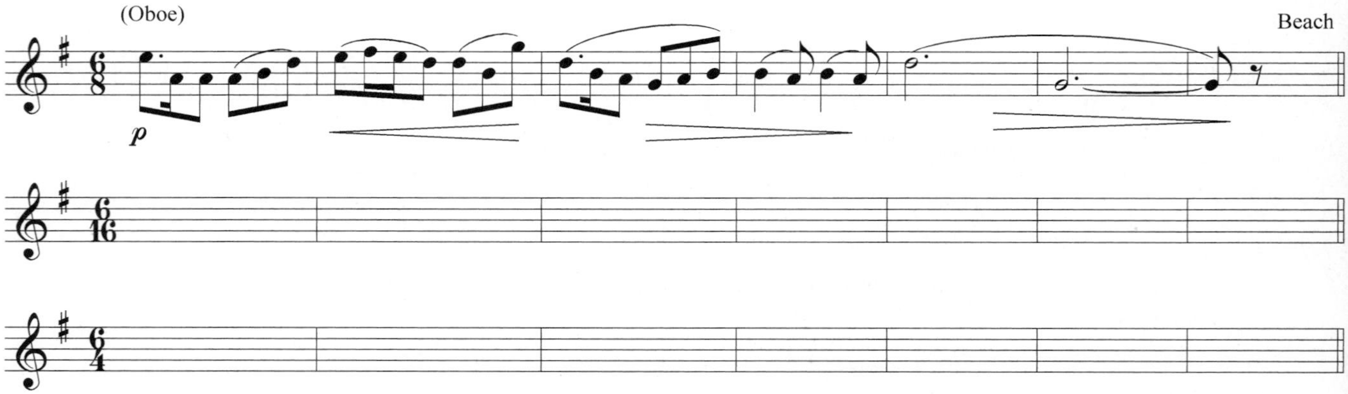

EXERCISE 8 In the following examples, mark every syncopation with an *x,* and draw a bracket over every hemiola.

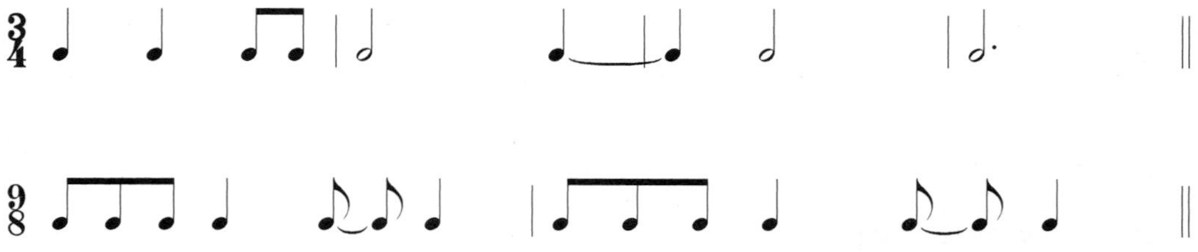

EXERCISE 9 Correct the notation of the following examples so that the beaming clarifies the meter and rhythm.

a.

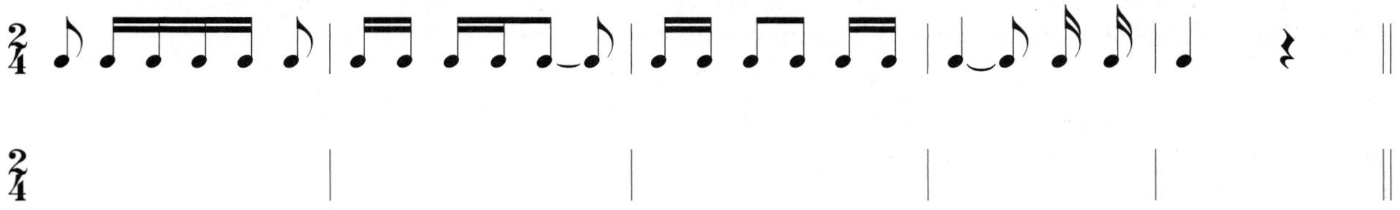

b.

Chapter C

Tonality: Scales and Keys

Sing or play the tune "The First Noël" (example C.1). There is no doubt that the pitches in this melody are organized according to some system. What intuitive observations can we make about this system, at least as it applies to this melody?

1. One pitch seems to be the most important of all, the **tonal center** around which other pitches are organized. We call this pitch the **tonic.** If you sing the tunes "Twinkle, Twinkle" and "Oh! Susanna," you will notice that both begin and end on a pitch that provides a sense of stability, repose, and, at the end, closure. These are characteristics of the tonic pitch.
2. What is the tonic in "The First Noël"? Sing the tune, and then sing the tonic. You should come up with the pitch C. In this case, the melody does not begin and end on the tonic, but the tonic feeling of C is nonetheless evident. Notice that the lowest and highest pitches are C4 and C5, respectively. The span between the lowest and highest pitches of a melody is called the **range.** In this case, the range is an octave, from tonic to tonic.
3. The space between C4 and C5 in mm. 1–3 of "The First Noël" is covered by means of an ascending succession of pitches moving by steps. As we saw in chapter A, the organization of a collection of pitches by successive ascending or descending steps is called a **scale.**
4. Another pitch that has a very prominent role in our tune is G (the pitch a 5th above C). G in emphasized as a "long pitch" (that is, by agogic accent) in mm. 2 and 4, where it splits the octave into two segments (C4–G4–C5). In mm. 4 and 6, moreover, the melody changes direction every time it touches on G. Measures 4–7 are built around the melodic segment G4–C5. The pitch a 5th above the tonic is called the *dominant* and it is indeed a very important pitch (second only to the tonic) in the system we are discussing.
5. Other than C and G, we see that E (a 3rd above the tonic) is a prominent pitch in "The First Noël," because the melody begins and ends on it. The 3rd above the tonic is called *mediant,* because it is halfway between the tonic and the dominant.

Example C.1 "The First Noël," mm. 1–8

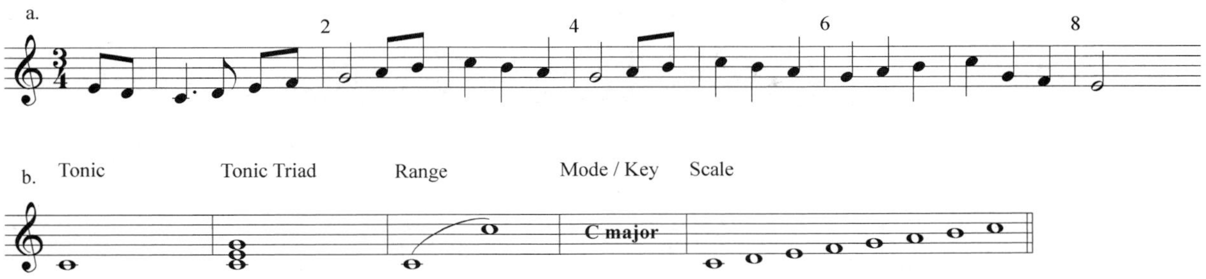

The three pitches, C–E–G, form what we call a **triad,** that is, a collection of three pitches which we call the **root,** the **third** (a 3rd above the root), and the **fifth** (a 5th above the root). Because C–E–G in this case is the triad built on the tonic, we call it the **tonic triad** (we will study triads in detail in chapter E). All of the above information is summarized in example C.1b.

We have discussed the basics of a system in which *pitches are organized hierarchically*. This type of system is called a **tonal system.** In principle, many different tonal systems exist in the world. The musics of India, Indonesia, medieval Christianity, and Mozart, to name just four different styles, are all based on different tonal systems. We have come to know the specific system on which Western music is based from about the mid-seventeenth to the late nineteenth centuries (the "common practice" period) as **tonality,** or also (somewhat abusively) as "*the* tonal system." Although other tonal systems are constructed mostly around melodic relationships (the Indian *rāga* system for instance), the Western tonal system is built on both *melodic* and *harmonic* relationships. Whereas in this book as a whole we will study in detail the harmonic relationships that define Western tonality, in this chapter we will review some of the basic principles of tonal melodic organization.

MODES AND SCALES

Western tonality is also known as **major-minor tonality** and as **functional tonality.** We call it major-minor tonality because it is based almost exclusively on two *types of scales*, or *modes:* the major mode and the minor mode. We call it functional tonality because each of the steps (or *degrees*) in these scales has a *tonal or harmonic function* with respect to the tonic, as we will study in chapters E and 3.

The Major Mode and the Scale Degrees

You will remember from chapter A that the standard Western collection of notes is made up of *seven pitches*. If a scale contains only the basic, unaltered pitches, we call it

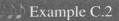

Example C.2

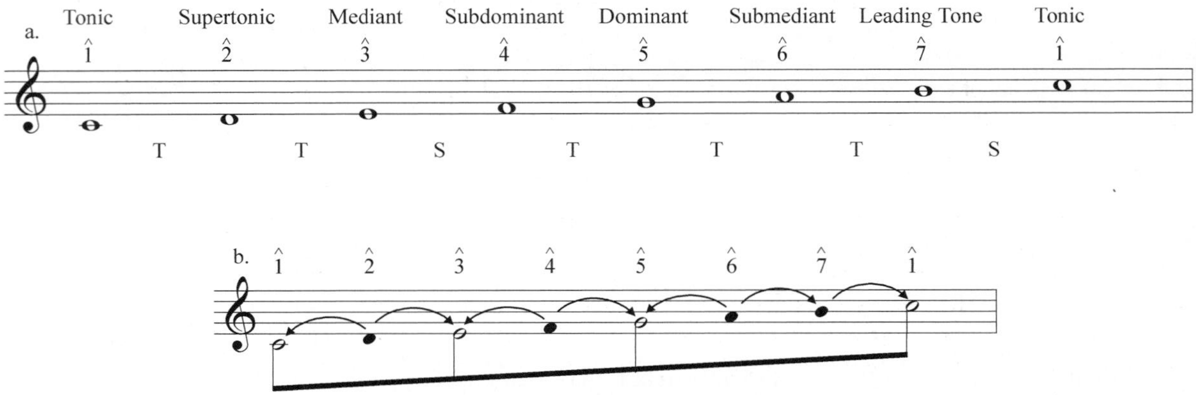

a *diatonic scale*. Example C.2a shows the diatonic **major scale** that begins on C, that is, which has C as the tonic. This is the C major (abbreviated CM) scale, which uses only the white keys of the keyboard (that is, it contains no accidentals). "The First Noël" is built on this scale, and as a matter of fact a passage of this song is based on the statement of the complete scale in ascending form (mm. 1–3). A composition based on this scale is said to be "in CM."

The pitch members of a scale, or its steps, are called **degrees.** In example C.2a we see that scale degrees are labeled in two ways. First, each degree is assigned a number with a little caret on it, such as $\hat{1}$, $\hat{2}$, and so forth. These symbols are read "scale degree 1," "scale degree 2," and so on, and they tell us the degree function of a specific pitch within a specific scale (that is, with respect to a specific tonic). Thus, D is $\hat{2}$ with respect to the tonic C, and F is $\hat{4}$. But D is also $\hat{4}$ with respect to the tonic A, and F is $\hat{6}$ with respect to A.

The other label for scale degrees is a **scale degree name.** We already know the names **tonic** ($\hat{1}$), **dominant** ($\hat{5}$), and **mediant** ($\hat{3}$). Now we add **supertonic** (the degree above the tonic, $\hat{2}$), **subdominant** ($\hat{4}$, the degree a 5th *below* the tonic, as opposed to the dominant, a 5th above the tonic), **submediant** ($\hat{6}$, a 3rd below the tonic, as opposed to the mediant, a 3rd above the tonic), and **leading tone** ($\hat{7}$, a half step below the tonic).

Melodic Tendencies of Scale Degrees

The **melodic tendencies of scale degrees** are an important component in the Western tonal system. Thus, although $\hat{1}$ is a stable degree and $\hat{5}$ and $\hat{3}$ are also relatively stable, the remaining degrees are all characterized by instability because of their melodic tendency to move to a different degree, in all cases to one of the adjacent, or neighbor, degrees. Thus, $\hat{2}$ tends to resolve down to $\hat{1}$ (or up to $\hat{3}$). Sing or play "Oh! Susanna," and verify what happens with each of the $\hat{2}$s in the tune. $\hat{4}$ tends to move up to $\hat{5}$ or down to $\hat{3}$. Can you think of any tune in which you can verify the motions from $\hat{4}$? $\hat{6}$ often functions as a melodic upper neighbor to $\hat{5}$, but also as a passing step in the motion $\hat{5}$–$\hat{6}$–$\hat{7}$–$\hat{1}$. How does $\hat{6}$ function in "Twinkle, Twinkle" and "Oh! Susanna"? And how does it function in "The First Noël"? Finally, $\hat{7}$ usually creates a strong pull toward $\hat{1}$, except when it is part of a descending scale from $\hat{1}$. Verify the role of all the $\hat{7}$s in "The First Noël," and then try hearing the motions from $\hat{7}$ in the opening phrase of both "Joy to the World" and "My Country 'Tis of Thee." The most common melodic tendencies for each of the degrees are represented in example C.2b. The stable pitches of the tonic triad are shown as white notes linked by a beam, the "active" degrees appear as black notes, and their melodic tendencies are shown by arrows.

An essential aspect of the major scale, which defines what we know as the **major mode,** is the major 3rd between the tonic and the mediant (C–E). Otherwise, all intervallic relationships between adjacent pitches shown in example C.2a are characteristic of the major mode. There are only two half steps in the diatonic major scale, marked S (for "semitone") in example C.2a, and they are always placed between $\hat{3}$–$\hat{4}$ and $\hat{7}$–$\hat{1}$, respectively. All other steps between degrees are whole steps, marked T (for "tone") in example C.2a.

The Minor Mode

Unlike the major mode, which features a single scale, the **minor mode** can be represented by several scale forms. The essential interval that defines the minor mode as opposed to the major mode is a lowered $\hat{3}$. The interval between the tonic and the minor mediant is thus a minor 3rd (C–E♭). There are, however, two other degrees that are also lowered in what we know as **the natural minor scale.** These are $\hat{6}$ and $\hat{7}$. The lowered 7th degree is called the **subtonic.** The natural minor scale on C, or the C minor scale (abbreviated Cm) is shown in example C.3a. The two half-step motions in this scale are found between $\hat{2}$–$\hat{3}$ and $\hat{5}$–♭$\hat{6}$ respectively.

In a harmonic context, that is, in chord progressions, $\hat{7}$ in minor is raised to become the leading tone. The minor scale with a lowered $\hat{6}$ and a raised $\hat{7}$ is called **harmonic minor scale,** and it is represented in example C.3b. Notice that the interval between $\hat{6}$ and raised $\hat{7}$ is a +2, which is usually avoided as a melodic interval.

NOTE

In general, we will refer to the diatonic $\hat{6}$ and $\hat{7}$ in minor (that is, lowered with respect to the major mode) simply as $\hat{6}$ and $\hat{7}$. If we need to be specific, however, and are referring to the lowered $\hat{6}$ or $\hat{7}$, we may use the terms "♭$\hat{6}$" and "♭$\hat{7}$" for clarity. Similarly, we will at times refer to "♯$\hat{6}$" or "♯$\hat{7}$" to refer to raised $\hat{6}$ or $\hat{7}$.

In a melodic context, a way of avoiding the +2 is to raise $\hat{6}$ when it ascends to $\hat{7}$. The resulting scale is called a **melodic minor scale,** and it features an ascending $\hat{5}$–♯$\hat{6}$–♯$\hat{7}$–$\hat{1}$ segment (example C.3c). Because in descending melodic passages $\hat{7}$ does

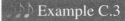

Example C.3

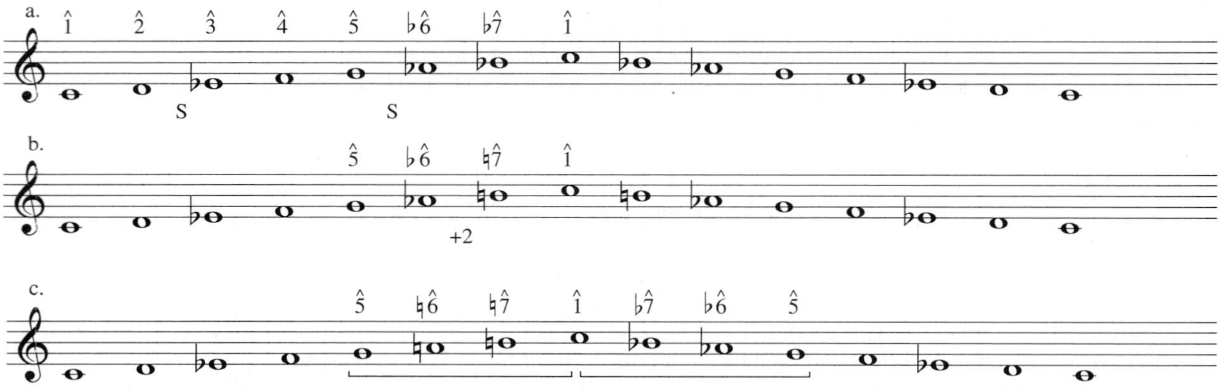

not function as the leading tone (it does not move up to $\hat{1}$), it does not need to be raised. Descending melodic segments from $\hat{1}$ are often $\hat{1}$–♭$\hat{7}$–♭$\hat{6}$–$\hat{5}$. The melodic minor scale, then, features raised $\hat{6}$ and $\hat{7}$ in its ascending form, and lowered $\hat{6}$ and $\hat{7}$ in its descending form.

A fun and useful exercise is to turn major tunes into minor. Try singing "Twinkle, Twinkle" and "Oh! Susanna" in minor. Try also with any other major-mode song you wish. Singing "The First Noël" in minor will provide you with some good chances to practice the melodic minor scale. What is the character of the minor mode, in contrast to the major mode? What does the minor mode do to the character of all these songs? Try, for instance, singing "Happy Birthday" in minor. Does it convey the type of mood you would expect in the circumstances in which that song is usually sung?

EXERCISE

To practice writing major and minor scales, refer to exercise 4 in worksheet C at the end of this chapter.

KEY SIGNATURES

Transposition

Compare examples C.4a and b with example C.la. In example C.4a, we have written the beginning measures of "The First Noël" one step higher than in example C.la. The tonic or tonal center is now D rather than C, and we are "in DM" rather than "in CM."

Example C.4

These are different keys. A **key** is a set of pitch relationships that establish a note as a tonal center. In our discussion of the major mode, we defined a set of scale degrees and intervallic relationships that we illustrated using the key of CM. That is, we applied these relationships to establish the note C as the tonic. In example C.4a we have transposed the tune one step up. This **transposition** has shifted the tonal center to D. In order to preserve the intervallic characteristics of the major scale, we need to add two sharps to the scale D–D (F♯ and C♯), This will allow us to establish the key of DM using the same scale degree and intervallic relationships that we previously applied to CM. In other words, we are transposing not only the tune, but also the key, from CM to DM. As a matter of fact, we can transpose the major scale to turn any of the twelve notes of the chromatic scale into a tonic. We can speak of twelve major keys, all of which have a different tonic, but all of which preserve exactly the same inner tonal relationships. In example C.4b the transposition is down a step, and the new scale requires two flats to preserve the intervals of the major scale. The new key is now B♭M.

The Major Key Signatures

Because the accidentals needed to define a key are an essential part of the key and its scale, we can write them at the beginning of the piece in the form of a **key signature.** Because there are twelve major keys, there will also be twelve major key signatures, without counting possible enharmonic spellings of the same key, such as D♭M and C♯ M. (Notice that, unlike meter signatures, key signatures are also notated along with clefs at the beginning of each staff.) You should learn all the key signatures by memory, and there are several ways to help you do so. In the first place, look at example C.5. This is the **circle of 5ths.** Pitches (or keys) are here organized by 5ths: if you move clockwise along the circle, you will see that keys move up by 5ths (C–G–D–A, etc.); counterclockwise motion will take you down by 5ths (C–F–B♭–E♭, etc.).

The outer circle in example C.5 shows the twelve major keys. Beginning with CM (no accidentals in the key signature), every step we move clockwise (up by 5ths) will add one sharp: GM (1♯)–DM (2♯)–AM (3♯), and so forth. Every step we move counterclockwise will add one flat: FM (1♭)–B♭M (2♭)–E♭M (3♭), and so on. Example C.6a shows

Example C.5

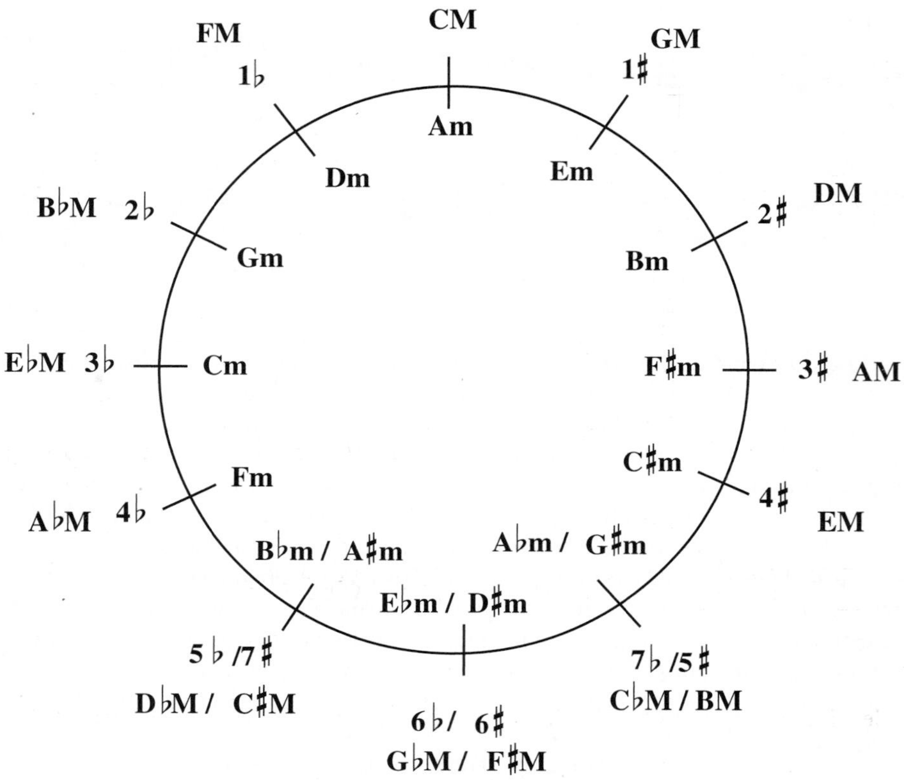

all the possible major key signatures. You will see a total of fifteen different key signatures, although there are only twelve major keys. What are the three keys that are duplicated enharmonically in this listing? Example C.6c shows the correct placement of sharps and flats in key signatures in C clefs.

Although the quickest way to identify key signatures is memory, another quick way to identify major key signatures is the following. First, you need to memorize the order of sharps and flats in key signatures.

- The **order of sharps** is: F–C–G–D–A–E–B (an ascending circle of 5ths).
- The **order of flats** is: B–E–A–D–G–C–F (a descending circle of 5ths).

After you have memorized these orderings, you can identify a key signature by the following rules:

- *Major keys with sharps in the signature:* The last sharp is the leading tone in our key. For instance, if the signature has four sharps (F♯–C♯–G♯–D♯), then D♯ is the

Example C.6

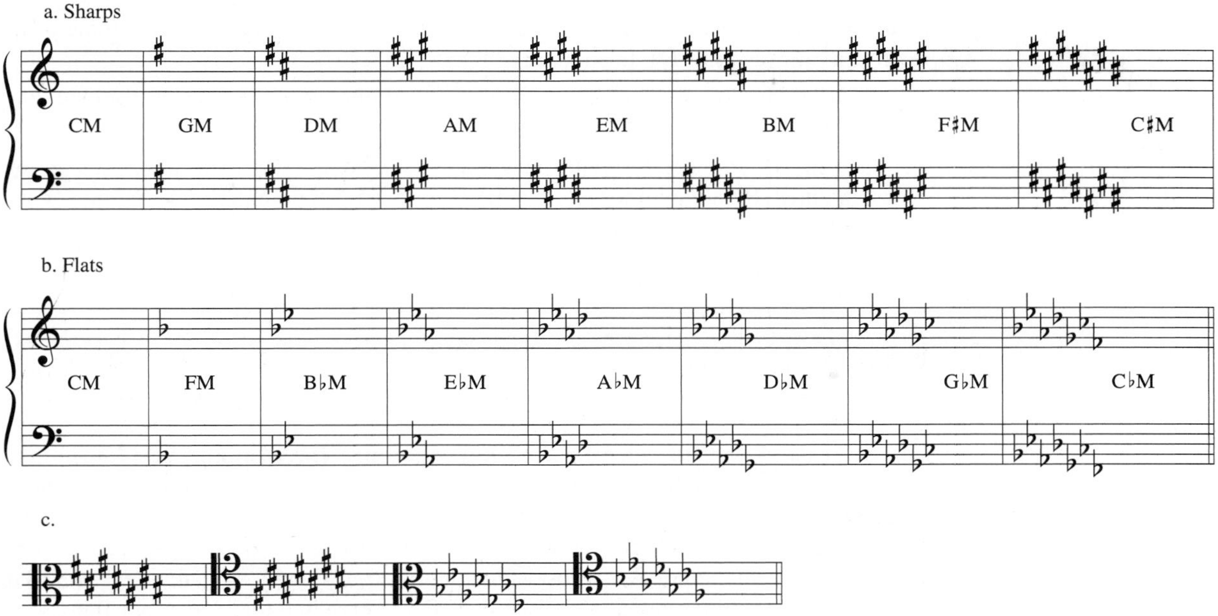

leading tone in our key. The key is then EM. What is the key if the signature has five sharps?

- *Major keys with flats in the signature:* The next to last flat is the actual key. For instance, if the signature has four flats (B♭–E♭–A♭–D♭), then the next to last flat, A♭, provides the name of the key, A♭M. What is the key if the signature has six flats?

EXERCISE

To practice writing and identifying major key signatures, refer to exercises 2.1 and 3.1 in worksheet C at the end of this chapter.

The Minor Key Signatures; Parallel and Relative Keys

In example C.3 the key of Cm is used to illustrate the minor mode. This permits us to see the parallelism between CM (example C.2) and Cm, the major and minor keys with the same tonic. These pairs of keys, which share a tonic, are indeed called **parallel keys.** We thus say, for instance, that the parallel minor of DM is Dm. Another possibility in example C.3 would have been to use the minor key with no accidentals in the key signature, Am, which is also closely related to CM. In their diatonic forms (that is, considering the natural minor scale), both use the same set of pitches, the white keys of the piano. Pairs of major-minor keys that use the same set of pitches in their scales, or, in other words, whose key signatures are identical, are called **relative keys.** We thus say that Bm is the relative minor of DM (they both feature two sharps in their key signatures). In all cases, the tonic of a relative minor is a minor 3rd below the tonic of its relative major (as in B–D). In summary,

1. *Parallel M/m keys:* Same tonic, different set of pitches in their scales, for example, CM–Cm.
2. *Relative M/m keys:* Different tonic, same set of pitches in their scales, same key signatures. Relative minor tonic: a m3 below corresponding relative major, for example, CM–Am.

EXERCISE

To practice determining relative major and minor keys, refer to exercise 1 in worksheet C at the end of this chapter.

The easiest way to determine the **key signature for a minor key** (other than memory) is to refer the key to its relative major, that is, to think of the major key whose tonic is a m3 above our minor key. For instance, the key signature for F♯m will be the same as the key signature for the major key a m3 above, AM, or three sharps. Conversely, what is the minor key whose signature has four flats? The major key with four flats is A♭M. The minor key a m3 below A♭ is Fm, which will then have four flats.

The inner circle of keys in example C.5 shows the circle of 5ths for minor keys. You can also see, in the correspondence between the outer and inner circles, all the relative M/m relationships among all 24 keys (12 major and 12 minor, without counting enharmonic spellings of keys).

EXERCISE

To practice writing and identifying minor key signatures, refer to exercises 2.2 and 3.2 in worksheet C at the end of this chapter.

OTHER MODES AND SCALES

Although the major or minor scales are the ones most often found in common practice Western music, other scales are at times also used. Among these, the medieval and Renaissance Church modes (often used in jazz) are especially important.

The Church Modes

In essence, the **medieval Church modal system** was based on four basic modes, to which two more were added in the Renaissance. The four original modes are **Dorian, Phrygian, Lydian,** and **Mixolydian.** The two added modes are **Aeolian** and **Ionian.**

Example C.7

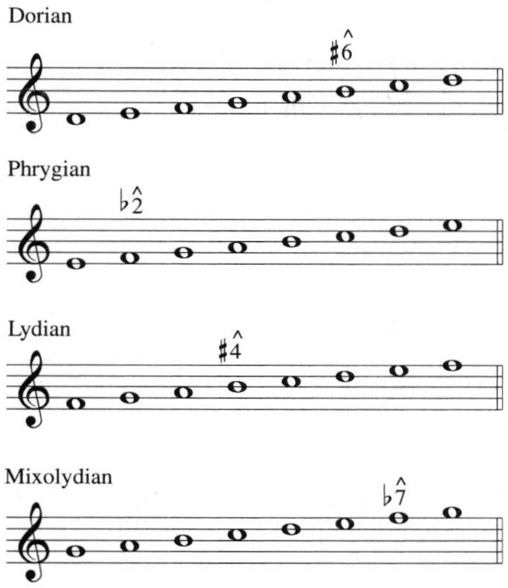

We can first think of these modes as using different white-key scales. Example C.7 shows the white key (no key signature) scale for each of the modes. Moreover, we can think of the modes in relation to the familiar major and natural minor scales, and remember which scale degree is different in each of the modes:

1. *Dorian (scale D–D):* a natural minor scale with a raised $\hat{6}$ (♯$\hat{6}$, or B♮).
2. *Phrygian (E–E):* a natural minor scale with a lowered $\hat{2}$ (♭$\hat{2}$, or F♮).
3. *Lydian (F–F):* a major scale with a raised $\hat{4}$ (♯$\hat{4}$, or B♮).
4. *Mixolydian (G–G):* a major scale with a lowered $\hat{7}$ (♭$\hat{7}$, or F♮).
5. *Aeolian (A–A)* is like natural minor (not included in example C.7).
6. *Ionian (C–C)* is like major (not included in example C.7).

To these modes we can add the modern mode **Locrian,** made up of the octave B–B (a minor scale with a lowered $\hat{2}$ and a lowered $\hat{5}$).

Identifying the Modes

The melody in example C.8a is modal. To identify the mode, we will first determine the tonic for the melody, in this case F. Then we will examine the scale used in the melody, which we will build on our tonic. The scale for this example is F–G–A–B–C, not covering a full octave. Then we'll compare this scale to the corresponding major or minor scales. Because of the A♮, this is a major scale on F. The B♮, or ♯$\hat{4}$, on the other hand, identifies this mode as Lydian.

Example C.8

a.

Adam de la Hale

b.

Lassus

The same procedure can be followed to identify transposed modes. Sing the phrase in example C.8b. You will hear that the tonic is G and that the scale is a G minor scale (because of the B♭) with an E♮, or $\sharp\hat{6}$. The mode is thus Dorian transposed to G.

Spelling Modal Scales

We can use this same system to spell modal scales beginning on any pitch. The Phrygian scale on D, for instance, will be the same as a D natural-minor scale with a $\flat\hat{2}$. D natural minor has a B♭ in the signature, to which we have to add an E♭ for $\hat{2}$. The scale will then be D–E♭–F–G–A–B♭–C–D, as shown in example C.9a. Similarly, Mixolydian on D will be the same as D major with a $\flat\hat{7}$. The key signature for DM has two sharps. But because we need $\flat\hat{7}$, we will have to lower C♯ to C♮. The scale is then D–E–F♯–G–A–B–C–D, as in example C.9b.

EXERCISES

To practice writing modal scales, refer to exercise 5 in worksheet C at the end of this chapter.

Example C.9

a. D-Phrygian b. D-Mixolydian

Example C.10

a.

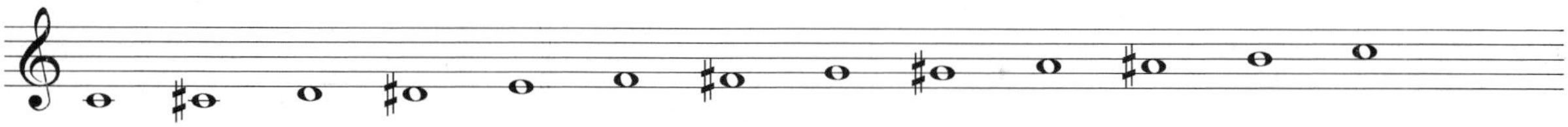

b.

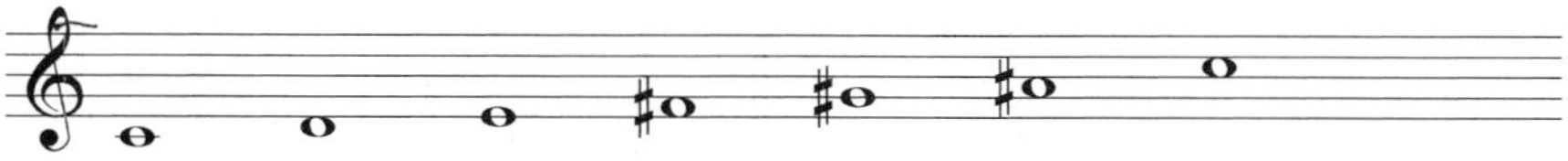

c.

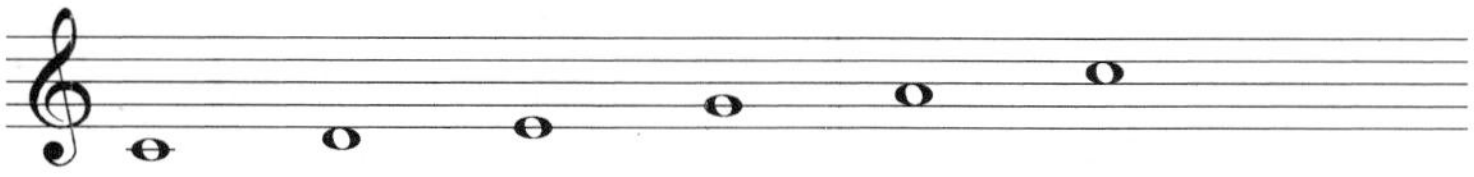

Other Scales

The number of different scales one could build with different combinations of twelve pitches is obviously enormous. Some tonal systems, like the Indian *rāga* system, use a truly astounding wealth of scales. South Indian, or Karnatic, music, for instance, is based on 72 reference scales (*mēlakartā rāgas*), from each of which one can further generate various other derived scales. The following three scales are commonly used in the Western musical tradition:

1. The **chromatic scale** contains all twelve pitches, and all motion is by half steps (example C.10a).
2. The **whole-tone scale** is made up only of whole tones and contains only six different pitches (example C.10b).
3. A **pentatonic scale** consists of only five different pitches. There are numerous types of pentatonic scales. Example C.10c shows the most usual type found in Western music. It is called "anhemitonic" because it lacks semitones.

EXERCISE

To practice identifying tonal characteristics and scale types for melodies from a variety of repertoires, refer to exercise 6 in worksheet C at the end of this chapter.

ASSIGNMENT

For an assignment based on the materials learned in this chapter, refer to chapter C in the workbook.

Terms for Review

- Tonal center
- Tonic
- Range
- Scale
- Triad
- Root, third, fifth
- Tonic triad
- Tonal system
- Tonality
- Major-minor tonality
- Functional tonality
- Major scale
- Scale degrees
- Scale degree names, tonic, supertonic, mediant, subdominant, dominant, submediant, leading tone
- Melodic tendencies of scale degrees
- Major mode
- Minor mode
- Natural minor scale
- Subtonic
- Harmonic minor scale
- Melodic minor scale
- Key
- Transposition
- Key signature
- Major key signatures
- Circle of 5ths
- Order of sharps and flats
- Parallel M/m keys
- Relative M/m keys
- Minor key signatures
- Medieval Church modes: Dorian, Phrygian, Lydian, Mixolydian, Aeolian, Ionian
- Locrian
- Chromatic scale
- Whole-tone scale
- Pentatonic scale (anhemitonic)

Worksheet C

EXERCISE 1

1. Write the relative minor for the following major keys:

   E♭M: Cm A♭M: Fm AM: F# EM: F♯M:

   DM: Bbm FM: Dm GM: Em BM: D♭M:

2. Write the relative major for the following minor keys:

   Gm: Dm: Bm: C♯m: Em:

   Fm: E♭m: Cm: B♭m: F♯m:

EXERCISE 2

1. Identify the *major* key signatures in exercise 2a.
2. Identify the *minor* key signatures in exercise 2b.

a.

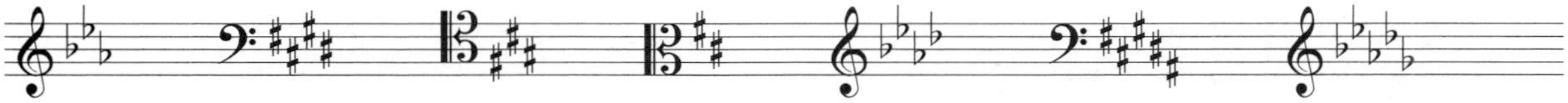

b.

EXERCISE 3

1. Write the *major* key signatures in exercise 3a. Make sure to write sharps and flats in the correct order and to place them in the correct location on the staff.
2. Write the *minor* key signatures in exercise 3b.

a.

FM DM GM EM B♭M G♭M

b.

F♯m B♭m Em Gm Dm Fm

EXERCISE 4 Write the following *major and minor* scales without using key signatures (use accidentals before each note as needed). The tonic for each scale is given.

Major

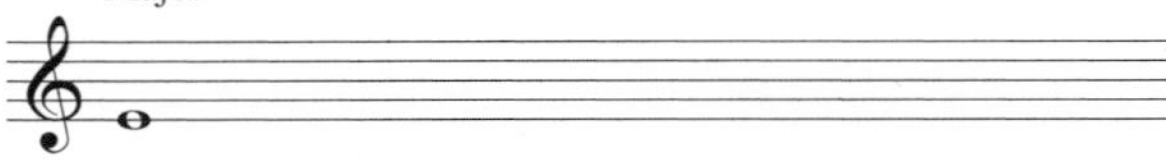

Melodic minor (ascending and descending)

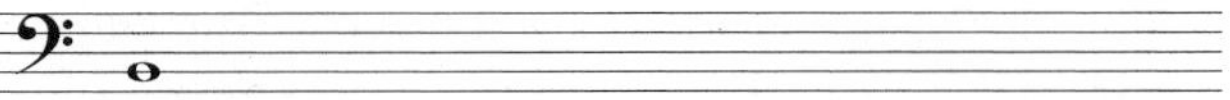

Harmonic minor

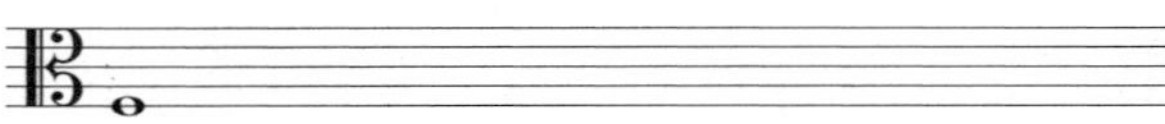

Natural minor

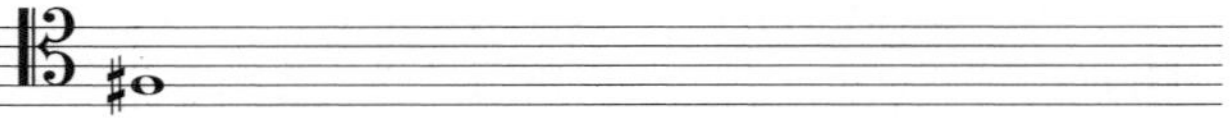

EXERCISE 5 Write the following transposed modal scales without using signatures (write accidentals before each note as needed).

Aeolian

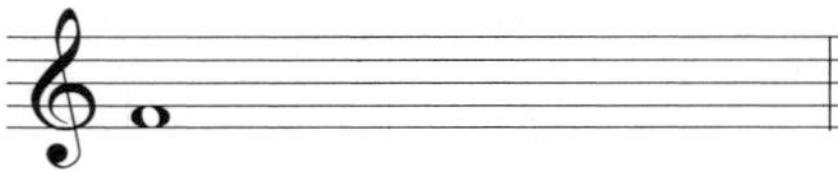

Dorian

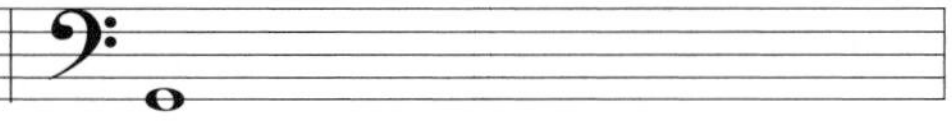

Mixolydian

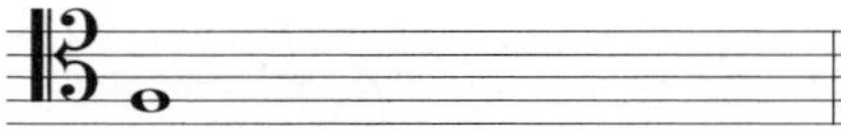

Lydian

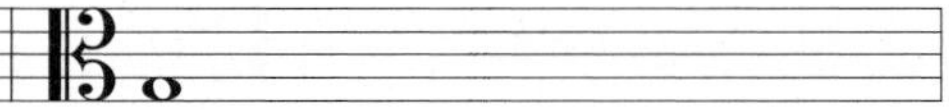

Phrygian

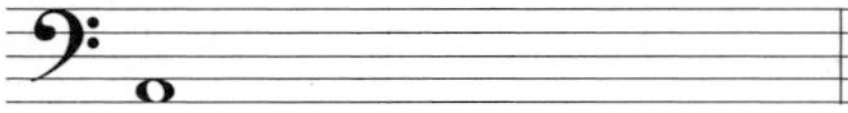

Ionian

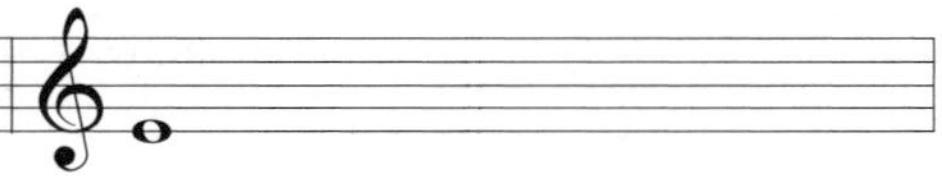

EXERCISE 6 Sing or play each of the following melodies. Then, analyze the melody to determine the following items: tonic pitch (or tonal center), tonic triad, range, mode or key, and scale. Write each of the items in the spaces provided under each melody. The answers for the first melody are provided as an example. This same process is also illustrated in example C.1.

For mode or key, the following options are possible: any major or minor key, any of the Church modes (Dorian, Phrygian, etc.), pentatonic, or whole tone. Because some of these melodies are not really based on the principles of major-minor tonality as we have presented them in this chapter, some of the items do not apply to them. You will find these items marked with the sign N/A.

a. Scandinavia

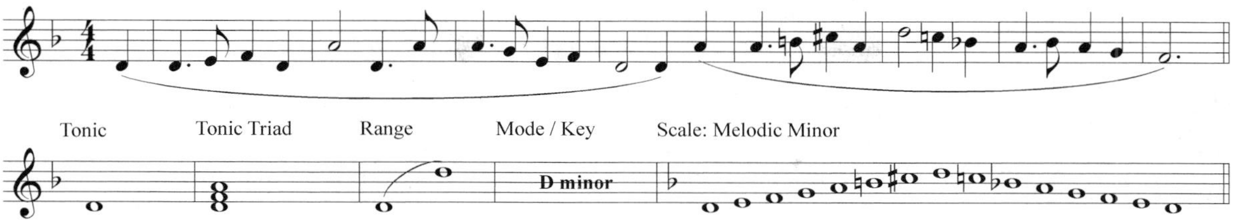

b. France

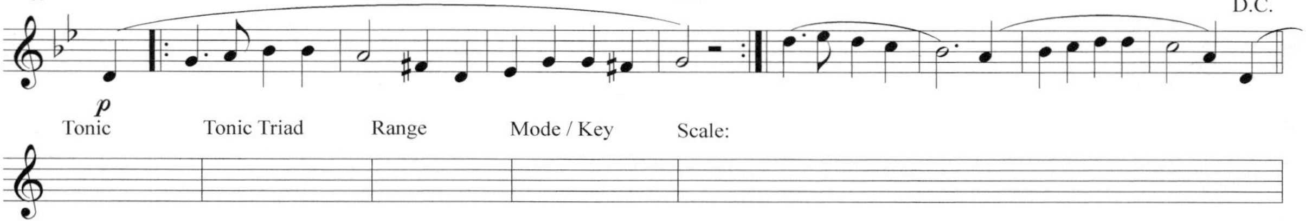

c. Mozart

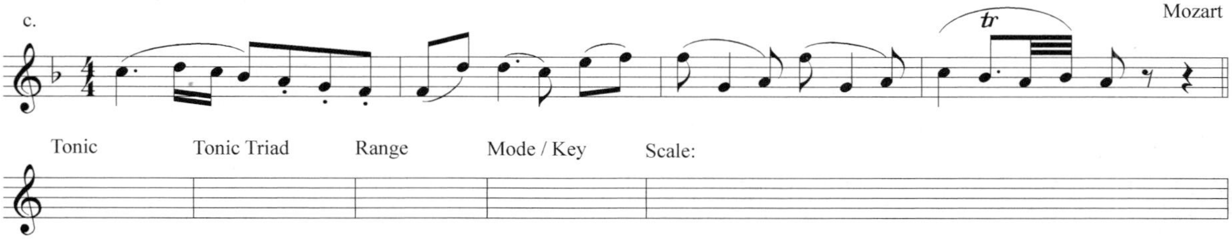

d. Plainchant

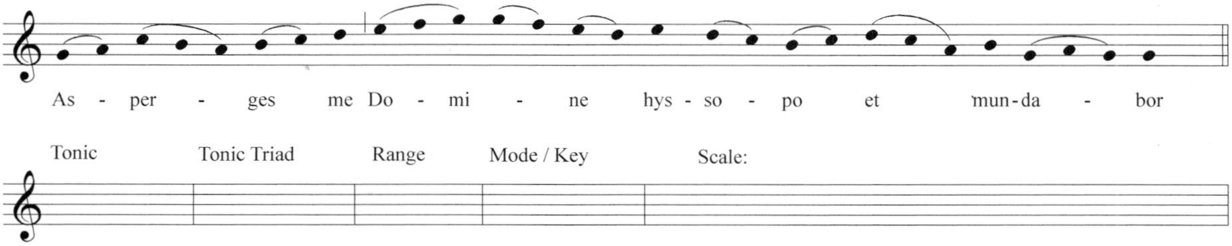

e. Bartók

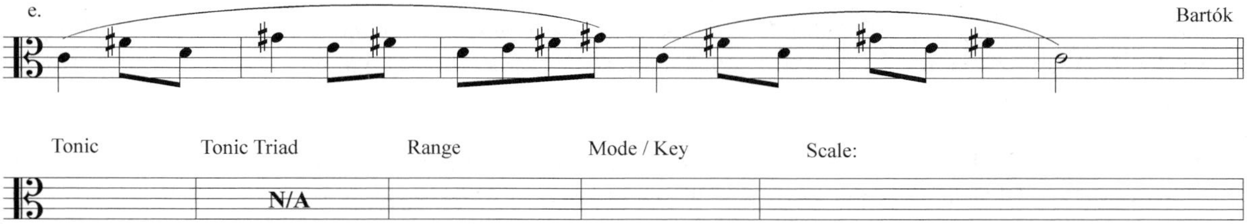

f.

Mussorgsky

Tonic | Tonic Triad | Range | Mode / Key | Scale:

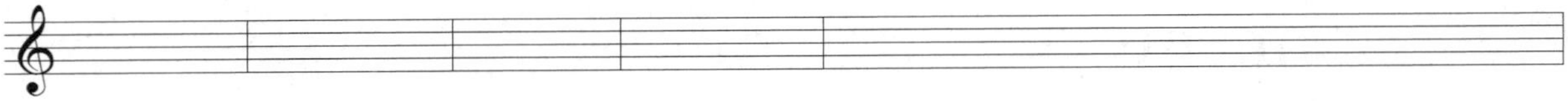

g.

Scotland

Tonic | Tonic Triad | Range | Mode / Key | Scale:

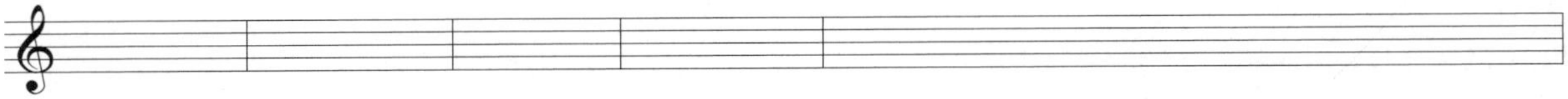

h.

Hassler

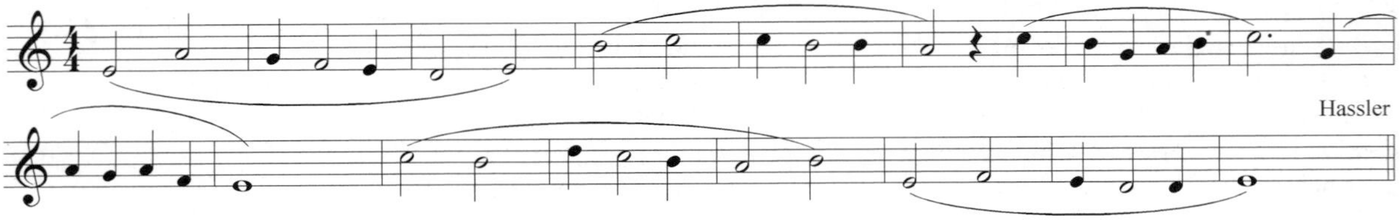

Tonic | Tonic Triad | Range | Mode / Key | Scale:

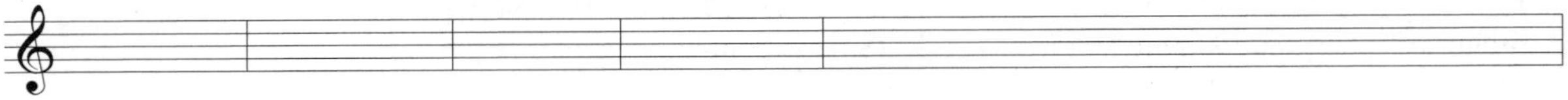

Chapter D

The Rudiments of Harmony I: Triads and Seventh Chords

When we listen to music, we hear two dimensions of sound. On the one hand, music moves forward in time. This is the horizontal dimension. On the other hand, we hear simultaneous sounds, musical "moments" in which several pitches sound at the same time. This is the vertical dimension. Horizontally, music is made up of melodies or lines; vertically, of chords or harmonies. Melodies and harmonies are totally interdependent. Harmonies result from several horizontal lines sounding together. Example D.1a demonstrates how four independent melodic lines create vertical harmonies. Melodies, in turn, are an elaborate linear or horizontal presentation of their underlying harmonies, as you can see in example D.1b. Notice that the melody in the upper staff is constructed mostly with the same pitches that constitute the harmonic accompaniment in the lower staff, along with some other ornamental pitches. The brackets in mm. 24–25, for instance, indicate the melodic and harmonic use of the pitches F–A–C, and the brackets in mm. 27–28 mark a similar use of the pitches C–E–G–B♭.

As a preparation for the study of tonal harmony (which we will begin in chapter 1), in this chapter we will focus on its vertical building blocks (triads and seventh chords), and in chapter E we will learn to label chords in a tonal context.

CHORDS

A group of three or more pitches sounded simultaneously is known as a **chord.** Example D.2a includes several chords in which all the pitches sound literally at the same time (**block chords**). The pitches in a chord, however, may also be sounded in close succession as in examples D.2b, c, and d. In this case we speak of **broken** or **arpeggiated chords.** The tonal system that we will study in this book is based almost exclusively on **tertian chords** (chords built of 3rds), and especially on triads and seventh chords.

Example D.1a J. S. Bach, Chorale 21, "Herzlich thut mich verlangen," mm. 1–4

Example D.1b Wolfgang Amadeus Mozart, Piano Concerto in CM, K. 467, II, mm. 23–29

In chapter A we discussed consonant and dissonant intervals. We can also speak of **consonant and dissonant chords.** A chord is consonant if each interval formed by any two of its pitches is consonant. The first chord in example D.2a is consonant because, taking any two of its pitches, the possible intervals are a M3, a m3, and a P5. Chords 2 and 3, on the other hand, contain at least one dissonance each; hence, they are both dissonant. Identify all the possible dissonant intervals in these chords.

Example D.2

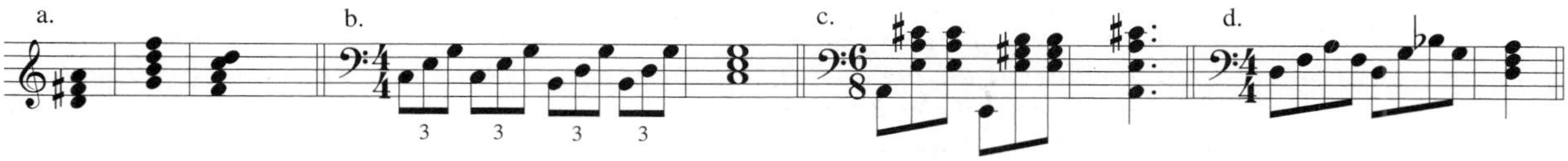

TRIADS

A **triad** is a chord made up of three pitches, which we call the **root** (the lowest pitch), the **third** (a M3 or m3 above the root), and the **fifth** (a P5, °5, or +5 above the root). The root is also called the **fundamental.** To differentiate triad members from intervals, in this book triad members will be fully spelled out (as in third and fifth), whereas intervals will be abbreviated (as in 3rd and 5th). Depending on the quality of the intervals involved, there may be four **triad types,** as illustrated by example D.3.

1. In a **major** triad (**M**) the third is a M3 above the root, whereas the fifth is a P5 above the root. If you think of the triad as a 5th divided into two 3rds, a major triad consists of a M3 at the bottom and a m3 at the top.
2. In a **minor** triad (**m**) the third is a m3 above the root, and the fifth is a P5 above the root. A minor triad consists of a m3 at the bottom and a M3 at the top.
3. In a **diminished** triad (°) the third is a m3 above the root, and the fifth is a °5 above the root. A diminished triad consists of two minor 3rds.
4. In an **augmented** triad ($^+$) the third is a M3 above the root, whereas the fifth is an +5 above the root. An augmented triad ($^+$) consists of two major 3rds.

All the triads in example D.3 are in *root position,* which means that the root is the lowest pitch (that is, the root is in the bass). A *triad is named after its root.* The major triad built on G (G–B–D), for instance, is the G major (GM) triad, and the minor triad built on D is the D minor (Dm) triad. We can similarly speak of the B diminished triad (B°) or the C augmented (C$^+$) triad.

Major and minor triads in root position are consonant and form the basic harmonic material in Western music since the Renaissance. Both diminished and augmented triads in root position, on the other hand, are dissonant because of the dissonant fifth.

Example D.3

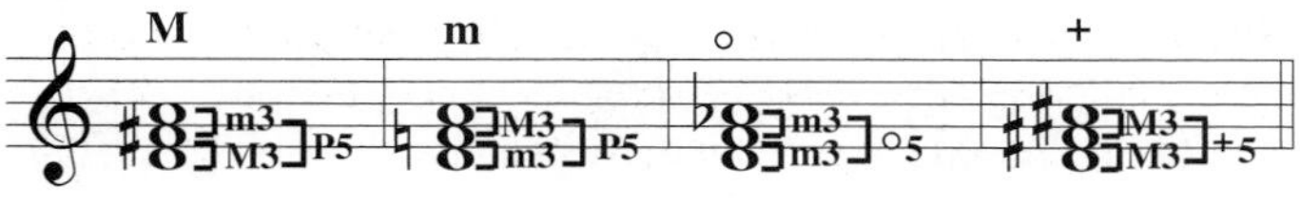

Play each of these triad types, and hear the stable character of M and m triads (for instance, you can end a piece on one of these triads) as opposed to the unstable character of ° and ⁺ triads.

EXERCISE

To practice identifying and writing triads in root position, refer to exercises 1 and 2 in worksheet D at the end of this chapter.

Diatonic Triads in the Major and Minor Keys

Chords and triads are diatonic if they are built using only notes that belong to a given diatonic scale. Triads can be built on each degree of a major or minor scale. The triads most frequently used in diatonic harmony, as well as their quality, are indicated in example D.4. Example D.4a shows the triads on each degree of the major scale. In chapter C we learned the scale degree names (tonic, supertonic, mediant, etc.). The same terms are used to refer to the triads built on each of these degrees. Thus, the triad built on $\hat{1}$ is the tonic triad, the triad built on $\hat{2}$ is the supertonic triad, and so forth, as indicated in example D.4a.

The minor scale normally used in harmony the harmonic minor scale (that is, the scale with $\flat\hat{6}$ and $\flat\hat{7}$). The chords in example D.4b, the most usual in minor-mode harmony, result from this scale (with the only exception of the chord on $\hat{3}$, which is most often major, and thus does not result from the harmonic minor scale because it includes a $\flat\hat{7}$). The occasional use of melodic or natural scales, however, may also produce other triads in the minor mode, as we will see in later chapters.

EXERCISE

To practice identifying the quality of triads built on each of the scale degrees, refer to exercise 3 in worksheet D at the end of this chapter.

Example D.4

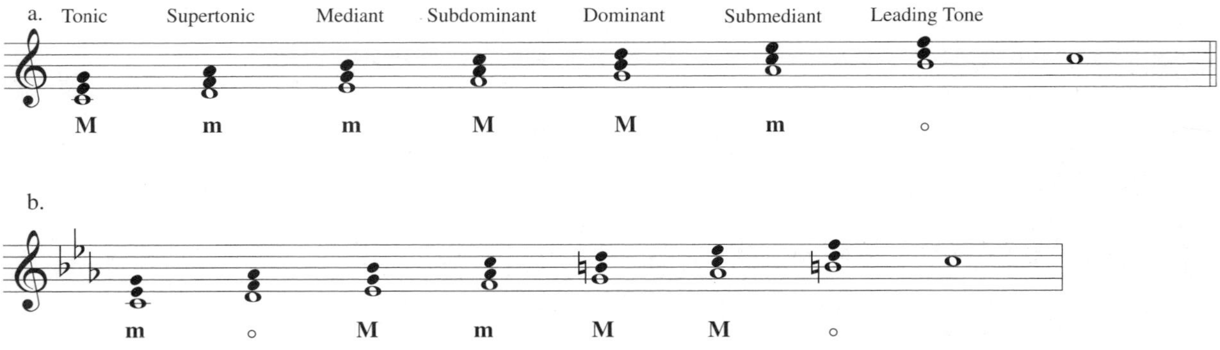

Example D.5

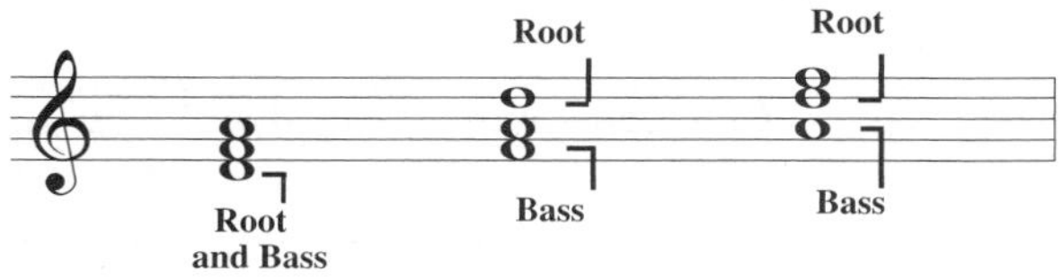

Bass and Root

Notice how the first two chords in example D.2b are different. In the first chord, C–E–G, the root (C) is in the bass. The **bass** is the lowest pitch in a sonority or texture, and it must not be confused with the **root** of a chord (the generating pitch on which a tertian chord is built). *The bass is not necessarily the root of a chord.* The second chord in example D.2b, ordered in 3rds, would be G–B–D. However, in example D.2b the root is not in the bass. Rather, the third (B) is in the bass. The diagram in example D.5 will help clarify the difference between root and bass: whereas the root of all three chords in this example is the same (the chord is always D–F–A, with D as its root), the bass in each case changes (D in the first chord, F in the second, and A in the third).

Chord Position: The Inversion of Triads

The **position** of a chord is determined by the chord member that is in the bass. The three positions of a triad are illustrated in example D.6a. Triad members in this example are indicated by the labels R (root), 3 (third), and 5 (fifth). Notice that what matters here is what triad member is in the bass. The pitches above the bass can appear in any order or register, regardless of the triad position:

1. A triad with the root in the bass is said to be in **root position.**
2. In the second triad we have moved the root up an octave, and the third is now in the bass. A triad with the third in the bass is in **first inversion.**
3. Finally, in the third chord in example D.6a we have also moved the third of the triad up an octave, and the fifth is now in the bass. This triad is in **second inversion.**

Example D.6

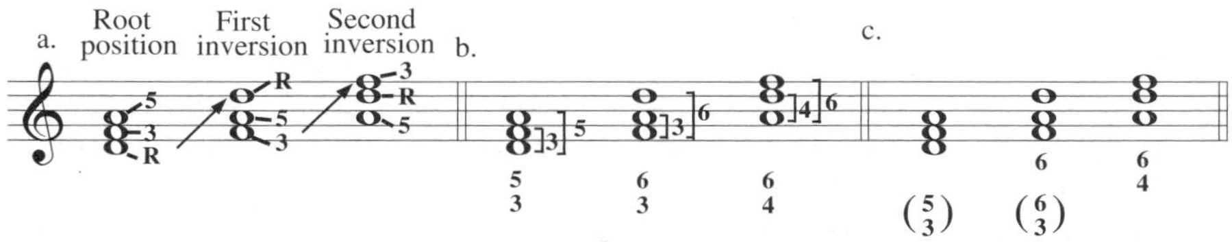

The following table summarizes all triad positions.

Triad Positions	Root is in the bass: triad in *root position*
	Third in the bass: triad in *first inversion*
	Fifth in the bass: triad in *second inversion*

The figures under the chords in example D.6b represent *intervals above the bass.* We can use this type of figure (which we call **figured-basss symbols**) to analyze or refer to chords and chordal positions (here again, pitches above the bass can be realized in any order or register).

1. A triad in $^5_3$ position is a root-position triad because the intervals above the bass are a 3rd and a 5th.
2. A $^6_3$ indicates a 3rd and a 6th above the bass, or a first-inversion triad.
3. A $^6_4$, a 4th and a 6th above the bass, represents a second-inversion triad.

In practice, some of these figures are usually abbreviated. Thus, no figures under a triad mean that the triad is in root position, and a 6 indicates a triad in first inversion. The figures under the chords in example D.6c represent both the symbols most frequently used in practice (without parentheses) and complete figured bass symbols (in parentheses).

NOTE

We have seen that major and minor triads in root position are consonant. Both types of triads in first inversion are also consonant. In second inversion, on the other hand, M and m triads feature a P4 that involves the bass. Whereas harmonic P4s in upper voices are consonant, P4s involving the bass are sometimes dissonant. *(In chapter F, for instance, we will learn that all P4s in two-voice counterpoint are considered dissonant.)* $^6_4$ chords often result from melodic motion, rather than from triadic inversion, and they may be consonant or dissonant depending on their context. *We will study the melodic processes that shape* $^6_4$ *chords, as well as their treatment as dissonant chords, in chapter 7.*

EXERCISE

To practice writing and identifying triads in first and second inversions, refer to exercises 4 to 6 in worksheet D at the end of this chapter.

SEVENTH CHORDS

A seventh chord is formed by adding one more 3rd on top of a triad. A seventh chord thus has four pitches: the root, the third, the fifth, and the seventh. The types of seventh chord are determined by the quality of the triad formed by the root, third, and fifth, and by the type of seventh. For instance, if the triad is major and the seventh is minor, we call the chord a "major-minor seventh chord," or Mm_7. A minor triad with a minor

Example D.7

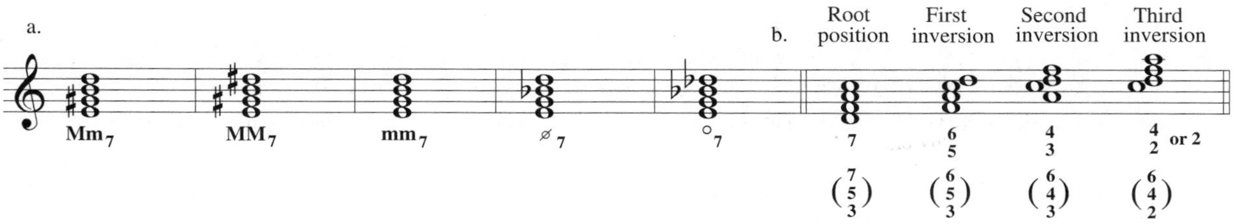

seventh is a "minor-minor seventh chord" (mm_7,), and so on. The most frequent **types of seventh chords** used in tonal harmony (and shown in example D.7a) are as follows:

1. **Major-minor** (Mm_7): major triad–minor 7th
2. **Major-major** (MM_7): major triad–major 7th
3. **Minor-minor** (mm_7): minor triad–minor 7th
4. **Half diminished** ($^{\varnothing}{}_7$): diminished triad–minor 7th
5. **Fully diminished** ($^{\circ}{}_7$): diminished triad–diminished 7th

Because seventh chords are made up of four pitches, they allow for three inversions. The four possible positions of a seventh chord are shown in example D.7b, with indication of both the complete figures for each (in parentheses), and the abbreviated figures more commonly used to indicate seventh chords in root position or inversion. The following table summarizes all **seventh chord positions** and their corresponding **figured-bass symbols.**

Seventh-Chord Positions Root in the bass: seventh chord in *root position* ($_7$)
Third in the bass: seventh chord in *first inversion* ($^6_5$)
Fifth in the bass: seventh chord in *second inversion* ($^4_3$)
Seventh in the bass: seventh chord in *third inversion* ($^4_2$)

Because in all cases the 7th is a dissonant interval (and so is its inversion, the 2nd), seventh chords are dissonant. Moreover, *the seventh of the chord usually results from linear (melodic) motion.* In chapters 8 and 15 we will study seventh chords in a harmonic context, and we will discuss both their linear nature and their role as dissonant sonorities.

Diatonic Seventh Chords in the Major and Minor Keys

Example D.8 shows the **diatonic seventh chords** that result on each of the scale degrees of major and minor scales. The seventh chords on the minor scale shown in this example are the most commonly used in minor keys, and, as in the case of triads, result from the harmonic minor scale, with the only exception of the seventh chord on $\hat{3}$. Scale degree $\hat{7}$ in this chord is not raised to become the leading tone.

Example D.8

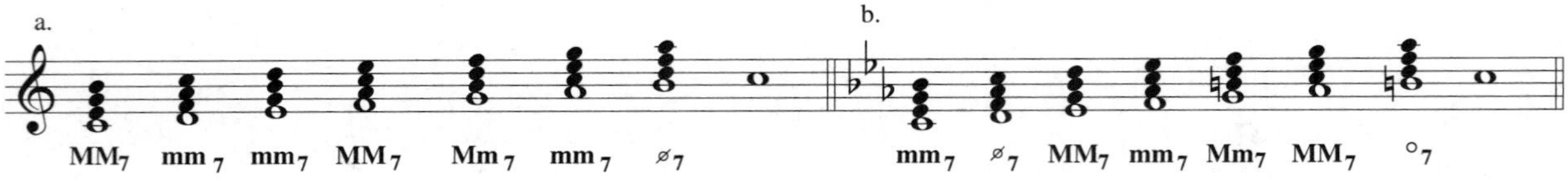

EXERCISES

To practice writing and identifying seventh chords in root position and inversions, refer to exercises 7 and 8 in worksheet D at the end of this chapter.

To practice identifying both triads and seventh chords in all positions, refer to exercises 9 and 10.

ASSIGNMENT

For an assignment based on the materials learned in this chapter, refer to chapter D in the workbook.

Terms for Review

- Chord
- Block chord
- Broken chord
- Arpeggiated chord
- Tertian chords
- Consonant and dissonant chords
- Triad
- Root, third, fifth, fundamental
- Triad types: M, m, °, +
- Diatonic triads on each scale degree
- Bass and root
- Chord position
- Root position
- First inversion
- Second inversion
- Figured-bass symbols for triad positions
- Seventh chord
- Types: Mm, MM, mm, ø, °
- Figured-bass symbols for seventh-chord positions
- Diatonic seventh chords on each scale degree

Worksheet D

EXERCISE 1 Identify and label the following triads by root and type (M, m, °, ⁺), and label each triad as shown in the example.

EXERCISE 2 Write and play at the piano the indicated triads in root position. A triad member (root, third, or fifth) is given. Identify the root for each triad, and notate it under the triad type, as indicated in the given examples.

Procedure: If the root is given, first write the third (a M3 or m3 depending on the triad type) and then the fifth (a P5, °5, or +5 depending on the triad type). If the third is given, first write the root (a M3 or m3 below the third depending on the triad type) and then the 5th above the root. If the fifth is given, first write the root (a P5, °5, or +5 below the fifth) and then the third.

Root given

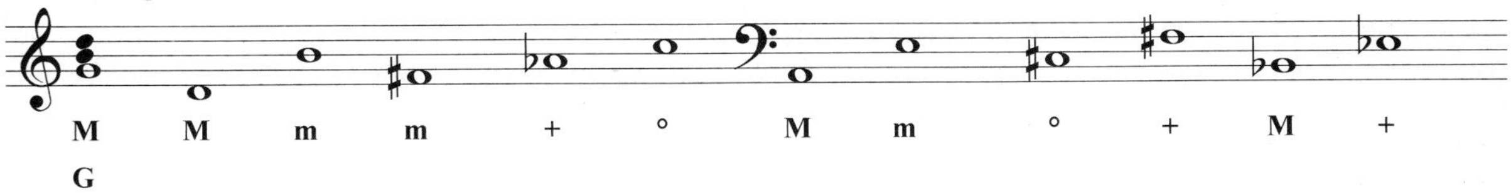

Third given

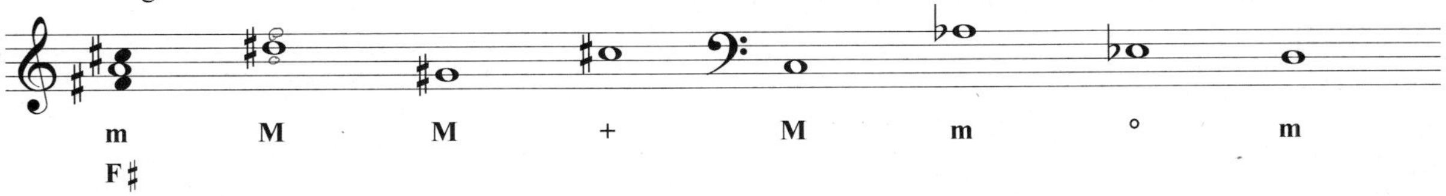

Fifth given

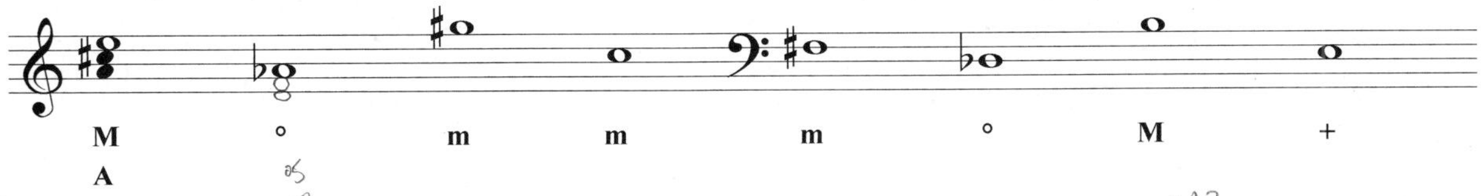

EXERCISE 3 In a major key, the diatonic triad on scale degree

$\hat{2}$ is: M / m / ° / + (*circle one*)

$\hat{7}$ is: M / m / ° / +

$\hat{3}$ is: M / m / ° / +

$\hat{1}$ is: M / m / ° / +

$\hat{6}$ is: M / m / ° / +

$\hat{5}$ is: M / m / ° / +

$\hat{4}$ is: M / m / ° / +

In a minor key, the following are the most usual diatonic triads, which result from the harmonic-minor scale (with the only exception of the chord on $\hat{3}$, which includes $\flat\hat{7}$):

The triad on

$\hat{2}$ is: M / m / ° / +

$\hat{7}$ is: M / m / ° / +

$\hat{3}$ is: M / m / ° / +

$\hat{1}$ is: M / m / ° / +

$\hat{6}$ is: M / m / ° / +

$\hat{5}$ is: M / m / ° / +

$\hat{4}$ is: M / m / ° / +

EXERCISE 4 Write and play the following M, m, or ° triads in *first inversion* on the given bass (the third of the chord). Identify the root for each triad, and notate it under the triad type, as indicated in the given example.

> **Procedure:** First determine the root of the triad (a M3 or m3 below the third depending on the triad type). Then, determine the fifth (a P5 or °5 above the root depending on the triad type). Write both pitches *above* the given bass.

EXERCISE 5 Write and play the following M or m triads in *second inversion* on the given bass (the fifth of the chord). Identify the root for each triad, and notate it under the triad type, as indicated in the given example.

Procedure: First determine the root of the triad (a P5 below the fifth in both M and m triads), and then the third. Write both pitches *above* the given bass.

EXERCISE 6 The following triads are in first or second inversion. Identify the root, the type, and the inversion for each of them, and label each triad as shown in the example. Your labels should be of the following type: Dm_6, GM^6_4, $\mathrm{E}^{\circ}{}_6$, $\mathrm{F}^{+6}_{\ 4}$, etc.

Procedure: First determine the triad position: Are the intervals above the bass a 6th and a 3rd (first inversion) or a 6th and a 4th (second inversion)? Then determine the root. In $^6_3$ position, the root is the 6th. In $^6_4$ position, the root is the 4th. Once you have the root, you can determine the triad type by imagining mentally the three pitches organized by 3rds above the root and checking the quality of the third and the fifth.

EXERCISE 7 Identify and label these seventh chords by type (Mm, MM, mm, ⌀, °).

EXERCISE 8 Write and play the indicated seventh chords in root position. The root is given.

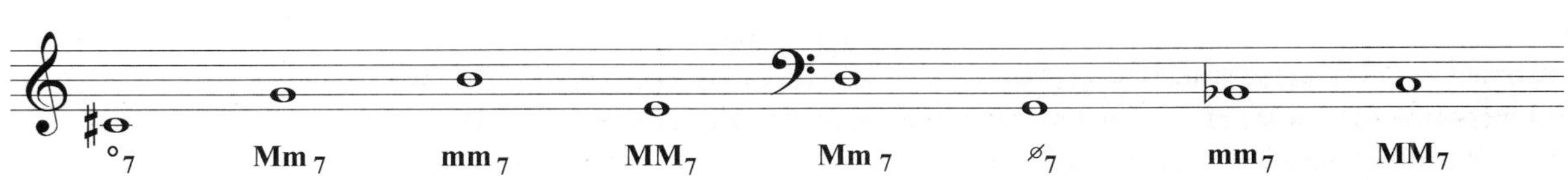

EXERCISE 9 Identify the following chord types and inversions. Notice that both triads and seventh chords are included in this exercise. Label each chord with the usual chord-type symbols and with figures to indicate inversion, and also write down its root (e.g., M^{6}_{4}/A, Mm^{4}_{3}/G, mm^{6}_{5}/D, m_{6}/F, etc.).

Procedure to identify a chord: The key to recognizing a chord is to organize its members in thirds. If the chord is in root position, its structure by thirds is likely to be evident (although an arrangement such as, from the bottom up, C–G–E, still requires some reorganization to become C–E–G, evidently organized by thirds). If the chord is in inversion, find the arrangement of pitches that reveals the chord's structure by thirds, determine the pitch on which the chord is built (the root), identify the chord member in the bass, and determine the chord position.

For instance, the pitches G♯–B–E (always reading from the bottom up), when organized in thirds as E–G♯–B, reveal a M triad on E. Because the third, G♯, was in the bass, the original chord was in first inversion. The chord F–B♭–D becomes B♭–D–F, a M triad; with the fifth, F, in the bass, the chord was in second inversion. Finally, the pitches A–C–D–F♯ can be organized in thirds as D–F♯–A–C, a Mm_7 chord; because the fifth, A, was in the bass, this is a seventh chord in second inversion ($^{4}_{3}$). Now practice by identifying the following chords (identify type and inversion, and notate it, for instance, as M^{6}_{4}, Mm^{6}_{5}, m_{6}, etc.):

D♯–F♯–B:	E–G–A–C:
B–E–G:	B♭–G–E♭:
C♯–E–G–A:	G–E–B:
B–D–G♯:	B♭–E–C–G:

EXERCISE 10 Refer to the passage by J. S. Bach reproduced in example D.9. Eighteen chords are numbered. Study each of the chords and determine whether it is consonant or dissonant, a triad or a seventh chord, the root and type of chord (DM, Cm, EMm_7, Fmm_7, etc.), and the appropriate figures to indicate the chord's position ($^{5}_{3}$, $^{6}_{3}$, $^{6}_{4}$, $_7$, $^{6}_{5}$, $^{4}_{3}$, etc.). You may provide all the above information in the following table (the information for chord 1 has been provided as an example).

Example D.9 J. S. Bach, Chorale 298, "Weg, mein Herz, mit den Gedanken," mm. 1–9

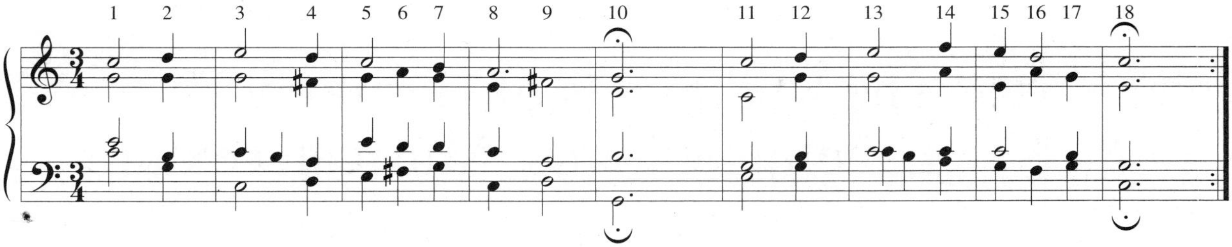

CHORD	1	2	3	4	5	6	7	8	9	10	11	12	13	14	15	16	17	18
Consonant (C)/ dissonant (D)	C	C	C															
Triad (TR)/ seventh (7th)	TR	TR																
Chord type/root	CM		CM	DM	CM	CM	GM		DM	GM								
Position ($^5_3$, $^6_3$, $^6_4$, 7, $^6_5$, $^4_3$, $^4_2$)	$^5_3$				$^6_3$	$^6_3$												

Chapter E

The Rudiments of Harmony II: Labeling Chords; Musical Texture

In chapter D we studied the fundamental material of harmony: triads and seventh chords. We should now learn how to refer to these chords in a tonal context. This means understanding the tonal hierarchy of chords, how they relate to the tonic, and how they relate to one another. In this chapter we will study two systems of chord reference and labeling that have been used by musicians and theorists in the past few centuries and are still widely used in harmonic instruction: Roman numerals and figured bass. We will also study musical texture, a term that refers to the relationship between the various horizontal and vertical components of music.

HARMONIC FUNCTION, ROMAN NUMERALS

The term **harmonic function** refers to the relationship of a chord with the other chords in the same key, and specifically to its relationship with the tonic, the chord on $\hat{1}$. We already learned in chapter C that tonality is a hierarchical system based on a center (the tonic pitch and, harmonically, the tonic triad). Harmonic function determines the behavior of chords in relation to other chords, according to this hierarchy around the tonic. **Roman numerals** are used precisely to indicate the function of a chord with respect to tonic. Thus, no matter what the major key, the symbol I indicates the tonic triad (the triad built on $\hat{1}$); the symbol V indicates the dominant triad (the triad built on $\hat{5}$); IV indicates the subdominant triad (the triad built on $\hat{4}$), and so forth. The standard behavior and role of each of these chords within the system will be our focus of study throughout part 1 of this book

Roman Numerals for Diatonic Triads

Example E.1 shows the Roman numerals for each of the diatonic triads in major and minor keys. **Capital-letter Roman numerals** indicate a major triad; **lowercase Roman numerals** are used for minor triads (you can review the quality of triads on each degree in example D.4). The symbol ° next to a lowercase Roman numeral means diminished triad. Scale degree numbers in this example show the correspondence between Roman numerals and bass scale degrees. As we discussed in chapter D, scale degree $\hat{7}$ will

Example E.1

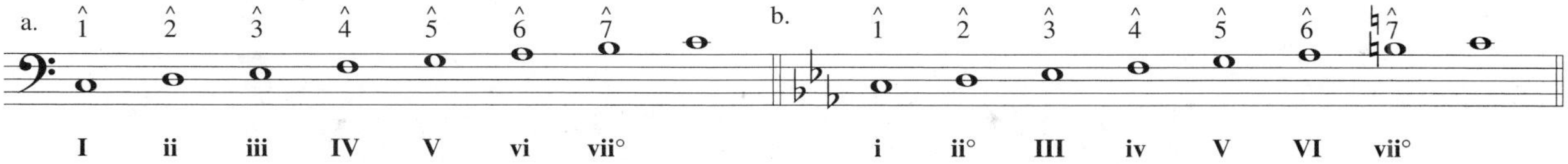

usually be raised in the minor mode, to become the leading tone, when the pitch is part of the V chord (the third) or of the vii° chord (the root). As part of the III chord in minor keys (the fifth), however, $\hat{7}$ is usually not raised, thus allowing for a major (rather than an augmented) chord on $\hat{3}$.

We will most often use a combination of Roman numerals and figures to refer to chords in a tonal context. In this system, a root position tonic triad in a major key is represented as I, and its inversions become I_6, and I^6_4, respectively. Similarly, the three positions for, say, the subdominant triad in a minor key are iv, iv_6, and iv^6_4. Example E.2 illustrates the use of some of these symbols, which provide us information about the quality, the inversion, and the function of a triad.

EXERCISE

To practice writing triads from given Roman numerals and labeling given triads with Roman numerals, refer to exercises 1 to 4 in worksheet E at the end of this chapter.

Roman Numerals for Diatonic Seventh Chords

In example E.3 you can see the Roman numerals for each of the diatonic seventh chords in major and minor keys. Here again, we use a combination of Roman numeral labels and figures to indicate both function and position. Thus, ii_7 is a mm_7 chord built on the supertonic, whereas the three inversions of this supertonic seventh chord will be notated as ii^6_5 (first inversion), ii^4_3 (second inversion), and ii^4_2 (third inversion). Notice that in Roman numerals for seventh chords, capital or lowercase symbols refer to the lower triad of the seventh chord, not to the seventh itself. Because both MM_7 (for instance, IV_7 in major) and Mm_7 (V_7) are built on major triads, they are represented with capital Roman numerals. Conversely, seventh chords built on minor or diminished triads are represented by lowercase Roman numerals.

Example E.2

Example E.3

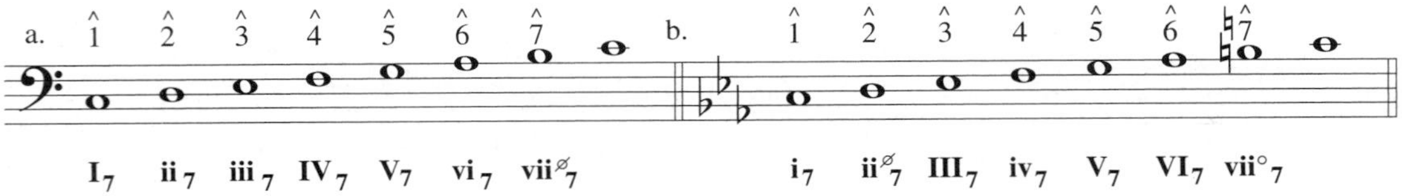

EXERCISE

To practice writing seventh chords from given Roman numerals, refer to exercise 5 in worksheet E at the end of this chapter.

FIGURED BASS

The system of numerical symbols used in the baroque period (approximately 1600–1750) to indicate harmonies above a bass is known as **figured bass** or **thoroughbass.** The system provides a notational shorthand, allowing a performer of a keyboard instrument to play complete harmonies from only a notated bass with added Arabic numerals (figures). The same system is still used in harmonic instruction to indicate harmonies that the student must fully realize in four voices from a given bass line with added figures.

The figures, which are notated below (or above) bass notes, represent *intervals above the bass.* In chapter D you were already introduced to figured bass in the discussion of triad and seventh chord positions. You learned that a $\begin{smallmatrix}5\\3\end{smallmatrix}$ means that the chord consists of a 3rd and a 5th above the bass, hence it is a root-position triad. A $\begin{smallmatrix}6\\3\end{smallmatrix}$ (a 3rd and a 6th above the bass) represents a first-inversion triad, and $\begin{smallmatrix}6\\4\end{smallmatrix}$ (a 4th and a 6th above the bass) represents a second-inversion triad. You also studied the abbreviated figures for both triads and seventh chords in root position or inversion, as summarized in the following tables.

Figured-Bass Symbols for Diatonic Triads

Triad in root position: $\begin{smallmatrix}5\\3\end{smallmatrix}$ or no figures

Triad in first inversion: $\begin{smallmatrix}6\\3\end{smallmatrix}$ or 6

Triad in second inversion (or linear $\begin{smallmatrix}6\\4\end{smallmatrix}$ chord): $\begin{smallmatrix}6\\4\end{smallmatrix}$

Figured-Bass Symbols for Diatonic Seventh Chords

Seventh chord in root position: $\begin{smallmatrix}7\\5\\3\end{smallmatrix}$ or 7

Seventh chord in first inversion: $\begin{smallmatrix}6\\5\\3\end{smallmatrix}$ or $\begin{smallmatrix}6\\5\end{smallmatrix}$

Seventh chord in second inversion: $\begin{smallmatrix}6\\4\\3\end{smallmatrix}$ or $\begin{smallmatrix}4\\3\end{smallmatrix}$

Seventh chord in third inversion: $\begin{smallmatrix}6\\4\\2\end{smallmatrix}$, $\begin{smallmatrix}4\\2\end{smallmatrix}$, or 2

Example E.4

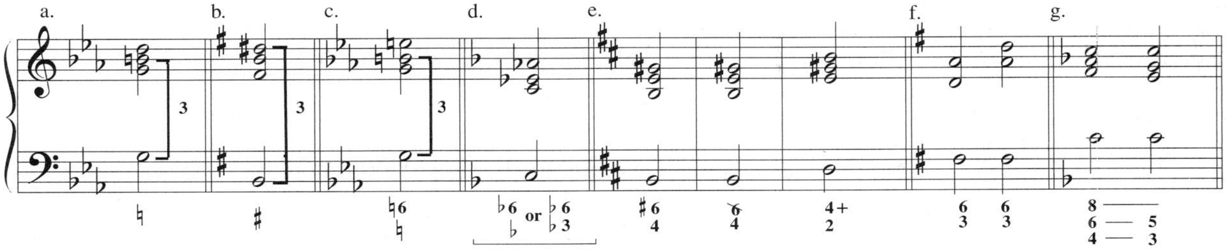

Accidentals in Figured Bass

Accidentals are also indicated in figured basses.

1. An accidental alone applies to the 3rd above the bass (examples E.4a and b).
2. Other accidentals precede or follow the numeral that represents the affected note (examples E.4c and d).
3. A slash across a number or a + sign after it have the same meaning as a ♯ next to that number—the note must be raised a half step (example E.4e).

NOTES

Figures do not determine the specific arrangement of upper voices. Although, for instance, in a $^6_3$ chord there must be a 6th and a 3rd somewhere above the bass, it does not matter whether the 6th is above the 3rd, or vice versa (see example E.4f).

Notice also that 8ve doublings are usually not indicated by figures, although they may be if the composer wants a particular pitch to be doubled. In example E.4g the 8 means that the bass of the first chord (the C) must be doubled; the line after the 8 indicates that the C must be sustained in the same voice into the next chord. Otherwise, in a $^{6-5}_{4-3}$ figure the 6th and 5th above C should be in the same voice, as indicated by the dash between the 6th and the 5th (6– 5, or A– G), and the same for the 4th and 3rd above C (4– 3, or F– E).

An Example by Handel

Example E.5 reproduces two fragments of a composition by George F. Handel, a sonata for flute and continuo. Handel wrote only the flute part and the figured bass, from which the keyboard player would improvise a right-hand realization. This type of texture or technique is called ***continuo*** or ***basso continuo.*** Example E.5 shows a possible realization of the figured bass for a keyboard instrument. A different realization might feature different arrangements of the right-hand chords, different 8ve doublings, or different ornamental pitches or *nonchord tones* (pitches, such as passing tones or neighbor notes, that are not part of the chord with which they sound, as we will study in chapters F and 6). Examine the realization and verify the interpretation of the figures provided in the keyboard's upper staff.

A FIGURED-BASS CHECKLIST

1. $^5_3$ or no figures indicates a root-position triad.
2. $^6_3$ or 6 indicates a first-inversion triad.
3. $^6_4$ indicates a second-inversion triad or a linear $^6_4$ chord.
4. A single accidental applies to the 3rd above the bass.
5. Other accidentals precede or follow the numeral that represents the affected note (as in ♮4 and ♭6, or 4♯ and 6♭).
6. A ♯ before or after a number, a slash across a number, or a + sign after the number all mean that the note should be raised by a half step.
7. The figures 7, $^6_5$, $^4_3$, and $^4_2$ indicate seventh chords in root position and each of the three inversions, respectively.

Example E.5 George Frideric Handel, Sonata for Flute and Continuo, op. 1, no. 7

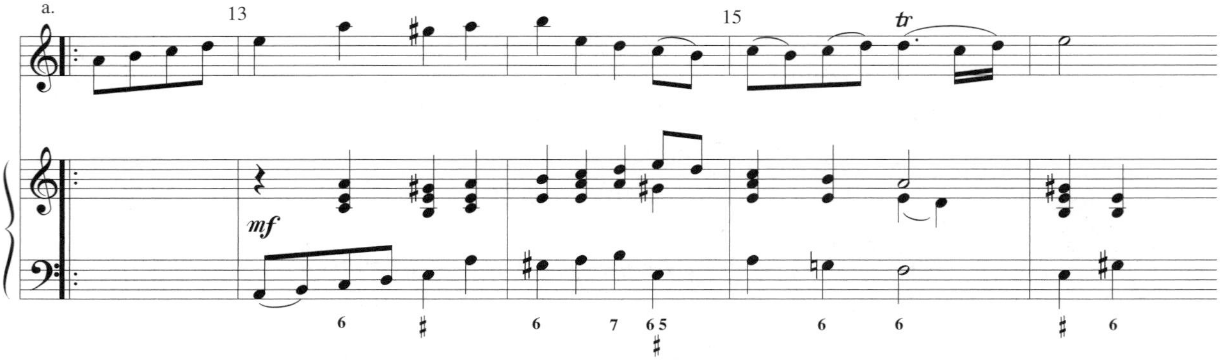

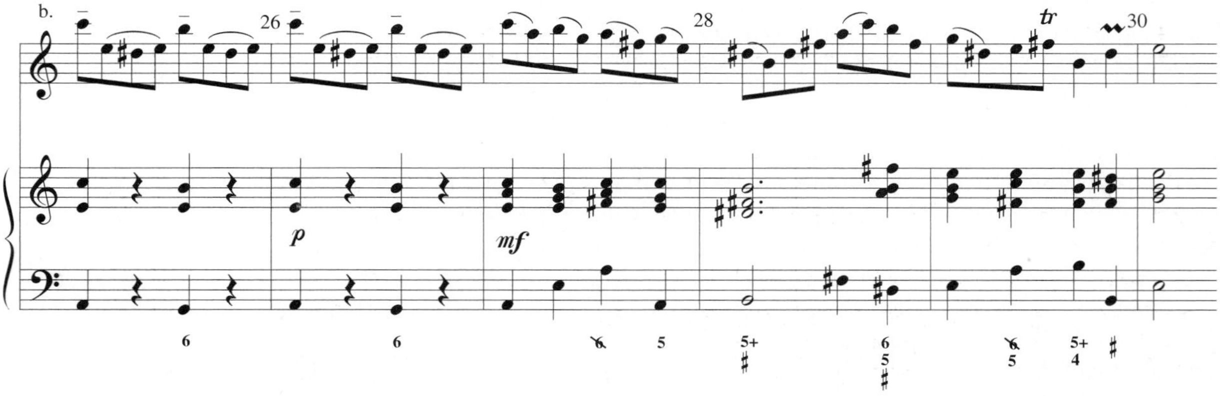

Example E.5a features only triads in root position or first inversion, and a seventh chord. The following comments will help you in your study of the realization.

1. Taking m. 13 as an example, you will see that a C with a 6 means an Am triad in first inversion, an E with a ♯ means a root position chord on E with a raised 3rd, and an A with no figure means a root position Am triad.

2. Notice also that the first two measures of the keyboard's left hand imitate the flute melody. Because of this melodic nature of the initial eighth notes in the bass, not all notes need to be harmonized (the B and the D are *passing tones* between the members of the Am triad, A–C–E).
3. The 7th in m. 14 (A) is prepared (by the same pitch in the same voice in the previous chord) and resolved down by step (to G♯). The 6–5 in the same measure indicates a melodic motion (in the flute) of a 6th and a 5th over the bass. The flute figure is accompanied in 3rds by the keyboard's upper voice (the eighth-note D in the keyboard is also a passing tone).

The figures in example E.5b are more complex. Try to understand their meaning, and then read the following comments.

1. The slash across the 6 in m. 27 means that the 6th over the A needs to be raised (F♯).
2. The symbol 5+ in m. 28 also means a raised 5th over B, hence the F♯. Why is the D also raised?
3. In mm. 28–29 you will see two $^6_5$ labels. Verify that both cases indicate seventh chords in first inversion. Identify the complete seventh chord in each case, as well as the 6th and the 5th above the bass. What does the slash across the 6 in the second $^6_5$ chord refer to?
4. Explain the 5+ symbol in m. 29, beat 3. The 4–♯ figures represent a 4–3 suspension, a type of nonchord tone that we will study in chapter F.

EXERCISES

To practice figured-bass realization and analysis, refer to exercises 6 and 7 in worksheet E at the end of this chapter.

To practice chord and Roman numeral analysis, refer to exercise 8.

MUSICAL TEXTURE

The term **texture** refers to the relationship between different musical lines and between the horizontal and vertical components of music. Music in which there is a single, unaccompanied line is said to be **monophonic.** In example E.6a, on the other hand, two voices are presented simultaneously. Music that has more than one voice is **polyphonic.** In the type of polyphony illustrated by our example, voices are independent, and they are equally important. Because polyphonic textures are ruled by the principles of **counterpoint** (the art of combining two or more melodic lines), they are also called **contrapuntal textures.** In example E.6a, not only are the voices independent (in contour, rhythm, type of motion, etc.), but so is the thematic material. This is an example of **free counterpoint,** as opposed to the fragment in example E.6b written in **imitative counterpoint.** In the latter type of polyphony, voices share the same motives or themes, and hence "imitate" each other. Although voices here are still independent, their thematic material is the same. **Imitation** in example E.6b is present not just at the beginning.

Example E.6a J. S. Bach, Sarabande, from Partita no. 2 in Cm, for Harpsichord, mm. 9–12

Example E.6b Orlande de Lassus, "Benedictus," from *Missa pro defunctis*

Example E.6b Continued

The first three entries of the initial motive are marked with brackets on the score. Find and mark all the subsequent statements of this motive. Beginning with the bass in mm. 9–10, moreover, a second motive is repeatedly stated in all voices. Mark all the entries of this second motive from m. 10 to the end of the piece. The words mean: "Blessed is He who comes in the name of the Lord." Do the words have anything to do with the motivic content of the piece? That is, are the two motives we have identified related to specific words?

In example E.7a, on the other hand, there is only one melody (the top line), while the function of the left-hand lines is to provide a chordal accompaniment (the parallel sixths added for two beats in m. 3 do not constitute an independent line, but simply a **supporting parallel melody**). The accompanying lines are thus subordinate to the melody. Such a texture is called **homophonic.** In a homophonic texture the accompaniment may be in the form of block chords, as in example E.7a (in which some of the pitches that complete the chord are presented by the right-hand melody), or the chords may be broken into a variety of figurations. In example E.7b, the chordal accompaniment is arpeggiated, but the texture is still purely homophonic.

Chorale Texture

A particular type of texture, which we will call **chorale texture,** is found in chorale-style harmonizations. These are four-part vocal harmonizations of hymn tunes, in which the actual tune is usually placed in the upper voice, thus becoming the main voice. This type of composition started being widely used in Lutheran services in the baroque period (to be sung by the congregation) and is still used in the same context. You can find examples of complete chorale harmonizations by J. S. Bach in anthology, nos. 8–10. Chorale harmonizations feature four independent lines, and as such they are contrapuntal. At times, chorale harmonizations are **homorhythmic;** that is, all voices have the same or nearly the same rhythm. In such cases, the effect is of a chordal texture, and it is clearly apparent that harmonies result from the simultaneous presentation of independent lines, as in the chorale fragment we discussed in example D.1a.

Example E.7a Joseph Haydn, Piano Concerto in DM, Hob. XVIII:11, II, mm. 1–4

Example E.7b F. Schubert, *Phidile,* mm. 1–4

EXERCISE

To practice analysis of a variety of textures, refer to exercise 9 in worksheet E at the end of this chapter.

ASSIGNMENT

For an assignment based on the materials learned in this chapter, refer to chapter E in the workbook.

Terms for Review

Harmonic function
Roman numerals
Roman numerals for diatonic triads
Capital and lowercase Roman numerals
Roman numerals for diatonic seventh chords
Figured bass
Thoroughbass
Continuo
Basso continuo
Figured-bass symbols for triads and seventh chords in all positions

Texture
Monophonic
Polyphonic
Counterpoint
Contrapuntal texture
Free counterpoint
Imitative counterpoint
Imitation
Supporting parallel melody
Homophonic
Chorale texture
Homorhythmic

Worksheet E

EXERCISE 1 Write the triads represented by Roman numerals in the given keys.

> **Procedure:** First write the root of the triad (the correct scale degree in the given key, as given by the Roman numeral). Then, determine the remaining two pitches, making sure that the triad type is correctly spelled (in some cases, you will need to use accidentals for this purpose).

B♭M: ii V vii° iii **Cm:** ii° iv vii° i

C♯m: III V iv VI **GM:** vi I ii V

EXERCISE 2 Write the following diatonic triads above the given bass notes. Triads are here represented by a Roman numeral (and a figure to indicate an inversion) in a given key. Identify the root for each triad, and notate it under the Roman numeral, as indicated in the given example.

GM: V_6 (D) I^6_4 $vii°_6$ IV **Dm:** iv_6 V i_6 iv^6_4

EXERCISE 3 Write the following diatonic triads, indicated by Roman numerals, in the given key.

Cm: III V_6 iv^6_4 $ii°_6$ **A♭M:** ii IV_6 $vii°_6$ I^6_4

EXERCISE 4 Provide the Roman numeral and position for the triads in this exercise in the given keys. Triads may appear in root position or inversion. Your labels should be of the following types, as shown in the example: V$^6_4$, ii$_6$, IV, vii$^\circ_6$, etc.

> **Procedure:** Once you have determined the root of the triad, you can figure out what scale degree that root represents in the given key, and that will tell you the Roman numeral, including the triad type (which, however, you can confirm by checking the triad intervals). The triad member in the bass will determine the position.

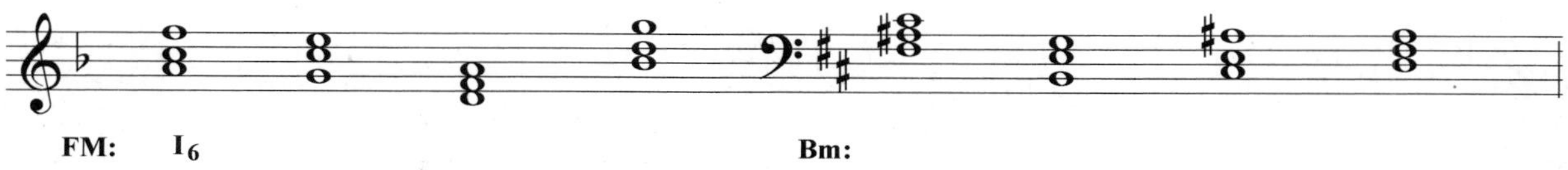

EXERCISE 5 Write the seventh chords represented by Roman numerals in the given keys.

EXERCISE 6 Realize the following isolated figured-bass chords. Exercises E.6a and b are all triads, and you will need only two upper voices, as in the example, to notate a complete chord. Items c and d are all seventh chords, and you will need three upper voices for complete sonorities.

> **Procedure:** You could notate these chords intervallically by simply realizing in the upper voices the intervals indicated in the figures. Thus, a $^6_5$ below an A in Em requires a 5th and a 6th in the upper voices (E and F♯) plus, of course, a 3rd which is omitted from the figures (C). At this stage, however, it is better to think of the chord type and position represented by the figures. Thus, $^6_5$ below A means a seventh chord in first inversion, in which A is the third. The complete chord is thus F♯–A–C–E, and my upper-voice pitches will then be F♯–C–E. After you determine the pitches, be sure to add whatever accidentals are required in the figured bass. Accidentals are best calculated intervallically: a ♮4 affects the 4th above the bass, a ♭6 affects the 6th, etc.

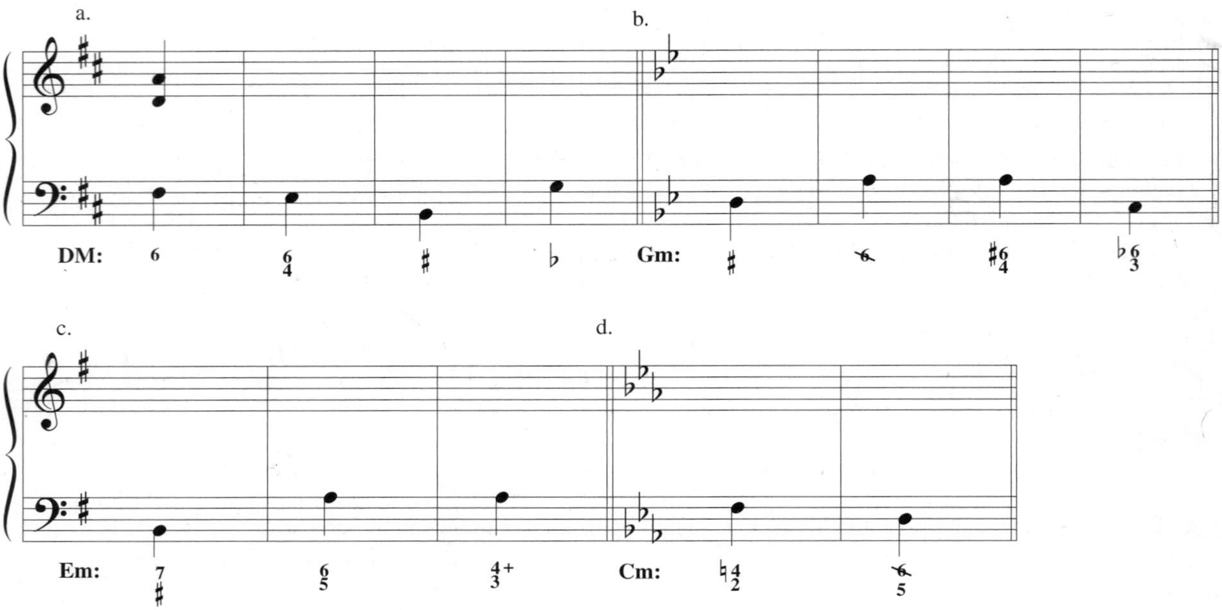

EXERCISE 7 Analyze the chorale by J. S. Bach with figured-bass symbols (example E.8). That is, imagine that you want to write a figured-bass reduction of this chorale for a keyboard player, using exactly Bach's harmonies. Under the chorale, notate the exact figures you would need to have in your figured bass.

Example E.8 J. S. Bach, Chorale 217, "Ach Gott, wie manches Herzeleid"

Procedure: First determine the type of chord you are labeling. Is it a triad or a seventh chord? In what position is it? That will give you the basic figures you need to write under the chord. Then, make sure that all upper-voice accidentals are incorporated into your figures, preceding the figure that represents the note with the accidental. Of course, accidentals in the bass will not be notated in the figures.

EXERCISE 8 Refer to the passage by Mozart reproduced in example E.9. Fifteen chords are boxed and numbered. Although some chords are complete in the left hand, others need to include some pitches from the upper staff to be complete. Not all right-hand pitches, however, are chord members. Some of them are nonchord tones, with a melodic, ornamental function. When a pitch of this type falls within one of the circled chords, it has been marked with an X, and you should ignore it for purposes of identifying the chord.

Study each chord, and determine whether it is consonant or dissonant, a triad or a seventh chord, its position, and, for chords 1–7, provide the complete Roman numerals (with figures indicating position, e.g. ii_6) in the key of DM. You may provide all the above information in the following table (the information for chord 1 has been provided as an example).

Example E.9 W. A. Mozart, Piano Sonata in DM, K. 284, III, mm. 1–8

Example E.9 Continued

CHORD	1	2	3	4	5	6	7	/	8	9	10	11	12	13	14	15
Consonant (C)/ dissonant (D)	C															
Triad (TR)/ seventh (7th)	TR															
Chord type	M															
Position ($^5_3$, $^6_3$, $^6_4$, 7)	$^5_3$															

CHORD	1	2	3	4	5	6	7	/	8	9	10	11	12	13	14	15
Roman numeral in DM (chords 1–7)	I							/	X	X	X	X	X	X	X	X

EXERCISE 9 Texture. Briefly discuss the texture of the following examples:

a) Anthology, no. 31, Maria Theresia von Paradis, *Sicilienne.*

b) Anthology, no. 34, Beethoven, op. 13, III, mm. 1–17.

c) Anthology, no. 37, Friedrich Kuhlau, Sonatina, mm. 1–8.

d) Anthology, no. 12, J. S. Bach, Gavotte, from *French Suite* no. 5.

e) Anthology, no. 14, J. S. Bach, *The Well-Tempered Clavier,* I, Fugue no. 2 in Cm.

In each of these examples, answer the following questions:

1) Is it homophonic or polyphonic (contrapuntal)?
2) If it is homophonic, what kind of accompaniment does it feature?
   a. Melody with block chords.
   b. Melody with broken (arpeggiated) chords.
   c. Melody, chords, and a parallel supporting melody.
   d. Accompaniment is (mostly) homorhythmic with melody.
   e. Other (explain).
3) If it is polyphonic, explain the exact relationship among voices.
   a. Chorale texture.
   b. Free counterpoint: voices unrelated, nonimitative counterpoint.
   c. Imitative counterpoint: voices share same thematic material.
   d. All voices are similar in importance.

Chapter F

Introduction to Species Counterpoint

As we studied in chapter E, music made up of several different melodic lines or voices is known as **polyphony.** The term **counterpoint** refers to both the art of combining two or more melodic lines and to the set of technical principles that regulates such combination of voices. All music in which different independent voices are presented together is contrapuntal. Composers in some musical periods, however, have been particularly inclined to writing in contrapuntal style. It is usually considered that the two high points of contrapuntal art were reached in the late Renaissance (second half of the sixteenth century, by composers such as Giovanni Pierluigi da Palestrina, Tomás Luis de Victoria, and Orlande de Lassus) and the late baroque (first half of the eighteenth century, notably by J. S. Bach). Of these, modal Renaissance counterpoint presents one of the most strict and rigorous sets of principles and technical regulations of any style in the whole history of music. For this reason it has been used throughout the centuries, to this day, as an excellent pedagogical tool to teach the craft of voice leading.

In 1725, Austrian composer and theorist Johann Joseph Fux published a treatise on counterpoint, *Gradus ad Parnassum* ("Steps to Parnassus") in which he presented a gradual, pedagogical approach to teaching counterpoint based on the principles of sixteenth-century contrapuntal style.[1] For a glimpse into the style of Renaissance music that was composed following these principles of counterpoint, you may listen to Victoria's *Kyrie* from the Mass *O magnum mysterium* (anthology, no. 1). Fux's method is usually known as **species counterpoint.** Because it teaches strict control of the musical material, and because it provides the foundation for all tonal voice leading, species counterpoint has been a staple component of a composer's craft-building education since it was first used by Fux. As a valuable example, Beethoven's studies of species counterpoint with his

[1]For a modern edition of Fux's *Gradus ad Parnassum,* refer to Johann Joseph Fux, *The Study of Counterpoint,* by Alfred Mann (New York: Norton, 1971). More specifically stylistic approaches to the study of sixteenth-century counterpoint (including the study of melody, rhythm, and text setting) can also be found in any of the following books: Knud Jeppesen, *Counterpoint* (New York: Dover, 1992); Robert Gauldin, *A Practical Approach to Sixteenth-Century Counterpoint* (Prospect Heights, IL: Waveland Press, 1995); and Peter Schubert, *Modal Counterpoint, Renaissance Style.* (New York: Oxford University Press, 1999).

teacher, Haydn, are reproduced in 54 pages of the book *The Great Composer as Teacher and Student* by Alfred Mann (New York: Dover, 1994). Although the study of species counterpoint is not indispensable to the study of harmony and voice leading, it provides a very strong musical and technical foundation on which to begin the studies of harmony. We will study, throughout this book, a variety of harmonic and linear concepts and techniques that can be referred back to species counterpoint, such as the good shape of melodic lines, the relationship between outer voices in a four-voice harmonic setting, the theory of nonchord tones, and especially the theory of suspensions.

In this chapter we will provide an introduction to species counterpoint. A full coverage of all five species in two, three, and four voices would require several chapters. We will limit our introductory study to four species (first, second, third, and fourth) in only two voices.

THE MELODIC LINE IN SPECIES COUNTERPOINT

In the Middle Ages and the Renaissance, polyphony was often built on preexistent melodies, usually borrowed from plainchant or other sources. A preexistent melody used as the basis for polyphonic composition is known as ***cantus firmus.*** Species counterpoint is usually also written on *cantus firmi.* We will then write our counterpoint on given melodies.

Because one of the functions of counterpoint is to preserve the independence and quality of individual lines, we will first practice writing single good lines. We will write for one of the four usual voice types: soprano, alto, tenor, or bass. You should keep your melodies within the acceptable range for each of these voices. You will find the vocal ranges in chapter 1, example 1.6.

In our counterpoint exercises we will write modal melodies using the modal scales we learned in chapter C. We will avoid, at this stage, the complexities of the medieval and Renaissance modal system. In its simplified form, sufficient for our purposes, the system is made up of the six basic modes we know from chapter C. The melodies in example F.1 are Fux's examples of modal melodies for each of these six modes. Examine and sing each of them. Then notice the following characteristics common to all of these melodies.

1. Fux's melodies are diatonic. Most of the melodic motion is by steps or small leaps. There are no repeated notes.
2. Each of Fux's single leaps is preceded or followed by motion in the opposite direction (the only exception to this observation is the opening leap in the Ionian melody; it is acceptable to begin a melody with a leap of a 3rd followed by stepwise motion in the same direction). Leaps larger than a 5th are rare, but if they occur (as in the 8ve leap in the Phrygian melody), they are both preceded and followed by motion in the opposite direction.
3. Two successive leaps in the same direction (or double leaps) outline the pitches of a major or minor triad, and in all cases they are both preceded and followed by motion in the opposite direction. You will find double leaps in the Lydian and Mixolydian melodies.

Example F.1 Johann Joseph Fux's Modal *cantus firmi*

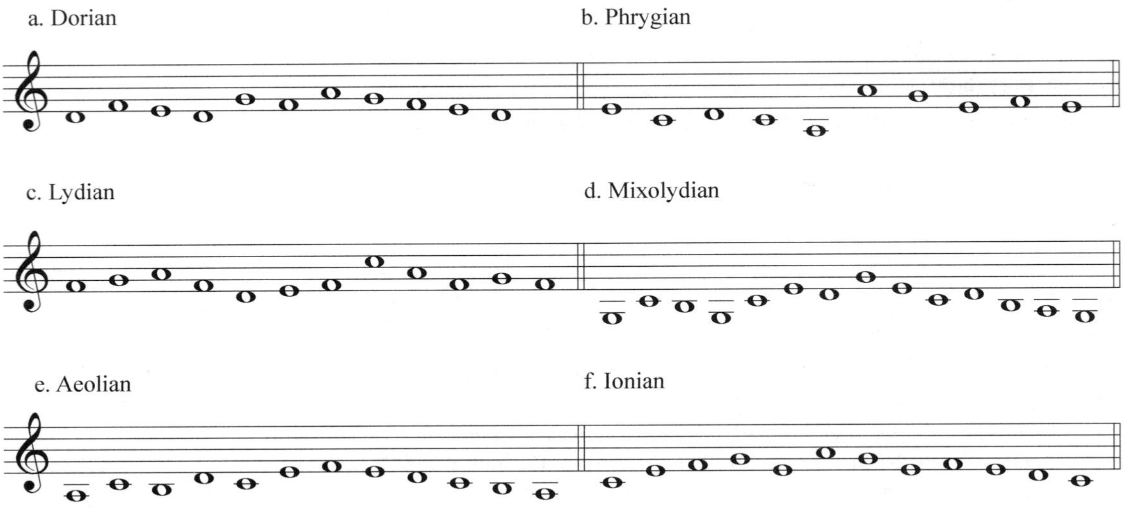

4. Each of Fux's melodies has a single focal point (a high or a low point). Verify the single focal point in each of the melodies. Do the melodic lines build up toward their focal points?
5. Each of Fux's melodies begins and ends on the tonic pitch. Final tonic pitches are approached by step from above or below. These are musical points of arrival or **cadences,** in this case articulated melodically by step ($\hat{2}$–$\hat{1}$ or $\hat{7}$–$\hat{1}$).

We can organize these observations in the form of the following guidelines, which you should carefully follow when you write your melodies. These principles are based on the melodic style of sixteenth-century sacred polyphony. To begin with, we will write melodies in whole notes, without bar lines.

Melodic Guidelines in Species Counterpoint

1. Your melodies should be *diatonic* (except for the leading tone at cadences in minor modes and G modes, and in the ascending fragment $\hat{5}$–$\sharp\hat{6}$–$\sharp\hat{7}$– $\hat{1}$ in minor). Always raise $\hat{7}$ at cadences (not within phrases) in minor modes and Mixolydian, but *not* in Phrygian.
2. Notes are *rarely repeated.*

3. Melodic motion will be mostly *by steps.*
4. Leaps are acceptable, with the following limitations:
   a) No *augmented or diminished* intervals are allowed.
   b) In general, leaps should not be *larger than a P5* (except for P8).
   c) Occasionally you may write an *ascending m6* (not descending, not a M6).
   d) All leaps should be *preceded or followed* by motion in the opposite direction.
   e) The ascending m6 and all P8s should be *both preceded and followed* by motion in the opposite direction.
   f) Occasionally you may write *two successive leaps in the same direction.* In this case:
      1) Both leaps should be preceded and followed by motion in the opposite direction.
      2) Both leaps may outline only a major or minor triad (not a diminished triad) or an 8ve (divided, from the bottom, as 5th + 4th, not 4th + 5th: D–A–D, not D–G–D).
5. Your melody should have a *single climax* or *focal point.* A high point is called a **zenith,** and a low point a **nadir.** A focal point should not be an isolated pitch. Rather, you should build up (or down) toward it progressively.
6. The last three or four notes of a passage in a single direction should not stress a tritone (although a diminished 5th is acceptable).
7. Your melodies should end on suitable *melodic cadences.* All your melodies should end on $\hat{1}$. Approach the final $\hat{1}$ by step from above or from below.

Verify that all the melodies in example F.1 follow the above guidelines. Example F.2, on the other hand, shows several faulty melodic segments. Identify the problem or problems in each of the melodies.

Example F.2 Melodies for Error Detection

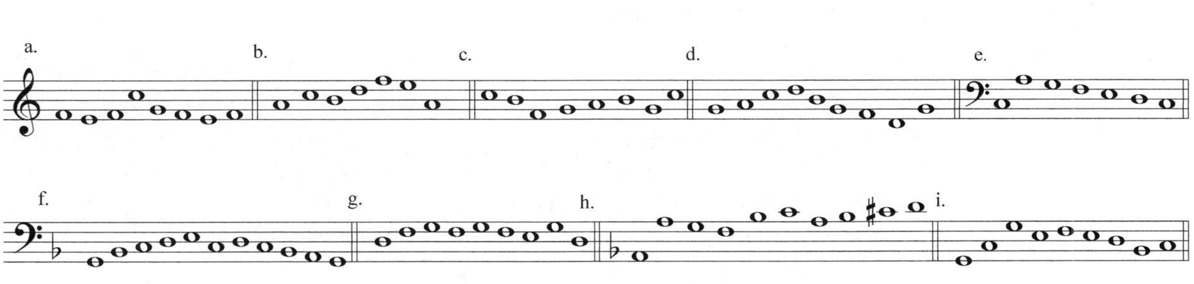

EXERCISE

To practice writing melodies in each of the modes, refer to exercise 1 in worksheet F at the end of this chapter.

GENERAL GUIDELINES FOR TWO-PART COUNTERPOINT

Before we begin studying the species one by one, consider the following guidelines, which apply equally to all species in two voices.

1. Counterpoint is made up of *equally good independent voices* in opposition: There should be no static voices. Do not "sit on a pitch."
2. Climaxes in both voices should be at different times, or of different types.
3. Begin the counterpoint with a PU (unison), P5, or P8.
4. End on a PU or a P8 only.
5. You will write counterpoint on a given *cantus firmus.*
   a) If the counterpoint (CTP) is above the *cantus firmus* (CF), then CF begins on $\hat{1}$, and CTP on $\hat{1}$ or $\hat{5}$.
   b) If CTP is below CF, then CTP begins on $\hat{1}$ (and so does CF).

You may verify each of the above points in the two-voice examples in example F.4. In example F.4a, moreover, we can see all four possible **types of motion** between two voices (*dyads,* or pairs of simultaneous pitches, are numbered in example F.4 for easy reference) as discussed below:

1. **Oblique motion:** A voice moves (up or down), the other voice stays on the same pitch. The motion between dyads 1 and 2 is oblique.
2. **Parallel motion:** Voices move in the same direction preserving the harmonic interval between them. See dyads 2 and 3.
3. **Contrary motion:** Voices move in opposite directions, as between dyads 3 and 4.
4. **Similar motion:** Voices move in the same direction, but the harmonic interval between them is not preserved. See dyads 4 and 5.

FIRST SPECIES (1:1)

In **first-species** counterpoint we write a note of counterpoint against each *cantus firmus* note. For this species we will use the same notation of whole notes with no bar lines. Keep in mind the general principles of both melodic writing and two-voice counterpoint that we outlined in the previous sections. Otherwise, the following criteria apply to first species in particular.

1. In first species we use *only consonances* as harmonic intervals: P5, P8, m3, M3, m6, M6.

2. *The* **harmonic P4** *is a dissonance in two-voice counterpoint.* It should be avoided, along with all other dissonances.
3. The PU is used *only to begin or to end* a phrase in first species, not within the phrase.
4. Perfect intervals (PU, P5, and P8) should be approached only by *contrary* or *oblique* motion, not by parallel or similar motion (examples F.3a and b).
5. **Parallel perfect unisons, 5ths, or 8ves** *are always incorrect,* even if they are approached by *contrary motion* (as in P5–P12 or PU–P8). See example F.3b.
6. The only exception to rule no. 4 is what we know as **horn 5ths** (similar motion descending from a 3rd to a P5, or ascending from a 6th to a P5) if the top voice moves by steps (example F.3c). Similar motion into a perfect interval with the top voice leaping produces the incorrect motion known as **direct** or **hidden unison, 5th, or 8ve,** as we indicated in example F.3b.
7. *Voices should not overlap.* **Voice overlap** takes place when the higher voice is on a lower pitch than the lower voice's immediately preceding note, or vice versa. Overlap results, for instance, from a faulty direct unison (see example F.3b).

Example F.3 Motions into Perfect Intervals

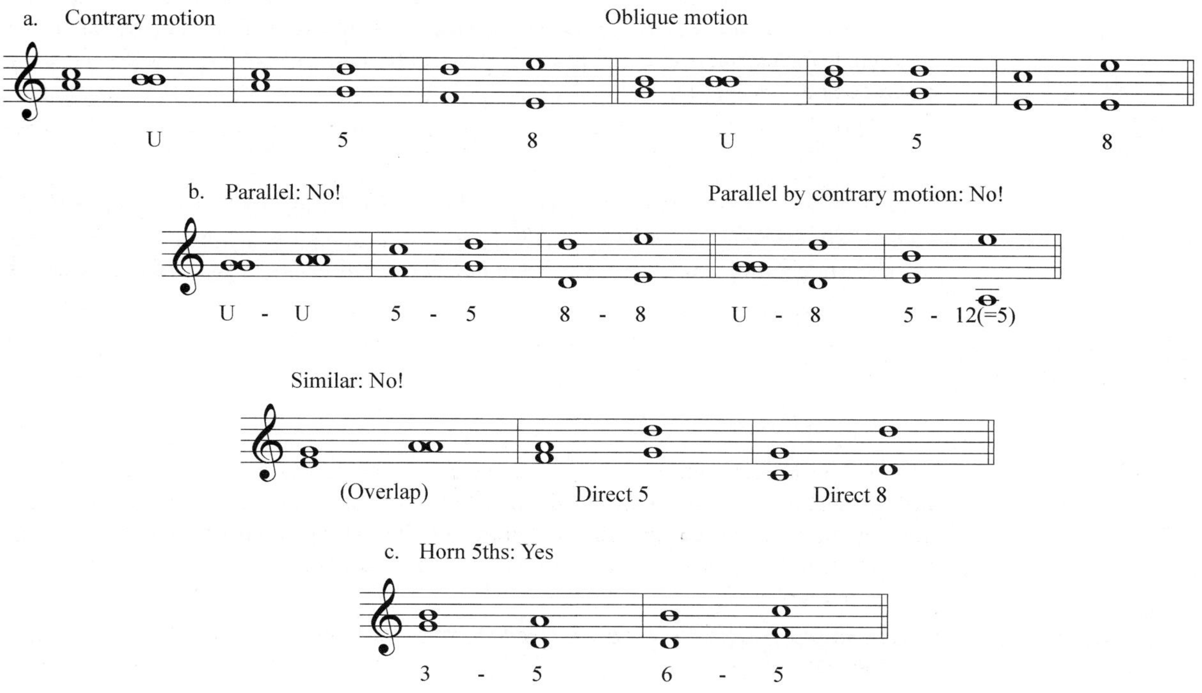

Example F.4

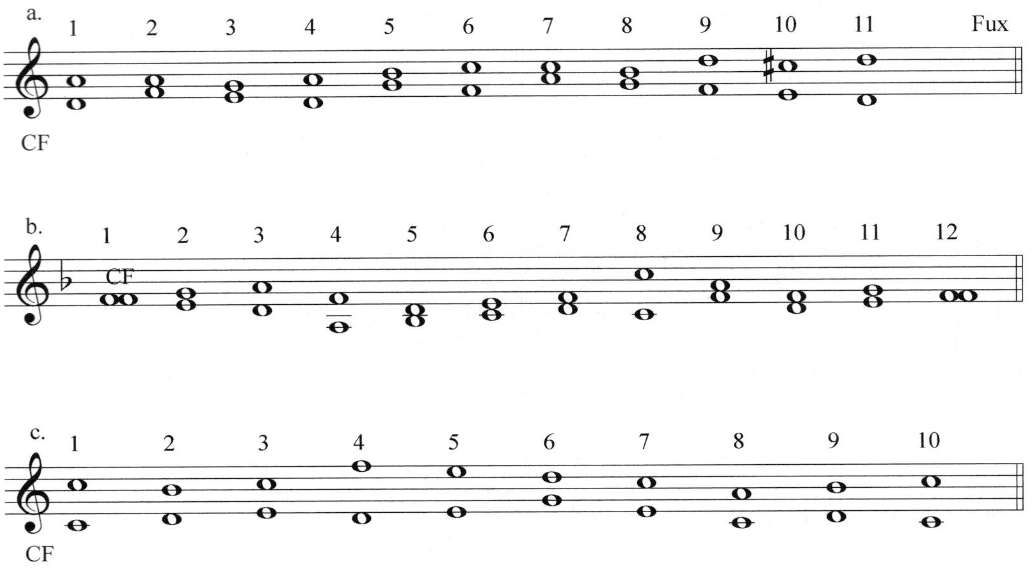

8. *Voices should not cross.* In **voice crossing** the upper voice moves below the lower voice, or vice versa.
9. You should not write more than *three parallel 3rds or parallel 6ths* in succession.

Three examples of correct first-species counterpoint appear in example F.4. Sing through them in class or with a friend. Then analyze and verify the consonances, the motion between dyads, the quality of the individual voices, and their contour and independence. After you do this, analyze the two phrases in example F.5, which include several melodic or contrapuntal errors. Mark and identify all the errors in these two examples.

Example F.5 Exercises for Error Detection

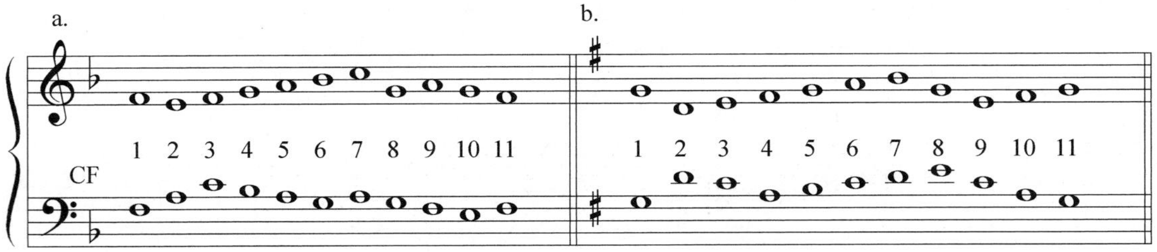

EXERCISE

To practice writing first-species counterpoint, refer to exercise 2 in worksheet F at the end of this chapter.

SECOND SPECIES (2:1)

In **second-species** counterpoint we write two notes of counterpoint against each *cantus firmus* note. We will notate second species in cut time, with bar lines. In this meter, the counterpoint consists of a metrically stressed half note (beat 1) and a metrically unstressed half note (beat 2) per measure. Second species allows for the first type of dissonance in our studies of counterpoint, as we explain in the following guidelines.

1. The *stressed half note* may only be consonant.
2. The *unstressed half note* may be consonant or dissonant (examples F.6a–b).
3. The only possible dissonance in second species is the **passing tone** (PT). A PT fills in a melodic gap of a 3rd by steps (examples F.6b–c).

Example F.6

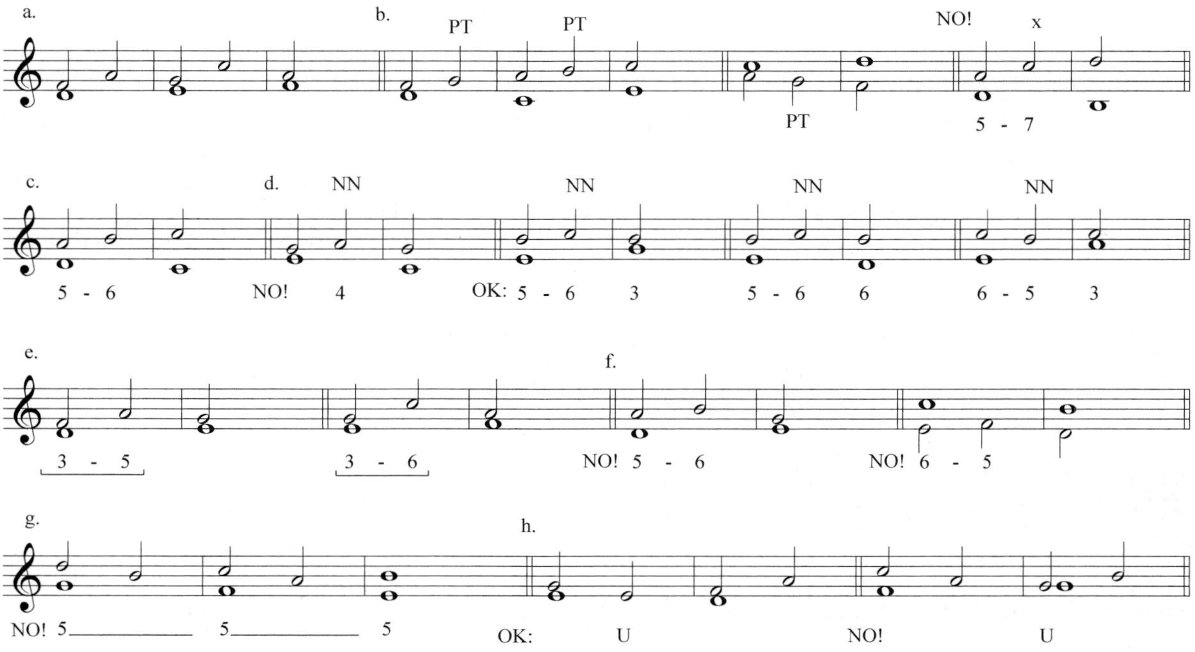

4. A PT may be *consonant* or *dissonant.* A consonant PT is, for instance, a 5–6 figure (example F.6c).
5. The unstressed half note should not be a *dissonant* **neighbor note** (NN), although it may be a *consonant neighbor note.* A neighbor note moves up (upper NN) or down (lower NN) one step from a given pitch and returns also by step to the same pitch. A dissonant NN as well as consonant NN figures involving 5–6 or 6–5 motions are illustrated in example F.6d.
6. If the second half note is consonant, it should stay *within the same triad* that was implied by the first half note. In other words, you should not write a 5–6 or 6–5 figure unless the second half note is a PT or a NN. In example F.6e, all three notes in the 3–5 figure belong to the same triad (D–F–A), and so do the three notes in the 3–6 figure (C–E–G). In Example F.6f, on the other hand, both the 5–6 and the 6–5 figures imply two different triads per measure.
7. Avoid parallel 5ths or 8ves *between strong beats* (example F.6g).
8. A *unison on a weak beat* is acceptable. But a unison on a strong beat (in 2 voices) is not (example F.6h).
9. Avoid repeated notes in the voice in half notes (the counterpoint).
10. You may begin the counterpoint with a half-note rest.
11. The last two notes (the cadence) may be in whole notes.

Sing, in class or with a friend, the two examples of second species in example F.7. Verify the consonances and dissonances in these phrases, and the quality of the individual lines. Notice that in example F.7b the zenith in the counterpoint is reached in the

Example F.7

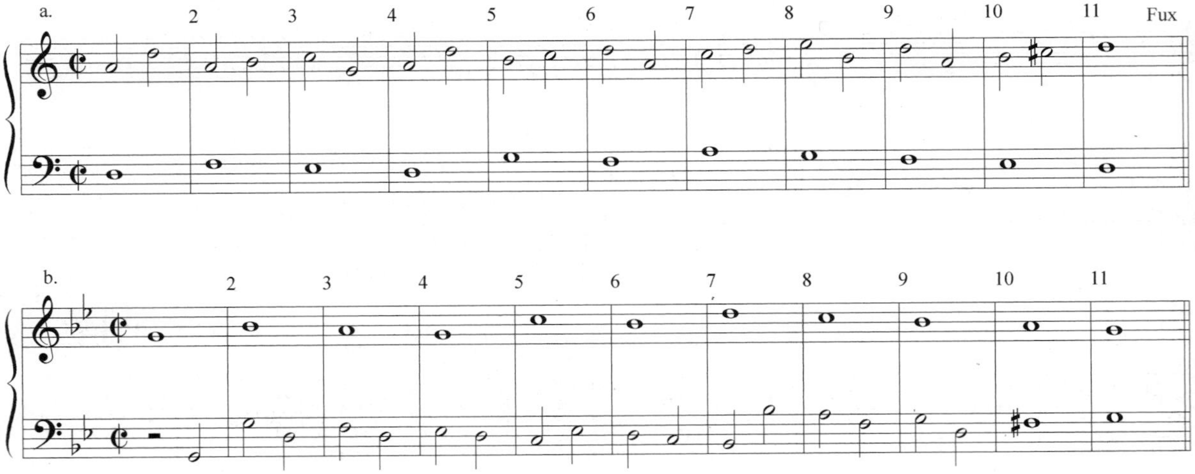

same measure as the zenith in the *cantus firmus*. But because the zeniths are not actually simultaneous (they take place in different beats), the phrase is perfectly acceptable.

EXERCISE

To practice writing second-species counterpoint, refer to exercise 3 in worksheet F at the end of this chapter.

THIRD SPECIES (4:1)

In **third-species** counterpoint we write four notes of counterpoint against each *cantus firmus* note. We will notate this species in $\frac{4}{4}$, with beats 1 and 3 being strong and beats 2 and 4 weak. In this species we will use two types of dissonance: the passing tone (PT), which we already know from second species, and a new dissonance, the neighbor note (NN). The following guidelines will rule our practice of third species.

1. The *first quarter* may only be consonant.
2. The *remaining three quarter notes* may be consonant or dissonant, regardless of their strong or weak metric placement.
3. The two possible dissonances in third species are as follows:
   a. *Passing tone* (PT), filling in a gap of a 3rd by steps (see example F.8a). It is also possible to use two consecutive passing tones to fill in a gap of a 4th by steps (example F.8b).

Example F.8

b. *Neighbor note* (NN). A NN moves up or down one step from a given pitch, then returns also by step to the same pitch (example F.8c).

4. As in second species, you should not have a unison on beat 1.
5. Avoid approaching a unison by means of a PT from a second (3rd-2nd-U), and also avoid writing a NN from a unison (U-2nd-U). Both of these faulty figures are shown in example F.8d.
6. You may begin with a quarter-note rest.
7. Avoid parallel 5ths or 8ves *on consecutive first beats.* Also avoid parallel 5ths or 8ves *on consecutive strong beats* (beats 3–1 on consecutive measures). Both of these types of faulty parallels are illustrated in example F.8e.
8. You should stay *within the same triad* for the whole measure. Neither of the two one-measure fragments shown in example F.8f can be explained as belonging to the same triad; in both cases you need two triads to account for all the pitches that are neither PTs nor NNs. These are both faulty examples.
9. *Do not outline a $^{6}_{4}$ chord between the two voices.* A $^{6}_{4}$ chord will result (and will be heard) if the chordal fifth is the lowest pitch in the measure. The first two measures in example F.8g show a $^{6}_{4}$ (G–C–E) that results from having the fifth (G) as the lowest pitch. In the first measure, moreover, we hear a P4 between the two voices, treated as a consonance. A harmonic P4 is never a consonance in two-voice species counterpoint. In the third measure, on the other hand, the chordal fifth is not the lowest pitch, neither do we hear a harmonic P4. This is a perfectly acceptable measure.

You will find that writing correct next-to-last measures in third species is not always easy. To help you with this task, you can see a number of standard third-species closings, or cadential formulas, in example F.9. Sing and play the two examples in third species in example F.10 and verify the correct use of PTs and NNs, as well as the correct application of all the previous guidelines. Finally, example F.11 contains numerous errors. As an exercise in error detection, find as many of them as you can.

Example F.9 Cadential Formulas

Example F.10

a.

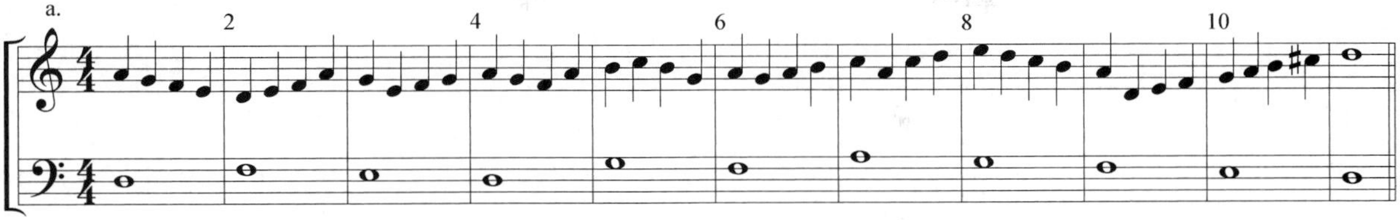

b.

Example F.11 Error Detection

EXERCISE

To practice writing third-species counterpoint, refer to exercise 4 in worksheet F at the end of this chapter.

FOURTH SPECIES (SYNCOPATED)

In **fourth species** the counterpoint is a *syncopated voice.* Fourth-species syncopes are written across the bar line, so they span beat 2 of a measure (weak) and beat 1 of the next measure (strong). The syncopes may be *consonant* or *dissonant.* If a syncope is *consonant,* both beats are consonant with the CF. If the syncope is *dissonant,* its weak half is consonant, but its strong half is dissonant. In other words, *the weak beat of a syncope must always be consonant.*

Example F.12

Suspensions

The only possible dissonance on the strong beat of a syncope is a **suspension.** Refer to example F.12. First, you will see two thirds in first-species counterpoint (example F.12a). Then the upper voice is delayed by one beat, in such a way that the motion from A to G does not come until beat 2 (example F.12b). Instead of a 3–3 counterpoint, we now have a 3–4–3 counterpoint, which includes a dissonance (the 4th) on the strong beat, resolving to a consonance (the 3rd) on the weak beat. Then, the lower voice is delayed by one beat (example F.12c). Instead of a 3–3 counterpoint we now have a 3–2–3 figure, in which the dissonance on the strong beat (a 2nd) resolves to a consonance on the weak beat.

A suspension thus creates a dissonance on a strong beat by delaying the motion between two consonances. A suspension figure actually has three parts: a **preparation** (P), always consonant and on a weak beat; the **suspension** (S), dissonant and on a strong beat; and the **resolution** (R), consonant and on a weak beat. *The resolution of a suspension is always by step and always descending.*

Suspension labels state the dissonant interval followed by the interval of resolution, both always counted from the bass upward. The suspension in example F.12b is, then, a 4–3 suspension, and in example F.12c we have a 2–3 suspension. There are three types of dissonant suspension when the syncopation is in the upper voice, as you can see in example F.13. These are the **9–8, 7–6, and 4–3 suspensions.** The **6–5 suspension** is not considered a real suspension by some authors because it is not dissonant. We have nevertheless listed it in example F.13 because it functions as a suspension, albeit consonant. The **2–1 suspension** is similar to the 9–8 suspension, but instead of a 9th resolving to an 8ve, we have a 2nd resolving to a unison. *There is only one possible suspension when the syncopated voice is in the bass.* This is the **2–3 suspension,** or its compound version, the **9–10 suspension.** Beware that 4–5 and 7–8 bass suspensions are not possible or correct.

EXERCISE

To practice writing suspensions, refer to exercise 5 in worksheet F at the end of this chapter.

Example F.13

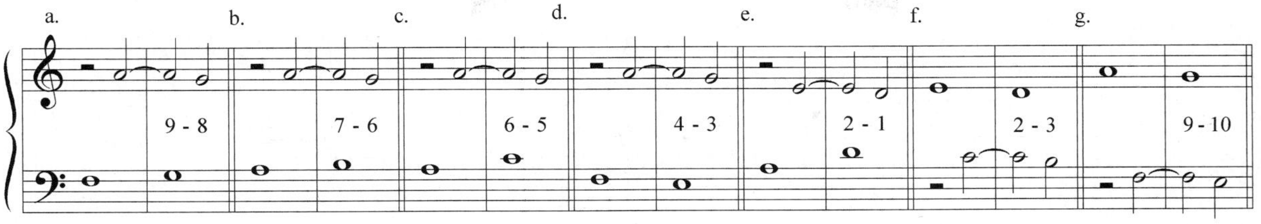

Syncopated Counterpoint

Example F.14 shows two fragments of fourth-species counterpoint by Fux. In the first fragment, only consonant syncopes are used. The second fragment uses a string of dissonant syncopes, all 7–6 suspensions. To write a consonant syncope, you must find a note that is consonant with two adjacent notes of the CF. To write a dissonant syncope, you must be able to resolve the dissonant note to a consonance by means of a descending second. Study now examples F.15a and b, and write in the intervals between voices for every beat. Verify that all dissonances are treated as correct suspensions, and that all suspensions in example F.15b are of the 2–3 type or its compound.

In example F.16a we see that, because a suspension is a retardation of note-against-note counterpoint, a string of 4–3 suspensions (4–3–4–3–4–3) can be reduced to a series of parallel 3rds (3–3–3). Similarly, a string of 9–8 suspensions (9–8–9–8–9–8) amounts to a series of parallel 8ves (8–8–8), and thus should be avoided (example F.16b). A string of 6–5 suspensions, on the other hand, is perfectly acceptable because the 5ths are separated by consonant intervals (the 6ths), and so they do not amount to a series of parallel 5ths (example F.16c). Parallel 5ths between strong beats are correct in fourth species as long as they are separated by consonances, as in example F.16d. The same is true for 8ves, but you should not write more than two in a row (more would weaken the sonority of the passage).

Example F.14

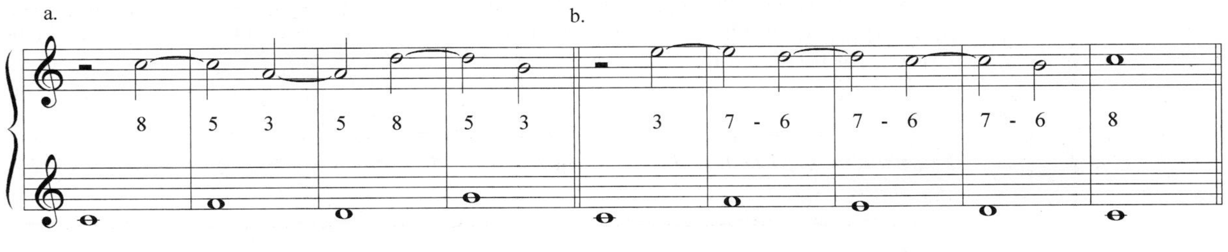

Example F.15

The *best suspensions* are 7–6 and 4–3, because both resolve to imperfect consonances. 9–8 is acceptable, although weaker in two voices (it resolves to an octave), and 2–1 is tolerable, although it is the weakest of all (the unison within the phrase, however, is acceptable in fourth species).

Cadences should feature what is known as a ***clausula vera,*** "true cadence." In a *clausula vera,* a M6 formed by degrees $\hat{2}$–$\hat{7}$ (with $\hat{2}$ in the bass, and a leading-tone $\hat{7}$ in all modes except for Phrygian) resolves to the octave $\hat{1}$–$\hat{1}$, or the inversion of the M6, a m3 ($\hat{7}$–$\hat{2}$, with $\hat{7}$ in the bass) resolves to a unison $\hat{1}$–$\hat{1}$ (or an octave if the m3 is compound).

If the cadence is of the M6 type, it will be approached with a 7–6 suspension. The m3 type will include a 2–3 suspension. These two standard cadential types appear in example F.16e, both in first and fourth species. In this example you will also find another standard cadential type, the **Phrygian cadence,** a *clausula vera* on E. In this type of cadence, $\hat{2}$–$\hat{1}$ is usually in the bass, and we do not raise 7 to make it a leading tone. The half-step motion in this cadence takes place as the "Phrygian $\hat{2}$–$\hat{1}$" in the bass, and not as an upper-voice leading tone.

Finally, you will have noticed that in example F.15 the chains of syncopations are occasionally broken. It is acceptable to do so, only occasionally, and if no better solution can be found. Do not break the chain, however, more than once or twice in an exercise of this length.

EXERCISE

To practice writing fourth-species cadences, refer to exercise 6 in worksheet F at the end of this chapter.

Example F.16

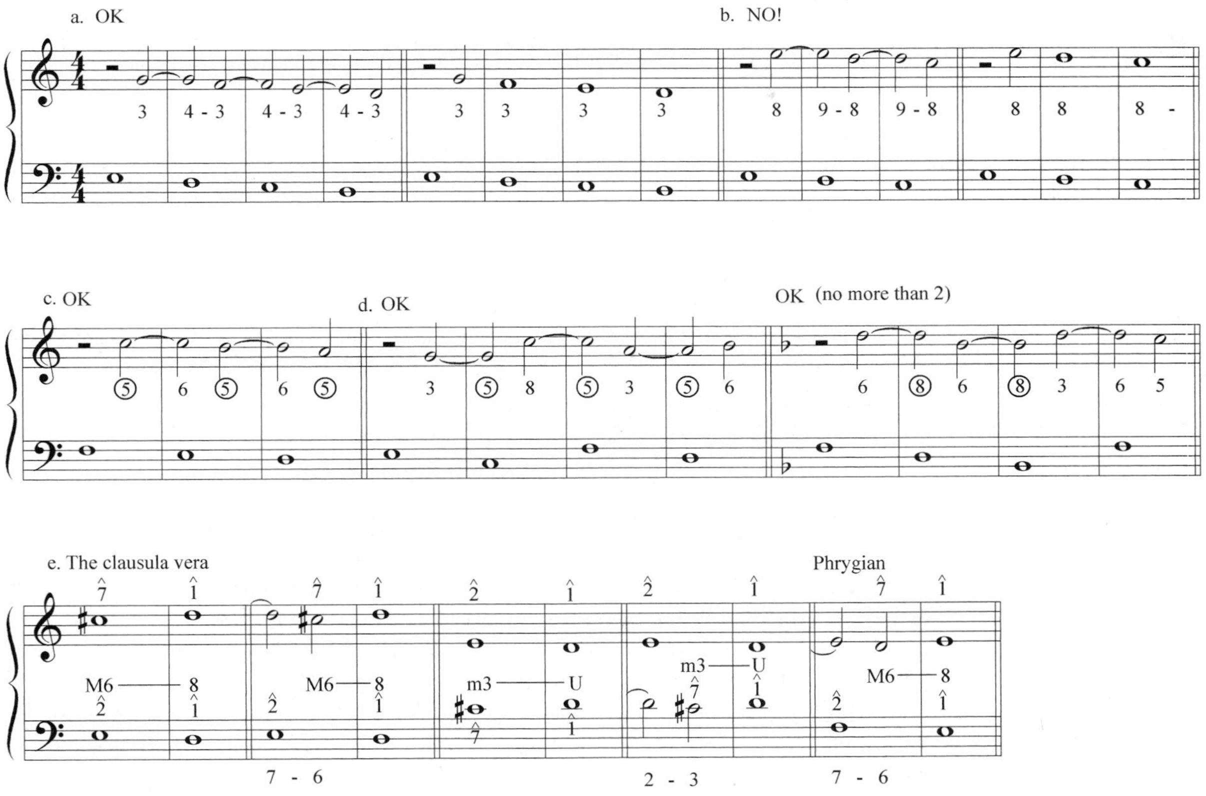

The following points summarize what we have discussed regarding fourth species:

1. Syncopes: Consonant or dissonant.
2. Dissonant syncopes: suspensions.
3. Suspension: preparation (consonant, weak beat); suspension (dissonant, strong beat); resolution down by step (weak beat).
4. Suspensions: 9–8, 7–6, 4–3, and their compounds; only suspension in the bass: 2–3; consonant suspension: 6–5.
5. A suspension is a retardation of 1:1 counterpoint. 3–3–3–3 thus becomes 4–3–4–3–4–3 (example F.16a). Then, 9–8–9–8 is wrong; it amounts to //8–8 (example F.16b). But 6–5–6–5 is correct (both intervals are consonant, example F.16c).

Example F.17 Error Detection

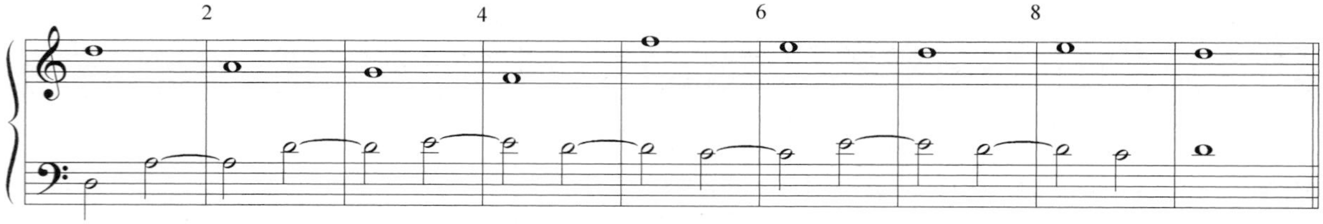

6. Parallel 5ths on strong beat separated by consonances are fine: 3 | 5 8 | 5 3 | 5 6 | (example F.16d). The same applies to octaves, but to no more than two in a row: 6 | 8 6 | 8 3 | 6.
7. Best suspensions: 7–6 and 4–3 (and 2–3 in the bass); 9–8 is acceptable; 2–1 is tolerable (unison may be used within the phrase in fourth species).
8. Cadences: only 7–6 or 2–3, with both voices resolving to $\hat{1}$ (example F.16e).
9. It is possible to break the chain of syncopes, only occasionally and if no better solution is available.

Example F.17 contains *numerous* errors. Analyze this example carefully, mark all the errors, and identify the type of problem each of them represents.

EXERCISES

To practice writing fourth-species counterpoint, refer to exercise 7 in worksheet F at the end of this chapter.

For further practice in any of the species, use any of Fux's cantus firmi *in example F.1.*

ASSIGNMENT

For an assignment based on the materials learned in this chapter, refer to chapter F in the workbook.

FOR FURTHER STUDY

For an additional introductory chapter, titled "Musical Style," refer to chapter G in the *Harmony in Context* Web page at www.mhhe.com/roigfrancoli2e.

Terms for Review

Polyphony
Counterpoint
Species counterpoint
Cantus firmus
Cadence
Zenith, nadir
Types of motion: oblique, parallel, contrary, similar
First species
Harmonic P4
Parallel perfect intervals
Horn 5ths
Direct or hidden unison, 5th or 8ve
Voice overlap
Voice crossing
Second species
Passing tone
Neighbor note
Third species
Fourth species
Suspensions
Preparation, suspension, resolution
4–3, 7–6, and 9–8 (or 2–1) suspensions
6–5 suspension
2–3 (or 9–10) suspension
Clausula vera
Phrygian cadence

Worksheet F

EXERCISE 1 Write six melodies, one in each of the modes, following the guidelines discussed in the section, "The Melodic Line in Species Counterpoint," and the models provided in example F.l.

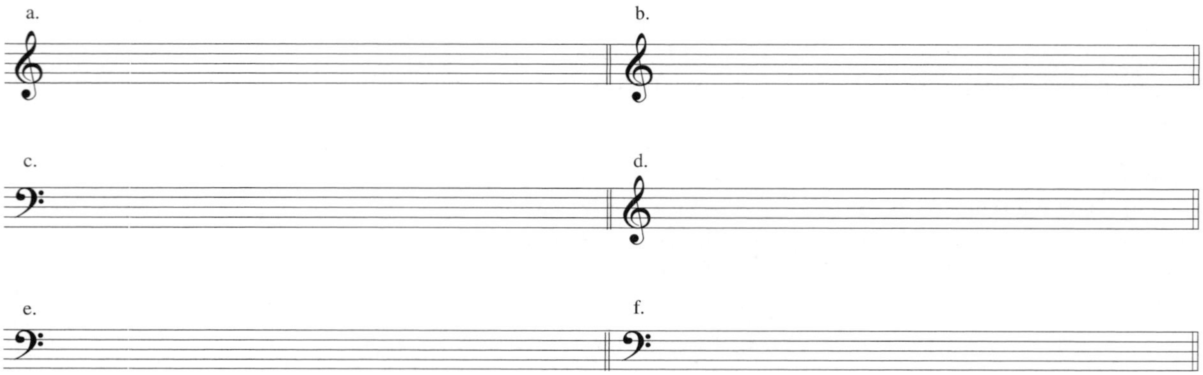

EXERCISE 2 Write first-species counterpoints above and below the following *cantus firmus.* As a suggestion, you may find it helpful to first write the opening pitches, then the cadence, and then plot a curve for your melody before you realize the rest of the counterpoint.

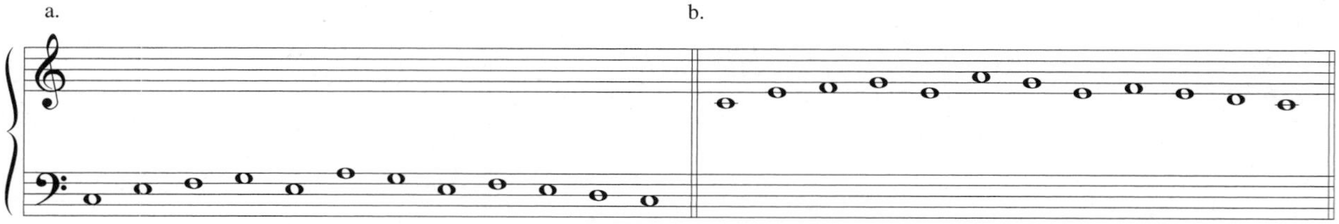

EXERCISE 3 Write second-species counterpoints above and below the following *cantus firmus.*

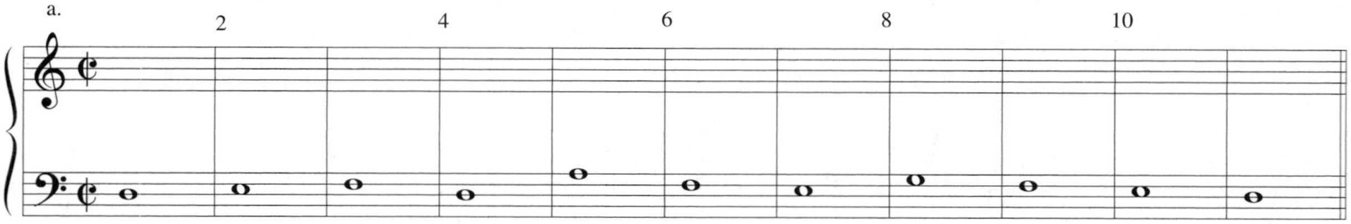

b.

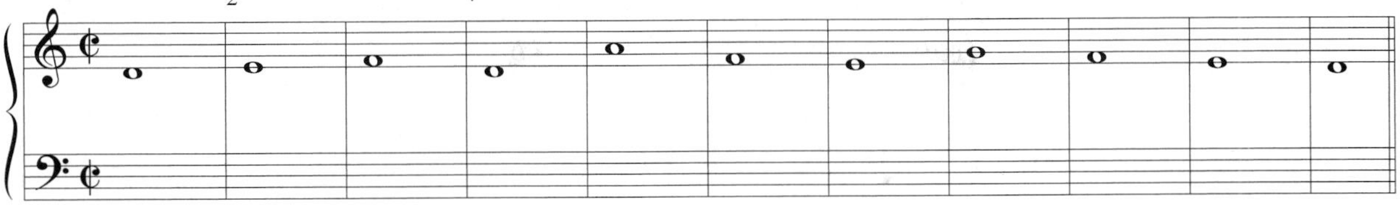

EXERCISE 4 Write third-species counterpoints above and below the following *cantus firmus.*

a.

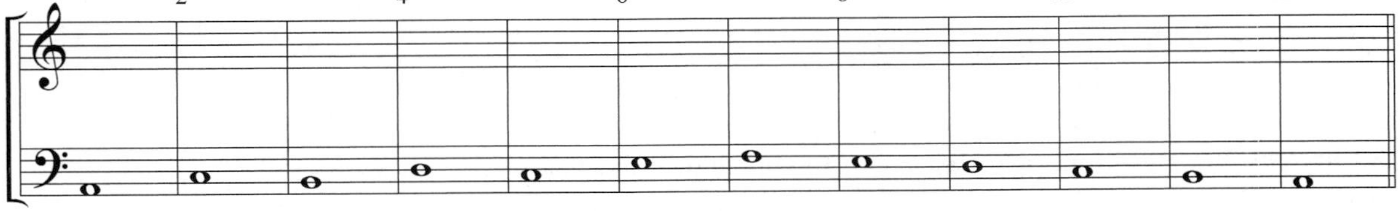

b.

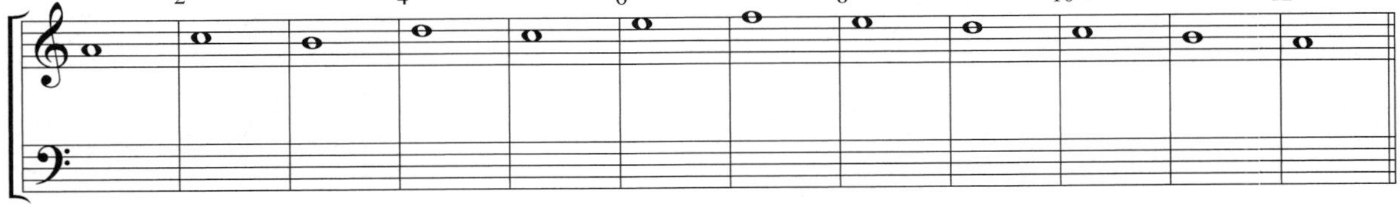

EXERCISE 5 Complete the suspensions in this exercise in two voices, including always a preparation (P), a suspension (S), and a resolution (R) above a *cantus firmus* note (CF). Some of the given notes are marked P for "preparation" or R for "resolution."

Procedure: If P is given, provide S (the same note as P), R, and the CF note (as indicated by the figures under the staff). If R is given, provide P and S (a step above R) and the CF note. If the CF note is given, write a complete P–S–R figure above it.

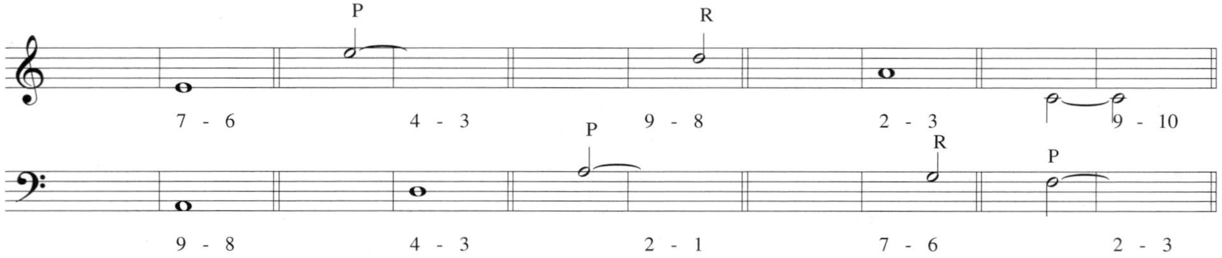

EXERCISE 6 Complete these cadences in two voices, following the *clausula vera* and Phrygian cadential models in example F.16e.

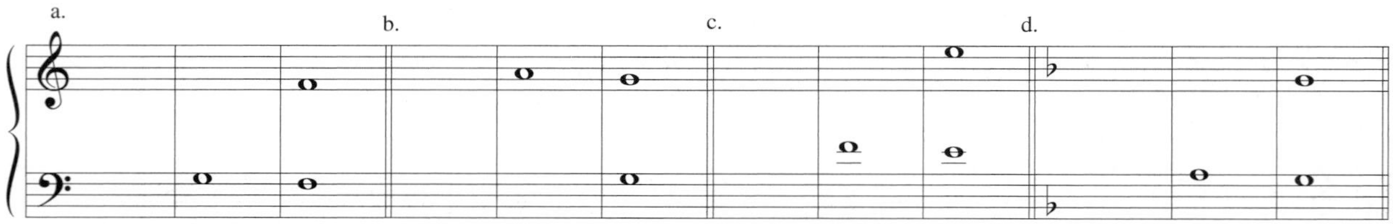

EXERCISE 7 Write fourth-species counterpoints above and below the following *cantus firmus.* As a suggestion, you may find it helpful to work from both ends toward the middle. First write the opening pitches and the cadence, and then plan a tentative curve for your melody before you realize the rest of the counterpoint.

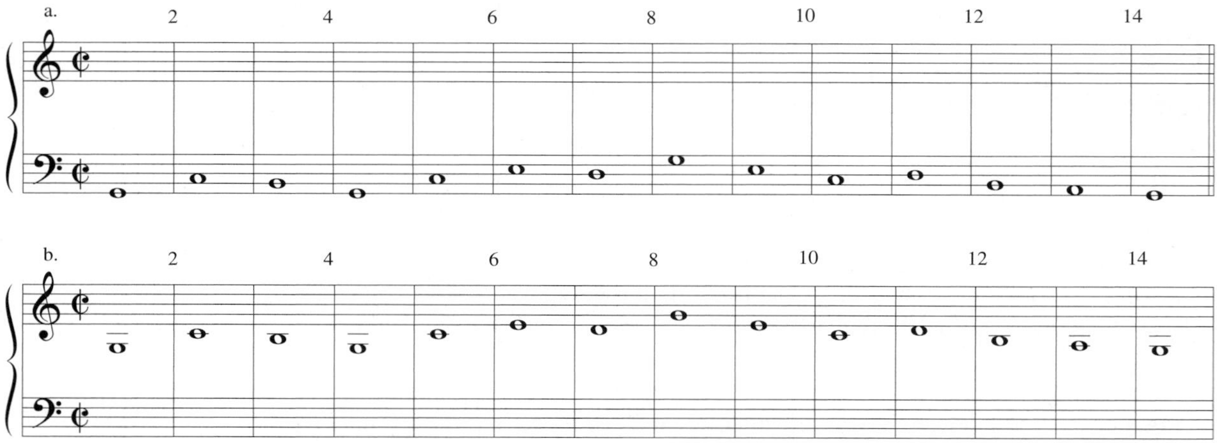

PART 1

Diatonic Harmony

Chapter 1

The Connection of Chords

If you listen to a recording of the opening fanfare of Claudio Monteverdi's *Orfeo* (1607), you will hear that it is based on a single chord. Tonality is here defined by the assertion of this single chord, the tonic triad. This is, however, a very unusual musical occurrence. Music is normally based on more than one chord, and tonality established by means other than assertion. In this chapter we will first examine the most frequent root relationships among successive chords, and then we will study the principles of part writing that regulate the connection of chords in tonal harmony.

HARMONIC PROGRESSION

A **harmonic progression** is a succession of two or more chords. In the tonal system, a given chord is not allowed to follow randomly any other chord. Some progressions are better than others, some are more idiomatic or typical than others, and conversely some chord successions are so atypical that, in principle, they sound "wrong" in the tonal language, and hence should be avoided. If chords constitute our harmonic vocabulary (like words in a spoken language), harmonic progressions are sentences, which we put together according to the correct syntax of the tonal language. Throughout this book we study both the harmonic vocabulary and the tonal syntax.

Basic Types of Progression

Taking into account the relationship between chord roots, there are three basic types of chord progression: *by 5th, by 2nd, and by 3rd.* Listen to the ***ritornello*** (the refrain, or recurring musical idea) from movement I of Antonio Vivaldi's "Winter" (*The Four Seasons*). The main melodic line, the bass line, and the Roman numerals for this musical phrase are reproduced in example 1.1. This is a progression in which all roots (also bass notes, in this case) are *related by 5th:* C–F–B♭–E♭–A♭–D–G–C–F.

The **progression by 5th,** in which chord roots are a 5th (or its inversion, a 4th) apart, is the most essential root relationship in tonal music. The root motion *down a 5th*

Example 1.1 Antonio Vivaldi, *The Four Seasons,* "Winter," I, *Ritornello*

or up a 4th has the property of propelling the music forward, of creating a harmonic motion that calls for continuation. The fundamental progression in tonal music, I–V–I, is based on this relationship: the root of V is a 5th above (or a 4th below) the root of I. Moreover, V is frequently preceded by ii, whose root ($\hat{2}$) is itself a 5th above $\hat{5}$. Any chord may be preceded by the chord a 5th above it; ii may thus be preceded by vi, and if we continue this same process, after seven chords we will use up all the available diatonic triads in a key (example 1.2). The bass line of the resulting progression, the **circle of 5ths** progression, contains, in its complete form, all the pitches of the diatonic scale

Example 1.2

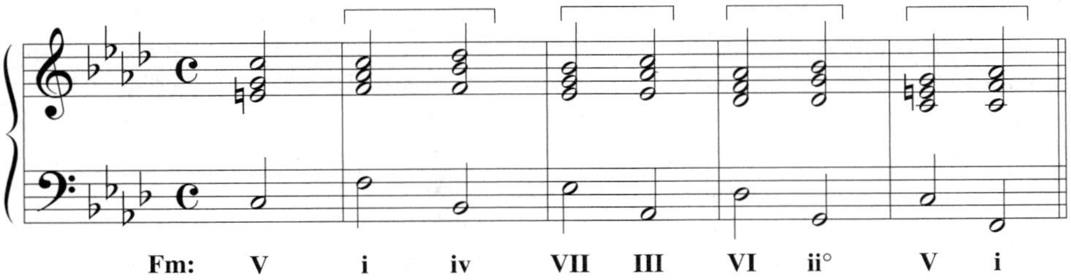

organized in descending 5ths, or ascending 4ths, or, as it is found most often in music, in descending 5ths alternating with ascending 4ths. Such is the case of the Vivaldi phrase and of the circle of 5ths triadic progression reproduced in example 1.2.

Both example 1.1 and example 1.2 illustrate the specific type of harmonic progression we call **sequence.** A sequence is a melodic-harmonic pattern that is restated, literally or with slight modifications, at different tonal levels, often up or down a step. In example 1.1, both the upper voice and the bass feature **melodic sequences.** In example 1.2, however, we see that the realization of the Roman numerals (the harmonies) from the Vivaldi example also displays a **harmonic sequential pattern** in which a pair of chords (the second and third chords) is restated in each of the following measures, and each statement is a step lower than the previous one. The circle of 5ths usually supports this type of sequence descending by steps, as we will often see in this book.

NOTE

In a diatonic circle of 5ths not all the 5ths or 4ths are perfect. Which 5th or 4th is not perfect in example 1.2, and what kind of 5th or 4th is it?

Example 1.3, on the other hand, features several cases of **progression by 2nd,** in which roots move by step. Beginning with the second chord (iii), the progression iii–IV–V–vi–V is all by 2nds. Stepwise progressions are also very common in tonal music, although not all progressions by 2nd are equally idiomatic. The step progressions shown in example 1.3 (marked with brackets) are all standard: iii–IV, IV–V, V–vi, and vi–V. I–ii is also found in the literature, although less often. Progressions such as ii–iii, IV–iii, and stepwise progressions to or from vii° in root position (vi–vii°, vii°–vi, I–vii°, or vii°–I) are seldom found and may be considered unidiomatic. Finally, the progression V–IV is very unusual in common practice harmony, although it is quite common in blues and rock music.

Example 1.4a illustrates the third type of standard progression, a **progression by 3rds,** in this case descending. An ascending progression by 3rds also appears in m. 1 of example 1.3. Here again, not all progressions by 3rds are equally idiomatic.

Example 1.3

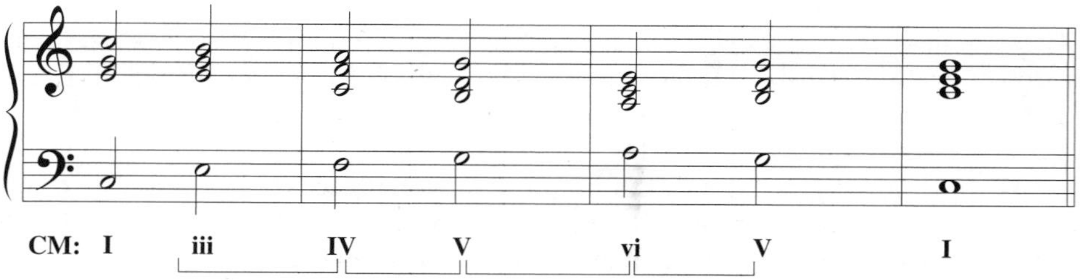

Example 1.4a

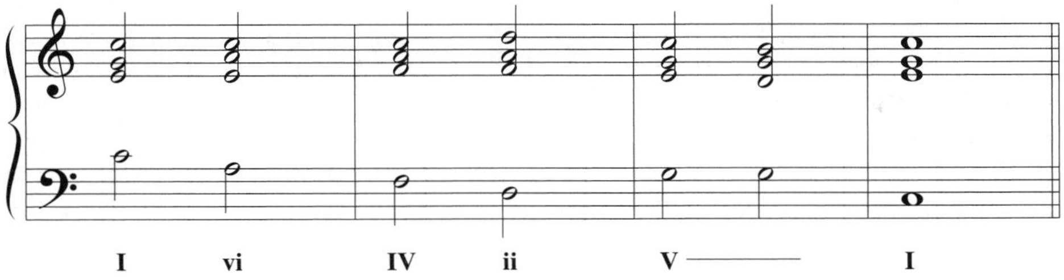

Example 1.4b John Lennon–Paul McCartney, "All My Loving," from the album *With the Beatles*

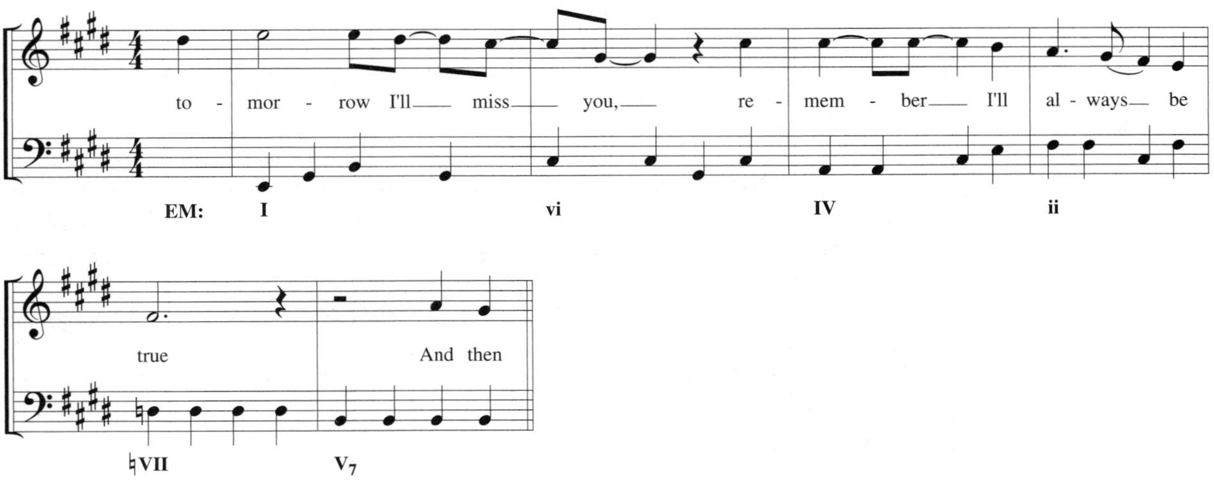

The two most frequent cases are the ascending progression I–iii–V or the descending progression I–vi–IV, which can be extended to I–vi–IV–ii, as in example 1.4a. Example 1.4b illustrates a progression by descending 3rds moving all the way from I to V: I–vi–IV–ii–♮VII–V_7.

Although examples 1.2, 1.3, and 1.4 illustrate progressions largely based on a single type of root motion, the three types are usually combined in music. Example 1.5 shows a progression combining root motion by 5th, 2nd, and 3rd.

Example 1.5

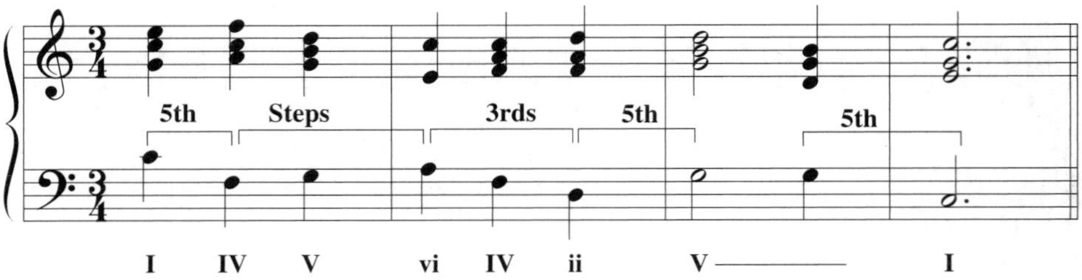

The detailed study of specific diatonic triads and the idiomatic progressions they are associated with in a musical context will be taken up in various chapters throughout part 1 of this book. In the remainder of this chapter we review the general principles of chord connection and discuss specific guidelines to connect chords whose roots are related by 5th, 2nd, or 3rd.

NOTATING, VOICING, AND SPACING CHORDS

Notation of Triads in Four Voices

We will begin by notating triads in *four voices* (or *parts,* as voices are often called) on two staves, according to the notational and musical conventions of vocal ensemble style in chorale texture. To begin with, we must keep each of the voices within possible (and comfortable) ranges. The four voices are called, from top to bottom, **soprano, alto, tenor,** and **bass (SATB).** Their ranges are represented in example 1.6. In chorale texture, soprano and alto are notated in the upper staff in treble clef, tenor and bass in the lower staff in bass clef. The direction of the stems, as illustrated in example 1.7a, is essential to the immediate visual identification of each of the four voices.

Voicing a Triad in Four Voices: Doublings

The term *voicing* refers to the distribution of pitches among the four voices, SATB. Because triads have three pitches and we write in four voices, a pitch must always be doubled. Once we connect several chords in harmonic progressions, *doubling will be determined mostly by voice leading.* If you have a choice, however, preferably double the root of the chord (example 1.7b). Doubling the fifth is your second choice (example 1.7c), followed by doubling the third (example 1.7d). These doubling preferences refer to *major and minor triads only.* The strongest and most stable interval in M and m triads is the P5,

Example 1.6

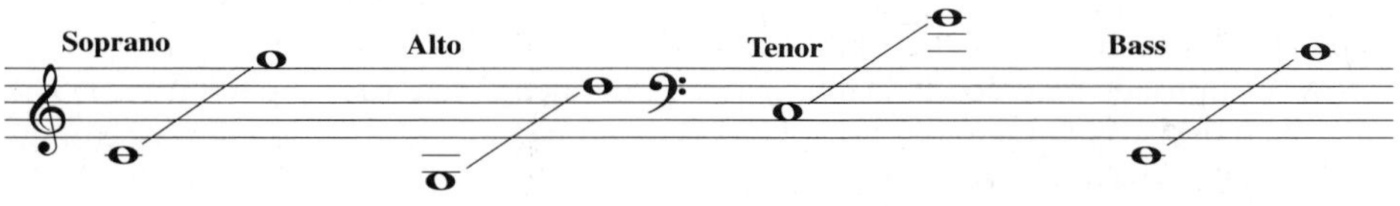

which frames them. For this reason, it is preferable to stress the root (the main pitch in a triad) or the fifth, rather than the third (unnecessarily stressing the third usually weakens the sound of a triad, an effect which, however, may be used to good advantage for expressive purposes).

NOTE

Because of the dissonant 5th that frames them, diminished and augmented triads present specific voicing problems that often depend on their harmonic context. Different criteria apply to doublings in these two types of triads, as will be discussed later in the book.

Example 1.7

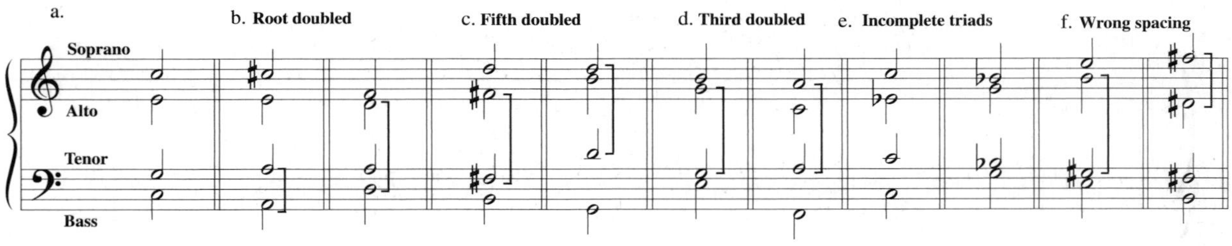

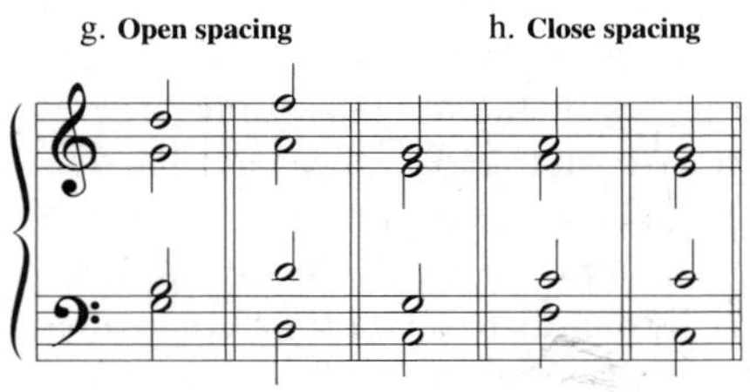

Do not double the leading tone (LT). Because it has a strong melodic tendency toward the tonic, the LT (the third of V, or the root of vii°) usually resolves to $\hat{1}$. Doubling it not only stresses a pitch which, because of its tendency, needs no additional emphasis, but also is likely to result in parallel 8ves if both LTs are resolved to $\hat{1}$ (see discussion of parallel 8ves in rule 5 in the next section).

M or m triads may occasionally, if rarely, be incomplete (one pitch left out). The only pitch that may be omitted is the fifth. The root and the third should never be omitted. (Omitting the root would create an identity crisis for the triad, and omitting the third would turn the triad into an open 5th, a perfect interval that may sound quite hollow in a triadic context.) If a chord has no fifth, you may either double the third or triple the root (example 1.7e)

Spacing

There should be no more than one 8ve between soprano and alto or alto and tenor. Tenor and bass, however, may be more than one 8ve apart (see example 1.7f).

Triads may be in open or close spacing. In **open spacing** there is one 8ve or more between soprano and tenor (example 1.7g). In **close spacing** there is less than an 8ve between soprano and tenor (example 1.7h). In other words, in open spacing you should be able to insert one or more chord notes between some of the adjacent three upper voices. For instance, in the first chord in example 1.7g you could insert a D between tenor and alto, and a B between alto and soprano. What pitches could you insert between adjacent upper voices in the second and third chords? In close spacing, on the other hand, you cannot insert any chord notes between any of the adjacent three upper voices. Verify whether this is true in example 1.7h.

EXERCISE

To practice notating triads in four voices, refer to exercise 2 in worksheet 1 at the end of this chapter.

CHORD CONNECTION: THE PRINCIPLES OF PART WRITING

We will now focus on the techniques of chord connection. A smooth, stylistically correct connection between two chords follows a number of principles, which we will summarize in the following paragraphs. These principles reflect *general harmonic conventions in common practice tonal music.* But even within this stylistic frame, some of the usual conventions of chord connection and melodic style are closely linked to vocal music, and specifically to **chorale-style harmonizations.** As we studied in chapter E, these are four-part vocal harmonizations of hymn tunes, in which the actual tune is usually placed in the soprano. You should keep in mind that some of the conventions you will study below do not necessarily apply to, say, instrumental music. Because of idiomatic writing, for instance, instrumental lines often include numerous large leaps of types that you will not find in chorale textures (or in choral music in general), and which you will need to avoid in your vocal four-part harmonizations.

In the anthology, nos. 8–10, you can examine some of the 371 chorale harmonizations by J. S. Bach that have reached us. In these chorales you can clearly hear the two simultaneous dimensions of sound: the horizontal dimension provided by the independent lines and the vertical dimension that results from pitch simultaneities among the four lines, which produces chordal sonorities. In our chord connections we need to keep both dimensions in mind. The motion of voices between chords is regulated by the principles of **part writing.** But at the same time we need to think of all four voices as interacting, independent lines—an element of harmony we refer to as **voice leading.**

Basic Voice-Leading Conventions

Example 1.8 shows several connections between tonic and dominant chords. Although the principles of part writing and voice leading apply to all types of chord connections regardless of their root motion, we will begin by illustrating these principles with

Example 1.8

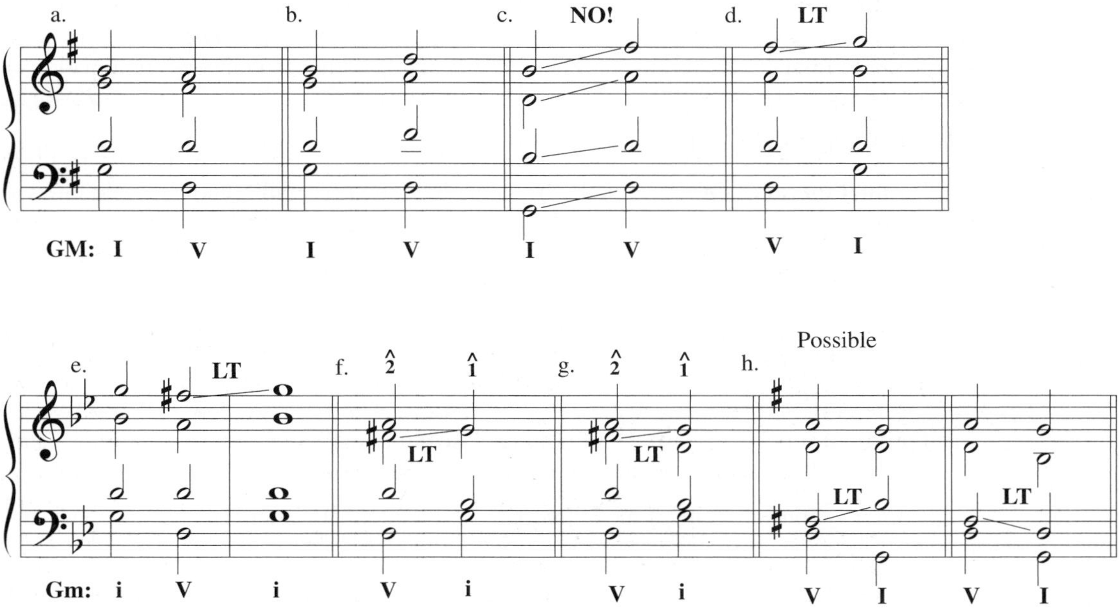

progressions based only on the tonic and the dominant triads. **Nine basic rules of voice leading** follow.

1. *General principle.* When connecting two chords, leave any *common tone(s)* between the chords in the same voice(s); take all other voices to the nearest possible pitch from the second chord, as long as doing so does not create some other kind of voice-leading problem, such as faulty parallel 5ths or 8ves (examples 1.8a, d, and e).
2. *Leaps.* Melodic motion by step (conjunct motion) is preferred. Avoid large leaps whenever possible, unless they are musically justified. Although leaps of 3rd, P4, and P5 are frequent in the bass (and so is the 8ve), leaps larger than a P4 or P5 should rarely be used in the upper voices. Leaps of a 7th should especially be avoided. The part writing in example 1.8b, although less smooth than example 1.8a because of leaps in three voices, is quite acceptable. Example 1.8c, on the other hand, presents some seemingly unnecessary large leaps in all four voices, which result in quite faulty part writing. Because a part-writing flaw often engenders other troubles, example 1.8c illustrates two more problems we will point out below.
3. *Augmented and diminished intervals.* Melodic augmented intervals should in principle be strictly avoided. Beware especially of the augmented second, $\flat\hat{6}$–$\natural\hat{7}$, in the minor mode. Diminished intervals, usually descending and most often in the bass (such as the diminished fifth $\hat{4}$–$\hat{7}$, the diminished fourth $\hat{3}$–$\sharp\hat{7}$ in minor, and even the diminished seventh $\hat{6}$–$\sharp\hat{7}$ also in minor), are possible in some progressions. They usually resolve by step in the opposite direction of the leap ($\hat{4}$–$\hat{7}$–$\hat{1}$ or, in minor, $\hat{3}$–$\sharp\hat{7}$–$\hat{1}$ or $\hat{6}$–$\sharp\hat{7}$–$\hat{1}$).
4. ***Contrapuntal motion** between voices.* As we studied in chapter F, the simultaneous presentation of independent lines (melodies) is known as *counterpoint.* The term also refers to the technical principles that regulate the simultaneous combination of voices.

   In chapter F we also saw four possible types of motion between voices.

Parallel motion: Voices move in the same direction preserving the harmonic interval between them. In example 1.8a, soprano-alto move in parallel motion (they preserve the 3rd, even though the first one is a M3 and the second a m3), as they do in example 1.8d, now preserving the 6th.

Similar motion: Voices move in the same direction, but the harmonic interval between them is not preserved. Both the soprano-tenor and alto-bass pairs in example 1.8f move in similar motion.

Oblique motion: A voice moves (up or down) and the other voice stays on the same pitch. The tenor-bass motion in examples 1.8a and d illustrates oblique motion.

Contrary motion: Voices move in opposite directions. In example 1.8b, the tenor and bass move by contrary motion.

Contrapuntal motion among the four voices. Try to avoid moving all four voices in the same direction, as in example 1.9a. If possible, at least one of the voices

Example 1.9

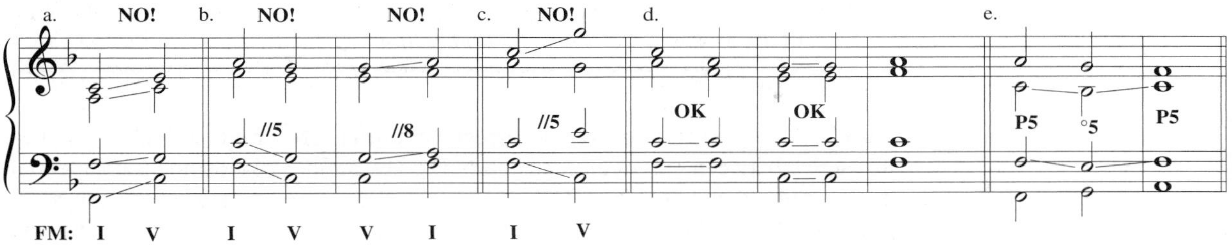

should move in contrary or oblique motion with respect to the other three (although at times a perfectly acceptable voice leading will include motion of all voices in the same direction). All the progressions in example 1.8 follow this voice-leading principle, except for example 1.8c. Not only do all voices leap, but they all do so in the same direction, contributing to the poor realization of the part writing.

5. *Forbidden parallels.* **Parallel 5ths** or **parallel 8ves** result when two voices move by parallel motion from a P5 to another P5, or from an 8ve to another 8ve. Parallel perfect 5ths (//5) and 8ves (//8) are strictly forbidden (example 1.9b). Consecutive **P5s or P8s by contrary motion** are equally forbidden (example 1.9c). This is a strong stylistic feature in tonal music and is based on the principle of voice independence: If two voices move in parallel 8ves (and, to a certain extent, also in parallel 5ths), their individuality and independence are lost. Moreover, because the 5th is a very stable and strong interval, the sound of parallel 5ths is particularly characteristic, and in a triadic texture of independent voices it tends to stand out as unstylistic. We mentioned previously that voice-leading woes rarely come alone. All voices leaping in the same direction in the faulty I–V progression in example 1.8c results in some problematic parallels. Can you find them?

NOTE

5ths or 8ves repeated *in the same voices, without motion, are not incorrect parallels (see example 1.9d).*

Consecutive 5ths are allowed only if one of them is diminished (*unequal 5ths*), although even then they should be avoided between the outer voices (bass and soprano). Example 1.9e illustrates a progression that features two sets of acceptable unequal 5ths in succession (P5–°5 and °5–P5).

NOTE

Instrumental or choral 8ve doubling is totally correct and is not of the same nature as voice-leading parallel 8ves. It is commonly used to strengthen a voice (as in 8ve doubling of a melody or bass at the piano) or for coloristic purposes (an oboe melody doubled at the upper 8ves by a flute and a piccolo).

6. *Direct or hidden 5ths or 8ves.* A **direct or hidden 5th or 8ve** results when a P5 or an 8ve between *outer voices* is approached by similar motion and with a leap in the soprano (example 1.10a). If the soprano is approached by step, the 5th or 8ve is perfectly acceptable (example 1.10b). This latter case happens frequently in what is called "horn 5ths." In example 1.10c, from Mozart's Sonata in FM, K. 332, I, brackets indicate two standard cases of horn 5ths. In the first type, a 5th is preceded by a 3rd, in a descending motion in which the soprano moves by step. The second type features an ascending motion from a 6th to a 5th, also with a soprano moving by step. (The 8ves between the top and middle voices in this example are not a case of faulty "parallel 8ves," but rather of correct 8ve doubling of a melody.)
7. *Leading tone.* As a general principle, **resolve the leading tone** up a half step, to the tonic, especially when the LT is in one of the outer voices. See examples 1.8d, e, and f; see also the section "Voicing a Triad in Four Voices: Doublings" on pages 110–112.

   If the LT is in an inner voice, however, exceptions to this principle are possible. If the voice above the LT moves to $\hat{1}$ in the same octave as the LT, then we hear the resolution to $\hat{1}$ in the upper voice as a satisfactory resolution. This allows the LT to move down a 3rd, as illustrated by example 1.8g. Occasionally a LT in an inner voice leaps up a 4th or down a 3rd, as demonstrated in example 1.8h. Although both of these LT motions are possible and found in Bach chorales, you should use them with moderation because they contravene the strong melodic tendency of $\hat{7}$ toward $\hat{1}$.

Example 1.10

Example 1.11

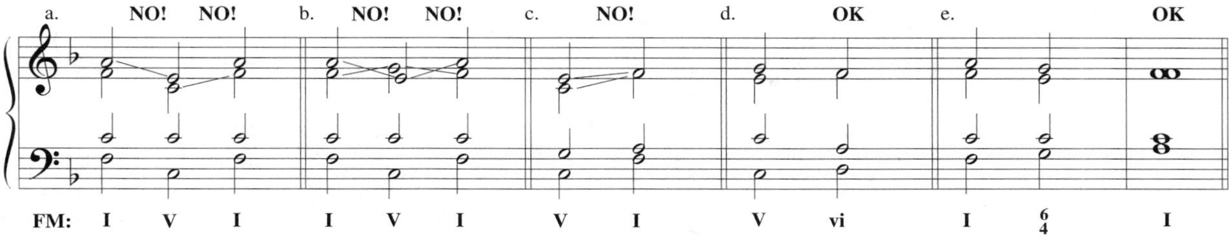

8. *Voice overlap and voice crossing.* In example 1.11a, the soprano moves to a pitch (E) lower than the adjacent voice (alto, F) in the previous chord. The alto then moves from C to F, a pitch higher than the adjacent voice (soprano, E) in the previous chord. These are all examples of **voice overlap,** which in principle should be avoided in part writing. As a reminder that often troubles do not come alone, what else is dubious in the connection of these three chords?

   In example 1.11b, the soprano and alto cross twice. **Voice crossing** should also be avoided in part-writing exercises, especially when it involves one of the outer voices. In other words, you should try to keep the proper order of voices: soprano above alto above tenor above bass. Occasional and brief voice crossing between the tenor and alto is possible as long as it does not create other voice-leading problems.

   The reason for these guidelines concerning voice crossing and overlap has to do again with the independence of the parts: Voices that cross or overlap tend to get confused with each other, thus losing their individuality. These are not, however, absolute rules. You will find occasional overlaps and voice crossings in Bach chorales, and you can also use them occasionally if you have some musical reason for it.

9. *Unison.* **Unison** between two voices is correct as long as it is approached and left by contrary or oblique motion. Do not approach or leave it by similar motion. The result will be an awkward voice overlap, as in example 1.11c. Two unisons in a row in the same voices involving successive different pitches (*parallel unisons*) are strictly forbidden, as much as parallel 8ves are. (Unisons repeated in the same voices, without change of pitch, are perfectly acceptable.) Examples 1.11d and e show two cases of correct unisons that occur frequently in progressions we will study.

EXERCISE

To practice error detection in chord connections, refer to exercise 3 in worksheet 1 at the end of this chapter.

Example 1.12

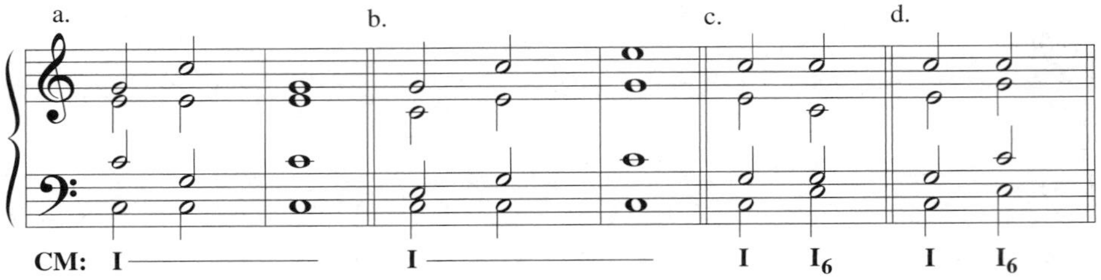

Changes of Voicing or Position

In a change of voicing, a chord remains the same, but its voicing changes. The change of voicing may affect one or more of the three upper voices, or it may affect the bass. If the bass position changes, the position of the chord changes (from root position to an inversion or vice versa, or from one inversion to another).

Examples 1.12a and b illustrate **changes of voicing** in the upper voices on a static bass. In example 1.12a only two voices change, whereas in example 1.12b all three voices change.

In four-voice connections involving a **change of position** (from root position to first inversion, for instance), at least one voice should remain static. Example 1.12c is an example of change of position in which only two voices change (including, of course, the bass). Example 1.12d illustrates a change of position in which three voices change.

EXERCISE

To practice changes of voicing and position, refer to exercise 4 in worksheet 1 at the end of this chapter.

VOICE-LEADING GUIDELINES FOR THE THREE BASIC TYPES OF PROGRESSION

At the beginning of this chapter, you learned that the three basic types of progression involve root motion by descending 5th, by step, or by 3rd, respectively. We will now review some general guidelines for voice leading in each of these progression types. The following guidelines assume that all chords are in root position and that the root is doubled in all chords. Many other voice-leading possibilities are afforded by different doublings and by chord inversions, as will become apparent to you as you begin writing progressions in the following chapters.

Example 1.13

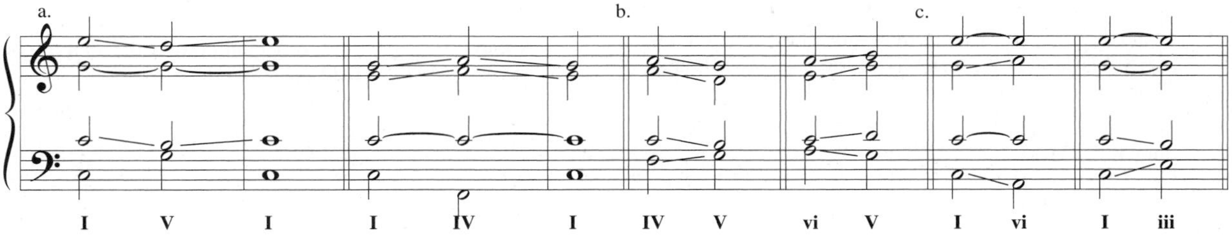

Roots by 5th

The voice leading for the 5th progression allows for several equally good possibilities. The most standard, and most smooth voice leading, however, is illustrated in example 1.13a: the common tone between the two chords remains in the same voice, while the other two upper voices move by step to the closest pitch in the next chord. This same principle applies to both the ascending 5th and the descending 5th progression, as both examples in example 1.13a illustrate (I–V–I, ascending-descending, and I–IV–I, descending-ascending).

Roots by 2nd

Progressions by 2nd do not allow for various possibilities without risk of parallel 5ths and 8ves. The best and safest voice leading is shown in example 1.13b: all three upper voices move in contrary motion with the bass (two of them by steps, one by 3rd). The same principle applies to roots ascending by step (such as IV–V) or descending by step (such as vi–V).

Roots by 3rd

Diatonic triads whose roots are related by a 3rd have two common tones. The smoothest voice leading in this progression keeps both common tones in the same voices, while the remaining voice moves by step. A descending 3rd progression (I–vi) and an ascending 3rd progression (I–iii) appear in example 1.13c.

EXERCISE

To practice part writing in four voices, refer to exercise 5 in worksheet 1 at the end of this chapter.

VOICE-LEADING GUIDELINES

1. Common tones between two chords preferably remain in the same voice(s). In 5th and 3rd progressions, the other pitches move to the nearest possible pitch in the second chord. In step progressions upper voices move in contrary motion with the bass.
2. Avoid unnecessary leaps. Conjunct motion is preferred.
3. Avoid augmented melodic intervals. Diminished intervals are acceptable, especially in the bass, and usually resolve by step in the opposite direction.
4. Try not to move all four voices simultaneously in the same direction.
5. Parallel perfect 5ths, 8ves, and unisons are forbidden. P5s and 8ves by contrary motion are also forbidden.
6. Avoid direct 5ths or 8ves between outer voices, unless the soprano moves by step.
7. It is best to resolve the LT up a half step to $\hat{1}$, especially in the outer voices.
8. Avoid crossing voices, especially above the soprano or below the bass. Avoid voice overlap.
9. Approach and leave unisons by contrary or oblique motion (not by similar motion).

MELODIC STYLE

As much as possible, your individual lines should be melodically satisfying. This applies especially to the *soprano line.* You should also craft the shape of your voices, especially the outer voices (soprano and bass). Some of the criteria for doing so are similar to those you studied in chapter F with reference to melody in species counterpoint. Because Renaissance style, however, was more strict than common practice style, the following melodic principles in four-part, chorale-style harmony are not quite as rigorous as those in species counterpoint.

Basic Melodic Conventions

1. *Stepwise motion* is always preferred. If possible, it is desirable to balance a leap in the melody with motion in the opposite direction before or after the leap, although this is considered a stricter guideline in counterpoint than in harmonic part writing. We have already seen that large leaps and augmented intervals should be avoided. Diminished melodic intervals, on the other hand, are acceptable. The bass line is likely to have more leaps than the upper voices, including frequent skips of 3rd, P4, P5, and 8ve.
2. Two *consecutive leaps* in the same direction are awkward unless they outline a triad (or, in the bass, an 8ve split by a 5th, as in $\hat{1}$–$\hat{5}$–$\hat{8}$), and in all cases it is best to balance them with motion in the opposite direction *before and after* the leaps.
3. Melodies should have a smooth (not jagged) contour. The best melodies have a single focal point (highest or lowest pitch). Repeating a pitch more than twice results in a static, uninteresting line. This may often happen, however, in the alto and tenor; inner voices will tend to be more static because of the preference to leave common tones in the same voice if possible. Avoid excessive or unmusical pitch repetition in the soprano.

All the preceding principles of good melodic style are illustrated in the four chorale melodies in example 1.14. Read the melodies carefully, sing them, and verify the application of the guidelines. Observe especially how leaps are balanced and how consecutive leaps in the same direction outline a triad or an 8ve split by a 5th. Basic contours are indicated under three of the melodies, and focal points are marked with arrows.

Example 1.14

EXERCISE

To practice critical analysis of melodic style, refer to exercise 6 in worksheet 1 at the end of this chapter.

VOICE INDEPENDENCE

Voices, especially outer voices (soprano-bass) must be as independent as possible. This principle is not different from what you learned in chapter F regarding voice independence in species counterpoint. Contrary or oblique motion is preferred, whereas parallel motion should be limited to three or four consecutive pitches. Contours should be independent, and focal points should, if possible, not happen at the same time. The outer voices of a phrase from a chorale by J. S. Bach are reproduced in example 1.15a.

Example 1.15a J. S. Bach, Chorale 80, "O Haupt voll Blut and Wunden," mm. 1–4

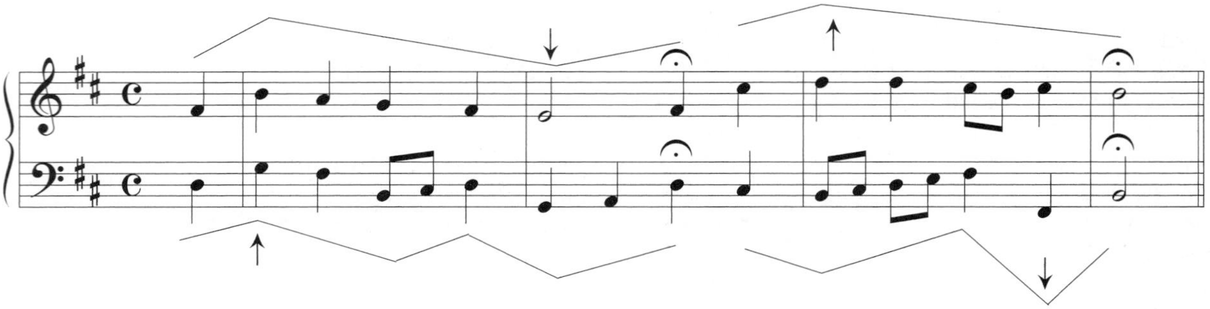

Example 1.15b J. S. Bach, Chorale 160, "Gelobet seist du," mm. 1–4

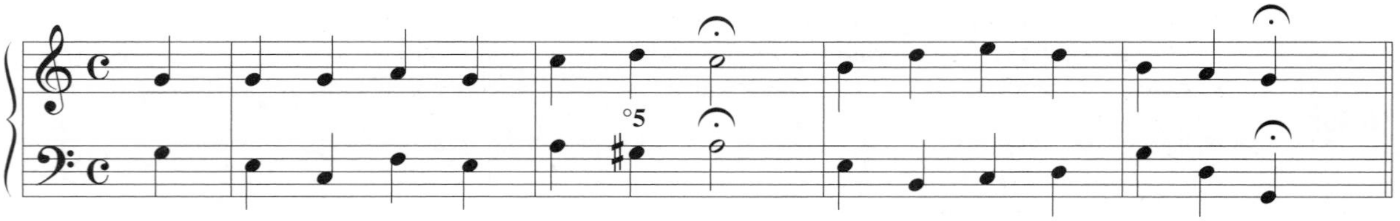

Example 1.15c J. S. Bach, Chorale 181, "Gott hat das Evangelium," mm. 1–4

Examine them for independence of contour and focal points. Notice that the leap of a 5th in the soprano after the first fermata is not balanced by motion in the opposite direction before or after the leap. This is quite acceptable in this case because the F♯ and the C♯ belong to different phrases, as indicated by the fermata, and hence are not heard as a melodic unit.

Voice Leading and Species Counterpoint

Most of the voice-leading principles we have just studied have their origin in Renaissance counterpoint and its pedagogical adaptation, species counterpoint. In chapter F you were introduced to species counterpoint, and you must certainly have recognized, in the present chapter, such principles as moving the voices mostly by steps, balancing leaps with motion in the opposite direction, avoiding parallel perfect intervals, avoiding direct 5ths and 8ves, and so forth.

As soon as we start realizing harmonic progressions, you will observe that *outer-voice motion is usually ruled by the principles of first- or second-species counterpoint.* This is often true also of inner voices, but in four-part harmonic realizations the shape of inner voices may have to be sacrificed to achieve smooth overall voice leading, especially if we are to keep common tones in the same voice as much as possible. Your focus should be mostly on outer-voice independence and shape.

In example 1.15b you can see the outer-voice frame for a fragment of a Bach chorale. Verify that it is written according to the principles of first-species counterpoint, Here again, some of the conventions of common practice counterpoint are slightly different from those of the Renaissance. In chapter F, for instance, you learned that, in first species, all harmonic intervals should be consonant. In the Bach example, a harmonic °5 has been marked. Both harmonic and melodic diminished intervals, such as °5 or °7, are quite idiomatic, and hence quite acceptable, in common practice harmonic style. Refer to example D.1a, another Bach chorale fragment in which outer voices are ruled by first-species counterpoint, and identify two correct harmonic diminished intervals in the outer-voice frame.

EXERCISE

To practice critical analysis of part writing, voice leading, and melodic style, refer to exercise 1 in worksheet 1 at the end of this chapter.

WHY ALL THESE RULES?

To be effective, the principles and conventions of voice leading and chordal connection must be understood in their proper context.

1. Voice-leading rules reflect conventions that for centuries have been considered the foundation of compositional craft.
2. The rules are stylistic in nature, and limited to a relatively short historical period. Although most voice-leading principles were already in effect in the sixteenth century, the style of chordal functional harmony that this book represents was practiced from mid- to late seventeenth to mid- to late nineteenth centuries. It is still practiced to the present day in most commercial music: Music composed for movies, television, musicals, and entertainment or background music in general is usually solidly grounded on the principles of tonal voice leading.

   Tonal music is written according to a number of conventions of good craft, which make it "sound as it does," that is, which make it sound "stylistically correct."

A fifteenth-century 8ve-leap cadence sounds very different than a Mozart cadence because of the different conventions involved. And, to use another example, frequent series of parallel 5ths are stylistically correct in the music of Debussy, whereas they would be totally out of place (stylistically wrong) in the music of Haydn or Mozart.

3. Even in the stylistic time span mentioned above, we find numerous exceptions to the rules in actual music by composers of the period. The reasons are multiple: (1) Four-part, chorale-style harmony reflects mostly a vocal style. Instrumental styles may at times be less strict in their observance of some rules. (2) Harmony and its principles, as studied in a book like this, are pedagogical in nature. Rules have an important function for beginning musicians, in helping them acquire technique, discipline, and control over the music they write. (3) All composers of the past acquired their solid craft through elaborate studies that included many more rules than the ones presented in this book. Once they possessed technique and control, at times they consciously ignored some convention for good musical reasons. But although good musical reasons always have priority over rules and conventions, careless craft only reflects (and produces) poor musicianship.

ASSIGNMENT

For a written assignment on the materials learned in this chapter, refer to chapter 1 in the workbook.

Terms for Review

Harmonic progression
Ritornello
Progression by 5th
Circle of 5ths
Sequence (melodic and harmonic)
Progression by 2nd
Progression by 3rd
Soprano, alto, tenor, bass (SATB)
Voicing a triad in four voices; doublings
Spacing:
    open, close
Chorale-style harmonizations
Part writing and voice leading
Voice leading conventions
    (nine basic rules)
Contrapuntal motion: parallel, similar, oblique, contrary
Parallel 5ths and 8ves
5ths and 8ves by contrary motion
Direct (hidden) 5ths and 8ves
Leading-tone resolution
Voice overlap, voice crossing
Unison
Changes of voicing or position
Melodic style
Voice independence

Worksheet 1

EXERCISE 1 Analysis.

a) Analyze example 1.16 with Roman numerals. What is the key of the passage? Notice that chords are presented in a characteristic keyboard figuration (the *bass afterbeat* pattern typical of waltzes and marches) in which a chord is broken into a bass note on the downbeat and the remaining pitches as a block chord in the following beats. The *complete measure* is analyzed as one chord, with the position determined by the bass on the downbeat.

Procedure to analyze progressions with Roman numerals: First determine the key for the passage. Then, identify the root and type of each chord by organizing its pitches in thirds. After you know the root of the chord, determine on what scale degree the chord is built in the specific key for the passage, and assign the correct Roman numeral (capital or lowercase) depending on the chord type.

b) How does the voice leading in the left hand reflect the guidelines studied in this chapter?

c) How does the melody reflect the changes of harmony? Does it also display good voice leading in its motion from chord 1 to chord 2?

d) Comment on the melody. Although it is an instrumental melody, is it "well written" by our vocal melodic standards?

Example 1.16 Franz Schubert, *Walzer, Ländler und Ecossaisen,* op. 18, Ländler, no. 3, mm. 1–8

e) Admitting that Schubert certainly knew what he was doing, could you comment critically on the melody in mm. 1–5?

EXERCISE 2 Write root-position triads in four voices with the requested spacing (o for open, c for close), without key signatures (write only the necessary accidentals before each triad).

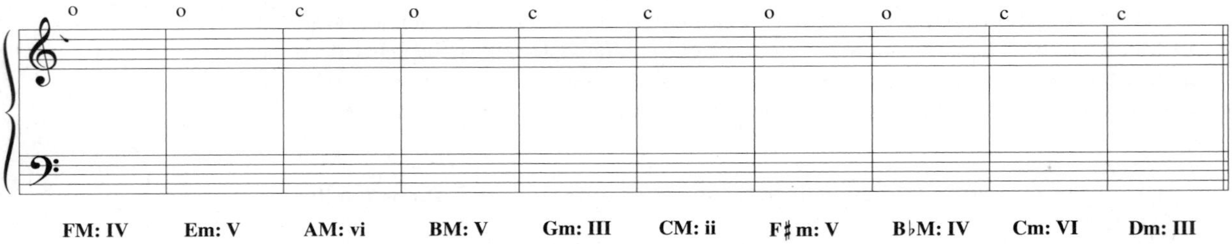

EXERCISE 3 Identify and mark all the voice-leading mistakes in the following progressions.

EXERCISE 4 Complete the following changes of voicing or position in four voices.

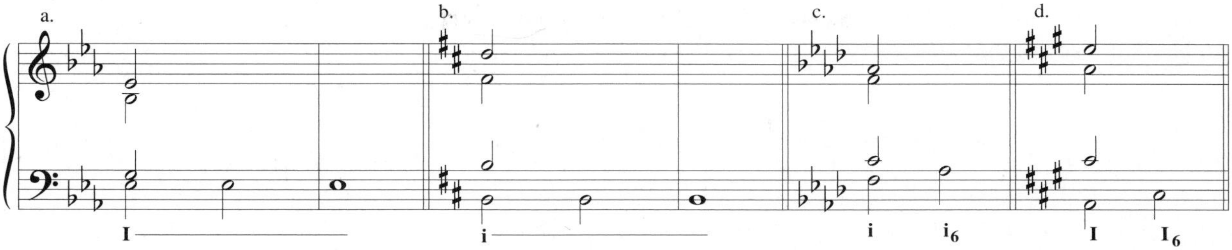

EXERCISE 5 Complete the following progressions in four voices on the given bass notes, following the provided models. All your chords should be in root position, and you should apply the principles of voice leading according to root motion, which you studied earlier (see example 1.13).

a. Root motion by 5th

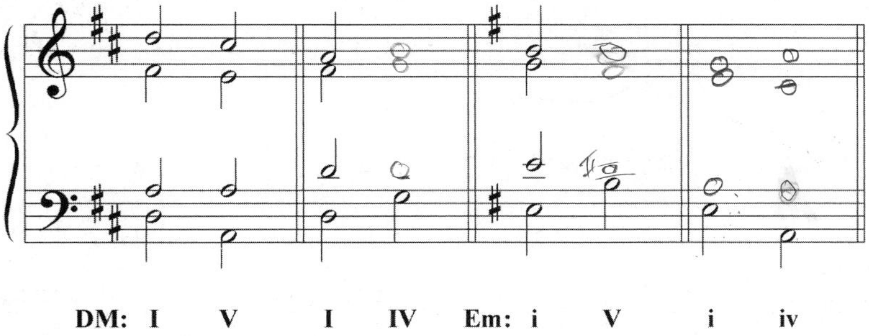

b. Root motion by 2nd

c. Root motion by 3rd

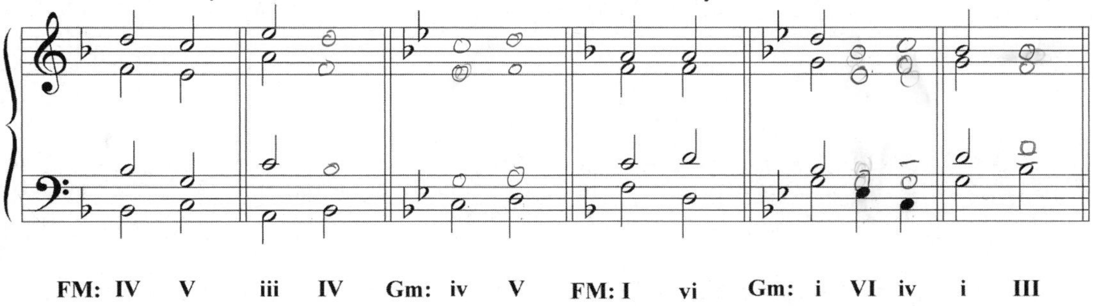

EXERCISE 6

The following melody is very weak according to the criteria for melodic style discussed in this chapter. Criticize the melody, circle all the faulty spots, and annotate the specific problem for each of the weak spots.

Chapter 2

The Tonic and Dominant Triads in Root Position

The tonic and the dominant triads (I and V in major keys, or i and V in minor keys) constitute the basic two-chord unit of the tonal system. The tonic is the tonal goal to which musical tensions and processes are ultimately directed, as well as the element of stability and release in which these tensions resolve. The dominant harmony, on the other hand, provides the most immediate factor of harmonic tension that requires resolution to the tonic. **Structural chords** are those that can have the role of beginning or ending musical units such as phrases, sections, or complete movements. The tonic and dominant harmonies are structural chords: only the tonic triad is a true point of departure; both the dominant and the tonic may function as points of arrival.

Many musical units are based on only these two chords. Listen to the opening of Giuseppe Verdi's drinking song from *La traviata* ("Libiamo ne' lieti calici," see anthology, no. 52). The section is based only on I and V_7 in the key of B♭M. The accompaniment features a chordal figuration that was discussed in worksheet 1—the **bass afterbeat figuration** typical of waltzes and marches. In this figuration, the chord is broken into a bass note on the downbeat and a block chord in the following beats. The *complete measure* is analyzed as one chord, with the position determined by the bass on the downbeat.

NOTE

You will notice that, in actual music, the dominant chord often appears as a seventh chord, V_7*, rather than a triad, V. Although we must first learn how to connect triads before we can deal with seventh chords, you will have to recognize the dominant seventh in actual musical examples from the outset. Chapter 8 will be entirely devoted to* V_7 *and its inversions.*

Examine now example 2.1, and identify the key and the chords on which the piece is based. To help you recognize the chords and to understand their relationship within the key, label each of them with the correct Roman numeral.

All of example 2.1 is based on two chords, I and V_7. Here the chords are presented in an **arpeggiated keyboard figuration,** rather than as block chords. (This

Example 2.1 Ludwig van Beethoven, *Seven Peasant Dances,* WoO 168, no. 4, mm. 1–8

type of arpeggiated keyboard figuration follows the pattern low note—high note—middle note—high note and is called **Alberti bass.**) Measures 1–2, left hand, contain only three pitches, D–F♯–A, the tonic triad (I) in DM. The right-hand melody in these measures is based on these pitches exclusively. Measures 3–4, left hand, feature also three pitches, A–E–G. These pitches do not form a triad, but they outline a seventh chord, and if we infer the missing pitch, A–C♯–E–G, we have the complete V_7 harmony in DM. We need not assume the missing pitch, though. The descending scale in the right hand actually contains all of the pitches in V_7, including our "missing" C♯, plus a few more. If we circle the V_7 pitches in this scale (in descending order, G–E–C♯–A–G–E–C♯), we see that the remaining pitches connect the chord tones by steps. They are, as you know from chapter F, **passing tones.** Passing tones belong to a general melodic category of pitches we call **nonchord tones,** which we will study at length in chapter 6. Nonchord tones are not part of the chord in which they appear, and they have a melodic, embellishing function. Measures 5–8 should be easy to figure out after mm. 1–4, especially because there are no new chords here, and these measures contain no nonchord tones at all. Notice that in m. 7, V_7 is now very clearly stated, if we consider all pitches in both hands.

In the two preceding examples, you will have observed that V (V_7) has a tendency to resolve to I and, in these particular examples, does indeed invariably resolve to I. This tension-resolution pattern between V and I is the defining harmonic force underlying the tonal system. In this chapter we will examine what creates this tension-resolution pattern, and we will review specific voice-leading issues regarding these two chords.

THE TONIC TRIAD

The tonic is the central pitch in a key, and the triad built on the tonic (the **tonic triad**, made up of scale degrees $\hat{1}$, $\hat{3}$, and $\hat{5}$) is the central triad in the tonal system. The tonic triad provides a sense of stability as well as a sense of resolution of tonal tension. Because of its stability, the tonic functions as a strong tonal point of departure. And because it provides resolution to tension, it functions as a strong tonal goal or point of arrival. Self-contained musical units, such as phrases, periods, or complete pieces, frequently begin and end on the tonic. Beginning on the tonic provides the listener with a sense of tonal center. Ending on the tonic provides a sense of conclusion: formal units that end on the tonic are said to be **closed.**

THE DOMINANT TRIAD

The **dominant triad** (scale degrees $\hat{5}$–$\hat{7}$–$\hat{2}$) follows the tonic in importance within the hierarchy of the tonal system. The leading tone, contained in the dominant triad, is a **tendency tone:** It creates a tension because it has a tendency to resolve to $\hat{1}$ by half-step motion. This tendency and its resolution are two of the fundamental tenets of tonality. Another member of V, scale degree $\hat{2}$, is also an unstable tone because of its dissonance with $\hat{1}$. Although not properly a tendency tone, $\hat{2}$ is melodically directed toward $\hat{1}$ or $\hat{3}$, both members of the tonic triad. Because of the tonal tension created by these melodic tendencies, V requires resolution to a more stable harmony. For the time being, V will move exclusively to I (or i), thus resolving the tonal tension created by the leading tone and by $\hat{2}$.

EXERCISE

To practice harmonic analysis of tonic-dominant progressions, refer to exercise 1.1 in worksheet 2 at the end of this chapter.

THE I–V–I PROGRESSION

Because the I–V–I progression is essential in defining common practice tonality, we call it the **fundamental progression** of tonal music. The tonic and dominant chords can be combined at several levels of musical activity and structure. In the first place, the I–V–I progression is often found as a harmonic unit of adjacent chords at the local level. Tonic and dominant, on the other hand, constitute the basic harmonies in several types of cadences. (As you remember from chapter F, a cadence is a musical point of arrival.) In this category, they have a role in the articulation of form. Finally, the I–V–I progression underlies larger formal and compositional spans, and from this point of view these harmonies represent the structural pillars on which larger formal units and complete compositions are built. In the following sections we will examine these three levels of harmonic activity involving the tonic and dominant chords.

Neighbor Motion in the I–V–I Progression

Several realizations of the fundamental progression appear in example 2.2. In example 2.2a, we see a I–V–I progression in which the bass affects the $\hat{1}$–$\hat{5}$–$\hat{1}$ motion characteristic of this progression, and the upper voice moves from $\hat{1}$ down by half step to $\hat{7}$ and back to $\hat{1}$. The type of melodic motion featured in the soprano, which was already introduced in chapter F, is called **neighbor motion:** A note moves stepwise to the closest note above or below it, and then back to the original note. The $\hat{1}$–$\hat{7}$–$\hat{1}$ motion is a **lower-neighbor figure,** and $\hat{7}$ functions here as a **neighbor note** to $\hat{1}$ (marked with an N). The I–V–I progression in example 2.2b, on the other hand, features an **upper-neighbor figure** in the soprano, $\hat{1}$–$\hat{2}$–$\hat{1}$.

Passing Motion in the I–V–I Progression

In example 2.2c, the same bass now supports a descending $\hat{3}$–$\hat{2}$–$\hat{1}$ line in the soprano. The motion here takes us from one member of the tonic triad, $\hat{3}$, to another member, $\hat{1}$, by means of a descending stepwise motion through $\hat{2}$. This type of stepwise motion in which a note fills in the space of a 3rd between two other notes is called **passing motion.** The $\hat{3}$–$\hat{2}$–$\hat{1}$ motion is a *passing figure,* and $\hat{2}$ functions here as a *passing tone* (marked with a P).

Example 2.2

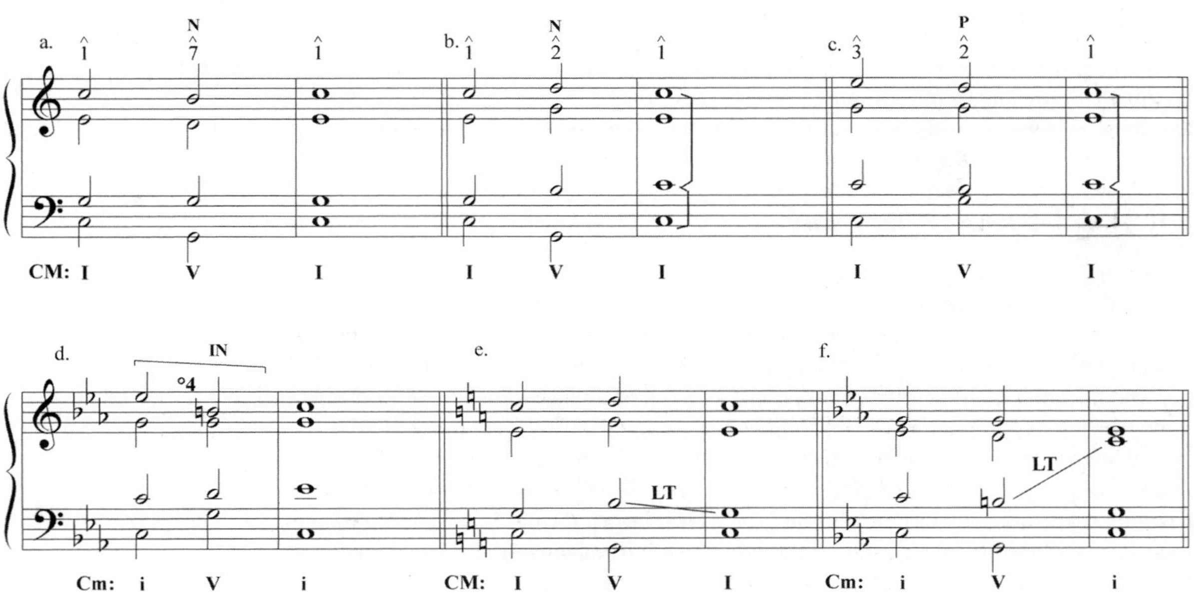

Incomplete-Neighbor Motion in the I–V–I Progression

In a neighbor-note motion, the embellished note is both approached and left by step. Melodic motion in which the embellished note is either approached *or* left by step, but not both, results in what is known as an **incomplete neighbor** (IN). Whereas a neighbor figure embellishing the pitch C, for instance, is C–B–C, incomplete-neighbor figures are either C–B or B–C (with B being the IN in both cases). The soprano in example 2.2d illustrates a case of incomplete-neighbor figure (B♮–C) in the context of a i–V–i progression.

The I–V–I Progression as a Linear Prolongation of I

In all of the preceding cases, the soprano can be understood as a melodic or *linear* elaboration of tonic triad members. Similarly, the bass motion $\hat{1}$–$\hat{5}$–$\hat{1}$ represents a melodic **bass arpeggiation** of two members of the tonic triad, $\hat{1}$ and $\hat{5}$. The I–V–I progression can thus be understood as a harmonic elaboration or extension of the tonic triad, by means of arpeggiation in the bass, and by either neighboring or passing motion in the soprano. These are examples of **prolongation.** By prolongation we mean the extended influence of a pitch or a chord that remains in effect regardless of whether it is actually sounding. Some frequent means of prolongation are arpeggiation, neighbor and incomplete neighbor motions, and passing motion, all of which are illustrated in examples 2.2a, b, c, and d. If in these examples you think of the outer-voice frame as a unit, we can also say that *the tonic triad is prolonged by contrapuntal means:* Arpeggiation and N, IN, or P figures are here presented simultaneously in a two-voice contrapuntal structure. We will often refer to chords with a contrapuntal, prolongational function as **linear chords,** because they result from melodic motion (lines) rather than vertical processes.

Connecting the Tonic and Dominant Chords

Example 2.2 shows several possible connections between I and V. More are possible, especially with different doublings (all the illustrations in example 2.2 begin with a tonic triad in which the root is doubled). These are, however, the most standard voice-leading possibilities. We will now comment briefly on each of them.

Voice Leading in the I–V–I Progression

1. Because the I–V–I progression is made up of two *root motions by 5th,* the simplest and smoothest voice leading follows the principles for this type of progression discussed in chapter 1. In the "lower-neighbor progression" represented in example 2.2a, the soprano effects a lower-neighbor motion, $\hat{1}$–$\hat{7}$–$\hat{1}$. As you can see in example 2.2a, in the three upper voices of both the I–V and V–I connections, the common tone remains in the same voice, while the other two voices move by steps.
2. Remember to avoid doubling the leading tone (LT) in V. In the V–I or V–i connection, in principle the leading tone *resolves* up a half step to the tonic. Remember also that in minor you need to raise $\hat{7}$ so it becomes the LT.

3. The progression in example 2.2b is an "upper-neighbor progression" because the soprano effects an upper-neighbor motion, $\hat{1}$–$\hat{2}$–$\hat{1}$. If we want to resolve the LT, we end up with three voices on $\hat{1}$ in the last I chord. This tripled root is acceptable as long as we include the third of the chord as part of the incomplete triad. The alto moves from $\hat{5}$ to $\hat{3}$ for this purpose.
4. Example 2.2c features a "passing progression," with a $\hat{3}$–$\hat{2}$–$\hat{1}$ passing figure in the soprano, as we discussed previously. Here again, we end up with an incomplete final triad if we want to resolve the LT to $\hat{1}$.
5. A possible alternative to the incomplete triads from examples 2.2b and c is shown in example 2.2e. Here the LT leaps down to $\hat{5}$ and is thus left unresolved, in exchange for a complete final triad. Unresolved LTs should be used only when they are in an inner voice. This is a type of voice leading often found in Bach chorales.
6. The solution in example 2.2f is perfectly acceptable, as we saw in chapter 1. In this voice leading we can hear the LT resolve to $\hat{1}$ in the adjacent upper voice.
7. Example 2.2d shows an "incomplete neighbor" V–I progression in which one voice (here the soprano) leaps down a 4th from $\hat{3}$ to $\hat{7}$. In minor modes, this voice leading features an acceptable diminished-fourth leap, which, as we saw in chapter 1 and as illustrated by our example, should be balanced with motion by step in the opposite direction of the leap.

CHARACTERISTIC SOPRANO-BASS PATTERNS

We mentioned previously that the outer-voice frames of the progressions in example 2.2 can be considered contrapuntal structures. Example 2.3 provides a summary of typical soprano-bass patterns in the I–V–I progression. The soprano patterns include three neighbor figures (examples 2.3a, b, and c), two passing figures (examples 2.3d and e), a sustained $\hat{5}$ figure (example 2.3f), and an incomplete-neighbor figure (example 2.3g).

Example 2.3

You should keep in mind that, as we discussed in chapter 1 and you can verify in examples 2.2 and 2.3, the voice-leading principles you learned in species counterpoint are present in harmonic progressions, even in such short instances as the ones in this example. In chapter 1 we also noted that one of the adjustments made to species counterpoint in common practice voice leading is a more liberal treatment of diminished intervals, both melodically and harmonically. The melodic °4 in the soprano in example 2.2d, although perfectly acceptable in this harmonic context, would be objectionable in a strict species-counterpoint context.

Typical Errors to Avoid:

1. Doubling the LT (and resolving both of them to $\hat{1}$, with resulting parallel 8ves).
2. Not raising $\hat{7}$ in minor modes.
3. Not resolving the LT, especially when it is placed in the soprano.
4. Omitting the third in an incomplete triad (instead of omitting the fifth).

EXERCISES

To practice realizing I–V–I progressions in four voices, refer to exercise 2 in worksheet 2 at the end of this chapter.

To practice specific voice-leading models in I–V–I progressions, refer to exercise 3 in worksheet 2 at the end of this chapter.

THE I–V–I PROGRESSION AS A FORM-GENERATING STRUCTURE

The I–V–I progression is the fundamental harmonic unit of the tonal system. It represents the statement of a tonal center (I), the momentary departure from that center and the creation of a tension (V), and the return to the center by means of the resolution of the tension. The I–V–I progression unequivocally *defines and establishes a key.*

The I and V chords (the latter usually in the more frequent form of V_7) provide sufficient harmonic support for short, simple compositions, such as Franz Schubert's "Originaltänze," op. 9, no. 26 (anthology, no. 40). Listen to this piece, examine the score, and analyze the chords with Roman numerals. (Beware of the first chord: What is the key of the piece? On what chord does it begin?)

The significance of I and V in tonal music goes much beyond the immediate chord-to-chord type of progression we first think of in chord connections. The I–V–I progression also has an essential long-range, formal significance in music. Complete compositions and formal structures are built on the harmonic structure provided by the tonic and dominant relationship. In this section we will examine some of the formal aspects of I and V, beginning with their cadential functions.

Cadences Involving I and V

Musical formal units (such as phrases, periods, sections, or complete pieces) are usually articulated by means of **cadences,** musical points of arrival defined both melodically and harmonically. We will study cadences in more detail in chapter 10, and basic formal units in chapter 11. As a preview of chapter 10, however, we can observe that several cadence types involve tonic and dominant harmonies.

The familiar V–I cadence, the most common closing gesture in the tonal system, is known as an *authentic cadence* (AC). An authentic cadence in which both chords are in root position and $\hat{1}$ is in the top voice in the final chord (approached by step from $\hat{2}$ or $\hat{7}$) is called a **perfect authentic cadence** (PAC) and has a conclusive effect (examples 2.4a and b). A V–I cadence in which at least one of the two chords is not in root position, or in which $\hat{1}$ is not in the top voice in the final chord, is called an **imperfect authentic cadence** (IAC) and has a less conclusive effect (examples 2.4c to e). A musical statement, however, may also end on V (usually with $\hat{2}$ or $\hat{7}$ in the top voice). Because V is not a stable harmony, such a statement is inconclusive, and continuation is necessary (such formal units are said to be **open**). A cadence on V is called a **half cadence** (HC) (example 2.4f).

We can appreciate the different effects of the cadential progressions V–I or I–V by comparing the cadences in examples 2.4g and h. In the verse of Nilsson's 1969 hit "Everybody's Talkin'," we hear a V_7–I authentic cadence (which is actually an IAC; why?). In the song from the show *Roberta* reproduced in example 2.4h, on the other hand, the verse ends with a I–V_7 cadence. What kind of a cadence is this, and what is its effect?

Cadence, Phrase, and Period

The two fragments by Bach reproduced in example 2.5 illustrate all of the preceding types of cadences, as well as two primary types of formal unit—the phrase and the

Example 2.4a–f

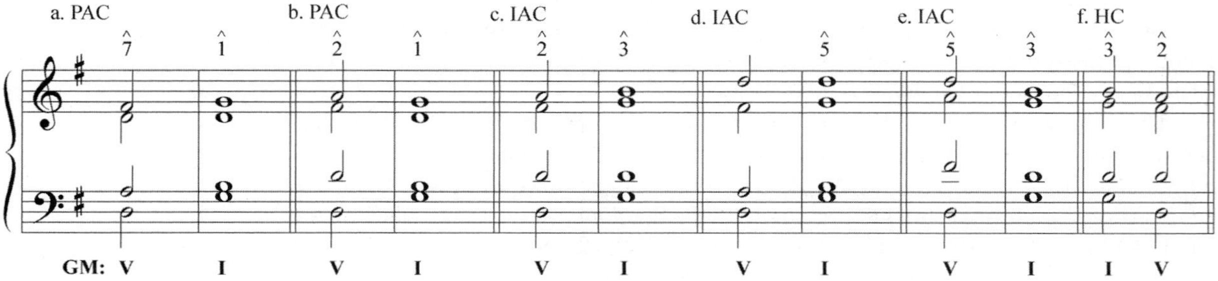

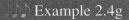

Example 2.4g Fred Neil, "Everybody's Talkin'"

Example 2.4h Otto Harbach-Jerome Kern, "Smoke Gets in Your Eyes," from *Roberta*

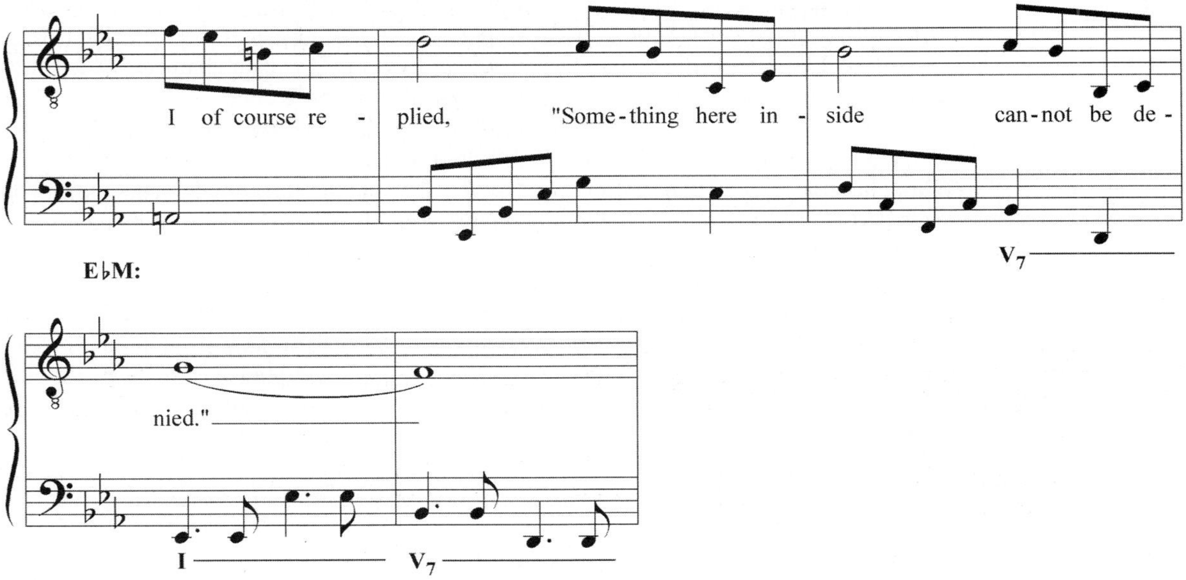

Example 2.5a J. S. Bach, Chorale 14, "O Herre Gott, dein göttlich Wort," mm. 1–5

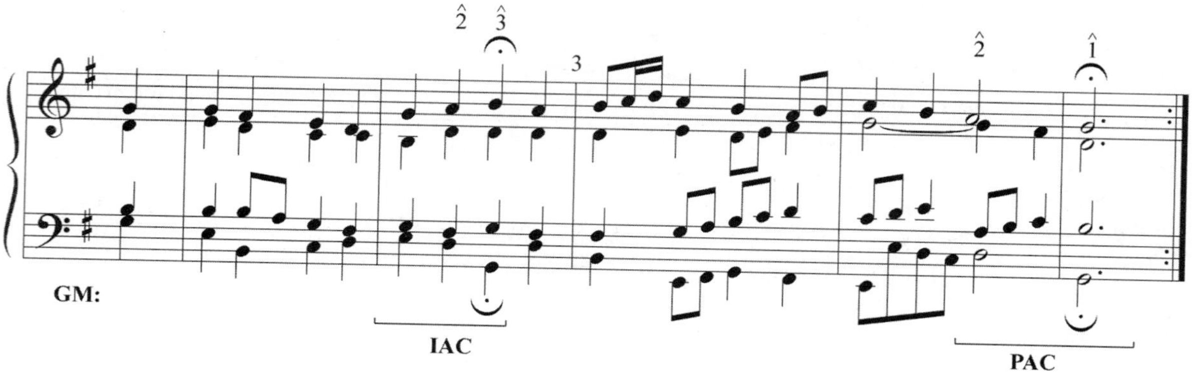

period. A **phrase** has been defined as "a directed motion in time from one tonal entity to another."[1] A phrase is a self-sufficient musical statement that traces a clear motion between two tonal points and ends with a cadence. In example 2.5a you can hear two phrases, indicated by the fermatas. The first phrase begins on I in GM and ends on an IAC on G. The tonic in this V–I cadence functions as a tonal goal for the phrase, but it does not sound like a conclusive tonal goal because $\hat{3}$, not $\hat{1}$, is in the upper voice. Compare the ending of the first phrase with the ending of the second phrase, which closes with a PAC on G. This time the tonal goal has a clearly conclusive character because of the $\hat{2}$–$\hat{1}$ motion in the soprano. Both phrases together constitute a formal unit we call a **period.** A period consists of at least two phrases, the last of which closes with a PAC.

Example 2.5b features another two-phrase period. The open character of the first phrase is even more evident in this case because of the HC on D (V in GM). The long-range tonal motion of the first phrase is I–V. The closing cadence in this period is, again, a conclusive PAC with a $\hat{2}$–$\hat{1}$ motion in the soprano. Considering the beginning harmony, the temporary tonal goal at the HC, and the final tonal goal at the end of the period, the long-range tonal motion in this example is I–V–I, a tonic-dominant-tonic progression at the formal level.

Listen now to mm. 1–8 of Mozart's Piano Sonata in AM (anthology, no. 27), a period that begins on I and ends with a V–I PAC. You will hear that the period consists of two phrases, that the melodic material is the same in both phrases, and that the first phrase (mm. 1–4) seems inconclusive, whereas the second phrase (mm. 5–8) reaches the sense of completion not achieved at m. 4. What kind of cadence closes the first phrase in m. 4?

---

[1] William Rothstein, *Phrase Rhythm in Tonal Music* (New York: Schirmer, 1989), p. 5.

Example 2.5b J. S. Bach, Chorale 67, "Freu'dich sehr, o meine Seele," mm. 1–4

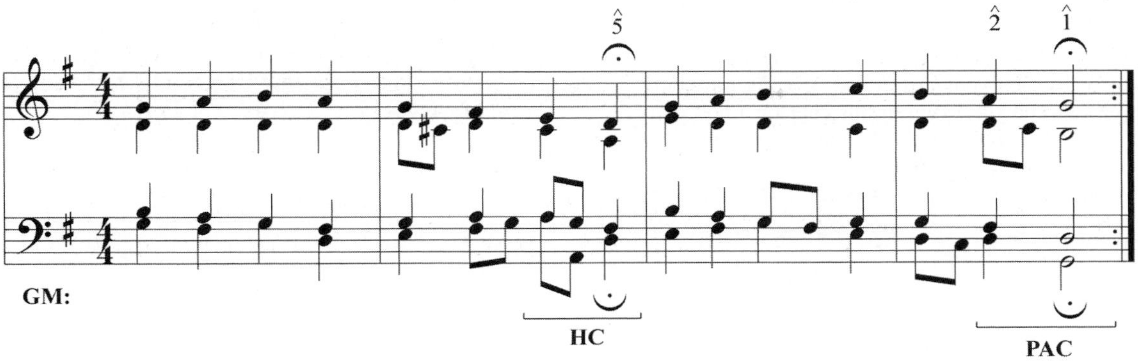

Identifying Cadences and Phrases

Because cadences and phrases are largely defined by harmonic criteria, identifying them should ideally involve examining both melody and harmony. We can tell a lot, however, from melody alone. The following steps will help you identify cadences and phrases in either a melodic/harmonic context, or also if you have only an unaccompanied melody.

1. Look for places in the score where the music seems to reach some kind of momentary repose: a fermata; a melodic long note perhaps followed by a rest; the end of a sentence or verse in the text if the music is vocal; or a clear melodic point of arrival after a musical statement, perhaps indicated by such elements as melodic shape or direction, or phrasing slurs and articulation.
2. Verify whether the point of repose you have identified is supported by a harmonic cadential gesture: an arrival on V or a clear cadential V–I. Keep in mind that not all V–I or I–V progressions are cadences. Inside a phrase, these harmonies simply constitute noncadential harmonic progressions. At the end of a phrase, they are cadences.
3. Melodic cadences can also be confirmed by the scale-degree motion involved. In a conclusive PAC, the melody will effect a $\hat{2}$–$\hat{1}$ or $\hat{7}$–$\hat{1}$ motion (examples 2.4a and b). In a less conclusive IAC, frequent melodic gestures will be $\hat{2}$–$\hat{3}$, $\hat{5}$–$\hat{5}$, or $\hat{5}$–$\hat{3}$ (examples 2.4c to e). Finally, a HC will probably feature a $\hat{3}$–$\hat{2}$ melodic motion (example 2.4f), or possibly also $\hat{1}$–$\hat{7}$.
4. Sing "Oh! Susanna" without any harmonic accompaniment. As you sing, hear the phrases and the melodic cadences that close each of them. What kind of cadences are you hearing? What scale degrees does the melody feature in each of the cadences?

PRACTICAL APPLICATION AND DISCUSSION

1. Discuss the formal role of the I–V–I progression in the following two complete pieces: anthology, no. 27 (Mozart, Piano Sonata in AM, I, theme) and anthology, no. 6 (Minuet from *Notebook for Anna Magdalena Bach*). Play or listen to the pieces, determine their phrase and cadential structures, and explain how they are shaped by the tonic and dominant harmonies.
2. Examine the compositions you are presently practicing or performing on your instrument, looking for examples of concepts discussed in this chapter. Look preferably at some short pieces such as minuets or other dance types. Answer the following questions:
   a) Do the main formal units begin and end on the tonic?
   b) Do main formal units conclude with a PAC?
   c) Are there any important cadences on V (HCs)?
   d) Do PACs and HCs affect your sense of phrasing?
   e) Identify some I–V and V–I progressions and examine their voice leading, comparing it with the normative voice leading studied in this chapter.
   f) How does the material studied in this chapter affect your musical experience both as a listener and as a performer?

EXERCISES

To practice cadence identification in musical contexts, refer to exercise 1 in worksheet 2 at the end of this chapter.

To practice analyzing the role of I and V as structural harmonies in a formal context, refer to exercise 1.2 in worksheet 2 at the end of this chapter.

FOR FURTHER STUDY

For additional chapter 2 materials, refer to the *Harmony in Context* Web page at www.mhhe.com/roigfrancoli2e.

ASSIGNMENT AND KEYBOARD PROGRESSIONS

For analytical and written assignments and keyboard progressions based on the materials learned in this chapter, refer to chapter 2 in the workbook.

PITCH PATTERNS

Sing (and listen to while you sing) the pitch patterns in example 2.6, in both the major and minor modes, as an aural practice of the tonic and dominant triads and their connections. Notice the leading tone and hear its resolution. Singing these patterns with scale degree numbers will help you understand their relationship to harmonic degrees and chordal functions. You may also use *solfège* syllables (do-re-mi-fa-sol-la-ti-do) if you want, depending on what sightsinging system is used at your school.

Example 2.6

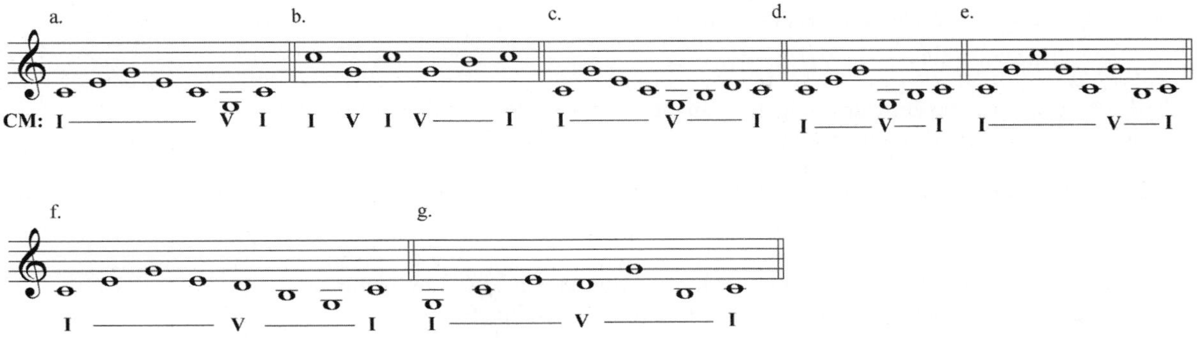

Terms for Review

I and V as structural chords
Bass afterbeat figuration
Arpeggiated keyboard figuration
Alberti bass
Passing tone
Nonchord tone
Tonic triad and its function
Closed formal units
Dominant triad and its function
Tendency tone
Fundamental progression
Neighbor motion
Upper- and lower-neighbor figures
Neighbor note
Passing motion
Incomplete-neighbor motion
Bass arpeggiation
Prolongation
Linear chords
Voice leading in the I–V–I progression
Cadence
Perfect authentic cadence
Imperfect authentic cadence
Open formal units
Half cadence
Phrase
Period

Worksheet 2

EXERCISE 1 Analysis

1. a) Analyze example 2.7 with Roman numerals.

   b) What types of cadences can you identify in mm. 4 and 8? How are they different, and what are their different effects?

   c) Granting that melody and harmony are always interdependent, how is this dependence or relationship even more evident than usual in this fragment?

2. Discuss the structural role of the I–V–I progression in the following two fragments: anthology, no. 7 (Bach, Polonaise from *Notebook for Anna Magdalena Bach),* mm. 1–8, and anthology, no. 21 (Haydn, Piano Sonata in DM, Hob. XVI:37, III), mm. 1–20. Play or listen to these examples. Determine their phrase and cadential structures, as well as the role of I and V in shaping the form of these fragments.

Example 2.7 L. v. Beethoven, *Für Elise,* mm. 1–8

EXERCISE 2 Write the following progressions in four voices, with correct voice leading. Always play and listen to your part-writing exercises before you turn them in to your teacher.

General procedure for realizing a progression from given Roman numerals:

1. If the bass is not given, write out the complete bass line for the progression.
2. Write the first chord with correct doubling and spacing.
3. You will want to ascertain that your outer-voice frame is made up of independent, satisfactory lines. For this purpose, you might want to sketch out the soprano right after you write the bass, making sure that you have a good upper line and that the outer-voice duet follows the principles of first-species counterpoint.
4. Fill in inner voices chord by chord with the smoothest possible connection between chords: think of all the pitches for each chord, leave common tones in the same voices, take the remaining pitches from one chord to the closest possible pitches from the next chord, and check the resolution of the LT.
5. Double-check the connection for possible mistakes (parallel or hidden 5ths or 8ves, augmented melodic intervals, failure to raise $\hat{7}$ in minor keys, doubled LT, etc.).

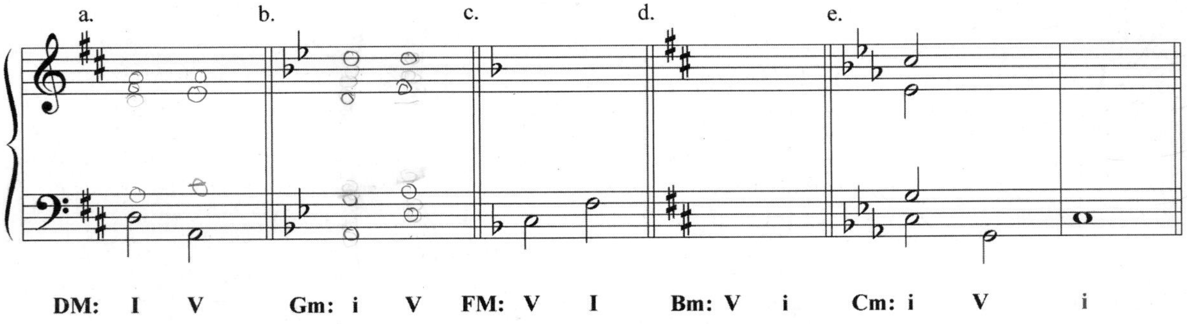

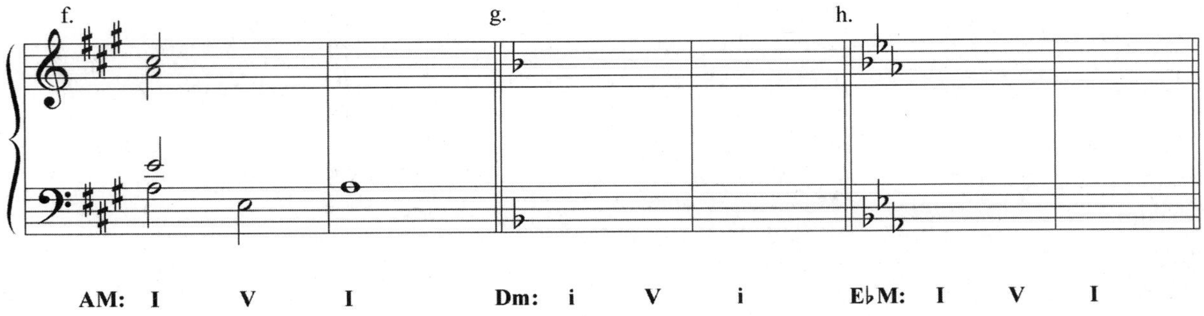

EXERCISE 3 Realize the following I–V–I (or i–V–i) progressions in four voices. In each of the progressions, use the required voice-leading model.

3a: Lower neighbor progression.

3b: Upper neighbor progression.

3c: Passing progression.

3d: Resolve the LT in the voice above it.

3e: Upper neighbor progression with an unresolved LT (and a complete final triad).

3f: A descending °4 leap in the soprano.

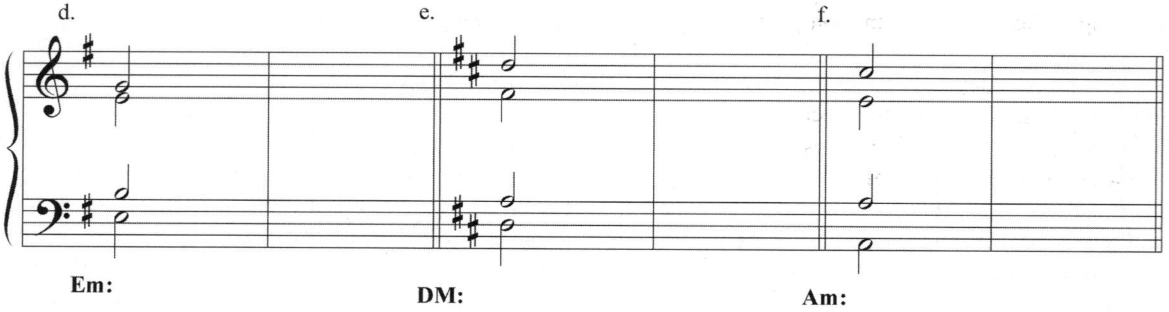

Chapter 3

Harmonic Function; The Subdominant Triad in Root Position

THE BASIC HARMONIC FUNCTIONS

In chapter E we defined **harmonic function** as the relationship of a chord with the other chords in the key, and especially its relationship with the tonic. Functions may be grouped according to their type. The three basic functions are tonic, dominant, and pre-dominant. Whereas the tonic is the only chord in the system that provides conclusive repose (the **tonic function,** abbreviated as T), several chords that contain the leading tone provide a tension that needs to resolve. Some of these chords are V, V_7, vii°, vii°_7, and $vii^{ø}_7$. We will refer to all these chords as having a **dominant function** (abbreviated as D). A number of other chords can precede a chord with a dominant function. Chords in this group, which have the function of preparing the dominant, include mainly IV, ii, and ii_7. We refer to this function as **pre-dominant** (abbreviated as PD).

Some chords function at times as **substitutes** for other chords. Although V must in principle resolve to I, in the "deceptive progression," V-vi, it resolves to a tonic substitute, vi. Finally, chords at times have the function of extending or embellishing other chords contrapuntally. This is a frequent function, as we will see throughout part 1, of first- and second-inversion chords, as well as of such chords as IV, vi, and iii. We refer to this extending or embellishing function as **prolongational function.** The most common functions of all seven diatonic triads are summarized in the chart that follows.

NOTE

Chordal function is entirely dependent on context; one chord can have different functions in different contexts. In this chapter we will see that IV can function as a pre-dominant, but, in a different context, it can also function as a tonic prolongation. Chords in the dominant family (such as V_6 *or* vii°_6*), on the other hand, often appear as linear chords, as we will study in chapters 4, 8, and 9. Thus, a chord can also have two simultaneous functions (such as a member of the dominant family actually functioning as a contrapuntal chord prolonging the tonic).*

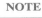

Summary of the Most Common Harmonic Functions of the Diatonic Triads

I (i)	Tonic
ii (ii°)	Pre-dominant (precedes V)
iii (III)	Tonic prolongation
IV (iv)	Tonic prolongation (subdominant) or Pre-dominant (precedes V)
V	Dominant
vi (VI)	Tonic prolongation or Tonic substitute or Pre-dominant (precedes V)
vii°	Dominant

THE SUBDOMINANT TRIAD

The **subdominant triad** (IV in major keys, iv in minor) is built on $\hat{4}$. It comprises scale degrees $\hat{4}$–$\hat{6}$–$\hat{1}$. The tonic, dominant, and subdominant triads can be considered the basic chords in the tonal system, and they illustrate all the main functions that have been defined previously (tonic, dominant, pre-dominant, and prolongation). For this reason they are known as the **primary triads.**

IV as Pre-dominant

The most common function of IV is to precede V. The I–V–I progression is often elaborated by the introduction of IV between I and V: I–IV–V–I. Because the step progression $\hat{4}$–$\hat{5}$ in the bass from IV to V creates a melodic drive toward V, IV is a particularly strong pre-dominant chord (and, as we will see in chapter 5, so is ii_6, a chord very close to IV that also features $\hat{4}$ in the bass). In example 3.1a, both subdominants in mm. 23 and 25 function as pre-dominant chords because they precede (and prepare) the authentic cadences that follow.

The second part of Schubert's "Ecossaise" no. 2 (example 3.1b) is based only on the I–IV–V_7–I progression. Analyze this complete little piece, writing the correct Roman numerals under each measure.

IV as Prolongation of I

In the opening measures of example 3.2a, the harmonic progression is V_7–I–IV–I–V_7–I–V_7–I. The phrase is thus based mostly on dominant-tonic progressions; the only

Example 3.1a Robert Schumann, "War Song," from *Album for the Young,* op. 68, mm. 21–26

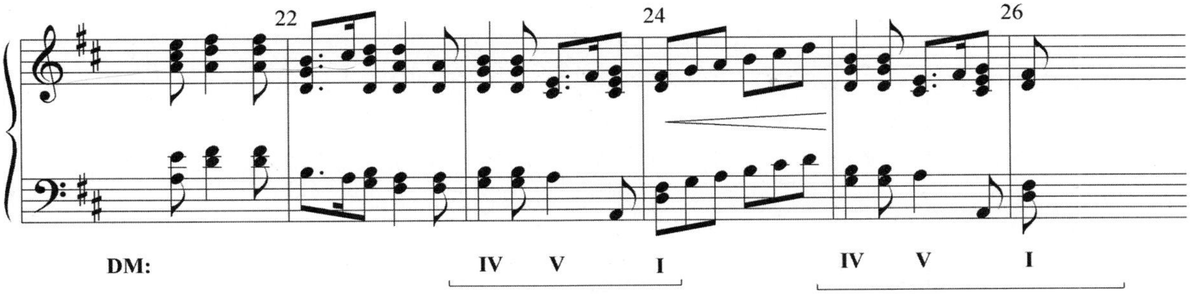

Example 3.1b F. Schubert, *Walzer, Ländler und Ecossaisen,* op. 18, Ecossaise no. 2

exception is the third chord, a subdominant triad that follows and precedes tonic triads. Examine the voice leading of this I–IV–I progression, as shown in the harmonic reduction in example 3.2b (where the left hand from example 3.2a has been reduced to block chords): the roots are related by descending 5th; one pitch (scale degree $\hat{1}$, B♭) is common to both chords, and remains in the same voice; the other two pitches in I, F–D,

Example 3.2a F. Chopin, Mazurka in B♭M, op. 7 no. 1, mm. 1–8

Example 3.2b

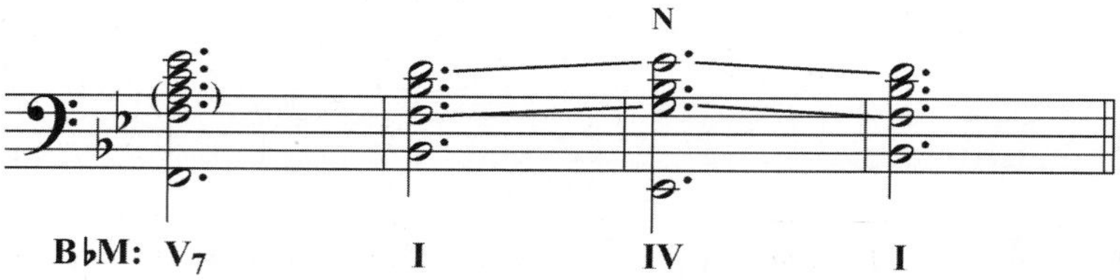

move up by steps to their upper neighbors, G–E♭, and down by steps again. IV functions here as a prolongation of the tonic, as opposed to a pre-dominant. In this function, IV embellishes the tonic triad and extends the tonic harmony by means of an upper-neighbor progression. This is an example of **IV as a prolongational chord.**

The Plagal Cadence

Sometimes composers write an authentic cadence at the end of a piece, and prolong the final I by means of a IV–I cadence (the complete progression may thus be V–I–IV–I). A IV–I (or iv–i) cadential progression is called a **plagal cadence,** and is often sung to the word *Amen* at the end of Protestant hymns. In example 3.3, Gaetano Donizetti ends the "Introductory Chorus" of *Don Pasquale,* act III, with a PAC followed by a reiterated plagal cadence. Observe that, in mm. 40–42, the repeated cadential I–IV–I progression in the orchestra (the piano reduction in our example) harmonizes an extended scale degree $\hat{1}$ in the chorus.

Example 3.3 Gaetano Donizetti, *Don Pasquale,* act III, "Introductory Chorus," mm. 39–44

EXERCISES

To practice analyzing musical fragments based on I, IV, and V harmonies, refer to exercise 1 in worksheet 3 at the end of this chapter.

To practice realizing progressions using IV as a prolongation of I, refer to exercises 2a to d and 3a in worksheet 3 at the end of this chapter.

To practice realizing progressions using IV as a pre-dominant chord, refer to exercises 2e to g and 3b to d in worksheet 3 at the end of this chapter.

To practice harmonizing melodic fragments with I, IV, and V chords, refer to exercise 4 in worksheet 3 at the end of this chapter.

CHARACTERISTIC SOPRANO-BASS PATTERNS

Example 3.6 provides a summary of some typical soprano-bass contrapuntal patterns that can be harmonized with the two progressions we have studied in this chapter. Examples 3.6a to c show outer-voice patterns for the I–IV–V–I progression, including the conclusive $\hat{1}$–$\hat{1}$–$\hat{7}$–$\hat{1}$ and $\hat{3}$–$\hat{4}$–$\hat{2}$–$\hat{1}$ soprano patterns, the less conclusive $\hat{3}$–$\hat{4}$–$\hat{2}$–$\hat{3}$ and $\hat{5}$–$\hat{6}$–$\hat{5}$–$\hat{5}$, and the ascending $\hat{5}$–$\hat{6}$–$\hat{7}$–$\hat{1}$ pattern. Examples 3.6f to h show three patterns for the I–IV–I progression, including the sustained $\hat{1}$ soprano pattern and two neighbor figures, $\hat{5}$–$\hat{6}$–$\hat{5}$ and $\hat{3}$–$\hat{4}$–$\hat{3}$.

VOICE-LEADING GUIDELINES

1. The IV chord includes two tonally strong degrees ($\hat{4}$ and $\hat{1}$, the root and fifth, respectively), either of which is perfectly suitable for doubling. Doubling the third ($\hat{6}$), produces a weaker sonority.
2. In the I–IV–I progression, the roots are a 5th (or a 4th) apart. The chords have one common tone, which remains in the same voice. The other two pitches move by steps in the same direction (example 3.4a).

   This voice leading reflects the fact that this progression is a prolongation of the tonic: $\hat{1}$ is retained as the common tone, while the voices with $\hat{3}$ and $\hat{5}$ are embellished with *upper neighbor-note figures* (up a step, and return to the original note). From a voice-leading point of view, IV functions here as a **neighbor chord** (a chord that results from linear neighbor-note motion).

   The I–IV–I progression can be used to harmonize a soprano that repeats or holds $\hat{1}$ (as in example 3.4a) or one that features either of two neighbor figures: $\hat{5}$–$\hat{6}$–$\hat{5}$ or $\hat{3}$–$\hat{4}$–$\hat{3}$ (example 3.4b).
3. Example 3.4b illustrates a plagal cadence in block-chord style. A V–I authentic cadence is followed by a IV–I cadence in which the voice leading follows the same guidelines as in no. 2.
4. The IV–V connection, however, presents new difficulties. This progression features root motion by 2nd. As you learned in chapter 1, to connect chords whose roots are a second apart, *the three upper voices should move in contrary motion with the bass* (two of the voices by step, one by leap of a 3rd). This connection is illustrated in example 3.5a.
5. Several soprano melodic patterns can be harmonized with a IV–V–I cadential progression. Among them, $\hat{1}$–$\hat{7}$–$\hat{1}$ and $\hat{4}$–$\hat{2}$–$\hat{1}$ provide a conclusive effect appropriate for PACs, while $\hat{4}$–$\hat{2}$–$\hat{3}$ and $\hat{6}$–$\hat{5}$–$\hat{5}$ are used in IACs or in progressions inside phrases (examples 3.5a to c). Here again, notice that the outer-voice frames in these examples follow the principles of first-species counterpoint.
6. If you want to harmonize a $\hat{6}$–$\hat{7}$–$\hat{1}$ motion in the soprano with a IV–V–I progression, you must beware of multiple voice-leading problems. Parallel 8ves and 5ths are a frequent error in such harmonization (example 3.5d). Example 3.5e shows a possible voice-leading solution to this problem.
7. In the minor mode, however, the same progression from example 3.5e would be flawed by a melodic augmented 2nd (♭$\hat{6}$–♯$\hat{7}$) in the soprano (example 3.5f). Examples 3.5g and h illustrate two ways of avoiding the augmented 2nd in minor. Example 3.5g features identical voice leading as does example 3.5c (the normative voice leading in progressions with roots a 2nd apart): ♭$\hat{6}$ and ♯$\hat{7}$ are simply placed in different voices. At other times the melodic minor scale is used in its ascending form ($\hat{5}$–♯$\hat{6}$–♯$\hat{7}$–$\hat{1}$), thus avoiding the awkward melodic augmented 2nd. As you will see in example 3.5h, such use of the melodic minor scale results in a major IV (rather than iv) in a minor key, with the same voice leading as in example 3.5e.

Example 3.4

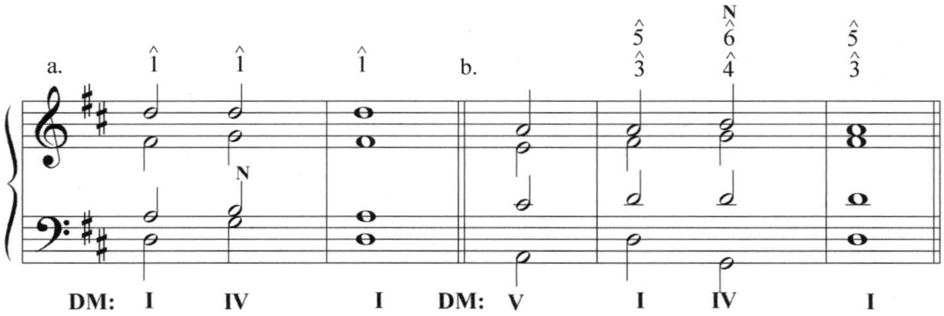

Example 3.5

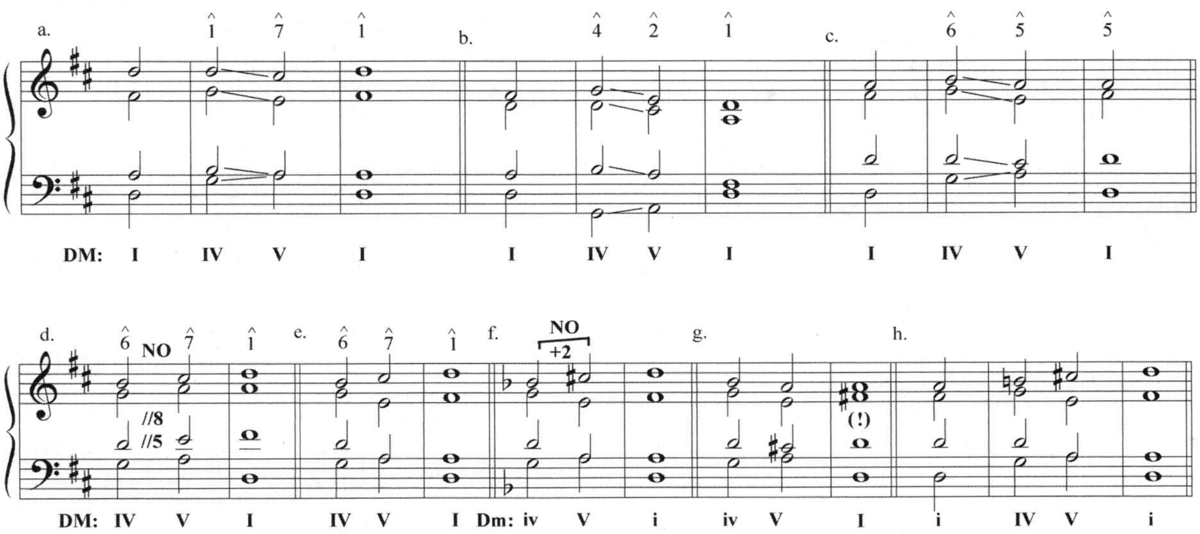

NOTE

The last chord in 3.5g, shown by an exclamation mark, is a major tonic triad (notice that the third has been raised) in a minor mode. This is a device frequently used by composers (especially during the Renaissance and Baroque periods) to close a piece in the minor mode, and it is called ***Picardy third.*** *Ending a minor mode piece with a major tonic triad gives the final cadence a stronger sense of conclusion.*

Typical Errors to Avoid

1. Writing parallel 5ths or 8ves in the IV–V connection.
2. Writing an augmented 2nd in the iv–V connection (minor modes) if ♭$\hat{6}$ and ♯$\hat{7}$ are left in the same voice.
3. Writing the bass of the IV–V progression ($\hat{4}$–$\hat{5}$) as a 7th rather than a 2nd.

A MODEL TO ELABORATE THE FUNDAMENTAL PROGRESSION

We have defined the I–V–I progression as the fundamental progression of tonal music. In this and the following chapters we will learn many ways of elaborating the fundamental progression. Summarizing chordal functions into three major categories

Example 3.6

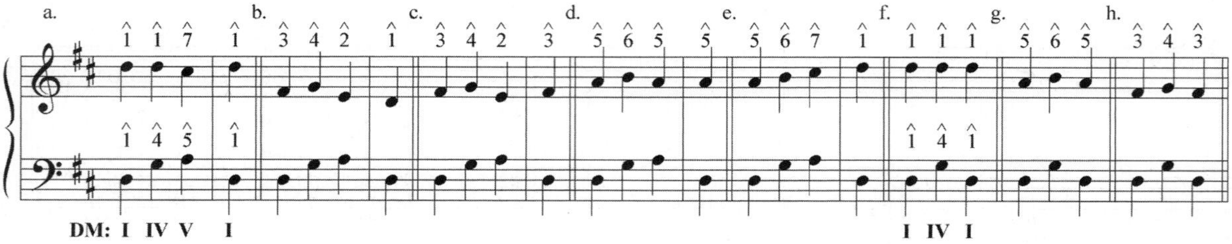

will help our definition of a model to elaborate the tonic-dominant-tonic (T–D–T) progression:

1. *Structural chords* are those that can have a beginning or ending function within musical units. Only I (i) and V are truly structural in functional tonality.
2. *Pre-dominant chords* have the function of preparing the dominant. ii, IV, and vi can function as pre-dominant chords.
3. *Prolongational chords* have the function of extending the structural frame in time or of extending other nonstructural chords. We will study a variety of prolongational structures throughout this book

The fundamental progression comprises only chords in the first category: I–V–I, or T–D–T. The first elaboration of the fundamental progression entails the addition of a pre-dominant (PD) chord from category 2: T–PD–D–T. Any of the four harmonies in this progression can be extended by means of chords from category 3, the prolongational chords. The most common type of prolongation, however, involves the opening tonic. Thus, our basic model progression will consist of *TONIC//tonic prolongation//pre-dominant//DOMINANT//TONIC*. The fundamental progression I–V–I (shown in capitals) frames this model. Possible extension of the pre-dominant, the final dominant, and the final tonic will also be discussed throughout this book. The following chart illustrates the three levels for our basic model progression as we have just defined them.

TONIC			DOMINANT	TONIC
TONIC		Pre-dominant	DOMINANT	TONIC
TONIC	Tonic prolongation	Pre-dominant	DOMINANT	TONIC

Example 3.7

Elaborating the I–V–I Progression with Subdominant Harmonies

We can expand the I–V–I progression in several ways using the harmonic elements we have learned in this chapter. First, we can prepare the V–I cadence with a pre-dominant IV, as shown in example 3.7a. Then, we can prolong the initial I with a contrapuntal I–IV–I progression, as in example 3.7b. Finally, we can also extend the final tonic by means of a plagal cadence, as shown in example 3.7c. The lower line of Roman numerals under these examples demonstrates that *we can hear two levels of harmony in these progressions*. At one level, we hear each chord in isolation, as indicated by the upper Roman numerals. At the next, deeper level, the initial or final tonic triads and their prolongations are heard as single harmonies extended by neighboring motions.

NOTE

The progressions in example 3.7 are written in keyboard texture, rather than four-part vocal texture. In chordal keyboard texture, the bass is usually played alone with the left hand, and the remaining voices are played in close position with the right hand. Voice-leading rules and guidelines are the same as for vocal texture.

ASSIGNMENT AND KEYBOARD EXERCISES

For analytical and written assignments and keyboard exercises based on the materials learned in this chapter, refer to chapter 3 in the workbook.

PITCH PATTERNS

Sing the pitch patterns in example 3.8, both in major and minor modes. Listen to the chords and progressions that are either implied (as in patterns a and b) or actually spelled out linearly (as in pattern h, where the tonic and subdominant chords have been "horizontalized").

Example 3.8

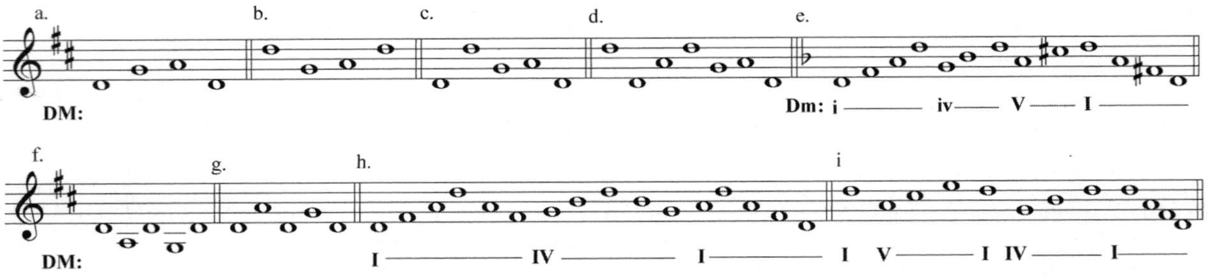

Terms for Review

Harmonic function
Tonic function
Dominant function
Pre-dominant function
Substitution
Prolongational function
Subdominant triad
Primary triads
IV as pre-dominant
IV as a prolongation chord
Plagal cadence
Picardy third
Neighbor chord

Worksheet 3

EXERCISE 1 Analysis.

1. a) Analyze example 3.9a with Roman numerals (RNs). The second sixteenth note in each of the sixteenth-note figures should be analyzed as a nonchord tone, an ornamental pitch foreign to the chord against which it sounds as a dissonance. In this case, the second sixteenth note is always a melodic lower-neighbor note (a note a step below a chord tone).

   b) On the other hand, the chord on m. 2, beat 1, is also an ornamental chord with a similar function. Study the voice leading to and from this chord, and explain its function with precise musical terms. Show the voice-leading structure of mm. 1–2 (using only chord tones) in the staves in example 3.9b. With what kind of cadence does the passage close? Explain.

Example 3.9a F. Schubert, Ecossaise D.158

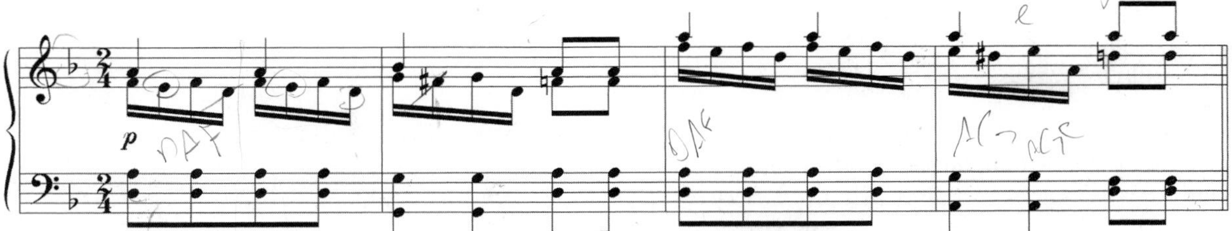

Example 3.9b

2. a) Analyze the complete example 3.10 with RNs (one chord per measure, except for m. 15, which has two chords). Beware of—and for the time being ignore—the numerous nonchord tones.

Example 3.10 F. Schubert, *Zwanzig Walzer,* op. 127, no. 13

b) Section 1 (mm. 1–8). On what progression is this section based?

c) Chords in section 1 change every measure. How does Schubert achieve a sense of motion within mm. 1–2 and 5–6?

d) How does the bass reflect the melody in mm. 1–2 and 5–6?

e) The most dissonant beat in this section (m. 3, beat 1) is a dominant ninth chord (a V_7 chord with one more third on top of the seventh) resulting from the melodic line. How does Schubert stress this dissonant spot?

f) The resolution of the progression, in mm. 4 and 8, also receives a special articulation treatment. How?

g) Section 2 (mm. 9–16). On what progression is this second section based?

h) Chords change here every two measures. By what means does Schubert extend each chord for two measures?

i) Changes of harmony, as well as dissonance, and also harmonic function (tension/release) are all reflected in this section by specific articulation marks. Explain.

j) Compare the cadences in mm. 8 and 16. What are their types, and how are they different?

EXERCISE 2 Realize the following progressions in four voices. First add RNs if missing, then write the bass line if it is not provided. Next, write a good soprano line, making sure that it forms a good contrapuntal frame with the bass. Finally, add inner voices using correct voice leading. Use only, in all cases, tonic, dominant, or subdominant chords in root position. *Remember*: Before turning in a part-writing exercise, play it and listen to it.

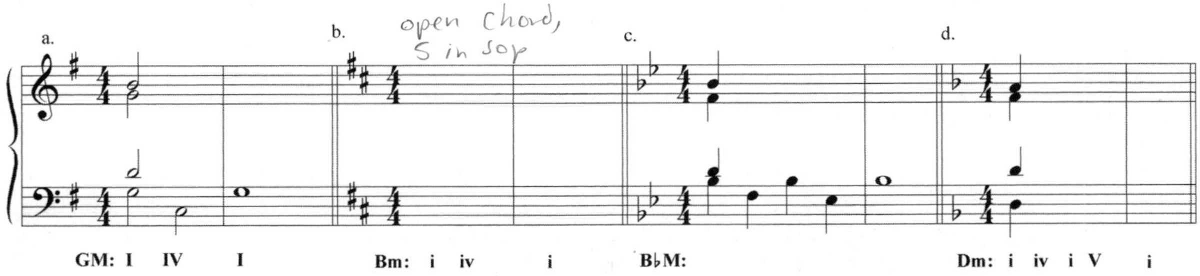

EXERCISE 3 Write four-voice harmonizations for the following melodic fragments. Write the bass first, and then fill in with the inner voices. Sing each melody before writing the harmonization, and after writing it play the complete harmonization at the piano.

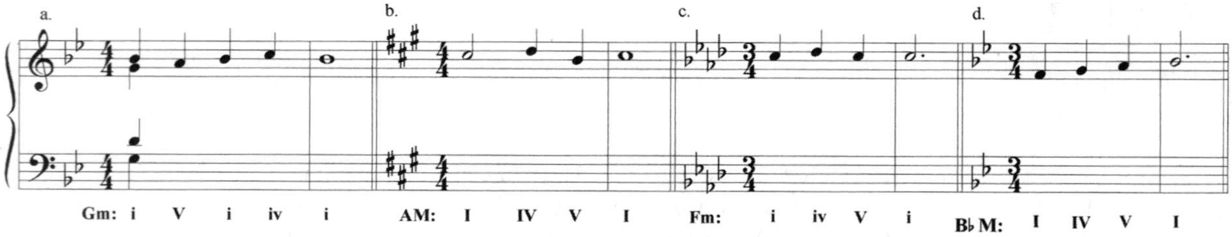

EXERCISE 4 The following soprano fragments are made up of melodic tonal patterns that in this chapter have been associated with specific harmonic patterns. Harmonize each fragment with the corresponding harmonic pattern or patterns. First, write scale degrees over the melodic fragments. Then, provide the *bass line and RNs* for your harmonization. You need not fill in the inner voices, although you may do so for additional practice. The melody in 3.4d is made up of two segments that you can harmonize with two different patterns. To connect both segments, harmonize m. 1, beats 3–4 with a single chord.

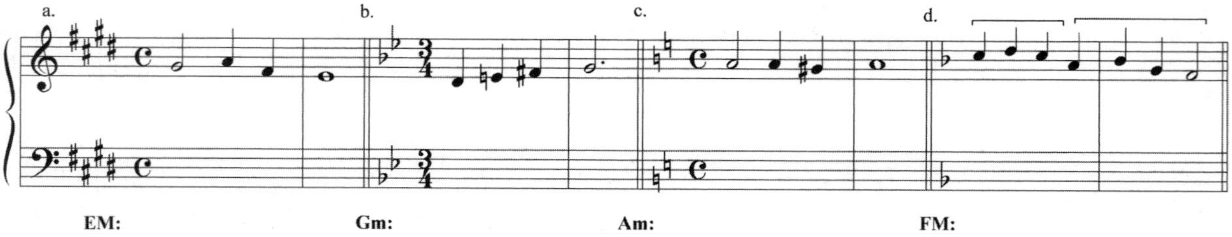

Chapter 4

Triads in First Inversion

In this chapter we will study triads in first inversion in their harmonic and musical contexts. We will see that by using triads in first inversion we increase the available options for both chordal sonorities and bass notes. We can create richer harmony, more varied voice leading, and more melodic bass lines.

As an introductory example, analyze anthology, no. 9 (Bach, "Was Gott tut"), mm. 1–4, with Roman numerals. When the beat is subdivided into eighth notes in this particular example, the first eighth note is always the actual chord, and the second one is either a nonchord tone or a change of voicing. Analyze, then, the first eighth note for each chord. You will notice that, other than the third chord from the end (a ii^{6}_{5}), all the other chords are either I, IV, or V. They are not all, however, in root position. If this were the case, there would be only three possible different bass notes for these three chords. Counting root position and first inversion, on the other hand, we have six possible bass notes, which allow for a much more interesting bass line.

EXERCISE

To practice writing isolated triads in first inversion from given Roman numerals, refer to exercise 2 in worksheet 4 at the end of this chapter.

THE TRIAD IN FIRST INVERSION: USES AND FUNCTION

First-inversion triads may be used to provide for better voice leading, to increase the number of available pitches for the bass (and thus to allow for a more melodic bass line), or to provide variety to the types of chordal sonorities in a texture. In "Was Gott tut," we just saw that the chords in first inversion introduce an element of variety in a passage that contains basically only three triads. By using I_6, IV_6, and V_6, the number of both sonorities and pitches for the bass are doubled. In example 4.1, on the other hand, we can see the logic of voice leading as a reason to use inverted triads. The I_6 in m. 14 is the tonic chord keyboard position closest to the IV in m. 13 (following our voice-leading guideline 1 in chapter 1), whereas the tonic at m. 16 is approached through a V_6 (also the closest dominant position), thus stressing the $\hat{7}$–$\hat{1}$ voice leading by exposing it in the bass.

Example 4.1 W. A. Mozart, Piano Sonata in B♭M, K. 570, I, mm. 1–20

Because triads in first inversion are less stable than root-position triads, composers have used them for expressive or formal purposes, when the stability of a root position triad is not desired. In a PAC, for instance, both V and I are in root position. If the composer wants to have a V–I cadence without a fully conclusive effect, one of the two chords may be used in first inversion. The V_6–I or V– I_6 cadences, known as **imperfect authentic cadences** (IACs), are often used for this purpose because they are less conclusive and stable than a PAC. We will study IACs in more detail in chapter 10.

Prolongation as a Function

As you will remember from chapter 3, a prolongational chord extends or embellishes another chord contrapuntally. One of the most direct ways of extending a harmony in time is to change the position of the chord from root position to first inversion. *Prolongation is indeed the most frequent function of triads in first inversion.* In example 4.2 you can see how first inversion chords (marked with a 6) extend two of the harmonies: the initial i and the iv that precedes the final HC. (The circled bass pitches are nonchord tones.) In other words, first-inversion triads are usually *prologational chords*.

Example 4.2 J. S. Bach, Chorale 111, "Herzliebster Jesu, was hast du verbrochen," mm. 1–3

Positions: 5 6 6 6 6
Chords: Am: i —— V —— i vii° i —— iv —— V

Arpeggiation and Voice Exchange

In examples 4.3a and b, which summarize the voice leading of the first inversion chord used as a **prolongation,** a i_6 extends the previous i: The chord (the harmony) does not change between chords 1 and 2; only the position changes. The tonic function is thus prolonged by means of **arpeggiation** or chordal skip, as indicated by the lower line of Roman numerals. In example 4.3a the main (or only) voice-leading motion within the chord is what we call a **voice exchange,** produced by arpeggiation in two voices: the soprano and bass lines (C–A and A–C, respectively) exchange pitches, while $\hat{1}$ and $\hat{5}$ are sustained in the other two voices. Voice exchange is indicated graphically by a cross symbol showing the exchange of pitches between two voices in this type of voice leading. The same voice leading and function apply if the first inversion precedes the root position, as in example 4.3c.

Example 4.3

Am: i i_6 V i | i i_6 V i | i_6 i iv i
i —— V i | i —— V i | i ——

Example 4.4

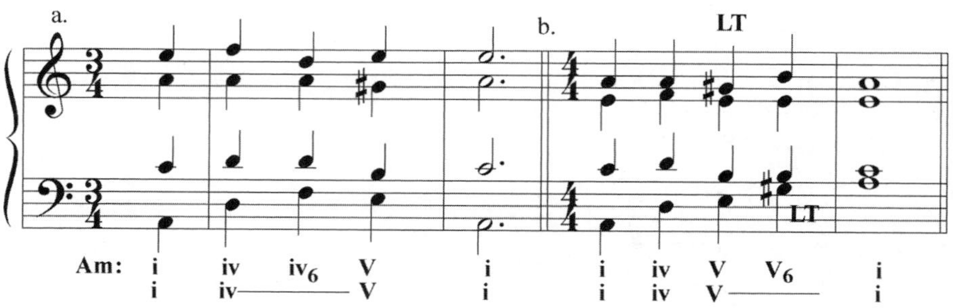

In example 4.4a, the subdominant triad is similarly extended by a iv_6, in a prolongation of the pre-dominant function. In example 4.4b, V_6 extends the dominant chord and function. In both examples 4.4a and b, the lower line of Roman numerals reminds us that, as we saw in chapter 3, we can hear two levels of harmony in these progressions. At one level, we hear each chord in isolation. At the next, deeper level, the root position triad and its inversion are heard as a single harmony in which a voice-leading change (a change of position or arpeggiation) is operated. (Identify and mark a case of voice exchange in one of these two examples.)

EXERCISE

To practice realizing short progressions using changes of position and voice exchange, refer to exercises 3a to c in worksheet 4 at the end of this chapter.

THE NEIGHBOR V_6

In chapters 2 and 3 we studied cases of dominant and subdominant harmonies that function as neighbor chords to I by means of neighbor figures. Example 4.5 shows a similar type of voice leading, this time featuring **V_6 as a neighbor chord:** In the progression I–V_6–I, one voice remains static while the other three perform neighbor-note figures (two lower neighbors—down a step, back up a step—and one upper neighbor—up a step, down a step). The function of V_6 here is to prolong the tonic, and so is the function of the following neighbor IV, which completes the progression in our example. An example by J. S. Bach illustrates the use of the I–V_6–I progression in a chorale texture, with slightly embellished voice leading (example 4.6). Compare Bach's realization with the model in example 4.5, and comment on the differences. Possible melodic patterns to be harmonized with the neighbor I–V_6–I progression and shown in these examples are $\hat{1}$–$\hat{2}$–$\hat{1}$ (example 4.5) and $\hat{3}$–$\hat{2}$–$\hat{3}$ or $\hat{5}$–$\hat{5}$–$\hat{5}$ (example 4.6).

Example 4.5

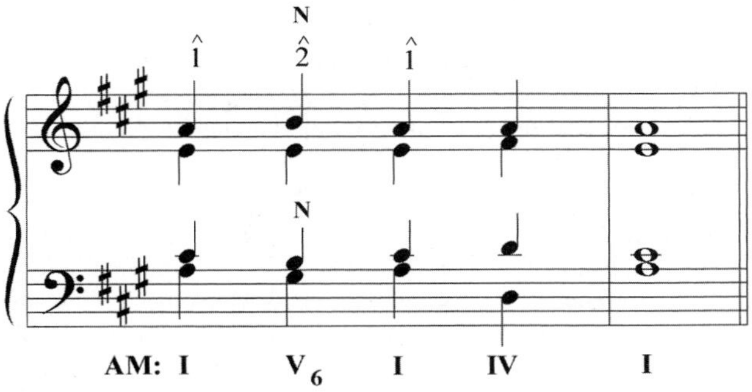

Example 4.6 J. S. Bach, Chorale 196, "Da der Herr Christ zu Tische sass," mm. 1–2

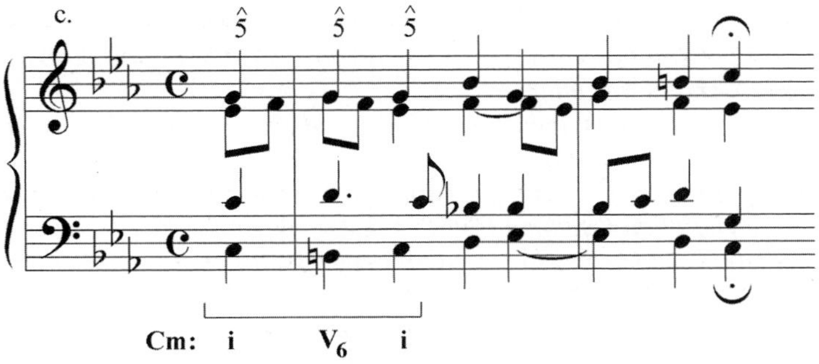

In an alternative, and very frequent, voice leading, the neighbor-note figure in the two upper voices is replaced by the *passing-tone figures* $\hat{1}$–$\hat{2}$–$\hat{3}$ or $\hat{3}$–$\hat{2}$–$\hat{1}$. The B in the soprano in example 4.7a functions as a passing tone (marked with a P) between A and C♯, and so does the B in the tenor. In this voice leading, the two voices that have the PT figures also feature voice exchange: The soprano and tenor exchange the pitches A–C♯, with an intervening passing tone B in each voice. Bach's chorale "Was Gott tut" (anthology, no. 9) opens with this type of realization of the I–V_6–I progression. A varied form of this progression, shown in example 4.7b, features an incomplete-neighbor figure in the bass (IN) created by the bass pattern $\hat{3}$–$\hat{7}$–$\hat{1}$ in the progression I_6–V_6–I.

VOICE-LEADING GUIDELINES

1. *Doubling*. In primary triads in first inversion it is preferable to double the root or the fifth. Double the third only if doing so produces the best possible voice leading. Otherwise, double the root or the fifth. Doubling the bass in a $^6_3$ chord (especially if it is doubled by the soprano) strongly emphasizes the third of the chord, an effect which, unless specifically desired by the composer, unnecessarily weakens the sound of the triad.
2. Do not double the LT (the bass) in a V_6 chord. Because the LT is in the bass, the V_6 chord will always resolve to a root-position tonic chord.
3. The best voice leading in a change of position (from root position to first inversion or vice versa) is illustrated in example 4.3a: A voice exchange is effected between the bass (A–C) and another voice (in this case the soprano, C–A). In such a voice exchange, two voices exchange pitches, while the other two do not move. An alternative voice leading can be seen in 4.3b: One voice remains static, while the other three move in the same direction. Other combinations are also possible. In all cases, the voice leading involves chordal skips in one or more voices.
4. To avoid parallel 8ves between two different chords, one of which is in root position and the other in first inversion (as in I–V_6, V_6–I, IV_6–V, IV_6–I, etc.), approach and leave the doubled note in the $^6_3$ chord by contrary or oblique motion. The lines in example 4.8 show how the doubled notes in both V_6 in example 4.8a (B) and iv_6 in example 4.8b (D) are approached and left by contrary motion. Without changing the voice leading in the remaining voices, try approaching or leaving any of the doubled notes in these two examples by parallel motion, and verify the resulting parallel 8ves.
5. Chordal figuration, such as changes of position or voicing, can be used to *prevent parallel 5ths or 8ves,* as illustrated by examples 4.8c and d. In example 4.8c, a chordal skip in the tenor prevents what otherwise would have been parallel 8ves between bass and tenor. Similarly, a change of position (a chordal skip in the bass) prevents parallel 5ths in example 4.8d. On the other hand, the same type of chordal skips can *produce parallel 5ths or 8ves,* as illustrated in examples 4.8e and f. In example 4.8e, a change of position produces parallel 8ves and a direct 5th; in example 4.8f the chordal skip in the alto results in parallel 5ths.

EXERCISES

To practice realizing short progressions using V_6 as a neighbor chord, refer to exercises 3d to f in worksheet 4 at the end of this chapter.

To practice analysis of musical fragments including triads in first inversion, refer to exercise 1 in worksheet 4 at the end of this chapter.

To practice realizing figured basses using first-inversion triads, refer to exercises 4a–b in worksheet 4 at the end of this chapter.

To practice harmonizing melodic fragments with progressions that include first-inversion triads, refer to exercise 5a to c in worksheet 4 at the end of this chapter.

Example 4.7

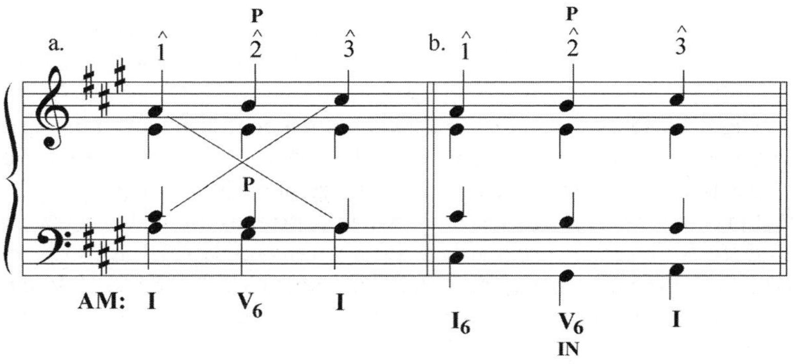

Example 4.8

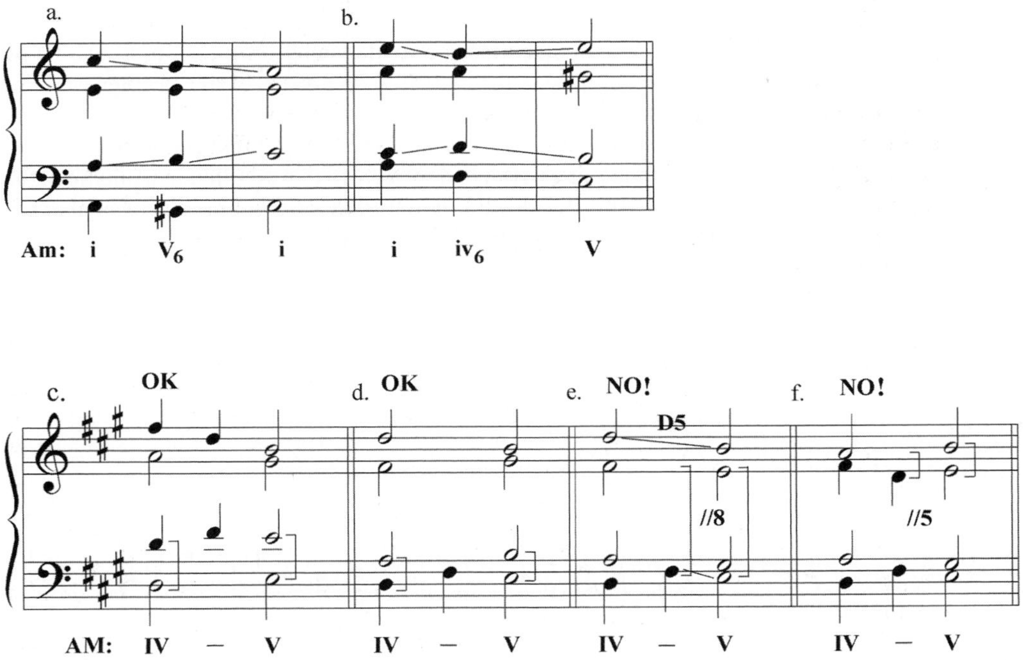

Typical Errors to Avoid:

1. Doubling the LT in V_6.
2. Not approaching and leaving the doubled note in the $^6_3$ chord by contrary or oblique motion, with resulting parallel 8ves.
3. Writing parallel 5ths or 8ves as a result of a chordal skip in the bass or any other voice.

CHARACTERISTIC SOPRANO-BASS PATTERNS

Example 4.9 provides a summary of some typical soprano-bass contrapuntal patterns that can be harmonized with first-inversion tonic and dominant chords. Examples 4.9a and b show changes of position with voice exchange. The change of position in example 4.9c features parallel 10ths between the outer voices. Examples 4.9d and e show two neighbor progressions using V_6, and examples 4.9f and g demonstrate two passing progressions using V_6. The I–V_6–I progression can also be used to harmonize a sustained $\hat{5}$, as shown in example 4.9h. Finally, example 4.9i illustrates an incomplete-neighbor pattern in the bass, harmonizing $\hat{1}$–$\hat{2}$–$\hat{3}$ in the soprano. Play each of these outer-voice patterns at the piano, adding inner voices in keyboard texture.

ELABORATING THE I–V–I PROGRESSION

In chapter 3 we saw that we can elaborate the fundamental progression by extending the initial tonic triad and by preparing the cadential dominant. In this chapter we have learned more means to extend not only the initial tonic triad, but also actually any triad. Example 4.10 shows some of the elaborations of the I–V–I progression that we can write at this point. The initial tonic is extended by a change of position in example 4.10a and by a neighbor V_6 in 4.10b. Besides the initial tonic, the pre-dominant is also extended by a change of position in example 4.10c, and the cadential dominant is extended in the same way in 4.10d.

Example 4.9

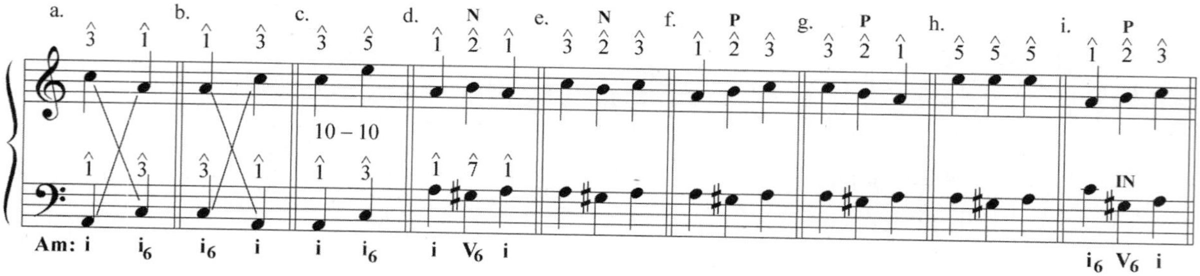

Example 4.10

First-inversion triads allow us to write longer progressions than the ones possible so far, as shown in example 4.11. In this example we first extend the initial tonic by means of two first-inversion triads (a passing V_6 and a I_6). Note the two voice exchanges that result from our voice leading. Then, we continue with a complete cadential gesture, IV–V–I. Finally, we extend the final tonic triad by means of a neighbor I–IV–I progression (a plagal cadence). What do the Roman numerals in the bottom line tell us as compared with the upper line of Roman numerals?

In example 4.12, the primary progression I–IV–V–I has also been elaborated by means of first-inversion triads and by a closing plagal cadence. Analyze this figured-bass progression: Find the basic root-position chords, and understand how our three fundamental functions are prolonged to generate this nine-chord harmonic phrase. Write Roman numerals under each of the bass notes, and then a second set of Roman numerals under the first one, to indicate the deeper level of prolonged harmonies. Finally, add a soprano line to this bass, and include voice exchanges for two of the three changes of position.

Example 4.11

Example 4.12

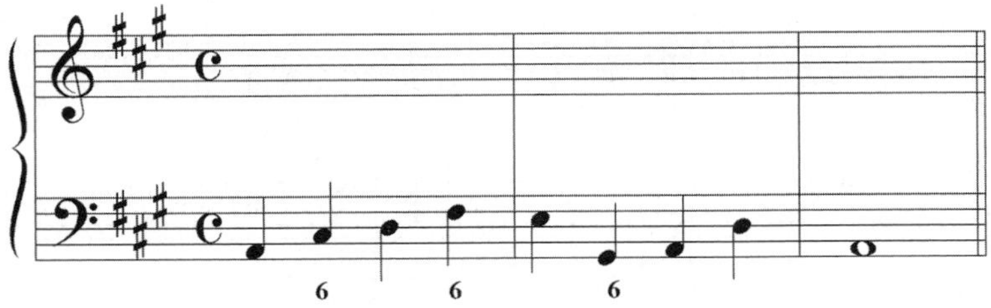

PRACTICAL APPLICATION AND DISCUSSION

1. Identify all first inversion triads in anthology, no. 8 (Bach, "Was mein Gott will"), mm. 1–5, and discuss their function within the passage.
2. J. S. Bach's Chorales 29 and 64 (anthology, nos. 10a and b) provide two different harmonizations of the same chorale melody. Compare how the initial $\hat{1}$–$\hat{2}$–$\hat{3}$ melodic gesture is harmonized in each chorale, and discuss the details of voice leading in each case. In Chorale 29, identify the cadence types in mm. 6, 8, and 13.
3. Find several first-inversion triads in a composition you are currently performing (or in its piano accompaniment). What is the function of each of them? Why do you think that the composer chose to use each of them instead of a root-position triad? How do these inverted triads make the music more interesting?

ASSIGNMENT AND KEYBOARD EXERCISES

For analytical and written assignments and keyboard exercises based on the materials learned in this chapter, refer to chapter 4 in the workbook.

PITCH PATTERNS

1. Practice singing triads in first inversion up from various pitches. The ascending scale-degrees (assuming a tonic triad) and intervallic patterns for M and m triads in first inversion are as follows:

   M triad in first inversion: $\hat{3}$–$\hat{5}$–$\hat{1}$ (m3 + P4)

   m triad in first inversion: $\flat\hat{3}$–$\hat{5}$–$\hat{1}$ (M3 + P4)

2. Sing the pitch patterns in example 4.13 (and hear the horizontalized harmonies) in the major and minor modes.

Example 4.13

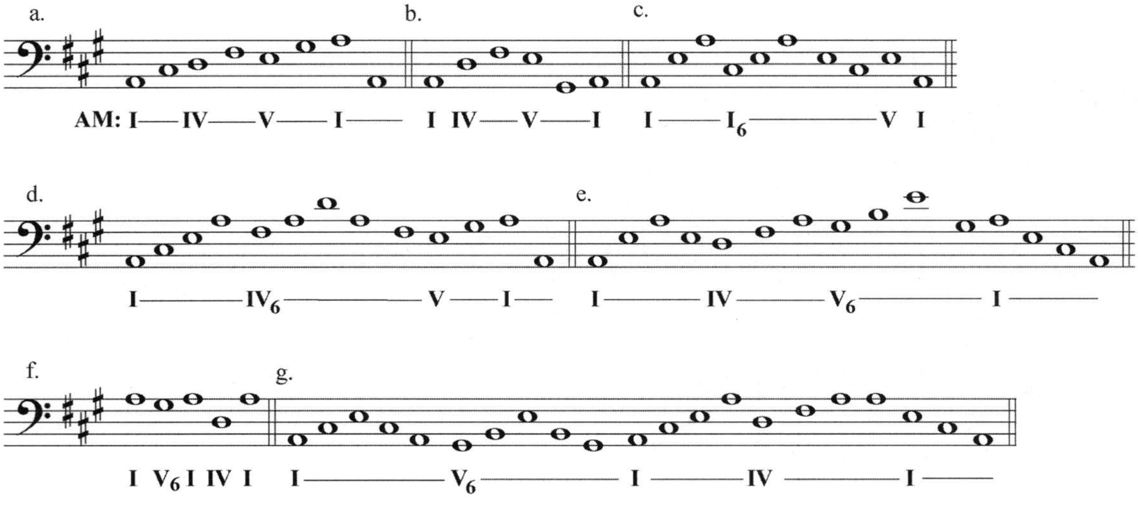

Terms for Review

Imperfect authentic cadence
Triads in first inversion:
functions and voice leading
$^6_3$ chords as prolongation (arpeggiation)
Voice exchange
V_6 as a neighbor chord

Worksheet 4

EXERCISE 1 Analysis.

1. Provide a RN analysis of example 4.14 and explain the function of the chords in this passage. Comment briefly on the voice leading. How can the passage be explained as a prolongation of the tonic triad?

NOTE

Although the key signature in this example indicates B♭M, this passage is actually in B♭m because of the accidentals in the music. Compositions do not stay in the same key throughout, and a fragment reproduced in a particular example may not be in the key indicated by the piece's key signature. In such cases, you will have to determine the key of the passage by examining the accidentals present in the music.

---

2. Analyze example 4.15 with RNs. Remember our definition of *passing tone* (PT): a pitch that fills in a gap of a 3rd by steps. A PT is an ornamental melodic pitch, and it does not change the harmonic nature of a chord.
   a) Circle all the PTs in the fragment.
   b) Mark all the changes of position with a bracket. Explain their role, especially in view of the soprano line Bach is harmonizing.

   c) Mark any voice exchange with the usual cross sign.
   d) Study the voice leading in the last three chords. Does the IV–V connection feature our standard voice leading? What about the V–I connection? Does Bach allow himself any voice-leading license? After you find it, make sure you first scream the customary, "If Bach does it, why can't I do it too ???" ☺ Then, explain why you think Bach chose this particular voice leading. His alternative could have been to write a B in the tenor for the last chord. What advantage did he find in writing a D instead?

Example 4.14 Maria Szymanowska, Nocturne in B♭M, mm. 17–19

Example 4.15 J. S. Bach, Chorale no. 54, "Lobt Gott, ihr Christen allzugleich," mm. 1–2

EXERCISE 2 Write the following triads in four voices with correct doubling.

FM: I_6 Cm: iv_6 F♯m: V_6 D♭M: IV_6 EM: I_6 Gm: V_6 A♭M: I_6 Dm: V_6

EXERCISE 3 Realize the following progressions in four voices. Use voice exchange where possible. *Always verify (and enjoy) the sound of what you write* by playing and listening to it.

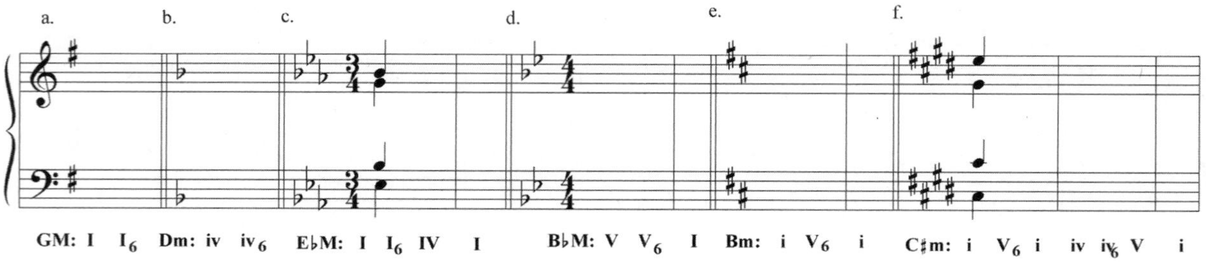

EXERCISE 4 *Figured bass realization.* Provide a RN analysis and a four-voice realization of the following figured basses.

Procedure to realize a figured bass: Review the section titled "Figured Bass" in chapter E.

1. First provide a RN analysis of the figured bass.
   a) Bass notes with no figures (or with a $^5_3$, a 5 or a 3) indicate root position chords.
   b) Accidentals alone refer to the third above the bass.
   c) A note with only an accidental indicates a root position triad with an altered third. For instance, a ♯ under a $\hat{5}$ in a minor key reminds you to raise $\hat{7}$ in a root position V chord; a ♯ under a $\hat{1}$ in a minor key indicates a Picardy third.
   d) A 6 (or a $^6_3$) indicates a first inversion triad.
2. Then realize the figured bass with your RNs as you have already been doing. Remember to write a good soprano line first, and to check your outer-voice first-species contrapuntal frame.

EXERCISE 5 Analyze the progression with RNs and realize the figured bass in four voices. Always play the exercises you write to know what they sound like. Remember to double-check your outer-voice frame for good first-species counterpoint.

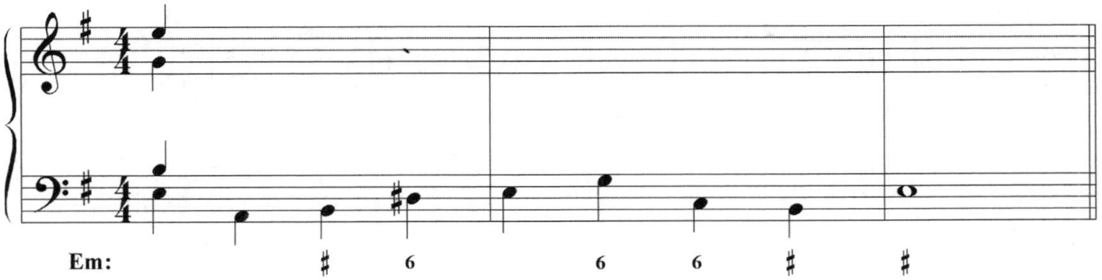

EXERCISE 6 Harmonize the following melodic patterns with a bass line and RNs, using standard harmonic patterns that correspond with each of the melodic patterns. Exercise 6a is made up of three 3-note overlapping patterns, whereas exercise 6b consists of two 3-note patterns.

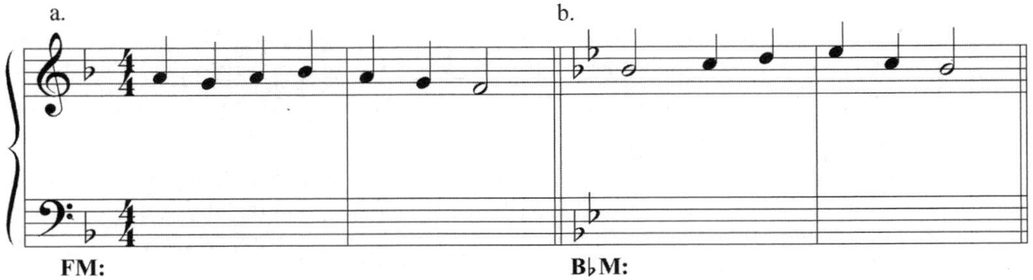

Chapter 5

The Supertonic; Melody Harmonization

You are already familiar with the concept of pre-dominant function, and with IV as a pre-dominant chord. The **supertonic triad** is another chord whose function is almost exclusively to precede and prepare the dominant. The supertonic (ii in major, ii° in minor) is the triad on $\hat{2}$, and it contains scale degrees $\hat{2}$, $\hat{4}$, and $\hat{6}$.

THE SUPERTONIC IN ROOT POSITION

In example 5.1 you can observe the most characteristic harmonic context for **ii in root position,** which may be summarized as follows:

1. Because ii has two common tones with IV ($\hat{4}$ and $\hat{6}$), the two chords are very closely related tonally and functionally; ii often follows IV (examples 5.1 and 5.2a).
2. Because of the 5th relationship with V, **ii functions as a very strong pre-dominant chord.** Whereas the relationship between IV and V is melodically strong (the roots are related by 2nd, and that provides a melodic tendency of IV toward V), ii and V have the strongest harmonic relationship (roots related by 5th; examples 5.1 and 5.2a).
3. The cadential progression ii–V–I is often used to harmonize the melodic patterns $\hat{2}$–$\hat{2}$–$\hat{1}$ or $\hat{2}$–$\hat{7}$–$\hat{1}$ as shown in examples 5.2a and b.
4. The progression I–ii (both in root position), although quite possible and correct, is not very frequent in the tonal repertoire because of its weak harmonic nature (roots by second). More often, ii is preceded by I_6 (as in I–I_6–ii–V–I, example 5.2c) or by IV (I–IV–ii–V–I, example 5.2a). I–ii–I_6, or the even weaker I–ii–iii, are not suitable progressions to harmonize a $\hat{1}$–$\hat{2}$–$\hat{3}$ bass. If you do write a I–ii progression, beware of parallel 5ths or 8ves: As in any progression by steps, the best voice leading results from moving the three upper voices in contrary motion with the bass; see example 5.2d.

Example 5.1 F. Schubert, Originaltänze, op. 9, no. 3, mm. 1–8

5. ii° (root position supertonic in a minor key) is a dissonant chord—it contains a °5th—and it is rarely found in root position. The supertonic in minor is more likely to appear as ii°$_6$.

Doubling and Voice Leading

The usual progressions with ii do not present any special doubling or voice-leading difficulty, as illustrated by example 5.2. Any of the members of ii in root position may be doubled, and doubling should be determined by voice leading. In ii° (root position in minor), an infrequent but possible chord, it is better to double the third (the root and the fifth form a dissonant °5th, and dissonant pitches should not be doubled).

IV and ii have two common tones, which in principle should be left in the same voices while the other voice moves up by step. ii and V have one common tone. In example 5.2a (soprano pattern $\hat{2}$–$\hat{2}$–$\hat{1}$), the common tone is sustained while the other two upper voices move up by step. An alternative and correct voice leading is shown in example 5.2b (soprano pattern $\hat{2}$–$\hat{7}$–$\hat{1}$), where all voices move down in contrary motion with the bass. I and ii have no common tones, and all three voices should move down in contrary motion with the bass (example 5.2d).

Example 5.2

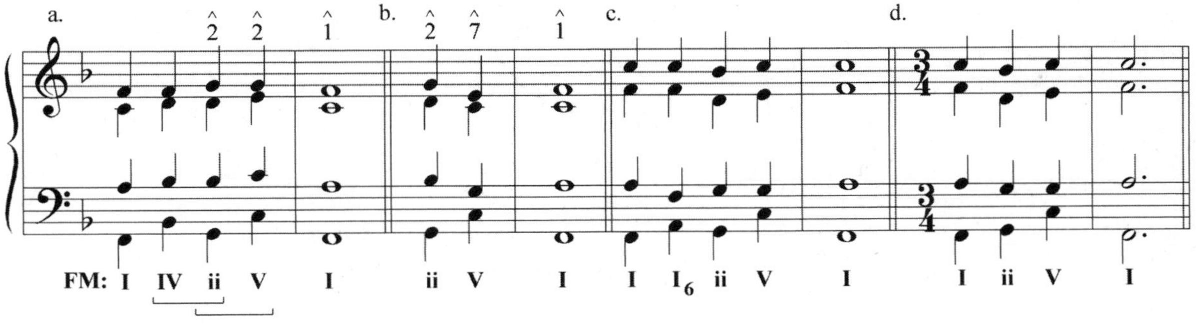

EXERCISE

To practice realizing short progressions using supertonic chords in root position, refer to exercises 2a and b in worksheet 5 at the end of this chapter.

THE SUPERTONIC IN FIRST INVERSION

The supertonic chord appears most often in **first inversion.** ii_6 ($ii°_6$ in minor) may be found even more frequently than IV as the chord preparing the dominant. ii_6 is indeed a very effective pre-dominant harmony because it has both the harmonic strength of the ii–V relationship (roots by 5th) and the melodic strength of the IV–V progression (a bass by steps, $\hat{4}$–$\hat{5}$). The close relationship between ii and IV, as well as their identical function, is best understood by comparing the ii_6–V and IV–V progressions, which differ in only one note (see examples 5.4a to c). In fact, IV and ii_6 may appear in succession over a sustained bass note $\hat{4}$, in such a way that IV is transformed into ii_6 by means of a simple **5–6 melodic motion** (the 5th above the bass turns into a 6th above the bass) in one of the upper voices, as illustrated by example 5.4b. The progression ii_6–V–I (or $ii°_6$–V–i) is a common cadential formula, as illustrated by the Verdi phrase shown in example 5.3.

Doubling and Voice Leading

ii_6 (in major) appears very often with a doubled third ($\hat{4}$, a tonally strong scale degree), as in example 5.4c. Doubling the root (example 5.4d) is perfectly acceptable, whereas doubling the fifth (example 5.4e) is possible but less frequent. In the minor mode, $ii°_6$ normally appears with a doubled third (example 5.4f), possibly with a doubled root. Doubling the fifth in $ii°_6$ is likely to result in an augmented 2nd, $\flat\hat{6}$–$\natural\hat{7}$ (compare examples 5.4e and h), so in general it should be avoided.

Example 5.3 Giuseppe Verdi, *Rigoletto,* act I, no. 9, "Caro nome"

NOTES

Compare examples 5.4f and g. In the progression I–ii$_6$, parallel 5ths may easily result if the root of I is doubled, as in example 5.4g. The problem can be avoided by doubling the third in I, as in example 5.4f (although the problem arises only in major keys; in minor, the consecutive 5ths in the same progression would be perfectly acceptable unequal 5ths, P5–°5). This is an example of doubling of the third in a root position triad totally justified by voice-leading considerations.

Compare also examples 5.4d and g. In 5.4d, the parallel 5ths are avoided by switching the position of the voices involved (that is, the soprano line from example 5.4g is taken an octave lower in example 5.4d and becomes the alto line, and the alto in example 5.4g

Example 5.4

becomes the soprano in example 5.4d). Parallel 5ths thus become correct parallel 4ths. In general, parallel 5ths among upper voices can often be avoided (and turned into parallel 4ths) by switching the voices that produce the faulty voice leading.

Typical Errors to Avoid:

1. Doubling the fifth in ii°$_6$, with a resulting augmented 2nd in the ii°$_6$–V progression.
2. Writing parallel 5ths in the I–ii or I–ii$_6$ progression.

EXERCISES

To practice realizing short progressions using supertonic chords in first inversion, refer to exercises 2c and d and 3 in worksheet 5 at the end of this chapter.

To practice analyzing musical examples that include supertonic chords, refer to exercise 1 in worksheet 5 at the end of this chapter.

CHARACTERISTIC SOPRANO-BASS PATTERNS

Example 5.5 shows some typical soprano-bass patterns that can be harmonized with the supertonic as a pre-dominant chord. Examples 5.5a to d feature melodic patterns harmonized with progression involving a root-position ii, with the cadential gesture $\hat{2}$–$\hat{5}$–$\hat{1}$ in the bass. Examples 5.5e and f show two common melodic patterns harmonized with the cadential $\hat{4}$–$\hat{5}$–$\hat{1}$ in the bass. All these patterns feature ii and ii$_6$ as additions to our repertoire of chords that elaborate the I–V–I progression with a pre-dominant function. Play each of these outer-voice patterns at the piano, adding inner voices in keyboard texture.

Example 5.5

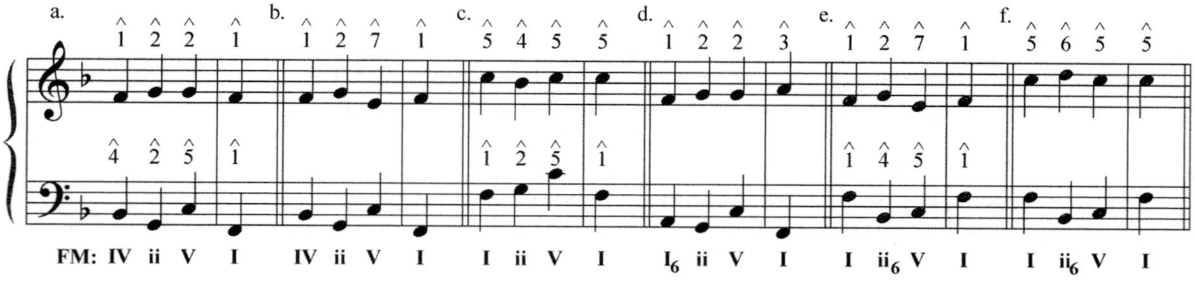

Example 5.6

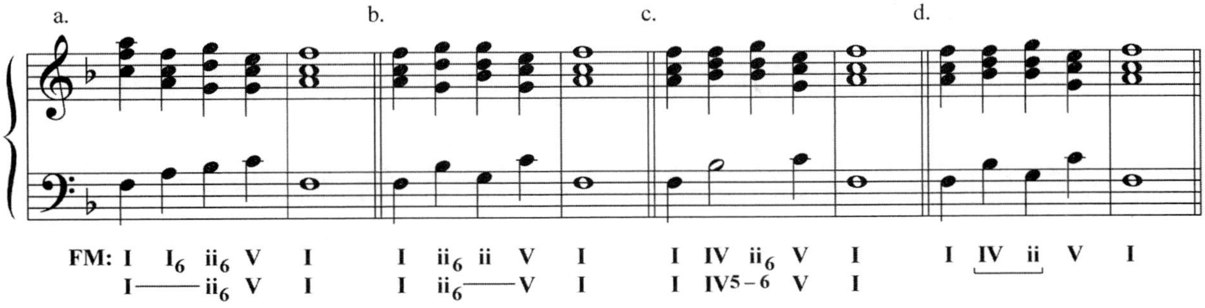

ELABORATING THE I–V–I PROGRESSION

The chords and progressions we have studied in this chapter add some new possibilities to our elaboration of the I–V–I progression. In the first place, we now have the choice between IV or ii as a pre-dominant. Example 5.6a shows an extension of the opening tonic by a change of position, followed by a pre-dominant ii_6. The pre-dominant can now also be extended in various ways. In example 5.6b, a change of position extends a pre-dominant ii_6 harmony, whereas in 5.6c the pre-dominant harmony is extended by a 5–6 motion over $\hat{4}$ in the bass. Finally, in example 5.6d the pre-dominant harmony includes two root-position chords, IV and ii, harmonizing the same melodic gesture that we just identified as 5–6 over $\hat{4}$ in 5.6c.

HARMONIZING A MELODY

So far, you have written chordal realizations in four voices of given bass or soprano lines with Roman numerals (the harmonization) also provided, or harmonizations of brief melodic patterns that we have associated with standard harmonic patterns. In this chapter you will start to compose your own harmonizations of longer soprano lines. For the time being, you will write *only the bass line and Roman numerals,* omitting the two inner voices.

Harmonic Rhythm

The rhythmic pattern created by the change of chords is known as **harmonic rhythm.** (We will study harmonic rhythm in detail in chapter 13.) The rhythmic phrase under the Roman numerals in example 5.8f, for instance, indicates the harmonic rhythm (HR) for the progression. Notice that a change of position is not counted as a change of chord ($I–I_6$ is the same chord). The harmonic rhythm for the melodies you will harmonize will be given. Sometimes you will be asked to write a chord for each soprano note (example 5.7a). Sometimes, however, two soprano notes belong to the same chord and can be

Example 5.7

harmonized with a single chord, as in example 5.7b. In most of these cases, using a change of position within the same chord contributes to the melodic motion and variety of the bass (example 5.7c). Conversely, if a soprano note is long (two or more beats, or, in compound meter, a dotted quarter or longer) you may be able to harmonize it with two different chords (example 5.7d), or you may need to use only one chord and its first inversion (example 5.7e).

Procedure

The basic procedure for harmonizing a melody is as follows:

1. For the time being, progressions will begin and end on the tonic chord.
2. First, try to identify any possible melodic patterns we may have associated with standard harmonic patterns. A scale degree analysis of the melody will help you in this process. In example 5.7a, for instance, we recognize two familiar scale degree patterns, $\hat{1}$–$\hat{2}$–$\hat{3}$ and $\hat{4}$–$\hat{2}$–$\hat{1}$, and both are harmonized with corresponding harmonic patterns that we have already studied. The same $\hat{4}$–$\hat{2}$–$\hat{1}$ pattern also appears in examples 5.7b, c, and e. In example 5.7d we see the $\hat{1}$–$\hat{2}$–$\hat{3}$ pattern that we can harmonize with the I–V_6–I progression, except in this case the initial I can itself be extended by means of a i–iv–i neighbor progression.
3. In example 5.8 you can see a detailed illustration of an alternative (and complementary) method to the identification of patterns. This method is more laborious,

Example 5.8

but it will be useful when you do not recognize any particular standard pattern in a passage. First, think what possible chords each given note belongs to in the given key, using only chords and inversions you have already studied in this book.

4. From the possible chords, choose the ones that result in a *good progression,* that is, in a progression that follows the criteria that we have studied so far: V should resolve to I and not to IV, IV may follow I and precede V, and so forth. If the HR is given, look for melodic fragments that may be harmonized by a single chord with change of position (two notes that belong to the same chord, or a long note).
5. Avoid sustaining a chord over the bar line, or, in quadruple meter, over beats 2 and 3. In both cases, the chord would begin on a weak beat and end on a strong beat, creating a **harmonic syncopation** that produces a blurring of meter and a conflict between meter and harmony.
6. When you have the correct progression, write a bass line for it. If your line is monotonous or repetitive because you are using only root-position triads, try to enrich your bass by using some first inversions in the spots that you previously identified as possible for changes of position. Think of the outer-voice frame you are writing in terms of first-species counterpoint, and remember to check for voice-leading errors.

Practicing the Process

Let us try the latter process with a melody, following the steps illustrated in example 5.8.

Example 5.8a—We will harmonize the melody shown in example 5.8a, following the given harmonic rhythm. First, sing or play the melody several times.

Example 5.8b—As an initial exercise, we will practice melody harmonizations using only I, IV, and V. After singing the melody, list the possible chords for each note, as in example 5.8b.

Example 5.8c—Assume for a moment that you were not given the HR and that you could choose freely from the possible chords. The circled chords in example 5.8c seem to be a possible good progression, for which we write a bass line. The progression is correct but produces a poor and repetitive bass because the progression itself has several repeated connections (as the two I–IV pairs). The last measure is too simple.

Example 5.8d—Look now at the harmonization in example 5.8d. The bass is not only weak melodically, but there are several obvious errors: two harmonic syncopations (marked with asterisks) and a V–IV progression. We mentioned before that harmonic syncopations blur the sense of meter. The lower staff in example 5.8d illustrates this point: Because the HR in this progression creates a grouping of chords in 3, we may hear this bass line as if it were in $\frac{3}{4}$, as notated in the lower staff, thus producing a conflict with the $\frac{4}{4}$ meter of the given melody.

Example 5.8e—Considering the lack of success of our attempted harmonizations, we might as well go back to the given HR. According to it, three pairs of notes should be harmonized with the same chord, as shown by the brackets in example 5.8e.

Example 5.9

These same fragments indicated by brackets are all subject to harmonizations using a change of position. The progression circled in this example follows the given HR and makes sense harmonically, although the bass that results from it is quite poor because of the various repeated notes.

Example 5.8f—For the final version in example 5.8f, we have improved the bass by changes of position, and we have also taken advantage of two possible voice exchanges. The last measure, with its plagal cadence, is now also much improved.

The outer-voice frame we have written works just fine as a first-species counterpoint duet. In example 5.8f we could be picky about the unbalanced leap in the bass, m. 2, but considering the various problems we have had to deal with, this seems a very minor flaw in this context, and we can let it pass. Sing all four versions in class or with some friend (examples 5.8c, d, e, and f), and notice the different points we have discussed. Now try your own harmonization of the following melody (example 5.9), using only I, IV, V, and their first inversions.

EXERCISE

To practice harmonizing melodies, refer to exercises 4 and 5 in worksheet 5 at the end of this chapter.

ASSIGNMENT AND KEYBOARD EXERCISES

For analytical and written assignments and keyboard exercises based on the materials learned in this chapter, refer to chapter 5 in the workbook.

PITCH PATTERNS

Sing the pitch patterns in example 5.10, listening to and understanding the various uses of the linearized supertonic chords.

Example 5.10

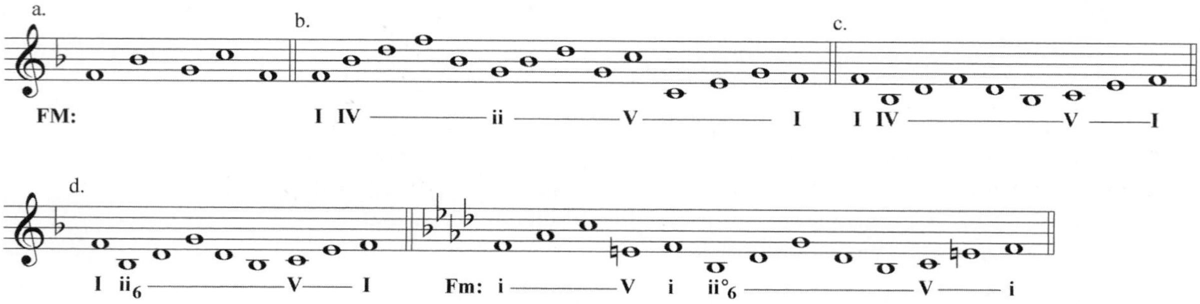

Terms for Review

The supertonic triad
Function of the supertonic triad
ii in root position
Relationship of ii with IV and V
ii and ii° in first inversion
5–6 melodic motion
Harmonic rhythm
Harmonic syncopation

Worksheet 5

EXERCISE 1 Compare the cadences in examples 5.11a, b, and c. What do they have in common? How do they differ? (Take into account the complete pre-dominant/dominant/tonic pattern.)

Example 5.11a G. Verdi: *Il trovatore,* act II, no. 15, "E deggio e posso crederlo?"

Troubadour.
16
Nè m'eb - be il ciel, nè l'or - ri - do var - co in - fer - nal sen - tie - ro.

Example 5.11b W. A. Mozart, Piano Sonata in CM, K. 330, III

168

Example 5.11c Notebook of Anna Magdalena Bach, "Aria di Govannini"

EXERCISE 2 Realize the following short progressions in four voices. Add Roman numerals (RNs) where missing.

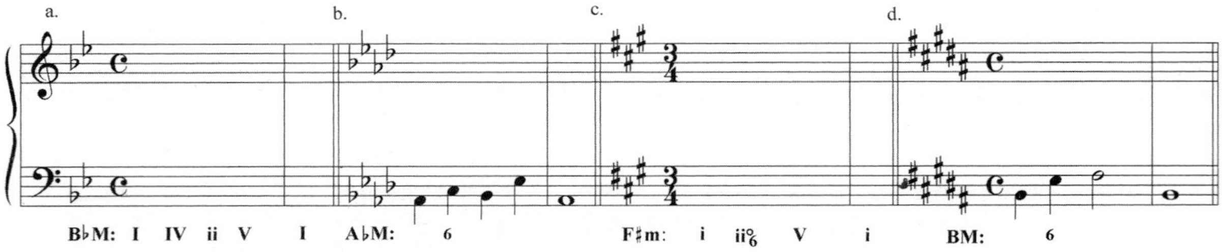

EXERCISE 3 Realize the following progression in four voices. Remember to double-check your outer-voice frame for good first-species counterpoint.

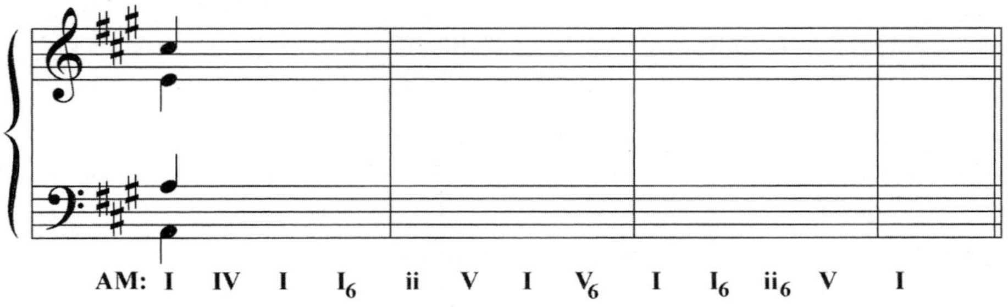

EXERCISE 4 *Melody harmonization.* Write a bass and RNs (no inner voices) harmonizing the following melodies. The harmonic rhythm (HR) is given.

1. Sing each melody several times before writing the harmonization.
2. Use only I, IV, or V in root position or first inversion.
3. First try to identify any melodic patterns that may be harmonized with some of the harmonic patterns you have learned.
4. Harmonize the notes marked with a 6 with first inversion triads. (If necessary, a 5 is used to indicate a root position triad.)
5. Check your two-voice contrapuntal frame to verify good voice leading.
6. Always *play your harmonizations* (as well as all your other exercises) before you turn them in. Make sure you are satisfied with them, and enjoy them!

EXERCISE 5 Harmonize the following melodies with bass and RNs (no inner voices). Use I (i), IV (iv), V, or ii (ii°) in root position or first inversion. Remember to double-check your outer-voice frame for good first-species counterpoint.

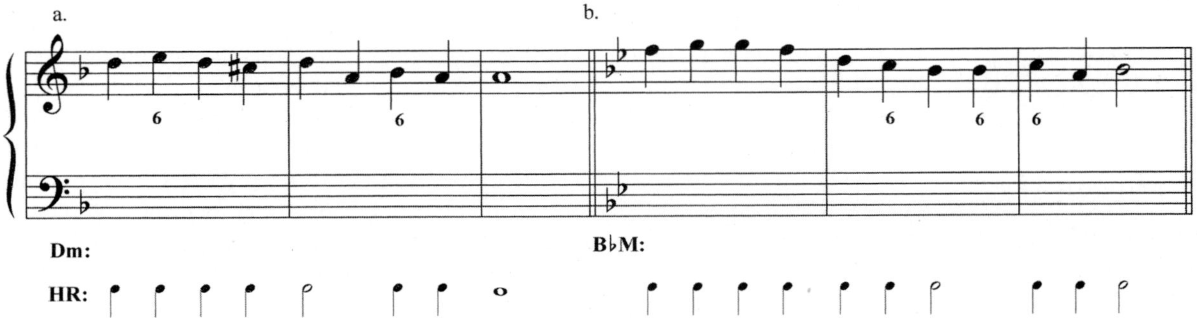

Chapter 6

Nonchord Tones

Refer to anthology, no. 9 (Bach, "Was Gott tut"). You will remember that when you analyzed this fragment with Roman numerals in chapter 4, you were told to consider the first eighth note in each beat as the actual chord, while the second eighth note was, in this example, either a nonchord tone or a change of voicing. Examine, for instance, the first chord. It is a tonic GM triad, G–B–D, with the root doubled. The pitches A–C do not belong to the chord and create dissonances with some of the chord tones. A and C are here nonchord tones. **Nonchord tones** (NCT), also called *nonharmonic tones,* are pitches foreign to the chord with which they sound simultaneously. Nonchord tones may be consonant or dissonant but, most often, they create dissonances within the chord that contains them, and for this reason they cannot be used freely in tonal music. Rather, their use is regulated by a number of conventions to control dissonance. In general, the tenets of dissonance control require *resolution to a consonance* and, in many cases, also *preparation* (that is, a predetermined way of approaching the dissonant pitch).

In previous chapters we have already introduced both the concept of nonchord tones and some specific types of nonchord tones. In chapter F, for instance, we discussed the passing tone and the neighbor note in the context of second- and third-species counterpoint (see examples F.6b to d and F.8a to c), and we studied suspensions as part of fourth species. In this chapter we will study the most common types of NCTs and their normative behavior within the consonant frame of the tonal system. The most common NCTs fall into one of the following categories: passing tones, neighbor notes, anticipations, incomplete neighbors, or suspensions. *NCTs are melodic in nature.* That is, they are not harmonic (vertical) events, but rather linear (horizontal) events. NCTs provide both tonal variety (by introducing pitches foreign to the harmonic framework) and musical tension (by introducing dissonances that need to resolve to consonances).

NOTE

An important factor to consider in the study of nonchord tones is their placement on metrically strong or weak beats or beat divisions. As you will remember from chapter B, in duple meter beat 1 is strong and beat 2 is weak. In quadruple meter, beats 1 and 3 are strong, and 2 and 4 weak. And in triple meter, only beat 1 is strong. The same principles apply to beat divisions or fractions. In a beat divided into two eighth notes, the first one is strong, the second one weak. If the division is into four sixteenth notes, notes 1 and 3 are strong, and notes 2 and 4 are weak. In beats divided into three notes (in triplets or compound meters), note 1 is strong and notes 2 and 3 are weak.

THE PASSING TONE

A **passing tone** (PT) is a NCT that fills in the gap between two chord tones (normally a 3rd). Example 6.1 features a PT in every measure but the last (the circled notes). In all six cases you will see that PTs are approached and left by step (both in the same direction), and that regular PTs fall on a weak beat or beat fraction.

PTs may occur simultaneously in two voices (**double passing tones**). Find several instances of double PTs in anthology, no. 9 ("Was Gott tut").

NOTE

The passing tones we are studying in this section are purely melodic nonchord tones. You should not confuse this type of passing tone with the type of linear passing motion that results in some harmonic progressions. In examples 2.2 and 4.7 we discussed this type of linear passing motion in the context of chordal voice leading. The same comment applies to the difference between melodic neighbor notes, which we will study later in the chapter, and linear neighbor motion in a chordal context, which we also discussed in examples 2.2 and 4.5. The nonchord tones and the chordal voice-leading types of passing or neighboring motion result from interpretations of melodic motion at different musical levels.

A PT that fills in a 3rd is usually diatonic. A **chromatic PT,** on the other hand, fills in a whole-step gap by means of two half steps. In Beethoven's Sonata in Cm, op. 10/1, II (anthology, no. 33), chromatic PTs can be found in the top voice, mm. 2 and 4. The D♯ circled in m. 3 of example 6.3 is a chromatic PT closing the step between D and E.

An **accented passing tone** (APT) is a passing tone that falls on a strong beat or beat fraction. All the circled pitches in example 6.2a are APTs. If the gap to be filled is a 4th rather than a 3rd (as in a melodic fragment $\hat{5}$–$\hat{6}$–$\hat{7}$–$\hat{1}$ filling a $\hat{5}$–$\hat{1}$), two PTs are needed. Two such successive PTs are shown in example 6.2b, m. 8, beat 2. In this case, the first PT is unaccented and the second one accented. (The same figure in compound meter or a triplet results in two successive unaccented PTs.)

A final example by the Beatles will help you review all the different types of PTs we have discussed previously. The initial harmonic progression in example 6.2c is

Example 6.1 J. Lennon–P. McCartney, "Lucy in the Sky with Diamonds," from the album *Sgt. Pepper's Lonely Hearts Club Band* (Verse)

Some - bo - dy calls you, you an - swer quite slow - ly a girl with kal -
AM:
eid - o - scope eyes.

Example 6.2a W. A. Mozart, Piano Sonata in B♭M, K. 333, I, mm. 1–4

Example 6.2b W. A. Mozart, Piano Sonata in AM, K. 331, I, Var. VI, mm. 9–10

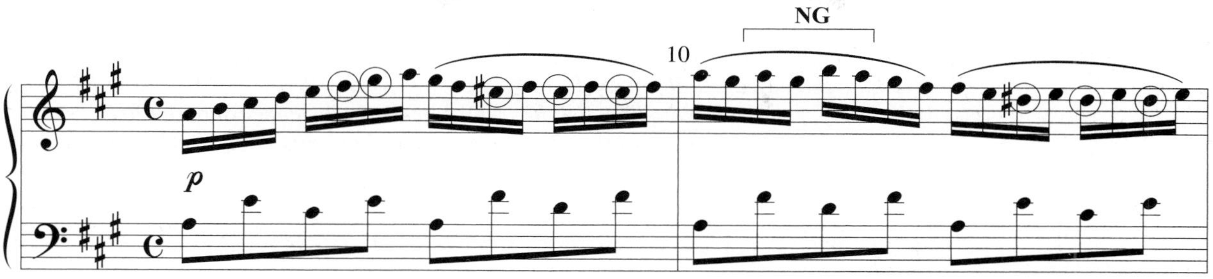

Example 6.2c J. Lennon–P. McCartney, "A Hard Day's Night," from the film and album *A Hard Day's Night* (Final Cadence of Verse)

simply I–IV–V–I in GM. And yet this simple harmony is greatly enriched by a variety of double PTs in the two vocal parts in parallel 3rds. Examine the vocal parts, circle the chord tones, and then determine whether each PT is diatonic or chromatic, accented or unaccented. What kind of cadence closes this phrase?

NOTE

Whereas parallel 5ths and 8ves have been considered unstylistic in Western "art music," and we know that common practice composers have, as a general principle, avoided them, popular music often revels in the bald expressive power of parallel perfect intervals. Thus, parallel 5ths and 8ves are not unstylistic or avoided in popular music. Examine the voice leading from IV to V in example 6.2c. If you disregard the PTs, you will discover that avoiding parallel 5ths was indeed not the concern of the Beatles! This type of voice leading is certainly fully acceptable in the stylistic context of a rock song.

THE NEIGHBOR NOTE

A **neighbor note** (NN) is a NCT that departs by step from a pitch and returns, also by step, to the same pitch. The NN is thus a step above (upper NN) or below (lower NN) the embellished pitch. NNs usually fall on weak beats or beat fractions, although they may also fall on accented metric divisions (**accented NN**). The initial motive of Mozart's Sonata in AM, K. 331 (anthology, no. 27) is based on an upper NN figure.

NNs may also be *chromatic* (a half step above or below the embellished pitch). In example 6.3, m. 3, the pitch D is first embellished by a diatonic upper NN, and then by a chromatic lower NN, followed by a chromatic PT between D and E. Notice that at m. 5, the pitch A is also embellished by two NN figures.

Examine now the successions of NNs circled in example 6.2b, in the second half of each measure. You will see that each of them falls on either the beat or the third sixteenth note of the beat. In other words, these are all *accented NNs* (ANN).

Example 6.3 F. Chopin, Mazurka in Am, op. 7, no. 2

Example 6.4 W. A. Mozart, Piano Sonata in AM, K. 331, I, Var. III, mm. 1–2

Neighbor Group

You may have seen that in example 6.2b, m. 2, beats 1 to 2, the melodic turn A–G♯–B–A contains a lower NN of A immediately followed by the upper NN, before the figure returns to the chord tone, A. Such a figure is called a **neighbor group** (NG) or *double neighbor,* and it consists of two NNs (one upper and one lower, or vice versa) immediately following each other. The passage in example 6.4, from Mozart's AM sonata, features two NGs. Identify and circle them on the score.

THE ANTICIPATION

An **anticipation** (ANT) is a nonchord tone that anticipates a pitch from the next chord. An ANT is approached by step and left by repeating the same note, and is placed on a weak beat or beat fraction.

The period by Beethoven reproduced in example 6.5 opens with two anticipation figures. In the anacrusis (pickup) to m. 1, the F♯ sounded against the GM chord anticipates the F♯ in m. 1, where it is a member of the V_7 chord. Similarly, the nonchord tone G at the end of m. 1 anticipates the chord tone G in m. 2.

INCOMPLETE NEIGHBORS

We know that a neighbor note is approached by step from the note it embellishes and then returns to the same note also by step. Now examine the three examples in example 6.6. In example 6.6a, a nonchord tone (E in the alto) is approached by leap and left by step, whereas in example 6.6b the nonchord tone C in the soprano is approached by step and left by leap. Both of these NCTs are placed in metrically weak beat divisions. The G in the alto in example 6.6c, on the other hand, is also approached by leap and left by step, but its position is metrically strong. All three NCTs have in common that they function as neighbor notes to a chord tone which they approach *or* leave by step. In other words, they are all neighbor notes which do not effect the complete two-step neighbor motion we are familiar with, and for this reason we call them **incomplete neighbors** (IN). The

Example 6.5 L. v. Beethoven, Sonata in GM, op. 49, no. 2, II, mm. 1–8

first example (example 6.6a) is the least frequently found in music. Examples 6.6b and c, on the other hand, represent two types of incomplete neighbors that are found more often and that are usually called escape tone and appoggiatura, respectively.

The Escape Tone

An **escape tone** (ET) is a type of incomplete neighbor approached by step and left by leap, normally in the opposite direction (example 6.6b). It occurs on a weak beat or beat fraction. Refer to anthology, no. 9 ("Was Gott tut"), m. 3. The chord on beat 4 is IV_6 in GM (a CM chord in first inversion). The NCT in the bass is, of course, a familiar PT. The D in the soprano, on the other hand, is an ET, approached by step up and left by leap down.

Example 6.6

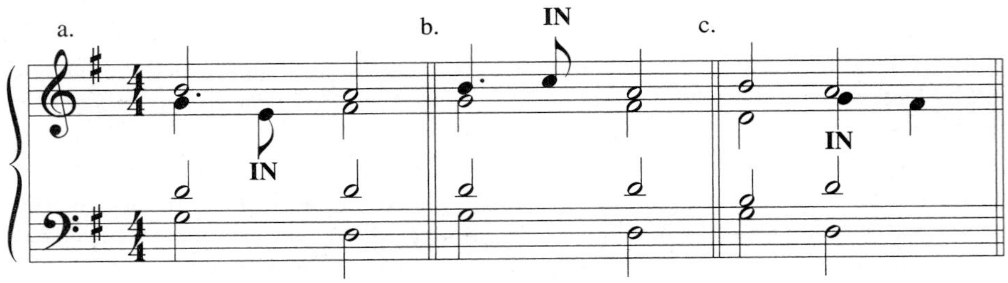

The Appoggiatura

An **appoggiatura** (AP) is a type of incomplete neighbor approached by leap and left by step (normally in the opposite direction from the approaching leap), and usually falls on a strong beat or beat division (although metrically weak appoggiaturas are also possible, as illustrated by example 6.6a).

The opening phrase in anthology, no. 33 (Beethoven's Sonata op. 10/1, II) contains two APs. In m. 1, the C in the top voice does not belong to the underlying chord (a V^6_5 in A♭M, which includes the pitches E♭–G–B♭–D♭, with G in the bass), and it is approached by leap and left by step in the opposite direction. Examine and discuss the equivalent AP in m. 3. Instances of APs may also be found in example 6.2a, m. 2, and 6.3, m. 4. Identify and circle them.

Examples 6.7a and b will allow you to compare (and to make sure you do not confuse) the opposite characteristics of the escape tone (weak placement, approached by step, left by leap, as in example 6.7a) and the appoggiatura (strong placement, approached by leap, left by step, as in example 6.7b).

Example 6.7a J. Haydn, Piano Sonata in CM, Hob. XVI:3, II, mm. 1–2

Example 6.7b W. A. Mozart, Piano Sonata in CM, K. 309, I, mm. 54–56

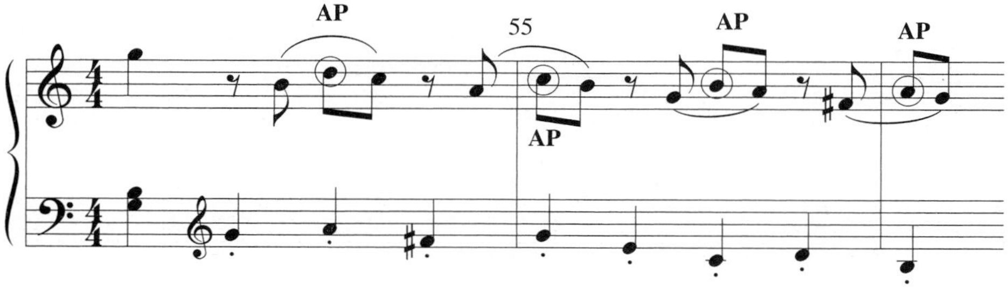

VOICE-LEADING GUIDELINES

1. NCTs do not prevent or hide faulty parallel perfect intervals, although they may easily create them. The poor voice leading in example 6.8a is not hidden or improved by a few passing tones: The parallel 5ths between bass and tenor (beats 1 and 2), between bass and soprano (beats 2 and 3), and the 8ves in contrary motion between bass and tenor (8ve C–C in m. 1, beat 3, followed by unison G in m. 2, beat 1) are incorrect in spite of the intervening passing tones. On the other hand, the passing tone in example 6.8b creates parallel 5ths in a chord connection that otherwise would be correct.
2. Simultaneous NCTs in different voices are possible and occur frequently in chorale textures. Simultaneous NCTs, however, sound better if they are *consonant among themselves* (although, of course, they may be dissonant with the chord tones that sound at the same time). Anthology, no. 8 (Bach, "Was mein Gott will") features a variety of simultaneous NCTs. Examine this example, and notice how NCTs are indeed consonant among themselves.
3. As a summary of the NCTs studied previously, each of them is briefly demonstrated in example 6.9.

Example 6.8

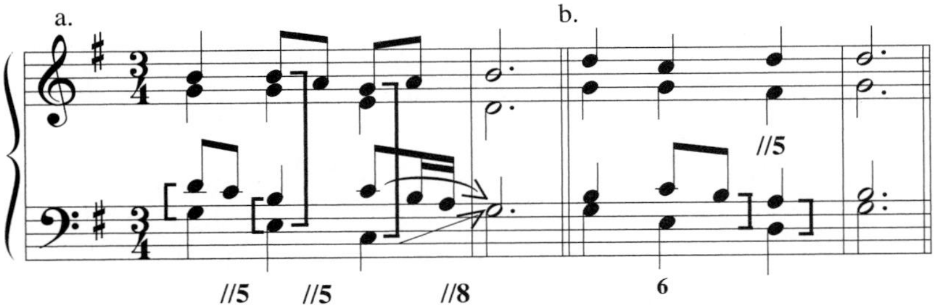

Example 6.9

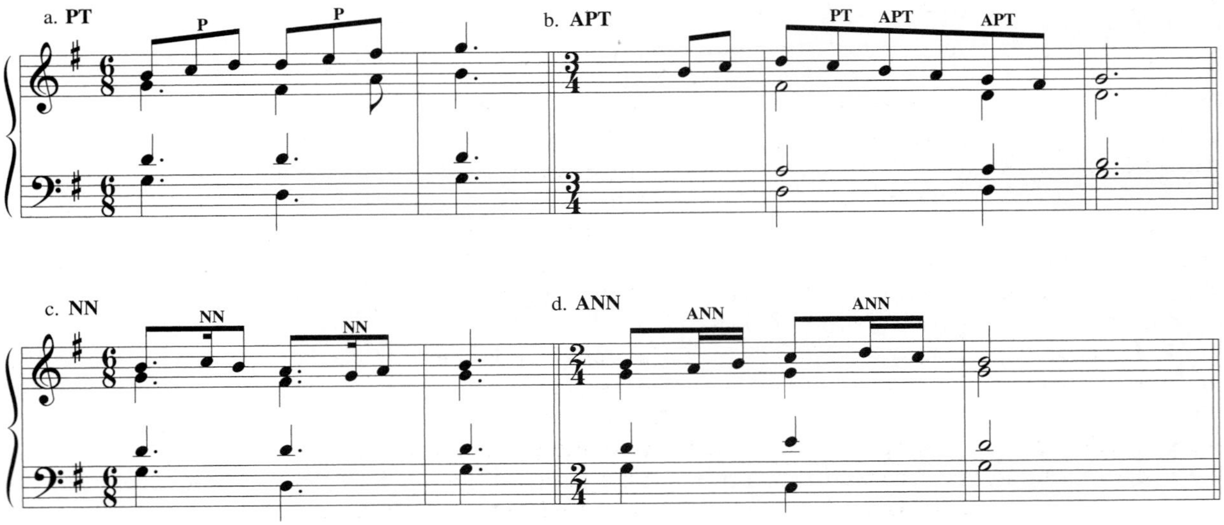

Example 6.9 Continued

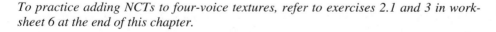

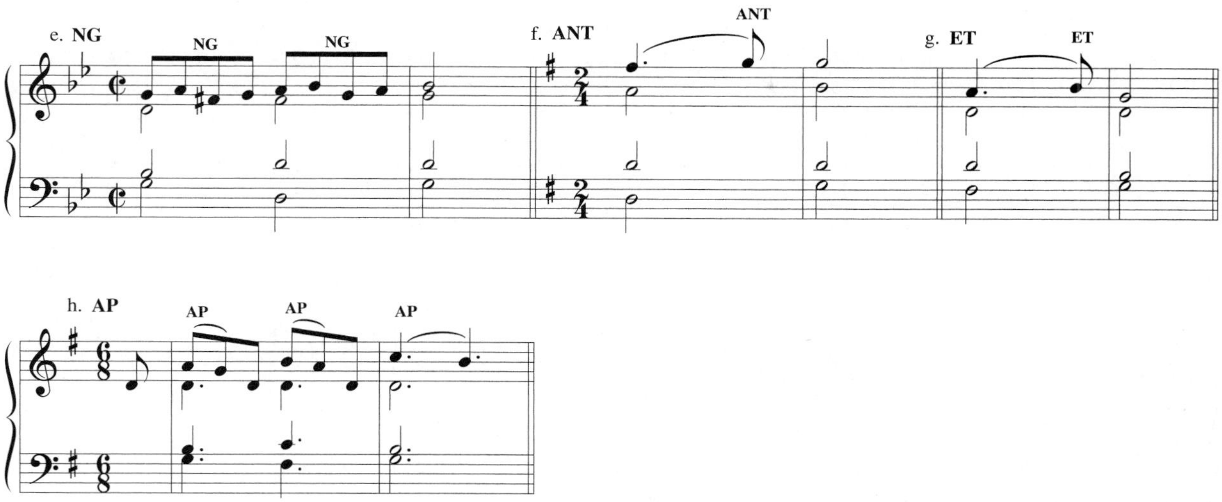

EXERCISE

To practice adding NCTs to four-voice textures, refer to exercises 2.1 and 3 in worksheet 6 at the end of this chapter.

SUSPENSIONS

In chapter F you were introduced to the study of **suspensions.** You learned that, for instance, if in two consecutive thirds in first species you delay the upper-voice motion by one beat, the 3–3 counterpoint becomes 3–4–3, a figure that includes a 4–3 suspension, as was illustrated in examples F.12a and b. If you examine example 6.10a, you will see a similar process, only now it takes place in a four-voice chordal frame. First, we see a plain I–V–I progression. Then, the motion from $\hat{1}$ to $\hat{7}$ in the upper voice is delayed by one beat. Counting intervals from the bass, we see that the delayed pitch and its resolution form a 4–3 suspension with the bass note A.

A suspension thus involves two chords (in our example, the D and A chords in m. 1). A note from the first chord is sustained and then resolved into the second chord. The actual suspension (marked S in our example), which occurs over the second chord, is the *sustained note.* The **preparation** (P) and the **resolution** (R), however, are required components that precede and follow a suspension. Example 6.10a illustrates the parts in a suspension figure: the pitch D, which belongs to the DM triad, is suspended

Example 6.10

over the AM triad as a NCT, and then resolved down to C. The components are as follows:

1. *Preparation (P).* The suspended note must be a chord tone in the previous chord and must appear in the same voice as (and usually, but not necessarily, tied to) the suspension. The preparation will generally be at least as long as (or longer than) the suspension.
2. *Suspension (S).* The preparation note is suspended, or delayed, into the second chord, where it usually creates a dissonance. The suspension must fall on a *strong beat.* It is often tied to the preparation, but it may also be rearticulated and still be a suspension, as long as it is prepared by the same pitch in the same voice.
3. *Resolution (R).* The suspension resolves *downward* to a member of the second chord.

Types of Suspension

Suspensions are labeled by means of two Arabic numerals which indicate *intervals with the bass.* The first numeral refers to the interval between *the bass and the suspension;* the second numeral indicates the interval between *the bass and the resolution.*

1. In a **4–3 suspension** (example 6.10a), the suspension is a 4th above the bass, and resolves down to the pitch a 3rd above the bass.

2. In a **7–6 suspension** (example 6.10b), the suspension is a 7th above the bass, and resolves down to the pitch a 6th above the bass. Because the chord of resolution contains a 6, a 7–6 suspension does not resolve to a root-position triad, but rather to one of the chord inversions that contain a 6 (for the time being, only a triad in first inversion).
3. A **9–8 suspension** (example 6.10c), features a suspension a 9th (*not* a 2nd) above the bass, resolving to the 8ve.
4. The **2–3 suspension** is the only one in which a suspension is actually *in the bass.* Look at example 6.10d carefully to understand how the 2–3 suspension works. The suspended C, in the bass, creates a dissonance of a 2nd (or a 9th) with another voice (in this case, the tenor). The bass dissonance resolves down to a pitch which forms a 3rd with the tenor, hence the 2–3 label (in which, of course, intervals are still counted from the bass upward). The 2–3 suspension often resolves to a first-inversion triad, as in our example. The $\substack{5-6 \\ 2-3}$ figures simply indicate that the A in the alto is a 5th over the delayed D, which then becomes a 6th over the pitch of resolution, C.
5. A different category of suspension (one that is often not considered a true suspension) is represented in example 6.10e. The **6–5 suspension** is different from the previous four types in that it is a *consonant* suspension, and therefore its musical effect is much less dramatic than in the case of dissonant suspensions.

NOTE

The note of resolution should not sound at the same time as the suspension, except in a 9–8 suspension. Example 6.10f illustrates an incorrect version of the 7–6 suspension from example 6.10b: The note of resolution (G) is present in the soprano at the same time as the suspension (A). In example 6.10b, it is not. The problem in example 6.10f is that while we are delaying the motion to G in one voice (creating an expectation), we hear the delayed pitch in another voice (thus frustrating the expectation). The suspension and its resolution sounding at the same time, moreover, make for an unclear sonority. The effect is similar to giving away the punch line beforetime. In a 9–8 suspension, on the other hand, the note of resolution (D in example 6.10c) is present in the bass, by definition, at the same time as the suspension, because the resolution is to the 8ve above the bass (that is, to the same note as the one in the bass, in a higher 8ve).

EXERCISE

To practice writing suspensions, refer to exercises 2.2, 3b, and 4 in worksheet 6 at the end of this chapter.

Embellished Suspensions

Suspensions are often **embellished** with some of the NCTs we have studied. In example 6.11a, the suspension presented in its plain version in example 6.10a has been embellished with an anticipation of the resolution. Example 6.11b features an

Example 6.11a to e

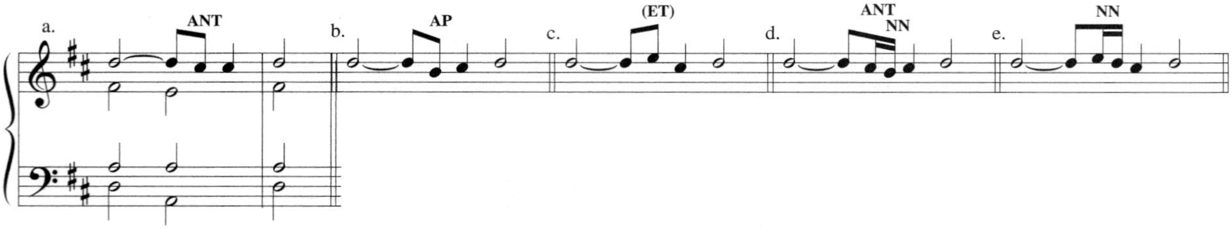

Example 6.11f J. S. Bach, Chorale 32, "Nun danket alle Gott," mm. 2–4

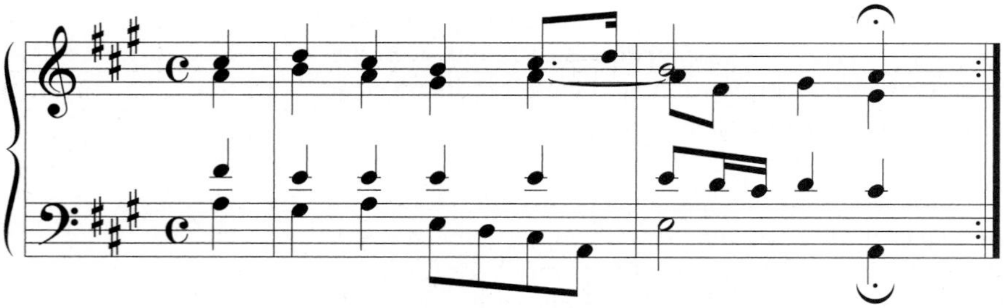

appoggiatura to the resolution; example 6.11c, an escape tone (which, however, in this case is a chord tone); example 6.11d, a neighbor note to the anticipation-resolution; and example 6.11e, a neighbor note (also a chord tone in this particular example) to the suspension. An embellished suspension appears in the last measure of example 6.11f. Discuss the suspension and its embellishment, as well as all the other NCTs in this phrase.

Suspensions with Change of Bass (or Change of Part)

Occasionally the bass note changes between the suspension and the resolution. This produces a rearrangement of the interval between the bass and the resolution, but the basic frame of the suspension remains unchanged. The suspension, which in example 6.10c was a 9–8, becomes a 9–6 in example 6.12a because of a change of chord position and hence of bass note. The 7–6 suspension from example 6.10b, on the other hand, becomes a 7–3 in example 6.12b because of a complete change of chord between the suspension and the resolution. Similarly, the 4–3 suspension from example 6.10a turns into a 4–6, involving a complete change of chord, in example 6.12c. Notice, though,

Example 6.12

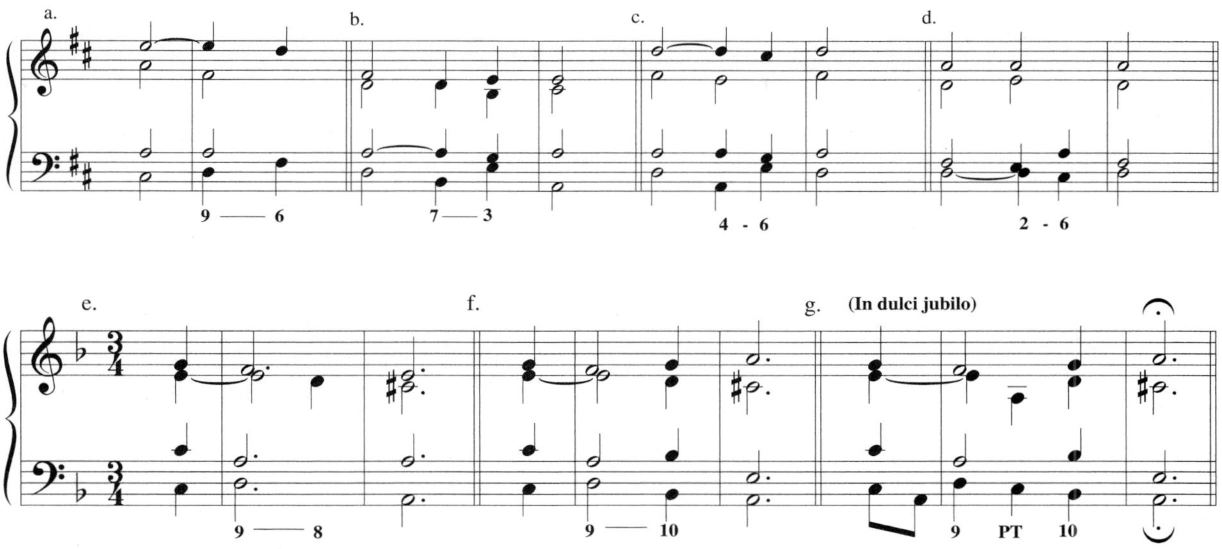

that the structure of the suspension (P–S–R) has not changed in any of these cases. Finally, a similar process turns the 2–3 suspension from example 6.10d into a 2–6 suspension in example 6.12d. Notice, however, that the voice that changes here is not the bass (which carries the 2–3 suspension in both examples), but one of the upper voices, in this case the tenor. Rather than "change of bass," in 2–3 suspensions we speak of "change of part."

A complex example of embellished suspension with change of bass is illustrated by examples 6.12e to g. A simple frame for a 9–8 suspension appears in example 6.12e. In example 6.12f the same suspension is resolved with a change of bass (and a change of chord). Finally, example 6.12g reproduces a passage from Bach's chorale "In dulci jubilo," in which the suspension is ornamented with a chord tone (A), and a passing tone is added in the bass.

Chain of Suspensions

A **chain of suspensions** is an uninterrupted succession of several suspensions. In a chain of suspensions the resolution of a suspension becomes the preparation for the next one. In the excerpt by J. S. Bach reproduced in example 6.13, the resolution of a 9–8 suspension on F becomes the preparation for a 4–3 suspension on C, and the resolution of the latter becomes the preparation for a 9–8 suspension on D.

Sequences are often based on chains of suspensions of the same type. The most frequent sequential series of suspensions is the *chain of 7–6 suspensions.* The Handel

Example 6.13 J. S. Bach, Chorale 34, "Erbarm dich mein, O Herre Gott"

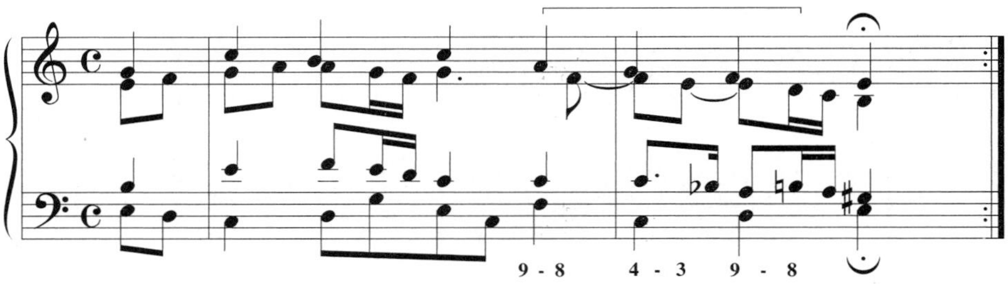

fragment in example 6.14 is based on such a chain. In three voices, the third voice in this sequence doubles the bass in parallel 10ths, as shown in the Handel fragment by the circled pitches. In four voices, the voice leading (illustrated in example 6.15a) also includes a voice which alternates doubling each of the voices in parallel 10ths (avoiding always to double the suspension resolution). Notice that *parallel 5ths on weak beats resulting from a chain of suspensions are perfectly acceptable* (as in the 5ths between tenor and alto in our example). The octaves on strong beat (alto-soprano) are not a problem because they are separated by chordal skips, which, as we saw in chapter 4, prevent parallel 5ths and 8ves.

Chains of 2–3 suspensions are also common. The chain in example 6.15b results from a series of parallel $^5_3$ chords. Here again, the 5ths on weak beat (bass-tenor) separated by a suspension are not objectionable. In example 6.15c, the chain of 2–3 suspensions results from a series of parallel $^6_3$ chords. The parallel 5ths on strong beats (bass-tenor) are not a problem because they are separated by consonant intervals, and neither are the 8ves on strong beat (tenor-soprano) because of the chordal skips in the tenor.

Finally, although parallel 5ths on weak beats resulting from suspensions are not considered faulty, parallel 8ves resulting from a chain of 9–8 suspensions are more

Example 6.14 G. F. Handel, "Chaconne," from *Trois Leçons,* Var. 9, mm. 1–5

Example 6.15

objectionable (example 6.15d). Because a series of 9–8 suspensions is too close to a series of parallel octaves, chains of 9–8 suspensions are usually avoided.

EXERCISE

To practice writing chains of suspensions, refer to exercise 5 in worksheet 6 at the end of this chapter.

Retardation

A suspension figure that resolves upward is called a **retardation.** In example 6.2a the C on the downbeat in m. 4 would be a 9–8 suspension over B♭ if it resolved down by step. Its upward resolution to D, however, makes it a retardation. Examine the cadence in anthology, no. 33, m. 16 (Beethoven, Sonata in Cm, op. 10/1, II). Three NCTs sound on the final A♭. What kinds of NCTs are they? How does each of them resolve?

PEDAL POINT

A **pedal point** is a tone that is sustained, usually in the bass (although it may occur in any other voice), while a variety of changing harmonies (some consonant, some dissonant) sound over it. Most often, pedal points have the function of prolonging the tonic or

Summary of Nonchord Tones

NCT	Approached by	Left by	Metric Position
Passing tone	Step	Step (same direction)	Weak
Accented PT	Step	Step (same direction)	Strong
Neighbor note	Step	Step (opposite dir.)	Weak
Accented NN	Step	Step (opposite dir.)	Strong
Anticipation	Step	Repeated note	Weak
Escape tone	Step	Leap (normally opposite direction)	Weak
Appoggiatura	Leap	Step (normally opposite direction)	Strong (sometimes weak)
Suspension	Repeated note (from preparation)	Step down (to resolution)	Strong
Retardation	Repeated note (from preparation)	Step up (to resolution)	Strong

dominant harmonies (pedals on $\hat{1}$ and $\hat{5}$, respectively). A pedal on $\hat{1}$ usually comes as a cadential extension after a PAC, whereas a pedal on $\hat{5}$ often leads to an important return of the tonic, toward the end of a composition, usually after a developmental excursion away from the tonic.

Example 6.16 shows a characteristic tonic pedal point in the bass, closing a fugue by J. S. Bach. The pedal in this example begins after a PAC on C in m. 29. As is usually the case, the material over the pedal begins and ends with statements of the chord that is being prolonged, hence with consonances. To analyze harmonies over a pedal, you

Example 6.16 J. S. Bach, Fugue no. 2 in Cm, from *The Well-Tempered Clavier,* I, mm. 28–end

PRACTICAL APPLICATION AND DISCUSSION

1. Find examples of as many as possible of the types of NCTs studied in this chapter in compositions you are practicing or performing on your instrument.
2. How do NCTs affect performance? How do you perform different NCTs? For instance, how does the way you approach the performance of a passing tone or a neighbor note differ from the way you perform an appoggiatura or an accented passing tone? Composers often stress this by means of articulation marks. How? Use the initial period from anthology, no. 28 (Mozart, Sonata in B♭M, III, mm. 1–8) as a reference for your discussion. Notice that in the cadential $^6_4$ at the HC (m. 4), the D and the B♭ can actually be interpreted as APTs.
3. Composers through the centuries have been very fond of suspensions. Why? What is the effect of a suspension as perceived by the performer and the listener? What effect do suspensions have on musical motion? Do you perform suspensions in any specific way?

should in principle ignore the pedal note and think of the lowest voice in the chordal texture above the pedal as the bass voice. After you have identified the type of harmonies over the pedal, however, it is useful to verify their level of consonance or dissonance against the pedal tone.

EXERCISES

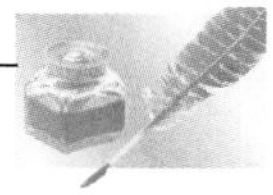

To practice harmonizing melodies that include a variety of NCTs, refer to exercise 6 in worksheet 6 at the end of this chapter.

To practice identifying and labeling NCTs, refer to exercise 1.

FOR FURTHER STUDY

For additional analysis using materials studied in this chapter, refer to the *Harmony in Context* Web page at www.mhhe.com/roigfrancoli2e.

ASSIGNMENT

For analytical and written assignments based on the materials learned in this chapter, refer to chapter 6 in the workbook.

Terms for Review

Nonchord tone
Passing tone
Double PT
Chromatic PT
Accented PT
Neighbor note
Accented NN
Neighbor group
Anticipation
Incomplete neighbors
Escape tone
Appoggiatura
Suspension
Preparation and resolution
4–3 suspension
7–6 suspension
9–8 suspension
2–3 suspension
6–5 suspension
Embellished suspension
Suspension with change of bass or change of part
Chain of suspensions
Retardation
Pedal point

Worksheet 6

EXERCISE 1 Analysis. Identify and label all NCTs in the two excerpts by Bach reproduced in example 6.17. Label suspensions with the correct figures.

Example 6.17a J. S. Bach, Chorale 29, "Freu dich sehr, o meine Seele," mm. 1–4

Example 6.17b J. S. Bach, Chorale 76, "Freu dich sehr, o meine Seele," mm. 1–5

Note: At this stage, you will not be able to analyze and understand all the chords and harmonic processes in these excerpts. This should not hinder you, however, from identifying and understanding most of the NCTs and their function.

EXERCISE 2

1. Add NCTs (no suspensions yet) to the chorale in example 6.18a.

Procedure for embellishing a given texture with NCTs:

1. Identify spots where you may use PTs (filling a 3rd).
2. Identify spots where you may use NNs (such as repeated notes in the given texture).
3. Locate other possible places for other NCTs. For an ANT, for example, you need a voice ascending or descending by step. Write one in the next-to-last chord (**).
4. Be sparing in your use of NCTs. An overloaded texture may turn unmusical. You may use simultaneous NCTs in different voices, but only as long as they are consonant among themselves. Some suggested spots for simultaneous NCTs are marked with a +.

Example 6.18a (Based on Bach, Chorale 72)

2. Add three suspensions to the phrase in example 6.18b, as required.

Procedure for embellishing a given texture with suspensions: You first need to identify spots where you may use a suspension. For this purpose you will need a voice that descends by step, in such a way that the second note of the step is an 8ve (for a 9–8), a 6th (a 7–6), or a 3rd (4–3 or 2–3) above the bass. In example 6.18a, m. 5, the chord marked with an asterisk (*) allows for a 7–6 suspension. Why? Write it. Can you add a suspension to the second chord in m. 1 in example 6.18a? And to the second chord in m. 2?

Example 6.18b (Based on Bach, Chorale 64)

EXERCISE 3 Realize the following two progressions in four voices. Then, add NCTs to both of them (no suspensions in exercise 3a; include a suspension in exercise 3b, m. 3).

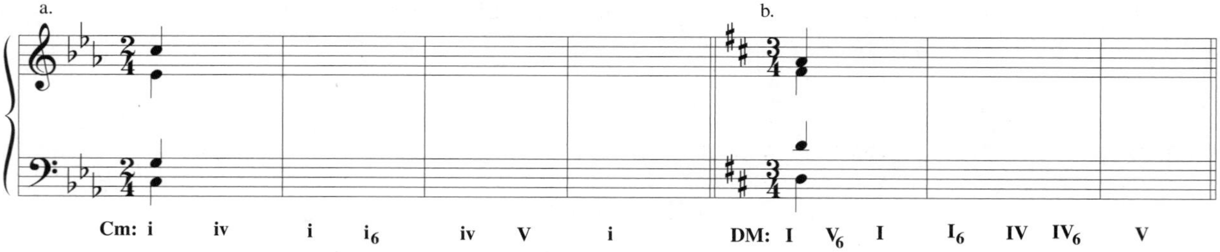

EXERCISE 4 Realize the following suspensions in four voices. Write the actual suspension in the specified voice. Remember not to double the note of resolution (except in 9–8 suspensions). Notice that the Roman numeral V^{5-6}_{2-3} simply refers to a V_6 with a 2–3 suspension in the bass.

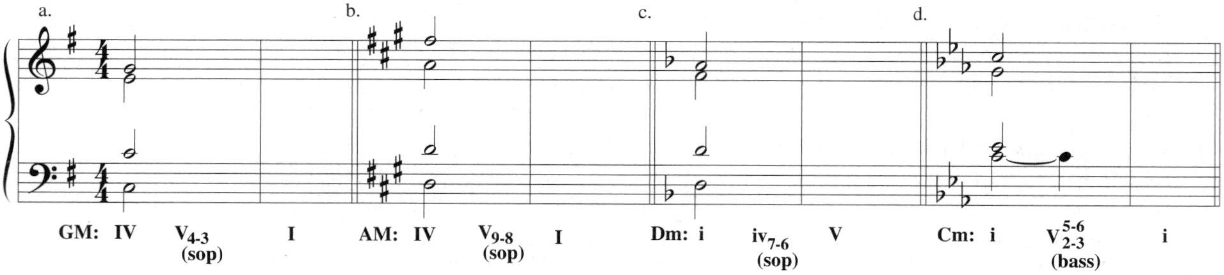

EXERCISE 5

1. Complete the chain of 4–3/9–8 suspensions that has been started for you in exercise 5a. The first four suspensions are part of the chain and will all be in the same voice. The last 4–3 suspension will be in a different voice.
2. Complete the chain of 7–6 suspensions that has been started for you in exercise 5b.

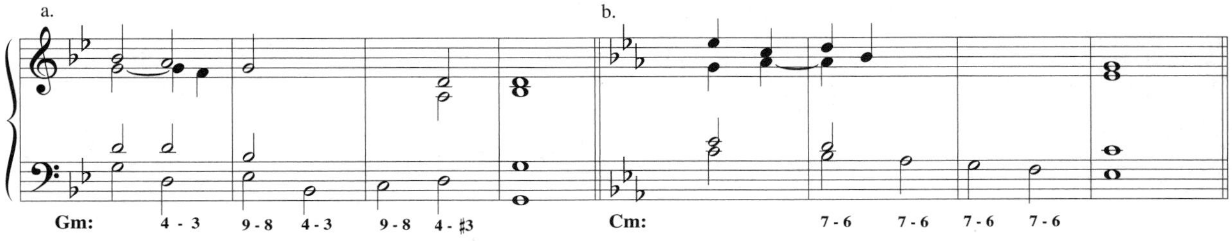

EXERCISE 6 Harmonize the melody in exercise 6 in four voices, using only i, iv, V, and their first inversions, following the given harmonic rhythm (HR) (harmonize the notes marked with a 6 with a first inversion of the previous chord). Sing the melody and the harmonization in class or with friends.

Procedure to harmonize a melody with NCTs:

1. Sing the melody, and identify (or verify the given) HR.
2. Identify, mark, and label the NCTs in the melody. In m. 2, for instance, all three pitches on beat 1 may not belong to the same chord; but pitches 1 and 3 may, which leaves pitch 2 as a likely PT. Beat 2 in the same measure, however, features a melodic figure that is part of the same triad.
3. Harmonize the melody as if it did not have NCTs (that is, base your harmonization on the chord tones). In m. 2, for example, the beat 1 chord will include the pitches C–E♭ (a likely iv). Write Roman numerals for your chords, then write a bass line and fill in the inner voices according to the rules of correct voice leading and doubling.

Chapter 7

$^6_4$ Chords

In chapter D we studied that a triad is in second inversion if its fifth is in the bass. The two intervals above the bass in this position are a 6th and a 4th, hence the figured bass $^6_4$ to indicate second inversion. The category of chords that we know as "$^6_4$ chords," however, presents some conceptual difficulties. In the first place, although they all *look* like triads in second inversion, most of them *do not function or sound* like triads in second inversion. In most cases, $^6_4$ chords *behave linearly and not functionally.* Hence, we hear them melodically rather than as a harmonic inversion. In chapter F, moreover, we learned that the P4 is a dissonant interval if it involves the bass, as is the case in $^6_4$ chords. As a result, $^6_4$ chords *may be dissonant chords,* because they contain a dissonance—the P4 between the bass and another voice.

Indeed, both of the above criteria are true for most types of $^6_4$ chords: they are linear and hence do not funtion like second inversion triads, and they are dissonant. These criteria, however, do not apply to a category of $^6_4$ chords that we will study first, the *consonant* $^6_4$s. We will then study three types of *dissonant* $^6_4$s: the *neighbor,* the *passing,* and the *cadential* $^6_4$s. All $^6_4$ chords that you write should belong to one of the above categories, and their voice leading should follow the conventions for each of the types that will be studied in this chapter. In any case, whether they are consonant or dissonant, $^6_4$ chords always function as *prolongational chords.*

EXERCISE

To practice spelling single $^6_4$ chords in four voices, refer to exercise 2 in worksheet 7 at the end of this chapter.

CONSONANT $^6_4$ CHORDS: THE ARPEGGIATED $^6_4$

Sometimes a $^6_4$ chord is heard as an inversion of a root-position triad, which it actually extends. Because this type of $^6_4$ chord sounds like triadic inversions in the context of an extended consonant harmony, we do not think of them as dissonant chords.

Example 7.1 L. v. Beethoven, Symphony no. 3. in E♭M, op. 55, III, mm. 167–173 (Trio)

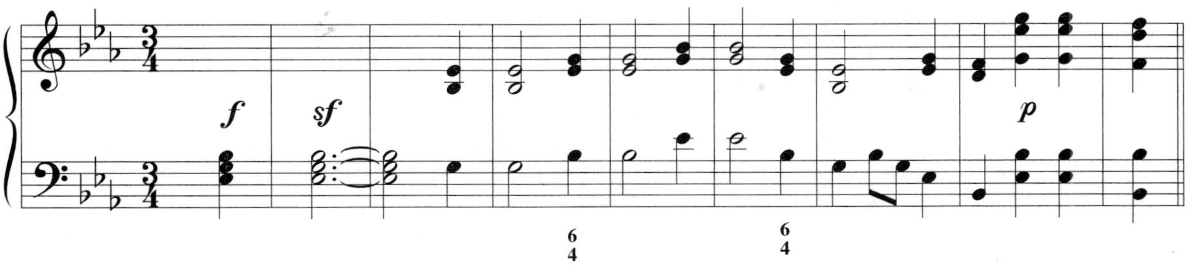

Listen to the beginning of Beethoven's Symphony no. 3 (*Eroica*), III, mm. 167–173 (example 7.1). The phrase is based on an arpeggiation of the tonic triad in all voices. The bass arpeggiation produces an obvious unfolding of the tonic harmony, which may be read as I–I_6–I^6_4–I–I^6_4–I_6–I, or simply as an extended I. Because the role of I^6_4 in this context (the **arpeggiated $^6_4$**) is clearly to extend a consonant harmony by means of triadic inversion, without actually departing from the consonant frame established in m. 1, we hear it as a **consonant $^6_4$**.

A type of consonant arpeggiated $^6_4$ also results from a common accompaniment figure in which the bass of a tonic chord alternates between $\hat{1}$ and $\hat{5}$, a pattern frequently found in waltzes and marches. The song "Die Beschwörung," by Viardot-García, begins with such a left-hand pattern (example 7.2). Here again, we hear all of m. 1 in this example as a consonant tonic chord.

Example 7.2 P. Viardot-García, "Die Beschwörung," mm. 1–3

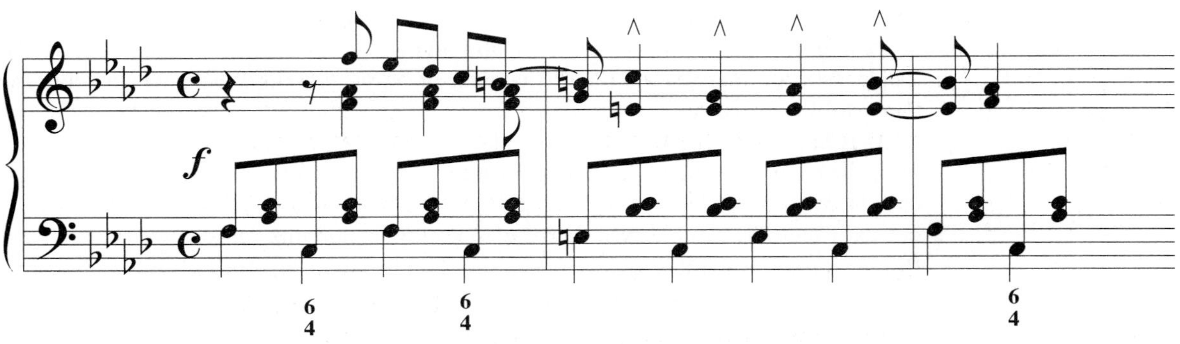

DISSONANT $^6_4$ CHORDS

In this section we will discuss the three most common types of **dissonant** $^6_4$ chords. All these $^6_4$ chords are *linear* in nature (that is, they result from contrapuntal and melodic processes), and they do not constitute independent harmonic entities. Their function is to embellish or intensify other, more important harmonies. In other words, they are all *prolongational chords.* Because of their linear nature, we do not hear them as triads in second inversion in a consonant context. The 4th with the bass results here from melodic, contrapuntal processes, and for this reason we treat it as a dissonance. Thus, *these* $^6_4$ *chords are dissonant* themselves. As we learned in the chapter on nonchord tones, dissonances may not be used freely in tonal music. They must resolve, and normally also be prepared, according to standard voice-leading principles. Such is also the case with dissonant $^6_4$ chords. Because they are treated as dissonances, they may not be used freely. We will now study the voice-leading conventions that regulate the normative behavior of linear $^6_4$ chords.

THE NEIGHBOR $^6_4$

Examine the phrase by Elton John in example 7.3a. The first three measures feature a bass pedal on $\hat{1}$. The only harmonic change occurs briefly in m. 1, and then again in the complete next measure. In both cases, two of the tones from the tonic triad ($\hat{3}$ and $\hat{5}$) move to their upper neighbors ($\hat{4}$ and $\hat{6}$), and then back, in a motion over the bass that we can represent as $^{5-6-5}_{3-4-3}$. In chapter 3 we studied that when IV functions as a prolongation of I (in the progression I–IV–I), one of the upper voices sustains the common tone $\hat{1}$, while the other two voices feature neighbor-note (NN) figures. If the common tone is also left in the bass instead of only one of the upper voices, a I–IV$^6_4$–I progression results, as in example 7.3a. This is a very common progression, which clearly functions as a linear prolongation of I. $\hat{1}$ is present in the bass as a pedal (and also usually doubled in one of the upper voices), while the other two voices realize a double NN figure. For this reason, this type of $^6_4$ chord is known as a **neighbor** $^6_4$ (N$^6_4$) or also *embellishing* $^6_4$ or *pedal* $^6_4$. Identify the N$^6_4$ chord in example 7.3b, and verify its voice leading. The standard voice leading for the N$^6_4$ is summarized in example 7.4a.

The most frequent occurrence of the N$^6_4$ is as an elaboration of the tonic. Other similar progressions are possible, as illustrated by the N$^6_4$ elaboration of IV which appears in example 7.3a, m. 4, and the elaboration of V illustrated in example 7.4b. Example 7.4c summarizes the linear character of N$^6_4$ progressions: rather than "chords," these are linear harmonies that result from two nonchord tones (two NNs). Although using Roman numerals for these progressions can be practical because they help determine the exact pitches in the $^6_4$ chord, Roman numerals distort the linear nature of these chords. We do not really hear a N$^6_4$ to I as a subdominant in second inversion (IV$^6_4$), but as a melodic double NN figure elaborating I. For this reason, we will not use Roman numerals to refer to dissonant $^6_4$ chords. The label "N$^6_4$" (as in I–N$^6_4$–I) describes much better the musical process taking place in the neighbor $^6_4$ progression, as shown in example 7.4.

Example 7.3a Elton John, "Candle in the Wind," from the album *Live in Australia* (1987)

Example 7.3b F. Schubert, *Valses Sentimentales,* op. 50, no. 3, mm. 1–8

Example 7.4 The Neighbor $^6_4$

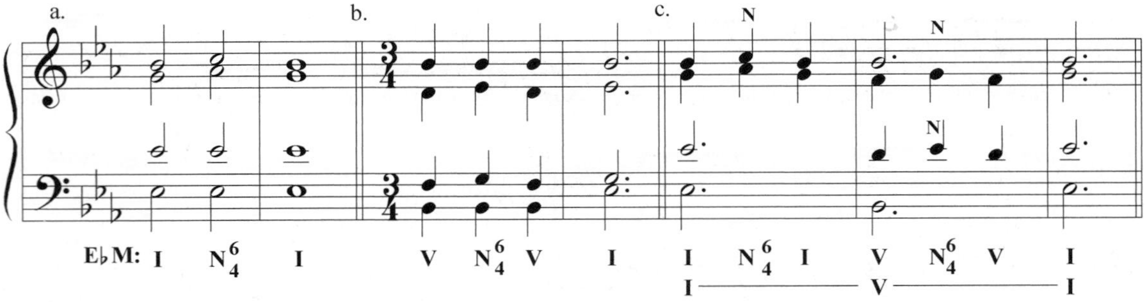

THE PASSING $^6_4$

In example 7.5, m. 2, you will see another case of a dissonant $^6_4$ chord resulting from linear motion. I and I_6 in this example are connected by means of an intervening PT in the bass and another one in the top voice ($\hat{2}$ in both cases). The resulting V^6_4 is an example of a **passing** $^6_4$ chord (which we will label as P^6_4), a chord normally used to connect melodically two chords with the same function, most often a root-position triad and its first inversion (or vice versa). Notice that the two voices with PT figures (the outer voices in this case) perform a voice exchange. Another voice sustains $\hat{5}$, while the fourth voice features a leading-tone NN figure, $\hat{1}$–$\hat{7}$–$\hat{1}$. Study carefully the voice leading in both examples 7.5 and 7.6, noticing the linear character of each voice,

Example 7.5 Meredith Willson, "Goodnight My Someone," from *The Music Man*

Example 7.6 The Passing $^6_4$

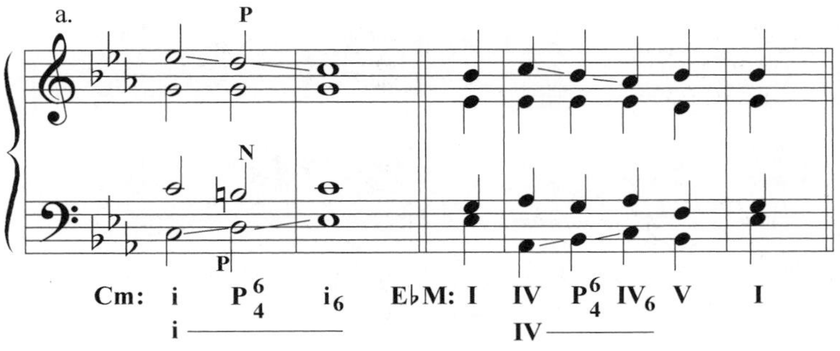

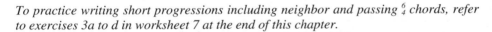

the voice exchange, the doubled bass (fifth) in the P$^6_4$, and the prolongational function of the complete i–P$^6_4$–i$_6$ progression. Because the P$^6_4$ (a *passing chord*) has the same linear function as a PT, it normally appears on a *weak beat.* Besides the P$^6_4$ linking I and I$_6$, other passing $^6_4$ progressions may possibly be found, such as IV–P$^6_4$–IV$_6$ (example 7.6b).

EXERCISE

To practice writing short progressions including neighbor and passing $^6_4$ chords, refer to exercises 3a to d in worksheet 7 at the end of this chapter.

THE CADENTIAL $^6_4$

The last type of $^6_4$ chord that we will study in this chapter, and also the type most commonly found in the literature as a familiar cadential gesture, is known as the **cadential $^6_4$**. Examine and play the PAC cadence from Donizetti's *Lucia di Lammermoor* reproduced in example 7.7. You will recognize the basic frame for a PAC: a V$_7$–I in DM (mm. 4–5) preceded, in m. 3, by IV. In m. 4, left hand, notice that above the A in the bass, a voice effects a 4–3 motion (D–C♯), while another voice effects a 6–5 motion (F♯–E). If we consider both of these motions together, we come up with the intervals $^{6-5}_{4-3}$ above $\hat{5}$ in the bass. Although this voice leading produces a $^6_4$ sonority (in the first half of m. 4) that looks like a I$^6_4$, this chord does not function at all as a tonic. It is a dissonant linear sonority over $\hat{5}$ resulting from NCTs, and its function is to intensify and embellish melodically the dominant chord that follows it and to which it resolves (that is, the V$^5_3$ to which the linear $^6_4$ resolves).

Example 7.7a G. Donizetti, *Lucia di Lamermoor,* act III, Final Aria, "Tu che a Dio spiegasti l'ali"

Examples 7.7b and c

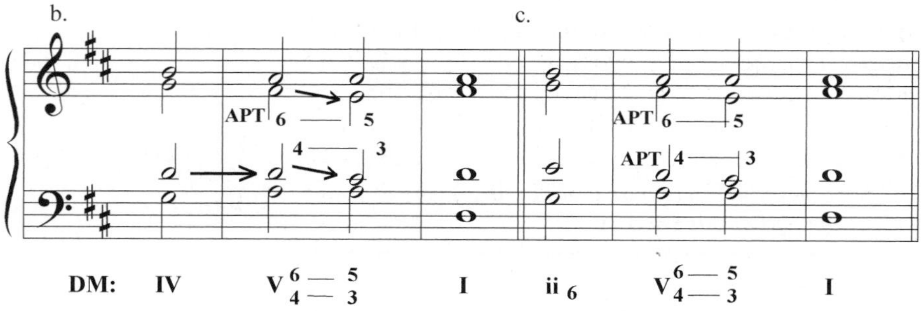

NOTE

In four-voice realizations of the cadential, $^6_4$, it is customary to double the bass ($\hat{5}$).

The voice leading for the cadential $^6_4$ is summarized in examples 7.7b and c and in the following points:

1. When the cadential $^6_4$ is preceded by IV, as in example 7.7b, *the 6th above the bass,* which *always resolves down to the 5th above the bass* (6–5), functions as an accented PT in the figure $\hat{4}$–$\hat{3}$–$\hat{2}$; *the 4th above the bass,* which *always resolves down to the 3rd above the bass* (4–3), functions as a 4–3 suspension ($\hat{1}$–$\hat{7}$), *including its correct preparation*. The fourth voice holds the doubled bass, $\hat{5}$.

Example 7.8 G. Donizetti, *Lucia di Lammermoor,* act I, no. 3, "Regnava nel silenzio," final cadence

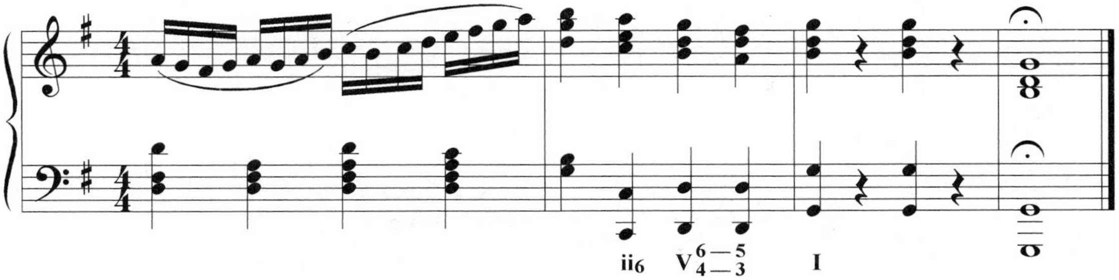

2. When the cadential $^6_4$ is preceded by ii or ii_6, both the 6th and the 4th above the bass function as accented passing tones and thus should be approached by step, as illustrated by example 7.7c. Another cadence from Donizetti's *Lucia di Lammermoor,* reproduced in example 7.8, shows this cadential figure and its voice leading in a musical context.
3. According to the linear explanation of the cadential $^6_4$, the **voice leading,** *which intensifies V, can be summarized by the figures* $^{6-5}_{4-3}$. The notation V^{6-5}_{4-3}–I, which we will use in this book, expresses more accurately the nature of this progression than the alternative notation I^6_4–V–I found in some books. The complete $^{6-5}_{4-3}$ figure, over $\hat{5}$ in the bass, has a *dominant function* (as expressed by the V^{6-5}_{4-3} notation) and not a tonic function, as could be misinterpreted from the I^6_4–V notation.

NOTE

Unlike the dissonant $^6_4$ chords we have studied previously, and because of its linear function as a suspension/accented PT figure, the cadential $^6_4$ usually falls on a strong beat, hence it is an accented $^6_4$ chord. In triple meters the cadential $^6_4$ is often found on beat 2, with the resolution to $^5_3$ on beat 3. As we studied in chapter B, beat 2 in triple meter may be perceived as either weak or strong depending on the context, and, in fact, beat 2 is sometimes stressed in a variety of ways (such as dynamic or agogic accents, or phrasing). Placing a cadential $^6_4$ (which we perceive as an accented harmonic event) on beat 2 is in itself a way of emphasizing this beat.

Numerous examples of the ii_6–V^{6-5}_{4-3}–I progression, perhaps the most common cadential formula, may be found in the literature. Examples 7.9 and 7.10 present two such cadences. Analyze both of them, labeling them with Roman numerals and discussing

Example 7.9 J. Haydn, Trio in FM, Hob. XV:6, I, mm. 142–49

Example 7.10 G. Donizetti, *Don Pasquale,* act II, scene IV, mm. 7–11

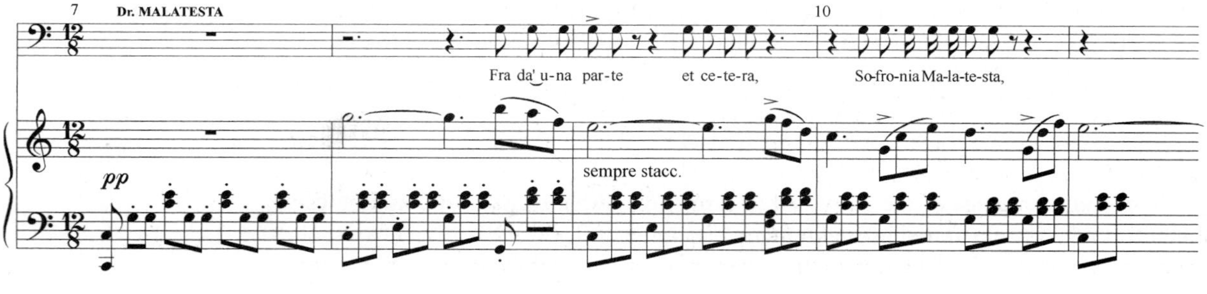

VOICE-LEADING GUIDELINES

1. *Doubling.* As a rule, **double the bass (the fifth) in a $^6_4$ chord.** You will rarely find any other triad member doubled in $^6_4$ chords. On occasions you may find the third of the chord (the 6th above the bass) doubled because of strong voice-leading reasons. The root (the 4th above the bass) is never doubled because it is the dissonant pitch, and dissonances are not doubled.
2. *Neighbor $^6_4$.* In the most common N^6_4 progression (I–N^6_4–I), the bass and the voice that doubles it sustain $\hat{1}$, while the other voices perform NN figures ($\hat{3}$–$\hat{4}$–$\hat{3}$ and $\hat{5}$–$\hat{6}$–$\hat{5}$). In the V–N^6_4–V progression, $\hat{5}$ is sustained and doubled, and the other two voices also perform NN figures over the $\hat{5}$ pedal.
3. *Passing $^6_4$.* Most often used to connect a triad and its first inversion (or vice versa). Because of its function as a passing chord, it is usually placed on a weak beat. In the most common passing $^6_4$ progression (I–P^6_4–I_6), the bass and one of the upper voices feature a voice exchange ($\hat{1}$–$\hat{2}$–$\hat{3}$ and $\hat{3}$–$\hat{2}$–$\hat{1}$), a third voice sustains $\hat{5}$, and the fourth voice performs a leading-tone neighbor figure, $\hat{1}$–$\hat{7}$–$\hat{1}$.
4. *Cadential $^6_4$.* It is normally placed on a strong beat (or in beat 2 in triple meter). In the V^{6-5}_{4-3} figure, $\hat{5}$ is in the bass and doubled. The $^6_4$ above $\hat{5}$ resolves to $^5_3$ in the V chord, following the voice-leading 6–5, 4–3. If the $^6_4$ is preceded by IV, the 4th must be prepared as a suspension by keeping $\hat{1}$ in the same voice in the IV and $^6_4$ chords. If it is preceded by ii or ii_6, both the 6th and the 4th function as accented PTs.
5. *Errors to avoid.* Because neighbor, passing, and cadential $^6_4$ chords are dissonant, their doubling, preparation, and resolution should follow the voice-leading conventions summarized previously. In principle, any departure from these conventions should be considered a voice-leading error to be avoided.

their voice leading. Make sure you identify both the 6–5 and the 4–3 in Haydn's cadential $^6_4$ progression in example 7.9 (the 4–3 is quite obvious, but where is the 6–5?). Discuss the harmonic/linear techniques used to prolong the final tonic chord in Haydn's example (mm. 145–49), as well as in example 7.10, mm. 8 and 9.

NOTE

Because of its linear function as a suspension/accented PT figure, the cadential $^6_4$ usually falls on a strong beat. In triple meters, however, the cadential $^6_4$ is often found on beat 2, with the resolution to $^5_3$ on beat 3. As we studied in chapter B, beat 2 in triple meter may be perceived as either weak or strong depending on the context, and, as a matter of fact, beat 2 is sometimes stressed in a variety of ways (such as dynamic or agogic accents, or phrasing). Placing a cadential $^6_4$ (which we perceive as an accented harmonic event) on beat 2 is in itself a way of emphasizing this beat.

EXERCISES

To practice writing short progressions including cadential $^6_4$ chords, refer to exercises 3e to g in worksheet 7 at the end of this chapter.

To practice analyzing musical examples including a variety of $^6_4$ chords, refer to exercise 1 in worksheet 7 at the end of this chapter.

To practice realizing a figured bass including all types of dissonant $^6_4$ chords, refer to exercise 4 in worksheet 7 at the end of this chapter.

CHARACTERISTIC SOPRANO-BASS PATTERNS

A variety of melodic patterns may be harmonized with $^6_4$ chords. Some of the most common patterns and their harmonizations are illustrated in example 7.11.

1. In example 7.11a you can see a string of melodic neighbor patterns, all of which allow harmonizations using N^6_4 chords. In the most frequent N^6_4 progression (I–N^6_4–I), the melodic patterns may be $\hat{5}$–$\hat{6}$–$\hat{5}$ or $\hat{3}$–$\hat{4}$–$\hat{3}$, but other patterns and progressions are possible, as shown by mm. 3–4 in the same example.
2. Example 7.11b shows possible patterns to be harmonized with P^6_4 progressions. In general, the melodic patterns will be either a lower-neighbor figure or a passing figure. In the I–P^6_4–I_6 progression, such patterns will be $\hat{1}$–$\hat{7}$–$\hat{1}$ and $\hat{3}$–$\hat{2}$–$\hat{1}$ (or $\hat{1}$–$\hat{2}$–$\hat{3}$, depending on the direction of the bass). A sustained $\hat{5}$ can also be harmonized with this same progression.
3. Finally, example 7.11c shows patterns that may be harmonized with a cadential $^6_4$. The possibilities for the actual cadential $^6_4$ figure are $\hat{3}$–$\hat{2}$–$\hat{3}$ (or $\hat{3}$–$\hat{2}$–$\hat{1}$), $\hat{1}$–$\hat{7}$–$\hat{1}$, or $\hat{5}$–$\hat{5}$–$\hat{5}$. Notice how the approach to the $\hat{1}$–$\hat{7}$–$\hat{1}$ pattern changes depending on whether we use a IV to precede the $^6_4$ (and then the pattern is $\hat{1}$–$\hat{1}$–$\hat{7}$–$\hat{1}$) or a ii_6 (and then the pattern is $\hat{2}$–$\hat{1}$–$\hat{7}$–$\hat{1}$).

Example 7.11

Example 7.12

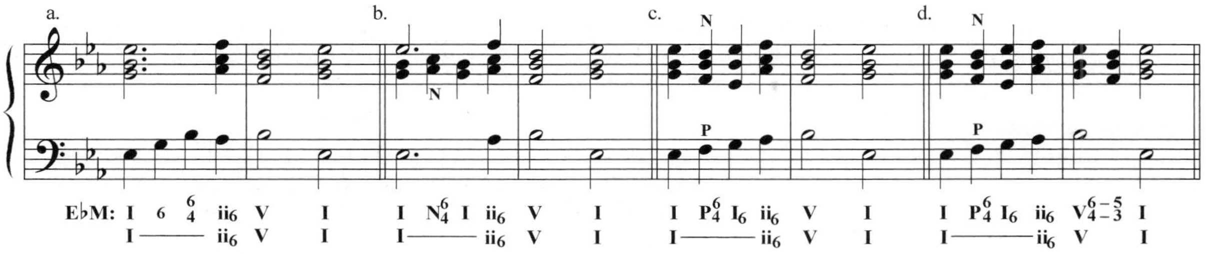

EXERCISE

To practice harmonizing a melody including all types of dissonant $^6_4$ chords, refer to exercise 5 in worksheet 7 at the end of this chapter.

ELABORATING THE I–V–I PROGRESSION

Because of their linear nature, all of the $^6_4$ chords can function as contrapuntal elaborations of the I–V–I progression. Examine the four progressions in example 7.12, all of which feature a basic I–V–I framework elaborated with a predominant ii_6 chord. Then, in example 7.12a, the opening tonic is extended by means of an arpeggiation in the bass that produces a $I–I_6–I^6_4$ elaboration. In 7.12b, the opening tonic is extended by means of a N^6_4, and in 7.12c by a P^6_4 and a I_6. Finally, the I–V–I progression in example 7.12d is first elaborated with a P^6_4 that extends the opening tonic, and then by a cadential $^6_4$ that embellishes the cadential dominant.

Neighbor and passing $^6_4$ chords can be used to extend not only the tonic, but also the dominant or other harmonies. If you look back at example 7.11a, you will see that both the initial tonic and the dominant in the I–V–I progression have been extended by means of N^6_4 chords. In example 7.11b we see extensions of both the I and IV harmonies by means of P^6_4 chords.

FOR FURTHER STUDY

For additional analysis using materials studied in this chapter, refer to the *Harmony in Context* Web page at www.mhhe.com/roigfrancoli2e.

ASSIGNMENT AND KEYBOARD EXERCISES

For analytical and written assignments and keyboard exercises based on the materials learned in this chapter, refer to chapter 7 in the workbook.

PITCH PATTERNS

Sing the pitch patterns in example 7.13. As you sing, understand the harmonies that are linearized in them. Hear the various $^6_4$ chords, as well as their characteristic voice leading and linear function.

Example 7.13

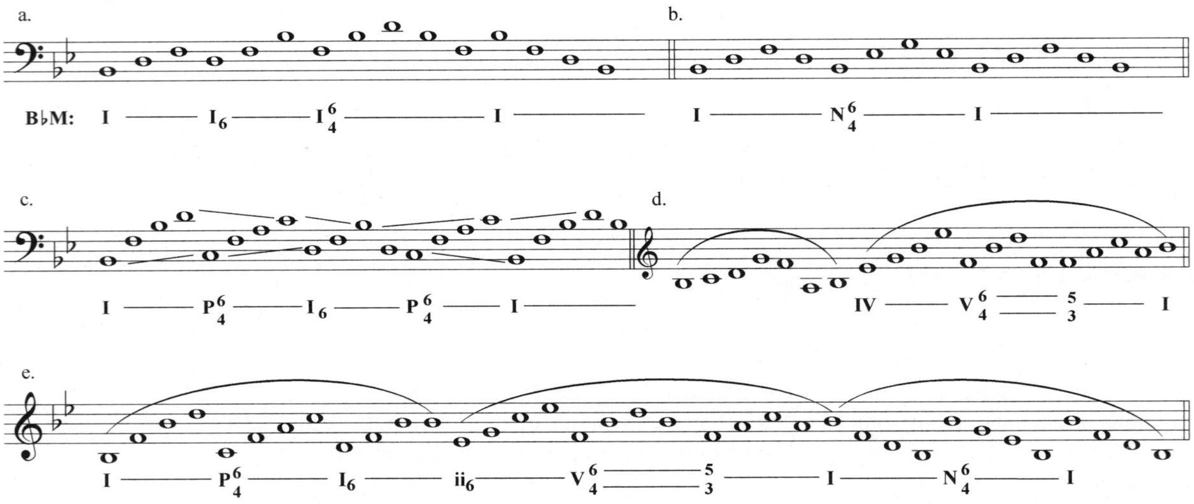

Terms for Review

Arpeggiated $^6_4$
Consonant $^6_4$ chords
Dissonant $^6_4$ chords
Neighbor $^6_4$
Passing $^6_4$
Cadential $^6_4$
$^{6-5}_{4-3}$ voice leading
Doubling in $^6_4$ chords

Worksheet 7

EXERCISE 1 Analysis.

1. Identify and list in the spaces below the type of $^6_4$ chords used in each of the following short excerpts by Florence Price, F. Schubert, and Gioachino Rossini.

   a) Example 7.14a (list type and measure numbers).

Example 7.14a Florence Price, *Fantasie Negre,* mm. 141–148

   b) Example 7.14b: For this example, mark on the score—with lines—the characteristic voice leading for this type of $^6_4$ chord. Does the melody also reflect the voice leading?

Example 7.14b F. Schubert, *Valses Nobles,* op. 77, no. 6, mm. 1–8

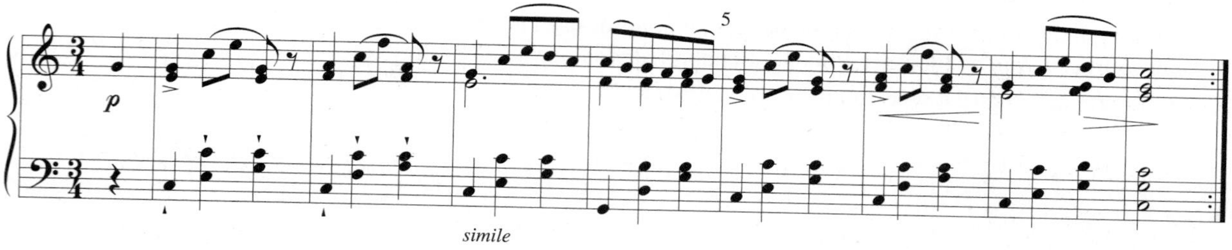

c) Example 7.14c: Identify and mark on the score the characteristic voice leading for the type of $^6_4$ represented by this example.

Example 7.14c G. Rossini. *Il barbiere di Siviglia,* act I, no. 3, mm. 139–144

2. Compare the following three cadences by Mozart: Piano Sonata in CM, K. 309, III, mm. 18–19 (anthology, no. 26); Piano Sonata in AM, K. 331, I, mm. 7–8 (anthology, no. 27); and Piano Sonata in B♭M, K. 333, III, mm. 7–8 (anthology, no. 28). Are they all of the same type? What are the exact RNs for each? Can you identify any familiar voice-leading figures?

EXERCISE 2 Write the following triads in four voices with correct doubling.

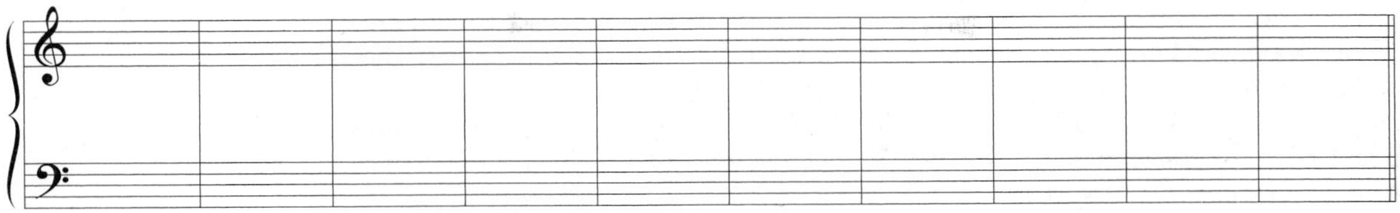

EXERCISE 3 Realize the following short progressions in four voices. Provide RNs where needed.

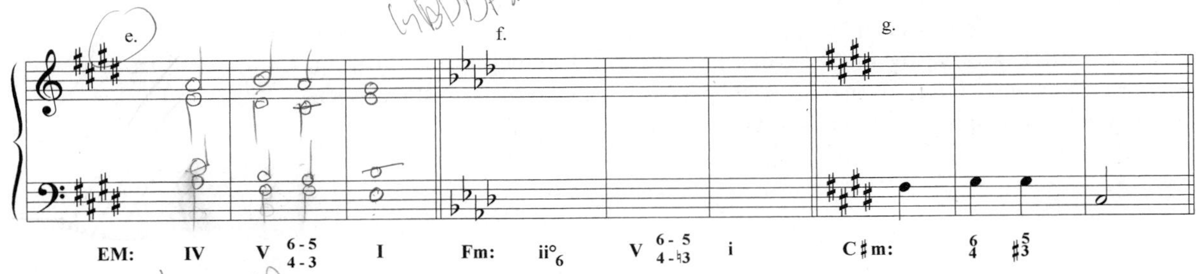

EXERCISE 4 Analyze the following progression with RNs and realize it in four voices, using only i, iv, ii, V, and their inversions. Remember to double-check your outer-voice frame for good first-species counterpoint.

EXERCISE 5 Provide a four-voice harmonization of the following melody. As a practice of $^6_4$ chords, this melody allows you to use one in each measure (including m. 4), except for mm. 7 and 8 (an unlikely situation in the music literature, to be sure). First, write a good bass line, taking into account the possible $^6_4$ chord in every measure. Then, add the inner voices, following the voice-leading guidelines for $^6_4$ chords studied in this chapter. Indicate all the $^6_4$ chords you use, and provide a RN analysis of your harmonization. Notice that, other than m. 7, which will require three different RNs, all other measures require only one RN each.

Note:

1. Always listen to everything you write: Play through your exercises, or have a friend play through them while you listen.
2. When you listen to progressions, do not listen chord by chord. Rather, hear (a) harmonic patterns (bass patterns), and (b) linear patterns in the upper voices. In the I–P$^6_4$–I$_6$ pattern, for instance, first hear the $\hat{1}$-$\hat{2}$-$\hat{3}$ in the bass and then the voice exchange between the bass and an upper voice. In the I–N$^6_4$–I pattern, focus on the double-neighbor motion over the static bass.

Chapter 8

The Dominant Seventh and Its Inversions

In previous chapters we have often seen musical examples utilizing dominant seventh chords. It is indeed common for the dominant triad to appear with an added seventh. The resulting chord, the dominant seventh, is a dissonant chord that creates a strong tension toward a resolution. In this chapter we will study the dominant seventh and its inversions.

V_7 IN ROOT POSITION

This chord comprises the dominant triad (a M triad) and an added minor seventh (a diatonic seventh above the root). V_7 is always a Mm_7 sonority including scale degrees $\hat{5}$–$\hat{7}$–$\hat{2}$–$\hat{4}$, and it contains two dissonant intervals: the m7 between $\hat{5}$ and $\hat{4}$, and the °5 (or +4, depending on the voicing) between $\hat{7}$ and $\hat{4}$. Because of its dissonant quality, V_7 is a very effective chord in which the tendency of V to resolve to the tonic is further enhanced by the tendency of dissonance to resolve to consonance. V_7 thus contains *two tendency tones* (example 8.1a): the *leading tone,* (LT) which, as we know, has a tendency to resolve *upward to* $\hat{1}$, and the dissonant *seventh* ($\hat{4}$), which in V_7 will as a principle resolve *down to* $\hat{3}$. Example 8.1b summarizes the linear tendencies in this chord. Example 8.1c shows the melodic origin of the seventh in the V_7 chord: Originally, the seventh resulted from a passing 8–7 motion within a V triad. Only later (in the seventeenth century) did the seventh become an independent chordal dissonance as part of the V_7 chord.

Identify the V_7 chord in the cadence reproduced in example 8.1d, and verify the resolution of the two tendency tones. Notice also the unusual voice leading in the resolution of the cadential $^6_4$ in this example. Is the dramatic change of register in both the vocal part and the cadential $^6_4$ voice leading justified in any way by the text?

Doubling

A four-pitch chord in principle requires no doubling in four voices. As we will see immediately, though, V_7 appears sometimes in an incomplete form, with the fifth ($\hat{2}$) omitted (the fifth is the only member of a seventh chord which may be omitted: We already

Example 8.1a to c

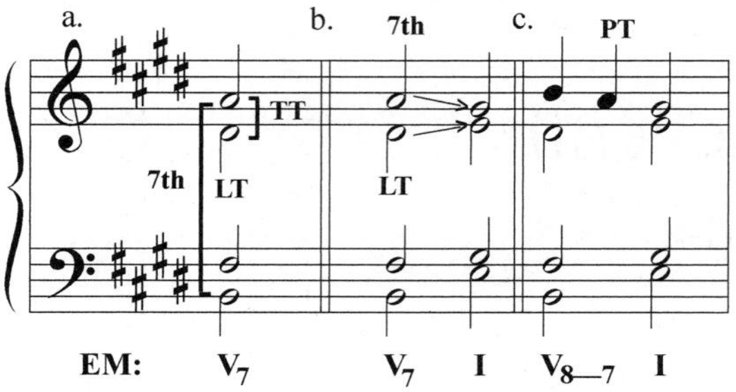

Example 8.1d M. Willson, "I Ain't Down Yet," from *The Unsinkable Molly Brown* (Final Cadence)

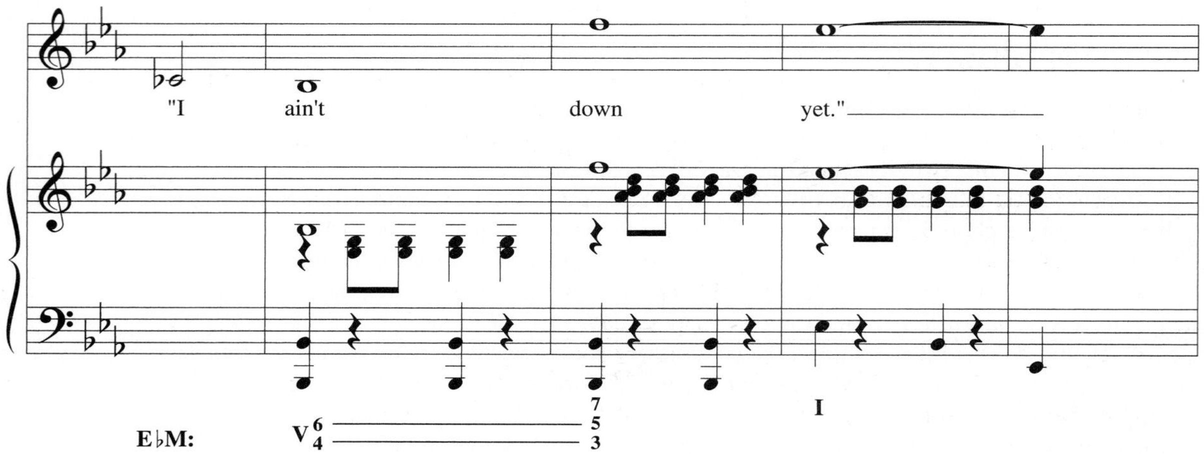

know that the root and third of any chord may not be left out, and the omission of the seventh in a seventh chord is obviously a contradiction in terms). Because tendency tones and dissonant pitches should not be doubled, the only member of V_7 that may be doubled if the fifth is omitted is the root.

EXERCISE

To practice spelling Mm_7 chords in root position, refer to exercise 2 in worksheet 8 at the end of this chapter.

The V_7–I Progression: Voice-Leading Guidelines

The two phrases from R. Schumann's "Ein Choral" reproduced in example 8.2 illustrate the most important aspects regarding the voice leading of V_7. In example 8.2a (m. 7) we see again *the melodic nature (and origin) of the seventh in V_7*: the voice that doubles the root of the V triad. $\hat{5}$, moves to $\hat{3}$ by means of a dissonant passing tone, $\hat{4}$. In example 8.2b (m. 31), the seventh is not a passing tone (PT), but rather a member of the harmonic sonority, V_7. Because it is a dissonance, Schumann prepared it by presenting the same pitch ($\hat{4}$) in the same voice as a consonance in the previous chord. By preparing it in this way, the seventh is here treated as if it were a suspension. Although it may not always be possible, *it is preferable to prepare the seventh* when you write in vocal chorale style by approaching it either by step or by repetition, as in the Schumann examples. (Can you identify an example of voice overlap in one of these phrases?)

Both examples 8.2a and b depict the same type of resolution of V_7, which may be summarized as follows:

1. The third ($\hat{7}$ or LT) moves up to $\hat{1}$, especially when it is in an outer voice.
2. The seventh ($\hat{4}$) moves down to $\hat{3}$.
3. The fifth ($\hat{2}$) may move up to $\hat{3}$ or down to $\hat{1}$.

Example 8.2 R. Schumann, "Ein Choral," from *Album for the Young,* op. 68

4. The same melodic fragments which you learned could be harmonized with a V–I progression can also be harmonized with a V_7–I progression ($\hat{2}$–$\hat{1}$, $\hat{2}$–$\hat{3}$, $\hat{7}$–$\hat{1}$, and $\hat{5}$–$\hat{5}$). To these, you can now add $\hat{4}$–$\hat{3}$ as a characteristic melodic pattern for a V_7–I harmonization.

Complete and Incomplete V_7–I Voicings

If you apply these guidelines to the resolution of a complete V_7, as Schumann does, you will necessarily end up with an incomplete I as a chord of resolution (see both cadences in example 8.2). *In the V_7–I progression, one of the two chords is usually incomplete* in order to exercise correct voice leading. Example 8.3 presents all the standard resolutions of V_7 to I, beginning with the one that you must *avoid:* If you insist on resolving a complete V_7 to a complete I following the guidelines listed previously, you will end up with parallel 5ths (example 8.3a). If the V_7 is complete, the resolving I will usually be incomplete. This **complete-incomplete (C–IN)** voice leading includes two possibilities: If you resolve the fifth up, the incomplete I will include a doubled root and a doubled third (example 8.3b); if you resolve the fifth down, the incomplete I will include a tripled root and a single third (as in the Schumann example, and in example 8.3c). In another correct voice leading, V_7 is incomplete and resolves to a complete I (**incomplete-complete, IN–C,** example 8.3d).

The "complete-incomplete" issue is most crucial when the $\hat{7}$–$\hat{1}$ motion is in the soprano. *If the LT is in an inner voice* some alternative voice-leading possibilities allow for two complete chords. In example 8.3e, for instance, we see that by resolving the LT in an inner voice to the voice immediately above it, we can allow the voice with $\hat{7}$ to leap down to $\hat{5}$, thus completing the tonic triad (**complete-complete, C–C).** In yet another possible voice leading illustrated by example 8.3f (acceptable, if less desirable), we see that we can also come up with two complete chords by not resolving the inner-voice LT at all. (To review the options regarding the resolution of the LT, refer to chapter 2 section, "Connecting the Tonic and Dominant Chords," points 5 and 6.)

Example 8.3

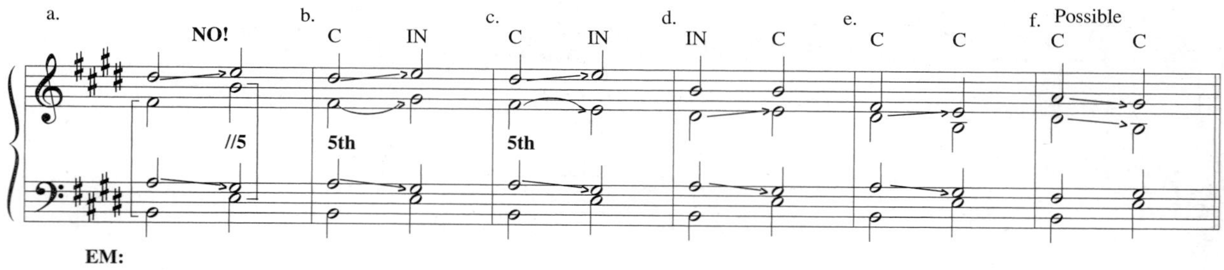

EXERCISE

To practice realizing V_7–I progressions, refer to exercise 3 in worksheet 8 at the end of this chapter.

Preparing the Seventh in V_7

Although numerous approaches to V_7 are possible, we will examine here some of the most frequent cases involving the chords we have already studied. In both the IV–V_7 (or iv–V_7) and ii_6–V_7 ($ii°_6$–V_7) progressions, the seventh may be properly prepared by repetition (examples 8.4a and b). In the IV–V_7 connection you should still pay attention to the same parallel fifths that we learned to avoid in the IV–V connection (chapter 3). In the ii_6–V_7 progression, it is possible to have scale degrees $\hat{6}$–$\hat{7}$–$\hat{1}$ in the same voice in the major mode. The same progression in the minor mode, on the other hand, will result in an objectionable melodic +2 (examples 8.4c and d).

V_7 often follows a V triad, in such a way that the only harmonic or voice-leading chang is the addition of the seventh. The best voice leading in this case is demonstrated in example 8.4e: the only voice that moves is the one that is *doubling the root of V.* This voice approaches the seventh by step, in an 8–7 motion over the bass. A similar voice leading is also the best for the cadential $^6_4$ progression with V_7 (example 8.4f): The

Example 8.4

PRACTICAL APPLICATION AND DISCUSSION

Many examples of V_7 can easily be found throughout the musical literature, especially in authentic cadences. As a sample of various uses of V_7, look at these excerpts from the anthology: no. 24 (Mozart, Sonata in DM, mm. 7–8 and 15–17); no. 27 (Mozart, Sonata in AM, Theme, mm. 7–8 and 17–18); no. 19 (Haydn, Divertimento, mm. 1–3); no. 31 (Paradis, *Sicilienne,* mm. 3–4 and 8–10); and no. 52 (Verdi, "Libiamo").

In studying these examples, first identify the key of each passage (note that the keys are different in the two passages from the Mozart DM sonata, as well as in the two passages from Paradis's *Sicilienne*). After you know the correct key, label the chords with exact Roman numerals. Then, observe the doubling and voice leading of the progressions. Are the chords complete or incomplete? Do tendency tones resolve as expected? Are all the voice-leading guidelines studied on pages (229–230) followed?

Pay special attention to the two passages in Mozart's DM sonata. Because chord tones are presented melodically in the right hand, the voice leading may not be immediately obvious. Make sure, though, that you identify the complete voice-leading figure $\begin{smallmatrix}8-7\\6-5\\4-3\end{smallmatrix}$ in both cadences. Does the seventh resolve? Where? Notice that the line $\hat{5}$–$\hat{4}$–$\hat{3}$ (the preparation of the seventh, the seventh, and its resolution) is interrupted by a change of register, or a ***register transfer:*** By displacing the pitch D down an octave, the line has been brought to (and continued in) a lower register. What kind of double nonchord tone takes place on the final tonic in each of the two cadences?

doubled $\hat{5}$ in the $^6_4$ chord moves down by step to the seventh of V_7 (in an 8–7 motion over the bass). Notice the complete voice leading indicated by the figures $\begin{smallmatrix}8-7\\6-5\\4-3\end{smallmatrix}$. In a possible alternative to this voice leading, the 6th in the cadential $^6_4$ moves *up* to the 7th, in the $\begin{smallmatrix}6-7\\4-3\end{smallmatrix}$ motion shown in example 8.4g.

EXERCISE

To practice realizing short progressions using V_7 in root position, refer to exercise 4 in worksheet 8 at the end of this chapter.

INVERSIONS OF THE DOMINANT SEVENTH

Listen to example 8.5 and analyze all its chords. (Remember to transpose the horn in E♭ as you read the passage: In this transposing instrument a notated C sounds as an E♭—a M6 below. You can study transposing instruments in Appendix 1. You will see that the opening phrase (mm. 1–4) has a familiar bass line ($\hat{1}$–$\hat{7}$–$\hat{1}$–$\hat{2}$–$\hat{3}$–$\hat{4}$–$\hat{5}$) which could be harmonized using only triads. The chord in m. 2 ($\hat{7}$ in the bass) could be a V_6, prolonging the initial I with a neighbor motion. The first three bass notes in m. 3 could be harmonized with a passing $^6_4$ progression, I–P^6_4–I_6. Mozart, however, used inversions of V_7 in both m. 2 and m. 3: V^6_5 instead of V_6, and V^4_3 instead of P^6_4. (In the second phrase, mm. 7–8, you will also find two V_7 chords. Review doubling and voice leading in both of them.)

All three inversions of V_7 are frequently used in tonal music. They normally appear in complete form and resolve to a complete tonic triad following the same guidelines we studied for V_7. As the following comments will show, *all three inversions usually function as linear chords.*

First Inversion

In the first inversion of V_7, V^6_5 (complete figures: $\begin{smallmatrix}6\\5\\3\end{smallmatrix}$), the leading tone is in the bass. Its standard resolution is thus to a tonic triad in root position, with the bass moving up to $\hat{1}$.

Example 8.5 W. A. Mozart, Concerto in E♭M for Horn and Orchestra, K. 447, II, mm. 1–8

The most common functions of V_5^6 (as those of V_6) are to prolong the tonic as a neighbor chord (example 8.5, mm. 1–2 and example 8.6a), or to approach I from below as a passing chord between vi or IV_6 and I, in a progression which also prolongs I: I–IV_6–V_5^6–I (example 8.6b).

Second Inversion

In the second inversion of V_7, V_3^4 (complete figures: $\begin{smallmatrix}6\\4\\3\end{smallmatrix}$), the fifth is in the bass, which allows for two possible resolutions: down to tonic in root position or up to tonic in first inversion. Its most frequent function is to prolong the tonic, either as a neighbor chord (example 8.6c) or as a passing chord between I and I_6, or vice versa (example 8.6d).

Example 8.6

An example of the latter (I_6–V^4_3–I) may be seen in the Schumann chorale reproduced in example 8.2, m. 30. This passing function of V^4_3 is equivalent to the passing function of P^6_4, and thus V^4_3 is an alternative to P^6_4 in the harmonization of a $\hat{1}$–$\hat{2}$–$\hat{3}$ or $\hat{3}$–$\hat{2}$–$\hat{1}$ bass segment.

NOTE

Study the resolution of V^4_3 in m. 3 of Mozart's horn concerto (example 8.5). The outer voices in the I–V^4_3–I_6 progression (bass and horn/violins) move in parallel 10ths, with the result that the seventh (D♭) resolves upward. When V^4_3 moves to I_6, ***the seventh may resolve upward*** *as in the Mozart example. This exception to the downward resolution of the seventh is justified by the linear voice-leading pattern in parallel 10ths or 3rds. The 5ths that may result in this progression are perfectly acceptable unequal 5ths, as illustrated by example 8.6e.*

Third Inversion

In the third inversion of V_7, V^4_2 (complete figures: $^6_4{}_2$), the seventh is in the bass. Because the seventh must resolve downward, V^4_2 will always resolve to I_6, as shown in the Haydn excerpt reproduced in example 8.7 (mm. 26–27). A frequent function of V^4_2 is to prolong V by means of a passing tone in the bass, in the progression V–V^4_2–I_6 (example 8.6f). The Haydn example depicts another standard application of V^4_2: A pre-dominant chord with $\hat{4}$ in the bass (IV or ii_6) moves to V^4_2 on a repeated $\hat{4}$ in the bass, as in example 8.6g. (Find two other inversions of V_7 in example 8.7 and observe their resolutions.) It is also common to find V^4_2 approached directly from I in the progression I–V^4_2–I_6, as shown in example 8.6h. The chordal seventh in this progression ($\hat{4}$, the A in the bass in our example, approached by leap from E) is unprepared and functions as an incomplete neighbor.

EXERCISES

To practice spelling Mm_7 chords in inversion, refer to exercise 5 in worksheet 8 at the end of this chapter.

To practice realizing short progressions using inversions of V_7, refer to exercise 6 in worksheet 8 at the end of this chapter.

To practice harmonizing a bass line, realizing a figured bass, and harmonizing a melody using V_7 chords in various positions, refer to exercises 7 to 9 in worksheet 8 at the end of this chapter.

Typical Errors to Avoid

- Not resolving the seventh of V_7 downward by step (or the LT in an outer voice up to $\hat{1}$).
- Writing parallel 5ths in a V_7–I progression if both chords are complete.
- Not resolving V^4_2 to I_6.

Example 8.7 J. Haydn, Trio in GM, Hob. XV:5, III, mm. 25–28

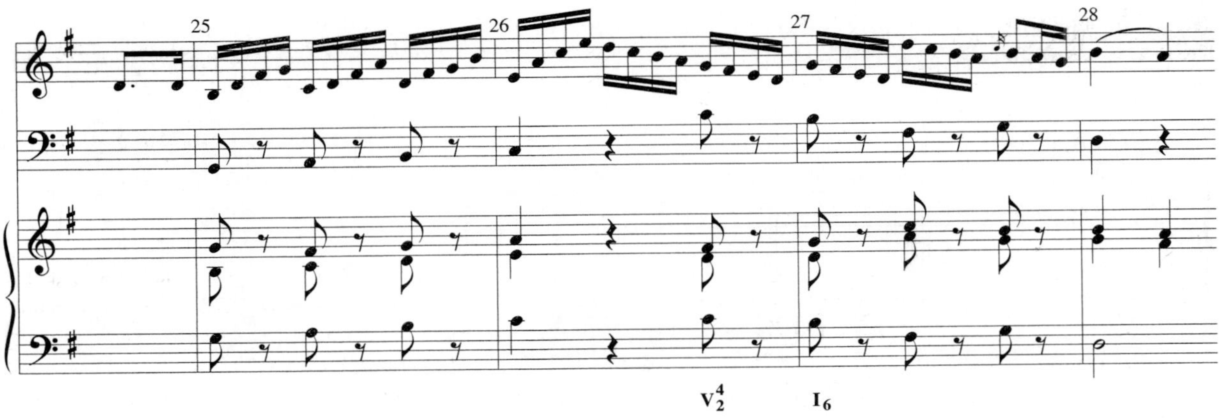

CHARACTERISTIC SOPRANO-BASS PATTERNS

Numerous soprano patterns can be harmonized with progressions involving V_7 or its inversions. We will first examine some of the patterns that can be harmonized with the I–V_7–I progression. (Note that other patterns are possible, but here we will discuss only some of the most characteristic examples.)

Patterns with the I–V_7–I Progression

Any of the soprano patterns that can be harmonized with a I–V–I progression can also be harmonized with a I–V_7–I progression. This includes the patterns we learned in example 2.3, all of which are listed again in example 8.8. A new pattern has been added to that list: example 8.8f shows the soprano fragment $\hat{5}$–$\hat{4}$–$\hat{3}$, which can be harmonized with a I–V_7–I, but not with a I–V–I progression. If we consider melodic motion in the soprano, we see that patterns 8.8a to c feature neighbor figures, patterns 8.8d to f feature passing figures, and 8.8g shows an incomplete-neighbor figure.

Patterns with Inversions of V_7

Here again we will illustrate only a sample of the numerous possible melodic patterns that can be harmonized with progressions using inversions of V_7. Example 8.9 shows three neighbor and two passing melodic patterns harmonized with I–V^6_5–I progressions. In example 8.10, two neighbor figures, a passing figure, and two incomplete-neighbor patterns are harmonized with I–V^4_3–I_6 progressions. Example 8.11 illustrates five melodic patterns harmonized with progressions involving V^4_2. The melodic patterns include three neighbor figures, a passing figure, and an incomplete-neighbor pattern. The latter pattern (example 8.11e) consists of two incomplete-neighbor figures, one in each voice (soprano and bass). Play each of the outer-voice patterns in examples 8.8 to 8.11 at the piano, adding inner voices in keyboard texture.

Example 8.8

Example 8.9

Example 8.10

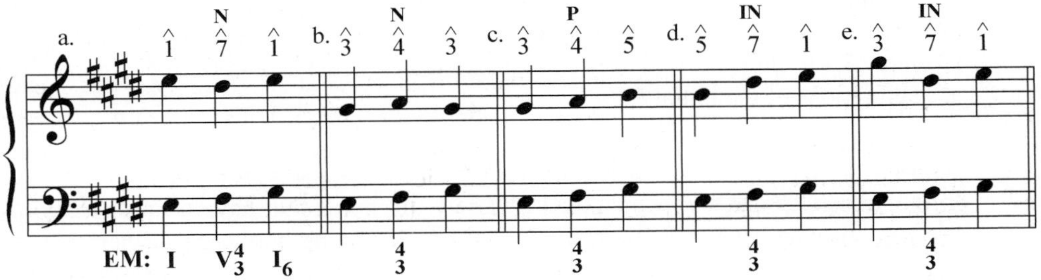

Example 8.11

ELABORATING THE I–V–I PROGRESSION

Because of their linear nature, all three inversions of V_7 can be used to elaborate the initial tonic in a I–V–I progression, as shown in example 8.12. The V^6_5 in example 8.12a functions as a neighbor-chord extension of I, just as V_6 would function on the same

Example 8.12

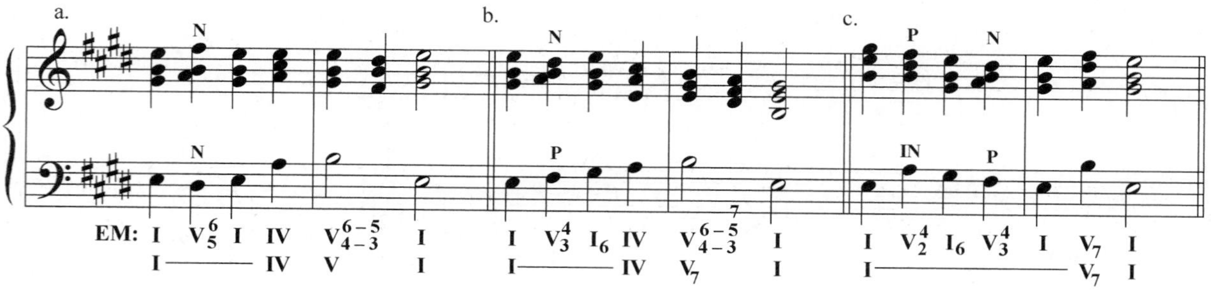

$\hat{1}$–$\hat{7}$–$\hat{1}$ bass pattern, as we learned in example 4.9. The V^4_3 in example 8.12b, on the other hand, functions as a passing-chord elaboration of I, in the same way that a P^6_4 does when harmonizing the same bass line ($\hat{1}$–$\hat{2}$–$\hat{3}$), as was shown in example 7.14c. Example 8.12c shows both V^4_2 (as an incomplete neighbor) and V^4_3 (as a passing chord) as elaborations of the initial I.

Combining Prolongational Chords

In the preceding chapters we studied a variety of chords that have a linear function. We have usually seen such chords in isolation, illustrating how each of them is used to prolong a previous chord, normally a tonic or a dominant. Examples of isolated harmonic linear patterns are I–IV–I, I–N^6_4–I, I–P^6_4–I_6, V–N^6_4–V, IV–P^6_4–IV_6, I–V^6_5–I, I–V^4_3–I_6, V–V^4_2–I_6, etc. By combining several of these chords or patterns, composers may extend (and provide variety to) passages of harmonic prolongation. In example 8.13a we hear a

Example 8.13

V^4_3 followed by a V^6_5, resulting in a melodic upper neighbor followed by a lower neighbor (that is, a neighbor group). These two chords function as a single prolongation of the opening tonic. This is the same prolongational progression that we can hear in both the Haydn and Granados fragments reproduced in examples 8.14 and 8.15. Identify the progression and the prolongational chords in these two examples.

Example 8.14 J. Haydn, Piano Sonata in CM, Hob. XVI:20, I, mm. 32–35

Example 8.15 Enrique Granados, *Escenas Románticas,* no. 5, mm. 40–42

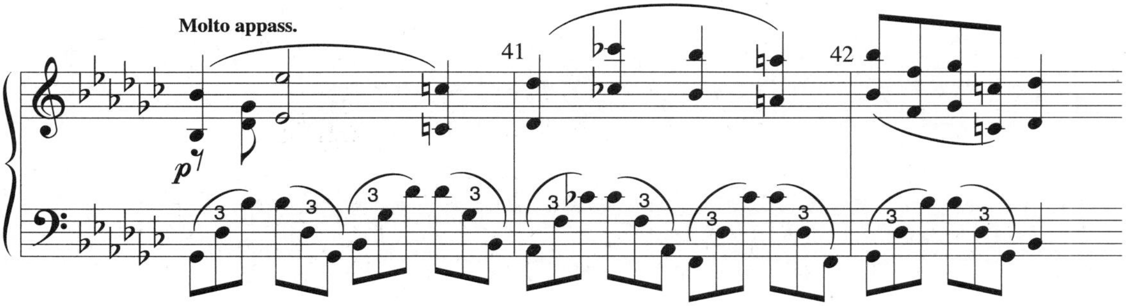

PRACTICAL APPLICATION AND DISCUSSION

As an application of concepts that you have learned so far, you may analyze the following two excerpts from the anthology: no. 33 (Beethoven, op. 10, no. 1) and no. 37 (Kuhlau, Sonatina).

1. Anthology, no. 33 (Beethoven):
   a) What is the linear function of the inverted V_7 chords in mm. 1–3?
   b) The first of these inverted V_7 chords is on a weak beat; the second one on a strong beat. What causes the discrepancy?
   c) What is the harmonic rhythm in mm. 5–8? How is harmonic motion achieved in mm. 5–6? Does Beethoven do something in mm. 6–7 (a harmonic-metric event) which you have been told to avoid? What is the effect of this event, and how does Beethoven emphasize it by other means (consider the dynamic and performance indications for the second chord in m. 6)?
   d) What is the linear function of the inverted V_7 in m. 7?
   e) In spite of its complex appearance because of contrapuntal activity in the upper voices, the cadence at mm. 15–16 is of a simple and familiar type. Identify the type, and mark on the score the specific $\begin{smallmatrix}8-7\\6-5\\4-3\end{smallmatrix}$ voice leading.
2. Anthology, no. 37 (Kuhlau):
   a) Find two inverted V_7 chords in mm. 1–8, and discuss their linear functions.
   b) The complete phrase in mm. 9–16 may be considered a harmonic prolongation of the tonic, which was reached at m. 8. What is the chord used for this prolongation, and how is it used linearly? Pay special attention to mm. 14–15 and to the means used to prolong I in these measures.

How would the points raised in this discussion affect your perception and your performance of these pieces? For instance, could your phrasing be affected by hearing groups of chords as linear prolongations of a tonic harmony, rather than as individual entities? Does the concept of harmonic prolongation help you understand better the harmonic coherence and function (as well as the long-range direction) of these phrases?

Think, for example, of the Kuhlau phrase in mm. 9–16. Where does it come from? Where does it lead? How does it do so? And, in the opening phrase of the Beethoven example (mm. 1–4), how does the shift of the dominant harmony from a metrically weak to a metrically strong beat affect you as listener or performer? Where does it direct your attention, and hence toward what goal does it direct the phrase?

Example 8.13b shows another combination of two familiar neighbor chords used in succession to prolong I: N^6_4 and V^6_5. Listen to and analyze example 8.16, and explain how these two same chords create a single prolongation of the opening tonic.

EXERCISE

To practice analysis of musical fragments including V_7 chords in various positions, refer to exercise 1 in worksheet 8 at the end of this chapter.

Example 8.16 Chevalier de Saint-Georges, Sonata no. 2, for Violin and Piano, mm. 13–16

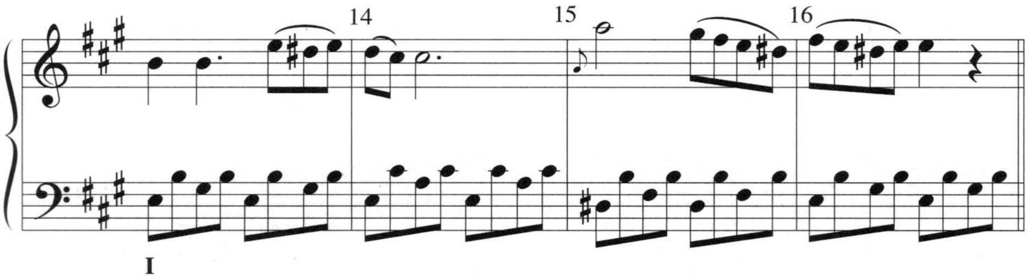

ASSIGNMENT AND KEYBOARD EXERCISES

For analytical and written assignments and keyboard exercises based on the materials learned in this chapter, refer to chapter 8 in the workbook.

PITCH PATTERNS

Sing the pitch patterns in example 8.17; as you sing, listen to the linearized V_7 chords in root position or inversion and to their resolution.

Example 8.17

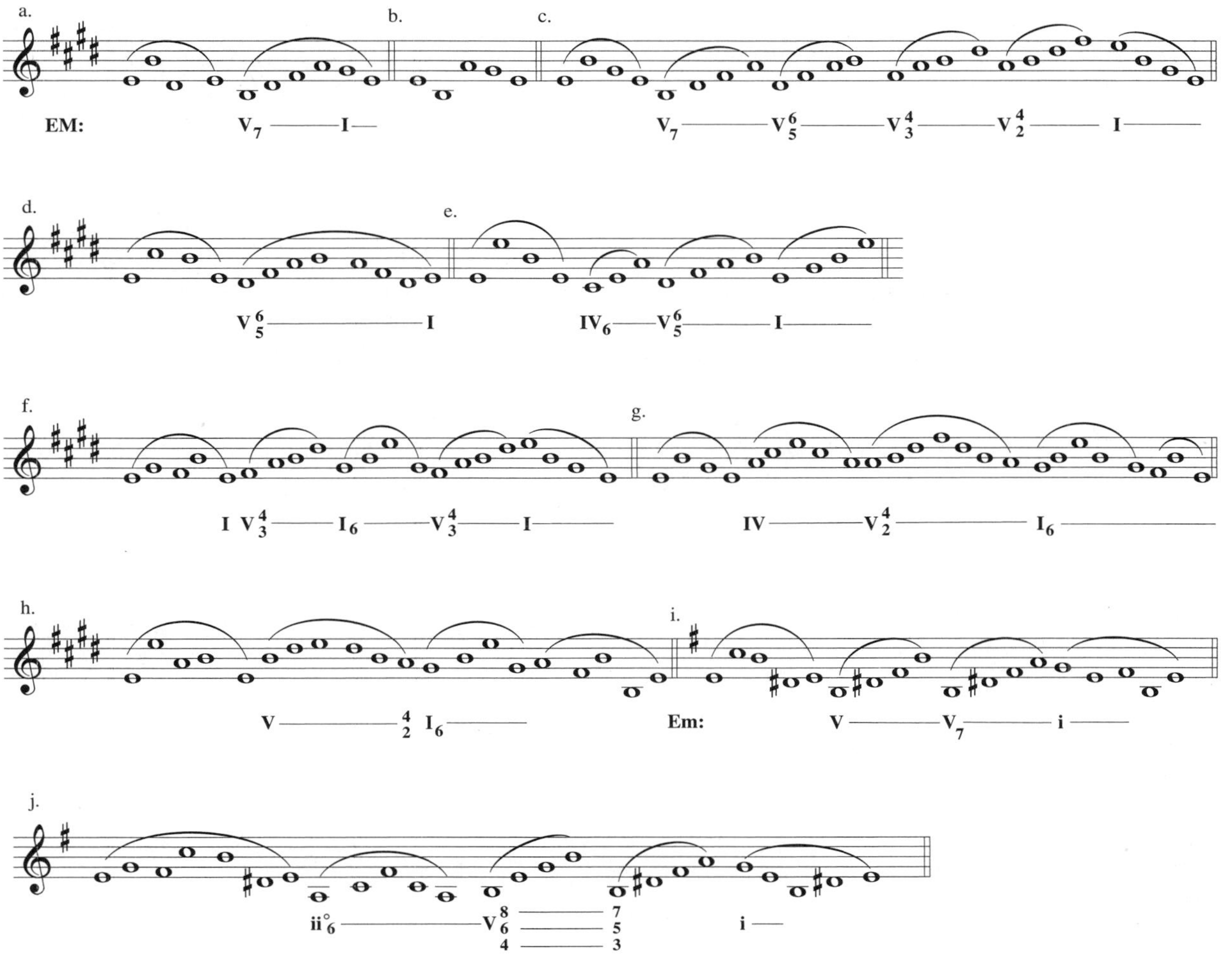

Terms for Review

Resolution and function of V_7
Resolution of the seventh
Doubling in V_7
Preparation of the seventh
Voice-leading possibilities: C–IN, IN–C, C–C
$V–V_7$
$V^{8-7}_{\substack{6-5\\4-3}}$
Register transfer
Resolution and function of V^6_5
Resolution and function of V^4_3
Upward resolution of the seventh in V^4_3
Resolution and function of V^4_2
Harmonic prolongation by combination of several linear chords

Worksheet 8

EXERCISE 1 Analysis.

1. a) Provide a Roman numeral (RN) analysis for example 8.18.
   b) Explain the linear function of each inversion of the dominant seventh used in this passage.

   c) Comment on the textural and instrumental variations between mm. 1–8 and 9–16.

Example 8.18 W. A. Mozart, Sonata for Violin and Piano, K. 377, II, mm. 1–16

2. a) Analyze with RNs the passage from Edvard Grieg's *Peer Gynt* reproduced in example 8.19. (Beware of transposing instruments!)

   b) The complete passage functions like a harmonic prolongation of i. In the space below, explain the linear function of each chord and how it contributes to this extended prolongation.

Example 8.19 Edvard Grieg, "The Rape of the Bride (Ingrid's Lament)," from *Peer Gynt,* Suite II, op. 55, I, mm. 35–42

V_7 in Root Position

EXERCISE 2 Write Mm_7 chords in root position (in four voices, with correct spacing) above the following pitches. Indicate under each chord the key in which it functions as V_7.

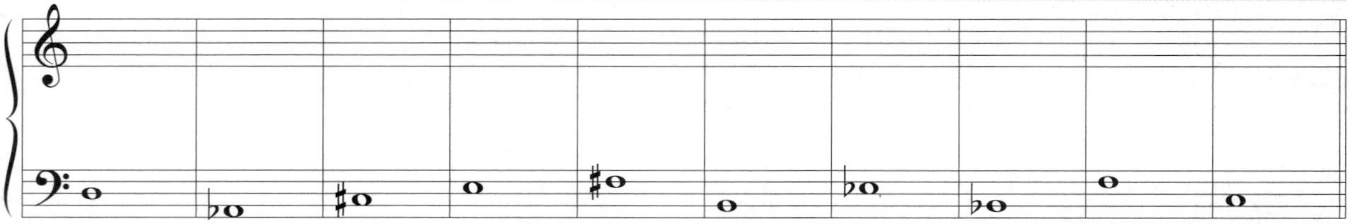

Key:

EXERCISE 3 Resolve each of the following V_7 chords three times, illustrating each of the three possible ways of resolving V_7 to the tonic (C–IN, IN–C, C–C).

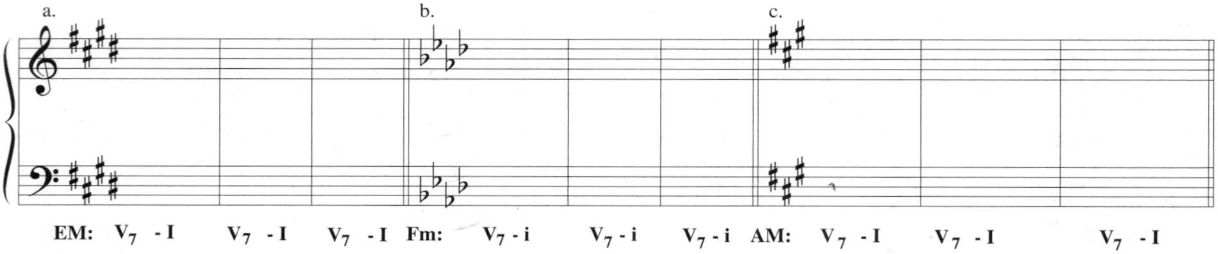

EXERCISE 4 Realize the following short progressions in four voices.

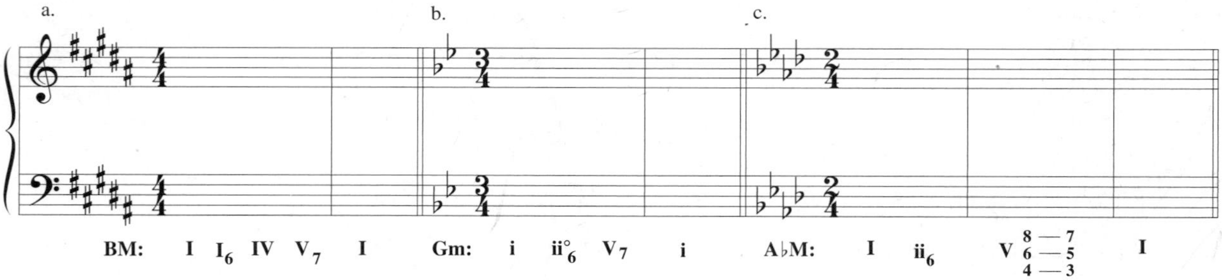

Inversions of V_7

EXERCISE 5 Write the following inverted V_7 chords and indicate the key for each of them.

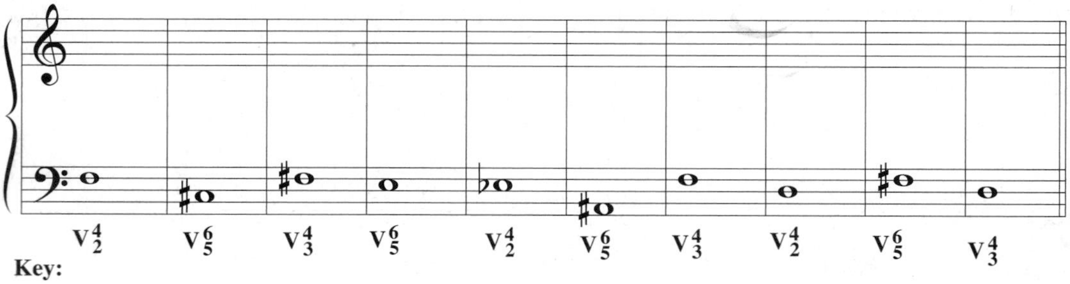

Key:

EXERCISE 6 Realize the following short progression in four voices.

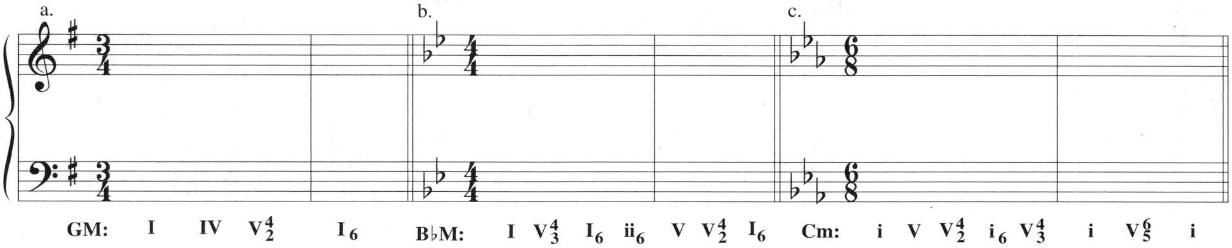

EXERCISE 7 Provide correct RNs for the following bass. Include three types of $^6_4$ chords and all three inversions of V_7.

EXERCISE 8 Analyze the bass with RNs and realize in four voices. Remember to double-check your outer-voice frame for good first-species counterpoint.

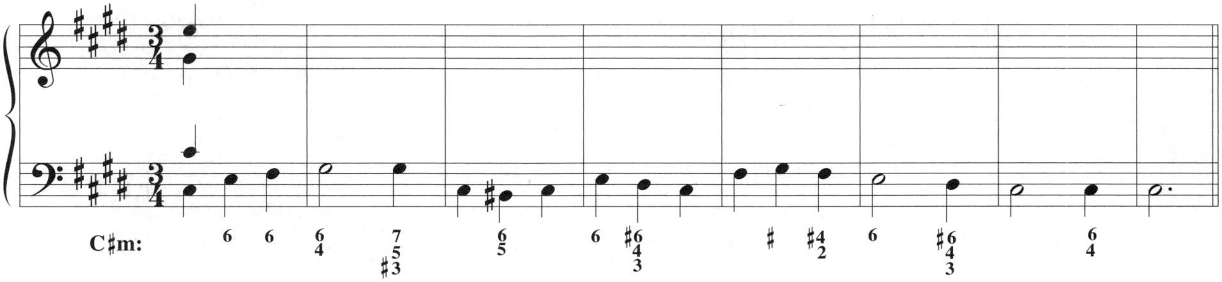

EXERCISE 9 Harmonize the following melody with a bass and RNs (no inner voices). Include a passing and a cadential $^6_4$, and harmonize the notes marked with an X with inversions of V_7 (all three inversions should be present). The harmonic rhythm is one chord per note, except for the two notes marked with a bracket, which will be harmonized with a change of position (a voice exchange). Remember to double-check this outer-voice frame for good first-species counterpoint.

Chapter 9

The Leading-Tone Triad

The triad built on the leading tone (LT), vii° (in both major and minor keys), comprises scale degrees $\hat{7}$–$\hat{2}$–$\hat{4}$. It thus has two common tones with V and three common tones with V_7. The **leading-tone triad** has a dominant function, and as such may substitute for V, V_7, or for some of their inversions. Unlike V or V_7, however, vii° is not a structural chord, but functions as a *prolongational chord.* vii° contains the same two tendency tones as V_7, $\hat{7}$ and $\hat{4}$, which produce a harmonic dissonance (°5, or +4 when inverted). Because it is a dissonant chord, doubling and resolution in vii° follow the usual conventions: Dissonant tones should not be doubled, and dissonant intervals should be resolved.

DOUBLING AND VOICE LEADING

1. The leading-tone triad usually appears in first inversion. Whereas in the root-position vii° the bass is part of the dissonant °5, in **vii°$_6$** the dissonance does not involve the bass, but rather two upper voices.
2. Because the root (the LT) and the fifth (the dissonant tone) form a °5, neither is usually doubled. As a norm, **double the third (the bass) in vii°$_6$.**
3. The °5 (or +4) may be resolved as a dissonance. $\hat{7}$ must resolve to $\hat{1}$ as usual, whereas $\hat{4}$ may resolve by step down to $\hat{3}$. This **resolution of the tritone** (°5 or +4) is desirable and is the same as the resolution of the same tritone, $\hat{7}$–$\hat{4}$, in V_7. Example 9.1 shows three cases in which the tritone is resolved. (Notice that when the tritone is spelled as a °5, the resolution is inward to a 3rd; when the tritone is presented as an +4, it resolves outward to a 6th.) In all these cases the chord of resolution is incomplete (doubled root and third).
4. The **resolution of the tritone,** although desirable, is not indispensable. In example 9.2, both $\hat{7}$ and $\hat{4}$ move upward by step. This voice leading is found very frequently in the literature, and it allows for a complete chord of resolution. The 5ths in example 9.2b are acceptable unequal 5ths (°5–P5).
5. In all cases, $\hat{2}$ may move down to $\hat{1}$ or up to $\hat{3}$.

Examples 9.1 and 9.2

9.1. Tritone Resolves **9.2. Tritone Does Not Resolve**

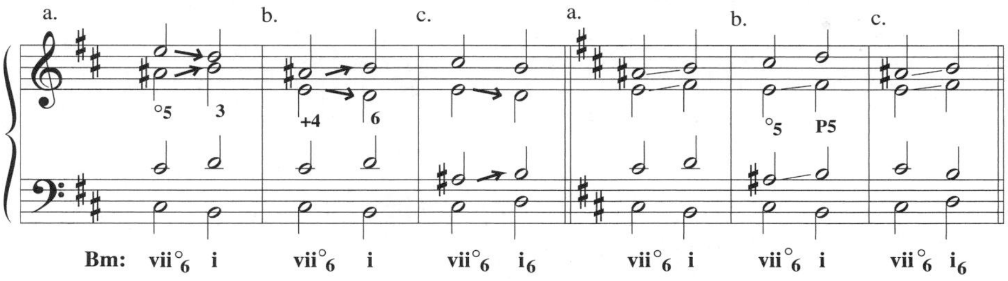

THE PASSING vii°_6

The function of vii°_6 is most frequently linear, connecting I and I_6 (or I_6 and I) as a passing chord. In example 9.3a Bach uses vii°_6 in this contrapuntal context between i and i_6 in Am. (The phrase is indeed in Am, although the ♯ in the key signature suggests a modal scale on A; what mode on A has an F♯ in the key signature?) Study the voice leading in this example. In the first place, you will see that this progression is built on a $\hat{1}$–$\hat{2}$–$\hat{3}$ (or $\hat{3}$–$\hat{2}$–$\hat{1}$) bass segment connecting i and i_6. This is, then, the third possible alternative that we learn to harmonize this bass line, along with i–P^6_4–i_6 and i–V^4_3–i_6. *All three progressions prolong the tonic harmony by means of a passing chord of the dominant family*. Moreover, you will notice in example 9.3a that the outer voices feature a *voice exchange,* and that another voice carries a $\hat{1}$–$\hat{7}$–$\hat{1}$ leading-tone figure. Both voice-leading properties are common to the passing vii°_6 and P^6_4 progressions.

Example 9.3a J. S. Bach, Chorale 3, "Ach Gott vom Himmel, sieh darein," mm. 1–2

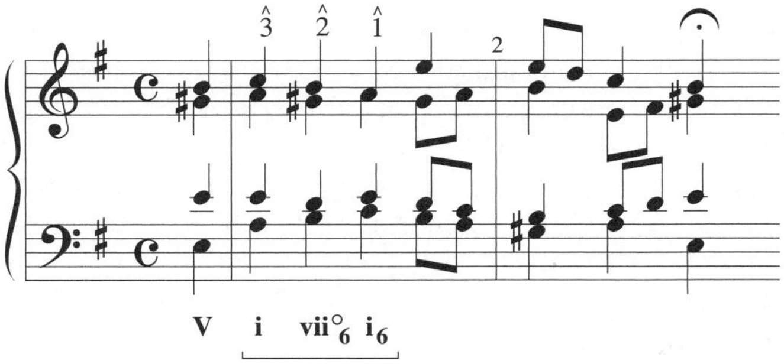

The same as the P^6_4 progression, the passing vii°$_6$ can be used to harmonize $\hat{1}$–$\hat{2}$–$\hat{3}$ or $\hat{3}$–$\hat{2}$–$\hat{1}$ melodic segments. Two instances of passing vii°$_6$ in keyboard texture appear in examples 9.3b and c. Analyze both passages with Roman numerals (RNs) and study their voice leading.

Example 9.3b M. Martínez, Sonata in AM, I, mm. 1–2

Example 9.3c W. A. Mozart, Sonata in FM, K. 280, mm. 136–142

EXERCISE

To practice realizing short progressions using the passing vii°_{6}*, refer to exercises 2a to c in worksheet 9 at the end of this chapter.*

vii°_{6} AS A DOMINANT SUBSTITUTE

vii°_{6} functions as a dominant substitute (an alternative to P^{6}_{4} and V^{4}_{3}) in the passing vii°_{6} progression. The function, however, is all the more evident when vii°_{6} substitutes for V in such a standard progression as IV–V–I, which with the substitution becomes **IV–**$\mathbf{vii^{\circ}_{6}}$**–I.** Bach's Chorale 42 opens with this progression, which clearly establishes the AM key with a tonic/pre-dominant/dominant/tonic harmonic phrase (example 9.4a). This progression is used especially to harmonize ascending $\hat{1}$–$\hat{2}$–$\hat{3}$ or $\hat{6}$–$\hat{7}$–$\hat{1}$ segments in the soprano. Examples 9.4b and c illustrate correct voice-leading possibilities for this progression. In minor, the melodic segment $\hat{6}$–$\hat{7}$–$\hat{1}$ may produce an +2 between ♭6 and ♯7, as in example 9.4d. The solution to avoid the +2 is to place ♭6 and ♯7 in different voices, or to use an ascending melodic minor scale (♯$\hat{6}$–♯$\hat{7}$–$\hat{1}$), with the resulting major subdominant chord in a minor key (IV–vii°_{6}–i), as in example 9.4e.

EXERCISE

To practice realizing short progressions using vii°_{6} *as a dominant substitute, refer to exercises 2d and e in worksheet 9 at the end of this chapter.*

Example 9.4a J. S. Bach, Chorale 42, "Du Friede fürst, Herr Jesu Christ," mm. 1–4

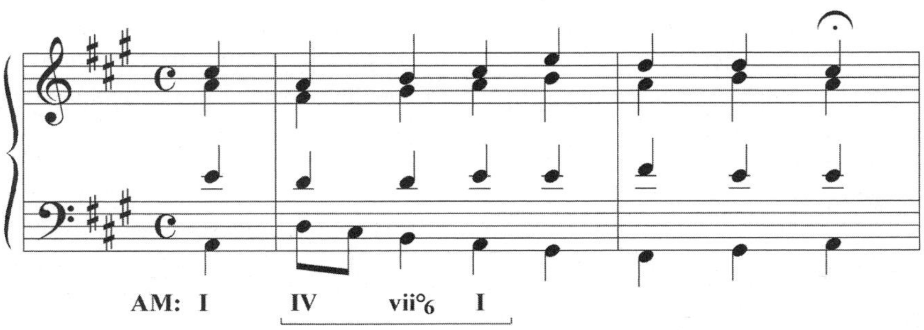

Example 9.4b to f

THE LEADING-TONE CADENCE

The progression vii°_{6}–I, when used as a cadential gesture, is called the **leading-tone cadence.** This type of cadence is not very common in music after the seventeenth century. In the fifteenth and sixteenth centuries (the Renaissance), however, it was one of the standard cadential formulas. The structural frame in this cadence is the $\hat{2}$–$\hat{1}$ motion in the bass and the $\hat{7}$–$\hat{1}$ motion in one of the upper voices. In example 9.5, the structural frame is found in the alto-bass voice pair. Notice the 7–6 suspension at the cadence between these two voices. This "cadential suspension" (effected by the voice which carries the $\hat{1}$–$\hat{7}$–$\hat{1}$ figure) is a characteristic stylistic feature of this cadence in the Renaissance. Study the reductions of this passage in example 9.4f, including a version without the cadential suspension and one with it.

Typical Errors to Avoid

- Doubling the LT.
- Not resolving the LT in vii°_{6}.
- Writing an +2 between ♭6 and ♯7 in the progression iv–vii°_{6}–i (in minor).

1. In vii°$_6$ it is best to double the bass (the third of the chord, $\hat{2}$). It is permissible to double the fifth ($\hat{4}$), but you should never double the root ($\hat{7}$).
2. It is desirable to resolve the tritone $\hat{7}$–$\hat{4}$ to the 3rd $\hat{1}$–$\hat{3}$ (or $\hat{4}$–$\hat{7}$ to the 6th $\hat{3}$–$\hat{1}$). It is also possible to move $\hat{4}$ upward by step to $\hat{5}$. In the first case, the tonic of resolution is incomplete. In the second case, it is complete.
3. The most frequent use of vii°$_6$ is as a passing chord between I and I$_6$, or vice versa. Standard voice-leading patterns for this progression appear in example 9.6. The bass and another voice (in this example the soprano) feature a voice exchange; all the other voices carry neighbor-note or passing figures.

Example 9.5 G. P. da Palestrina, *Missa Quam pulchra es,* "Sanctus," mm. 8–10

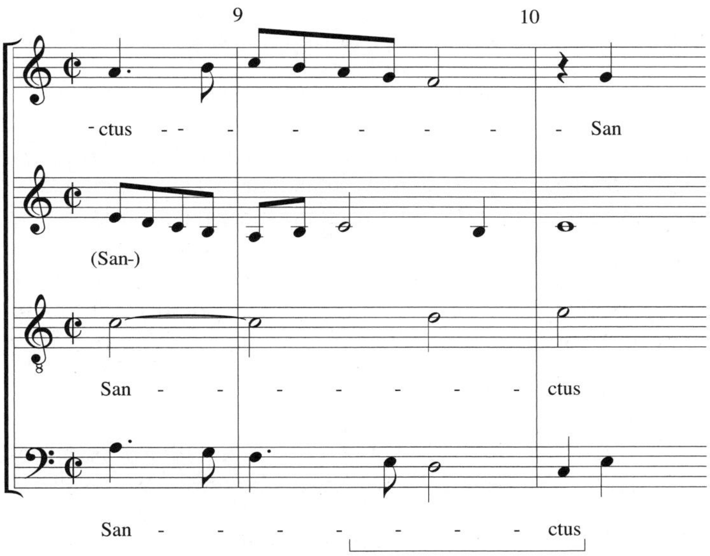

Example 9.6

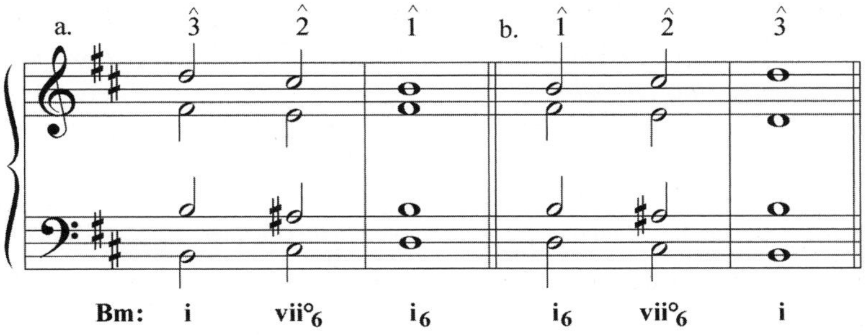

Example 9.7

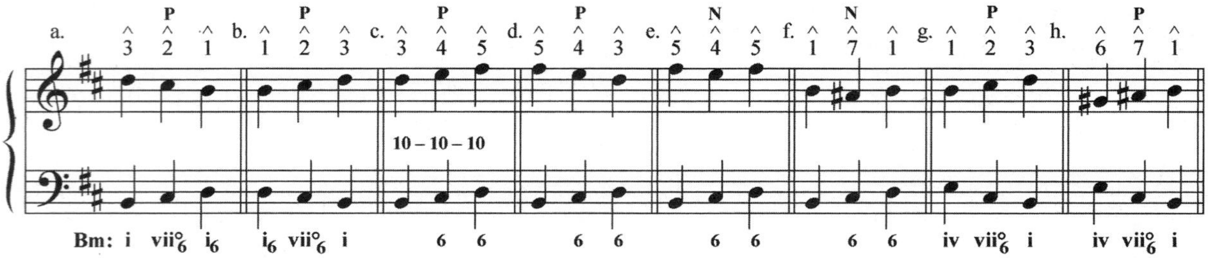

CHARACTERISTIC SOPRANO-BASS PATTERNS

As we have already discussed, the passing vii°$_6$ progression may be used to harmonize $\hat{1}$–$\hat{2}$–$\hat{3}$ or $\hat{3}$–$\hat{2}$–$\hat{1}$ fragments in either the bass or the soprano, as shown in examples 9.7a and b. Two other common soprano passing figures harmonized with a passing vii°$_6$ are $\hat{3}$–$\hat{4}$–$\hat{5}$ (a pattern in which soprano and bass move in parallel 10ths) and $\hat{5}$–$\hat{4}$–$\hat{3}$, as shown in examples 9.7c and d. Examples 9.7e and f, on the other hand, show two soprano neighbor figures harmonized with the passing vii°$_6$ progression. The progression iv–vii°$_6$–I, shown in examples 9.7g and h, can be used to harmonize $\hat{1}$–$\hat{2}$–$\hat{3}$ or $\hat{6}$–$\hat{7}$–$\hat{1}$ (♯$\hat{6}$–♯$\hat{7}$–$\hat{1}$ in minor) in the soprano. Play each of these outer-voice patterns at the piano, adding inner voices in keyboard texture.

ELABORATING THE I–V–I PROGRESSION

The passing vii°$_6$ chord elaborates the tonic in a similar way as the P^6_4 and passing V^4_3 progressions do. In fact, we now have three possible passing progressions to elaborate the opening tonic in a I–V–I progression by means of a $\hat{1}$–$\hat{2}$–$\hat{3}$ motion in the bass. The three options are illustrated in example 9.8. Play and compare these three passing progressions and hear how all three share the same function (prolonging the opening tonic harmony).

EXERCISES

To practice realizing a progression using various vii°$_6$ chords, refer to exercise 3 in worksheet 9 at the end of this chapter.

To practice harmonizing a melody using vii°$_6$ and other chords, refer to exercise 4.

To practice analysis of musical fragments including vii°$_6$ chords, refer to exercise 1 in worksheet 9 at the end of this chapter.

ASSIGNMENT AND KEYBOARD EXERCISES

For analytical and written assignments and keyboard exercises based on the materials learned in this chapter, refer to chapter 9 in the workbook.

Example 9.8

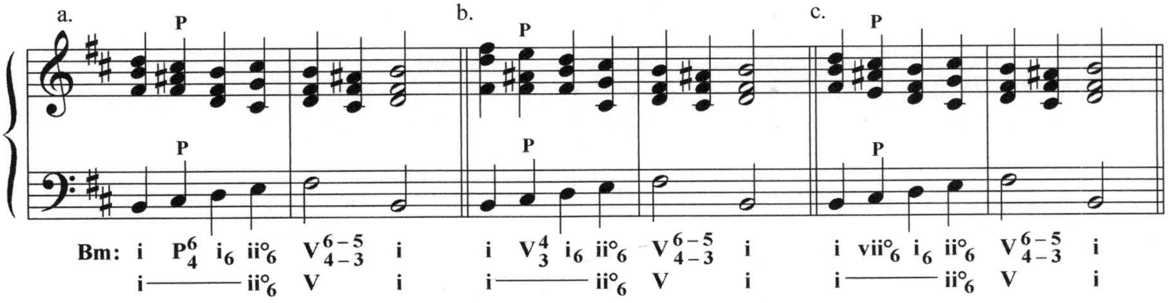

PITCH PATTERNS

Sing the pitch patterns in example 9.9, listening to the vii°$_6$ chords, their function within the phrase, and their resolution.

Example 9.9

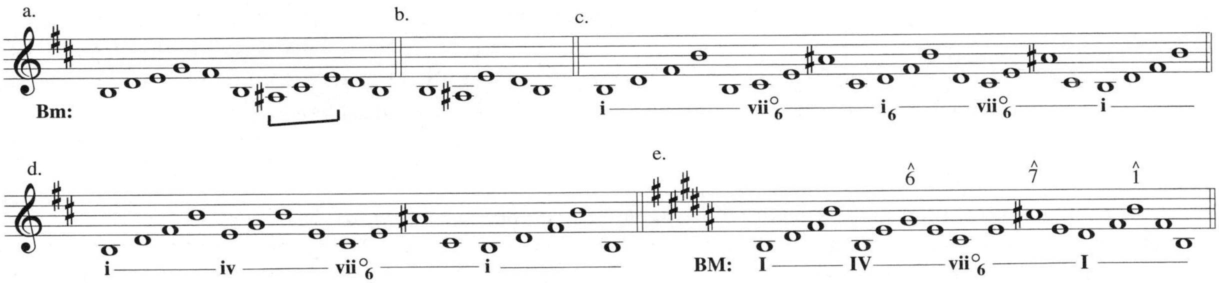

Terms for Review

Leading-tone triad

vii°$_6$

Doubling and resolution of vii°$_6$

The passing vii°$_6$

vii°$_6$ as a dominant substitute

IV–vii°$_6$-I progression

Leading-tone cadence

Worksheet 9

EXERCISE 1 Analysis

1. Study mm. 21–29 of Chevalier de Saint-Georges's *Adagio* (example 9.10).
   a) Analyze the complete passage with RNs.
   b) Measures 21–24 are a prolongation of the tonic triad, and mm. 25–29 prolong the dominant. Mark prolongational chords with an N or a P, depending on their neighbor or passing function.

Example 9.10 Chevalier de Saint–Georges, *Adagio*, mm. 21–29

2. Analyze the passage by Antonio Caldara reproduced in example 9.11. Provide RNs for the complete passage and answer the following questions.
   a) Identify two harmonic patterns studied in this chapter, in mm. 23–26.

   b) What harmonic/linear means are used to prolong the tonic in mm. 23–24?

   c) And in mm. 27–28?

d) What dissonance type do you identify in the keyboard's right-hand part, m. 29, beat 1? (Provide the exact label.)

e) Circle and label all the nonchord tones (NCTs) in the voice part.

Example 9.11 Antonio Caldara, "Alma del core," from *La constanza in amor vince l'inganno,* mm. 23–30

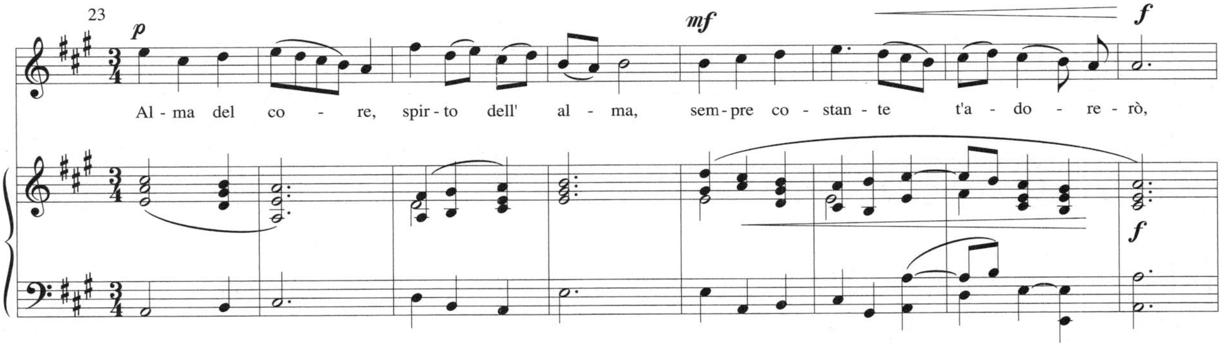

3. Identify and circle passing vii°$_6$ in example 9.12. Explain (and provide the exact label for) the dissonance that is also present in the same measure.

Example 9.12 Elizabeth Jacquet de la Guerre: Suite in Am, Sarabande, mm. 1–8

4. Identify a leading-tone triad in anthology, no. 19 (Haydn, Minuet in CM), Trio. What is its function? What NCT is used to embellish both the leading-tone triad and the chord it resolves to?

EXERCISE 2 Realize the following short progression in four voices.

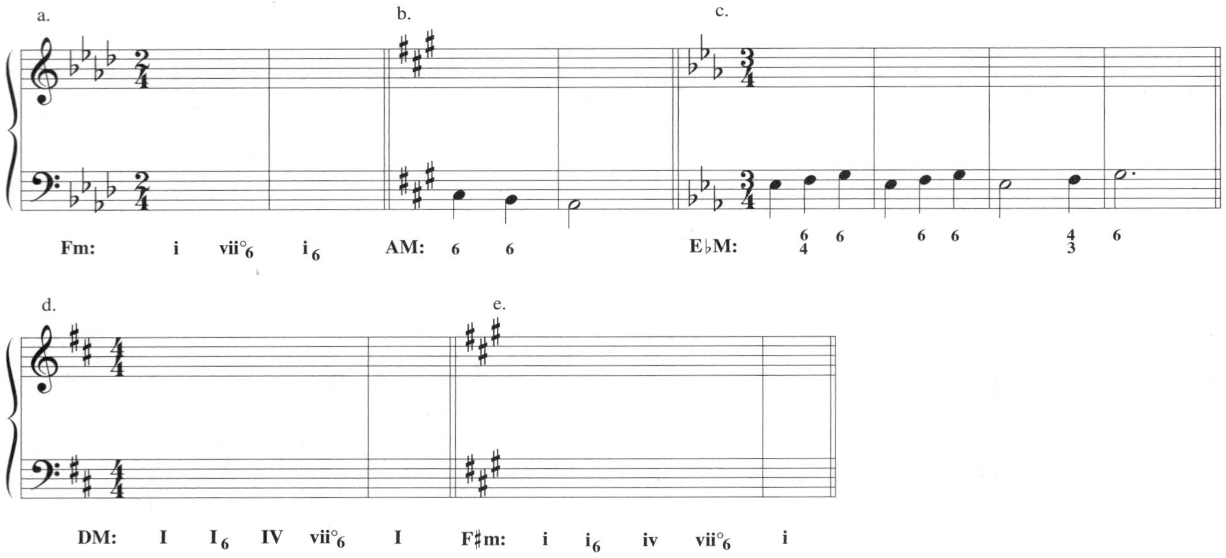

EXERCISE 3 Realize the following progression in four voices. Remember to double-check the outer-voice frame for good first-species counterpoint.

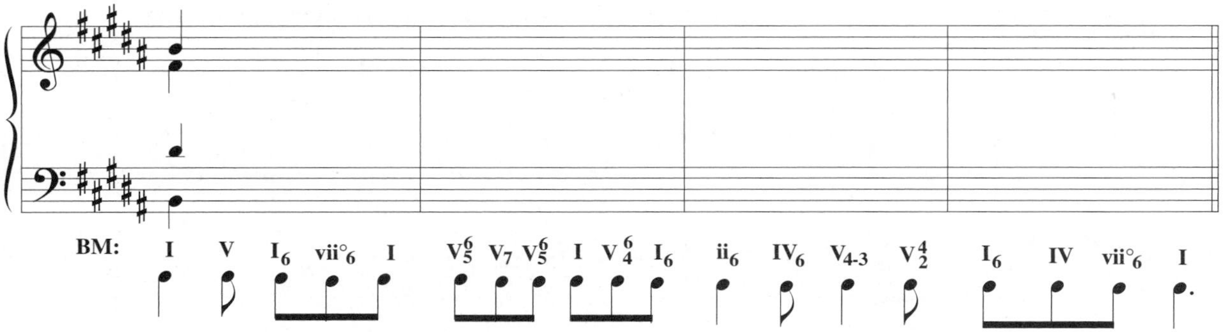

EXERCISE 4 Harmonize the following melody with bass and RNs. Use i, iv, V, ii, and their inversions. Include one or more of each of these: passing vii°$_6$, neighbor $^6_4$, cadential $^6_4$. Remember to double-check your outer-voice frame for good first-species counterpoint.

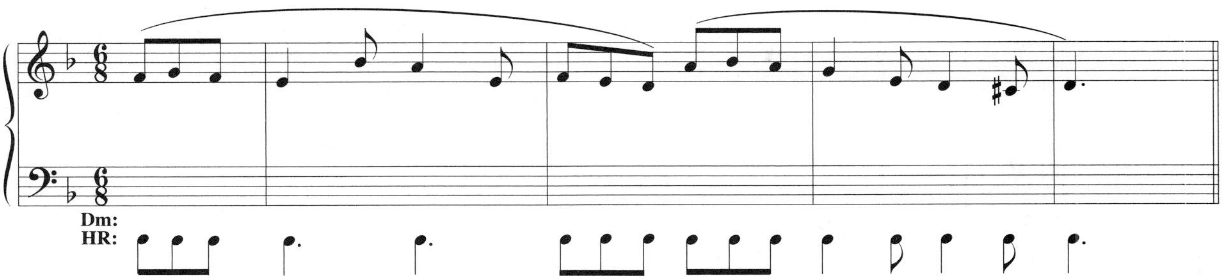

Chapter 10

Cadences

A **cadence** is a musical point of arrival, normally produced by harmonic and melodic means, which articulates the end of a musical group (such as a phrase, a period, a section, or, of course, a complete movement or piece). Cadences provide musical punctuation, and their function is similar to the function of periods and commas in written language. Some are conclusive and final (like periods), some are conclusive in a weaker way (like semicolons), and others are used to confirm or reiterate a conclusion. Or, in some other cases, cadences are not meant to produce any kind of closing effect, but rather to suspend momentarily musical motion (like commas). Because they mark the end of phrases, periods, and other musical units, cadences have an essential role in defining musical sections. The tonal, rhythmic, and thematic relationships among units or sections (the "shape" of a composition) constitute musical **form.** As we will see in chapter 11, cadences are an element of *formal articulation:* They are sectional markers and also define the tonal goal or direction of sections. In this chapter we will study in some detail all the most frequent cadence types found in tonal music. Although we have already seen, in previous chapters, the authentic, half, plagal, and deceptive cadences, we will now discuss each of them more specifically.

AUTHENTIC CADENCES

An **authentic cadence** includes a chord of the dominant family resolving to a tonic chord (for instance, V–I, V_7–I, V_6–I, V–I_6, or vii$^\circ_6$–I). As we saw in chapter 2, authentic cadences can be of two types, perfect and imperfect, depending on the scale degrees in the upper voice and the position of the chords involved.

The Perfect Authentic Cadence

Mozart closes the last movement of his Piano Sonata in B♭M, K. 333 (anthology, no. 28) with a V_7–I cadence, in which both V_7 and I are in root position, $\hat{1}$ is in the top voice in the final tonic, and it is approached by step from $\hat{7}$. This type of V_7–I or V–I

Example 10.1 J. Haydn, Piano Sonata no. 32 in C♯m, Hob. XVI:36, I, mm. 94–97

cadence is the most conclusive of all authentic cadences, and it is known as a **perfect authentic cadence (PAC).** *In a PAC, $\hat{1}$ is in the top voice in the last chord, it is approached by step from $\hat{2}$ or $\hat{7}$, and both the dominant and the tonic chords are in root position.*

Many pieces and movements end with a PAC, and at times the cadence is reiterated several times to stress the sense of closure. To conclude the first movement of his Piano Sonata no. 36 in C♯m (example 10.1), Haydn wrote a string of five cadential gestures, all of the PAC type. Verify that these are all indeed PACs, and notice the strongly conclusive effect of the example.

EXERCISES

To study voice leadings for PACs, refer to examples 10.7a and b.

To practice realizing PACs in four voices, refer to exercises 2a and b in worksheet 10 at the end of this chapter.

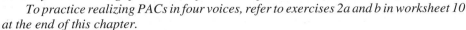

Perfect authentic cadences are often embellished with a cadential $^6_4$. Study the cadence in example 10.2. First, find the $^6_4$ pitches in the melody (m. 5 of the example, to the words "Ev'rythin's"). Does this melodic $^6_4$ resolve to $^5_3$ in the next measure ("goin' my")? Notice that the B♭ that doubles the bass in the melody in m. 5 moves to an A♭ in m. 6, the seventh of the V_7 chord. The complete melodic figure in mm. 5–6 can then be represented as $V^{8-7}_{\substack{6-5\\4-3}}$. If you look at the accompaniment you will see another frequent possibility for approaching the seventh in the V_7. First, find the $^6_4$ in the piano part (m. 5). Then, verify that, instead of moving down in a 6–5 figure, the 6th of the $^6_4$ moves up to the seventh in a 6–7 figure, hence the Roman numeral V^{6-7}_{4-3}.

Imperfect Authentic Cadences

Composers at times want to end a musical statement with a less-conclusive gesture than the PAC. In the section immediately before the PAC cadence by Mozart mentioned previously (anthology, no. 28), he avoids a conclusive cadence in order to

Example 10.2 Oscar Hammerstein II–Richard Rodgers, "Oh, What a Beautiful Mornin,'" from *Oklahoma!*

build up tension toward the end and also to achieve a stronger closing effect after he finally reaches the final PAC. The series of $V–I_6$ cadences that he writes (mm. 206–222; see especially mm. 207, 210, 213, 218, and 222) do not create a sense of conclusion because the tonic in first inversion is a weak sonority for ending a piece. These are **imperfect authentic cadences** (IAC). In an IAC, *one of the chords is not in root position (or both chords are not), or* $\hat{1}$ *is not in the top voice.* The cadences in mm. 206–222 of anthology, no. 28 illustrate the first type (a chord is in inversion). An example of the second type is found earlier in the same movement: Although in m. 20 Mozart closes a phrase with a V–I cadence and both chords are in root position, it is a nonconclusive IAC because $\hat{3}$ is in the top voice (the upper-voice cadential motion is here $\hat{5}$–$\hat{3}$). The vii°_6–I cadence (which we studied in chapter 9) is a special type of IAC called **leading-tone cadence,** and it is more common in Renaissance music than in the common practice repertoire.

EXERCISES

To study voice leadings for IACs, refer to examples 10.7d to h.

To practice realizing IACs in four voices, refer to exercises 2e to h in worksheet 10 at the end of this chapter.

THE HALF CADENCE

Examine now the opening period of the same sonata movement by Mozart (anthology, no. 28, mm. 1–8). The statement ends on a PAC. At m. 4, however, the first phrase ends on a V chord, creating a definite need to resolve the harmonic tension, and thus to continue to the second phrase, as in a question-answer structure. A *cadence on V* (often preceded by the tonic or by a pre-dominant chord) is called a **half cadence** (HC). The most frequent melodic motion at a HC is $\hat{3}$–$\hat{2}$. Instead of immediately effecting a melodic resolution down to $\hat{1}$, a phrase interrupted at a HC usually begins all over again and eventually reaches closure with the resolution of the melodic $\hat{2}$ to $\hat{1}$ in the PAC at the end of the period.

Half cadences are very effective musical "marks of punctuation": They allow for clear articulation of the musical flow (we can clearly finish a phrase on a HC), and yet they create a harmonic need to "move forward." Listen to the Fm phrase by Pauline Viardot–Garcia in example 10.3; although we realize that this is indeed a phrase, we also know that the music will go on. Further, we expect the next phrase to begin on an Fm tonic chord because the phrase ends on a dominant harmony in Fm, a half cadence.

The Phrygian Cadence

Refer to anthology, no. 50 (Schumann, *Album for the Young,* "Folk Song"). The first phrase ends at m. 4 with a half cadence (on V of Dm). Because V is preceded by iv$_6$, $\hat{5}$ in the bass is approached by half-step motion, B♭–A. This special type of half cadence

Example 10.3 Pauline Viardot-Garcia: "Die Beschwörung," mm. 60–63

in minor, in which V is preceded by iv_6, is called **Phrygian cadence** (Ph.C.), because of the prominent half-step motion in the bass (which, in the Phrygian mode, takes place both between degrees $\hat{1}$–$\hat{2}$ and $\hat{5}$–$\hat{6}$).

EXERCISES

To study voice leadings for HCs, refer to examples 10.7i to l.

To practice realizing HCs in four voices, refer to exercises 2i to l in worksheet 10 at the end of this chapter.

THE PLAGAL CADENCE

The IV–I cadence is known as a **plagal cadence** (PC). In chapter 3 we explained that the plagal cadence is sometimes used by composers to prolong the final tonic, following a more conclusive PAC. After a PAC, a plagal cadence has the effect of strongly confirming the conclusion of a piece. Such an extended prolongation of the final tonic can be seen in example 10.4. Brahms closes his Romance in FM, op. 118, no. 5 with a

Example 10.4 J. Brahms, Romance, op. 118, no. 5, mm. 53–57

PAC in mm. 53–54, followed by four measures of tonic prolongation, which include a prominent plagal cadence in mm. 55–56. Notice the unusual final sonority in this piece. In what position is the final tonic chord in m. 57?

THE DECEPTIVE CADENCE

A **deceptive cadence** (DC) is a cadential progression of the dominant to a chord other than the expected (and, in principle, prescribed) tonic. In example 10.5, Mozart first delays the PAC that eventually closes the Fantasia in Cm, K. 475, by means of a deceptive cadence, V_7–VI, in m. 179. (The V_7 chord is preceded by a slight elaboration of the standard cadential $^6_4$ figure.) A repeat an octave lower of the same cadential gesture leads to a PAC in m. 180, confirmed by a second PAC in mm. 180–181 (this time with a standard voice leading for the cadential $^6_4$, that is, $^{8-7}_{\substack{6-5\\4-3}}$).

The V–vi (or V–VI in a minor key) progression is the most frequent type of deceptive cadence. A slight variation of this progression is occasionally found in the literature: V may resolve deceptively to IV_6 instead of vi (see anthology, no. 9, m. 3). In a deceptive cadence the leading tone still resolves to the tonic ($\hat{7}$–$\hat{1}$), thus providing melodic closure, as in the top voice of the Mozart example. But because the $\hat{5}$ in the bass resolves to $\hat{6}$ instead of $\hat{1}$, we hear this cadence as an inconclusive (and usually unexpected and surprising) harmonic motion. Because it requires continuation to some kind of closure, it is often used to delay the end of a harmonic phrase as in example 10.5.

The passage by Palestrina in example 10.6 combines two of the cadences we just studied. In m. 40 we hear what might be the approach to a PAC. Instead, the dominant at the end of m. 40 resolves deceptively, to the VI in m. 41, which immediately turns into an extended iv chord. What kind of cadence, then, is the final cadence in mm. 42–44? What kind of tonic chord do we end on? This beautiful cadence, which

Example 10.5 W. A. Mozart, Fantasia in Cm, K. 475, mm. 179–181

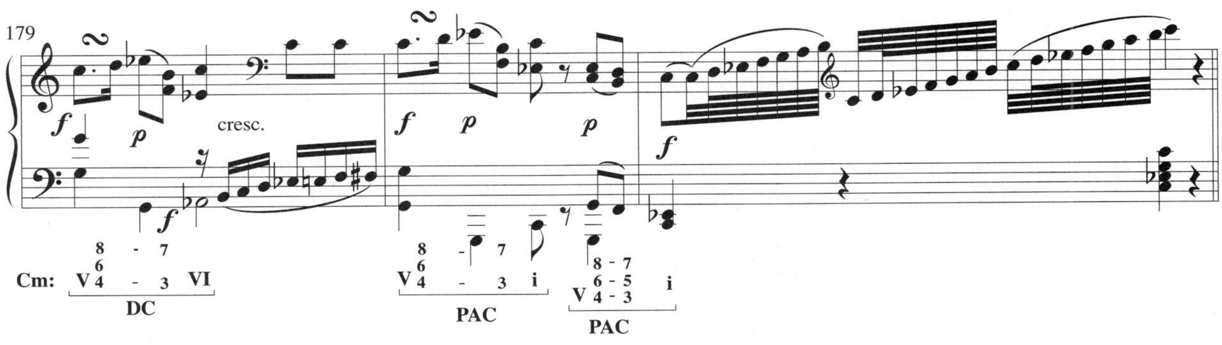

Example 10.6 Giovanni Pierluigi da Palestrina, "Hosanna in excelsis," from *Missa Gabriel Archangelus*, mm. 40–44

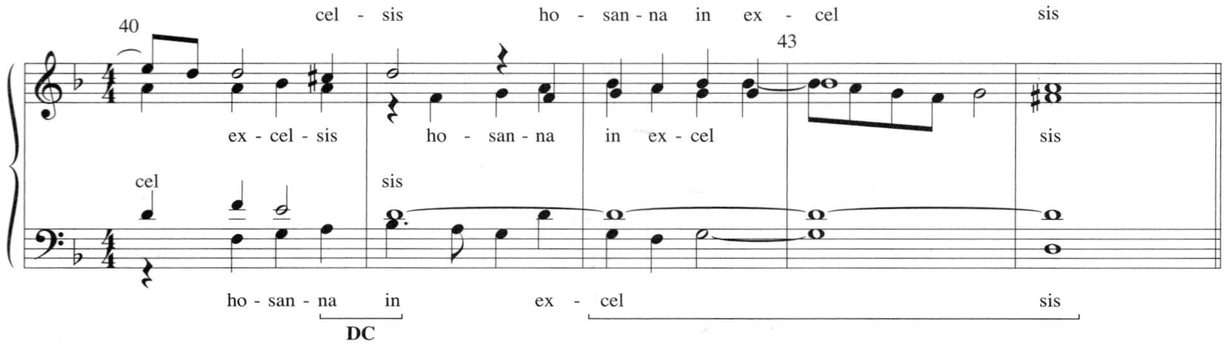

definitely has a conclusive effect, does not include a PAC at all. Moreover, although the movement could end on a PAC in m. 41 (we actually reach melodic closure in this cadence, with the $\hat{7}$–$\hat{1}$ in the soprano), the deceptive and plagal cadences that follow allow for a few measures of *cadential extension,* a concept we will study in more detail in chapter 12.

EXERCISES

To study voice leadings for plagal and deceptive cadences, refer to examples 10.7m to o.

To practice realizing plagal and deceptive cadences in four voices, refer to exercises 2m and n in worksheet 10 at the end of this chapter.

Typical Errors to Avoid

1. Doubling the LT (and resolving both of them to $\hat{1}$, with resulting parallel 8ves).
2. Not raising $\hat{7}$ in minor modes.
3. Not resolving the LT, especially when it is placed in the soprano.
4. Writing parallel 5ths or 8ves in progressions by step, such as IV–V and V–vi.
5. Writing parallel 5ths or 8ves in the progression IV_6–V_6 (double-check the part writing for this progression in example 10.7e).

Example 10.7

Perfect Authentic
a. 4̂ 2̂ 1̂
b. 1̂ 7̂ 1̂
c. 4̂ 3̂ 2̂ 1̂
B♭M: ii6 V I
IV V I
IV V 6-5 4-3 I
Imperfect Authentic
d. 4̂ 2̂ 1̂
e. 1̂ 2̂ 3̂
f. 4̂ 2̂ 3̂
g. 6̂ 5̂ 3̂
h. 6̂ 5̂ 5̂
ii6 V I6
IV6 V6 I
ii6 V I
IV V I
IV V I
Half
i. 1̂ 7̂
j. 3̂ 2̂
k. 3̂ 3̂ 2̂
I IV V
V6 I V
V6 I V 6-5 4-3
Phrygian
l. 1̂ 7̂
B♭m: i iv6 V
Plagal
m. 3̂ 2̂ 1̂
B♭M: I V I IV I
Deceptive
n. 7̂ 1̂
o. 7̂ 1̂
I V vi
I V IV6

CADENCES: SUMMARY AND VOICE LEADING

Example 10.7 provides a variety of voice-leading models for each of the cadences previously discussed. Authentic and half cadences are represented by three-chord progressions using only I, IV, and V. The following comments will help you understand these examples.

1. Examples 10.7a–c illustrate three frequent upper-voice figures in PACs: $\hat{4}$–$\hat{2}$–$\hat{1}$, $\hat{1}$–$\hat{7}$–$\hat{1}$, and, with a dominant embellished by a cadential $^6_4$, $\hat{4}$–$\hat{3}$–$\hat{2}$–$\hat{1}$. Notice that, in the cadential $^6_4$, $\hat{5}$ (the bass) is doubled.
2. Examples 10.7d–e show IACs in which one of the two cadential chords is in first inversion. In 10.7e, moreover, the upper voice cadential pattern, $\hat{1}$–$\hat{2}$–$\hat{3}$, does not end on $\hat{1}$.
3. Examples 10.7f–h feature root-position chords, but the upper voice does not end on $\hat{1}$ in the last tonic chord. All three melodic patterns, $\hat{4}$–$\hat{2}$–$\hat{3}$, $\hat{6}$–$\hat{5}$–$\hat{3}$, and $\hat{6}$–$\hat{5}$–$\hat{5}$, are typical of IACs.
4. Examples 10.7i–l show four HCs. The first two represent frequent melodic patterns in HCs, $\hat{1}$–$\hat{7}$ and $\hat{3}$–$\hat{2}$. The $\hat{3}$–$\hat{3}$–$\hat{2}$ pattern in example 10.7k results from a $^{6-5}_{4-3}$ embellishment of the cadential V. Finally, a Phrygian cadence appears in example 10.7l.
5. The plagal cadence in example 10.7m does not require any comment, other than noticing that, in this case, the sustained $\hat{1}$ appears in the upper voice.
6. Two deceptive cadences (V–vi and V–IV_6) appear in examples 10.7n–o. The progression V-vi is a progression by step, of the type in which, in principle, we recommended that all three upper voices move in contrary motion with the bass. The LT in this cadence, however, should still resolve. The root and third of V will thus move a step up, while the other two voices move down. This voice leading results in a *doubled third* in the vi chord (or a doubled fifth in the V–IV_6 variant).

EXERCISES

To practice analyzing a variety of cadences, refer to exercise 1 in worksheet 10.

To practice writing progressions ending on one of the cadences we have studied in this chapter, refer to exercise 3.

To practice realizing a figured bass and harmonizing a melody, refer to exercises 4 and 5.

FOR FURTHER STUDY

For additional analysis using materials studied in this chapter, refer to the *Harmony in Context* Web page at www.mhhe.com/roigfrancoli2e.

ASSIGNMENT AND KEYBOARD EXERCISES

For analytical and written assignments and keyboard exercises based on the materials learned in this chapter, refer to chapter 10 in the workbook.

PITCH PATTERNS

Sing the pitch patterns in example 10.8. Hear the different cadences as you sing them, and understand the characteristics that define each of the cadences, as well as their functions.

Example 10.8

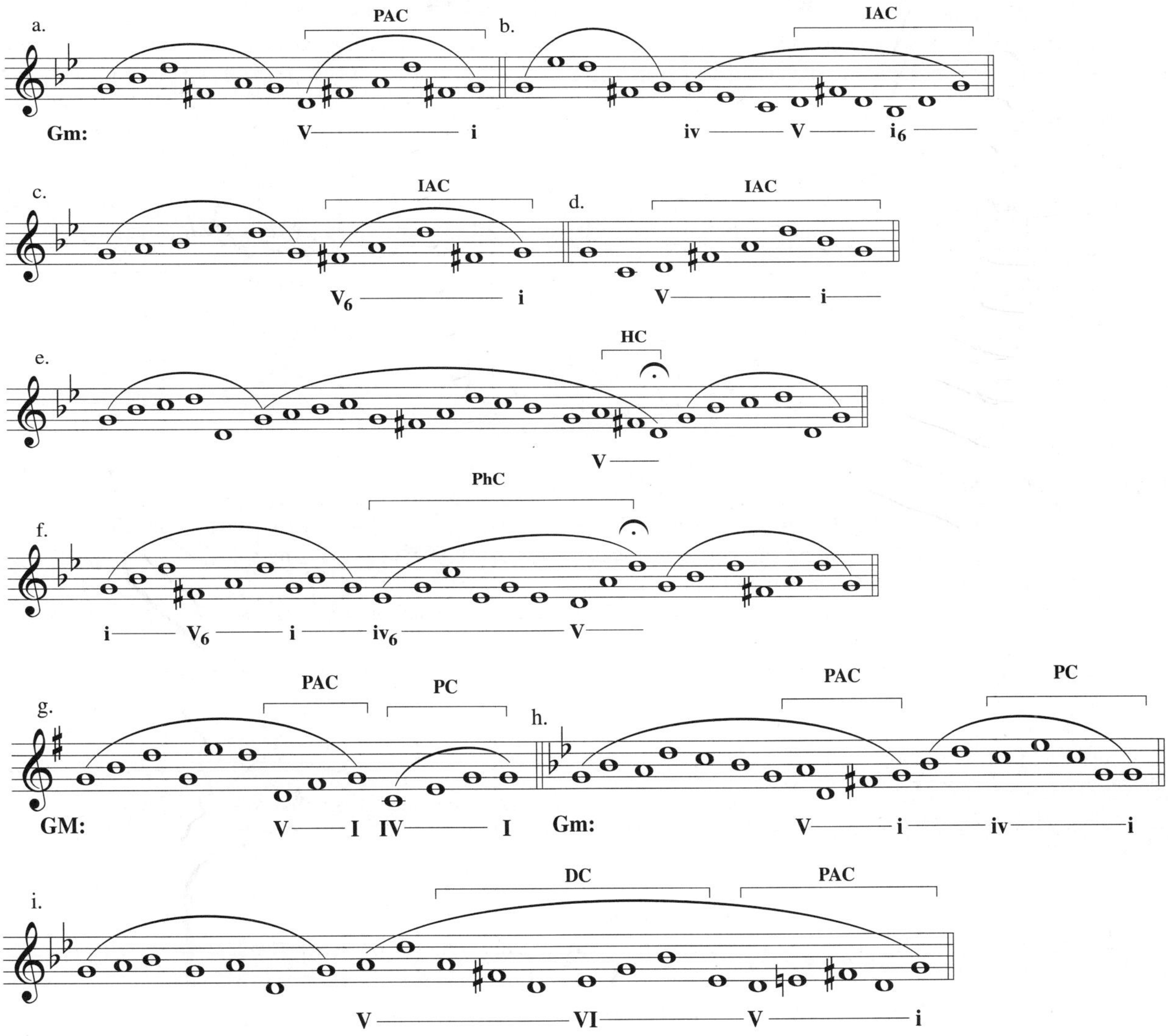

Terms for Review

- Cadence
- Form
- Authentic cadence
- Perfect authentic cadence
- Imperfect authentic cadence
- Leading-tone cadence
- Half cadence
- Phrygian cadence
- Plagal cadence
- Deceptive cadence

Worksheet 10

EXERCISE 1 Analysis. Study and label each of the following cadences. Name the cadence type and provide specific (Roman numerals) RNs and other characteristics (such as upper-voice melodic motion) to justify your choice.

1. Example 10.9.

Example 10.9 J. S. Bach, Chorale 143, "In dulci jubilo," mm. 29–32

2. Example 10.10.

Example 10.10 R. Schumann, "Wenn ich in deinen Augen seh," from *Dichterliebe,* op. 48, no. 4, mm. 8–12

3. Example 10.11.
   a) Identify the two cadences as marked.
   b) Comment on the resolution of the first cadence to the chord at the beginning of the next measure.

Example 10.11 J. S. Bach, Chorale 197, "Christ ist erstanden," mm. 27–29

4. Example 10.12.

Example 10.12 J. Lennon–P. McCartney, "Got to Get You into My Life," from the album *Revolver* (verse)

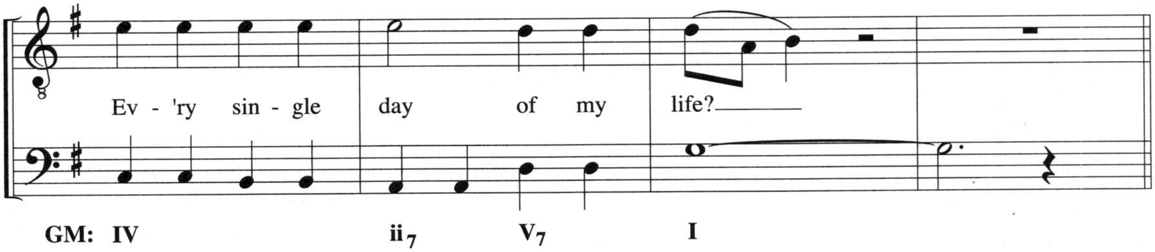

5. Anthology, no. 26, Mozart, Sonata in CM, III, m. 8.

6. Anthology, no. 18, Amalie, Sonata in FM, m. 21.

7. Anthology, no. 11, Bach, Minuet from *French Suite* no. 3, m. 8.

8. Anthology, no. 47, Schumann, "Ich grolle nich," mm. 11–12.

9. Anthology, no. 32, Beethoven, Sonata in Fm, op. 2, no. 1, m. 8.

EXERCISE 2 Realize the following cadences in four voices as required. Some soprano melodic patterns are provided, and so are some Roman numerals. Provide RNs where missing.

a. **PAC** $\hat{1}$ $\hat{7}$ $\hat{1}$ b. **PAC** $\hat{4}$ $\hat{2}$ $\hat{1}$ c. **PAC** $\hat{4}$ $\hat{3}$ $\hat{2}$ $\hat{1}$ d. **PAC** $\hat{4}$ $\hat{3}$ $\hat{2}$ $\hat{1}$

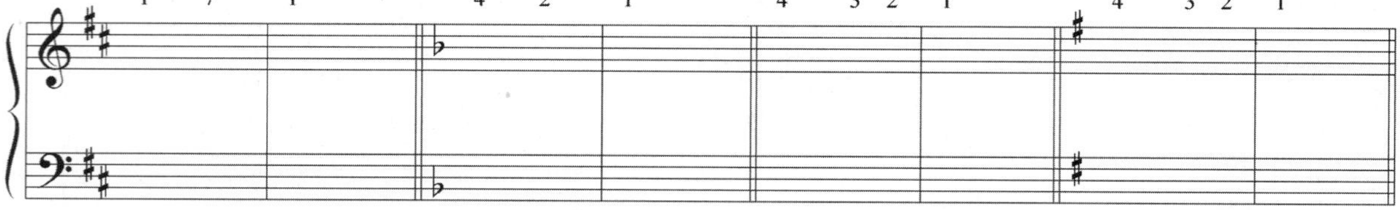

DM: **FM:** **Am: iv V^{6-5}_{4-3} i** **GM: ii_6 V^{6-5}_{4-3} I**

e. **IAC** f. **IAC** $\hat{4}$ $\hat{2}$ $\hat{3}$ g. **IAC** $\hat{6}$ $\hat{5}$ $\hat{3}$ h. **IAC** $\hat{1}$ $\hat{2}$ $\hat{3}$

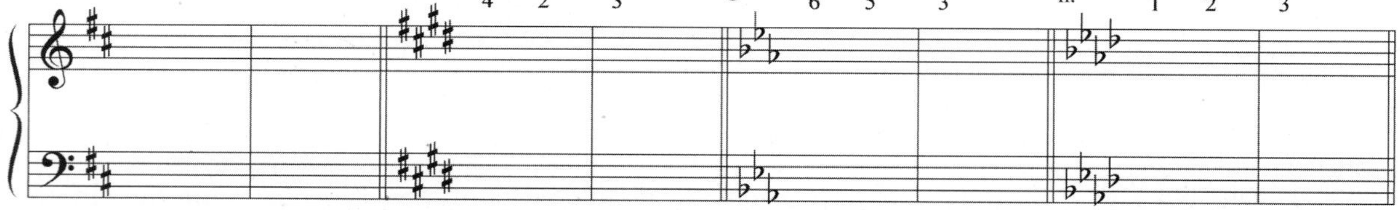

Bm: iv V i_6 **C♯m:** **E♭M:** **A♭M: IV_6 V_6 I**

i. **HC** $\hat{3}$ $\hat{2}$ j. **HC** $\hat{1}$ $\hat{7}$ k. **HC** $\hat{3}$ $\hat{3}$ $\hat{2}$ l. **PhC** $\hat{3}$ $\hat{4}$ $\hat{2}$

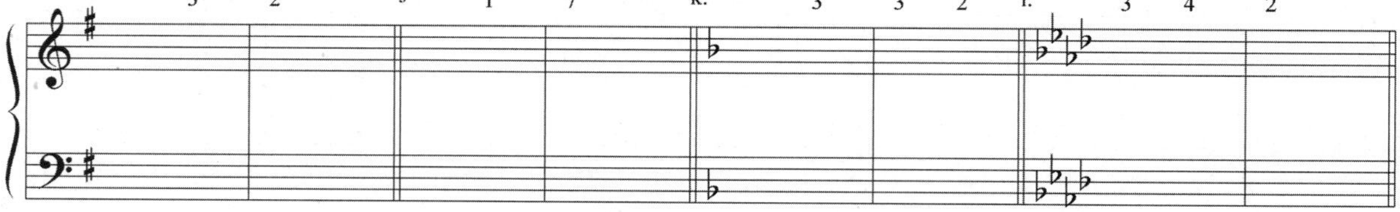

Em: V_6 i **CM: I IV** **Dm: V_6 i V^{6-5}_{4-3}** **Fm: i**

m. **DC** n. **PC** $\hat{3}$ $\hat{2}$ $\hat{1}$

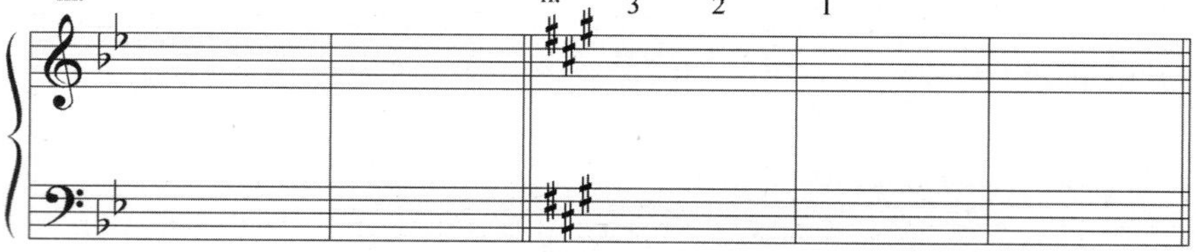

Gm: i V **AM: I V**

EXERCISE 3 Finish each of the following short progressions with the required cadence type (and realize the complete progression in four voices).

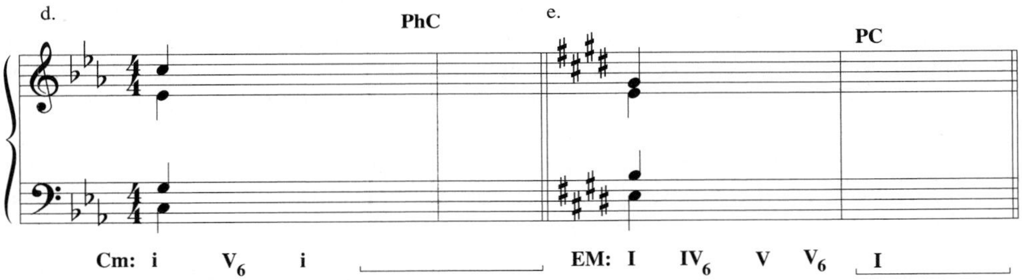

EXERCISE 4 Realize the following progressions in four voices. Remember to double-check your outer-voice frame for good first-species counterpoint.

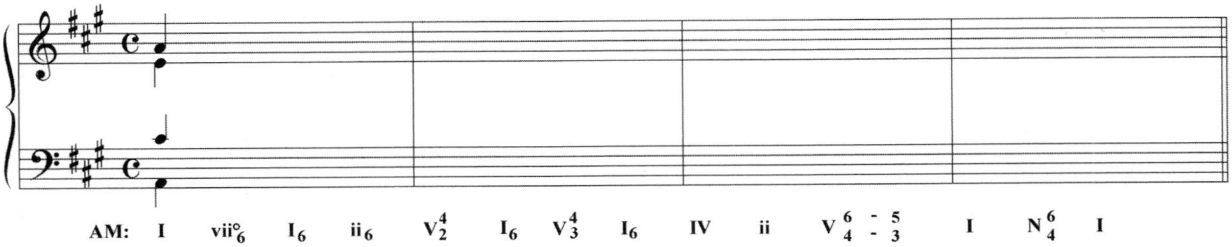

EXERCISE 5 Provide a RN analysis and realize in four voices.

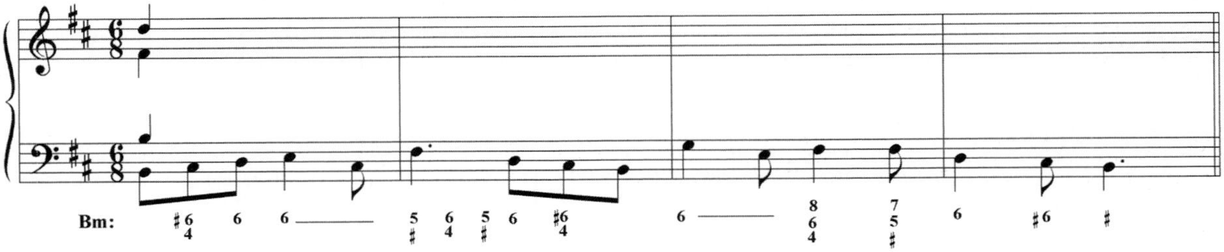

Chapter 11

Melodic Organization I: Phrase Structure

Similar to language syntax, musical thoughts and statements are grouped into units of varied length and function, in which melodic, rhythmic, and harmonic factors play a determining role, and in which cadences are an element of punctuation. As we noted in the previous chapter, the tonal, thematic, and rhythmic relationships among musical units constitute what we know as musical **form.** In this chapter we will study the basic types of musical statements and their groupings, with emphasis on melodic and tonal organization. You should keep in mind that music allows for an enormous variety of formal possibilities at any level. In this and other chapters we will discuss specific formal models that may be considered standard, at least in some repertoires. Not all the music you perform or listen to, however, conforms to these models. There are other possible models, and in many cases music does not conform to any preestablished formal type. The principles you will study in this and other chapters will provide you with criteria to approach the formal aspects of music, as well as a basis for comparison of specific formal arrangements with standard methods of musical organization.[1]

MOTIVE

A **motive** is a short, recurring musical figure, consisting of a characteristic rhythmic or pitch pattern, identifiable throughout a composition or a musical section. A **rhythmic motive** is a rhythmic figure that has, by its repetition, a structural role in a piece or passage. The accompaniment in anthology, no. 57 (Wolf, "Das verlassene Mägdlein") is based exclusively on the rhythmic motive quarter note/two eighth notes. The motive in example 11.1, on the other hand, presents both a clearly identifiable pitch pattern (a lower-neighbor-note figure) and a characteristic rhythmic pattern (two sixteenth notes/one eighth note).

[1] For further study of this chapter's topics, you can find a thorough coverage of phrase structure in Douglass Green, *Form in Tonal Music* (New York: Holt, Rinehart and Winston, 1979) and W. Rothstein, *Phrase Rhythm in Tonal Music*. For a study of phrase structure in the Classical period, see William Caplin, *Classical Form* (New York: Oxford University Press, 1998).

Example 11.1 J. S. Bach, Brandenburg Concerto no. 3, I, mm. 1–2

PHRASE

In our preview of phrase structure in chapter 2, we used the following definition of **phrase:** "a directed motion in time from one tonal entity to another" (W. Rothstein). In other words, a phrase takes us from a certain tonal point to another tonal point. A phrase presupposes *motion,* although the motion may well take us back where we started (motion from, say, I to I is perfectly acceptable within a phrase). Moreover, a phrase usually ends with a cadence of some type and gives us a sense of being a self-sufficient musical unit (although not necessarily a closed or conclusive one).

Refer, for instance, to example 11.2. Although mm. 1–2 display some degree of musical independence, at least melodically, we would not call this fragment a phrase because it does not feature any kind of harmonic motion (the linear neighbor figure in the piano's right hand, m. 1, beat 2, is certainly not what we consider "harmonic motion"). The same can be said of mm. 3–4. Whereas mm. 1–2 are a linear elaboration of I, mm. 3–4 constitute in turn a linear elaboration of V. We do hear, on the other hand, the complete mm. 1–4 as a self-sufficient unit that effects a motion from tonic to a half cadence (HC) on V. This is the first phrase in this example. But, of course, a HC is not conclusive, and the music continues until it reaches another tonal goal, in this case a more stable one, the tonic in m. 8. Measures 5–8 are also a phrase by our definition.

A NOTE ABOUT IMPLIED HARMONY

As we discussed in chapter 2, one should in principle examine both melody and harmony in order to identify cadences and phrases. At times, however, only a melody may be available. The harmony at the beginning or end of a phrase, if the melody alone is provided, may be implied from the melodic pitches (scale degrees). For structural purposes within a phrase, you will only need to identify implied tonic or dominant harmonies. The following suggestions will help you identify ***implied harmonies:***

1. *Is either I or V outlined melodically at the beginning or end of the phrase?*
2. *Is the beginning or end of the phrase built around (or based on) characteristic pitches of I or V?*
3. *Can you harmonize the beginning or the end with a I or a V?*
4. *A phrase ending on $\hat{1}$ indicates a perfect authentic cadence (PAC). Possible* ***melodic cadential patterns*** *will be $\hat{2}$–$\hat{1}$ or $\hat{7}$–$\hat{1}$.*

5. *A phrase ending on $\hat{3}$ indicates an imperfect authentic cadence (IAC). Likely cadential patterns will be $\hat{2}$–$\hat{3}$ or $\hat{5}$–$\hat{3}$. An ending on $\hat{5}$, with the pattern $\hat{5}$–$\hat{5}$, is more ambiguous and could mean both an IAC (V–I) or a HC (I–V).*
6. *A phrase ending on $\hat{2}$ ($\hat{3}$–$\hat{2}$) or $\hat{7}$ ($\hat{1}$–$\hat{7}$) is a clear sign of a HC.*

Phrase Segment

The two phrases in the Reichardt example (mm. 1–4 and 5–8) can each be broken up into smaller segments. We mentioned that mm. 1–2 display some degree of musical independence, at least melodically. The same is true for mm. 3–4, 5–6, and 7–8, as

Example 11.2 Louíse Reichardt, "Frühlingsblumen," mm. 1–8

indicated by the lower level of brackets. The divisions of a phrase are called **phrase segments** or **subphrases.** The second phrase (mm. 4–8) is equally made up of two phrase segments.

Sentence Structure

The first phrase of anthology, no. 50 (R. Schumann, *Album for the Young,* "Folk Song," mm. 1–4) also features two distinctive segments, mm. 1–2 and 3–4. Phrase segments may contain contrasting thematic material, as in Schumann's example, or similar material, as in anthology, no. 27 (Mozart, Sonata in AM, K. 331, I). The latter example also illustrates a particular type of phrase structure known as **sentence.** A sentence opens with a melodic segment (m. 1 in Mozart's K.331) which is immediately restated, transposed or untransposed (m. 2 in K.331, a transposition down a step of m. 1). This is usually followed by a passage twice the length of the original segment (mm. 3–4 in our case), which leads to a cadence. Refer now to anthology, no. 32 (Beethoven, Sonata in Fm, op. 2, no.1, mm. 1–8) and explain why this phrase is a sentence.

Phrase Connections: Elision

Phrases may be distinctly separated, or they may overlap. Musical factors such as rests, fermatas, or long notes can help in the determination of phrase length. In Reichardt's example above, the HC in m. 4 supports a long A in the melody followed by a rest, all of which stresses the cadence's role as a point of momentary repose. Each phrase in Bach's Chorale 29 (anthology, no.10a) closes with a fermata, leaving little doubt as to the length and number of phrases in this example.

The end of a phrase, however, may also overlap with the beginning of the next phrase (that is, end and beginning may share the same pitch) in what we know as an **elision.** In example 11.3, the first phrase ends on the downbeat of m. 5, whereas the second phrase begins on the same downbeat. The brackets above and below this excerpt show that the two phrases are connected by means of elision. Do the two-measure phrase segments also feature elision? You may also study the elisions in anthology, no. 25 (Mozart, Sonata in CM, K. 309, I, mm. 7–8) and example 2.1 (Beethoven, *Seven Peasant Dances,* no. 4).

EXERCISE

To practice the analysis of phrase and cadence structures, refer to exercise 1 (questions 1 to 3) in worksheet 11 at the end of this chapter.

PERIOD STRUCTURE

Phrases are often grouped into larger units. A **period** is a group of two or more phrases that ends on a conclusive cadence (normally PAC, occasionally IAC), and that contains one or more inner cadences (normally HC or IAC) *weaker* than the final one. Three of the examples we have previously discussed meet these conditions. In the Reichardt example (example 11.2), the first phrase ends on a HC, and the second phrase closes with

Example 11.3 J. S. Bach, Menuet I, from Partita no. 1 in B♭M, for Harpsichord, mm. 1–8

a PAC, thus confirming its periodic structure. Discuss how both R. Schumann's "Folk Song" fragment (anthology, no. 50) and Mozart's Sonata in AM (anthology, no. 27), mm. 1–8, are examples of periods.

Antecedent-Consequent Structure

Now refer back to Reichardt's example. We know that the first phrase reaches a HC in m. 4, which, of course, is inconclusive harmonically. You could think of this type of phrase as a "question." The second phrase, conclusive because of the PAC at the end of it, can be thought of as the "answer." Two phrases that form a period and that have this type of musical "question-answer" relationship because the first phrase ends on a HC, while the second one ends on a PAC, are called **antecedent** (the first phrase) and **consequent** (the second phrase). Antecedent-consequent structures are very common in music, especially in the Classical period. Are the Schumann and Mozart periods which we just mentioned also antecedent-consequent structures?

Parallel Period

The two phrases in a period do not necessarily need to be related thematically. In Mozart's AM sonata, however, they obviously are, at least for two measures (mm. 1–2 are the same as mm. 5–6). This is an example of a **parallel period.** A parallel period has two phrases that *begin* with the same (or similar) material. A parallel period appears in anthology, no. 28 (Mozart's Piano Sonata in B♭M, K. 333, III), mm. 1–8. Discuss the

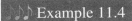

Example 11.4 S. Foster, "Gentle Annie" (Verse)

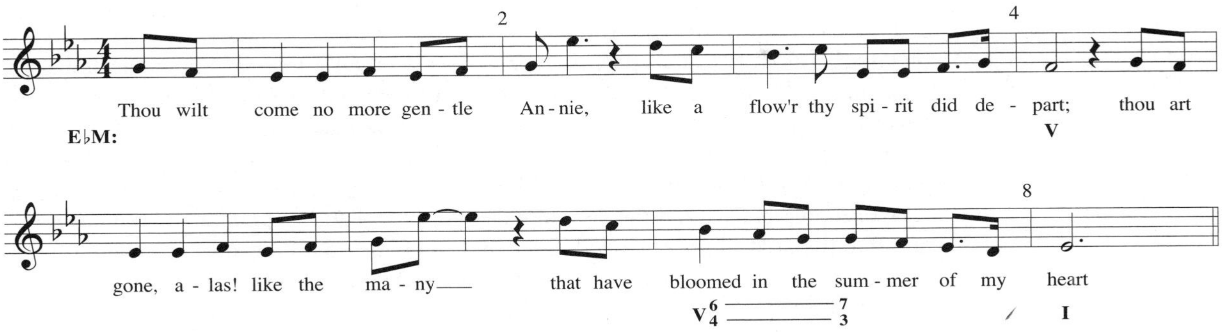

motivic, phrase (Are there phrase segments? Are they contrasting or similar?), and cadential structures in this example. Now sing the melody in example 11.4, and comment on its phrase structure. Is it an antecedent-consequent structure? And a parallel period? Why?

EXERCISE

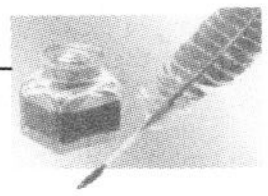

To practice writing a parallel period, refer to exercise 2 in worksheet 11 at the end of this chapter.

FORM DIAGRAMS

We will use graphic **form diagrams** of the type known as **line** or **bubble diagrams** to summarize visually the form and formal relationships of a composition or a section. Sections of a composition and their length are represented on a line, and slurs ("bubbles") are used for the same purpose as additional visual references. The bubbles, moreover, are hierarchical: A bubble may include other bubbles, which in turn may include other bubbles, and so on, to indicate different formal levels. We indicate thematic relationship between phrases by means of lowercase letters. Phrases with the same thematic material are designated with the same letter, whereas different letters indicate contrasting material. The diagram in example 11.5 refers to the period in anthology, no. 27 (Mozart, AM

Example 11.5 Form Diagram for Anthology, no. 27 (Mozart, AM Sonata), mm. 1–8

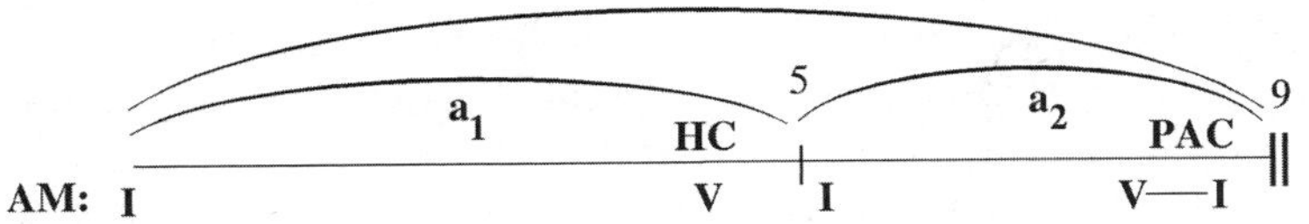

sonata, mm. 1–8): The letters a_1–a_2 indicate that the two phrases are related thematically. Capital letters will be used to indicate thematic relationships between formal units at a higher level than the phrase (phrase pairs, periods, etc.).

The long-range tonal motion of phrases and periods, essential to the articulation of form, is mostly determined by their beginning and cadential harmonies. In our diagrams, tonal motion is represented by Roman numerals under the line, and cadences will be labeled with the usual abbreviations (PAC, HC, etc.). You will find this type of graph very useful to express the main formal characteristics of a piece, and to compare different pieces among themselves at a glance. The graph in example 11.5, for instance, tells us that Mozart's period is made up of two phrases related thematically, that the first phrase begins on I and ends on a HC (antecedent), and that the second phrase also begins on I but ends on a PAC (consequent). Hence, the two phrases constitute a parallel period. Note that in this type of form diagram we can clearly see the form-generating role of I and V as structural chords, as we discussed in chapter 2.

EXERCISE

To practice realizing form diagrams, refer to exercise 1 in worksheet 11 at the end of this chapter.

MORE ON PERIOD STRUCTURE

Contrasting Period

Unlike a parallel period, the two phrases in a **contrasting period** are not based on the same thematic material, as illustrated by anthology, no. 37 (Kuhlau, Sonatina, op. 55/4, II, mm. 1–8). The letters a and b in example 11.6 indicate that the two phrases in this fragment are not related thematically. Harmonically, this is still an antecedent-consequent structure because the first phrase ends on a HC and the second on a PAC. You may remark that the second phrase does not begin on the tonic, but rather on the dominant. The chord at m. 5, a V_7 in third inversion (V^4_2), prolongs the dominant harmony on which the first phrase ends. The complete second phrase may actually be seen as a dominant prolongation, which does not fully resolve until the final tonic.

Example 11.6 Form Diagram for Anthology, no. 37 (Kuhlau, Sonatina), mm. 1–8

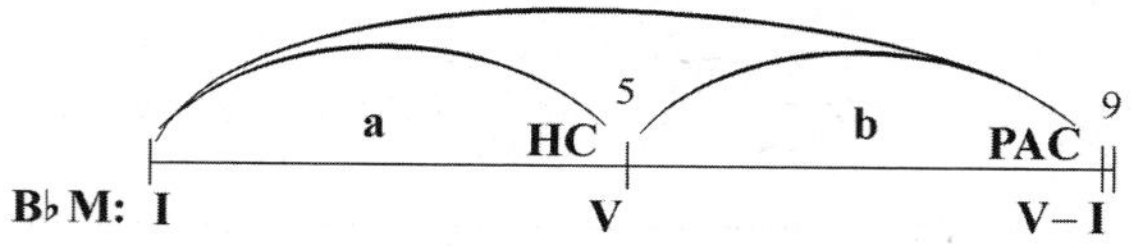

Example 11.7 W. A. Mozart, Sonata in FM, K. 332, I, mm. 1–12

Symmetrical and Asymmetrical Periods

In a **symmetrical period,** both phrases have the same length. Both examples 11.5 (Mozart, AM sonata) and 11.6 (Kuhlau, sonatina) represent symmetrical periods. Considering the number of measures in each of the phrases, we can describe both of these periods as having a 4 + 4 phrase structure. In an **asymmetrical period,** phrases are not of equal length. Example 11.7 illustrates a twelve-measure period, in which the two contrasting phrases (mm. 1–4 and 5–12) are, respectively, four and eight measures long (4 + 8).

Three-Phrase Period

Listen to anthology, no. 30 (Mozart, "Die Zufriedenheit"). The first phrase ends in m. 5, with an inconclusive cadence on D, V in GM. The second phrase ends again on a HC in m. 9. A third phrase finally brings the song to a conclusion, in m. 14, with a PAC on G. Because this final cadence is conclusive and the previous two are not, the three phrases constitute a period, in this case a **three-phrase period.** The diagram in example 11.8 shows the formal characteristics of this song. Because phrases 2 and 3 are related motivically (compare mm. 6–7 with mm. 10–11), we assign to them the letter symbols b_1 and b_2. The second phrase begins and ends on V, and thus we consider it a harmonic prolongation of the cadential V in m. 5.

EXERCISE

To practice writing a three-phrase period, refer to exercise 3 in worksheet 11 at the end of this chapter.

Example 11.8 Form Diagram for Anthology, no. 30 (Mozart, "Die Zufriedenheit")

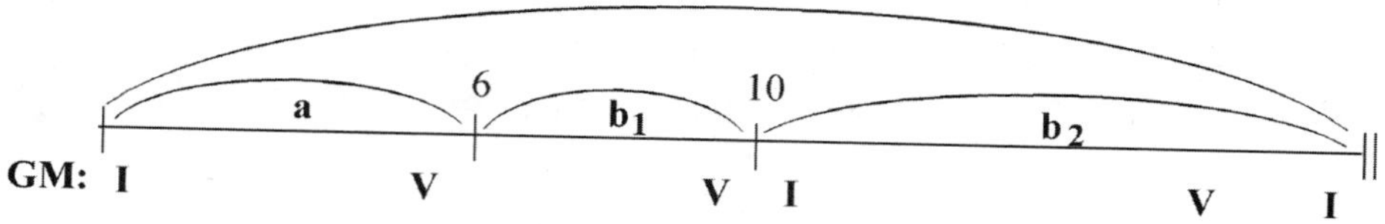

Double Period

Listen now to anthology, no. 33 (Beethoven, Sonata in Cm, op. 10/1, II, mm. 1–16), marking phrases and cadences on the score as you listen. You will hear and see that the complete passage forms a single period (the only PAC is at the end), and that it has four phrases, each four measures long. Moreover, you will hear that the four phrases are grouped in pairs. This type of four-phrase period with phrases grouped in pairs is called **double period.** The first part of such a period (which ends on a weak cadence) thus comprises two phrases. The second part consists of two more phrases and ends on a PAC. In anthology, no. 33, phrases 1 and 2 are contrasting (a_1 and b_1, mm. 1–4 and 5–8), and both end on HCs. Phrase 3 (a_2, mm. 9–12) is a varied repetition of the first phrase (the accompaniment changes), and phrase 4, b_2, is itself a variation of phrase 2, leading in this case to the conclusive PAC. Considering the two parts of the period (A_1 and A_2, mm. 1–8 and 9–16), this is an antecedent-consequent structure, as well as a parallel and symmetrical period. Study and understand the form diagram in example 11.9, and listen again to the fragment while following and "hearing" the diagram.

Modulating Period

Music does not always stay in the same key. The process of moving from one key to another is known as **modulation.** Examine the parallel period in example 11.10. The key signature and the beginning of the period establish the key of FM. The antecedent ends on a HC in FM (m. 4). The end of the consequent, however, features a PAC in CM (m. 8). Although the key signature is still FM because that is the main key of the

Example 11.9 Form Diagram for Anthology, no. 33 (Beethoven, Sonata op. 10/1)

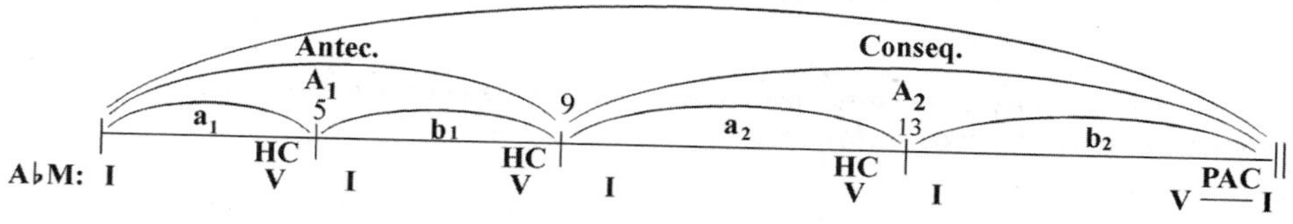

Example 11.10 S. Foster, "Jeanie with the Light Brown Hair" (Chorus)

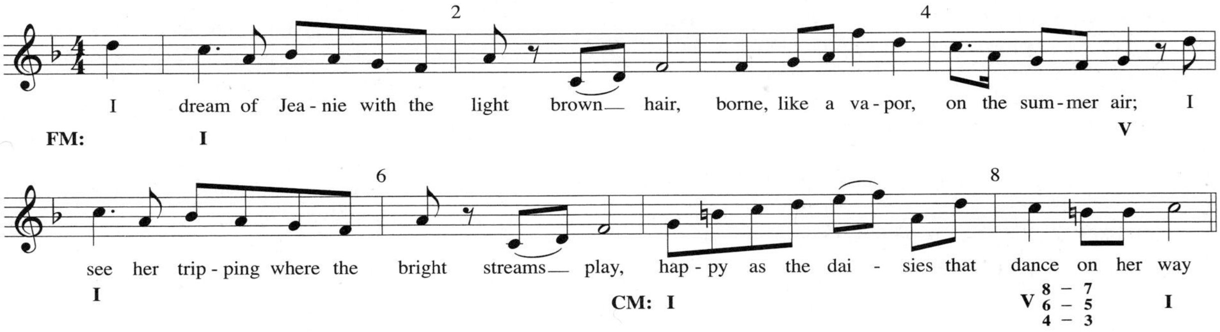
2
4
I dream of Jea - nie with the light brown— hair, borne, like a va - por, on the sum - mer air; I
FM: I
V
6
8
see her trip - ping where the bright streams— play, hap - py as the dai - sies that dance on her way
I
CM: I
V 8 6 4 – 7 5 3
I

complete song, by mm. 7–8 we have modulated to CM, as confirmed by the clear PAC in the new key. A period may indeed begin in a key, modulate to a different key, and end on a PAC *in the new key.* Such a period is a **modulating period.** Explain how this same process works in anthology, no. 24 (Mozart, Sonata in DM, K. 284, I, mm. 1–8) and in anthology, no. 12 (Bach, *French Suite* no. 5, "Gavotte," mm. 1–8).

EXERCISE

To practice analysis of a variety of period structures, refer to exercise 1 (questions 4 to 7) in worksheet 11 at the end of this chapter.

PHRASE GROUP

A group of two or more phrases that does not end on a PAC or a IAC is not a period. We refer to such a musical unit as a **phrase group.** Examine the two initial phrases in anthology, no. 57 (Hugo Wolf, "Das verlassene Mägdlein," mm. 5–12). The first phrase, in Am, closes on a HC, and so does the second phrase. Because both phrases end on half cadences and the unit does not end on a conclusive cadence, this is a phrase group and not a period.

FOR FURTHER STUDY

For additional chapter 11 materials, refer to the *Harmony in Context* Web page at www.mhhe.com/roigfrancoli2e.

ASSIGNMENT

For an analytical assignment based on the materials learned in this chapter, and for a variety of writing assignments, refer to chapter 11 in the workbook.

PRACTICAL APPLICATION AND DISCUSSION

1. The types of structures we have discussed in this chapter are best found in compositions of the Classical period (by composers such as Haydn, Mozart, Beethoven, and their contemporaries, and also by nineteenth-century composers such as Schubert, Mendelssohn, and Chopin) and in dance pieces by late-baroque composers (such as minuets, bourrées, gavottes, etc., by Bach, Handel, and many others). Try to find, in the pieces you perform (by these or any other composers), examples of some of the following items: a phrase (or larger unit) based on a motive, two phrases connected by an elision, a parallel period, an antecedent-consequent structure, a three-phrase period, a double period, a modulating period, and a phrase group. You will probably not find examples of all these in the pieces you play, but try to find as many as you can, and bring your findings to class for possible class discussion.
2. How does your understanding of cadences, phrase and period structure, and types of periods affect your appreciation of the music you listen to and perform? Why is the understanding of form and long-range tonal relationships among formal units important for a musician? Apply this discussion to one of the examples from the anthology you have analyzed in this chapter (such as the fragments from Mozart's AM sonata, I; Mozart's CM sonata, III; or Beethoven's Cm sonata, op. 10/1, II). How does the knowledge of form and tonal relationships affect the way you hear and would perform any of these examples?

Terms for Review

Form
Motive
Rhythmic motive
Phrase
Implied harmony
Melodic cadential patterns
Phrase segment, subphrase
Sentence structure
Elision
Period
Antecedent
Consequent
Parallel period
Form diagram
Line (bubble) diagram
Contrasting period
Symmetrical period
Asymmetrical period
Three-phrase period
Double period
Modulation
Modulating period
Phrase group

Worksheet 11

EXERCISE 1 Analysis. Study the phrase/period structure of the following examples. For each of the examples, provide a brief discussion of structure, including at least the following information:

1. Is the fragment based on a motive?
2. How many phrases are there? Provide measure numbers and phrase numbers for each. Are any phrases connected by elision?
3. Identify the cadences at the end of each phrase. In cases where only a melody is given, you can identify cadences on the basis of the given Roman numerals and the cadential melodic gestures.
4. Is there any antecedent-consequent phrase structure?
5. What kind of a period is this? One or several of the following may apply to each example: parallel, contrasting, symmetrical, asymmetrical, three-phrase (or four-phrase), double, modulating, phrase group (not a period).
6. Provide a line (bubble) diagram for each of the examples, indicating the following items: phrases/measure numbers; phrase relationship with letters; cadences at the end of each phrase (with a cadence-type abbreviation); and long-range harmonic motion from beginning to end of each phrase.

Examples for Analysis

1. Example 11.11. (Do not count phrase repetitions as independent phrases in this example.)

Example 11.11 J. Haydn, String Quartet, op. 76/3, II

Discussion:

Form diagram:

---

2. Example 11.12.

Example 11.12 Amy Beach, "Oh Were My Love Yon Lilac Fair!" from *Twenty-Three Songs,* op. 43, no. 3, mm. 3–10

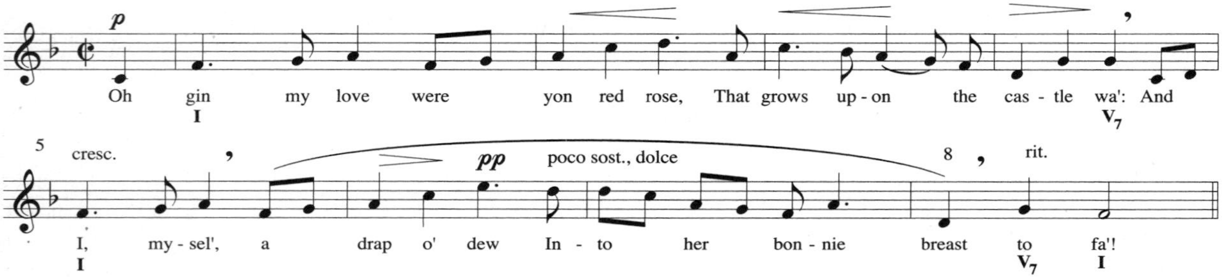

Discussion:

Form diagram:

---

3. Example 11.13.

Example 11.13 Manuel de Falla, *The Three-Cornered Hat,* "The Neighbor's Dance," mm. 1–16

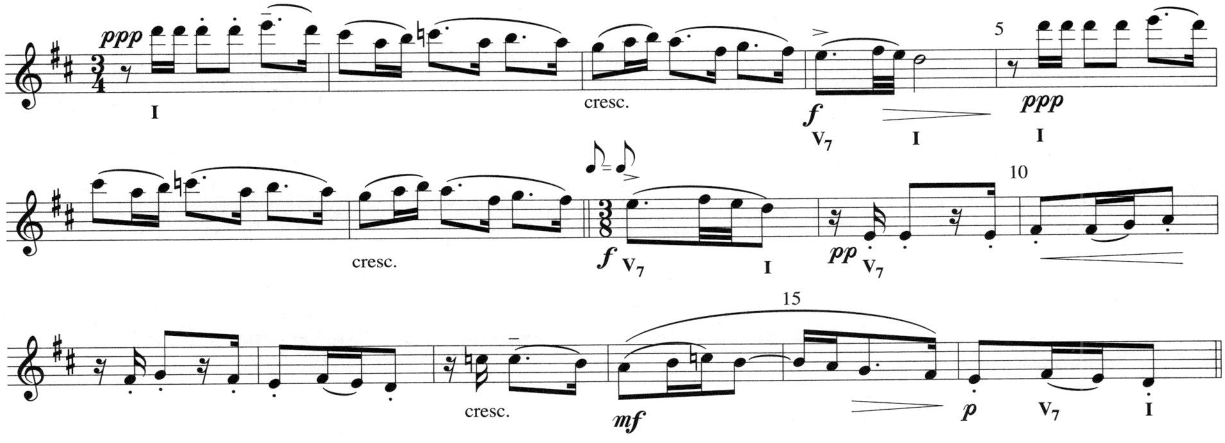

Discussion:

Form diagram:

4. Anthology, no. 31 (Paradis, *Sicilienne,* mm. 1–10)

Discussion:

Form diagram:

5. Example 11.14.

Example 11.14 Chevalier de Saint–Georges, Symphonie Concertante in AM, op. 10, no. 2, I, mm. 1–16

Discussion:

Form diagram:

6. Anthology, no. 23 (Chevalier de Saint–Georges, Symphonie Concertante, II)

Discussion:

Form diagram:

EXERCISE 2 Write a melody in antecedent-consequent form (a parallel period). The beginning is given. Be ready to sing or play your melody if asked by your instructor.

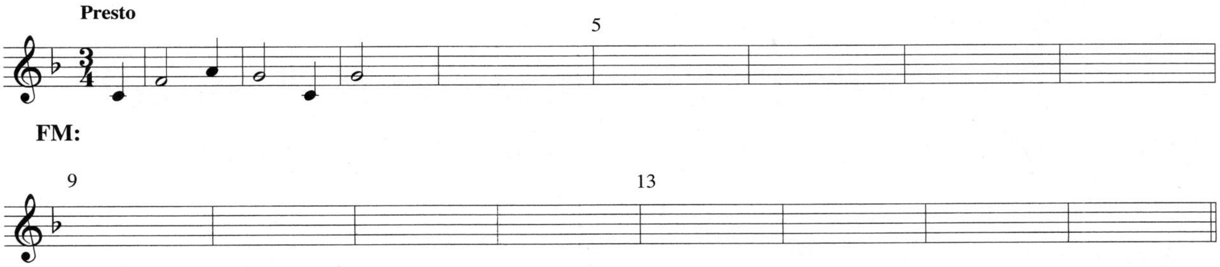

EXERCISE 3 Write a melody with the following characteristics: a three-phrase period, form a–b–a or a_1–b–a_2, twelve measures long. Make it musical, and be able to sing or play it. Indicate (with cadence-type abbreviations) what cadences are implied at the end of each phrase.

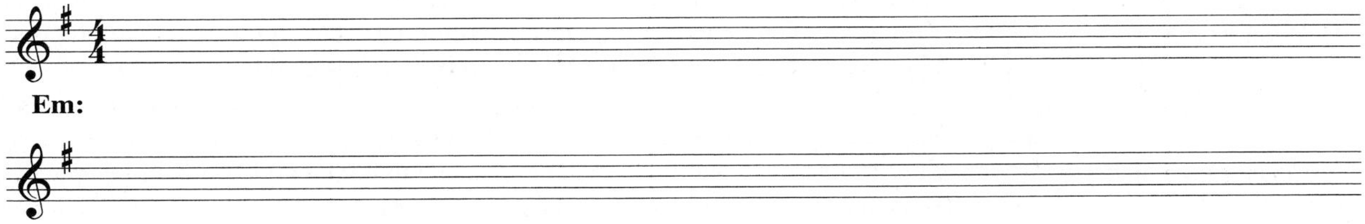

Chapter 12

Melodic Organization II: Thematic Development; Phrase Extension

Along with harmonic development, melodic or thematic development is one of the basic forces of musical growth. The term **thematic development** refers to the musical process by which melodic material is derived from a previously presented theme or melody, or to the process of musical growth by which themes or melodies generate extended sections. Such musical growth is effected by means of a variety of developmental techniques. Thematic development is both a melodic and a harmonic process, and both processes interact and influence each other. In this chapter we will first focus specifically on some of the standard techniques of melodic development. The techniques we will examine may be found even within the scope of a period (for instance, when the two phrases in a parallel period are related but not identical) or within a phrase (when, for instance, the phrase is derived from a single motive). After studying melodic developmental techniques, we will focus on *phrase extension*. Phrases can be expanded in a variety of ways, often using the same means of melodic development we will discuss in the first part of the chapter.

MELODIC DEVELOPMENTAL TECHNIQUES

Compositions or movements usually begin with one or more sections in which the musical materials on which the piece is based are presented. Later sections in the piece, however, often have the function of developing the material that was presented earlier. At times, the new material presented at the beginning is very brief, perhaps just a short motive (what Beethoven symphony is based on a very brief and well-known motive presented at the very outset?), and even the initial section is based on the immediate development of that motive. We will now examine some of the most common techniques of melodic and motivic development.

Repetition and Transposition

The **repetition** of a motive or a phrase is a basic means of formal growth. Repetition implies restatement of a segment at exactly the same tonal level. Examine example 12.1a

Example 12.1a J. S. Bach, Brandenburg Concerto no. 2, I, mm. 1–5

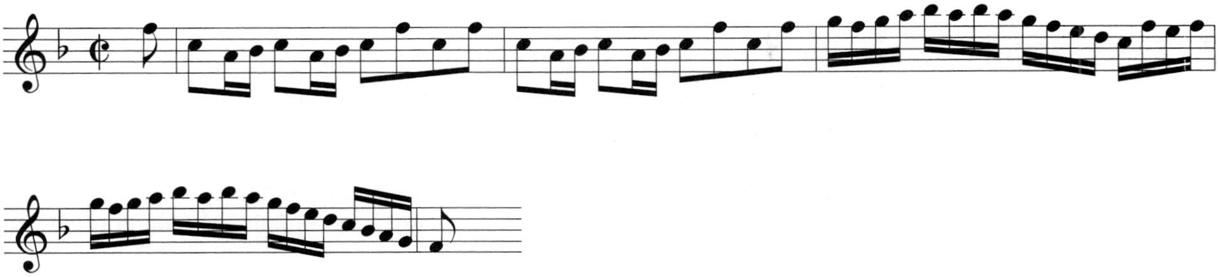

Example 12.1b J. S. Bach, Invention no. 1 in CM, mm. 1–2

Example 12.1c F. Chopin, Mazurka no. 45 in Am, op. posth. 67, no. 4, mm. 1–8

Example 12.1d Nikolay Rimsky-Korsakov, *Scheherazade,* III, mm. 1–4

and identify several instances of repetition of a motive or a melodic segment, in this case all within a single phrase. A repetition stated at a different tonal level than the original segment is a transposed repetition, or a **transposition.** In example 12.1b, the motive that begins Bach's Invention in CM is first stated at the level of the tonic (m. 1) and then repeated a 5th higher, at the level of the dominant. In chapter 11 we studied the sentence, a type of phrase structure that includes repetition or transposition (of the intial segment) as a means of formal growth. Example 12.1c shows a sentence by Chopin, in which the first phrase segment (mm. 1–2) is repeated a 3rd lower in mm. 3–4.

Variation

Repetition may be literal, as in example 12.1a, or varied. In a *varied repetition* (or **variation**) the basic frame of the melody is preserved, but the original motive or phrase is now altered in some way (embellished with added notes or figuration, simplified, rhythmically altered, etc.). An example of varied repetition by Nikolay Rimsky-Korsakov appears in example 12.1d. Circle, in m. 3 (the varied repetition of m. 1), the notes from the original statement in m. 1.

Melodic Sequence

In a **melodic sequence**, several immediate restatements of a melodic *segment* occur at a lower or higher tonal level. A melodic sequence thus involves transposition of a melodic segment several times in a row, in a pattern of transpositions that rises or falls by intervals of the same size (often, but not necessarily, by steps). Notice that in a sequence the restatement takes place *in the same voice,* as opposed to imitation, where a theme is restated in a different voice. The melody by George Gerswhin reproduced in example 12.2a includes a three-measure sequence descending by steps (each sequence segment, marked with brackets on the example, is a step lower than the previous segment).

Tonal and Real Sequences

In example 12.2a, the sequence goes down by steps following the diatonic scale of CM, which means that the exact relationships of steps and half steps between segments are not preserved. This type of sequence is called a **tonal sequence.** Look now at anthology, no. 24 (Mozart, Sonata in DM), m. 9, a two-segment sequence. Because some of the pitches have been altered, the first and second segments feature exactly the same intervallic relationships. This is a **real sequence,** in which the exact intervallic relationships are preserved. To clarify these concepts, compare the two sequences in example 12.2b. In the first one, a tonal sequence, we preserve the diatonic scale of Am, and hence the exact intervals are not preserved. In the second one, a real sequence, the exact intervals are preserved, and as a result of the necessary chromaticism, we soon get away from the diatonic Am scale.

Modified Sequence

A sequence in which the restatement of the segment is not literal, not because of the normal step and half-step diatonic relationships, but because some variation has been introduced, is called a **modified sequence.** Some intervals, for instance, may have been expanded or contracted (see "Intervallic Expansion and Contraction," on page 295). In anthology, no. 20 (Haydn, Sonata in DM), mm. 1–2 present an example of modified sequence: The 5th D-A in m. 1 turns into a°7, C♯-B♭, in m. 2.

Example 12.2a Ira Gershwin–George Gershwin, "Someone to Watch Over Me," from *Oh, Kay!*

There's a some - bo - dy I'm long - ing to see I hope that he turns out to be some - one to
watch o - ver me.

Example 12.2b

Tonal
Real

Change of Mode

The theme of Vivaldi's "Spring" (from *The Four Seasons*), III, as shown in example 12.3, mm. 58–61, is in EM. In m. 61, however, Vivaldi begins a sequence on this theme by stating the first sequence segment (derived from the theme) in Em rather than EM. Besides featuring repetition and descending sequence by steps, this example is thus also an illustration of **change of mode** as a technique of melodic development. In change of mode the key remains the same, but the mode changes from major to minor, or vice versa.

Fragmentation

Melodic development is often based on a fragment of the original theme rather than the complete unit. Such technique is known as **fragmentation.** The fragment may be repeated, presented as a sequence, or subjected to any other kind of developmental transformation. Example 12.4 illustrates Beethoven's use of fragmentation in his Symphony

Example 12.3 A. Vivaldi, *The Four Seasons,* "Spring," III, mm. 58–64

Example 12.4 From L. v. Beethoven, Symphony no. 6, I

no. 6 in FM, I. Example 12.4a presents the first theme of the movement. The theme begins with two characteristic motives, labeled "a" and "b" in example 12.4a. The initial motive of the theme (motive "a") is treated sequentially in example 12.4b,whereas motive "b" generates the repeated figure represented in example 12.4c. A similar instance of combined fragmentation and sequence appears in example 12.5 (Beethoven, Symphony no. 7 in AM, I). The phrase in example 12.5a (part of the first theme) includes the motive labeled "a" in the example. This motive later generates the sequence reproduced in example 12.5b. Taking into consideration the accidentals in example 12.5b, what other type of developmental technique is used in this passage?

Example 12.5 From L. v. Beethoven, Symphony no. 7, I

Example 12.6a

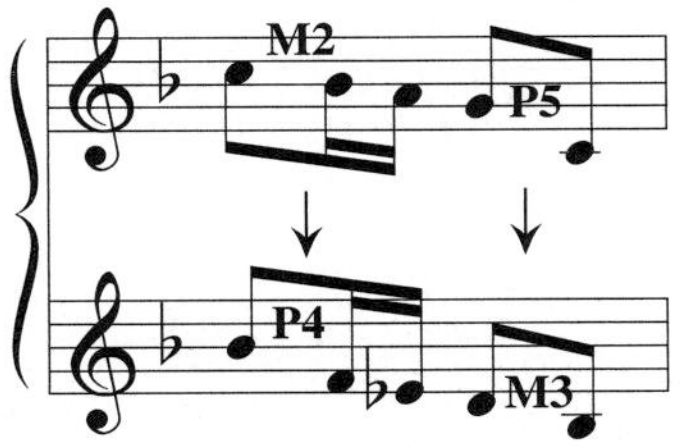

Example 12.6b Marianne Martínez, Sonata in AM, mm. 4–5

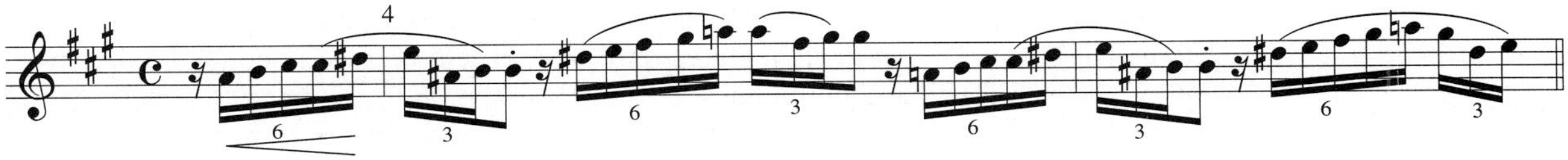

Intervallic Expansion and Contraction

Although example 12.4c is clearly derived from m. 2 in example 12.4a, you may have observed that the intervals are not at all the same. In thematic development, motives are at times immediately recognizable by their characteristic contour and rhythm, although some intervals may have been replaced by other larger or smaller intervals, in what we call **intervallic expansion** or **contraction.** Example 12.6a shows how the first interval in Beethoven's motive has been expanded from a M2 to a P4 and the last interval has been contracted from a P5 to a M3. Are there any examples of intervallic expansion or contraction in example 12.5b? The passage in example 12.6b is highly motivic, and it includes several cases of intervallic expansion or contraction. Explain what the exact transformation is in each case.

Inversion

An **inversion** is a mirror image of a melody. In an inversion the contour of the melody and the direction of intervals are reversed: ascending motion becomes descending, and vice versa. In Bach's Fugue in D♯m (*Well-Tempered Clavier,* I, no. 8), some statements of the subject (the main theme of a fugue) are presented in inversion. Compare the original form and its inversion, reproduced in example 12.7. Compare also the two phrases in the opening period of Mozart's Sonata in DM, K. 284, I (anthology, no. 24, mm. 1–8). The eighth-note figure in the second half of m. 5 and first half of m. 6 is an inversion of the equivalent figure in mm. 1–2. Inversion can thus also be used as a variation device between two parallel phrases.

Example 12.7 J. S. Bach, *The Well-Tempered Clavier,* I, Fugue no. 8 in D♯m, Subject

Melodic Retrograde

Whereas inversion involves reading a melody upside down, to **retrograde** a melody is to read it backward. Although melodic retrograde is seldom used in homophonic music, it is a device found in contrapuntal music. Example 12.8 is a two-voice **retrograde canon** by Bach. A **canon** is a "rule" by which a voice is derived from another voice (a **round** is a type of perpetual canon, in which several voices sing the same melody but

Example 12.8 J. S. Bach, *A Musical Offering* (Retrograde Canon)

Example 12.9

a.

b. Augmentation

each voice comes in when the previous voice reaches a certain point). Bach's original score provides only the top voice. The bottom voice is derived from the top by a canon (rule) which can be very simply expressed. Find the canon in this composition, and discuss in class why this is called a retrograde canon (or, also, a crab canon).

Augmentation

Augmentation and its equivalent, *diminution,* are examples of rhythmic transformations of motives or themes. Augmentation is the statement of a theme in proportionally longer rhythmic values. Most often, rhythmic values are doubled, tripled, or quadrupled. In the same fugue by Bach that we mentioned in example 12.7 (Fugue in D♯m), the subject is also presented in augmentation, with doubled values. Example 12.9 compares the original statement of the theme with its augmented version.

Diminution

The opposite process to augmentation, **diminution,** is the statement of a theme in proportionally shorter rhythmic values. Example 12.10 reproduces two instances of diminution from Beethoven's Symphony no. 3 in E♭M (*Eroica*), IV. In example 12.10a, one of the two main themes in the movement is first stated in its original form, and toward the end of the movement it appears in diminution. Example 12.10b reproduces a fragment by the second violins in which a three-note figure is stated four times in descending sequence, twice in original values, twice more in diminution.

EXERCISES

To practice the analysis and recognition of various techniques of melodic development, refer to exercise 1 (items 1 to 9) in worksheet 12 at the end of this chapter.

To practice writing various techniques of melodic transformation, refer to exercise 2 in worksheet 12 at the end of this chapter.

Example 12.10 From L. v. Beethoven, Symphony no. 3, IV

a.

b.

PHRASE EXTENSION

In chapter 11 we studied a variety of phrase and period structures. A phrase can be lengthened by adding a melodic fragment to it, and developmental techniques such as the ones we studied previously are often used in the process. A transformation that adds length to a phrase is called a **phrase extension.** Repetition, variation, and sequence are some techniques frequently found in phrase extensions. An extension may take place at the beginning of a phrase (*initial extension*), within a phrase (*internal extension* or *interpolation*), or at the end of a phrase (*cadential extension*). We will now study some specific examples of each of these three types of extension.

Initial Extension

A melodic unit may be lengthened by adding notes to its beginning, in what we call **initial extension.** The theme from Bach's Invention no. 3 in DM appears in example 12.11a. In later statements, this theme includes an initial extension, which lengthens its anacrusic (or pickup) segment (example 12.11b).

Initial extensions are not always melodic. Opening phrases, especially in songs, are often preceded by an introductory accompanimental figure that functions as a harmonic

Example 12.11 J. S. Bach, Invention no. 3 in DM, Theme

a. b.

prefix. Examples of this type of initial extension can be found in anthology, no. 42 (Schubert, "Auf dem Flusse") and no. 48 (Schumann, "Widmung").

Cadential Extension

Refer back to example 10.1, the closing passage for the first movement of a Haydn sonata. You will see that mm. 95–97 are made up of a series of cadential gestures. The cadence in m. 95 is a perfect authentic cadence (PAC), and it could have been the concluding cadence of the movement had Haydn wanted to stop there. Instead, he wrote four additional PACs, further strengthening the sense of final closure. The four additional cadences in mm. 95–97 are a **cadential extension** because their function is to expand the PAC cadence in m. 95. A cadential extension is a fragment added at the end of a musical unit, usually after the cadence. It may take the form, as in the Haydn example, of a few reiterations of the V–I cadence, as if to confirm that this is indeed the final cadence; it may also be a slightly longer addition (often called a **codetta**), including some thematic material; or it may be an extended section, sometimes of substantial length, at the end of a movement. We call the latter case a **coda.**

A common type of cadential extension by means of a deceptive resolution of V is illustrated by example 12.12. Instead of resolving the V_7 directly to I in a PAC, which could have ended the phrase in m. 2 of our example, Lennon and McCartney extended the phrase for three more measures by means of a deceptive resolution of V_7. (Notice that the specific type of deceptive cadence in this example involves an inverted seventh chord on ♭VI, the chromatic submediant, as indicated by the Roman numeral $\flat VI^6_5$, rather than the simpler type of resolution to the diatonic submediant, vi. ♭VI is a chromatic chord that we will study in chapter 23.)

Example 12.12 J. Lennon–P. McCartney, "I Will," from the Album *The Beatles* ("The White Album")

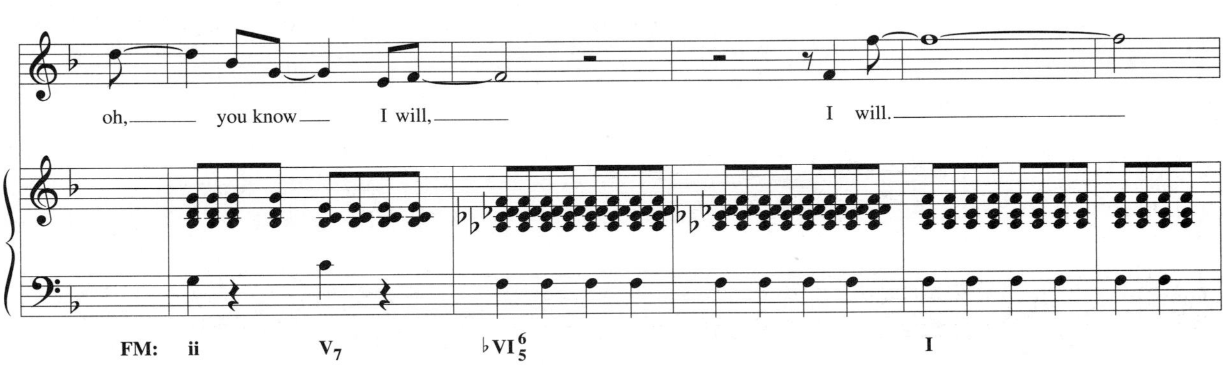

Example 12.13a L. v. Beethoven, Symphony no. 5 in Cm, op. 67, III, mm. 1–18 (violin 1 and cello parts)

Example 12.13b W. A. Mozart, Piano Sonata in CM, K. 279, III, mm. 1–10

PRACTICAL APPLICATION AND DISCUSSION

1. Find examples of thematic development in at least one of the compositions you play. Identify any of the developmental techniques you have just learned.
2. Comment on your findings in class, and discuss whether this chapter has helped you discover something interesting you did not know about the music you perform.

Internal Extension: Interpolation

An **interpolation** is an internal addition to a phrase. The clearest type of interpolation occurs when a phrase that has been previously stated is stated again, and this second statement includes material that has clearly been added to the original version. This is the case of example 12.13a. The opening phrase of Beethoven's Symphony no. 5, III, closes with a fermata in m. 8. The phrase is immediately repeated, but this time it closes with a fermata in m. 18. The second phrase, then, is ten measures long instead of the initial eight. The two added measures, bracketed in the example, constitute a clear interpolation.

Internal extensions provide a rich resource for a composer to vary and extend musical materials in unexpected ways, and to break the predictable balance of parallel periods and equal phrase lengths. In example 12.13b, for instance, a period by Mozart begins with a four-measure antecedent made up of two phrase segments (2 + 2 measures) and closing on the HC in m. 4. By analogy, we could expect the characteristic four-measure consequent of a parallel period, closing in m. 8 with a PAC. The PAC comes indeed, but in m. 10, not m. 8 as expected, because of the interpolation of two measures, mm. 7–8, bracketed in our example. If you play the consequent skipping from m. 6 to m. 9, you will hear the phrase as it would have been without the interpolation. Much more predictable and also less interesting, to be sure. Looking at the interpolation itself, what developmental technique does Mozart use in these two measures?

EXERCISE

To practice the analysis of various techniques of phrase extension, refer to exercise 1 (items 9 and 10) in worksheet 12 at the end of this chapter.

FOR FURTHER STUDY

For additional chapter 12 materials, refer to the *Harmony in Context* Web page at www.mhhe.com/roigfrancoli2e.

ASSIGNMENT

For an analytical and compositional assignment based on the materials learned in this chapter, refer to chapter 12 in the workbook.

Terms for Review

Thematic development
Repetition
Transposition
Variation
Melodic sequence
Tonal sequence
Real sequence
Modified sequence
Change of mode
Fragmentation

Intervallic expansion
Intervallic contraction
Inversion
Retrograde
Retrograde (crab) canon
Round
Augmentation
Diminution
Phrase extension
Initial extension
Cadential extension
Codetta
Coda
Internal extension (interpolation)

Worksheet 12

EXERCISE 1 Analysis. Identify and name the technique(s) of thematic development or phrase extension in the following examples. In the case of sequences, identify the exact type.

1. Anthology, no. 26 (Mozart, Sonata in CM, III), mm. 5–7.

2. Anthology, no. 32 (Beethoven, op. 2, no. 1, I):

   mm. 56–59:

   mm. 61–62:

   mm. 95–100 (compare to mm.1–2):

3. Example 12.14. How is fragment b related to fragment a?

Example 12.14 J. S. Bach, *The Well-Tempered Clavier,* II, Fugue no. 2 in Cm

a.

b.

4. Example 12.15. How is fragment b related to fragment a?

Example 12.15 J. S. Bach, *The Well-Tempered Clavier,* II, Fugue no. 3 in C♯M

a.

b.

5. Example 12.16. How is fragment b related to fragment a?

Example 12.16 J. S. Bach, *The Art of Fugue*

a.

b.

6. Example 12.17. Fragment b is a variation on fragment a. What technique(s) of thematic development can you identify?

Example 12.17 Sergei Rachmaninoff, *Rhapsody on a Theme of Paganini,* op. 43

a. **Allegro vivace**

b. **Andante cantabile**

7. Example 12.18.

Example 12.18 F. Chopin, Étude in E♭m, op. 10, no. 6, mm. 29–32

8. Example 12.19.

Example 12.19 W. A. Mozart, Symphony no. 40 in Gm, I, mm. 20–28

9. In anthology, no. 26 (Mozart, Sonata in CM, III), the antecedent has eight measures (mm. 1–8), and the consequent has eleven (mm. 9–19). Why? What is the formal role of mm. 16–18?

10. Refer to anthology, no. 31 (Paradis, *Sicilienne*).
    a) Phrase 1 (mm. 1–4) is four measures long; phrase 2 (mm. 5–10) is six measures long. A possible phrase proportion for this period would be 4 + 5 instead of 4 + 6. What measure has been clearly interpolated?
    b) How is the interpolated measure related with the previous one?
    c) What technique of formal growth is used in mm. 11–14?
    d) And in mm. 15–16?
    e) How is m. 17 related to the previous two?

f) Could the cadence at m. 23 have taken place in m. 21?

What is the formal function of mm. 21–22?

By what means is this function effected (that is, how are mm. 21–22 related to mm. 19–20)?

g) Could the cadence at m. 28 have taken place in m. 27?

What is the formal function of m. 27?

How is m. 27 related to m. 28?

EXERCISE 2 Write new versions of the following melodies using the devices specified in each case.

a. Bach, *The Art of Fugue*. Inversion.

b. Bach, *The Well-Tempered Clavier* II, Fugue no. 22 in B♭m. Inversion.

c. Bach, *The Art of Fugue*. Diminution.

d. Bach, *The Art of Fugue*. Inversion, augmentation.

e. Luther, "Ein feste Burg." Retrograde.

f. Mozart, Symphony no. 39 in E♭M, IV. Descending sequence on the given segment: Write three missing segments, and end on $\hat{1}$ in Cm.

a.

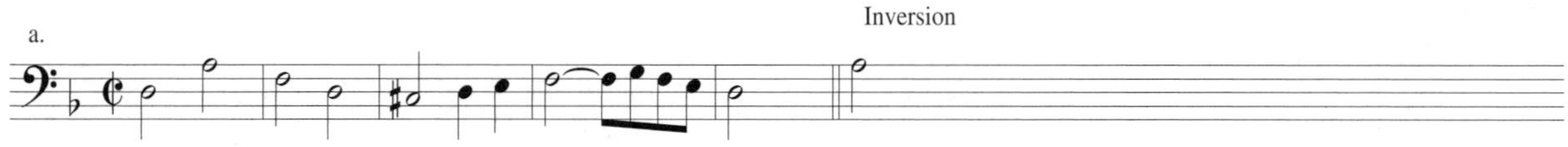

b.

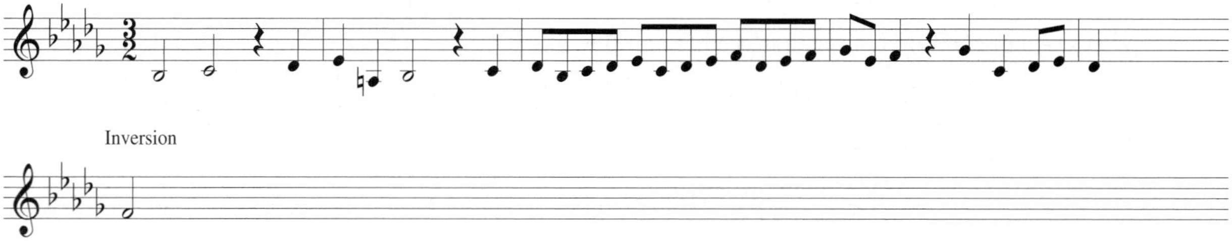

c.

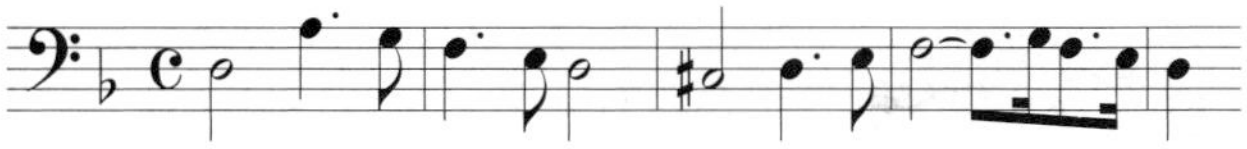

Diminution

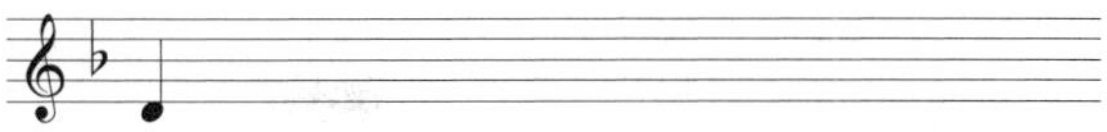

d.

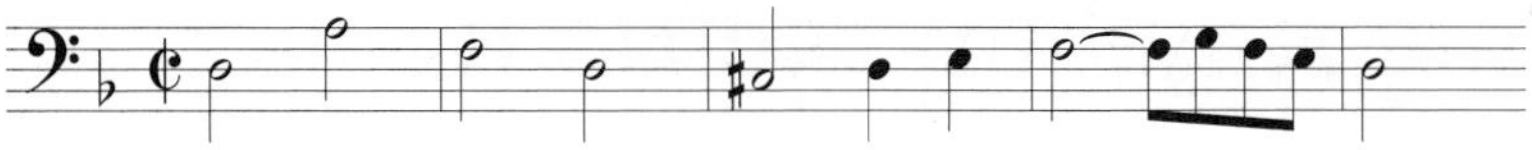

Inversion, augmentation

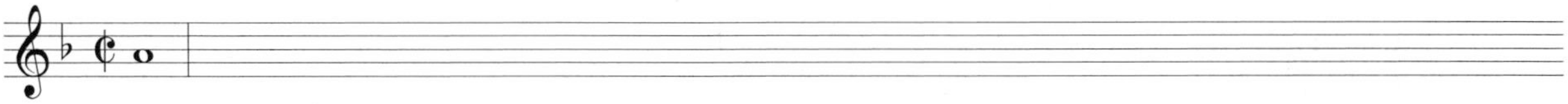

e.

Retrograde

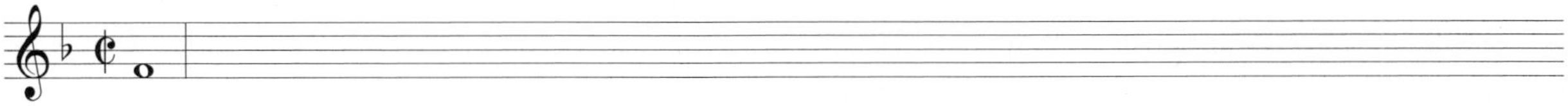

f.

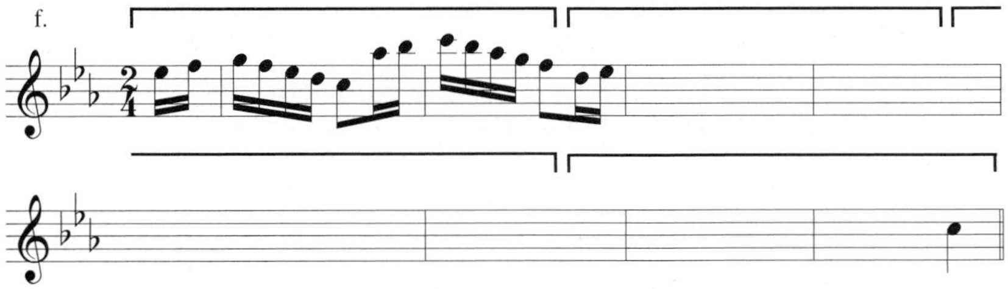

EXERCISE 3

1. Complete the following parallel period from Mozart's Symphony no. 39 in E♭M with a consequent. How was the sequence segment in exercise 2f derived from this theme?

Chapter 13

Harmonic Rhythm; Metric Reduction

In this chapter we will study some of the interactions between harmony, rhythm, and meter. Harmonic progressions do not occur in isolation. Rather, they form harmonic phrases that are usually part of a melodic/harmonic complex appearing in a rhythmic and metric context. Although the possible interrelations between harmony and the temporal aspects of music (rhythm, meter, and tempo) are endless, and good composers often surprise us with unexpected possibilities, we will examine some standard relationships commonly found in Western tonal art music. We will also learn the technique of metric reduction that will allow us to simplify complex harmonic textures. We will study compound melody, a type of melody that can be better understood with the help of metric reduction, and we will learn how to write good harmonic progressions in a metric context. All of this will enhance our understanding of harmony within its musical and temporal context.

HARMONIC RHYTHM

While listening to a recording of anthology, no. 52 (Verdi, "Libiamo ne'lieti calici," from *La traviata*), consider these questions: How many different chords are there in the complete excerpt? How often do chords change? We will refer to the rate of chord change with the term **harmonic rhythm** (HR). The harmonic rhythm in anthology, no. 52 is certainly very slow: Only four chord changes occur in twenty-one measures (using only two different chords), and the first chord does not change for eight measures. A diagram for the harmonic rhythm of this excerpt appears in example 13.1.

Now examine example 13.2a, the first period of Verdi's famous aria, "Sempre libera" (also from *La traviata*). Although the harmonic rhythm may still be considered slow, it is not quite as slow as in the previous example. The rate of change here is one chord per measure, except in mm. 12–13. Because m. 12 ends a phrase and m. 13 begins the next phrase, however, we do not really hear these two measures as being one single harmonic unit. Example 13.2b represents graphically the harmonic rhythm of this passage.

Example 13.1

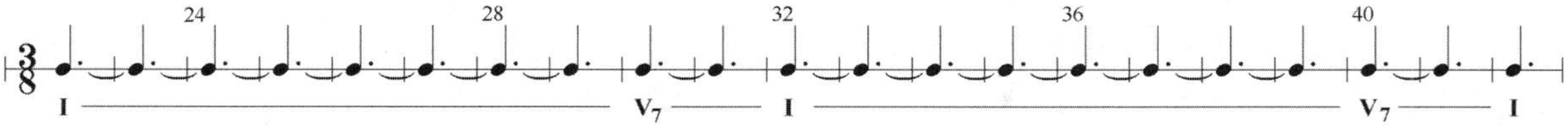

Example 13.2a G. Verdi, *La traviata*, "Sempre libera," mm. 8–16

Example 13.2b

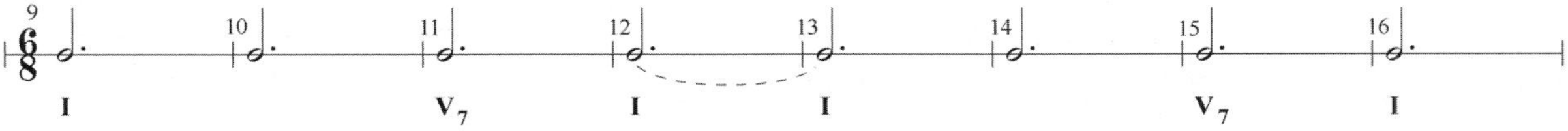

The harmonic rhythm in example 13.3a, on the other hand, is quite different from what we have seen in the two preceding examples. Throughout most of this excerpt, chords change every beat, producing a fast harmonic rhythm as indicated by the diagram in example 13.3b. Chorale harmonizations usually feature this same type of fast harmonic rhythm (a chord per beat).

Example 13.3a Josephine Lang, "Gott sei mir Sünder gnädig," mm. 5–10

Example 13.3b

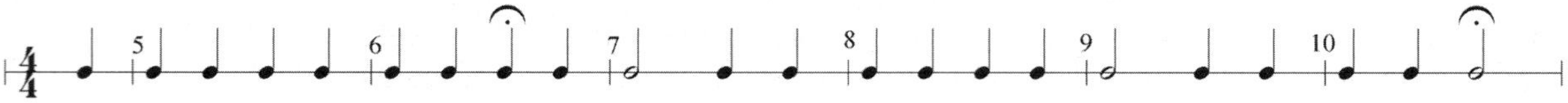

Notice that the terms *slow* and *fast* as applied to harmonic rhythm have nothing to do with how slow or fast the tempo of the music is. They refer to the rate of chordal change, and in this context *slow* means "not very often," whereas *fast* means "often or very often." We can also say that in a slow harmonic rhythm, chords usually (and approximately) change every measure or even less often, whereas in fast harmonic rhythms they change every beat or even more often, with numerous possible gradations in between. We discuss possible interactions between harmonic rhythm and tempo in the next section.

Harmonic Rhythm and Tempo

One may find fast or slow harmonic rhythms in a variety of contexts. In general, a fast harmonic rhythm creates a sense of harmonic activity that may enliven and add motion to the music, whereas a slow harmonic rhythm may produce a more static effect. Although no preestablished relationship exists between harmonic rhythm and tempo, faster tempos often feature slower harmonic rhythms (see example 13.2, and anthology, no. 52, Verdi, "Libiamo"), and slow tempos may display faster harmonic rhythms (see, for instance, anthology, no. 33, Beethoven, Sonata op. 10, no. 1, and anthology, no. 50, Schumann, "Folk Song"). A fast harmonic rhythm in a fast tempo may produce a blurred or crowded effect, whereas a slow harmonic rhythm in a slow tempo may result in a static musical passage.

Irregular Harmonic Rhythm

In examples 13.2 and 3, the rate of chord changes is quite regular (every measure, every beat). These are cases of **regular harmonic rhythm.** Harmonic rhythm is not always regular, though. Changes in harmonic rhythm are an element of musical variety, and they may be used to prevent predictability. Different sections in a composition often feature contrasting harmonic rhythms. Moreover, the harmonic rhythm may change within one single section.

Listen to the opening twenty-three measures of Mozart's *Jupiter* Symphony. As you listen, mark the chord changes on the keyboard reduction provided in example 13.4a. Then compare your notes with the diagram in 13.4b. This is an example of **irregular harmonic rhythm.** Comment on the different sections of the passage, and how the harmonic rhythm functions in each of them. The upper line of Roman numerals under the diagram indicates the rhythm of the basic tonic and dominant functions on which the excerpt is built at the surface level (other chords are not indicated by these Roman numerals). What kind of cadence does the passage end on? What happens to the harmonic rhythm, as we approach the cadence, in mm. 19–21? The *acceleration of harmonic rhythm* is a device often used by composers to create a *drive toward a cadence,* thus stressing the function of the cadence as a harmonic goal.

Levels of Harmonic Rhythm

Listen to the Mozart fragment again, listening to the harmonic rhythm indicated by the lower line of Roman numerals in example 13.4b. You are now hearing a deeper level of harmonic rhythm, one determined by the structural chords that are being prolonged

Example 13.4a W. A. Mozart, Symphony no. 41, K. 551, *Jupiter*, I, mm. 1–23 (Piano Reduction)

Example 13.4b

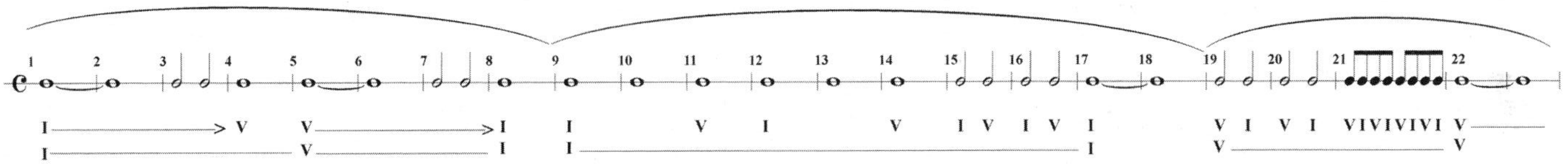

Example 13.5

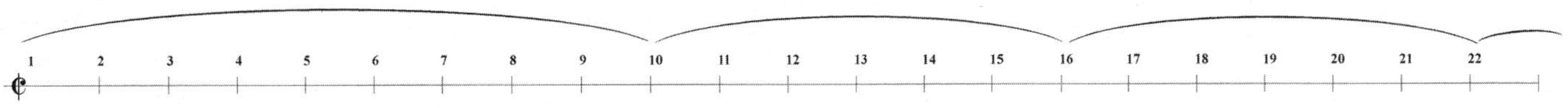

rather than by each particular chordal change at the surface level. At this deeper level of harmonic activity, we first hear a motion from I to V and back to I (mm. 1–8); then we hear an area in which I is prolonged (mm. 9–18), and finally a prolongation of V leads to the half cadence (mm. 19–23). At this level, the tonic harmony in mm. 9–18 is prolonged by several linear chords (functioning as passing and neighbor chords) over a tonic pedal, and the "tonic" chords in mm. 19–23 also have the function of embellishing the underlying dominant harmony by linear means (as neighbor chords). In other words, the diagram shows that we can hear **harmonic rhythm at various levels.** *At the surface level, the harmonic rhythm is often bound to melodic and rhythmic activity, whereas at the next deeper level it is associated with such formal factors as phrase and period structure.*

As an aural exercise, listen to the opening twenty-two measures of Mozart's Symphony no. 40 in G minor, K. 550. On the diagram provided in example 13.5, notate the harmonic rhythm of the passage (by ear) and also the long-range harmonic motion. Then discuss what you have heard in class. The slurs over the diagram should help you listen to this fragment and also determine its long-range harmonic motion.

EXERCISE

To practice analysis of harmonic rhythm, refer to exercises 1.1 and 1.2 in worksheet 13 at the end of this chapter.

METRIC REDUCTION

Musical textures are embellished with a variety of rhythmic figurations. Their underlying harmonic content is also often elaborated by means of nonchord tones, instrumental arpeggiation of chords, etc. It is useful, both for purposes of analysis and performance, to be able to simplify a more or less complex texture through some process of reduction. In this section we will learn about **metric reduction,** a process through which a musical texture is simplified to its *basic harmonic and melodic structure*. The essential process of reduction consists of removing NCTs and condensing arpeggiated chordal patterns into block chords. We refer to such harmonic reduction as metric reduction because the placement and duration of harmonies within the metric structure are preserved. Metric reduction has direct practical applications, such as helping a performer understand the underlying melodic and harmonic framework of a texturally complex passage and hence make decisions regarding grouping and phrasing.

The process of reduction involves several stages, which we will summarize in the following points.

1. Example 13.6a shows the score for the first period of Mozart's DM Sonata, K. 284. Our first step is to identify and circle nonchord tones in this passage (already circled on example 13.6).
2. In the first level of metric reduction shown in the system below the score (example 13.6b), NCTs have been removed and arpeggiated patterns have become block chords. This is the underlying harmonic and melodic frame of this passage, with register, metric placement, and durations preserved.

Example 13.6 W. A. Mozart, Piano Sonata in DM, K. 284, I

3. In a second level of reduction (example 13.6c) the pitches in the melody have been grouped (mostly in 3rds) following the harmonic structure provided by the left hand.

In the first level of reduction, we left pitches in the same register where they appear on the score. Occasionally, changing the octave of a pitch or a pattern may help construct a linear pattern that was otherwise concealed by a change of register. In example 13.6c, for instance, hearing the A in m. 2 in the upper register helps us understand the nature of this melody: The structural frame of the first phrase is an ascending arpeggiated tonic triad, A–D–F♯–A, with a passing tone G. The linear nature of the segment F♯–G–A–B (mm. 1–3) is best understood if we hear the A at m. 2 in the upper register. In a similar way, changing the register of the C♯ in m. 8 helps us hear the completion of the linear descending pattern F♯–E–D–C♯. Notice, finally, that although the G in m. 3 (right hand) moves down to E by steps (through the accented PT, F♯), the B does not resolve to A as you could expect, but is left "dangling" in its register, as indicated by the A in parentheses and the question mark in example 13.6c. When the high register is revisited in m. 6, however, the B does resolve to A, thus achieving closure in the high register, as shown by the arrow and the exclamation mark.

Let us review the process of metric reduction with a second example, the opening of Bach's Gavotte from French Suite no. 5, reproduced in example 13.7a (see also

Example 13.7 Bach, Gavotte, from French Suite no. 5 in GM, mm. 1–4

Metric Reduction and Performance

Simplifying a piece of music by means of metric harmonic reduction has immediate practical applications for the performer. In the first place, it helps understand the melodic and harmonic structure of the music, its voice leading, and its underlying linear patterns. In the second place, practicing a chordal reduction of a piece or fragment helps memorize it, phrase it, and, in the case of string instruments, work at intonation. Examples 13.6 and 13.7 illustrate these points as applied to a compositions for piano. Example 13.8 shows how a passage from the solo violin repertoire (Bach's "Chaconne") may be practiced in a reduced version to help improve musical understanding, intonation, and memorization. (To make it more idiomatic for the violin, the violinist would be likely to omit some of the notes in this reduction while practicing it.)

In example 13.8b we can see how a reduction helps us appreciate (and hear) the numerous sequential and linear patterns in all voices. The top voice features the sequence F–G/E–F/D–E, followed by another sequence F–D–B♭/E–C–A/D–B♭–G and a closing descending line (G–F–E–D). Each of the sequences (marked with brackets on the reduction), moreover, contains several linear designs. In mm. 57–60, notice the F–E–D–C♯ pattern (one pitch per measure, in parallel 3rds with the bass), and the G–F–E–D pattern mostly on the third beats. Identify the melodic linear patterns in mm. 61–65. Similarly, two basic linear patterns can be heard in the bass in mm. 57–60. The repeated **chaconne bass** on which Bach writes this composition (the descending melodic 4th D–C–B♭–A) comes out clearly in the reduction. If you consider all the bass notes in mm. 57–60 (D–G–C–F–B♭–E–[D]–A), what harmonic/melodic pattern do you recognize? (Note that both of the sequences marked on the reduction are not only melodic sequences, but also harmonic sequences.) Look now at the bass in mm. 61–65 and find the chaconne bass and other sequential and linear patterns. Finally, study the interesting voice leading in mm. 64–65. Do you see any voice exchange?

Example 13.8 J. S. Bach, "Chaconne," from Partita no. 2 in Dm for Violin Solo, BWV 1004, mm. 57–65

anthology, no. 12). This is a more polyphonic example than the previous one, featuring three distinctive voices. A reduction will enable us to understand the underlying harmonic structure for this polyphonic passage.

1. In example 13.7a we have circled all NCTs.
2. In example 13.7b, our first level of reduction, we group together some of the pitches that belong to the same chord. Mm. 1–2 display a harmonic rhythm of one chord per beat (the half note), whereas m. 3 includes a single dominant chord. This reduction allows us to make some interesting observations:
   a) The upper line begins with a sequence that outlines a melodic descending 6th twice. The third segment of the sequence presents a modified form of the motive, a descending 5th, E–A, instead of a 6th.
   b) The opening bass segment outlines a 5th descending by steps from G to C. This linear pattern is replicated in an inner voice in parallel 10ths. What we have here is not only a melodic sequence, but also a **harmonic sequence,** a sequence where the complete harmonic spacing and voice leading in all voices is preserved in each segment.
   c) The descending linear pattern in the bass leads to $\hat{4}$, pitch C in our example, over which we hear a 5–6 motion.
3. Example 13.7c shows a second level of reduction, where the linear sequential extension of I in mm. 1–2 is clearly indicated. The sequence leads to the pre-dominant IV_{5-6}, followed by a complete measure of V (with an 8–7 elaboration) leading to the I that closes the phrase.

This analytical reduction allows us to clarify the sequential framework of the opening measures of the Gavotte, and to hear the linear directed motion toward the final pre-dominant/dominant/tonic cadential gesture. We also see the importance of the predominant chord in m. 2, which functions both as the goal for the opening descending linear sequence and as the point of departure for the cadence that follows it. Knowing all this information helps us hear the unity, coherence, and motion of this phrase, to practice and memorize the essential framework of this passage, and to perform this beautiful passage in a way that transmits the linear sweep from I to IV followed by a cadence. Far from hearing or performing this phrase on a note-by-note basis, we can now interpret it as a harmonic and linear unit, and we understand why.

EXERCISE

To practice realizing metric reductions, refer to exercises 1.3 and 2 in worksheet 13 at the end of this chapter.

COMPOUND MELODY

Metric reduction is a useful tool to understand the type of melody we call compound melody. A **compound melody** comprises two (or three) strands in different registers, in such a way that it may be understood as several different, independent voices brought together into a single melody, as in "one-line counterpoint." Play the Bach theme in

Example 13.9 J. S. Bach, Fugue no. 3 in C♯M, from *The Well-Tempered Clavier,* I, subject

example 13.9a. Then, think of it as two independent melodies, and play it as in example 13.9b. This is a compound melody that contains the two hypothetical voices shown in example 13.9b.

Example 13.10a reproduces mm. 1–4 of Schubert's *Valses sentimentales,* op. 50, no. 3, a piece that we already studied in example 7.3b. Identify and label the nonchord tones (NCTs) in the piano's right hand, a compound melody. You will see that the explanation for some of them is not immediately obvious, especially for the A in m. 1 and the F♯–A in m. 3. Example 13.10b shows the melody and its two constituent voices (the upper voice is beamed upward, the lower voice downward). This reading of the

Example 13.10 Schubert, *Valses sentimentales,* op. 50, no. 3, mm. 1–4

phrase as a compound melody helps account for all the NCTs in the passage, which are explained in the following points.

1. In example 13.10b, we see that the upper voice, after the anacrusic D, basically consists of an ascending motion from G to B and descending back to G. In this context, the A in m. 1 is a passing tone, whereas the A in m. 3 is an accented passing tone.
2. The first half of the lower voice in example 13.10b is an extension of $\hat{5}$, elaborated by means of upper neighbors (D–E–D). The second half of the lower voice is a linear descent from G to D (G–F♯–E–D). We can now see that both the F♯ and A in m. 3 function as accented passing tones in two different voices.

EXERCISES

To practice analyzing and composing compound melodies, refer to exercises 3 and 4 in worksheet 13 at the end of this chapter.

WRITING YOUR OWN PROGRESSIONS

Beginning with this chapter, you will be asked to write your own progressions using the chords we have already studied. Being able to compose correct, musical harmonic progressions is an essential part of understanding and knowing tonal harmony. Your progressions should be metrical, and to avoid the needless four-voice realization of possibly faulty progressions, you will normally be asked to write only a bass line and Roman numerals. Before we discuss specific guidelines to write your own progressions, however, we will see how the relationship between metric and harmonic accents can affect the progressions you write.

Metric-Harmonic Relationships in Harmonic Progressions

In chapter B we studied the concept of **metric accent.** Metric accents result from the organization of pulses into regularly recurring patterns. Within a measure, beats are differently accented depending on specific meters. In essence, we learned that in duple meters the pattern of metric accents is strong-weak, in quadruple meters it is strong-weak-strong-weak, and in triple meters it is strong-weak-weak (although beat 3 is the weakest). These metric patterns are summarized in the following figures, where the symbol – means strong and ⌣ means weak.

– ⌣ – ⌣	– ⌣ – ⌣ – ⌣ – ⌣	– ⌣ ⌣ – ⌣ ⌣
$\frac{2}{4}$ 1 2 | 1 2 ‖	$\frac{4}{4}$ 1 2 3 4 | 1 2 3 4 ‖	$\frac{3}{4}$ 1 2 3 | 1 2 3 ‖

NOTE

In $\frac{4}{4}$, beat 3 is weaker than beat 1. Thus, if the harmonic rhythm is a half note, the second half note is weaker than the first one (the relationship that we are hearing, then, is the same as in $\frac{2}{2}$ – ⌣ for the whole measure).

The relationship between harmony and meter is free and flexible. To understand it better, we will define a new type of accent, which we will call harmonic accent. A **harmonic accent** is an accent that is created by harmonic progression. In the V_7–I progression, for instance, we hear the tonic as *rhythmically accented,* because after the unstable and dissonant V_7, the stable and consonant tonic is heard as a point of arrival or harmonic accent. *Harmonic accents are thus rhythmic rather than metric.* (You will remember that in chapter B we defined rhythmic accents as those that result from "grouping, note length, a sense of harmonic or tonal arrival, and other nonmetrical factors.") Whereas metric accents are regular and result from a metric structure that in some ways is superimposed to the music, harmonic accents result from harmonic events and hence come from the music itself. Harmonic accents are totally independent from metric accents, and as a result harmonic and metric accents may or may not coincide.

Examine, for instance, the progression in example 13.11a. In this progression all dominant chords fall on a metrically weak beat and resolve to I or vi on strong beats. Harmonic accents in this case correspond with metric accents, and thus we can speak of **metric-harmonic congruence.**

Now examine example 13.11b. Dominant chords are now on strong beats and resolve to I or vi on weak beats. Because metric and harmonic accents do not correspond in this progression, we perceive a **metric-harmonic conflict.** In example 13.11c, the same progression is renotated in $\frac{3}{4}$, and you can verify that the metric-harmonic conflict disappears. Compare and play the notations in examples 13.11b and c. The former

Example 13.11

creates ambiguity between harmonic accents and notated meter; the latter establishes an unequivocal correlation between the two types of accent.

Conflicts between harmonic and metric accents are abundant in music. When used skillfully, they are a powerful tool to create musical tension for expressive or formal purposes. Because writing such conflicts effectively, however, presupposes substantial skill, we will first concentrate on writing progressions in which *metric and harmonic accents correspond,* that is, progressions in which there is metric-harmonic congruence.

EXERCISE

To practice analyzing the relationship between metric and harmonic accents, refer to exercise 1.4 in worksheet 13 at the end of this chapter.

Harmonic Syncopation

In writing your own progressions, you should also be careful to avoid what we know as **harmonic syncopation.** The harmonic accents created by all chords in example 13.12a confirm the accentual metric pattern of triple meter. Although the V in m. 4 is on a strong beat, it does not resolve to a weak beat, but rather is prolonged in beat 3 to resolve in the next measure. A dominant such as this, beginning on a strong beat and resolving on the next strong beat, is perfectly correct. You can find a similar case in example 13.11c, m. 3, this time including a passing vi between V and V_6.

Now examine example 13.12b. The four brackets indicate chords that begin on a weak beat and continue to the next strong beat. Such metric events are called *harmonic syncopations* and should be systematically avoided for now because they have a weakening effect on the metric character of a progression. In other words, *do not write chords that begin on a weak beat and continue to a strong beat.* This applies also to changes of position, as in brackets 2 and 4 in example 13.12b.

Example 13.12

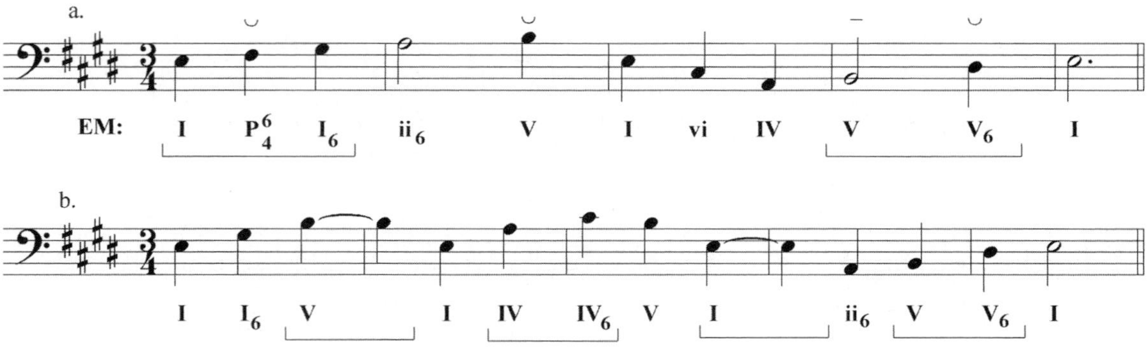

Guidelines for Writing Your Own Progressions

The following guidelines should be observed in writing your progressions:

1. Begin and end with tonic in root position (unless you choose to finish on a HC).
2. Establish a harmonic rhythm and keep it as regular as possible.
3. Avoid harmonic syncopation.
4. For the time being, strive for correspondence between harmonic and metric accents. Pay special attention to these points:
   a) Place chords with a dominant function preferably on a weak beat (or, if they are on a strong beat, prolong them through the next weak beat).
   b) Resolve chords with a dominant function to a strong beat.
   c) Passing and neighbor $^6_4$s will normally be placed on weak beats.
   d) The cadential $^6_4$ falls on a strong beat, whereas its resolution to $^5_3$ falls on a weak beat. The $^6_4$ may be on beat 2 of a $^3_4$ measure if it resolves to $^5_3$ on beat 3, because beat 3 is weaker than beat 2 in $^3_4$ (see example 13.13a, m. 4).
5. Think of your harmonic phrase as an elaboration of the basic I–V–I progression. Follow the fundamental principles of correct harmonic progression as we have learned them so far:
   a) Any chord may be used in root position or inversion to provide variety to the bass line. You may effectively use first-inversion chords to prolong (or precede) the same chord in root position.
   b) V, V_7, and their inversions resolve only to I, I_6, or (deceptively) to vi. Do not resolve V to IV or ii.
   c) V is usually preceded by a pre-dominant chord (IV or ii).
   d) All $^6_4$ chords should belong to one of the categories we have studied, and they should resolve accordingly.
   e) Finish your progression with one of the cadence types we have studied.
   f) Strive for harmonic and bass-line melodic variety.

Examples 13.13a and b

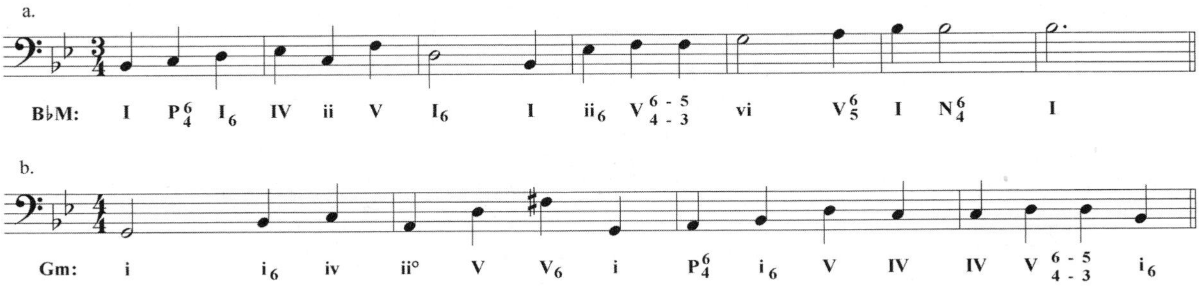

Example 13.13c J. S. Bach, Chorale 159, "Als der gütige Gott"

The progression in example 13.13a illustrates many of the points outlined previously. Discuss this progression, and remark on everything that is correct in it. On the other hand, many things in example 13.13b are wrong or dubious. Find the weaknesses in this progression, and learn to avoid these mistakes. Finally, analyze in class the Bach chorale reproduced in example 13.13c. Think about the succession of chords (after you have analyzed them with Roman numerals), their metric placement, and the relationships between metric and harmonic accents in this chorale. (The last chord in m. 6 is a secondary dominant of vi, a type of chord we will study in chapter 18.)

NOTES

1. *Harmonic syncopation involving the initial tonic is possible and frequently found in Bach chorales. Its function is to reinforce the tonality at the outset of a phrase.*
2. *Half cadences are often placed on strong beats. To prepare the arrival of V on a strong beat, the chords that lead to the HC may emphasize the dominant on strong beats (and then the tonic falls on weak beats). Example 13.14a illustrates a syncopated initial tonic and a HC on a strong beat, which, nonetheless, does not require any metric adjustments. The HC in example 13.14b, on the other hand, is preceded by a dominant on a strong beat and a tonic on a weak beat, thus preparing the strong arrival on V at the HC.*

EXERCISE

To practice writing your own progressions, refer to exercise 5 in worksheet 13 at the end of this chapter.

Example 13.14a J. S. Bach, Chorale 193, "Was bist du doch, O Seele, so betrübet"

Example 13.14b J. S. Bach Chorale 45, "Kommt her zu mir"

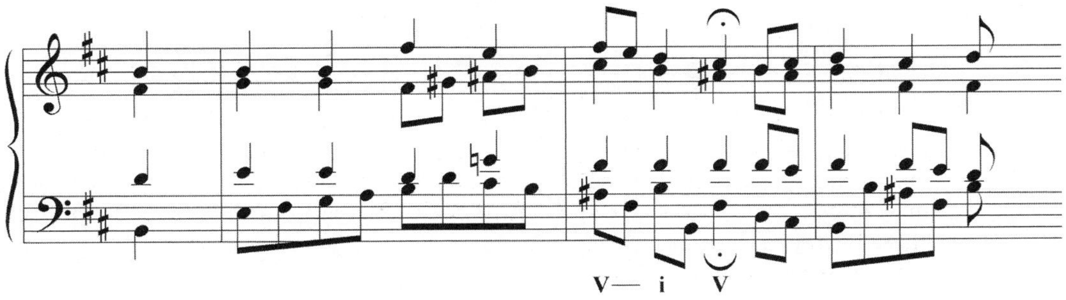

FOR FURTHER STUDY

For additional analysis using materials studied in this chapter, refer to the *Harmony in Context* Web page at www.mhhe.com /roigfrancoli2e.

ASSIGNMENT

For analytical and written assignments based on the materials learned in this chapter, refer to chapter 13 in the workbook.

Terms for Review

Harmonic rhythm (HR)
HR and tempo
Regular and irregular HR
Levels of HR
Metric reduction
Harmonic sequence
Metric reduction and performance
Chaconne bass
Compound melody
Metric accents
Harmonic accent
Metric-harmonic congruence and conflict
Harmonic syncopation

Worksheet 13

EXERCISE 1 Analysis.

1. Determine and notate the harmonic rhythm (HR) for Bach's Chorale 153 (example 13.15). Write note values for the length of each chord under the chorale's score. Beware that changes of position, suspensions, and other NCTs do not affect the harmonic rhythm.

Example 13.15 J. S. Bach, Chorale 153, "Alle Menschen müssen sterben"

2. Notate with note values the HR for Haydn's Sonata in DM, Hob. XVI: 24, II (anthology, no. 20), mm. 1–8. Is this a fast or slow HR?

2 4 6 8

3. Analyze anthology, no. 26 (Mozart, Piano Sonata in CM, K. 309, III).
   a) On the line below, provide a complete form diagram, including bubbles, measure numbers, cadences, and letters for form. What kind of period is this?

b) On the score, provide a complete Roman numeral (RN) analysis of mm. 1–8. What types of $^6_4$ chords can you identify?

c) What is the harmonic/linear function of each chord in mm. 1–8?

What is the overall harmonic motion from m. 1 to m. 8?

What is the long-range harmonic function of all the harmonies in mm. 1–7?

d) Analyze and explain the final cadence (mm. 18–19). Provide RNs and explain the voice leading.

e) Circle and label all NCTs in mm. 1–8.

f) Describe the texture of this passage. What is the term that best applies to this type of texture?

g) Using your own music paper, provide a metric reduction for this complete example.

4. Analyze the opening phrase from Bach's Chorale 1 (example 13.16) with Roman numerals. Then write strong and weak metric symbols on top of the score (– ◡ ◡) and comment briefly on the relationship between metric and harmonic accents in this passage. Why is the V in m. 4 on a strong beat? The dominant in m. 5, beat 1 is also on a strong beat. Considering that both the chords that follow in the same measure function as passing chords, where does the dominant on beat 1 resolve?

Example 13.16 J. S. Bach, Chorale 1, "Aus meines Herzens Grunde," mm. 1–7

EXERCISE 2 Metric reduction. On your own music paper, provide metric reductions for the following pieces:

1. Anthology, no. 27, mm. 1–8 (Mozart, Sonata in AM, K. 331, Theme).
2. Anthology, no. 6 (Minuet from *Notebook for Anna Magdalena Bach*). Your reduction should furnish an accurate account of the harmonic content for the complete piece.

EXERCISE 3 Example 13.17 reproduces a compound melody. In the staff below it, renotate the passage clearly showing the various voices that make up the compound melody. Refer to examples 13.9 and 13.10 for models of notation.

Example 13.17 Henryk Wieniawski, Scherzo-Tarantella, op. 16, mm. 4–13

EXERCISE 4 On your own music paper, write a compound melody using the examples studied in this chapter as models. A possible beginning is provided for you to use, although you may use your own beginning if you prefer.

EXERCISE 5 *Writing harmonic progressions.* Be careful with the correlation of metric and harmonic accents, and write harmonic phrases that are logical and musical. Play your progressions and make sure you like them!

1. Write a progression (bass and RNs only) in AM, in $^{2}_{4}$, using only I, IV, ii, and V, and their first inversions.

AM:

2. Write a progression (bass and RNs) in E♭M, in $^{3}_{4}$, using ii, V_7, a cadential $^{6}_{4}$, and a plagal cadence, besides any of the other chords we have already studied.

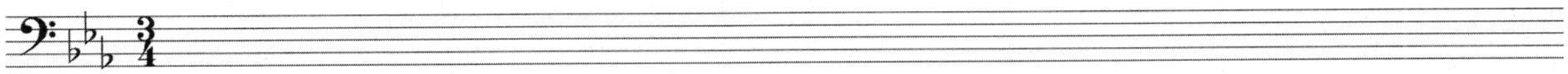

E♭M:

3. Write a progression in Dm, in $^{4}_{4}$, including, V^4_3, V^6_5, and a neighbor $^{6}_{4}$, besides any of the other chords we have already studied.

Dm:

Chapter 14

The Mediant, Submediant, and Subtonic Triads

The last diatonic triads we will study are the *mediant, submediant,* and *subtonic* chords. The mediant is built on $\hat{3}$, the submediant on $\hat{6}$: a 3rd above the tonic in the first case, a 3rd below in the latter case. Both chords have a weaker functional character than the triads we have studied so far, and both (especially iii) appear less frequently in tonal progressions. We will also see that the subtonic triad (built on $\flat\hat{7}$, and hence a diatonic triad in the minor mode) may be found at times associated with III in minor keys.

THE MEDIANT AND SUBMEDIANT TRIADS AS PROLONGATIONS OF THE TONIC

The triad built on $\hat{3}$ (the **mediant**) includes scale degrees $\hat{3}$–$\hat{5}$–$\hat{7}$; it is a minor triad (iii) in major keys, and a major triad (III) in its most frequent minor key form (notice that, in minor, the fifth of III is *not* the leading tone [LT], but rather $\flat\hat{7}$). The triad built on $\hat{6}$ (the **submediant**), on the other hand, includes scale degrees $\hat{6}$–$\hat{1}$–$\hat{3}$; it is a minor triad (vi) in major keys, and a major triad (VI) in minor keys. Because both iii and vi have two common tones with I, and because the root of each is a 3rd from $\hat{1}$, they are often used as chords prolonging the tonic by arpeggiation.

The Mediant

Two instances of *mediant chords prolonging the tonic* appear in examples 14.1a and b. In example 14.1a Bach prolongs i through all of m. 1 by means of arpeggiation of the bass: $\hat{1}$ moves a 3rd up to $\hat{3}$, then down a 5th to $\hat{6}$, and up a 3rd again to $\hat{1}$ (the 3rds are, of course, filled in by passing tones). Voice leading in the upper voices emphasizes the prolongational character of the complete measure: A passing tone (PT) connects two members of i in the soprano ($\hat{5}$–$\hat{4}$–$\hat{3}$), the alto moves also between two members of i ($\hat{3}$–$\hat{1}$), while the tenor moves from $\hat{1}$ to $\hat{5}$ by means of two PTs, $\hat{7}$–$\hat{6}$. Harmonically, the progression prolongs i by means of an arpeggiation *to* III, and another arpeggiation *from* iv_6 (i–III–iv_6–i).

Example 14.1a J. S. Bach, Chorale 138, "Jesu, meine Freude," mm. 1–2

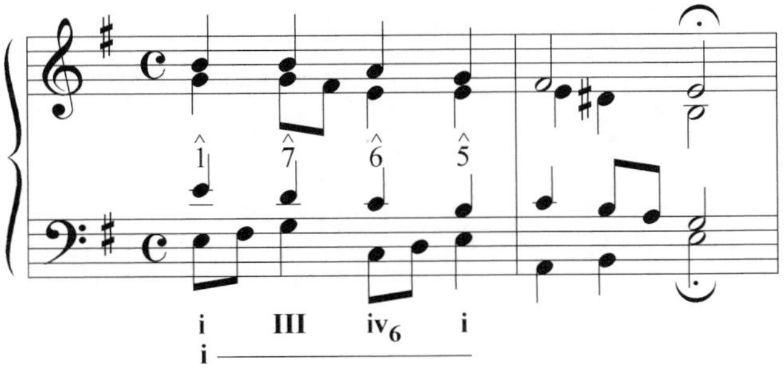

Example 14.1b J. Brahms, Symphony no. 4, op. 98, III, mm. 1–6

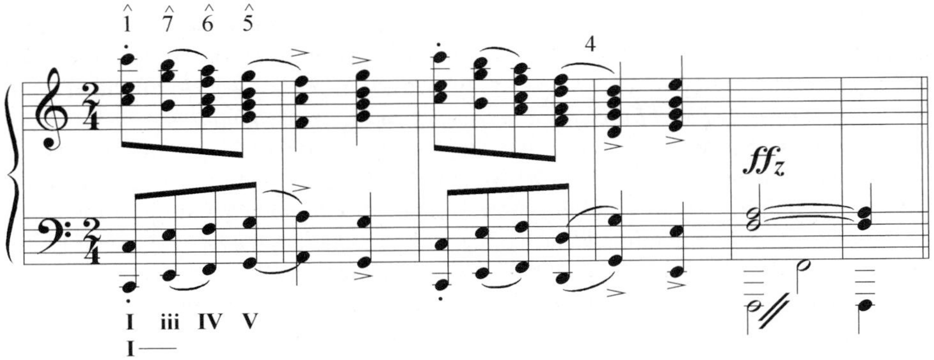

In example 14.1b we have a similar example by Brahms. In m. 1 the tonic is extended by a bass arpeggiation supporting a mediant chord, in the progression I–iii–IV–V. Observe that in both examples 14.1a and b one of the voices displays a descending line, $\hat{1}$–$\hat{7}$–$\hat{6}$–$\hat{5}$, and that in both cases $\hat{7}$ (actually ♭7 in minor) does not function or resolve like a leading tone. *The progression I–iii–IV, in which iii prolongs I and in which $\hat{7}$ does not resolve like a LT (it is not part of a dominant harmony), is often used to harmonize the melodic segment $\hat{1}$–$\hat{7}$–$\hat{6}$.*

Example 14.2 presents a summary of some usual progressions involving the mediant as a prolongation of I. In example 14.2a, the space between I and V is divided by iii. Compare this to example 14.2b, in which I is similarly prolonged by a I_6 which also divides the fifth by arpeggiation. In both examples 14.2c and d, a predominant chord has been added between iii and V; notice the characteristic descending $\hat{1}$–$\hat{7}$–$\hat{6}$–$\hat{5}$ in the soprano.

Example 14.2

The Submediant

Turning now to example 14.3, we see two instances of the *submediant as a prolongation of the tonic* by downward bass arpeggiation. This very common progression usually takes the form of a *succession of descending 3rds.* In its simplest form (two descending 3rds), the progression may be I–vi–IV–V, I–vi–ii$_6$–V, or I–vi–ii$^6_5$–V. In all three cases, *vi functions as a divider of the space between I and a pre-dominant chord.* Which of these progressions can you identify in examples 14.3a and b? Observe also the use of chromaticism in the bass in each of these examples. In example 14.3a, we can interpret the second chord in m. 4 as a passing chord including a chromatic passing motion in the bass (notice the passing motion in each of the voices), whereas the D♯ in example 14.3b, m. 43, also functions as a chromatic PT between the previous D and the E in m. 44.

Three **progressions in descending 3rds** using only triads appear in examples 14.4a, b, and c. In example 14.4c the progression is extended by the addition of one more third.

Example 14.3a L. v. Beethoven, Seven Variations on "God Save the King," mm. 1–6

Example 14.3b Chevalier de Saint–Georges, Symphonie Concertante in AM, op. 10, no. 2, I, mm. 41–45

NOTE

An important voice-leading principle in third-related chords (such as I–iii and I–vi), which, of course, have two common tones, is that you should retain both common tones in the same voices, *as you may verify in all such connections in examples 14.2 and 14.4.*

EXERCISE

To practice realizing short progressions using mediant and submediant chords, refer to exercises 2a to c in worksheet 14 at the end of this chapter.

Example 14.4

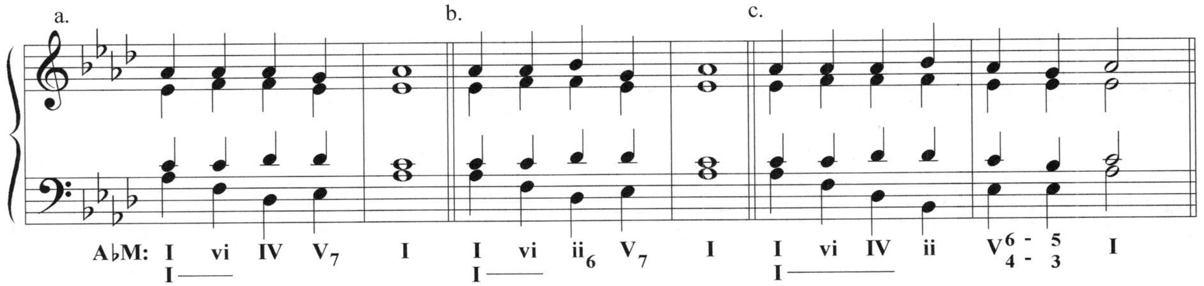

Example 14.5 J. S. Bach, Chorale 135, "Gott der Vater, wohn uns bei," mm. 1–4

OTHER USES OF THE MEDIANT AND SUBMEDIANT

vi as a Pre-dominant

Example 14.5 reproduces the first two phrases of Bach's Chorale 135. The vi in m. 3, beat 1, is not a tonic prolongation (it follows a ii chord). Its function is, rather, to precede a dominant harmony (V_6), and therefore it may be interpreted as a pre-dominant. The submediant may indeed function as a pre-dominant if it precedes the dominant. Its function, however, is often ambiguous, as shown in example 14.6a. Although vi precedes V and may be heard associated with the dominant, it still acts as a prolongation of the opening tonic, hence its ambiguous function. The vi in m. 2 of the same example is part of a $\hat{6}$–$\hat{7}$–$\hat{1}$ bass motion, and it moves to a dominant chord (V^6_5) that is itself a passing chord between vi and I. Here again the function of vi is ambiguous: It prolongs I (and proceeds to I through a passing chord), but it also precedes a dominant harmony.

iii and vi as 5th-Related Chords

Because of their root relationship by 5th (or 4th), iii and vi can effectively be paired in harmonic progressions. In example 14.7 (and example 14.6b), the standard I–vi–IV–V_7 progression is slightly altered by the insertion of iii between vi and IV: I–vi–iii–IV–V_7.

Example 14.6

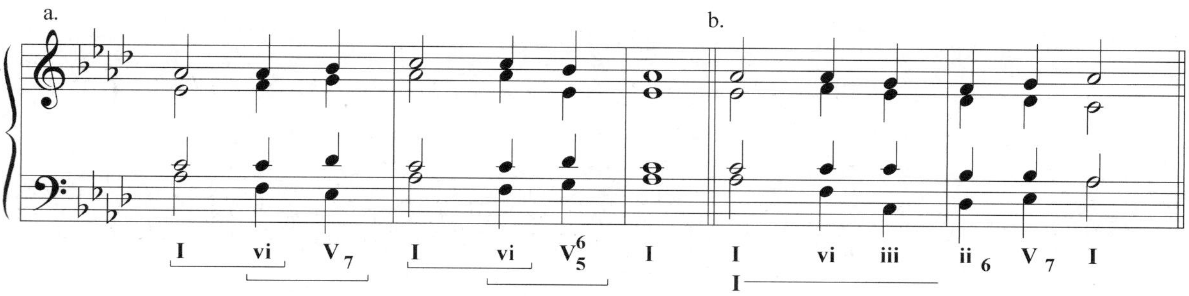

Example 14.7 J. S. Bach, Chorale 14, "O Herre Gott, dein göttlich Wort," mm. 1–2

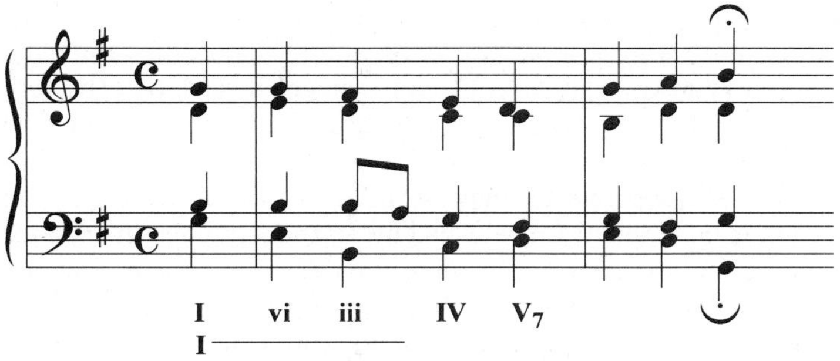

By doing so, Bach prolongs the tonic harmony one more beat (both vi and iii in this phrase prolong I by arpeggiation) while taking advantage of the strong root relationship (ascending 5th) between vi and iii. Moreover, notice that the melodic fragment that Bach harmonizes with this progression is the familiar $\hat{1}$–$\hat{7}$–$\hat{6}$–$\hat{5}$ and that iii allows for the standard harmonization of the descending $\hat{7}$, which we have studied previously.

The progression iii–vi–ii–V–I, on the other hand, is based on a pattern of roots related by descending 5ths (a fragment of the circle of 5ths). As we will see when we study the circle-of-5ths sequence in chapter 16, this progression can frequently be found as part of a larger descending-5ths pattern. Moreover, it often also appears in isolation (that is, without being part of a broader circle of 5ths), as you can see in example 14.8. This example features a slight variation of the above progression (notice the incomplete iii, the ii_6, and the cadential $^6_4$ figure), which is otherwise based on a pattern of roots related by descending 5ths, F♯–B–E–A, or $\hat{3}$–$\hat{6}$–$\hat{2}$–$\hat{5}$ in DM.

Example 14.8 Camille Saint-Saëns, *Christmas Oratorio,* no. 8, mm. 5–7

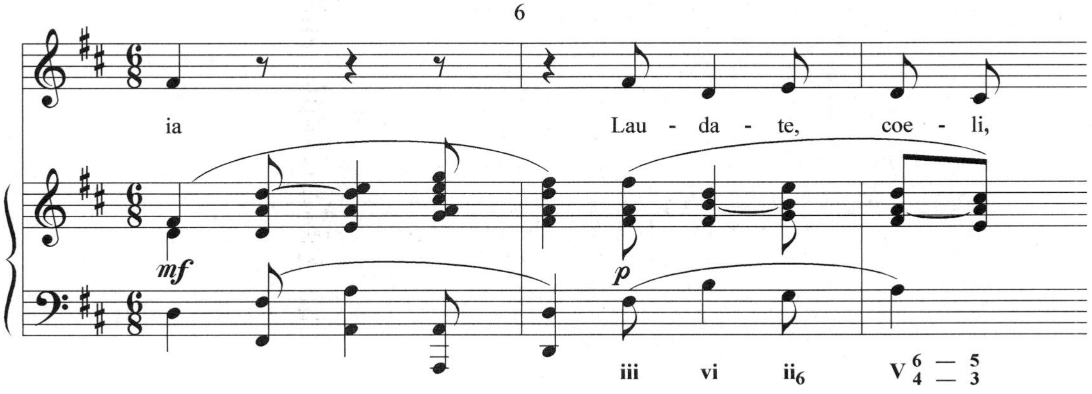

The Dominant as an "Apparent Mediant"

Occasionally, a chord that looks like a mediant in first inversion moves directly to a tonic chord. This is the progression represented in example 14.9a. In these cases, $\hat{5}$ is in the bass and it is doubled, and $\hat{7}$ does act as a LT. *We will not think of this chord as being a "mediant" at all, but rather a dominant harmony.* In major, this dominant chord looks like iii_6. In minor, however, it looks like an augmented triad, III^{+}_{6} (III with a raised $\hat{7}$: $\flat\hat{3}$–$\hat{5}$–$\hat{7}$, as in example 14.9b. You can find a clear example of an authentic cadence with an apparent "III^{+}_{6}–i" instead of the usual V–i in anthology, no. 50 (Schumann, "Folk Song"), m. 8. The apparent mediant in first inversion at a cadence can best be explained as a dominant harmony embellished by a nonchord tone. In example 14.9a, the soprano's $\hat{3}$ in iii_6 may be heard as an anticipation of the $\hat{3}$ in the following I chord. The voice leading in example 14.9b is very characteristic of this progression (see also the Schumann "Folk Song" cadence): $\hat{3}$ in the soprano can be heard as an escape tone (notice the $\hat{3}$–$\hat{1}$ motion in the soprano which replaces the familiar $\hat{2}$–$\hat{1}$ from the V–i

Example 14.9

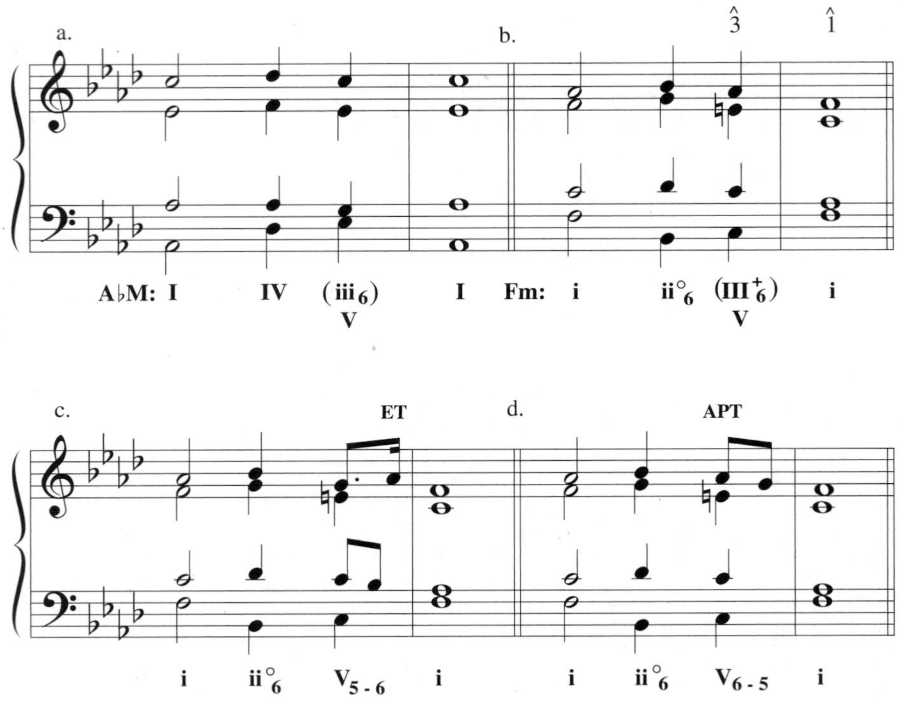

progression). In example 14.9c, the escape-tone function of the same $\hat{3}$–$\hat{1}$ figure (as part of a $\hat{2}$–$\hat{3}$–$\hat{1}$ motion) is perfectly apparent. Finally, in example 14.9d, $\hat{3}$ may be interpreted as an accented PT between $\hat{4}$ and $\hat{2}$, over a V chord (compare with example 14.9b). Notice that in both examples 14.9c and d, the "embellished dominant" figures result from a 5–6 or 6–5 motion over the bass $\hat{5}$.

The Deceptive Resolution of V: vi as a Tonic Substitute

In previous chapters we have already introduced the **deceptive cadence** (a V–vi cadence that usually delays momentarily an authentic cadence) or deceptive progression (a V–vi progression within a phrase, with no cadential function). In both cases, V resolves "deceptively" (that is, in an unexpected way) to vi, which functions here as a tonic substitute. Find a deceptive resolution of V or V_7 in each of the following examples: examples 14.1b and 14.7, and Schumann's "Folk Song" (anthology, no. 50). Notice, however, that in example 14.1b—Brahms—the deceptive progression is not V–vi, but rather an alternative form that we discussed in chapter 10. Refer now to anthology, no. 20 (Haydn, Sonata in DM) and study the closing section (mm. 20–24). Is there a deceptive resolution of V in the passage, and if so, what is its formal function?

The voice leading of the deceptive progression requires some considerations. As a principle, the LT should still resolve up to $\hat{1}$. To avoid possible parallel 8ves or 5ths, the other two voices should move in contrary motion with the bass. This correct voice leading, illustrated in example 14.10a, results in a vi with a *doubled third*. In the V_7–vi progression in example 14.10b, both the LT and the seventh should resolve as usual (the LT up, the seventh down), and the result is also a doubled third in vi.

EXERCISE

To practice realizing progressions using deceptive resolutions of V, refer to exercises 2d and 4 in worksheet 14 at the end of this chapter.

Example 14.10

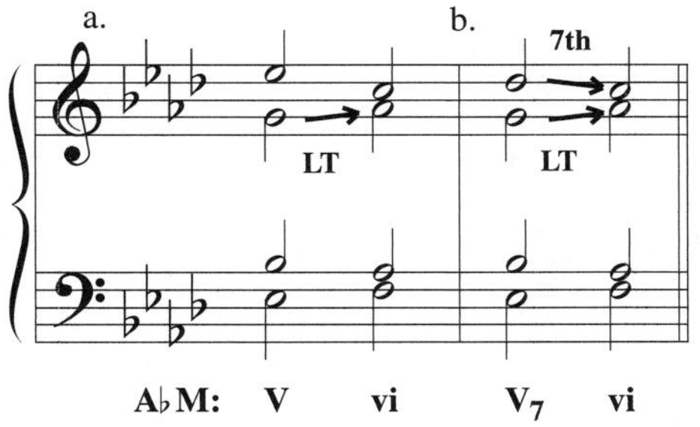

VOICE-LEADING GUIDELINES

1. In progressions by 3rds (I–iii, I–vi, vi–IV, etc.), retain common tones in the same voices.
2. Use the progression I–iii–IV to harmonize a descending melody, $\hat{1}$–$\hat{7}$–$\hat{6}$.
3. The "apparent" iii_6–I or III^+_6–i progressions are really dominant-tonic progressions with a nonchord tone embellishment. For this reason, you should double the bass ($\hat{5}$) and not the LT ($\hat{7}$).
4. In the deceptive resolution of V (V–vi), beware of parallel 8ves and 5ths: resolve the LT to $\hat{1}$, and move the other two voices in contrary motion to the bass. This will result in a doubled third in vi.

THE SUBTONIC

In the minor mode, III is often preceded by VII (the **subtonic triad,** made up of $\flat\hat{7}$–$\hat{2}$–$\hat{4}$), as illustrated by example 14.11a. In this progression, III divides the space between i and V, but it is now preceded by VII, which, in this context, sounds like a *momentary dominant of III*. If you play this progression and hear the VII–III motion as if III were a momentary tonic and VII its dominant, you will indeed get a taste of what's to come in chapters 17 and 18 (the concepts of tonicization and secondary dominant).

In m. 6 of example 14.11b, you can hear the VII–III progression in the context of a chorale by Johann Hermann Schein. In mm. 3–5 and 7–8, on the other hand, you can hear two progressions in which VII is preceded by III and followed by i (see brackets). The progression III–VII–i–V is a very common progression in the music of the sixteenth and seventeenth centuries. Notice that the VII between III and i prevents the parallel 8ves and 5ths that could result if the triads moved directly down a 3rd, from III to i. Two very popular **ground basses** (repeated harmonic phrases on which performers would improvise) from the sixteenth and seventeenth centuries, the **romanesca and folia** basses (example 14.11c), include this progression. The *romanesca* phrase is based exclusively on the III–VII–i–V progression, and the *folia* phrase includes the i–VII–III progression we just studied.

EXERCISES

To practice realizing short progressions using the subtonic triad, refer to exercises 2e and f in worksheet 14 at the end of this chapter.

Example 14.11a

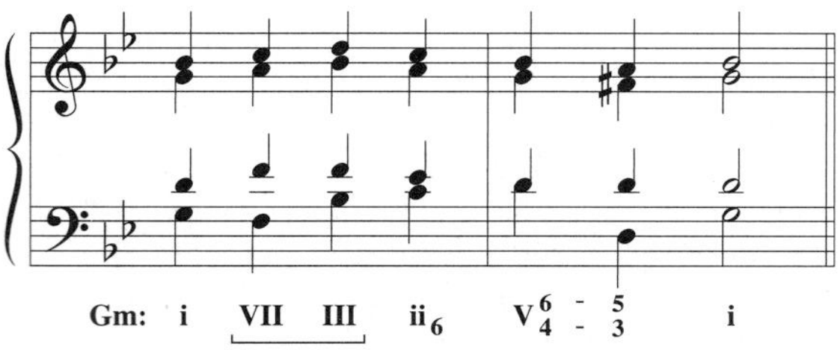

Example 14.11b Johann Hermann Schein, "Wir Christenleut," from *Cantional*

Example 14.11c The *Romanesca* and *Folia* Basses

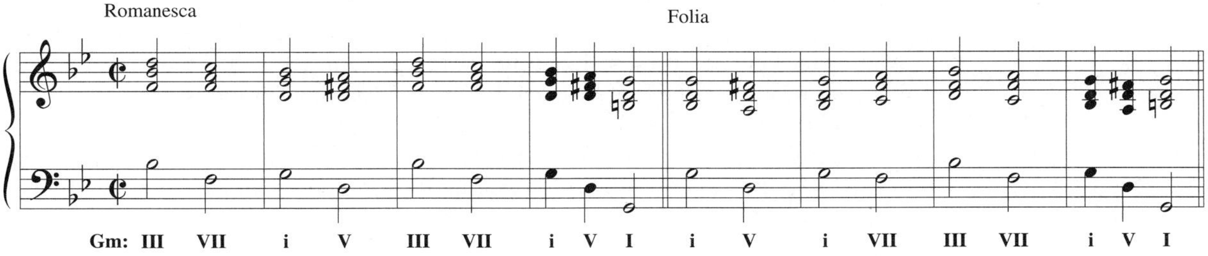

EXERCISES

To practice harmonizing a bass and a melody using mediant, submediant, and subtonic chords, refer to exercises 3 and 5 in worksheet 14 at the end of this chapter.

To practice writing your own progressions using mediant, submediant, and subtonic chords, refer to exercise 6 in worksheet 14 at the end of this chapter.

To practice analysis of musical fragments including mediant, submediant, and subtonic chords, refer to exercise 1 in worksheet 14 at the end of this chapter.

Example 14.12

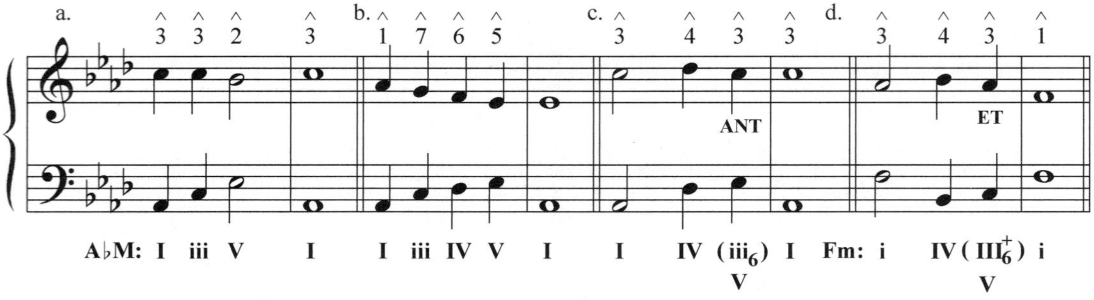

CHARACTERISTIC SOPRANO-BASS PATTERNS

The following examples illustrate some of the most characteristic soprano-bass patterns that can be harmonized with progressions we have studied in this chapter. Play each of the outer-voice patterns in examples 14.12 to 14.14 at the piano, adding inner voices in keyboard texture.

Patterns Using the Mediant

Example 14.12 shows four outer-voice patterns using progressions that include the mediant harmony. The patterns in examples 14.12a and b feature the mediant dividing the space between I and V. Example 14.12b presents the $\hat{1}$–$\hat{7}$–$\hat{6}$–$\hat{5}$ descending melodic pattern with its characteristic I–iii–IV–V–I harmonization. Examples 14.12c and d, on the other hand, include two patterns that use the dominant as an apparent mediant. In the context of the final V–I cadence in these examples, $\hat{3}$ functions as an anticipation (ANT) in example 14.12c and as an escape tone (ET) in example 14.12d.

Patterns Using the Submediant

Examples 14.13a to c show three melodic patterns harmonized with the bass by descending 3rds characteristic of the progression I–vi–IV–V–I. Two patterns using vi as a pre-dominant appear in examples 14.13d and e. Note that both of these feature ascending melodic lines that are typically cadential: $\hat{1}$–$\hat{1}$–$\hat{2}$–$\hat{3}$ and $\hat{5}$–$\hat{6}$–$\hat{7}$–$\hat{1}$. Two slightly longer patterns are shown in examples 14.13f and g, demonstrating melodic patterns harmonized with the progression I–vi–iii–ii$_6$–V$_7$–I. Finally, examples 14.13h to j show three melodic patterns featuring deceptive resolutions of V to vi.

Example 14.13

Patterns Using the Subtonic

Example 14.14a features the descending melodic segment $\hat{5}$–$\hat{4}$–$\hat{3}$–$\hat{2}$–$\hat{1}$ harmonized, as in the *romanesca* pattern, with a III–VII–i–V–i progression. Two melodic fragments derived from the *folia* pattern are illustrated in examples 14.14b and c, both harmonized with the progression i–VII–III–VII–i–V–I.

Example 14.14

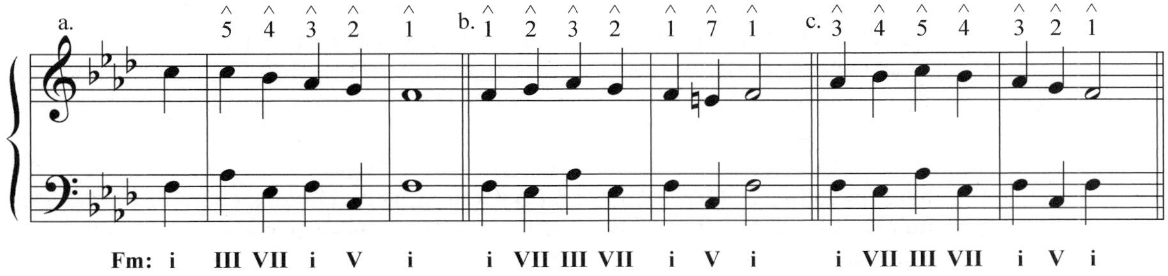

Example 14.15

ELABORATING THE I–V–I PROGRESSION

The main function of both the mediant and the submediant chords is to prolong the tonic by arpeggiation, up a 3rd in the case of iii, and down a 3rd in the case of vi. This function is illustrated in examples 14.15a and b, in the context of the I–IV–V–I progression. The function of the combined vi and iii chords in example 14.15c is also to prolong the initial tonic by arpeggiation in the bass and by neighbor motion in the soprano. In example 14.15d, both the initial tonic and the cadential dominant are prolonged by vi. The prolongation of the cadential dominant is effected by a change of position (V_7 to V^6_5) connected by a passing vi that provides a deceptive resolution of V_7. Finally, example 14.15e shows an inserted VII providing the connection between I and III by means of passing motion in the soprano and incomplete-neighbor motion in the bass. The combined VII–III chords are here a prolongation of the initial tonic in the i–V–i progression.

HARMONIZING A MELODY WITH KEYBOARD FIGURATION

Your melody harmonizations so far have been in vocal block-chord or chorale texture or in two voices (soprano and bass) with Roman numerals. Melodies are very often harmonized at the piano. Because simple sustained block chords are not a very idiomatic piano technique (the piano does not really sustain the sound, which is instead produced by a percussive attack), a variety of more active figurations are used to extend the sound of a chord, especially in slow harmonic rhythms. In all the fragments reproduced in example 14.16, for solo piano, a melody in the right hand is accompanied by some characteristic left-hand chordal figurations: **repeated block chords** in example 14.16a, the **bass afterbeat** pattern in example 14.16b (typical of waltzes and marches), a pattern of **repeated broken chords** in example 14.16c, **arpeggiated chords** in examples 14.16d and e, and a particular type of arpeggiation called **Alberti bass** in example 14.16f (in which the arpeggiation follows the pattern low note-high note-middle note-high note). In all these cases the principles of voice leading are preserved: Although chords may be broken, arpeggiated, and so on, their connections follow the familiar voice-leading guidelines as if we were dealing with block chords. (One may add, however, that you will find many more exceptions to the voice-leading norms in piano music and piano accompaniments in general than in four-voice vocal realizations.)

Example 14.16a L. v. Beethoven, Piano Sonata op. 14, no 1, I, mm. 1–4

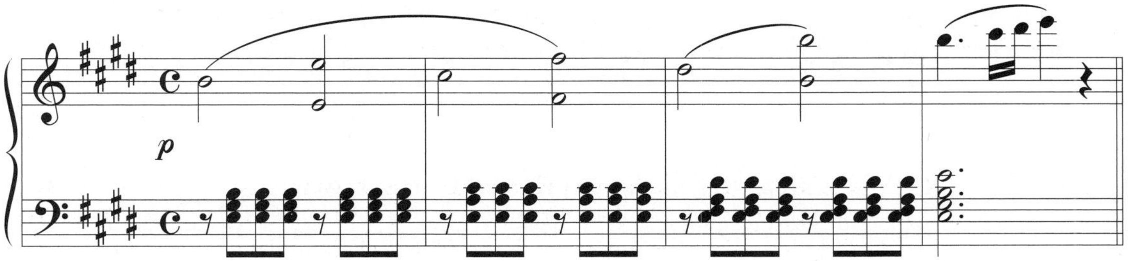

Example 14.16b F. Schubert, Waltz op. 9, no. 13, mm. 1–4

Example 14.16c L. v. Beethoven, Rondo op. 51, no. 1, mm. 1–2

Examples 14.16d and e W. A. Mozart, Piano Sonata K. 457, II, mm.1–2 and W. A. Mozart, Piano Sonata, K. 330, I, mm. 26–28

Example 14.16f W. A. Mozart, Piano Sonata K, 457, I. mm. 63–65

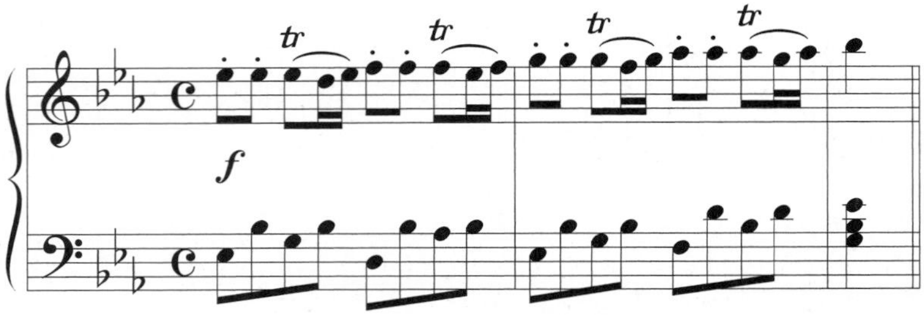

In all the fragments in example 14.16 the piano displays both the melody and the accompaniment. Very often, however, the melody is performed by a voice or a melodic instrument, while the piano provides only the accompaniment. In these cases, the chordal figuration is distributed between both hands, normally with the more active figuration in the right hand and a slower-moving bass in the left hand. The four fragments in example 14.17 are taken from Schubert songs and show the same techniques we saw in example 14.16, here performed with both hands: repeated chords in example 14.17a, bass afterbeat in 14.17b, repeated broken chords in example 14.17c, and arpeggiation in example 14.17d. Examine now the following examples in the anthology and notice the chordal figuration and the voice leading: anthology, no. 37, mm. 9–16 (Kuhlau, Sonatina); no. 24, mm. 7–8 (Mozart, DM sonata); no. 26 (Mozart,

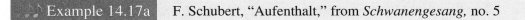

Example 14.17a F. Schubert, "Aufenthalt," from *Schwanengesang,* no. 5

Example 14.17b F. Schubert, "Ungeduld," from *Die schöne Müllerin,* no. 7

Example 14.17c F. Schubert, "Ständchen," from *Schwanengesang,* no. 4

3
3
3
Lei - se fle - hen mei - ne Lie - der durch die Na cht zu dir;

Example 14.17d F. Schubert, "Am Feierabend," from *Die schöne Müllerin,* no. 5

Hätt' ich tau - send Ar - me zu rüh - zen, könnt' ich brau - send die Rä - der füh - ren,

CM sonata, III); no. 32, mm. 1–8 and 125–131 (Beethoven, op. 2, no. 1); no. 34, mm. 1–8 (Beethoven, op. 13); 40 (Schubert, op. 9, no. 26); no. 52 (Verdi, "Libiamo"); no. 20, mm. 1–8 and 9–22 (Haydn, Hob. XVI: 24); no. 38 (Schubert, *Erlkönig*); and no. 47 (Schumann, "Ich grolle nicht").

Example 14.18

Writing a Keyboard Harmonization

We will now write a left-hand keyboard accompaniment for the melody given in example 14.18a. The procedure is as follows:

1. Write a Roman numeral harmonization of the melody on the basis of the given harmonic rhythm, taking into consideration the possible nonchord tones (NCTs) (marked with asterisks in example 14.18a). Anacrusic beginnings ("pickups") are not usually harmonized.
2. Examine the harmonic rhythm and think about what kind of rhythmic figuration may be used that would correspond with the duration of the harmonies.
3. Choose a figuration and realize the Roman numerals following the figuration and observing the usual voice-leading rules.

NOTE

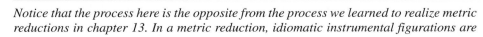

Notice that the process here is the opposite from the process we learned to realize metric reductions in chapter 13. In a metric reduction, idiomatic instrumental figurations are

reduced to block-chord style to simplify a texture for the sake of analysis or practice. When you write a keyboard harmonization, you first think of harmonies in a reduced form, such as Roman numerals or block chords, and then convert them into a more complex texture in the form of idiomatic keyboard figuration.

After singing or playing the melody in example 14.18a several times, and after thinking of possible chords for each measure, we realize that it may be harmonized with one of our standard progressions: I–IV–ii–V/V–I–V–I. Because the melody is in $\frac{3}{4}$, a bass afterbeat pattern would be appropriate (a waltz accompaniment), as illustrated by our realization in example 14.18b. If we want to provide an accompaniment with more rhythmic vitality than the bass afterbeat, an Alberti bass pattern like the one in example 14.18c would also be a good possibility.

You can now try to harmonize the melody in example 14.19, as a class exercise or on your own. A suggested pattern is provided, although you might prefer to use a different one. In m. 3, beat 1 (*), you may use an inversion of the chord from m. 2. In m. 5, beat 2, and m. 7, beat 1 (**), you may use $\frac{6}{4}$ chords.

Example 14.19

Paisiello, "Nel cor più non mi sento" (*La Molinara*)

ASSIGNMENT AND KEYBOARD EXERCISES

For analytical and written assignments and keyboard exercises based on the materials learned in this chapter, refer to chapter 14 in the workbook.

PITCH PATTERNS

Sing the pitch patterns in example 14.20. As you sing, listen to the chords we have studied in this chapter, and understand their function within the phrase.

Example 14.20

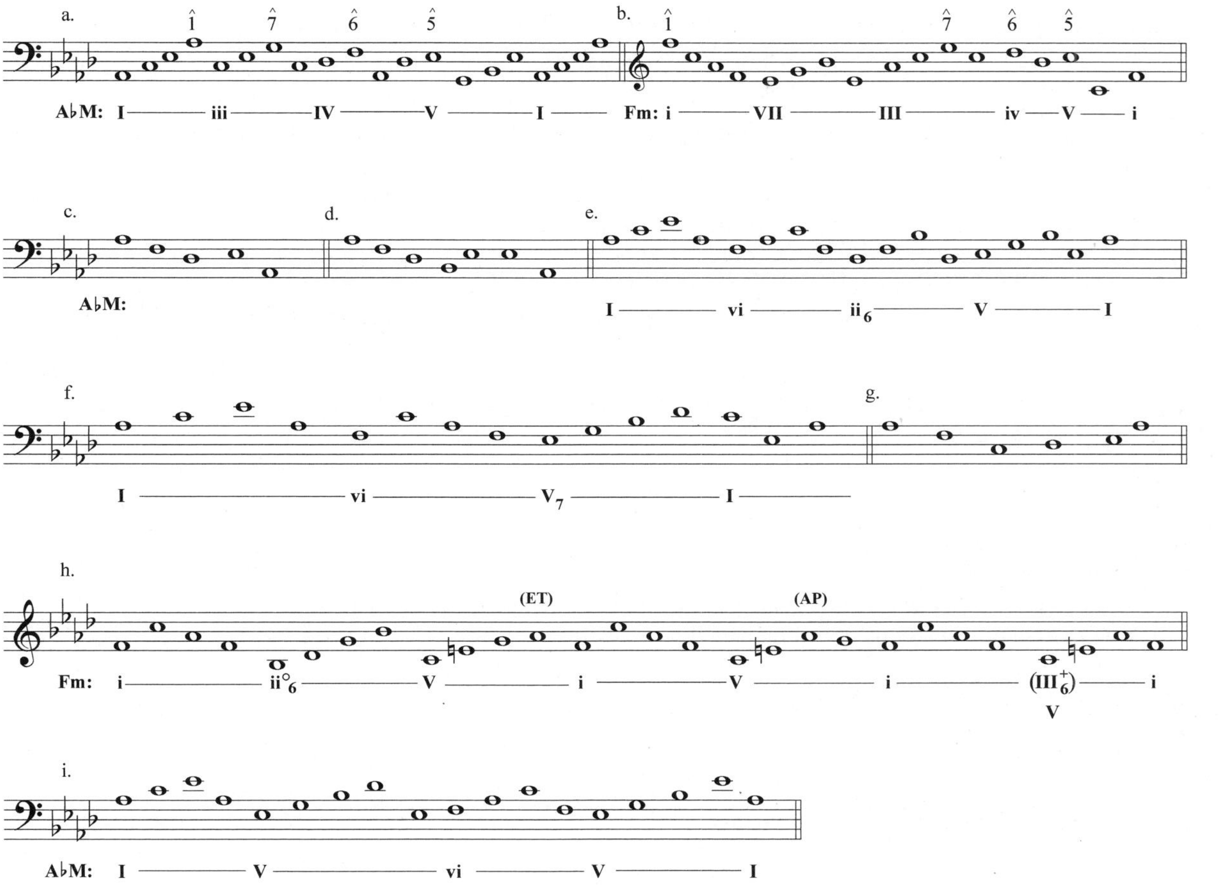

Terms for Review

- Mediant triad
- Submediant triad
- iii and vi as tonic prolongations
- Progression by 3rds
- vi as a pre-dominant
- iii and vi as 5th-related chords
- Dominant as an "apparent mediant"
- vi as a tonic substitute
- Deceptive cadence
- Subtonic triad
- Ground bass
- Romanesca and folia basses
- Keyboard figurations
- Repeated block chords
- Bass afterbeat
- Repeated broken chords
- Arpeggiated chords
- Alberti bass

Worksheet 14

EXERCISE 1 Analysis.

1. Identify the progression in example 14.21. What is the function of the second chord?

Example 14.21 F. Schubert, "Ständchen," from *Schwanengesang,* no. 4, mm. 1–4

2. a) Analyze example 14.22 with RNs.
   b) The complete passage is a harmonic prolongation of I. Explain very specifically how each chord functions in this extended prolongation.

   c) What kind of cadence closes the passage?

Example 14.22 J. S. Bach, Chorale 143, "In dulci jubilo," mm. 1–4

3. a) Analyze example 14.23 with RNs.
   b) How does vi function in this example?

   c) What kind of cadence closes the passage?

Example 14.23 J. S. Bach, Chorale 69, "Komm, Heilliger Geist, Herre Gott," mm. 1–2

4. Analyze example 14.24 with RNs.

Example 14.24 R. Schumann, "Armes Waisenkind," from *Album for the Young,* op. 68, mm. 1–4

EXERCISE 2 Realize the following short progressions in four voices. Provide RNs where missing.

EXERCISE 3 Provide a RN analysis for the following bass line. Include the following chords: III, two VIs (one of them as part of a deceptive candence), V_5^6, V_2^4, all three types of dissonant $^6_4$s (passing, neighbor, cadential), and a 4–3 suspension (you should not realize it, just write the figures under a bass note on which a 4–3 suspension would work).

EXERCISE 4 Realize the following figured bass in four voices. Provide a RN analysis. Remember to double-check the outer-voice frame for good first-species counterpoint.

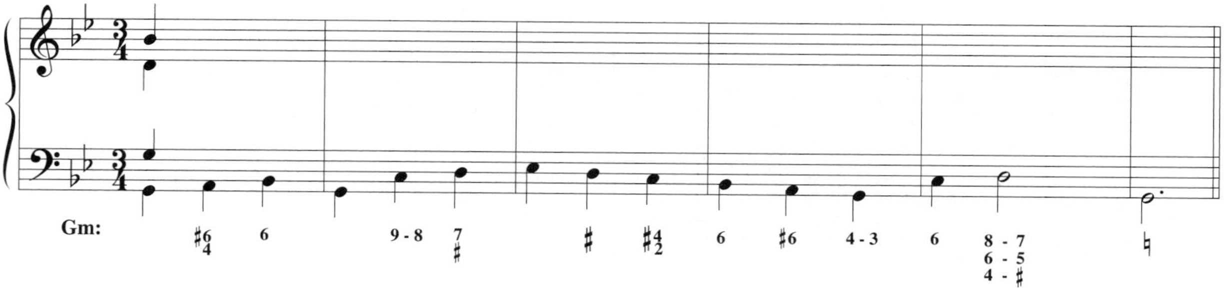

EXERCISE 5 Harmonize this melody in four voices, using the given HR. Include the following chords in your harmonization: iii, vii°_{6}, V^4_3, V^6_5, a cadential V^6_4, a deceptive resolution of V, and a neighbor $^6_4$. Use voice exchange between bass and melody wherever it is possible. Write your bass and RNs first, and make sure they make harmonic and metric sense. Then add the inner voices. Remember: Always play (and make sure you like) your exercises.

EXERCISE 6

1. Write progressions (bass and RNs) using the chords indicated in each case in the required meters. Be careful with the metric placement of your chords.
   a) iii, deceptive resolution of V, neighbor $^6_4$.
   b) Passing $^6_4$, V^4_2, a VII–III progression.
   c) V^6_5, V^4_3, a fragment of a circle of 5ths beginning on iii.

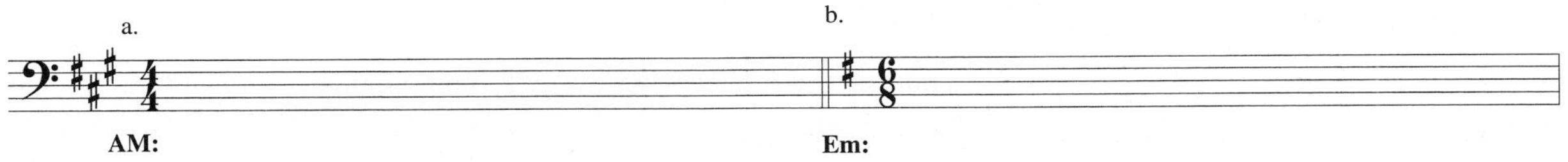

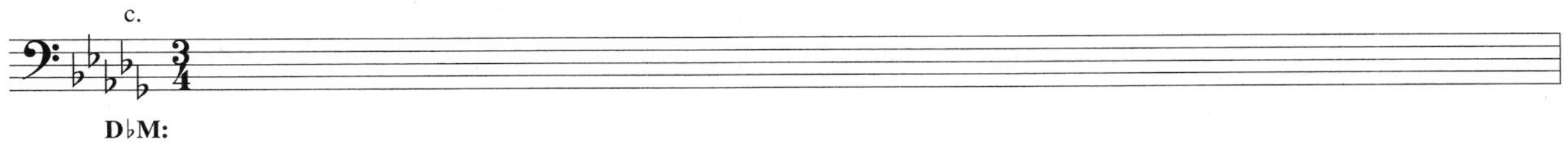

2. Choose one of your own progressions from above, and use it as a harmonic basis to compose a phrase for keyboard. Your phrase should consist of a simple melody (right hand) with a keyboard-style accompaniment (left hand).

Chapter 15

Other Diatonic Seventh Chords

We have now studied all of the diatonic triads and the dominant seventh chord. Seventh chords may also be built on any diatonic scale degree. You may want to review the quality of seventh chords on each of the diatonic degrees of major and minor keys in the chapter D section, "Diatonic Seventh Chords in the Major and Minor Keys." The function of seventh chords is usually the same as the corresponding diatonic triad. Although all seventh chords may be found in music, we will focus on those that appear most frequently: the leading-tone sevenths (vii$^{\circ}_{7}$ and vii$^{ø}_{7}$), the supertonic seventh (ii$_7$ or ii$^{ø}_{7}$), and the subdominant seventh (IV$_7$ or iv$_7$).

GENERAL DOUBLING AND VOICE-LEADING GUIDELINES

Because seventh chords in four voices will usually be complete, you need not double any pitch. If a seventh chord cannot be complete because of voice-leading considerations, you may omit the fifth of the chord. You should not double the seventh or the leading tone (LT). It is best to double the root unless it is the LT (as in vii$^{\circ}_{7}$). Two voice-leading conventions apply to all seventh chords:

1. The seventh must resolve downward by step.
2. It is better to prepare the seventh, if possible, by approaching it as a repeated note or by step. It is less desirable to approach it by leap, but if you must do so, it is better to approach it by ascending leap.

Doubling and voice-leading principles apply equally to seventh-chord inversions. For inversions we will use the same symbols we already learned as applied to the dominant seventh: $^{6}_{5}$ indicates first inversion (third in the bass), $^{4}_{3}$ indicates second inversion (fifth in the bass), and $^{4}_{2}$ indicates third inversion (seventh in the bass).

Example 15.1

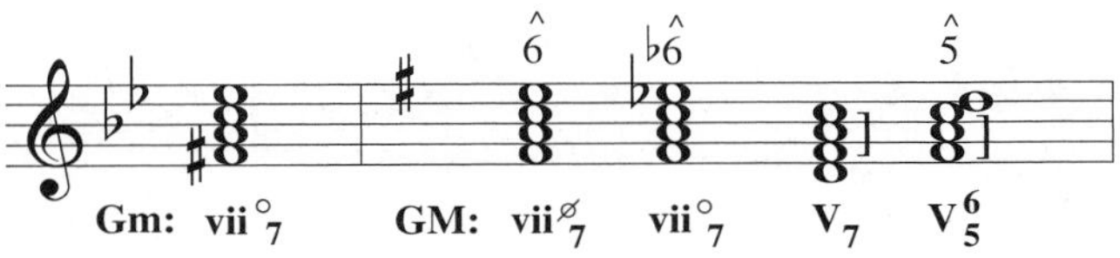

Example 15.2 A. Beach, "Barcarolle," from *Three Pieces,* op. 28, no. 1, mm. 1–6

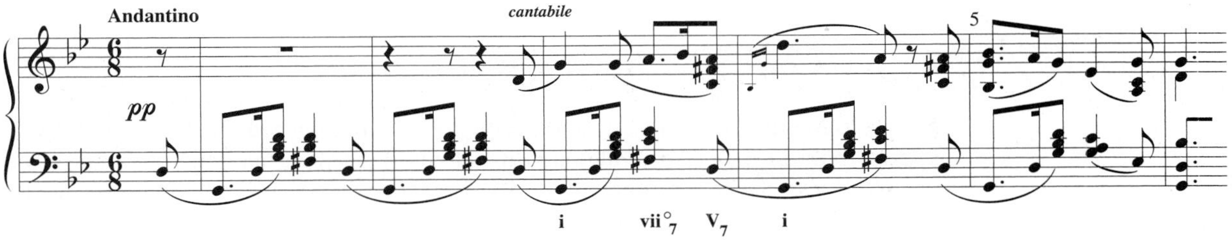

NOTE

The voice-leading guidelines we have just discussed are standard in common practice music, where sevenths are dissonant and are treated as such. In jazz and popular music, sevenths are not necessarily considered dissonant, and hence these voice-leading guidelines do not necessarily apply.

THE LEADING-TONE SEVENTHS

The diatonic seventh chord on the LT is half-diminished in major keys (**vii$^{ø}_7$**) and fully-diminished in minor keys (**vii°$_7$**). The fully-diminished chord, however, is also used in major keys, with exactly the same spelling as vii°$_7$ in minor. This is not properly a diatonic chord, because it requires a lowered $\hat{6}$ ($\flat\hat{6}$), a degree "borrowed" from minor. vii°$_7$ actually appears in major keys more often than the purely diatonic vii$^{ø}_7$, a fairly infrequent chord.

Both vii$^{ø}_7$ and vii°$_7$ resolve to the tonic, and both are chords with a dominant function, most often used as linear embellishments of the tonic. Both chords are **closely related to V$_7$:** The LT sevenths have three common tones with V$_7$ ($\hat{7}$–$\hat{2}$–$\hat{4}$, bracketed in example 15.1), and one pitch a step away from the root of V$_7$ ($\hat{6}$ in vii$^{ø}_7$, $\flat\hat{6}$ in vii°$_7$, $\hat{5}$ in V$_7$), as illustrated by example 15.1. The close relationship may best be observed by comparing the two LT sevenths with V$^6_5$: All three chords are built on the LT, and all three chords share the LT triad ($\hat{7}$–$\hat{2}$–$\hat{4}$). Because of this close relationship, LT seventh chords often move to V$_7$ before resolving to the tonic, as in the phrase by Beach reproduced in example 15.2 (see mm. 3–4).

Example 15.3 W. A. Mozart, Piano Sonata in DM, K. 284, III, Var. V, mm. 13–17

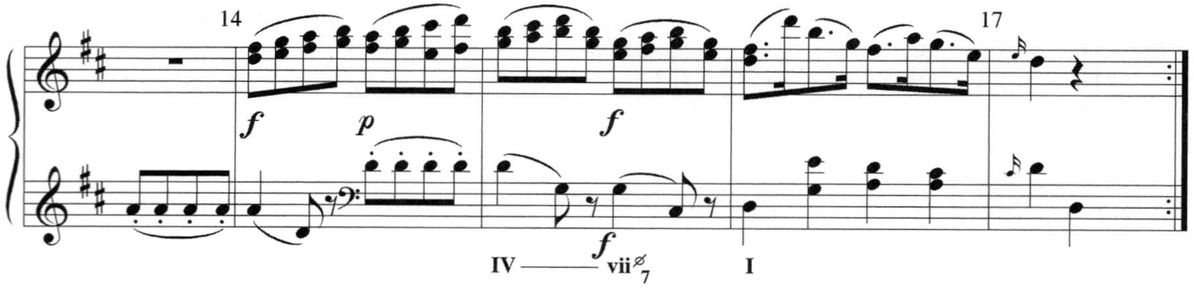

THE HALF-DIMINISHED SEVENTH

The *half-diminished seventh* sonority comprises a diminished triad and a m7. vii$^{\varnothing}_{7}$ appears only in major keys, although it is found less often than vii$^{\circ}_{7}$. Example 15.3 (m. 15) shows a standard context for vii$^{\varnothing}_{7}$: It functions as a dominant, it is preceded by a pre-dominant chord (IV), and it resolves to I.

Voice Leading

Example 15.4 illustrates the main voice-leading characteristics for this chord, as explained in the following points:

1. The °5, $\hat{7}$–$\hat{4}$ (common to both vii$^{\circ}_{7}$ and V_7) must be resolved inward to $\hat{1}$–$\hat{3}$ (or outward to $\hat{3}$–$\hat{1}$ if it appears as a +4, $\hat{4}$–$\hat{7}$ as in example 15.4d).
2. The seventh resolves down by step.
3. The third ($\hat{2}$) may in principle move up to $\hat{3}$ or down to $\hat{1}$. If it moves down to $\hat{1}$, however, parallel 5ths may result (as in example 15.4b); $\hat{2}$ should then move up

Example 15.4

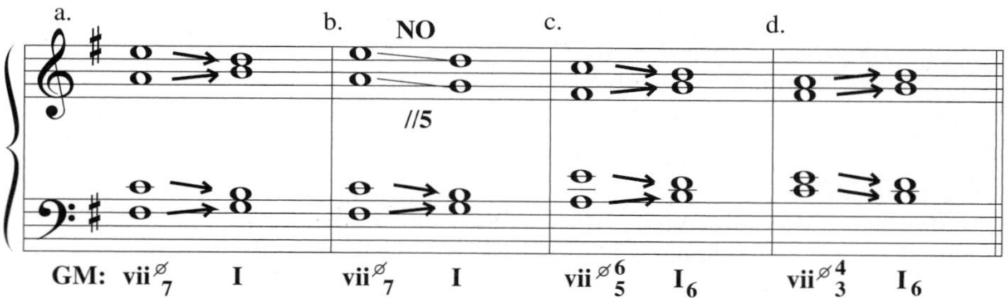

to $\hat{3}$, as in example 15.4a. (You could also switch the soprano and alto parts in example 15.4b to avoid the parallel 5ths.)

Inversions of vii$^{\varnothing}_{7}$

Examples 15.4c and d represent the two most usual inversions of vii$^{\varnothing}_{7}$: vii$^{\varnothing 6}_{5}$ and vii$^{\varnothing 4}_{3}$ (the 3rd inversion is much less frequent). vii$^{\varnothing 6}_{5}$ should not resolve to I in root position for the same reason we already discussed (the bass $\hat{2}$–$\hat{1}$ would produce parallel 5ths with another voice). And because the fifth of this chord ($\hat{4}$) resolves down by step to $\hat{3}$ as part of the tritone $\hat{4}$–$\hat{7}$, vii$^{\varnothing 4}_{3}$ will also usually resolve to I_6, as in example 15.4d. In all these examples you may note that in the normative resolution of this chord (which does not allow for much voice-leading freedom), the *third* of the tonic chord is doubled.

THE FULLY-DIMINISHED SEVENTH

The *fully-diminished seventh chord* is made up of a diminished triad and a diminished 7th. The **intervallic content** of this chord is highly uniform, as you can see in example 15.5a: You can indeed build a °7 chord by stacking *three minor 3rds*, or also by overlapping *two diminished 5ths*. The result is that you come up with the same intervals if you read from the bottom up or from the top down. We call this type of sonority a *symmetrical* sonority. Imagine the pitch F♯ placed on top of the °7 chord in example 15.5a. The resulting division of the octave into four minor thirds (F♯–A–C–E♭–F♯) is indeed symmetrical around the axis C; that is, the upper and lower halves of the sonority are, intervallically, mirror inversions of each other.

Because of its symmetrical nature and its highly uniform intervallic content, the °7th chord is a characteristic sonority with strong expressive power and a variety of harmonic possibilities, some of which we will study in the second part of this book. A result of this symmetrical intervallic content is that, although we can determine the position of a vii$_7$ chord by its spelling, the *sound* of each inversion is intervallically identical to any other inversion. In example 15.5b you can see the different spelling for each inversion. Play each of the chords and notice that you are still playing stacked 3rds (+2 = m3 in sound), overlapping tritones, and a °7th outer-voice interval.

Another property of °7th chords is that, if we consider their actual pitch content, regardless of possible enharmonic spellings, there are only **three possible different chords,** as illustrated by example 15.5c. Play a °7th chord on any pitch and on the two

Example 15.5

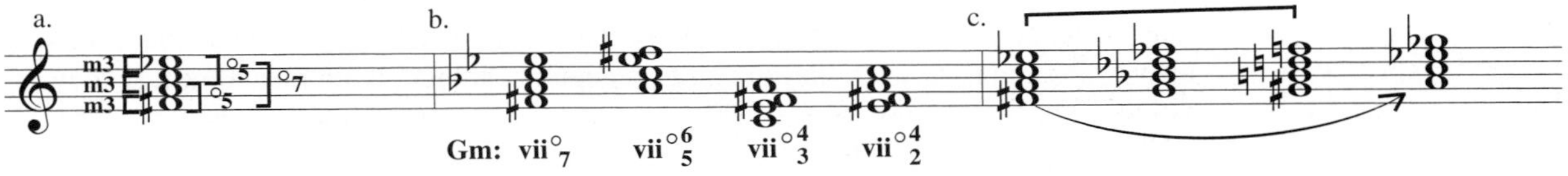

Example 15.6 J. Brahms, Ballade in BM, op. 10, no. 4, mm. 89–93

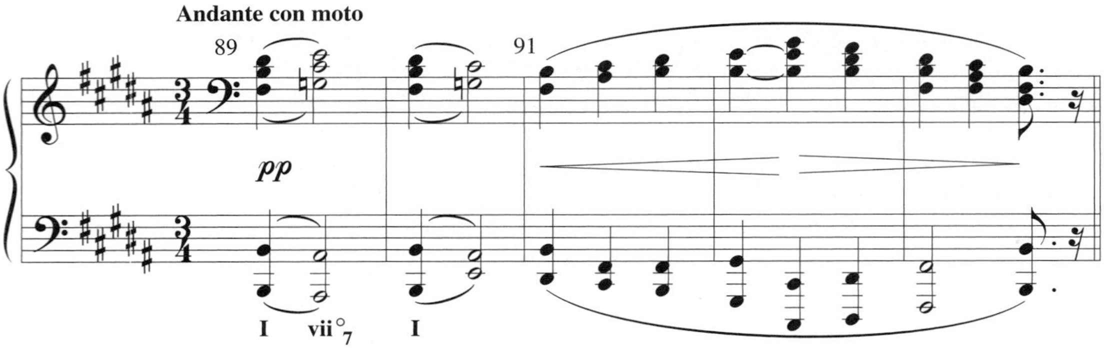

following pitches in the chromatic scale (such as F♯, G, and G♯). These are three different chords. The fourth chord, however, on A, contains exactly the same pitches as the first one, on F♯. All of these properties of the °7th chord have been widely used by composers as a means to modulate, to create harmonic ambiguity, and to create dramatic tension. For the time being we will limit our study of this chord to its most elementary function as a member of the dominant family often used as a linear prolongation of the tonic, in both major and minor keys.

Voice leading

Example 15.6 shows a frequent function of vii$^{\circ}_{7}$: It embellishes I as a linear neighbor chord (m. 1). Here you see the normative voice-leading principles in the resolution of vii$^{\circ}_{7}$: The LT (A♯) moves up to $\hat{1}$, the seventh (G♮) moves down (♭$\hat{6}$–$\hat{5}$), and the pitch that forms a °5 with the bass (E) also moves down ($\hat{4}$–$\hat{3}$). These standard voice-leading guidelines are clearly shown in example 15.7.

The third of vii$^{\circ}_{7}$ may either move up or down. If it moves up (as in example 15.7a), a satisfactory resolution of both °5ths occurs. In example 15.7b the third moves downward, producing unequal 5ths. This voice leading is often found in music and is quite acceptable. If the third moves down to $\hat{1}$, however, a more satisfactory voice leading results when the unequal 5ths appear inverted, as 4ths (example 15.7c).

vii$^{\circ 6}_{5}$

The first inversion of vii$^{\circ}_{7}$, vii$^{\circ 6}_{5}$, may then resolve *either to I or to I$_6$* (the third in the bass may move up or down). In the vii$^{\circ 6}_{5}$–I progression (as well as I–vii$^{\circ 6}_{5}$) unequal 5ths will also occur, and here again they are quite acceptable, although not ideal (because they involve the bass). The progression vii$^{\circ 6}_{5}$–I$_6$ produces a more satisfactory resolution of both tritones. Example 15.7d illustrates the use of vii$^{\circ 6}_{5}$ as a passing chord between I and I$_6$.

Example 15.7

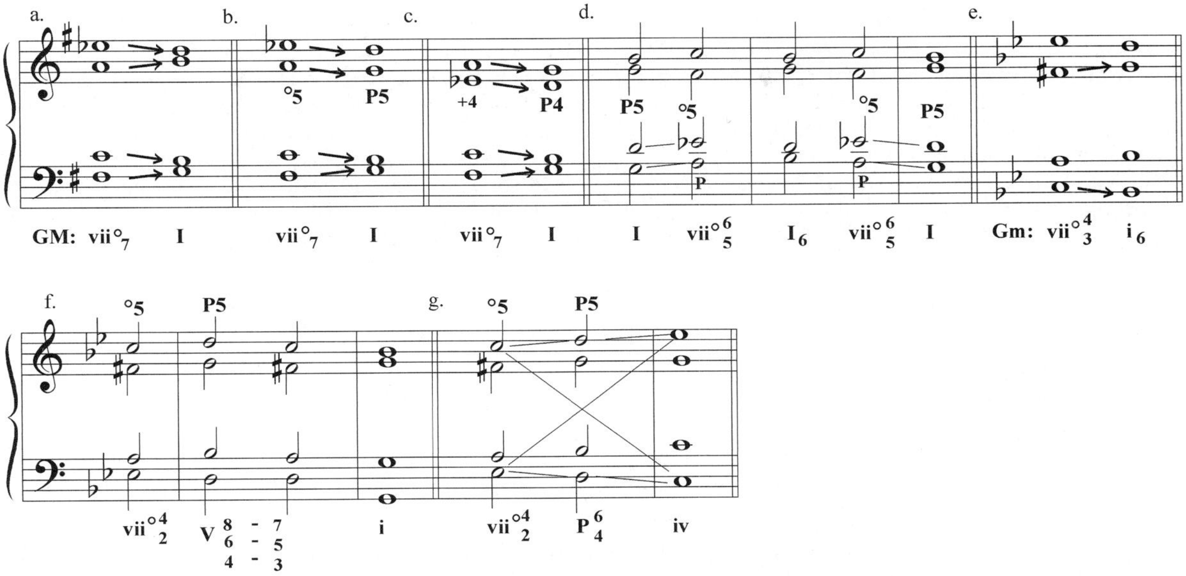

vii$^{\circ 4}_{3}$ and vii$^{\circ 4}_{2}$

Because the fifth of vii$^{\circ}_{7}$ ($\hat{4}$) must resolve down as part of the tritone $\hat{7}$–$\hat{4}$, the second inversion, vii$^{\circ 4}_{3}$, usually resolves to I_6 (or i_6, as in example 15.7e). In the third inversion (which is found less often than the other two inversions), on the other hand, the seventh ($\flat\hat{6}$) should resolve down to $\hat{5}$, resulting in a $^{6}_{4}$ chord which must be treated as one of the standard types of $^{6}_{4}$ chords. Most frequently, vii$^{\circ 4}_{2}$ resolves to a cadential $^{6}_{4}$, although it may also resolve to a passing $^{6}_{4}$. In both cases it is possible to find the voice-leading license used in examples 15.7f and g: in example 15.7f, in order to preserve the customary doubling in the $^{6}_{4}$ chord ($\hat{5}$ is doubled), the °5 in vii$^{\circ 4}_{2}$ (F♯–C, or $\hat{7}$–$\hat{4}$) does not resolve inward but rather moves up producing unequal 5ths; in example 15.7g the same unequal 5ths occur because of the voice exchange effected by the passing $^{6}_{4}$ figure.

Now go back to the Brahms passage in example 15.6 and study the resolution and voice leading of the fourth chord: What chord is it? To what chord does it resolve? How does Brahms avoid unequal 5ths? You may also notice some other harmonic aspects of the passage: How does Brahms prolong the tonic in m. 91? The second chord in m. 92 is also a seventh chord that we will study in this chapter. Which one? Does Brahms prepare the seventh in this chord?

vii$^{\circ}_{7}$ and V_7

vii$^{\circ}_{7}$ and V_7 have the same function, share three common tones, and by moving the fourth pitch by step, one of the chords may be converted into the other. Because of this close relationship, both chords often appear together. Example 15.8 shows several

PRACTICAL APPLICATION AND DISCUSSION

Example 15.9 begins with a statement of the tonic, a "dominant area," and a return to the tonic. How is the dominant area extended? Explain the linear relationships between the opening and closing tonic and the central dominant area (look at both the two upper voices and the left-hand chords).

Interesting linear designs involving vii°$_7$ chords may be found in two examples from the anthology. In anthology, no. 34 (Beethoven, Sonata op. 13, III), the first phrase ends at m. 4 on a V chord, and the beginning of the second phrase extends this dominant harmony to resolve it in m. 6. What is the chord at m. 5 that prolongs the V from m. 4?

Now turn to anthology, no. 56 (Clara Schumann, Trio). In mm. 269–270, two inversions of vii°$_7$ are connected linearly by a passing chord. What are the two inversions, what is the passing chord, and where is the voice exchange that connects the progression linearly? Look also at the resolution to I in m. 271. How is I prolonged in this measure? What seventh chord can you identify?

As a final example for this discussion, study example 15.10. First, think of mm. 1–8 as a single harmonic unit (underlying a phrase with two parallel phrase segments). The long-range motion is from i to i$_6$, hence a prolongation of i; how are i and i$_6$ connected? i$_6$ is itself extended through m. 14. How is i$_6$ extended linearly in mm. 9–14? What chord is used for this extension and how does it function? How does i$_6$ go back to i in mm. 15–18? In other words, all of mm. 1–18 are a prolongation of the tonic. Show the function of all the linear chords by marking them with a P or an N (for passing or neighbor, respectively).

Example 15.8

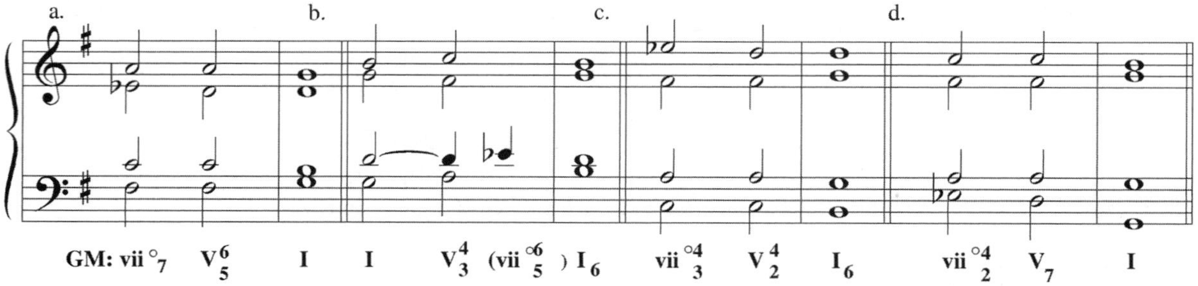

Example 15.9 W. A. Mozart, Piano Sonata in Cm, K. 457, I, mm. 1–8

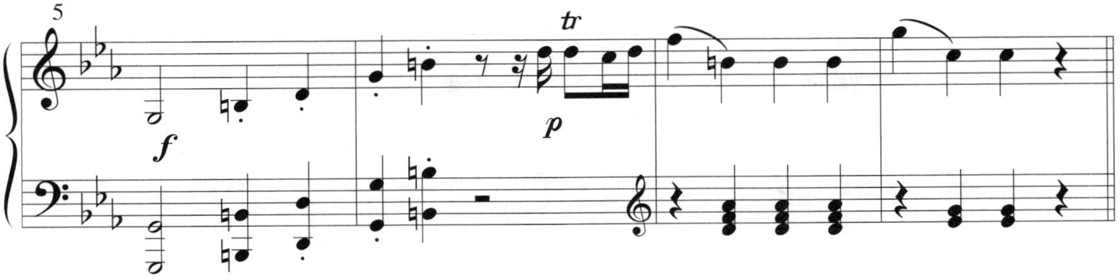

Example 15.10 L. v. Beethoven, Piano Sonata in Cm, op. 10, no. 1, I, mm. 1–22

possibilities of vii°$_7$ chords moving to V or V$_7$ chords (in either root position or inversion). In all these cases, the vii°$_7$ chord is heard as a contrapuntal elaboration of V$_7$, in which ♭$\hat{6}$ functions as a neighbor note or passing tone (depending on the context) moving to $\hat{5}$.

Example 15.10 Continued

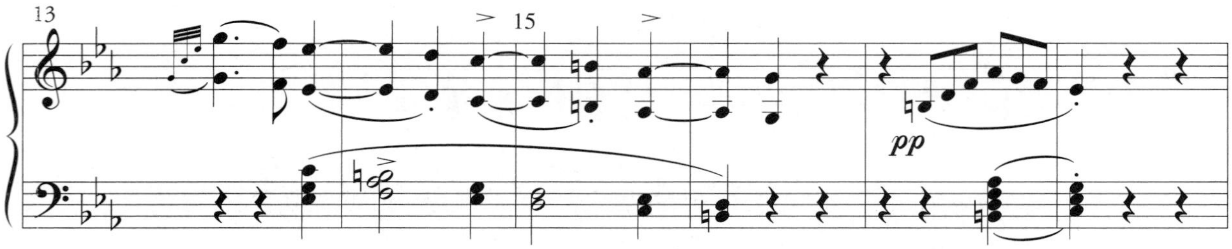

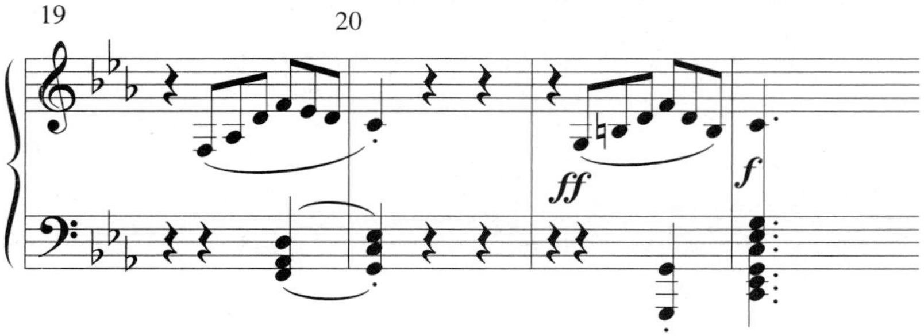

EXERCISES

To practice spelling and resolving leading-tone seventh chords, refer to exercise 2 in worksheet 15 at the end of this chapter.

To practice realizing short progressions using LT seventh chords, refer to exercises 3a and b in worksheet 15 at the end of this chapter.

THE SUPERTONIC SEVENTH

The seventh chord on $\hat{2}$, along with V_7, is one of the most commonly used seventh chords in the tonal literature. It is a mm chord in major keys (ii_7) and a half-diminished chord in minor keys ($ii^{ø}_7$). Its function is the same as the ii triad: to precede the dominant, most often in cadential gestures. Mendelssohn concludes the opening phrase of his violin concerto with an authentic cadence preceded by a $ii^{ø}_7$ dominant preparation (example 15.11). Note that the $ii^{ø}_7$ "grows" from the previous chord, iv (which has three common tones with it). The voice leading of the passage is as smooth as it can possibly be. The three common tones are retained in the same voices, including the seventh, which is thus prepared. The seventh resolves down to $\hat{7}$, and moreover the seventh in V_7 ($\hat{4}$) is also prepared (and, of course, resolved). Measures 1–8 in this phrase are a prolongation of the tonic. What harmonic/linear means does Mendelssohn use for this prolongation?

Example 15.11 Felix Mendelssohn, Concerto for Violin, op. 64, mm. 1–11

Even more common than ii_7 is its first inversion. $\mathbf{ii^6_5}$ is one of the strongest and most frequently used predominant chords. By combining the strong melodic bass motion ($\hat{4}$–$\hat{5}$) and the dissonant clash of a 2nd ($^6_5$ above the bass), this chord creates a powerful drive toward V. The cadential formula ii^6_5–V_7–I is one of Bach's favorites (as well as of most other composers). In Bach's realizations of this formula we can see the melodic origin of this chord (as of dissonance in general): The dissonance (the seventh of the chord) is normally prepared as a suspension that resolves in the next chord, with a change of bass. Two cadences by Bach reproduced in examples 15.12a and b confirm this voice leading.

The excerpt in example 15.12b is in Fm, despite the key signature. How do you explain the final FM chord? Observe that both examples illustrate the melodic origin of V_7: What is the function of the seventh in both final cadential dominants?

Examples 15.12a and b

J. S. Bach, Chorale 20, "Ein feste Burg ist unser Gott" (final cadence) and J. S. Bach, Chorale 25, "Wo soll ich fliehen hin" (final cadence)

Example 15.12c

Felix Mendelssohn, "Hexenlied," *Zwölf Gesänge*, op. 8, no. 8, mm. 71–74

Example 15.12d

M. Szymanowska, Nocturne in B♭M, mm. 53–55

Two examples by nineteenth-century composers show the use of ii^6_5 (or $\text{ii}^{\varnothing 6}_{5}$) in a keyboard texture (examples 15.12c and d). Even in this context in which dissonance is often treated with more freedom, both Felix Mendelssohn and Maria Szymanowska approach the seventh with careful voice leading. Study both passages, identifying the supertonic seventh chords, the chords that precede them, and the voice leading of both the preparation and the resolution.

Summary of Voice Leading; Other Inversions of ii_7

Example 15.13 presents a summary of standard resolutions of ii_7 and its inversions. In all of these cases the seventh ($\hat{1}$) is prepared, and it resolves down to $\hat{7}$. The ii_7–V_7–I progression is especially effective to harmonize the melodic patterns $\hat{4}$–$\hat{4}$–$\hat{3}$ (example 15.13b) and $\hat{1}$–$\hat{7}$–$\hat{1}$, whereas the ii^6_5–V–I or ii^6_5–V_7–I progressions are often used for the patterns $\hat{2}$–$\hat{2}$–$\hat{3}$ (example 15.13c), $\hat{6}$–$\hat{5}$–$\hat{5}$, or $\hat{1}$–$\hat{7}$–$\hat{1}$. Notice the close relationship of ii^6_5 as a pre-dominant (example 15.13c) with both IV and ii_6 (two chords that are contained in ii^6_5). In example 15.13d you will see another standard progression involving ii^6_5: Because ii^6_5 and V^4_2 have the same bass, $\hat{4}$, the progression ii^6_5–V^4_2 allows for very smooth voice leading over a stationary bass.

Example 15.13

The second inversion of ii_7, ii^4_3, is not found as frequently as ii^6_5. Example 15.13e shows the standard resolution of ii^4_3, down to V or V_7. The third inversion, on the other hand, is often used as part of the progression illustrated in example 15.13f. Because ii^4_2 is built on $\hat{1}$, it allows for a smooth connection with I. The seventh is thus prepared in the bass and, as usual, is resolved down to $\hat{7}$, and hence to V_6 or V^6_5. Study the harmonization of the opening period of Mozart's Gm Symphony (example 15.14). What are the only four chords used by Mozart? What is the complete progression? How does the second chord resolve?

Example 15.14 W. A. Mozart, Symphony no. 40 in Gm, K. 550, I, mm. 1–9

THE SUBDOMINANT SEVENTH

IV_7 is the most common among the remaining diatonic seventh chords. The subdominant seventh is a MM_7 sonority in major keys (IV_7) and a mm_7 sonority in minor keys (iv_7). IV_7 is also a chord that often illustrates the melodic origin of seventh chords. In example 15.15a you can find a IV_7 chord that results melodically from a PT in the soprano. (How do you explain each of the notes over the bass $\hat{5}$ in m. 4?) In example 15.15b, on the other hand, IV_7 appears as an independent chord. In both cases, however, the seventh over $\hat{4}$ ($\hat{3}$) is approached by step from above (prepared) and resolved by step downward. If IV_7 is preceded by I, as in example 15.15c, the seventh may be prepared as a repeated note. In any case, the progression IV_7–V_7–I works well to harmonize the melodic pattern $\hat{3}$–$\hat{2}$–$\hat{1}$.

Examples 15.15a and b J. S. Bach, Chorale 5, "An Wasserflüssen Babylon," mm. 3–4 and J. S. Bach, Chorale 117, "O Welt, ich muss dich lassen" (final cadence)

Examples 15.15c to e

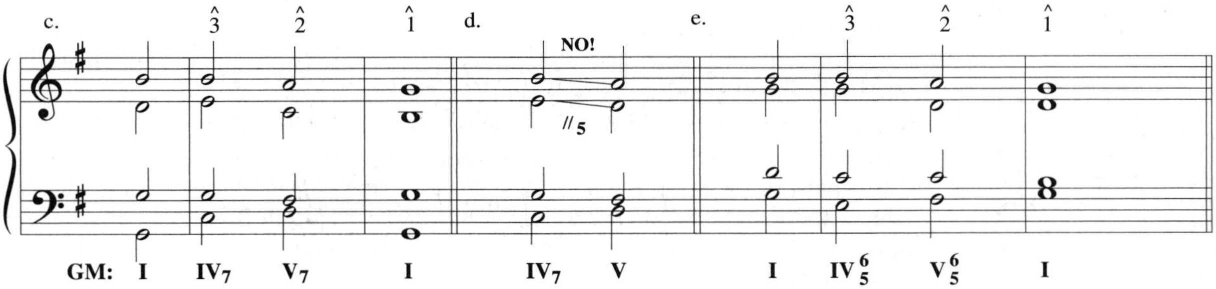

Example 15.15f G. F. Handel, "Surely He Hath Borne Our Griefs," from *Messiah*, mm. 19–24 (Simplified)

NOTE

Beware of parallel 5ths between IV$_7$ and V, as shown in example 15.15d.

IV$_7$ can often be found in first inversion, also harmonizing the $\hat{3}$–$\hat{2}$–$\hat{1}$ melodic pattern. The progression IV$^6_5$–V$^6_5$–I creates an effective contrapuntal motion toward I. Notice, in example 15.15e, the outer voices moving in contrary motion toward a common goal, $\hat{1}$: $\hat{3}$–$\hat{2}$–$\hat{1}$ in the soprano, and $\hat{6}$–$\hat{7}$–$\hat{1}$ in the bass. Identify, in example 15.15f, the same progression in the context of a well-known passage by Handel. In m. 23 of this same fragment, moreover, you will also find a IV$^6_5$ used as part of a two-beat pre-dominant complex. What chord does IV$^6_5$ move to in this measure?

IV$_7$, as well as all other diatonic seventh chords, can be found much more frequently in twentieth-century popular music (such as jazz, musical theater, or rock) than in common practice art music. Chordal dissonances in popular music are often more "harmonically" than "linearly" conceived. That is, they are often conceived more as an integral part of the chordal sonority, rather than as a result of linear voice leading. For this reason, the principles of preparation and resolution of sevenths in popular music are not always followed as strictly as in common practice art music. An example of a characteristic popular music progression involving IV$_7$ appears in example 15.16a.

Example 15.16b shows the final section of a well-known refrain based on the **blues progression.** The complete blues progression may include several seventh chords, as it does in the form it appears in this song: I$_{\flat 7}$–IV$_{\flat 7}$–I$_{\flat 7}$–V$_7$–IV$_{\flat 7}$–I–V. You may observe some interesting aspects in the blues harmonic phrase. First, the progression V–IV (with or without sevenths), so unusual in common-practice music, is an essential component of the blues progression. Second, the tonic and subdominant seventh chords in this example are not really diatonic. Although the diatonic seventh chords on both of these degrees are MM$_7$ sonorities, the ♭7th turns these chords into Mm$_7$ sonorities in which two chromatic degrees are used: ♭$\hat{7}$ in I$_{\flat 7}$, and ♭$\hat{3}$ in IV$_{\flat 7}$.

Example 15.16a Alan Jay Lerner–Frederick Loewe, "Almost Like Being in Love," from *Brigadoon* (Refrain)

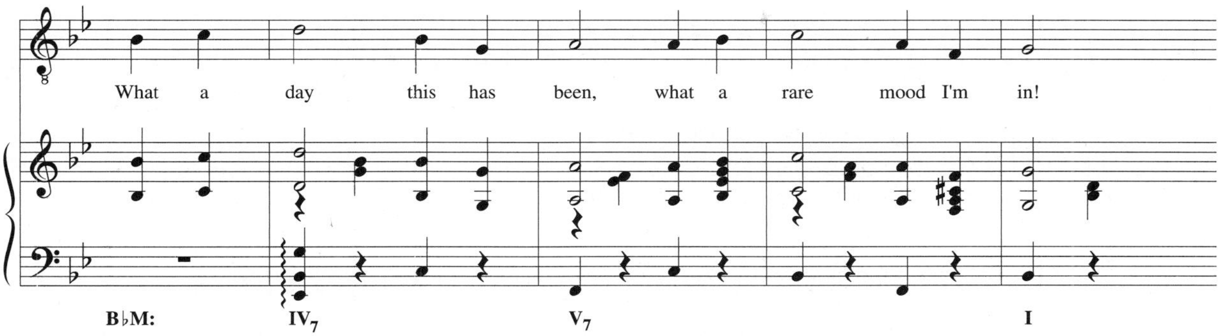

Example 15.16b J. Lennon–P. McCartney, "Can't Buy Me Love," from the film and album *A Hard Day's Night* (Refrain)

EXERCISES

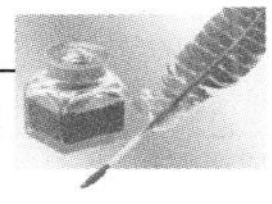

To practice realizing short progressions using supertonic and subdominant seventh chords, refer to exercises 3c to e in worksheet 15 at the end of this chapter.

To practice realizing a progression using a variety of seventh chords, refer to exercise 4 in worksheet 15 at the end of this chapter.

To practice harmonizing a melody using a variety of seventh chords, refer to exercise 5 in worksheet 15 at the end of this chapter.

To practice writing your own progressions using a variety of seventh chords, refer to exercise 6 in worksheet 15 at the end of this chapter.

To practice analysis of musical fragments including diatonic seventh chords, refer to exercise 1 in worksheet 15 at the end of this chapter.

Example 15.17

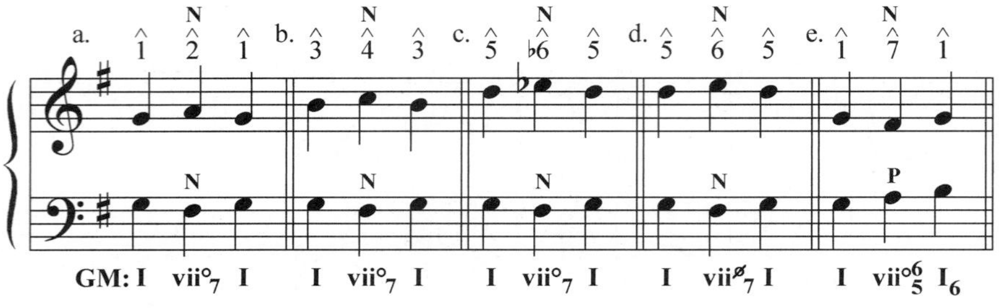

CHARACTERISTIC SOPRANO-BASS PATTERNS

The various chords we have studied in this chapter, including their inversions, allow for numerous soprano-bass patterns. Because a comprehensive list would be too extensive for our purposes, we will study only a few of the most characteristic patterns. Example 15.17 shows five patterns that use harmonizations with leading-tone seventh chords. All of them feature neighbor figures in both the soprano and the bass, except for pattern 15.17e, which includes a passing figure in the bass. Thus, all patterns in this example are linear figures that prolong the initial tonic.

Example 15.18 illustrates patterns that include pre-dominant seventh chords. These are all characteristic cadential patterns made up of pre-dominant/dominant/tonic progressions. Examples 15.18a to e feature supertonic seventh chords, whereas examples 15.18f and g include subdominant seventh chords. Play each of the outer-voice patterns in examples 15.17 and 15.18 at the piano, adding inner voices in keyboard texture.

ELABORATING THE I–V–I PROGRESSION

Because the most common function of leading-tone seventh chords is to prolong the tonic linearly, progressions using these chords are frequently used to extend the initial

Example 15.18

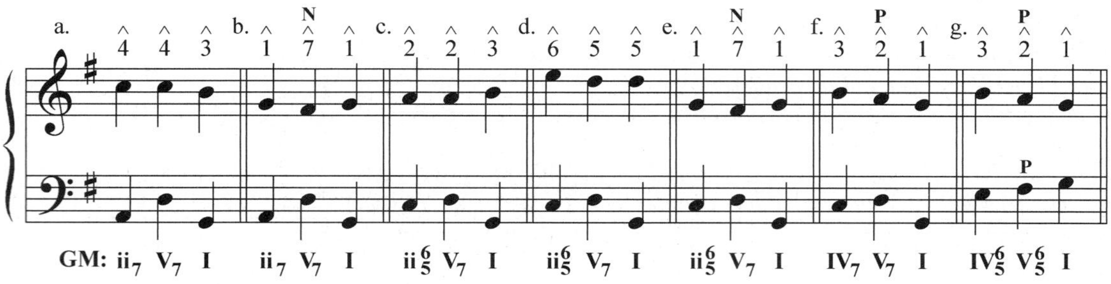

Example 15.19

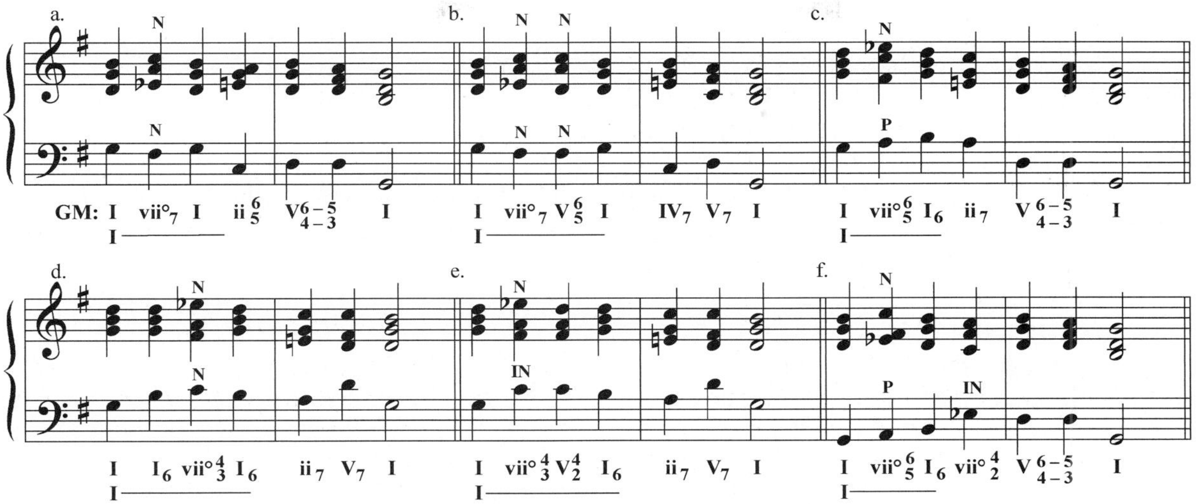

tonic in a I–V–I progression. This function is illustrated in each of the extended I–V–I progressions shown in example 15.19. Examples 15.19a to e also include pre-dominant seventh chords elaborating the closing cadence. In example 15.19f, the final dominant is approached from a vii$^{\circ 4}_{2}$ chord with an incomplete-neighbor function (IN). Otherwise, the extensions of the opening tonic by means of leading-tone seventh chords feature the familiar N or P motions, and, in one case (example 15.19e), an IN motion in the bass. All of these progressions may be played in M or m keys.

Besides their function as pre-dominant chords illustrated in example 15.19, the supertonic and subdominant seventh chords can also be used to prolong the initial tonic chord in the I–V–I progression, as shown in example 15.20. In all of these progressions the tonic is prolonged by means of N, P, or IN figures in the soprano and the bass, besides repeated notes (pedal figures, indicated as "Ped" in the examples) and, in example 15.20, an arpeggiation down a 3rd.

Example 15.20

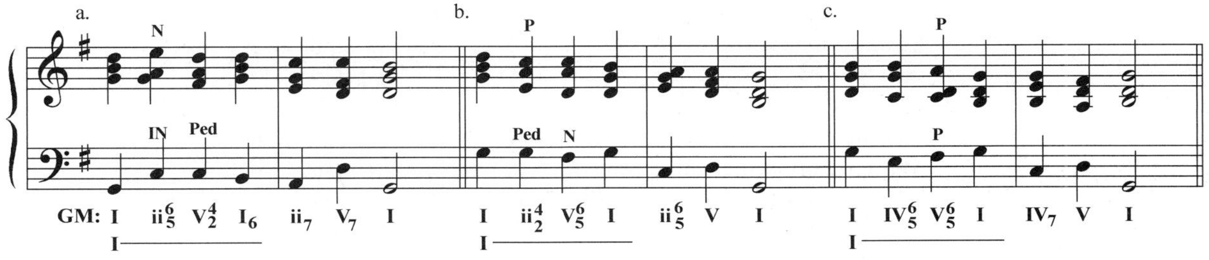

ASSIGNMENT AND KEYBOARD EXERCISES

For analytical and written assignments and keyboard exercises based on the materials learned in this chapter, refer to chapter 15 in the workbook.

PITCH PATTERNS

1. Be able to sing $^{\varnothing}{}_7$, $^{\circ}{}_7$, mm$_7$, and MM$_7$ sonorities in root position on any pitch.
2. Sing the pitch patterns in example 15.21, listening to the linearized harmonic progressions as you sing.

Example 15.21

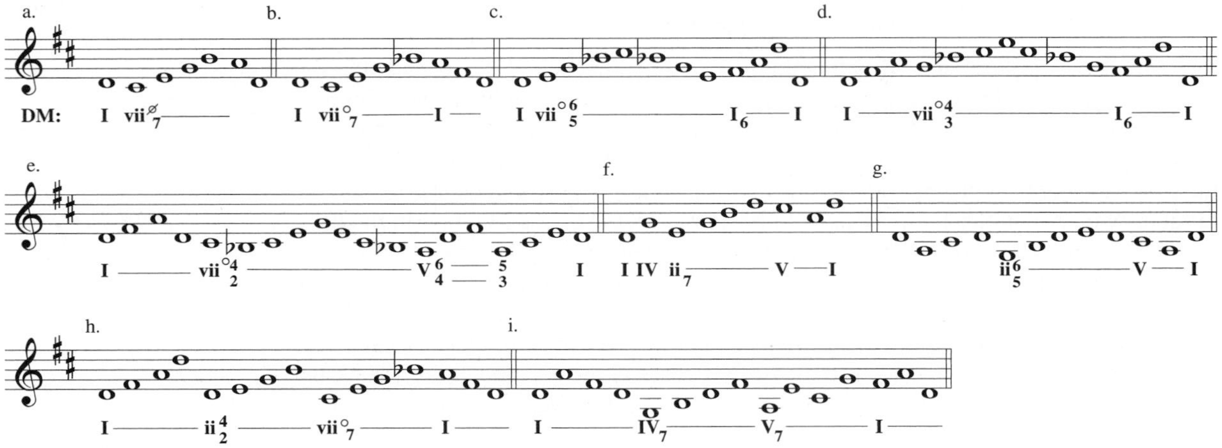

Terms for Review

Leading-tone sevenths
vii$^{\varnothing}{}_7$
vii$^{\circ}{}_7$
vii$^{\varnothing}{}_7$ and vii$^{\circ}{}_7$ as related to V$_7$
The $^{\circ}{}_7$ sonority: intervallic content, inversions, possible different $^{\circ}{}_7$ chords
Resolution of inversions of vii$^{\varnothing}{}_7$ and vii$^{\circ}{}_7$
Supertonic seventh
ii$^{6}_{5}$; other inversions of ii$_7$
Subdominant seventh
Blues progression

Worksheet 15

EXERCISE 1 Analysis.

1. Study example 15.22, focusing on the following aspects:
   a) *Texture.* Compare and discuss texture in mm. 1–4 and 5–9. What is the role of the harpsichord in mm. 1–4? And in mm. 5–9? What is the role of the flute in mm. 5–9 with regard to the harpsichord's right hand?

Example 15.22 J. S. Bach, Sonata no. 1 for Flute and Keyboard, BWV 1030, IV, mm. 1–9

   b) *Melody.* What kind of melody did Bach write in this example, if you consider the type of line (or lines)? Focus especially on mm. 1–2 and 3–4. How does the melody grow in mm. 1–2? Is it generated by a motive (comment on its rhythmic characteristics)? What technique of melodic growth does Bach use? Is this technique accompanied by a similar harmonic procedure?

c) *Harmony.* Analyze mm. 1–4 with RNs (focus on the keyboard part only).

1. What is the linear function of the seventh chord in m. 1, beat 2?

2. What are the two seventh chords in m. 2, beats 1–2? What is their linear function? What two chords do they connect, and by means of what voice leading (examine both the bass and the keyboard's top voice)?

3. The chord in m. 2, beat 3, has two nonchord tones that resolve in beat 4. Explain.

4. Measure 3, beat 3: What chord is this, and how does it resolve? The chord of resolution, in beat 4, is itself a dissonant chord. What is its linear function?

5. What is the basic progression in mm. 5–6, as outlined by the keyboard's left hand? What is the linear function of the chord at m. 6, beats 1–2?

2. Analyze example 15.23 with RNs. What familiar linear gesture opens the excerpt? What is the seventh chord in m. 13, and how does it function?

Example 15.23 L. Reichardt, *From Ariel's Revelation,* mm. 9–17

EXERCISE 2 Write the following leading-tone seventh chords in each of the indicated keys (provide key signatures) and resolve them appropriately. If the resolution is to a $^6_4$ chord, resolve the $^6_4$ chord, too.

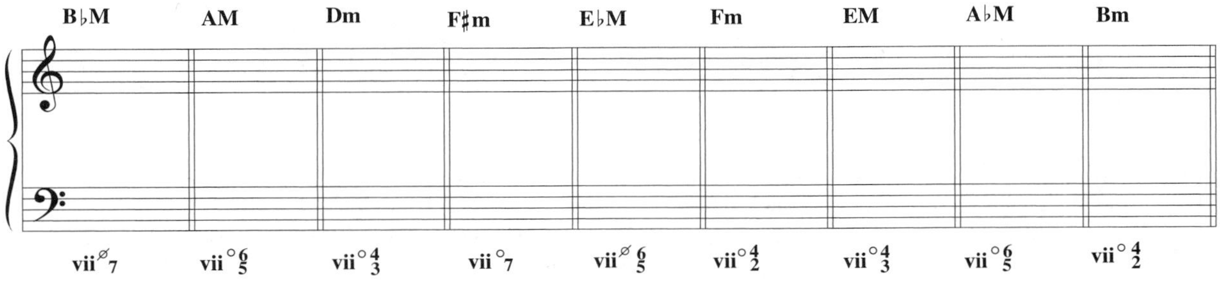

EXERCISE 3 Realize the following short progressions in four voices.

a. b.

FM: I $\mathrm{vii}^{\varnothing}_{7}$ I $\mathrm{vii}^{\varnothing 6}_{5}$ I_{6} V^{4}_{3} I Em: i $\mathrm{vii}^{\circ 4}_{2}$ P^{6}_{4} iv $\mathrm{vii}^{\circ 4}_{3}$ i_{6} $\mathrm{vii}^{\circ 6}_{5}$ i

c. d.

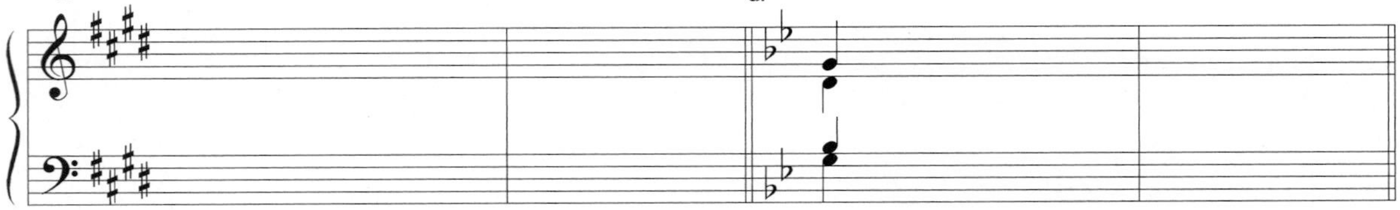

C♯m: i vii°_{7} i $\mathrm{ii}^{\varnothing 6}_{5}$ V^{6-5}_{4-3} i Gm: i $\mathrm{ii}^{\varnothing 4}_{2}$ V^{6}_{5} i iv_{7} V_{7} i

e.

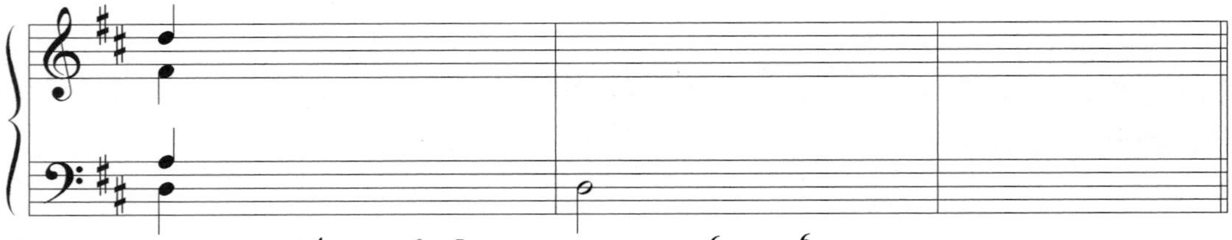

DM: I $\mathrm{vii}^{\circ 4}_{2}$ V^{6-5}_{4-3} I IV^{6}_{5} V^{6}_{5} I

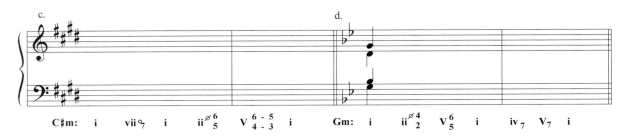

EXERCISE 4 Realize the following progression in four voices. Verify that your outer-voice frame follows the conventions of first-species counterpoint.

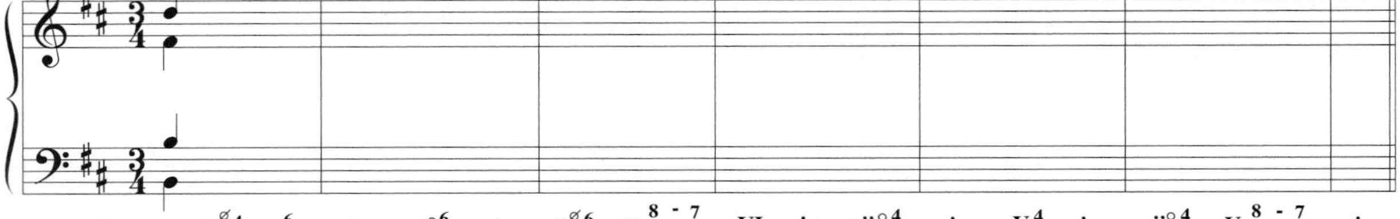

Bm: i $\mathrm{ii}^{\varnothing 4}_{2}$ V^{6}_{5} i $\mathrm{vii}^{\circ 6}_{5}$ i_{6} $\mathrm{ii}^{\varnothing 6}_{5}$ $\mathrm{V}\begin{smallmatrix}8-7\\6-5\\4-3\end{smallmatrix}$ VI iv_{7} $\mathrm{vii}^{\circ 4}_{3}$ i_{6} V^{4}_{3} i $\mathrm{vii}^{\circ 4}_{2}$ $\mathrm{V}\begin{smallmatrix}8-7\\6-5\\4-3\end{smallmatrix}$ i

EXERCISE 5 Harmonize the following melody with a keyboard texture. Include two leading-tone seventh chords, a deceptive cadence, and a cadential $^6_4$ preceded by a predominant seventh chord.

EXERCISE 6

1 Write progressions (bass and RNs) in the keys and meters indicated below. Use the following chords (in any order, but correctly resolved):

a) $ii^{ø6}_{5}$, vii^{o4}_{3}, vii^{o4}_{2}

b) ii^{4}_{2}, V^{4}_{2}, $vii^{ø4}_{3}$

c) $ii^{ø4}_{3}$, vii^{o6}_{5}, iv_7

a.

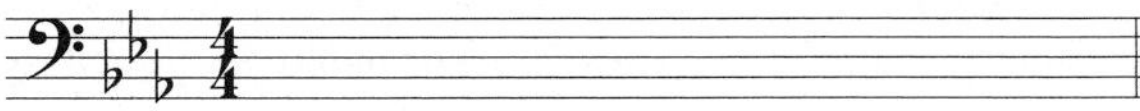

Cm:

b.

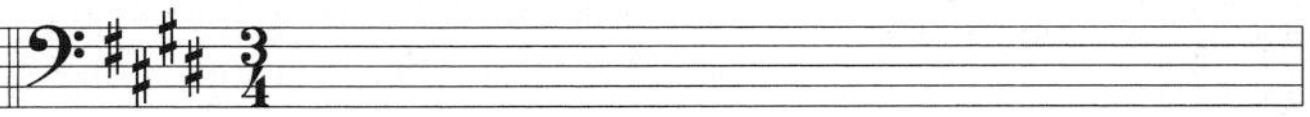

EM:

c.

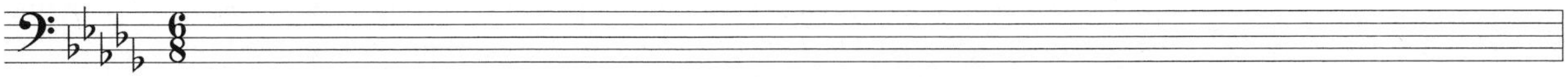

B♭m

2. Choose one of your own progressions from above, and use it as a harmonic basis to compose a phrase for the keyboard. Your phrase should consist of a simple melody (right hand) with keyboard-style accompaniment (left hand).

Chapter 16

Harmonic Sequences

In chapter 12 we studied melodic sequences, and we defined them as the restatement of a melodic segment at a higher or lower tonal level. A melodic sequence is often accompanied by a **harmonic sequence.** In example 16.1a, you will see that the violin performs a melodic sequence in which each segment is one measure long and is transposed a 3rd below the previous segment. You will also see that the sequence is diatonic: it stays within the key of FM, and has no accidentals outside this key. Now examine the accompaniment. Assign a Roman numeral (RN) to each chord and pay attention to the harmonic pattern for the complete phrase. Mozart wrote a harmonic diatonic sequence to accompany the melodic sequence. In each measure the root relationships (of descending 4ths) are preserved, and so are the exact spacing and voice leading, although each measure is *transposed a 3rd below the previous measure* (we will return to this sequence and this example later in this chapter when we study sequences by descending 3rds). In the staff provided under the example, write a four-voice metric reduction of the piano accompaniment; notice how each complete harmonic unit (one measure) is transposed as a whole, without any voice-leading alterations.

We will now study the most common types of harmonic sequences: by descending 5ths (the circle of 5ths), by ascending 5ths, by descending 3rds, and by steps (including parallel $^6_3$ chords and the 7–6 and 5–6 techniques). At this point, it may be useful for you to review the sections "Basic Types of Progression" and "Voice-Leading Guidelines for the Three Basic Types of Progression" in chapter 1.

NOTE

Harmonic sequences can best be understood as contrapuntal (rather than functional) events. What matters in a sequence is the exact transposed repetition of voice-leading or intervallic patterns that function linearly. This transposed repetition of patterns often results in the momentary suspension of functional relationships, as we will see in some of the sequences we will study in this chapter. In other words, sequences are not functional events, but rather linear events. Their role is to prolong a chord linearly, or to provide a contrapuntal path, based on transposed repetition, between two chords or two tonal points. In example 16.1a, the complete sequence extends the initial tonic and takes us from the initial tonic to the cadence in mm. 37–38.

Example 16.1a W. A. Mozart, Sonata for Violin and Piano, K. 372, I, mm. 34–38

Example 16.1b

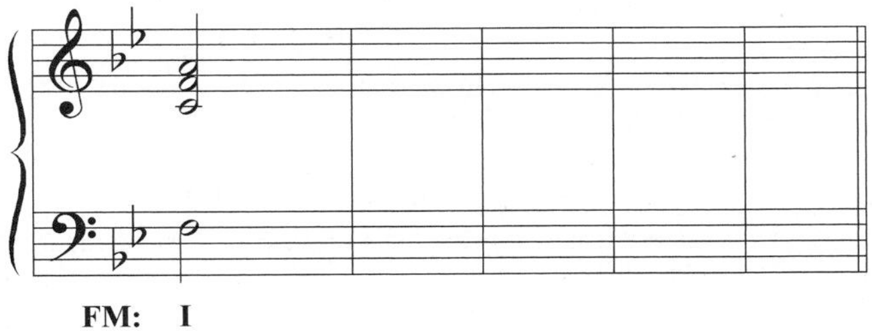

THE DESCENDING CIRCLE-OF-5THS SEQUENCE

The **descending circle of 5ths** is the harmonic sequence most widely used by composers of tonal music. It is a progression that provides a very strong harmonic support (root relationships by 5th) for melodic sequences descending by step. In example 16.2, a melodic sequence first begins with two two-measure segments, followed by two one-measure segments. The accompaniment (in the piano part) features a circle-of-5ths bass, first with a harmonic rhythm of a chord per measure, then a chord per beat. The complete circle-of-5ths bass line is A–D–G–C–F–B–E–A, with an added C–E–A cadential figure.

Rachmaninoff's lean harmonic realization of this bass as presented by the piano includes full chords only in mm. 18 and 20. Possible complete realizations of this progression in minor and major appear in examples 16.3a and b.

We should remark on several harmonic and voice-leading characteristics for the circle-of-5ths progression:

1. The descending-5ths bass most often appears as alternating descending 5ths and ascending 4ths.
2. In a complete diatonic circle of 5ths, one of the 5ths will be diminished (it may also appear as an ascending +4). In major, the °5 or +4 occurs between $\hat{4}$ and $\hat{7}$; in minor, between $\hat{6}$ and $\hat{2}$.
3. One of the triads in the diatonic circle of 5ths is diminished: vii° in major and ii° in minor.
4. Because the circle of 5ths is a descending harmonic sequence on a two-chord segment, the voice leading of chord pairs should be preserved.
5. In a harmonic sequence, preserving voice-leading patterns has priority over dealing with scale degrees functionally. In the major mode, vii° appears in root position, $\hat{7}$

Example 16.2 S. Rachmaninoff, *Rhapsody on a Theme of Paganini,* op. 43, Theme, mm. 17–24

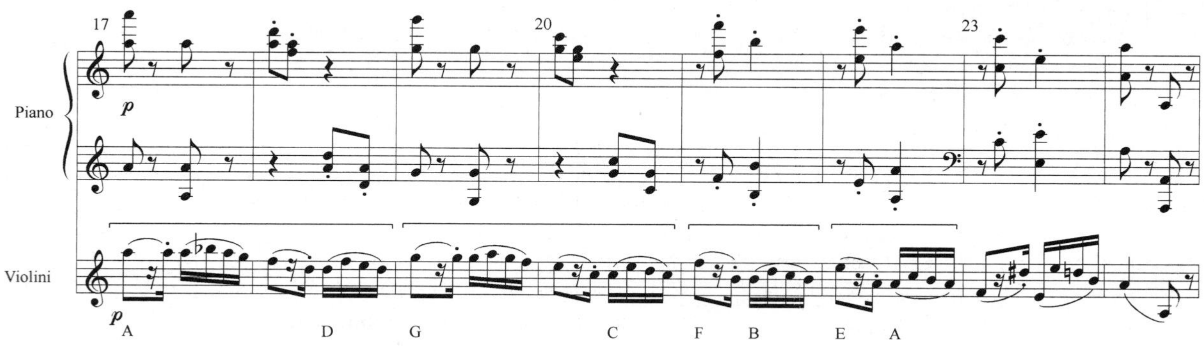

Example 16.3

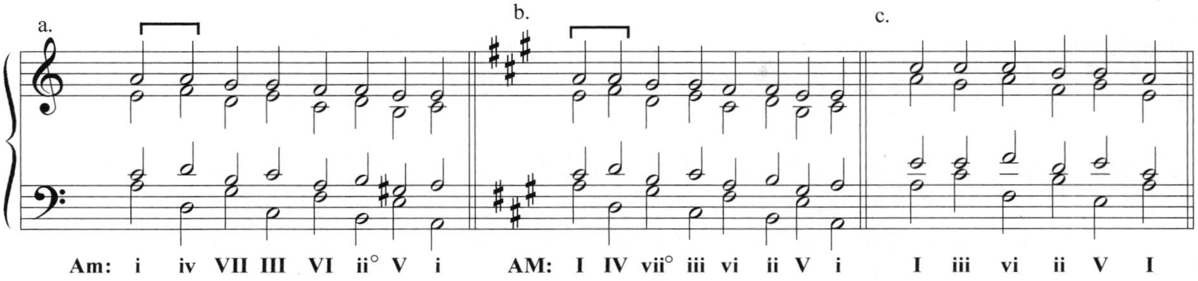

Example 16.4 J. S. Bach, Fugue 2 in Cm, from *The Well-Tempered Clavier,* I, mm. 22–25

is usually doubled, and it does not resolve to $\hat{1}$ (that is, it is not treated as a LT). vii°, moreover, proceeds to iii—not to I (see chords 3 and 4 in example 16.3b). In the minor mode, VII is usually major in this progression (on $\flat\hat{7}$, not on the LT), and ii° appears in root position.

Although the circle-of-5ths progression is often used in its complete form, it may also appear partially. A shorter circle-of-5ths segment sometimes found in music literature is I–iii–vi–ii–V–I. In this segment, all chords preserve the normative diatonic functions, and the chord on $\hat{7}$ is avoided (example 16.3c). Study example 16.4 and identify a complete circle-of-5ths progression underlying the contrapuntal texture.

Voice-Leading Variants for Circle-of-5ths Sequences

Example 16.5 shows four standard voice-leading paradigms for sequences based on the circle of 5ths with all triads in root position. Their differences affect mostly the **linear intervallic patterns** between outer voices. In example 16.5a, you can see a linear pattern of parallel 10ths every other chord, with octaves in between (resulting in a 10–8–10–8 design). Example 16.5b features parallel 10ths by contrary motion throughout, and

Example 16.5

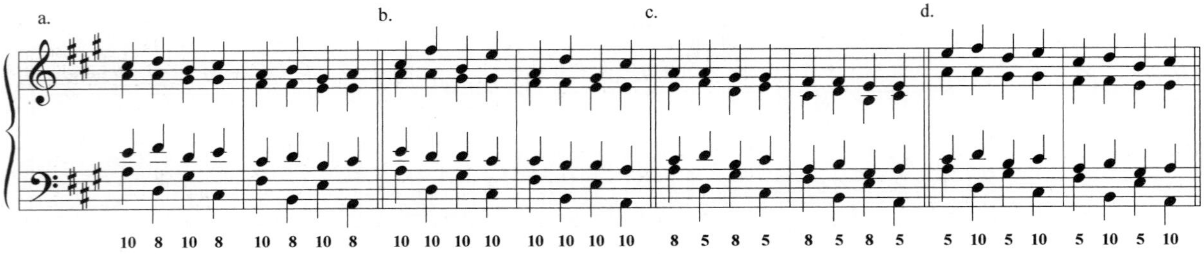

the outer-voice pattern in example 16.5c is 8–5–8–5. Finally, example 16.5d features a 5–10–5–10 pattern.

The Circle of 5ths with Inversions

A realization of the circle of 5ths frequently found in the literature alternates chords in $^5_3$ and $^6_3$ positions. Two voice-leading paradigms resulting from this alternation of root position and first-inversion triads appear in example 16.6. In the first of these, which begins with a $^5_3$ triad, the outer-voice pattern is 10–6–10–6, whereas the second paradigm, which begins with a $^6_3$ triad, displays the outer-voice pattern 6–5–6–5.

You can find an example of a circle-of-5ths sequence in which root-position and first-inversion triads alternate in anthology, no. 32 (Beethoven, Sonata in Fm, op. 2, no. 1, I), mm. 73–78. Which of the above voice-leading patterns can you recognize in this passage? An outer-voice paradigm in parallel 10ths, on the other hand, is illustrated by mm. 18–21 of example 16.7. Notice that in the upper voice a change of octave (a register transfer) occurs every two beats. For our outer-voice paradigm we assume that all pitches are in the same octave.

Example 16.6

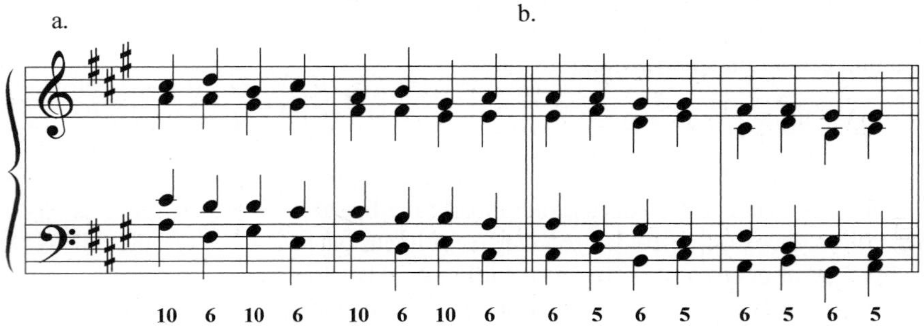

Example 16.7 W. A. Mozart, Piano Sonata in CM, K. 545, mm. 16–22

The Diatonic-Seventh Circle of 5ths

In the previous sections we have studied circle-of-5ths sequences exclusively made up of triads. A similar sequential progression results from a chain of diatonic seventh chords built on a circle-of-5ths bass, as in example 16.8a. The best voice leading for this progression consists of alternating complete (C) and incomplete (IN) chords, beginning with a complete one. This allows for preparation and resolution of all the sevenths. As you may see in example 16.8, all seven diatonic-seventh chords appear in this progression, and voice leading is treated as it is customary in harmonic sequences. As in all circle-of-5ths sequences, the sequence segment is here made up of two chords.

Example 16.8

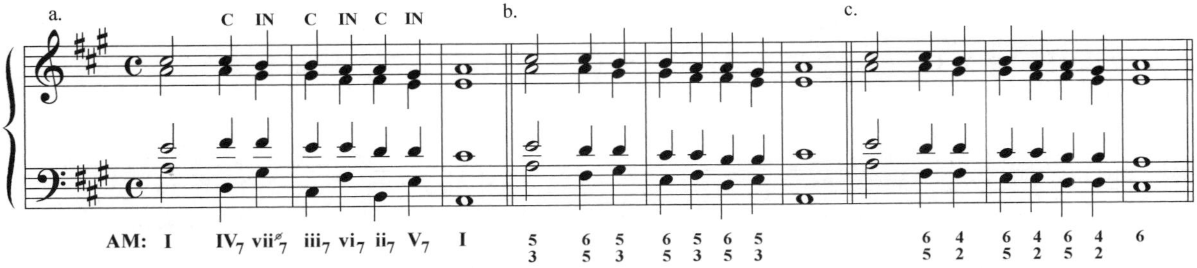

Examples 16.8b and c illustrate two common sequences using inversions of seventh chords. In example 16.8b, a triad in root position alternates with a seventh chord in first inversion (resulting in a succession of $^{5}_{3}$–$^{6}_{5}$ patterns). In example 16.8c we see an alternation of first inversion and third inversion seventh chords, in a repeated $^{6}_{5}$–$^{4}_{2}$ sequential pattern. Play all three sequences shown in example 16.8 at the piano and notice their great economy of voice-leading motion, as well as the very close relationship between examples 16.8b and c, where only every other note in the bass changes.

As in the case of the circle of 5ths with triads, the progression with seventh chords might appear complete, or, very often, only as a segment of the complete circle. The excerpt in example 16.9a is based exclusively on a circle of 5ths. Think of m. 22 as a tonic chord prolonged contrapuntally (embellished by a NN and two PTs—one in the violin and one in the keyboard's right hand); similarly, m. 23 functions as a iv chord with linear embellishments (two NNs, and a PT in the violin—notice that the second chord in m. 23 is actually a "dominant of iv," that is, a "secondary dominant" of the type we will study in the next chapter). If this accounts for the initial i–iv of the circle, analyze now the chords in mm. 24–25 for the rest of the progression, comparing it with example 16.8 for Roman numerals and voice leading. The circle of 5ths with seventh chords is as common in popular music as it is in common-practice art music. An example from the popular repertoire appears in example 16.9b. Play through this example and realize the Roman numerals either at the piano or on paper.

EXERCISES

To practice writing circle-of-5ths sequences, refer to exercises 2.1 and 2.2 in worksheet 16 at the end of this chapter.

Example 16.9a J. S. Bach, Concerto for Two Violins, BWV 1043, I, mm. 22–26

Example 16.9b Bart Howard, "Fly Me to the Moon (In Other Words)" (Opening)

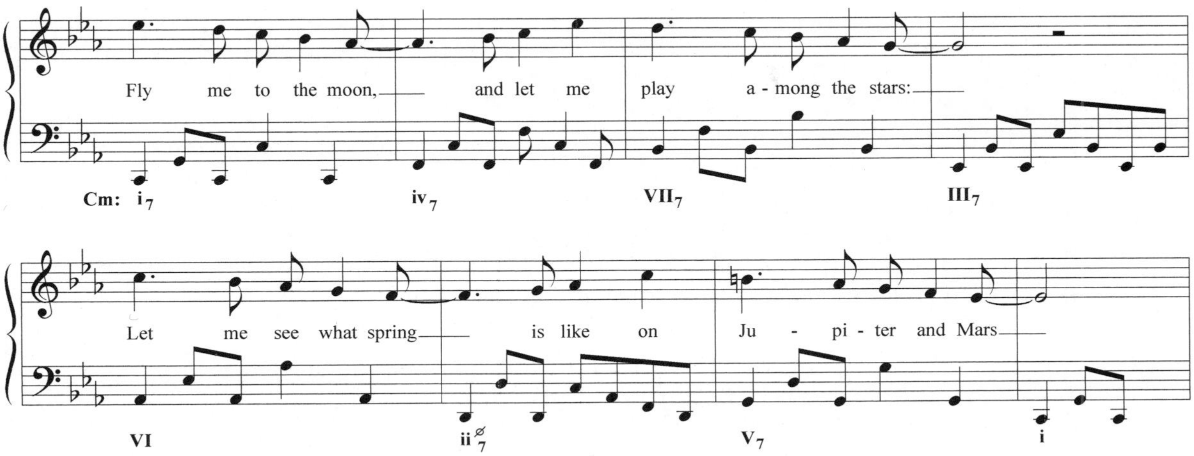
Fly me to the moon, and let me play a - mong the stars:
Cm: i7 iv7 VII7 III7
Let me see what spring is like on Ju - pi - ter and Mars
VI ii⌀7 V7 i

THE ASCENDING CIRCLE-OF-5THS SEQUENCE

Sequences based on the **ascending circle of 5ths** are also found in the literature, although much less frequently than the descending circle of 5ths. The passage by Bach reproduced in example 16.10 shows a sequence in which two-measure segments alternating between hands outline the pattern A–E–B–F♯, an ascending circle-of-5ths pattern, as shown with annotations on the example.

Example 16.11 shows two sequential paradigms based on ascending 5ths. In the first one, all triads are in root position. The second type alternates root-position and first-inversion triads. The ascending-5ths sequence is not usually found in minor, and when it appears in major it is often limited to the I to iii segment (that is, I–V–ii–vi–iii), thus avoiding the final vii°–IV–I segment, a very awkward cadential gesture, unlike the

Example 16.10 J. S. Bach, Invention no. 3 in DM, mm. 12–19

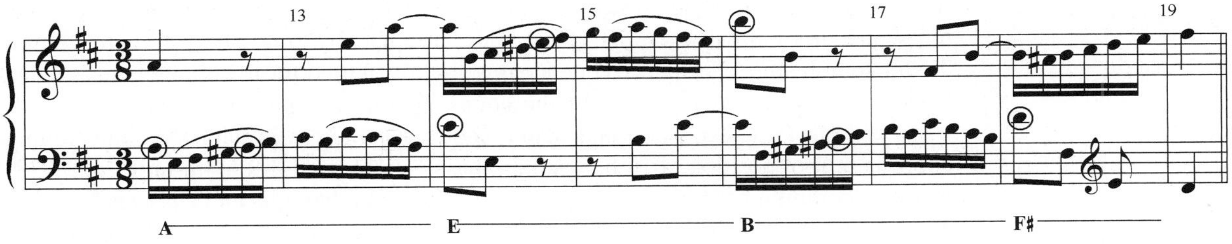
13
15
17
19
A
E
B
F♯

Example 16.11

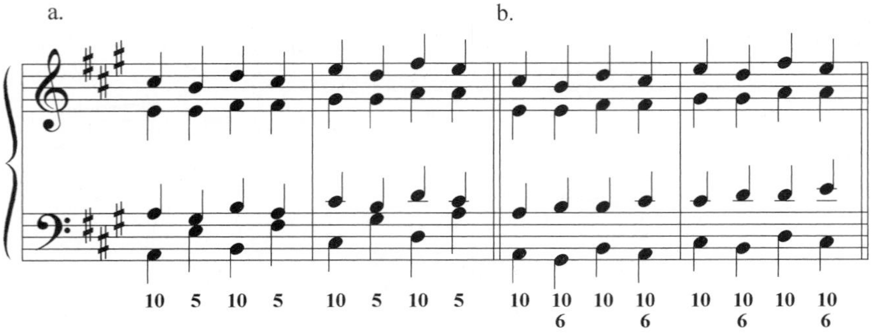

usual ii–V–I that closes the descending circle of 5ths. Even the I to iii segment includes the nonfunctional chord succession V–ii. This reversal of the functional ii–V progression (hence the term "retrogression" often used to describe it) reminds us again that harmonic sequences are linear patterns that do not necessarily behave according to the principles of functional progression.

EXERCISE

To practice writing an ascending circle-of-5ths sequence, refer to exercise 2.3 in worksheet 16 at the end of this chapter.

SEQUENCES BY DESCENDING 3RDS

In a **sequence by descending 3rds** based only on successive root-position triads, parallel 8ves and 5ths are likely to result, as illustrated by example 16.12a. Two common ways of avoiding the problem in this sequence are shown in examples 16.12b and c. In example 16.12b, a passing $^{6}_{3}$ chord connects the roots by 3rds (circled in the bass line). The resulting sequential pattern features an alternation of $^{5}_{3}$ and $^{6}_{3}$ chords over a bass descending by steps. Compare this sequential design with the passage by Carl Philipp Emanuel Bach reproduced in example 16.13. In this example, circle the roots by descending 3rds and label each of the intervening passing chords with a $^{6}_{3}$ below the corresponding bass note. Then study example 16.14. Whereas in the C. P. E. Bach example, the sequence by 3rds was quite literal both harmonically and melodically, the James Taylor song features the same sequence in a slightly altered form, both melodically and harmonically. What are these slight alterations and how are they produced?

Example 16.12c, on the other hand, shows a paradigm in which the intervening chord is in root position, and the resulting bass pattern is "down a 4th-up a 2nd." This is a very common harmonic paradigm, especially in the baroque and Classical periods. The Mozart passage that we discussed in example 16.1 is indeed based on this paradigm,

Example 16.12

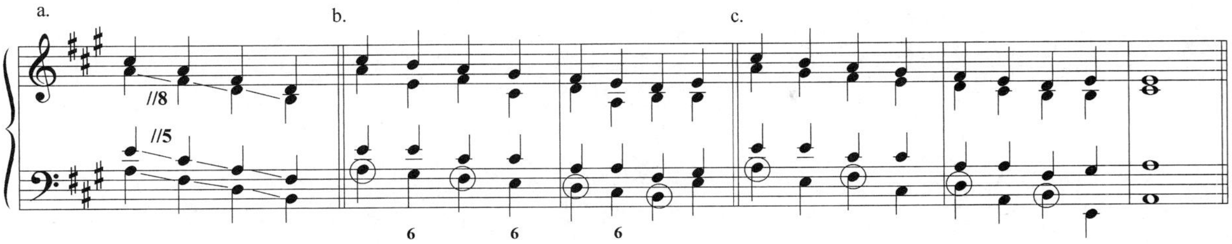

and so is the famous Canon in D by Pachelbel (listen to a recording of this piece to hear the repeated sequential pattern and the variations that Pachelbel writes on it).

EXERCISES

To practice writing sequences by descending 3rds, refer to exercises 2.4 and 2.5 in worksheet 16 at the end of this chapter.

Example 16.13

Carl Philipp Emanuel Bach, Piano Sonata no. 4, from *6 Sonaten für Kenner und Liebhaber,* I, mm. 5–8

Example 16.14 James Taylor, "Your Smiling Face" (beginning of verse)

When - ev - er I see your smil - ing face, I have to smile my - self,
EM: I
vi7
IV
be - cause I love you
ii7
V7
I

SEQUENCES BY DESCENDING AND ASCENDING STEPS

Parallel $^6_3$ Chords

Because a chord in first inversion (consisting of a 6th and a 3rd above the bass) does not contain a 5th if it is presented in close position, $^6_3$ chords may be used in succession without the difficulty of having to avoid parallel fifths. Composers have used **parallel $^6_3$ sequences** in passages in which the effect of a smooth, linear flow of parallel voices is desired. Parallel $^6_3$ sequences, which have a contrapuntal origin, momentarily suspend the functional character of harmony. Because they are perceived as parallel lines, their character is more melodic than harmonic. The passage in parallel $^6_3$ sonorities in anthology, no. 32 (Beethoven, Sonata op. 2 no. 1, III, Trio, mm. 59–62), shows indeed how a single melody (mm. 55–57) is first reinforced with a supporting melody in parallel 3rds (mm. 57–59), and finally with full parallel $^6_3$ chords.

Example 16.15 W. A. Mozart, Piano Sonata in GM, K. 283, III, mm. 9–14

The fragment by Mozart reproduced in example 16.15a (Piano Sonata K. 283, III, mm. 9–14) is a sequence based on parallel $^6_3$ sonorities, as you may see clearly in the chordal reduction of the passage that appears in example 16.15b.

Voice-Leading Issues in Parallel $^6_3$ Sequences

In three voices, the connection of parallel $^6_3$ chords does not present any difficulty as long as the 6th above the bass (the chordal root) is in the soprano (example 16.15c). If the 3rd above the bass (the chordal fifth) is in the soprano (open $^6_3$ position), parallel 5ths will result (example 16.15d). In four voices, because one of the voices must be doubled, parallel 8ves will result if the same voice is always doubled. This is exactly what happens in the Mozart example. Whereas the parallel 8ves in example 16.15a, however, either result from instrumental octave doubling (in the left hand) or are minimized by an instrumental broken-chord figuration (in the right hand), the octaves in the four-voice reduction (example 16.15b) have no justification. To avoid them, one of the voices will not move in parallel motion with the other three, and the doubled voice will not always be the same. Examples 16.15e and f illustrate this technique known as **alternate doublings.** Notice that in all cases the doubled notes (marked in the examples) are approached and left by similar or contrary motion, and the LT should still not be doubled if it appears in a chord that is followed by the tonic triad, as in the next-to-last chord in examples 16.15e and f.

The 7–6 and 5–6 Techniques

We will now study two sequential techniques that are based on the principles of fourth-species counterpoint (syncopated counterpoint). In chapter F we learned how to write a series of 7–6 suspensions (see example F.14b). We also learned that a string of 6–5 suspensions is perfectly acceptable because 5ths separated by a consonant interval (a 6th in this case) are not parallel 5ths, and that, by the same token, parallel 5ths between strong beats are correct in fourth species as long as they are separated by consonances (see example F.16c).

Refer first to example 16.16a. Without the syncopated upper voice, this sequential paradigm would simply be based on a descending series of parallel $^6_3$ chords of the type we just studied. By syncopating the upper voice (the 6th above the bass) we elaborate this sequence with a series of 7–6 suspensions in what we know as the **7–6 technique.** The Mozart fragment reproduced in example 16.17 is based on this paradigm, as you can verify in the metric reduction below it.

Example 16.16b, on the other hand, is based on an ascending succession of $^5_3$ chords. By moving one of the voices in syncopation by step, a 5–6 pattern is produced above the bass. This contrapuntal procedure, which we know as the **5–6 technique,** breaks the faulty parallel 5ths that would result if the successive $^5_3$ chords were not elaborated. Example 16.16c shows a variant of this sequence in which the bass moves down a third to the same pitch that forms the 6th in the 5–6 motion, thus turning the sequence into

Example 16.16

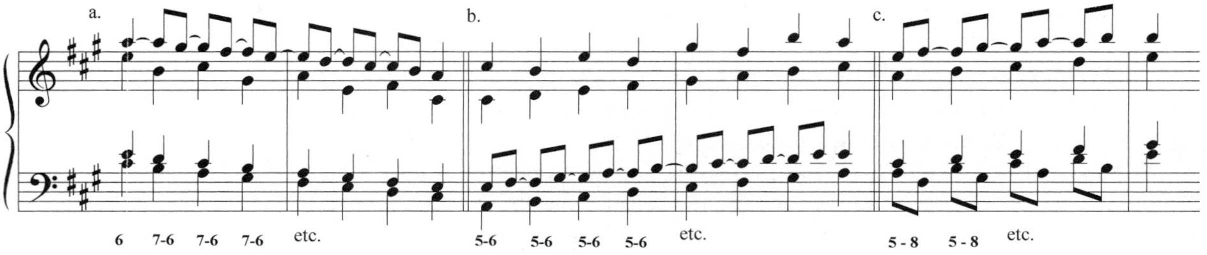

Example 16.17 W. A. Mozart, Piano Sonata in GM, K. 283, I, mm. 48–51

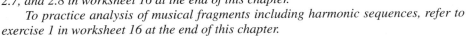

a succession of root-position triads with a "down a 3rd-up a 4th" bass pattern. The 5–6 sequence works best in major. It is also possible in minor, although the best segment in which to use it in this mode is usually from III to vi. An example of ascending 5–6 sequence appears in example 16.18.

EXERCISES

To practice writing sequences by ascending and descending 2nds, refer to exercises 2.6, 2.7, and 2.8 in worksheet 16 at the end of this chapter.

To practice analysis of musical fragments including harmonic sequences, refer to exercise 1 in worksheet 16 at the end of this chapter.

Example 16.18 E. Y. Harburg-Harold Arlen, "If I Only Had a Brain," from the film *The Wizard of Oz*

A SUMMARY OF HARMONIC SEQUENCES: ELABORATING THE I–V–I PROGRESSION

Example 16.19 shows a summary of all the sequence types we have studied in this chapter: the descending circle of 5ths (examples 16.19a to c); the ascending circle of

Example 16.19

5ths (example 16.19d); the sequence by descending 3rds (with a connecting passing $^6_3$ chord in example 16.19e and the "down a 4th-up a 2nd" bass pattern in 16.19f); and four sequences by steps, including the succession of parallel $^6_3$ chords (example 16.19g), sequences using 7–6 and 5–6 techniques (examples 16.19h and i), and the "down a 3rd-up a 4th" bass pattern (example 16.19j).

At the beginning of this chapter we saw that the function of harmonic sequences is to provide a linear contrapuntal prolongation of a chord (most often the tonic), or to provide a path leading from one chord to another. Each of the sequences in example 16.19 illustrates this function. All of them are set in the context of a I–V–I progression (in most cases with a pre-dominant preceding the cadential dominant), and each of them can be interpreted as a contrapuntal extension of the initial tonic, as well as a linear path leading from the initial tonic to the cadential V–I. Each of these sequences thus functions as an extended contrapuntal elaboration of the I–V–I progression.

ASSIGNMENT AND KEYBOARD EXERCISES

For analytical and written assignments and keyboard exercises based on the materials learned in this chapter, refer to chapter 16 in the workbook.

PITCH PATTERNS

Example 16.20 includes the most characteristic outer-voice linear intervallic patterns using the harmonic sequences we have studied in this chapter. Sing these two-voice pitch patterns in class or with a fellow student. As you sing, listen to both the sequential intervallic patterns and the underlying harmonic sequence represented in each of the examples.

Example 16.20

Terms for Review

- Harmonic sequence
- The descending circle-of-5ths sequence
- Linear intervallic patterns
- Sequence by ascending 5ths
- Sequences by descending 3rds
- Sequences ascending or descending by steps
- Parallel $^6_3$ sequences
- Alternate doublings
- The 7–6 and 5–6 techniques

Worksheet 16

EXERCISE 1 Analysis.

1. a) Identify the sequential progression in example 16.21, mm. 1–4. Analyze it with Roman numerals.

   b) Compare mm. 1–4 to the voice-leading paradigms studied in this chapter. What paradigm or paradigms do you recognize?

   c) The three phrases in example 16.21 present three different realizations of the same progression. How are they different?

   d) Using your own music paper, provide a metric reduction of mm. 9–12.

Example 16.21 G. F. Handel, Passacaglia, from *Suite de Pièces,* 1st coll., no. 7, IV, mm. 1–12

2. Study the contrapuntal sequence in example 16.22. In the staff under it, write a chordal metric reduction using the pitches circled in the example (the chordal tones). What voice-leading paradigm can you identify?

Example 16.22 J. S. Bach, Invention no. 4 in Dm, mm. 7–11

3. a) What are the underlying progressions in examples 16.23a and b? Identify the roots for each chord in the progressions and circle these roots in the bass. In example 16.23b, be sure to take into account the change of registers in the bass. What exact sequential type does this example represent?

Example 16.23a W. A. Mozart, Symphony no. 39, K. 543, in E♭M, IV, mm. 125–33

Example 16.23b J. S. Bach, Fugue no. 16 in Gm, from *The Well-Tempered Clavier,* I, mm. 24–26

b) Consider melodic/contrapuntal relationships in each of these passages. What are the basic principles of melodic growth in each individual line?

c) In example 16.23a, how are the lines related on a measure-by-measure basis? And how are they related as a whole, considering the complete example? What specific interval regulates this contrapuntal relationship?

4. Identify the exact sequence and voice-leading pattern in example 13.8, mm. 57–60. Then do the same for mm. 61–65. In the latter passage, the bass notes you should focus on for the sequential pattern appear on beats 2 and 3 of each measure. You will find that the metric reduction in that example will help you determine the voice-leading pattern.

EXERCISE 2 On your own music paper, realize the following harmonic sequences in four voices (three $\frac{4}{4}$ measures each, including the final cadence, as in example 16.24):

1. A root-position circle of 5ths with a 10–8–10–8 outer-voice pattern, in FM
2. A circle of 5ths alternating root-position and first-inversion chords, with a 10–6–10–6 outer-voice pattern, in Cm

3. An ascending circle-of-5ths sequence in GM
4. A sequence by descending 3rds with interpolated $\substack{6\\3}$ chords, in DM
5. A sequence by descending 3rds with interpolated root-position chords (with the bass pattern "down a 4th-up a 2nd"), in DM
6. A sequence of parallel $\substack{6\\3}$ chords, in CM
7. A sequence descending by steps using the 7–6 technique, in B♭M
8. A sequence ascending by steps using the 5–6 technique, in FM

Procedure to write harmonic sequences. As an example to illustrate the procedure to realize exercise 2, we will write a circle-of-5ths sequence in GM with a parallel 10th outer-voice pattern.

1. The basic framework for your sequences will be the outer-voice linear pattern. If the pattern is provided (as in our case), begin by writing the outer-voice frame. For our bass, we write a descending circle of 5ths. For our soprano, we write the pattern in parallel 10ths as we have learned it (in contrary motion with the bass). This is shown in example 16.24a. We change the harmonic rhythm for the last two chords to provide a suitable metric placement for the cadence.
2. If the outer-voice pattern is not provided, you can decide on one yourself, based on the examples we have studied in this chapter (see example 16.20 for a summary of common sequential outer-voice patterns). If you are requested to write a circle-of-5ths in GM, you can choose one of the possible outer-voice patterns we have studied (10–8, 10–10, 8–5, or 5–10) and then proceed as in point 1 above.
3. Given that you are going to be repeating a two-chord voice-leading pattern (the model), it is essential to write correct voice leading for your initial two chords. We do this in example 16.24b.
4. After we have the outer-voice frame and the opening two chords, all we need to do is to repeat the exact voice-leading pattern sequentially (in our case, down a step for each sequential segment), as shown in example 16.24c, and to write a correct cadence to close the phrase.

Example 16.24

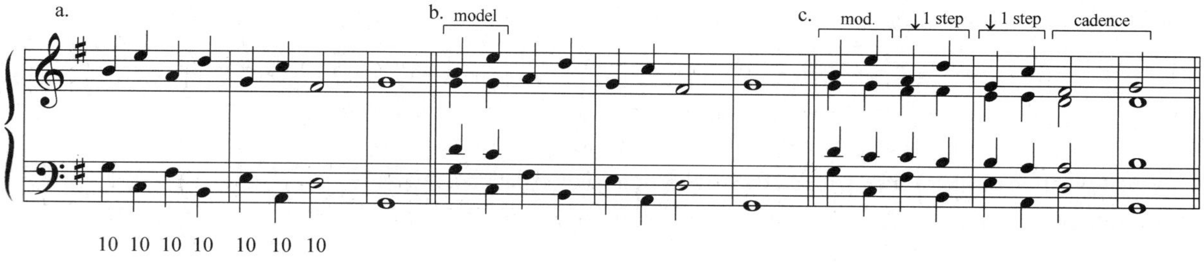

PART 2

Chromatic Harmony and Form

Chapter 17

Secondary Dominants I

CHROMATIC HARMONY

So far we have studied only chords constructed with pitches from the diatonic major or minor scales. The different types of minor scale (natural, melodic, and harmonic) are all considered diatonic in spite of the various alterations of $\hat{6}$ and $\hat{7}$. The only true **chromatic tones** (foreign to the diatonic scale being used) we have encountered are chromatic nonchord tones (NCTs) such as neighbor notes (NNs) and passing tones (PTs), and these are purely melodic in nature.

Beginning with this chapter, and for the remainder of the book, we will study **chromatic harmony,** that is, harmony in which chromatic alterations other than NCTs are introduced. At times these alterations result from **modulation,** the establishment of a new, different key. When music modulates, a new scale (with different accidentals than the original scale) is used, and this produces chromaticism with respect to the original key. The fragment in example 17.1a begins in DM and ends in Bm. The accidental in the second phrase, A♯, is the leading tone (LT) in the new key and results from the switch to the Bm scale.

Chromaticism, however, is very often present within a single key, resulting from **chromatic,** or **altered, chords,** chords that use a tone or tones foreign to the diatonic scale of the key they are used in. The passage in example 17.1b is all in Em, and yet in m. 7, beat 4, we see a chord that includes an A♯ and a C♯. Although these two pitches are part of a chord (A♯–C♯–E–G), this type of chromaticism is often a consequence of melodic, linear processes. *Chordal chromaticism often results from a linear elaboration of a diatonic framework.* Example 17.1c shows the diatonic framework the chorale phrase in example 17.1b elaborates. In this context, we see that the chromatic chord results from a chromatic passing-tone motion in the bass ($\hat{4}$–$\hat{5}$–$\hat{1}$ becomes $\hat{4}$–$\sharp\hat{4}$–$\hat{5}$–$\hat{1}$).

As illustrated in example 17.1, chordal or linear chromaticism may be used at the local level to provide pitch variety and to increase tonal "color" (the term *chromaticism* is derived from the Greek *chroma,* "color"). Moreover, chromaticism enhances voice-leading tension and direction. In example 17.1a, the A–A♯ line produces a strong pull

Example 17.1a J. S. Bach, Chorale 80, "O Haupt voll Blut und Wunden," mm. 1–4

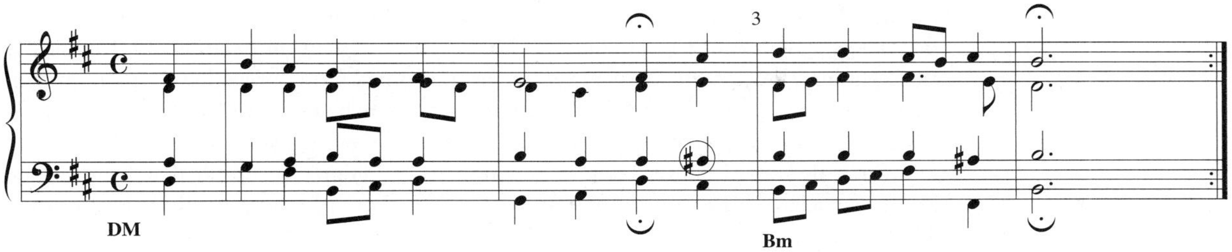

Examples 17.1b and c J. S. Bach, Chorale 167, "Du grosser Schmerzensmann," mm. 7–8, and Harmonic Reduction of Example 16.1b

toward B, the new tonic. In example 17.1b, the bass motion $\hat{4}$–$\sharp\hat{4}$–$\hat{5}$ is much stronger linearly than only $\hat{4}$–$\hat{5}$. Long-range chromaticism as represented by modulation, on the other hand, is an essential type of tonal process whose function is to define formal organization, as we will study in future chapters.

TONICIZATION: SECONDARY DOMINANTS

The first type of chromatic chord we will study results from the concept of **tonicization:** Any major or minor triad may become a momentary tonic if it is preceded by its dominant (that is, by the major triad or Mm_7 chord whose root is a 5th above—or a 4th below—the root of the tonicized chord). The fragment in example 17.2 is in CM throughout. The GM chord (V) in m. 1, beat 3, however, is preceded by its dominant (a Mm_7 chord on D, V_7 of G). Although we still hear the G chord as V in C (a half cadence), V is here momentarily tonicized because of the preceding chord.

Such dominant chords, whose function is to tonicize the triad that follows, are known as **secondary dominants** (some authors also call them **applied dominants**). Their Roman numeral (RN) abbreviation includes two symbols separated by a slash, as in V_7/V or V_7/IV. The first symbol indicates the secondary dominant function; the second symbol after the slash indicates the triad being tonicized. We read the slash as "of," thus V_7/V is "V_7 of V," and V_7/IV is "V_7 of IV." Although secondary dominants may appear as simple M triads (V/V of V/IV), most often they appear as Mm_7 chords (V_7/V).

Spelling Secondary Dominants

To spell the secondary dominant of a given degree, you build a M triad or a Mm_7 chord on the pitch a 5th above the given degree. Let's spell V_7/V in GM. The triad we are tonicizing is V in GM, and the degree we are tonicizing is $\hat{5}$ in GM, or D. That is, D becomes our momentary tonic. Think of the pitch a 5th above D. It is A (the dominant of D). Now build a Mm_7 chord on A: A–C♯–E–G. This is V_7/V in GM.

We can now try V_7/VI in Cm. VI in Cm is a triad on A♭, so we are tonicizing A♭. The pitch a 5th above A♭ is E♭. Now build a Mm_7 chord on E♭, and that will be V_7/VI in Cm: E♭–G–B♭–D♭.

Let's finish with a quick review of the process. We want V_7/ii in DM. We are tonicizing $\hat{2}$ in DM, or E. The pitch a 5th above E is B. The Mm_7 chord on B is B–D♯–F♯–A. This is V_7/ii in DM.

Example 17.2 J. S. Bach, Chorale 40, "Ach Gott und Herr," mm. 1–2

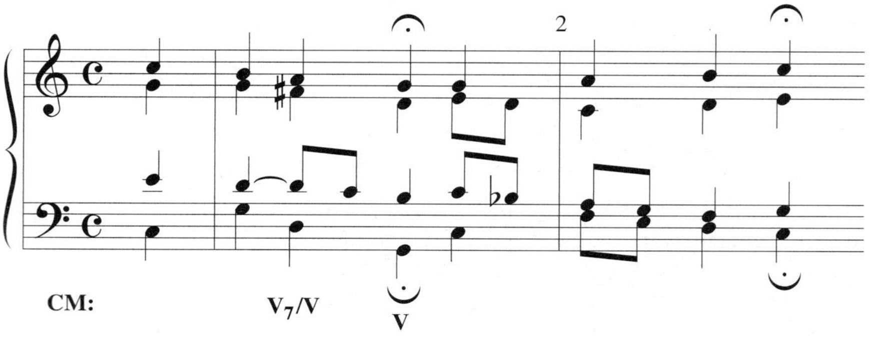

V_7 OF V

The degree most frequently tonicized is $\hat{5}$. V_7/V, the dominant of the dominant, is a Mm_7 chord built on $\hat{2}$ (the pitch a 5th above $\hat{5}$). The first "harmonic" accidental we introduce, as part of this chord, is $\sharp\hat{4}$ (by "$\sharp\hat{4}$" we mean "raised $\hat{4}$," regardless of whether the actual accidental is ♯ or ♮). $\sharp\hat{4}$ in this chord functions as a **secondary,** or *temporary,* **leading tone** of $\hat{5}$, and hence should not be doubled. Secondary dominants, in principle, resolve as regular dominant seventh chords (LT up, seventh down), so $\sharp\hat{4}$ will move to $\hat{5}$. Examples 17.3a and b illustrate the spelling and resolution of V_7/V in a major and a minor key. Notice that in minor, besides $\sharp\hat{4}$, we also need to raise $\hat{6}$ to $\sharp\hat{6}$, in order to have a Mm_7 sonority. Examples 17.3c to f present all the positions of V_7/V in the context of characteristic progressions. V_7/V, as well as V^6_5/V and V^4_3/V, can resolve to a V embellished by a cadential $^6_4$, as illustrated by examples 17.3g and h.

Example 17.3

In example 17.3 you can see a frequent melodic gesture that can be harmonized with a progression using V_7/V, $\hat{4}$–$\sharp\hat{4}$–$\hat{5}$. Other possible melodic fragments that can be harmonized with a secondary dominant of V and its resolution to V are $\hat{6}$–$\hat{5}$, $\hat{1}$–$\hat{7}$, and $\hat{2}$–$\hat{2}$ (which can be harmonized with an inverted secondary dominant of V). Among these, $\sharp\hat{4}$–$\hat{5}$, $\hat{6}$–$\hat{5}$, and $\hat{1}$–$\hat{7}$ can also be found as bass fragments in one of the progressions using an **inversion of V_7/V,** as you can verify in example 17.3.

EXERCISES

To practice spelling secondary dominants of V in root position and inversions, refer to exercise 2 in worksheet 17 at the end of this chapter.

To practice spelling and resolving secondary dominants of V, refer to exercise 3 in worksheet 17 at the end of this chapter.

V_7/V in root position is often found in cadential gestures. In example 17.3c, V_7/V precedes an authentic cadence. The bass $\hat{2}$–$\hat{5}$–$\hat{1}$, a very strong cadential gesture that we have previously harmonized diatonically as ii (or ii_7)–V–I, is strengthened by the chromatic tension provided by $\sharp\hat{4}$. As you will see, ii_7 and V_7/V differ only in one pitch: $\hat{4}$ in ii_7, or $\sharp\hat{4}$ in V_7/V. In this context, V_7/V functions as a chromatic pre-dominant chord.

In example 17.4 Haydn closes the phrase on a half cadence (HC), preceded by V_7/V that functions, in the way we have just discussed, as a chromatic pre-dominant chord. In m. 3 we see another very frequent form of the secondary dominant of V: V^6_5/V, which allows for the strong linear motion $\hat{4}$–$\sharp\hat{4}$–$\hat{5}$ in the bass. If V^6_5/V is preceded by ii^6_5, no motion is needed in any voice other than the bass chromaticism (see example 17.3d). The function of this type of secondary dominant is not harmonic, but rather linear, V^6_5/V is here a chromatic, embellishing chord with a passing function.

Because in V^4_2/V $\hat{1}$ is in the bass, the chord can be effectively used after I, with $\hat{1}$ carried over in the bass as a common tone between the two chords. Mozart does just that at the beginning of his Finale for Symphony no. 40, reproduced in example 17.5. Compare Mozart's opening progression (mm. 1–4) with example 17.3f (and remember that V^4_2/V

Example 17.4 J. Haydn, String Quartet op. 76, no. 5, I, mm. 1–4

VOICE-LEADING GUIDELINES

1. The principles for doublings and resolution that we applied to the dominant seventh chord also apply to secondary dominants.
2. Do not double the secondary LT ($\sharp\hat{4}$ in V_7/V).
3. Resolve the secondary LT up and the seventh down.
4. ***Cross relations.*** You may have observed that in examples 17.1a and b and example 17.4, at least one of the voices moves by chromatic half step (as in A–A♯ or C–C♯). When two adjacent chords include pitches related by chromatic half step, *it is better to keep the chromatic motion in the same voice.* Chromatically related pitches in different voices create what are known as cross relations. Although cross relations are found in music, they have not been used indiscriminately by composers. Because cross relations produce a dissonant clash between two voices, and because the smoothest voice leading results from keeping the chromatic motion in the same voice, as a principle we will avoid cross relations between outer voices.

   Sing or play the progressions in example 17.7, and hear the chromatic relationships among voices. Examples 17.7a and c illustrate cross relations between the outer voices. Listen to these realizations and compare them with the smoother realizations presented in examples 17.7b and d. Although in example 17.7b the cross relation between outer voices remains, its effect is softened by the chromatic motion in the bass.
5. ***The chromaticized voice exchange.*** The progression in example 17.7e shows a specific type of cross relation that, besides being quite acceptable, actually results in an especially effective voice leading. Notice the voice exchange between the figures D–B♮ in the soprano and B♭–D in the bass, indicated by the usual voice exchange cross. This is a *chromaticized voice exchange* that includes a cross relation (B♭–B♮). As shown in our example, this progression is often embellished with a passing $^6_4$, which makes the cross relation even less problematic.

resolves to V_6). Analyze Mozart's second phrase (mm. 5–8) harmonically. What kind of phrase structure can you identify in the complete passage? In the phrase by Andrew Lloyd Webber (example 17.6), on the other hand, V^4_2/V results from a passing motion in the bass (D–C–B, or $\hat{2}$–$\hat{1}$–$\hat{7}$) between V/V and V_6.

Example 17.5 W. A. Mozart, Symphony no. 40 in Gm, K. 550, IV, mm. 1–8

Example 17.6 Tim Rice–Andrew Lloyd Webber, "Don't Cry for Me Argentina," from *Evita* (Verse)

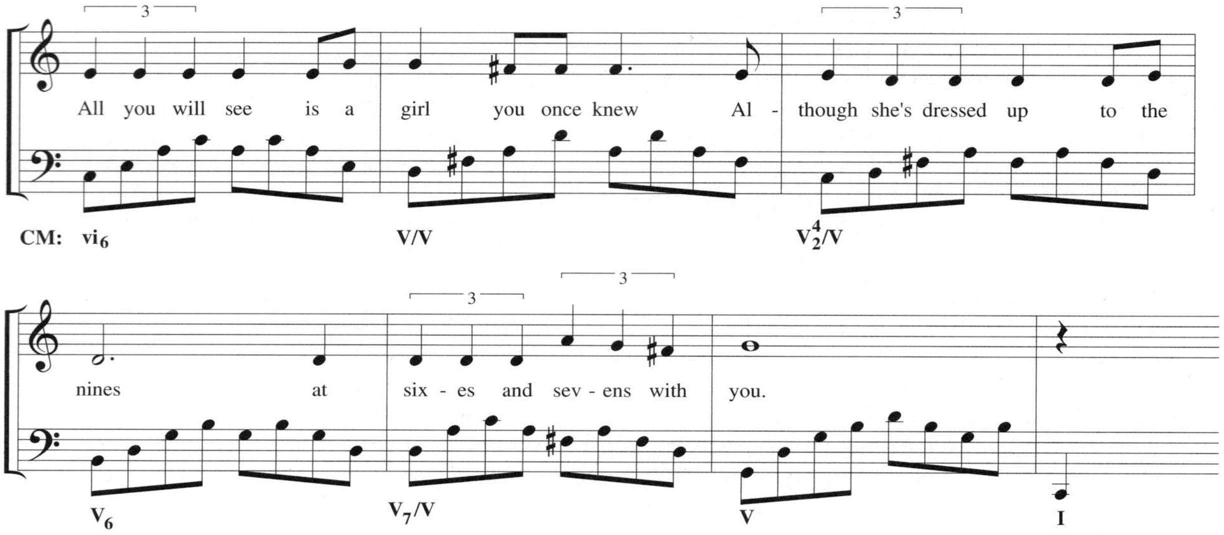

Example 17.7

V_7 OF IV (iv)

Along with V_7/V, the dominant of IV (iv in minor) is very frequently found in music. V_7/IV is the Mm_7 chord built on $\hat{1}$ (the pitch a 5th above $\hat{4}$). In major keys, V_7/IV consists of the I triad with an added m7. The new accidental introduced by this chord is thus $\flat\hat{7}$. In minor keys, $\flat\hat{7}$ is a diatonic pitch, and we need instead to raise the minor $\hat{3}$ to $\sharp\hat{3}$, the LT of $\hat{4}$. Examples 17.8a and b show the spelling and resolution of this chord in both M and m. Observe that in example 17.8b, $\flat\hat{3}$ and $\natural\hat{3}$ have been kept in the same voice, and the voice leading from example 17.8a has been changed in example 17.8b to avoid the +2 between $\flat\hat{6}$ and $\natural\hat{7}$ in the soprano.

The most frequent melodic pattern harmonized with a secondary dominant of IV and its resolution to IV is $\flat\hat{7}$–$\hat{6}$ (as part of the motion $\hat{1}$–$\flat\hat{7}$–$\hat{6}$), as shown in example 17.8a. Other possible patterns are $\hat{3}$–$\hat{4}$, $\hat{5}$–$\hat{4}$, or $\hat{5}$–$\hat{6}$.

EXERCISES

To practice spelling secondary dominants of IV in root position and inversions, refer to exercise 2 in worksheet 17 at the end of this chapter.

To practice spelling and resolving secondary dominants of IV, refer to exercise 3 in worksheet 17 at the end of this chapter.

Example 17.8

Examples 17.8a and b illustrate the use of the dominant of IV in the context of cadential progressions. V_7/IV in root position is also often used in opening progressions, with the function of both prolonging the opening I and of creating a pull toward the subdominant. In example 17.9 you will see how Beethoven begins his Trio, op. 1, no. 1, with a very effective use of such a progression. Analyze the complete passage.

Example 17.9 L. v. Beethoven, Trio op. 1, no. 1, I, mm. 1–9

Example 17.10 C. Schumann, Trio in Gm, op. 17, I, mm. 1–9

The prolongation of the tonic may be stressed even more by resolving V_7/IV to IV^6_4 (N^6_4) on a tonic pedal, as in example 17.8c. This is also a frequent opening progression because it establishes the tonic in a strong and colorful way. Study C. Schumann's use of this progression in the opening measures of her Gm Trio (example 17.10, mm. 1–3).

The most frequent **inversions of V_7/IV** are V^6_5/IV and V^4_2/IV, normally used in the standard progressions shown in examples 17.8d and e. V^4_2/IV usually follows I to create a very effective linear progression in which the upper voices do not move, as shown in example 17.8e. The bass moves down by step from $\hat{1}$ to $\flat\hat{7}$, and then to $\hat{6}$, and the other voices complete the IV_6 to which V^4_2/IV must resolve. Example 17.10, mm. 6–7 shows a version of this progression.

Example 17.11

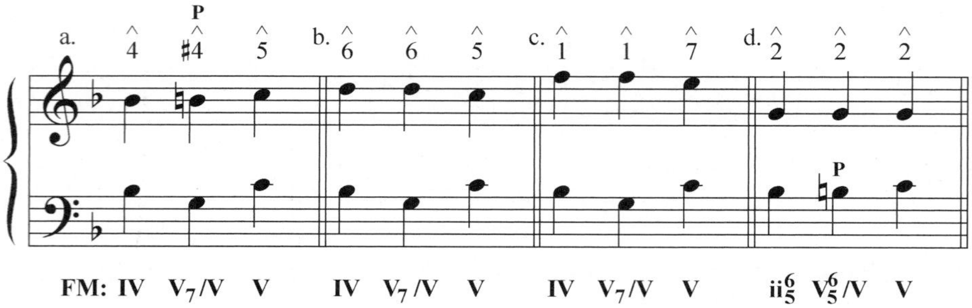

Example 17.12

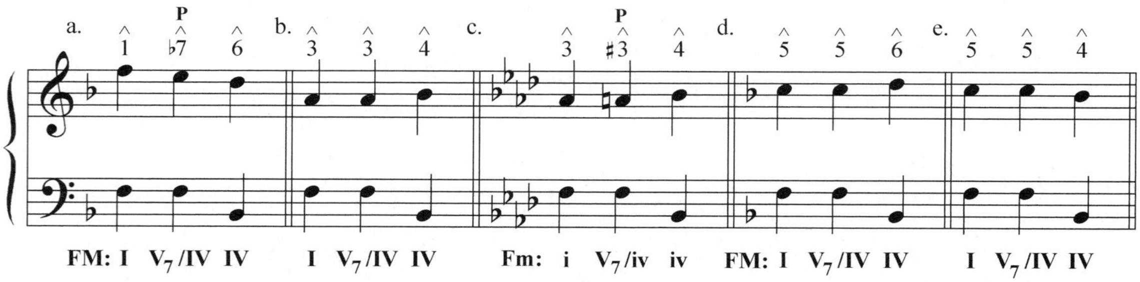

CHARACTERISTIC SOPRANO-BASS PATTERNS

Examples 17.11 and 17.12 present some of the characteristic soprano-bass patterns that can be harmonized with progressions using secondary dominants of V and IV. The most effective among these patterns are the ones that include chromatic passing motion (examples 17.11a and d, and 17.12a and c, the latter possible only in minor keys). Play each of these outer-voice patterns at the piano, adding inner voices in keyboard texture.

ELABORATING THE I–V–I PROGRESSION

The dominant of V functions most commonly as either a pre-dominant or as an extension of the tonic. Both functions are illustrated in example 17.13, in the context of the basic I–V–I progression. In examples 17.13a and b, the dominant of V provides an

Example 17.13

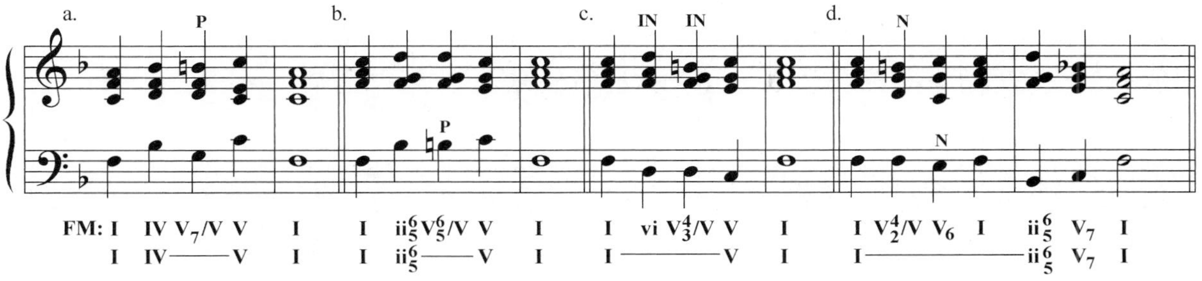

extension of a previous pre-dominant chord by means of a chromatic passing motion (in the soprano in example 17.13a and in the bass in example 17.13b). Examples 17.13c and d, on the other hand, show progressions in which the dominant of V functions as an extension of the initial tonic.

The dominant of IV normally functions as a prolongation of the tonic. In the three progressions shown in example 17.14, the dominant of IV extends the initial tonic in the I–V–I progression by means of a passing tone ($\flat\hat{7}$).

Elaborating a Diatonic Framework with Chromatic Harmony

At the beginning of this chapter we mentioned that chromatic chords often result from linear *elaborations of a diatonic framework.* Example 17.15 illustrates exactly that. We begin, in 17.15a, with the basic frame I–IV–V–I. In example 17.15b we extend the pre-dominant IV with an additional ii^6_5. In example 17.15c we see that a PT, E♭, between I and IV generates a V_7/IV. Moreover, another chromatic PT in the bass, B♮ (a simple chromatic alteration of the ii^6_5 chord) creates a V^6_5/V. As a final elaboration (in

Example 17.14

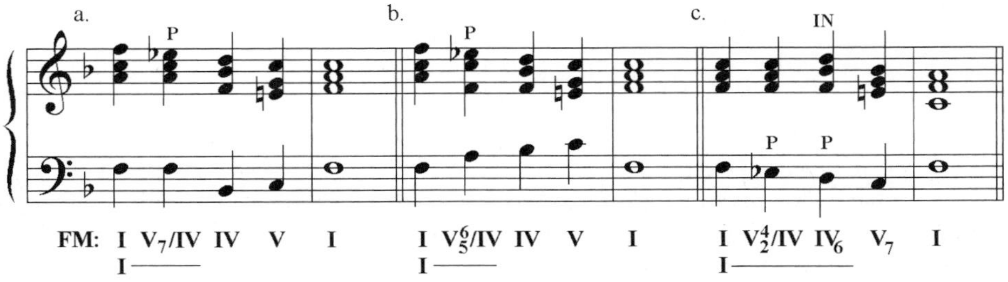

Example 17.15

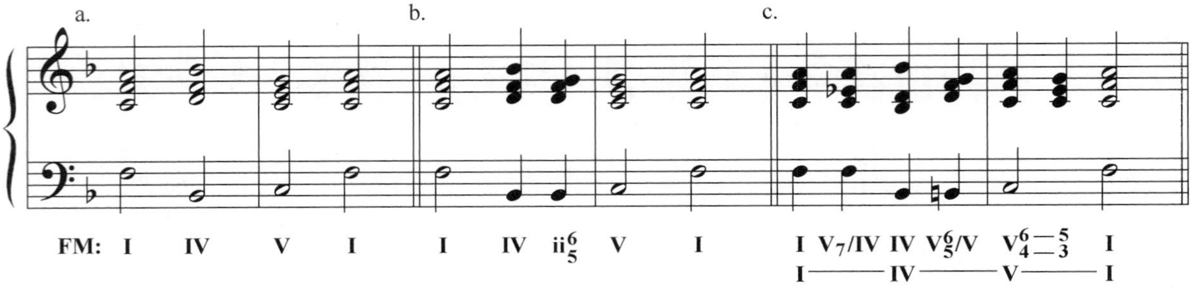

this case diatonic), we embellish V with a cadential $^6_4$ figure. Example 17.15c shows that the original I–IV–V–I diatonic framework remains, now elaborated with chromatic harmony and a cadential $^6_4$.

EXERCISES

To practice realizing progressions including tonicizations of V and IV, refer to exercises 4 and 5 in worksheet 17 at the end of this chapter.

To practice harmonizing a melody including tonicizations of V and IV, refer to exercise 6 in worksheet 17 at the end of this chapter.

To practice writing your own progressions using tonicizations of V and IV, refer to exercise 7 in worksheet 17 at the end of this chapter.

To practice analysis of musical fragments including tonicizations, refer to exercise 1 in worksheet 17 at the end of this chapter.

FOR FURTHER STUDY

For additional analysis using materials studied in this chapter, refer to the *Harmony in Context* Web page at www.mhhe.com/roigfrancoli2e.

ASSIGNMENT AND KEYBOARD EXERCISES

For analytical and written assignments and keyboard exercises based on the materials learned in this chapter, refer to chapter 17 in the workbook.

PITCH PATTERNS

Sing the melodic pitch patterns in example 17.16. As you sing, listen to the secondary dominants and their resolutions.

Example 17.16

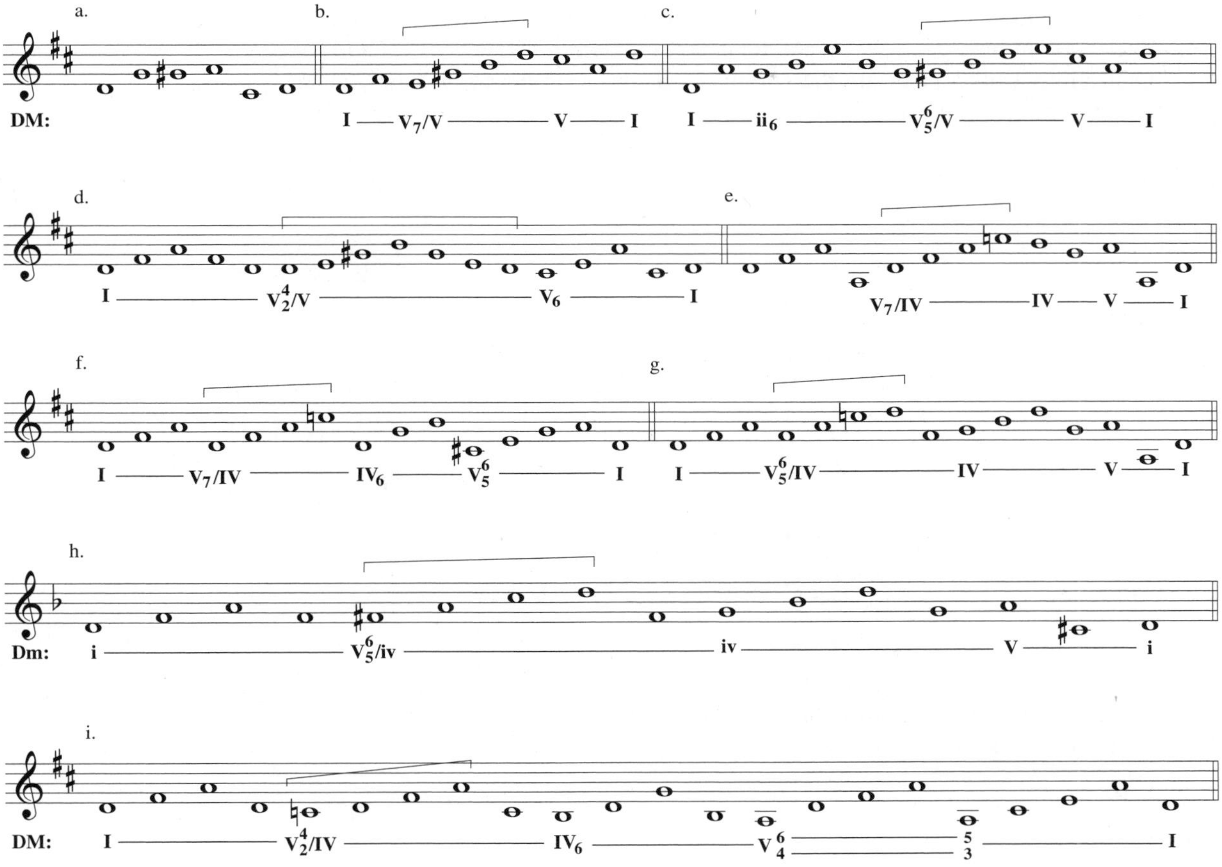

Terms for Review

- Chromatic tones
- Chromatic harmony
- Modulation
- Chromatic (altered) chords
- Tonicization
- Secondary dominants
- Applied dominants
- Secondary leading tone
- V_7/V and inversions
- Cross relations
- Chromaticized voice exchange
- V_7/IV and inversions

Worksheet 17

EXERCISE 1 Analysis.

1. Refer to anthology, no. 19, Haydn, Menuet and Trio in CM. Identify two cases of tonicization in mm. 9–12. What are the degrees tonicized? How does each of the tonicizations work? What are the chromatic degrees introduced and the Roman numerals in each of the tonicizations?

2. Play through the period in example 17.17.
   a) What degree is tonicized in the first phrase?

   b) How many times, and by means of which secondary chords?

   c) One of these tonicizations is linear and embellishing, whereas the other one is functional. Explain.

   d) Where do these tonicizations lead to within the period?

   e) Does the second phrase also include a similar tonicization?

Example 17.17 W. A. Mozart, "Là ci darem la mano," from *Don Giovanni,* m, 1–8

3. a) Two tonicizations take place in example 17.18. Identify both, provide exact RNs for each, and mark on the score any linear voice leading resulting from the tonicizations.

   b) This period features four clear harmonic units of two measures each. Comment on the formal/harmonic function of each of these units within the period. For instance, the first unit establishes the key (by what means?).

   c) On your own music paper, provide a metric reduction for the passage (both hands). Provide Roman numerals under the reduction, and show the form of the fragment by means of a bubble diagram over the reduction.

Example 17.18 L. v. Beethoven, Sonatina in GM, II, mm. 1–8

4. The opening of the chorale in example 17.19 features a tonicization. Explain what degree is tonicized, provide a RN analysis for the complete passage, comment on the voice leading for the tonicization, and explain the linear character of the complete example.

Example 17.19 J. S. Bach, Chorale 8, "Freuet euch, ihr Christen," mm. 1–2

EXERCISE 2

1. Write the following secondary dominants in root position, in four voices, with correct spacing. Provide key signatures.

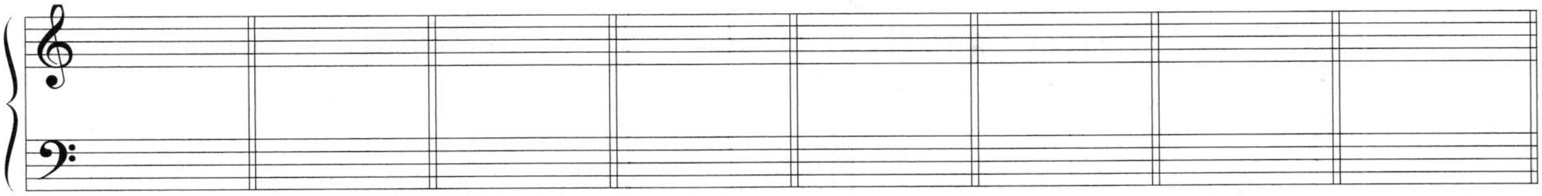

EM: V_7/V A♭M: V_7/V Am: V_7/V Cm: V_7/V Gm: V_7/iv B♭M: V_7/IV FM: V_7/IV C♯m: V_7/iv

2. Write the following secondary dominants in inversion, in four voices, with correct spacing. Provide key signatures.

Procedure for spelling secondary dominants:

a) The root of a secondary dominant is the pitch a 5th above (or a 4th below) the tonicized degree. The root of V_7/V, for instance, is $\hat{2}$, the pitch a 5th above $\hat{5}$.

b) On the root, you need to build a Mm_7 chord. Check carefully for possible accidentals you may need: the third should be major, the fifth perfect, and the seventh minor.

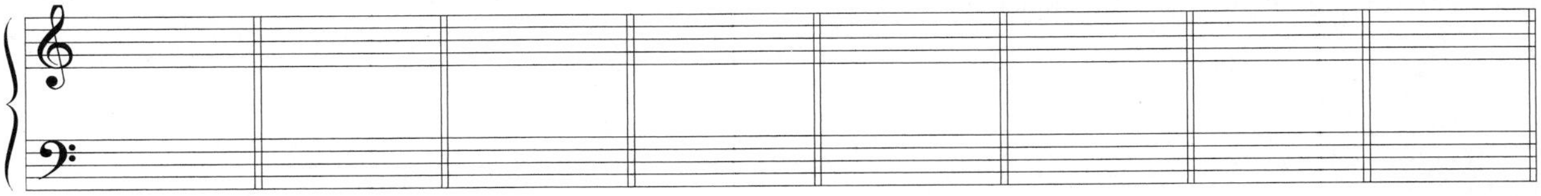

DM: V^6_5/V Bm: V^6_5/V AM: V^4_3/V GM: V^4_2/V Em: V^6_5/iv B♭M: V^4_3/IV Fm: V^4_2/iv F♯m: V^4_3/iv

EXERCISE 3 Spell and resolve the following secondary dominants of V and IV.

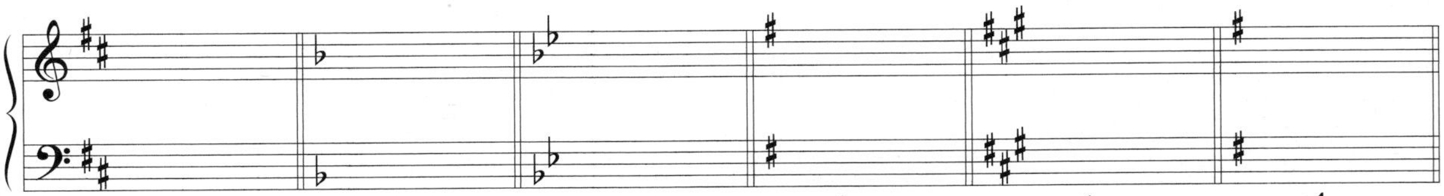

Bm: V_7/V V FM: V_7/V V B♭M: V^6_5/V V GM: V^4_3/V V F♯m: V^4_2/V V_6 Em: V^4_2/V V_6

Cm: V_7/iv iv   AM: V_7/IV IV   Gm: V^6_5/iv iv   Fm: V^4_2/iv iv_6 DM: V^6_5/IV IV   EM: V^4_2/IV IV_6

EXERCISE 4 Realize the following short progressions in four voices. Provide RNs for exercise 16.4b. Be careful to check the outer-voice frame for good counterpoint.

a. b.

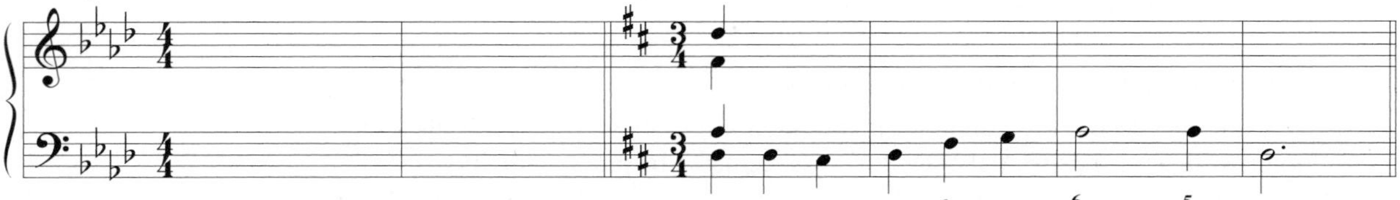

Fm: i V^4_2/iv iv_6 $ii^{\varnothing 6}_{5}$ V^6_5/V V_7 i   DM: $\sharp^4_2$ 6 $\natural^6_5$ $^6_4$ $^5_3$

EXERCISE 5 Realize the following progression in four voices. Be careful to check the outer-voice frame for good counterpoint.

E♭M: I ii^6_5 V^6_5/V V vi V^4_3/V $V^{6\,—\,5}_{4\,—\,3}$ I V^6_5/IV IV V_7 I

EXERCISE 6

1. Harmonize the following melody with a bass and RNs or a figured bass. Include a tonicization of iv and one of V. The harmonic rhythm is one chord per beat.
2. When you are sure that your harmonization is correct, copy the melody again on your own music paper and, below it, provide a left-hand keyboard realization of your harmonization.

EXERCISE 7

1. Write your own progressions (bass and RNs) in the keys and meters indicated below. Use the required chords, besides any of the other chords we have already studied. Make sure you resolve secondary dominants (and any other chords that require resolution) correctly.
   a) Gm; include V^6_5/iv and V_7/V.
   b) E♭M; include V^4_2/IV, V^6_5/V, and V^4_2/V.

2. Choose one of your own progressions from above and use it as a harmonic basis to compose a phrase for keyboard. Your phrase should consist of a simple melody (right hand) with keyboard-style accompaniment (left hand).

Chapter 18

Secondary Dominants II

In this chapter we will continue the study of secondary dominants. We will first examine the dominants of ii, vi (VI in minor), iii (III in minor), and the less frequent V_7/VII. We will also study the deceptive resolution of secondary dominants, the connection of consecutive secondary dominants and the irregular resolution resulting from this connection, and we will introduce secondary key areas.

The dominants of the supertonic, submediant, and mediant can frequently be found in music, and in principle they may appear in any inversion. To simplify our presentation, however, we will focus only on those inversions which appear most often in the form of standard harmonic patterns.

V_7 OF ii

Because the supertonic in minor keys is a diminished triad and only M and m triads can be tonicized, V of ii is found only in the major mode. It is a Mm_7 chord built on $\hat{6}$ (the pitch a 5th above $\hat{2}$), and it includes the accidental $\sharp\hat{1}$, the secondary leading tone (LT) of $\hat{2}$. In example 18.1, by nineteenth-century American composer Clara Scott, V_7/ii is used to approach the cadential gesture ii_7–V^{6-5}_{4-3}–I. The progression V_7/ii–ii–V–i (see also example 18.3) is especially strong because of the succession of 5th-related roots ($\hat{6}$–$\hat{2}$–$\hat{5}$–$\hat{1}$). Examine also Scott's voice leading: $\sharp\hat{1}$ (D♮) functions as a chromatic passing tone (PT) between $\hat{1}$ and $\hat{2}$.

The most frequent inversion of V_7/ii is V^6_5/ii, in which $\sharp\hat{1}$, the secondary LT, is emphasized in the bass (see example 18.3). The opening of Chevalier de Saint–Georges's Sonata no. 2 for violin and piano (example 18.2) shows an effective use of this inversion. Notice that while the chord in both m. 3 and m. 7 is V^6_5/ii, the root of the chord, F♯, appears only in the melody, thus further stressing $\sharp\hat{1}$ in the bass.

Example 18.1 Clara Scott, *Twilight Fancies,* mm. 1–8

Example 18.2 Chevalier de Saint–Georges, Sonata no. 2 for Violin and Piano, mm. 1–10

EXERCISE

To practice spelling and resolving secondary dominants of ii, refer to exercise 2 in worksheet 18 at the end of this chapter.

V_7 OF vi (VI)

The dominant of the submediant is found equally in major or minor modes. In major, V_7/vi is built on $\hat{3}$ (the pitch a 5th above $\hat{6}$) and includes $\sharp\hat{5}$, the LT of $\hat{6}$. In minor, V_7/VI includes the M triad III (diatonic), with an added m7, $\flat\hat{2}$. The opening phrase from the Étude-Mazurka "La Favorite," by nineteenth-century American composer Jane Sloman, illustrates the use of V_7/vi within a period in FM (example 18.4). After the first phrase establishes the key with a very standard diatonic progression, the V_7/vi at the beginning of the second phrase introduces an element of harmonic variety. Notice the tonally strong bass in this second phrase (two consecutive sets of P4-related pitches), the chromatic voice leading in the left hand, and the numerous chromatic nonchord tones (NCTs) in the right hand.

Example 18.3

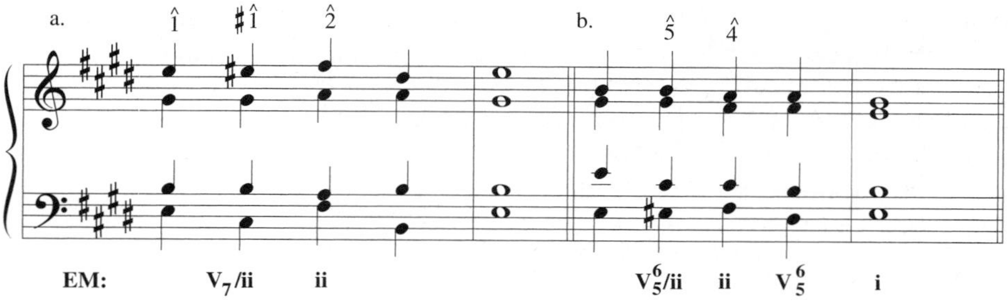

Example 18.4 Jane Sloman, "La Favorite," Étude-Mazurka, mm. 1–8

As with all secondary dominants, this chord is often found in first inversion (V^6_5/vi) because of the linear strength of the LT in the bass. Examine example 18.5, identify V^6_5/VI (the passage is in Dm), and verify its voice leading. What other secondary chords can you identify in the fragment?

The second inversion of V_7/vi, V^4_3/vi, allows for a good linear bass line descending by steps from $\hat{1}$. Another example by Mozart (example 18.6) demonstrates this progression on the bass $\hat{1}$–$\hat{7}$–$\hat{6}$, I–V^4_3/vi–vi. Analyze the first five chords in this passage (mm. 20–21; notice that the key here is E♭M, despite the key signature), paying attention not only to function and RNs, but also to voice leading. What is the linear function of the second chord? And of the fourth chord? The remainder of the passage presents some interesting challenges that we will discuss later in this chapter (see p. 432).

Consult example 18.7 for a summary of progressions involving the dominant of vi. Make sure you notice the difference between the V^4_3/vi progression (example 18.7d) and the progression with V^4_2/IV (example 17.8e). The last progression in this example (example 18.7e) shows a very effective use of V^6_5/vi as a chromatic passing chord embellishing a deceptive cadence. Play this progression, first omitting the V^6_5/vi (you will thus hear a simple deceptive cadence, I–V_7–vi), and then with the passing V^6_5/vi inserted between V_7 and vi.

Example 18.5 W. A. Mozart, String Quartet in Dm, K. 173, IV, mm. 73–77

Example 18.6 W. A. Mozart, Sonata for Violin and Piano, K. 481, II, mm. 20–24

Example 18.7

EXERCISE

To practice spelling and resolving secondary dominants of vi, refer to exercise 2 in worksheet 18 at the end of this chapter.

V_7 OF iii (III)

The secondary dominant of the mediant in the major mode is a Mm_7 chord on $\hat{7}$ (the pitch a 5th above $\hat{3}$), with two accidentals: $\sharp\hat{2}$ (LT of $\hat{3}$) and $\sharp\hat{4}$. In the minor mode, on the other hand, V_7/III is built on $\flat\hat{7}$, and it does not involve any chromatic alteration (the scale degrees are $\flat\hat{7}$–$\hat{2}$–$\hat{4}$–$\flat\hat{6}$, all members of the natural minor scale). Consult example 18.8 for spelling and resolution of this chord.

Because in minor modes the mediant key is the relative major (III), a key very closely related to the minor tonic key, the secondary dominant of the mediant appears more often in minor than in major. This chord also appears frequently in first inversion, although you will find examples of it in both root position and other inversions. The connection I–V_7/iii requires special voice-leading care because of the danger of parallel 5ths and a melodic +2 between $\hat{1}$ and $\sharp\hat{2}$ (try it and you will see; a solution is to

Example 18.8

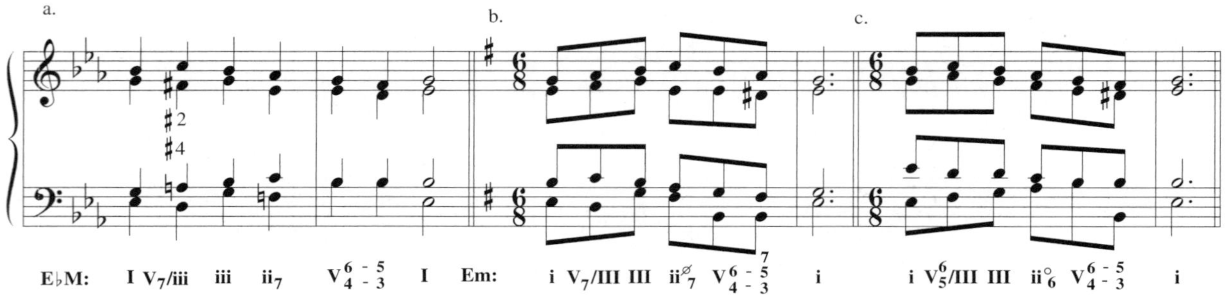

double the third in I, as in example 18.8a). In example 18.9a, Schubert partially avoids the problem by writing leaps in two voices (right hand). Does he avoid, however, the +2? Example 18.9b, on the other hand, illustrates a standard use of V_7/III in minor. By writing the chord in first inversion (V^6_5/III), Chopin can take advantage of the linear bass progression, $\hat{1}$–$\hat{2}$–$\hat{3}$. Notice also how natural and diatonic this chord sounds in the minor mode as compared to the equivalent progression in major.

EXERCISE

To practice spelling and resolving secondary dominants of iii, refer to exercise 2 in worksheet 18 at the end of this chapter.

V_7 OF VII

We do not tonicize vii because it is a diminished triad. As we studied in chapter 14, however, ♭$\hat{7}$ in minor is a diatonic degree, the root of a M triad, VII. This degree is

Example 18.9a F. Schubert, Symphony in Bm, "Unfinished," II, mm. 268–274

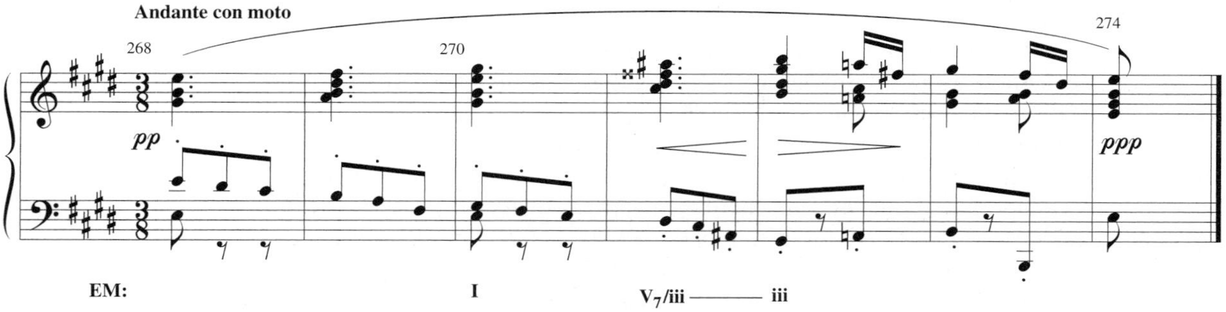

Example 18.9b F. Chopin, Mazurka 43 in Gm, op. posth. 67, no. 2, mm. 1–6

sometimes tonicized. The secondary dominant of VII is built on $\hat{4}$ and includes the raised $\hat{6}$. Although V_7/VII may be used as an independent tonicization, it is often found as part of a circle of 5ths of secondary dominants. Refer to anthology, no. 5 (Vivaldi, Concerto, op. 3, no. 3), mm. 15–22. This passage, in Em, begins with a sequence based on a circle-of-5ths bass: B–E–A–D. What harmonies does Vivaldi assign to the bass B–E–A in mm. 16–18? In mm. 19–20, we have an example of V_7/VII–VII to the bass A–D, $\hat{4}$–$\flat\hat{7}$. A four-voice realization of the same progression appears in example 18.10.

EXERCISES

To practice spelling and resolving secondary dominants of VII, refer to exercise 2 in worksheet 18 at the end of this chapter.

To practice realizing progressions including tonicizations of ii, vi, and iii, refer to exercise 3 in worksheet 18 at the end of this chapter.

To practice harmonizing a melody including various tonicizations, refer to exercise 4 in worksheet 18 at the end of this chapter.

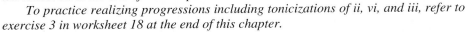

Example 18.10

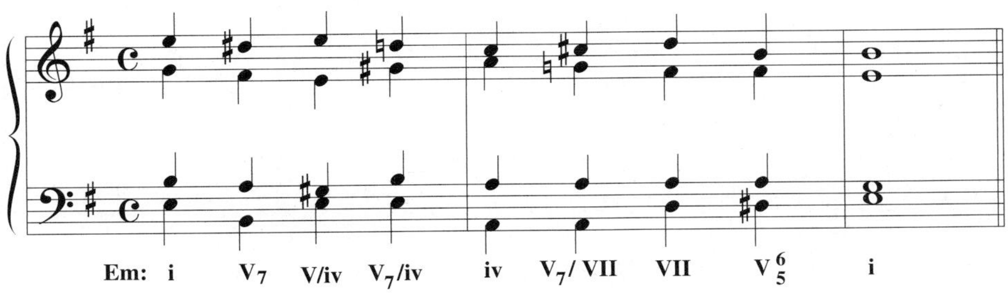

CHARACTERISTIC SOPRANO-BASS PATTERNS

The most characteristic soprano-bass patterns that are harmonized with secondary dominants of ii and vi involve chromatic passing motion in one of the voices. Examples 18.11a and b show two such patterns harmonized with the dominant of ii, and examples 18.11c to g show patterns using the dominant of vi (or VI in minor). Examples 18.12a to d, on the other hand, feature patterns harmonized with the dominant of iii (III in minor), including a passing figure in the soprano (examples 18.12 a and c) and a neighbor figure (examples 18.12b and d). Finally, example 18.12e features a chromatic passing figure harmonized with the dominant of VII. Play each of these outer-voice patterns, adding inner voices in keyboard texture.

ELABORATING THE I–V–I PROGRESSION

Each of the progressions shown in example 18.13 features an underlying I–V–I progression in which the opening tonic has been extended by means of a secondary dominant of ii (examples 18.13a and b), vi (examples 18.13c and d), iii (examples 18.13e and f), or VII (example 18.13g). Passing motion is used to extend the tonic in examples 18.13a

Example 18.11

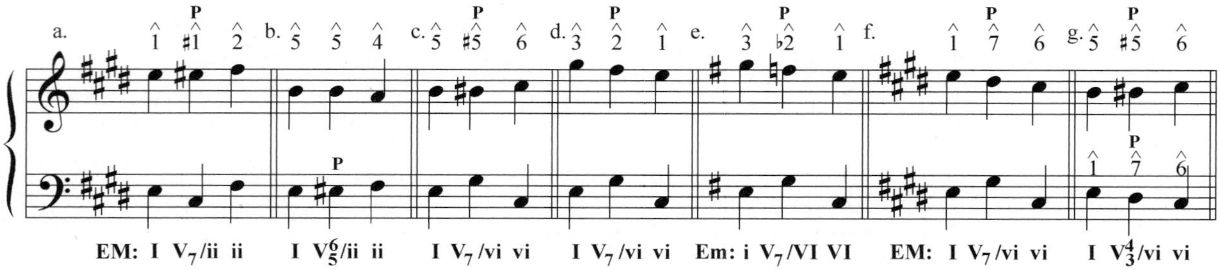

Example 18.12

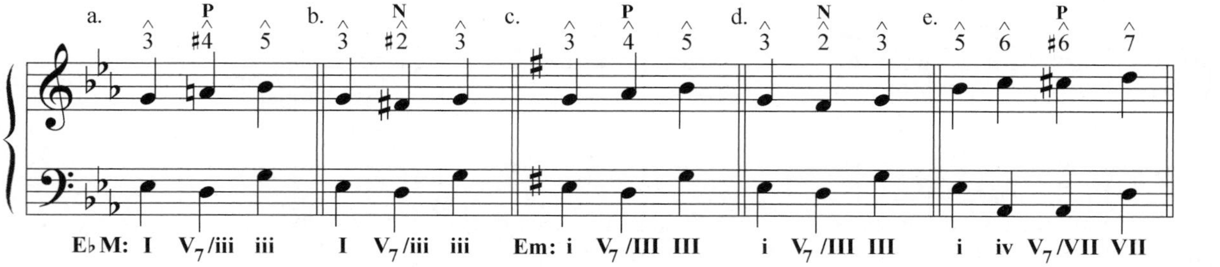

Example 18.13

to d and in example 18.13g, whereas neighbor motion is present in both examples with the dominant of iii or III (examples 18.13e and f).

DECEPTIVE RESOLUTIONS OF SECONDARY DOMINANTS

Just as a dominant chord may resolve deceptively to vi or VI, a secondary dominant may resolve deceptively by upward stepwise root motion to the triad that would function as vi or VI in the tonicized area. The Haydn fragment reproduced in example 18.14, for instance, illustrates a deceptive resolution of V_7/vi. The passage is in DM, and we first hear a deceptive resolution of V_7 to vi, followed by a tonicization of the submediant (V_7/vi). This chord also resolves deceptively to a GM chord, which, in the tonicized key area of the submediant, Bm or vi, is itself VI. The bracket under the Roman numerals V_7–VI should be read as "of vi," hence "V_7–VI of vi."

SEQUENCES WITH SECONDARY DOMINANTS

Various sequential patterns are possible using secondary dominants. We will now study patterns by descending 5ths, ascending 2nds, and descending 3rds.

Example 18.14 J. Haydn, String Quartet op. 77, no. 1, I, mm. 43–46

The Descending Circle-of-5ths Sequence

The following comments refer to example 18.15. Play through all the progressions if possible, listen to them, and sing them in class.

1. In example 18.15a you will recognize a succession of secondary dominants with their respective resolutions. The resulting bass pattern is a circle of 5ths.
2. In example 18.15b, we have deleted the intervening triad of resolution between secondary dominants. Each secondary V_7 now resolves to another secondary V_7

Example 18.15a

Example 18.15b

whose root is a 4th above (or 5th below). In chapter 16 we studied the circle of 5ths of diatonic seventh chords. Now we can write a chromatic circle of 5ths of secondary dominants.

3. The connection of two **consecutive secondary V_7s** requires an **irregular resolution** of the LT and the seventh. In the first place, notice that the chords in succession alternate between complete (C) and incomplete (IN). Then observe the voice leading (and see example 18.15c).
   a) The seventh of the first chord moves down chromatically to become the LT of the next chord.
   b) The LT of the first chord moves down chromatically to become the seventh of the next chord.

Observe, too, that in this progression (see example 18.15b) *two of the voices move chromatically* as long as you have successive V_7s.

Examples 18.15c, d, and e

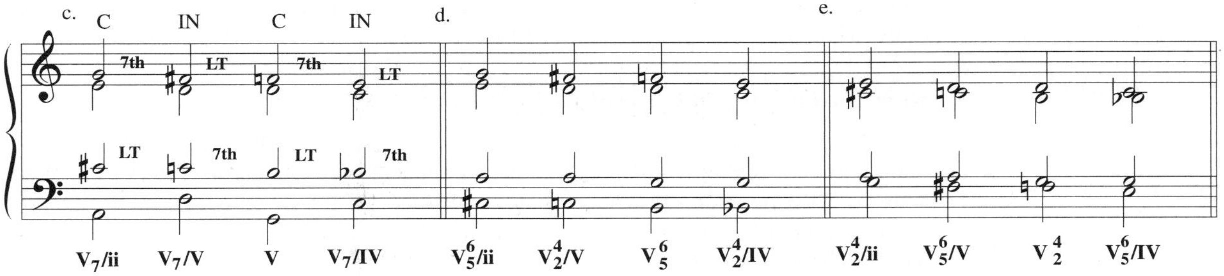

Example 18.15f

f.

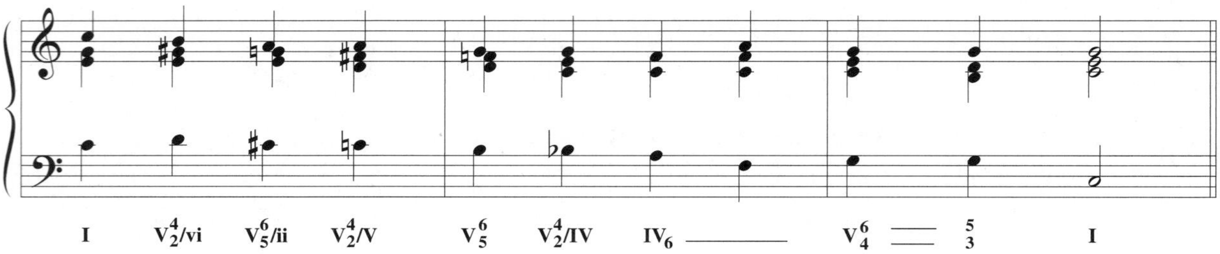

The Circle of 5ths with Inverted Secondary Dominants

If you place either of the chromatic voices in the bass, you will end up with a sequence of alternate secondary V$^6_5$s and V$^4_2$s, all of them complete. Compare example 18.15c (root position) with examples 18.15d and e. In the latter two, each of the chromatic voices has been placed in the bass, with the same results (in different order) in the inversions: $^6_5$–$^4_2$ or $^4_2$–$^6_5$. This is a common **sequential pattern,** as well as one of the most effective chromatic progressions.

In example 18.15f you can see this pattern applied to a closed progression in CM. Notice that we can now harmonize a **descending chromatic bass.** Moreover, we still think of this progression as being in CM—a very chromatic CM, to be sure, but CM nonetheless. So, what happened then to our good old white-key CM scale? After you introduce wholesale chromaticism, you will see that the chromatic scale ends up substituting for the diatonic scale (for any diatonic scale, in any key). These examples also show the harmonic power of secondary dominants. In only two chapters and with a single harmonic concept, we have gone from all-diatonic harmony to the type of thoroughly chromatic progression we are discussing now.

Example 18.16 illustrates several of the sequential techniques we have just discussed. The basic underlying progression is a circle of 5ths, indicated by the roots circled in each of the measures. The passage in mm. 104–106 is all made up of secondary dominants. The second and third eighth notes in each measure, connecting the circled roots, create a repeated $^4_2$–$^6_5$ pattern like the one we just discussed in example 18.15f.

Some Further Examples from the Literature

Refer to example 18.6, Mozart's violin sonata K. 481, and analyze mm. 2–3. The V$^6_5$/vi in m. 2, beat 1, resolves to a major VI, or V/ii, which immediately becomes V$^4_2$/ii. What does the V$^4_2$/ii move on to? What happens to the bass B♭, the seventh of V$^4_2$/ii, as it moves to the next chord? And to the E♮, the LT in V$^4_2$/ii? Complete the analysis of m. 3, tracing the voice leading of the LTs and sevenths.

Example 18.16 A. Vivaldi, "Laudamus Te," from *Gloria,* mm. 103–107

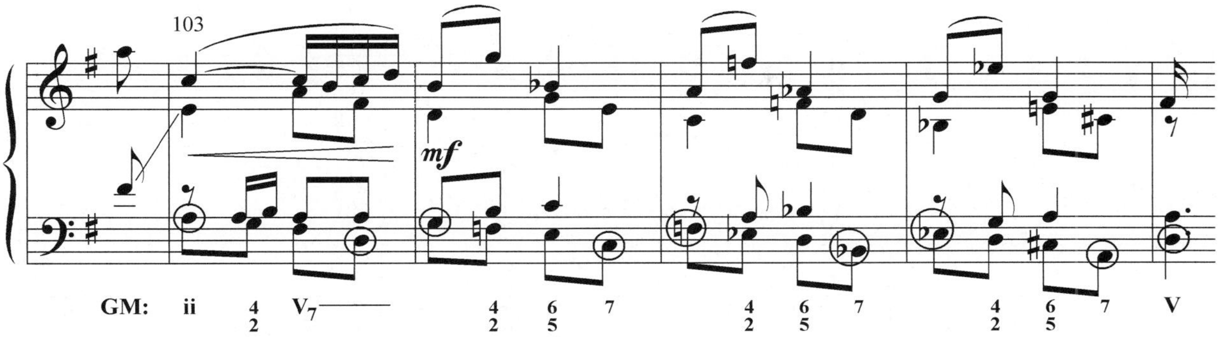

Refer now to anthology, no. 44 (Chopin, Mazurka 43). First, analyze mm. 25–32, in B♭M. You will find consecutive V_7s in mm. 25–26 (repeated in mm. 27–28), and especially in mm. 29–30, a circle-of-5ths fragment. In mm. 29–30, look at the right hand and trace the voice leading of the LTs and sevenths for each chord. Do they follow the criteria we have established above? What about the left hand in these measures: Does it follow our voice-leading principles? Well, composers *do* take liberties. In a case like this, with the left-hand parallel 5ths, Chopin is reinforcing the already strong bass by 5ths, in contrast to the smooth, chromatic right hand. Of course, Chopin did this in a deliberate way to emphasize musically an instrumental bass, and in no way are these 5ths "voice-leading errors."

The passage in mm. 29–30 tonicizes only diatonic degrees in B♭M. What about the similar but longer linear sequential passage in mm. 21–25? Some nondiatonic degrees are tonicized here, beginning with the V_7/♭VII in m. 23. The circle of 5ths leads from V_7/IV to V_7/♭VII, and after that on to the tonicization of $\flat\hat{3}$, $\flat\hat{6}$, $\flat\hat{2}$, and so forth. One could continue like this for the complete twelve-pitch cycle of the chromatic scale. To avoid this, Chopin breaks the circle of P5ths in m. 25 with a °5th from G♭ to C (instead of C♭), thus getting the sequence back into B♭M through V_7/V.

Sequences by Ascending 2nds: The 5–6 Technique

In chapter 16 we studied the diatonic sequence by ascending 2nds, and we saw that one way of avoiding the parallel 5ths resulting from triads ascending by steps was to alternate $^5_3$ and $^6_3$ chords using the "5–6 technique" illustrated in example 18.17a. We can turn this sequence into a chromatic sequence using secondary dominants by raising chromatically the repeated bass note in the bass, as shown in examples 18.17b and c. In example 18.17b, the secondary chords are triads in $^6_3$ position, whereas in 18.17c they are seventh chords in $^6_5$ position.

Notice that this sequence allows us to harmonize an **ascending chromatic bass line.** In a variant of this sequence, shown in example 18.17d, the secondary dominants

Example 18.17

are in root position, creating a "down a 3rd-up a 4th" bass pattern. This sequence allows for the ascending chromatic line to be in the soprano. Example 18.18 shows an example by Handel of this chromatic sequence ascending by steps.

Sequences by Descending 3rds

As we saw in chapter 16 (refer to examples 16.20e and f), by inserting a chord in either first inversion or root position, we avoid the parallel 5ths and 8ves that would result in a sequence descending by 3rds. Similarly, we can insert the secondary dominant of each 3rd-related chord, as shown in example 18.19a. Thus, the sequence I–vi–IV–ii becomes

Example 18.18 G. F. Handel, Minuet in F, mm. 9–14

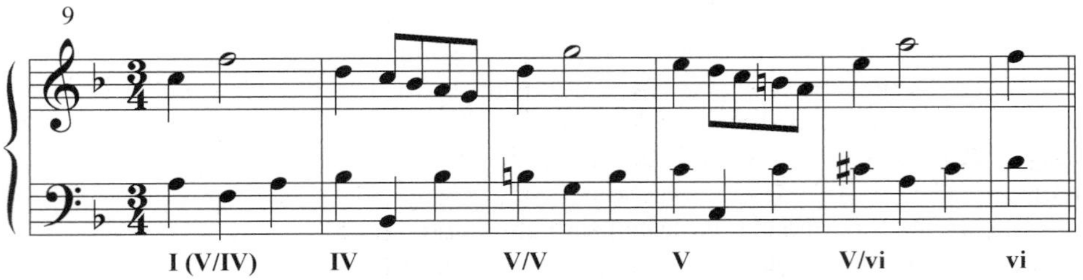

Example 18.19

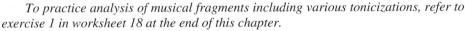

I–V_7/vi–vi–V_7/IV–IV–V_7/ii–ii. The same secondary dominants in second inversion ($^4_3$) result in a descending bass line, as shown in example 18.19b. Example 18.19c shows the same sequence, but now with the secondary dominants in $^6_5$ position. The resulting bass pattern ("down a 4th-up a 2nd") is particularly interesting because of the dissonant °4th intervals. If you refer back to example 18.5, mm. 74–75, you will hear a brief instance of exactly this sequence (from Mozart's String Quartet K. 173, IV), as shown in a reduced form in example 18.19d.

EXERCISES

To practice realizing chromatic sequences including secondary dominants, refer to exercise 5 in worksheet 18 at the end of this chapter.

To practice analysis of musical fragments including various tonicizations, refer to exercise 1 in worksheet 18 at the end of this chapter.

SECONDARY KEY AREAS

Listen to anthology, no. 54 (Verdi, *Il trovatore,* act II, no. 14, mm. 15–24). The fragment is in C: It begins in Cm and ends in CM. In mm. 19–21 we hear tonicizations of F ($\hat{4}$), and in mm. 21–22 we hear a tonicization of D ($\hat{2}$). The tonicization of $\hat{4}$ involves more than a single secondary dominant and its resolution to the tonicized F. In mm. 19–21

Example 18.20 G. Verdi, *Il trovatore,* act II, no. 14, mm. 17–24 (Anthology, no. 54), bass line

we hear V^4_2/IV followed by its resolution to IV_6, and then V^4_3/IV resolving to IV. We will use the concept of **secondary key area** to refer to short passages in which there is a progression that involves more secondary chords than just the dominant, or in which a degree is tonicized more than once. Mm. 19–21 of our example are, then, a secondary key area of IV. Example 18.20 presents the bass line for this passage (where the repetition of mm. 15–16 has been omitted) and shows our notation for secondary key areas. The length of the secondary key area is indicated by a line. The Roman numeral under the line refers to the degree tonicized (IV in our case), and the RNs above the line indicate the chords within the key area, analyzed and labeled in the secondary key, in this case FM (IV in CM).

Refer now to anthology, no. 34 (Beethoven, Sonata op. 13, III), mm. 18–25. The first period of the piece ends in m. 17 with a perfect authentic cadence (PAC) in Cm. Two brief secondary key areas (four measures each) follow, the first one in the Fm area (iv in Cm), the second one in the E♭M area (III in Cm). As it turns out, the second key area, of III, is here to stay: It proves to be a full modulation to E♭M, on which the second section of the piece is built, beginning in m. 25. But in mm. 22–24 we don't know this yet. We find out only after E♭M is established in m. 25, and we hear the new phrase continuing in E♭M. So, by analogy with mm. 18–21 (key area of iv), we will consider mm. 22–25 a secondary key area of III. Listen to the piece and notice the transitional character of these two passages in iv and III. Example 18.21 provides the bass line and the secondary-key-area indications. Fill in the specific RNs for each chord within the two key areas (above the key-area line).

ASSIGNMENT AND KEYBOARD EXERCISES

For analytical and written assignments and keyboard exercises based on the materials learned in this chapter, refer to chapter 18 in the workbook.

Example 18.21

PITCH PATTERNS

Sing the melodic pitch patterns in example 18.22, paying attention to the sound of the various secondary dominants marked by brackets.

Example 18.22

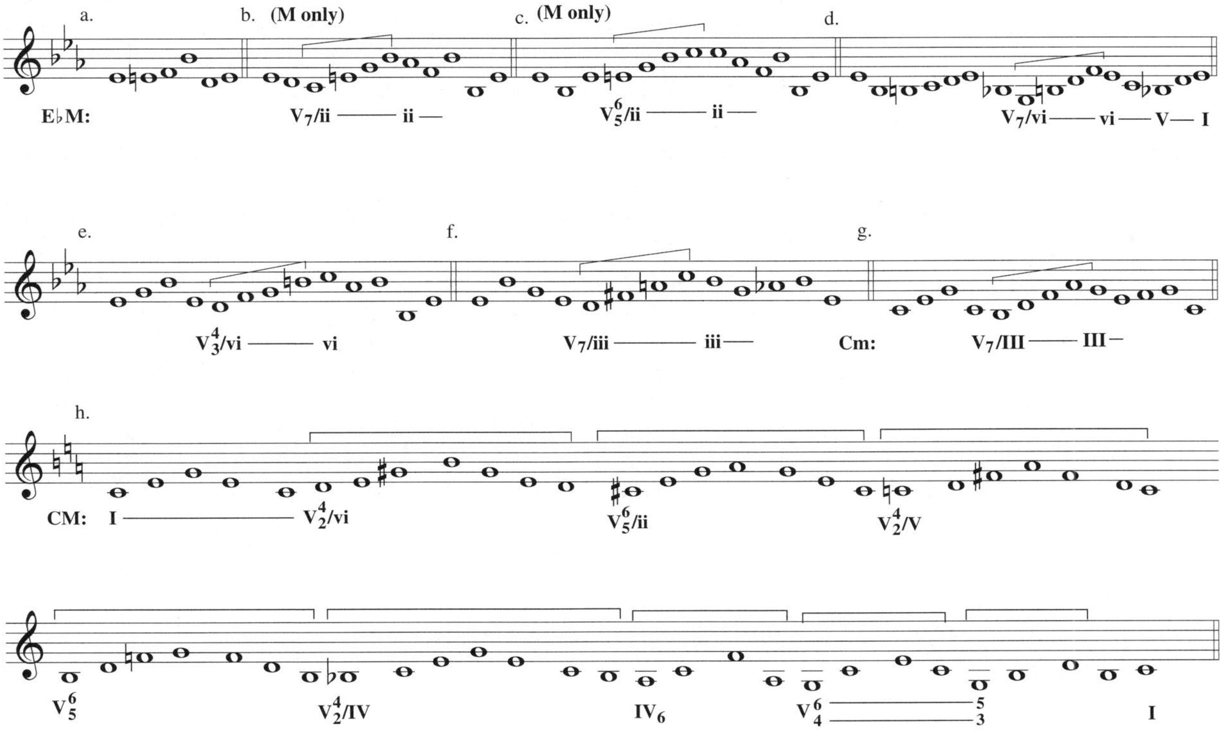

Terms for Review

V_7/ii and inversions
V_7/vi and inversions
V_7/iii and inversions
V_7/VII and inversions
Deceptive resolution of secondary dominants
Sequences with secondary dominants
The descending circle-of-5ths sequence
Consecutive secondary V_7s
Irregular resolution of V_7s
$^{6}_{5}$–$^{4}_{2}$ sequential pattern
Sequences by ascending 2nds: The 5–6 technique
Sequences by descending 3rds
Harmonizing the descending and ascending chromatic bass lines
Secondary key areas

Worksheet 18

EXERCISE 1 Analysis. The following examples include tonicizations of various degrees. Identify the degree or degrees tonicized in each case, and provide exact RNs if required.

1. Anthology, no. 31, Paradis, *Sicilienne,* mm. 7–8. Provide RNs for these two measures (the piece is in GM).

2. Example 18.23. Tonicization plays an essential role in this brief piece. What two degrees are tonicized in mm. 1–8? And what two degrees are tonicized in mm. 9–16? Provide RNs for all four secondary dominants. Comment on the melodic and harmonic sequential patterns that result in each of these two cases.

Example 18.23 F. Schubert, *Originaltänze,* op. 9, no. 16

3. Example 18.24. Which two degrees are tonicized in this example? Can you identify one or more linear patterns in the voice leading for one of these tonicizations?

Example 18.24 L. v. Beethoven, Piano Concerto no. 4, op. 58, II, mm. 1–13

4. Example 18.25. What progression is this passage based on? What kind of chords is the progression built on? Does it illustrate some special voice-leading properties we have studied in this chapter?

5. Example 18.26. Analyze this passage with RNs and identify the exact type of harmonic sequence on which it is based.

6. Example 18.27. The song from which this passage is taken is in CM. Provide a harmonic analysis for the passage. Analyze mm. 5–7 as a secondary key area, providing the correct analytical notation under the score.

Example 18.25 W. A. Mozart, String Quartet in Dm, K. 421, III, mm. 21–29

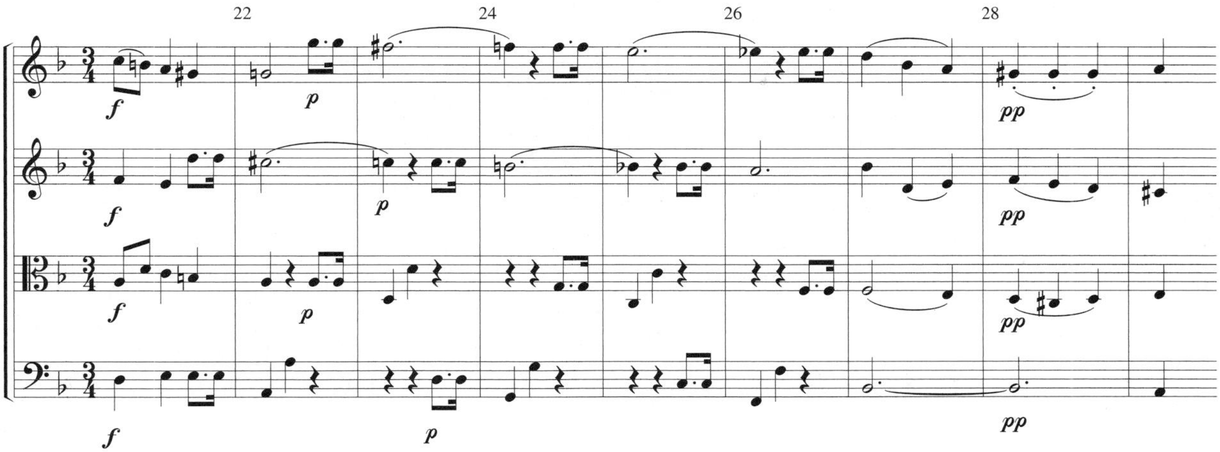

Example 18.26 G. Puccini, "Gloria," from *Messa di Gloria,* mm. 12–15

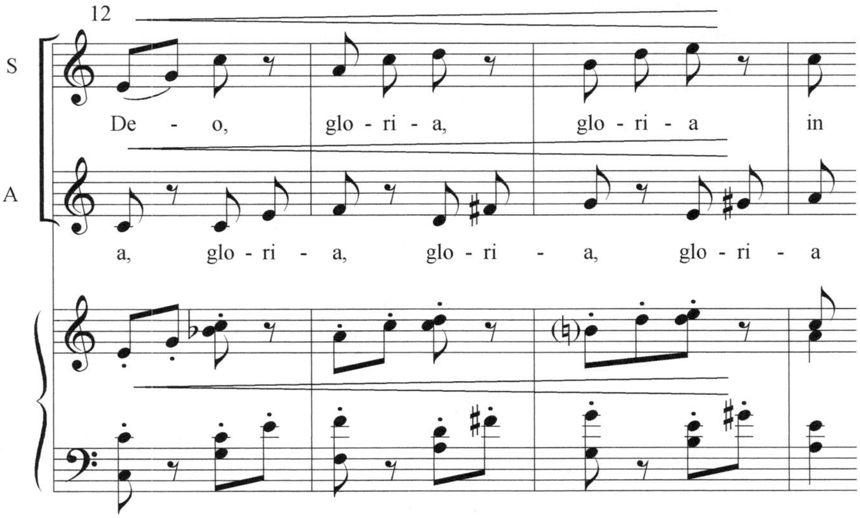

Example 18.27 Cole Porter, "Begin the Beguine," from *Jubilee* (end of refrain and beginning of bridge)

3
when they be - gin the Be - guine. To
live it a - gain is past all en - deav - or,

EXERCISE 2 Write and resolve the following secondary dominant chords. The resolution should be to the appropriate tonicized chord, in root position or inversion as required by the voice leading in the bass.

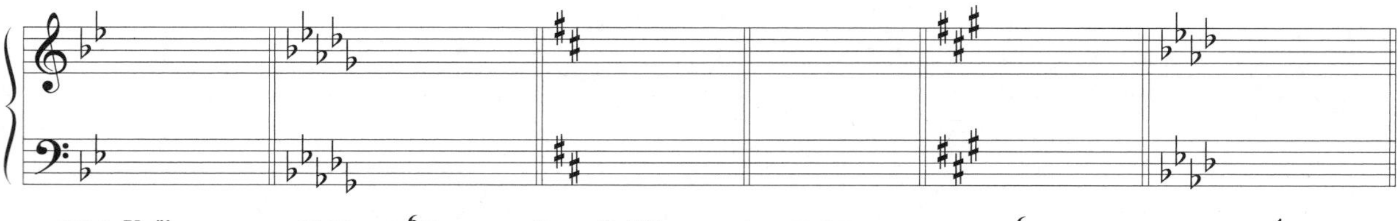

B♭M: V_7/ii __ D♭M: V^6_5/ii __ Bm: V_7/VI __ Am: V_7/VI __ F♯m: V^6_5/VI __ Fm: V^4_3/VI __

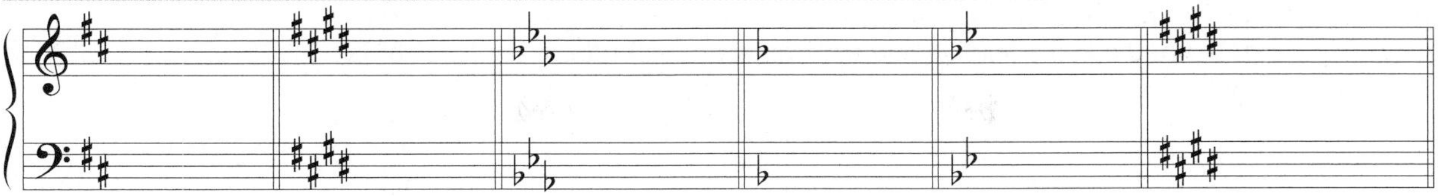

EXERCISE 3 Realize the following progressions in four voices and provide RNs for progression b.

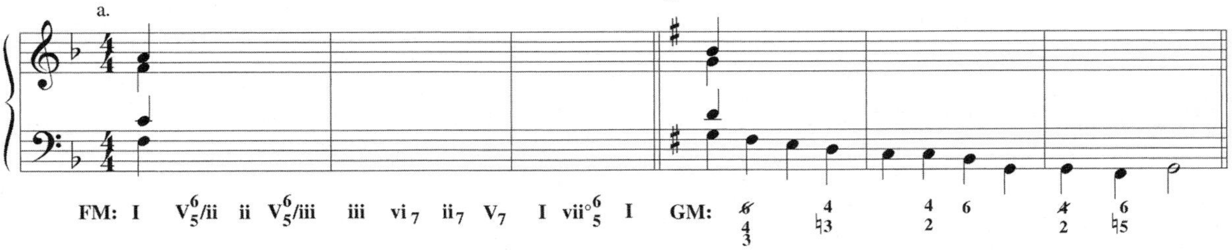

EXERCISE 4 Harmonize the following melody (based on Bach's Chorale 105) in four voices, in chorale style, and include a RN analysis of your harmonization. The notes marked with an asterisk should be harmonized with secondary dominants. Include tonicizations of III, iv, and V (although not necessarily in this order). Double-check your outer-voice frame for good counterpoint.

EXERCISE 5 Realize the following sequential patterns involving secondary dominants. Be careful with the voice leading and the irregular resolution of the LT and the seventh. Provide RNs for progression b.

Chapter 19

Secondary Leading-Tone Chords

In example 19.1 you will recognize a familiar harmonic structure: two phrases in Gm, the first one ending on a half cadence (HC), the second one on a perfect authentic cadence (PAC). In the approach to V at the HC, you will also recognize a familiar bass line, the secondary leading-tone figure $\hat{4}$–$\sharp\hat{4}$–$\hat{5}$. On the basis of our studies so far, we might expect $\sharp\hat{4}$ to be harmonized with V^6_5/V. A closer look will show that Bach chose to harmonize it with another familiar chord, a vii$^{\circ}_7$ chord, that close cousin and frequent substitute of V^6_5. In this case, vii$^{\circ}_7$ is not "of i" (Gm), but rather, because it is built on C♯, "of V" or "of D" in this example. (Incidentally, what unusual voice-leading event

Example 19.1 J. S. Bach, Chorale 19, "Ich hab' mein' Sach' Gott heimgestellt," mm. 1–4

do you see in m.1, in the right hand? To help explain it, remember that Bach was harmonizing a given, existing melody, which he was not going to change just because of a leading tone [LT] resolving in an unusual manner. Does the "voice overlap" help with the harmonic voice leading?)

SECONDARY LEADING-TONE SEVENTH CHORDS

The chord on $\sharp\hat{4}$ in example 19.1 is vii$^{\circ}_{7}$/V, a secondary vii$^{\circ}_{7}$ chord. Just as secondary dominants can tonicize any degree, the other members of the dominant family can also be used to tonicize chords. A **secondary leading-tone chord** is a triad or seventh chord built on a secondary LT (the pitch a half step below the degree we are tonicizing). vii$^{\circ}_{7}$/V, for instance, is a fully diminished seventh chord built on $\sharp\hat{4}$ (the pitch a half step below $\hat{5}$), and it will resolve to V as if V were a momentary tonic and as if $\sharp\hat{4}$ were a momentary LT resolving to its momentary tonic, $\hat{5}$. You will find secondary vii$^{\circ}_{6}$, vii$^{\varnothing}_{7}$, and vii$^{\circ}_{7}$ chords tonicizing the same degrees you can tonicize with V_7 chords. Secondary LT sevenths are more frequent than vii$^{\circ}_{6}$, and among them vii$^{\circ}_{7}$ is by far the most commonly found chord, in root position or inversion. You may refer to anthology, no. 18 (Amalie, sonata for flute) for an example of a secondary vii$^{\varnothing}_{7}$. In m. 8 you will see a HC on V, preceded by a $\sharp\hat{4}$ (B♮) in the bass. The complete chord is B♮–D–F–A, or vii$^{\varnothing}_{7}$/V. How does this LT chord compare with the other chord on $\sharp\hat{4}$ (B♮) in m. 11? What other secondary chord do you recognize in m. 10?

Spelling Secondary Leading-Tone Seventh Chords

*To spell the secondary leading-tone seventh chord of a given degree, you build a $^{\circ}_{7}$ or $^{\varnothing}_{7}$ chord on the pitch a half step below the given degree (that is, on the given degree's leading tone)***.** Let's spell vii$^{\circ}_{7}$/iv in Gm. The triad we are tonicizing is iv in Gm, and the degree we are tonicizing is $\hat{4}$ in Gm, or C. The pitch a half step below C (that is, the LT of C) is B♮. The $^{\circ}_{7}$ chord on B♮ is B♮–D–F–A♭. This is vii$^{\circ}_{7}$/iv in Gm.

To summarize the process, let's spell vii$^{\varnothing}_{7}$/III in Cm. We are tonicizing $\hat{3}$ in Cm, or E♭. The pitch a half step below E♭ is D. The $^{\varnothing}_{7}$ chord on D is D–F–A♭–C. This is vii$^{\varnothing}_{7}$/III in Cm.

Chord Types, Resolution, and Voice Leading

Example 19.2 illustrates the three possible seventh chord harmonizations of a secondary LT. Choosing V^6_5, vii$^{\varnothing}_{7}$, or vii$^{\circ}_{7}$ is totally up to the composer. vii$^{\varnothing}_{7}$ may be used to tonicize major triads (such as V or IV), but not usually for minor triads (such as ii or vi). vii$^{\circ}_{7}$, on the other hand, appears in tonicizations of both major and minor triads. All three chords stress the LT in the bass, with its strong linear pull. vii$^{\circ}_{7}$ has the advantage of, in some cases, introducing a new accidental. In example 19.2c, vii$^{\circ}_{7}$/V in M introduces $\flat\hat{3}$ besides $\sharp\hat{4}$; in example 19.4a, vii$^{\circ}_{7}$/IV includes $\flat\hat{2}$ besides $\flat\hat{7}$; and in example 19.4b, vii$^{\circ}_{7}$/ii adds $\flat\hat{7}$ to $\sharp\hat{1}$. These chords intensify the chromaticism of a passage and also create two strong linear tensions, the LT and the seventh.

Voice Leading

As usual, the secondary LT resolves up, and the seventh down. Otherwise, all the same voice-leading principles (and problems) we studied regarding leading-tone seventh

Example 19.2

chords apply to secondary LT sevenths. You may want to review chapter 15 to refresh your knowledge of these principles, especially the resolution of the tritone (root and fifth) and the possible parallel 5ths resulting from the downward resolution of the third in vii$^{ø}_{7}$ (see examples 15.4 and 15.7). Resolving the third upward in vii$^{\circ}_{7}$/V (or vii$^{ø}_{7}$/V), as in example 19.2d, results in a doubled LT in the V of the resolution, which you want to avoid. Example 19.2e shows a possible resolution with unequal 5ths (which, in vii$^{ø}_{7}$ would be faulty parallel 5ths), and example 19.2f shows the best possibility, with 4ths instead of 5ths. (Examples 19.2b and c avoid the problem altogether by voicing the chord differently.)

The resolution of vii$^{ø}_{7}$/V or vii$^{\circ}_{7}$/V to V$^{6-5}_{4-3}$, a very frequent occurrence, is illustrated in examples 19.2g to i. You may notice that the notation in example 19.2h is a bit awkward: The seventh, B♭, first has to go up a half step to B♮, before resolving down to A. Although awkward, the notation B♭–B♮–A is perfectly acceptable and found in many scores. At times, however, composers choose an alternative, and also perfectly correct, notation, which reflects the voice-leading motion better by using the enharmonic A♯ instead of B♭, as in example 19.2i.

Study Bach's use of vii$^{\circ}_{7}$/V in example 19.3. In m. 9, beats 2–3, the LT, seventh, and tritone (TT) are perfectly resolved as we would expect. How does Bach deal with the voice leading of the problematic third? Then, in m. 10, notice an interesting possibility: instead of preceding a V$^{6-5}_{4-3}$ figure, as in example 19.2h, Bach's vii$^{\circ}_{7}$/V acts as an ornamental neighbor chord between the $^{6}_{4}$ and the $^{5}_{3}$, creating a beautiful linear elaboration of V. One more observation before we leave this example: What secondary chord is used at the beginning of the phrase?

Example 19.3 J. S. Bach, Chorale 94, "Warum betrübst du dich, mein Herz," mm. 9–10

Example 19.4

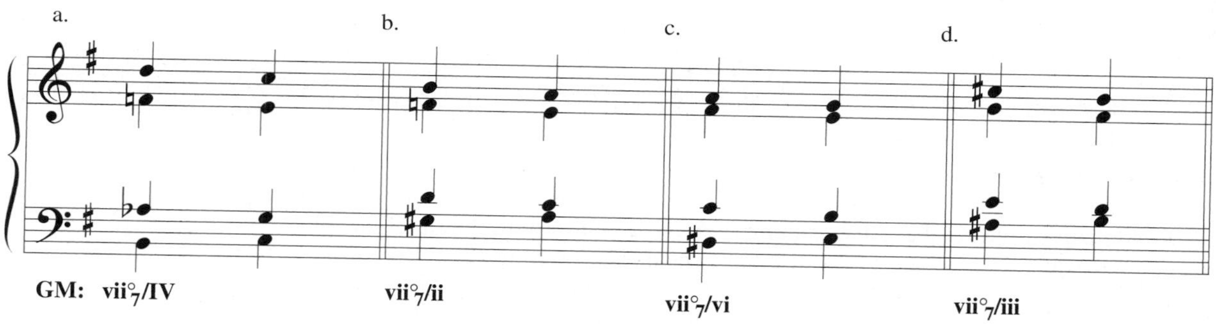

Example 19.4 shows some frequently found secondary vii°_{7} chords besides vii°_{7}/V. As we mention above, they all increase the chromatic intensity of the harmony, as well as the dissonant and linear tension of the voice leading. These are all dramatically effective chords.

EXERCISE

To practice spelling secondary diminished seventh chords in root position, refer to exercise 2 in worksheet 19 at the end of this chapter.

Examples from the Literature

The following examples demonstrate the use of the secondary vii°_{7} chord in a variety of contexts. In the Granados fragment (example 19.5), vii°_{7}/ii in m. 43 stands out as the only chromatic harmony in the passage. The voice leading in and out of this

Example 19.5 E. Granados, *Escenas Románticas,* no. 5, mm. 40–48

vii$^{\circ}_{7}$/ii is perfectly smooth in spite of the broad, open left-hand piano figuration. Notice also the linear function of vii$^{\circ}_{7}$/ii as a passing chord between the previous and following chords.

Example 19.6, on the other hand, features vii$^{\circ}_{7}$ chords in a more chromatic context. The first one, in m. 5, is also a vii$^{\circ}_{7}$/ii with a passing function. Now look at the resolution of the V_7 at the end of m. 6. Just by altering one pitch in the chord, $\hat{5}$ to $\sharp\hat{5}$, the chord becomes a passing vii$^{\circ}_{7}$/vi that connects V_7 with its deceptive resolution to vi (m. 7, beat 2). As we continue listening, however, we realize that all of m. 7 and m. 8 are actually *a secondary key area of vi.* Analyze these two measures as such, as if vi were the tonic. You will find a deceptive resolution within the secondary key area (in other words, a

Example 19.6 J. Lang, *Frühzeitiger Frühling,* mm. 5–11

Days of delight, are you here so soon?
Are you giving me the sun, hills, and forest?
The little brooks flow more fully.

Example 19.7 R. Schumann, "An Important Event," no. 6 from *Scenes from Childhood*, op. 15, mm. 1–4

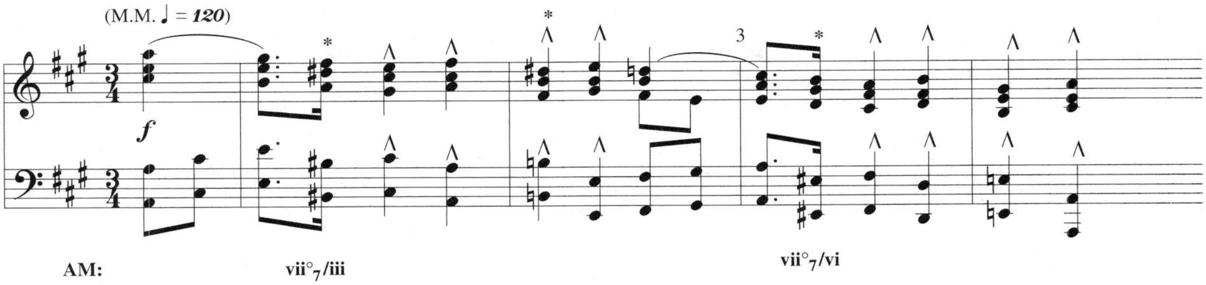

deceptive resolution of a secondary dominant, of the type we studied in the previous chapter), as well as a secondary function *within* the secondary key area (specifically, a dominant of the dominant of vi).

The phrase by Schumann in example 19.7 has two parallel phrase segments. What harmony is tonicized at the end of the first phrase segment? Both dotted figures include secondary vii°_{7} chords, of iii in m. 1, and of vi in m. 4. Verify the spelling and resolution of each of them and explain how they connect the previous and following chords linearly.

SECONDARY vii°_{7} CHORDS IN INVERSION

All inversions of the LT seventh chords may in principle be used, and they should all resolve according to the usual conventions of resolution of LT seventh chords. In summary, these are as follows:

1. The bass in $vii^{\circ 6}_{5}$ (the third of the chord) may resolve down to a root-position tonicized chord, or up to a chord in first inversion. In $vii^{\circ 6}_{5}$/V, however, the fifth of the chord resolves down, as part of the TT, to the LT, $\hat{7}$ (see example 19.8a). The bass must not, in this case, double $\hat{7}$, so it should not resolve up, but only down. The unequal 5ths that result are awkward, but possible. The same inversion as $vii^{ø6}_{5}$, however, is not possible because it would produce parallel 5ths.

   $vii^{\circ 6}_{5}$ tonicizing chords other than V does not present the problem of doubling the LT, so it may resolve up or down without difficulties. In example 19.8d, $vii^{\circ 6}_{5}$/ii resolves upward to ii_6. Compare this resolution with Haydn's identical resolution of the same chord in example 19.9.

2. According to the conventional resolution of the TT between the root and the fifth, $vii^{\circ 4}_{3}$, which has the fifth in the bass, should resolve downward to a tonicized chord in first inversion, as in example 19.8b. In example 19.10, Kreisler resolves a $vii^{\circ 4}_{3}$/ii

Example 19.8

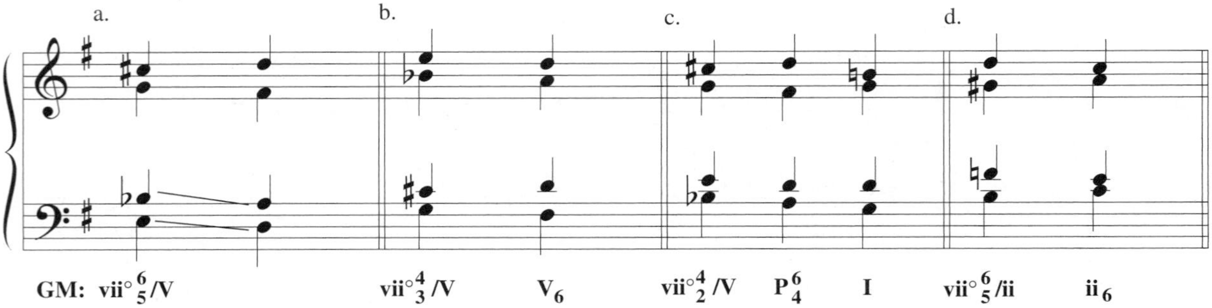

Example 19.9 J. Haydn, Piano Sonata in DM, Hob. XVI:37, III, mm. 110–114

to ii$_6$, following exactly the conventions we have studied. Study the voice leading of this chord's resolution, and notice also how Kreisler leads *into* the chord: He takes advantage of all common tones by keeping them sustained, and by introducing a passing chord between I and vii$^{\circ 4}_{3}$/ii (iii$_6$) he can write a nice descending chromatic line in an inner voice. Study the harmonies and voice leading in the passage and, as you play it or listen to it, hear the descending chromatic line in the inner voice.

3. vii$^{\circ 4}_{2}$ has the seventh in the bass, which resolves down to the fifth of the tonicized chord. The resulting $^6_4$ position will need to be treated as a dissonant $^6_4$ chord in one of the familiar ways. In example 19.8c, the V$^6_4$ moves on to I as a passing $^6_4$ chord. In example 19.11, on the other hand, vii$^{\circ 4}_{2}$/V resolves to V$^4_3$. Verify the spelling of vii$^{\circ 4}_{2}$/V in this phrase. Then, notice that, following the same voice leading we learned in irregular resolutions of secondary dominants, the leading tone in vii$^{\circ 4}_{2}$/V becomes the seventh in the following V$^4_3$. After you verify this, why do you think Maurice Jarre

Example 19.10 F. Kreisler, *Liebesleid,* mm. 73–80

Example 19.11 Paul Francis Webster–Maurice Jarre, "Somewhere, My Love," from the Film *Doctor Zhivago* (opening phrase)

chose to spell the secondary LT as D♭ instead of C♯? Does this enharmonic spelling make more sense from a melodic point of view?

EXERCISES

To practice spelling secondary diminished-seventh chords in inversion, refer to exercise 2 in worksheet 19 at the end of this chapter.

To practice analyzing figured basses including secondary diminished-seventh chords, refer to exercise 4 in worksheet 19 at the end of this chapter.

To practice realizing progressions including secondary diminished seventh chords, refer to exercises 3 and 5 in worksheet 19 at the end of this chapter.

THE vii$^\circ_7$ OVER A PEDAL POINT

vii$^\circ_7$ chords are often used over pedal tones, creating a very expressive multiple dissonance. The fragment in example 19.12, from a Bach Prelude in B♭m, features a pedal point on $\hat{5}$. As he does in many other pedal points, Bach writes a vii$^\circ_7$/V over the pedal at the end of m. 20. Notice the delayed resolution of the right-hand pitches. If you disregard the pedal, what is the inversion of vii$^\circ_7$ that Bach writes? Does he resolve this inversion as we have learned we should? To what position of V (again, disregard the

Example 19.12 J. S. Bach, Prelude 22 in B♭m, from *The Well-Tempered Clavier,* I, mm. 20–24

pedal) does he resolve it? Finally, notice that the fermata in m. 22 indicates a dramatic stop on a dominant harmony (a HC). On what dominant harmony does Bach pause?

In anthology, no. 56 (C. Schumann, Trio) you may see examples of vii$^{\circ}_{7}$ over a $\hat{1}$ pedal. What degree does the vii$^{\circ}_{7}$ over $\hat{1}$ in m. 265 tonicize? What is the inversion of this vii$^{\circ}_{7}$? Find the two appearances of the same secondary chord, also over $\hat{1}$, in mm. 275–278. What other vii$^{\circ}_{7}$ chord does Clara Schumann use repeatedly, over the same tonic pedal, in mm. 276–281?

ELABORATING THE I–V–I PROGRESSION

As it was the case with secondary dominants, secondary leading-tone seventh chords usually function as chromatic elaborations of a diatonic chordal frame. As an illustration, the progressions in example 19.13a to c show three root-position secondary leading-tone seventh chords elaborating the I–V–I progression. In examples 19.13a and b, the secondary vii$^{\circ}_{7}$ chords function as passing chords, and in 19.13c it functions as an incomplete neighbor chord. Examples 19.13d and e feature elaborations of the I–V–I progression by means of vii$^{\circ}_{7}$ chords in inversion. Finally, a variety of chromatic sequences can use secondary leading-tone seventh chords. Examples 19.13f and g show two cases of chromatic linear extension of the opening tonic in the I–V–I progression by means of sequences using secondary leading-tone seventh chords.

Example 19.13

A CHROMATIC HARMONIZATION OF A DIATONIC TUNE: BACH, CHORALE 21

As a summary of secondary LT chords, we now go back to an example we looked at a long time ago: example D.1a, reproduced again as example 19.14. Now we have all the tools we need to understand this beautiful chorale phrase. First sing the tune (the soprano line) and notice how simple and diatonic it is. Then play or listen to the harmonization and notice how chromatic it is, and how much intensity and drama is added to the melody through this chromaticism. First analyze the chorale harmonically, and *then* continue reading.

1. The beginning and end of the phrase tell us that it is in Am. In m. 1, beat 2, a vii°_7 chord tonicizes iv. Does the tonicization of iv continue? How do you hear the cadence in m. 2? It sounds like a HC in the key of iv (Dm). What specific kind of HC (consider the previous chord and bass note!)? The whole fragment from m. 1, beat 2, to the first fermata is, then, a *secondary key area of iv*. What kind of tonicizing chord appears in m. 1, beat 4, and how does it function linearly?
2. The chords in m. 3, beats 1–3, tonicize V. What is the first of these chords? The third one? What chord is used to connect them, in what position is it, and how does it function linearly? Notice the voice exchange figure characteristic of this type of linear function.
3. The annotations under example 19.14 show the long-range tonal plan for the phrase. Seen from this perspective, the tonal motion is an extended i_6–iv–V–i, in which iv and V appear as tonicized secondary areas. This phrase thus represents an extended chromatic elaboration of the i–iv–V–i progression.

EXERCISES

To practice harmonizing a melody including secondary diminished seventh chords, refer to exercise 6 in worksheet 19 at the end of this chapter.

To practice analysis of musical fragments including secondary diminished seventh chords, refer to exercise 1 in worksheet 19 at the end of this chapter.

Example 19.14 J. S. Bach, Chorale 21, "Herzlich thut mich verlangen," mm. 1–4

PRACTICAL APPLICATION AND DISCUSSION

Secondary Functions in Context: Two Songs by Mozart

1. Telling a story through harmony: "Wie Unglücklich bin ich nit" (anthology, no. 29).

We will use this Mozart song to illustrate the role of secondary functions in a long-range tonal structure and their relationship to the text. First, read the text. Then, analyze the complete song harmonically (use Roman numerals). Break the song into harmonic phrases (units). What is their tonal direction? How do they correspond with textual units and phrases? Can we tell a story through harmony? How does Mozart use chromaticism as a dramatic means?

a) *Harmonic unit 1, mm. 1–4.* This phrase establishes the key, by means of mostly diatonic progressions leading to the PAC in m. 4. The words in mm. 3–4 are "how languishing are my steps." How does the voice leading depict these words musically? See, for instance, the static lines, the dragging half-step motion in the bass (the only chromaticism in the whole phrase), and also the repeated G in the voice part, the lowest point in the section.

b) *Harmonic unit 2, mm. 5–6.* What happens harmonically in this section? It is all a secondary key area of V, leading to a PAC on a tonicized V in m. 6. The music has *turned away* from the tonic and moved *toward* the dominant. The text in these measures is: "When I turn them (my steps) toward you"!

c) *Harmonic unit 3, mm. 7–10.* "Only my sighs console me." The music is chromatic, with half steps in the bass and the voice part (the sighs, of course), and with the expressive vii°_{7} tonicizing ii. Notice, in m. 7, the change of position within vii°_{7}/ii by means of a voice exchange and a passing $^{6}_{4}$. Tonally, this unit takes us back toward the tonic. The "moving toward you" was short-lived; there does not seem to be much of a response from "you"! When we get back to the tonic, however, the words are "all my pains multiply." So the tonic that we reach in m. 9 is in minor mode, a sad and chromatic tonic, with numerous half-step sighs. The section closes on a tonicized HC on V (perhaps a sign of hope?).

d) *Harmonic unit 4, mm. 11–15.* So, is there hope? If I cannot be with "you," at least I can think of "you," and that is apparently as positive as things will get. So, to the words "when I think of you," the mode becomes major again, and the harmony diatonic, to the end of the song.

e) *In summary,* this song (1) *establishes* I, (2) *moves away* from I to V, (3) *returns* to the tonic, now minor, through a tonicization of ii, and (4) *reaffirms* I diatonically in a closing phrase. And all of this is telling a story through harmony, through chromaticism, and by means of secondary functions, tonicization, and changes of mode. Listen again to the song, or even better perform it, hear the long-range tonal motions, the tonal direction of phrases, and, most important, *hear the story* as it is told by the music!

2. Long-range tonal plan in "Die Zufriedenheit" (anthology, no. 30).

We can now study in more detail a piece which we already discussed in chapter 11. Analyze "Die Zufriedenheit" harmonically and formally, and review example 11.8 and the brief discussion of the song's phrase structure that accompanies that example in chapter 11. You will remember that the song has three phrases, clearly delineated by rests. Sing the melody several times, and discuss the form of the song motivically and thematically (assign letters to the phrases, indicating their formal relationship). If you consider the beginning and ending harmonies (cadences) for each phrase, what is the long-range tonal plan for the song? Within this harmonic plan, what harmonies are tonicized? After you think about these matters, you may discuss them in class and read the following notes.

a) *The song has three phrases (mm. 1–5, 6–9, and 10–14).* Phrases 1 and 2 are unrelated thematically. Phrases 2 and 3 are related motivically (see mm. 6–7 and 10–11). We can express the form by the letter scheme a–b_1–b_2.

b) *Phrase 1* begins with a prolongation of I: on a $\hat{1}$ pedal, I is prolonged by a N^{6}_{4} and V^{4}_{3}. V is tonicized at the cadence (m. 5) by means of a brief secondary key area of V, a cadential figure ii_6–V^{6-5}_{4-3}–I "of V" (or "in DM"). The long-range motion of phrase 1 is then I–V.

c) *Phrase 2* begins and ends on V, and it all can be interpreted as a prolongation of V leading to the HC in m. 9. ii is tonicized in mm. 6–7.

d) *Phrase 3* begins and ends on I. The phrase is a prolongation of I, including two tonicizations of IV in mm. 10–11.

e) *The long-range tonal plan* is, then, as follows:

I——V V——V I——I

In other words, in phrase 1 I is *established,* and we *move away* to V by the end of the phrase. In phrase 2, V is prolonged throughout, creating a central area of *tonal contrast* (and also of tonal tension) ending on a HC. In phrase 3, we *return* to I and we stay there. This short song is thus based on the same general tonal plan that may be found underlying most of the formal schemes in the music of the eighteenth and nineteenth centuries: **establishment** of the tonic, **departure** from the tonic, **return** to the tonic.

f) *Listen to the song* and/or perform it in class if possible. Hear the three phrases as harmonic/tonal units, hear their long-range motion, and the general tonal plan of the song. How is this discussion helping you understand the unity of this composition? If you perform it, how is it helping you with the interpretation and rendition of the phrases? Does it help you be aware, for instance, that all of phrase 2 is an extension of the V cadence in m. 5 (hence a "departure from"), creating a tension toward the return in phrase 3? Does it help to hear in this way the *direction* of the music?

g) If you are currently performing some short piece or movement on your instrument in which you can identify the same basic tonal scheme (establishment, departure, return), bring it to class, perform it, explain how you hear its overall tonal plan, and discuss how being aware of the plan might affect your performance.

ASSIGNMENT AND KEYBOARD EXERCISES

For analytical and written assignments and keyboard exercises based on the materials learned in this chapter, refer to chapter 19 in the workbook.

PITCH PATTERNS

Sing the pitch patterns in example 19.15, hearing the secondary LT seventh chords and their tonicizing effect. In examples 19.15f and g, hear the bracketed fragments as secondary key areas of IV and V, respectively.

Example 19.15

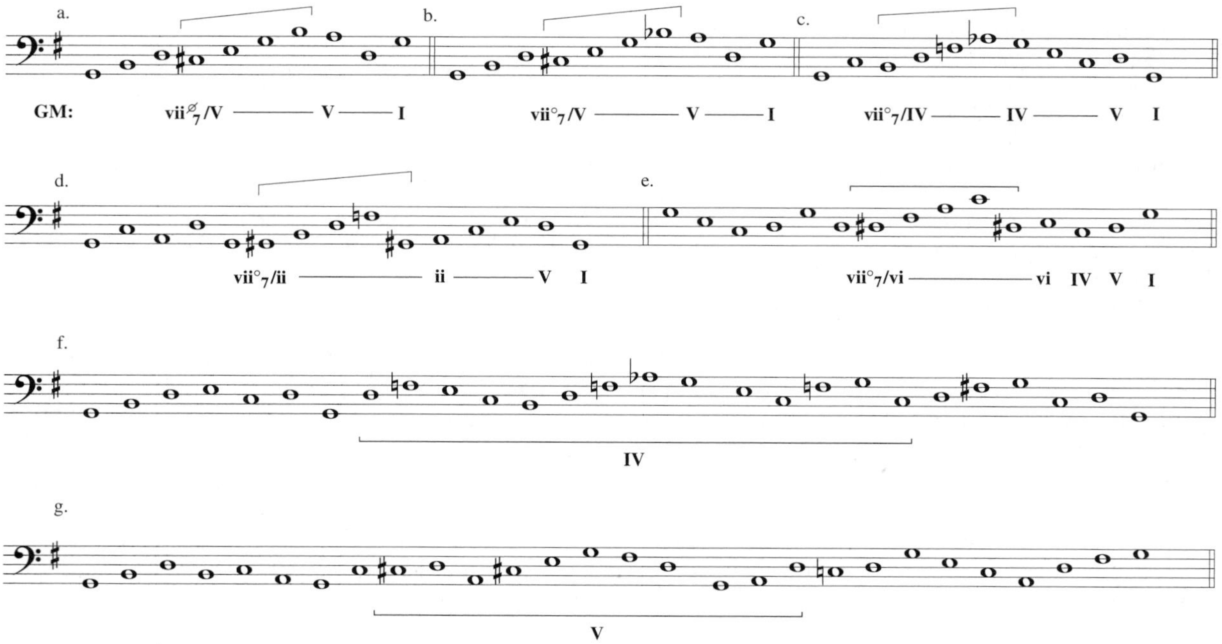

Terms for Review

Secondary leading-tone chords
Secondary leading-tone seventh chords: spelling, resolution, voice leading, inversions
vii°_{7} over a pedal point
The "establishment-departure-return" tonal paradigm

Worksheet 19

EXERCISE 1 Analysis.

1. Refer to anthology, no. 25 (Mozart, Sonata in CM, I).
   a) What two degrees are tonicized in mm. 13–14? Provide Roman numerals (RNs) for each secondary chord and its resolution in each measure.

   b) The key beginning in m. 35 is GM. In this key, what is the secondary chord in m. 50, and how does it resolve?

   c) Think of mm. 73–74 as a secondary key area of vi, or Am. *In this key,* provide RNs for the tonicization in m. 74.

   d) The key in mm. 103–108 is Cm. Provide RNs for the complete passage. Be careful to identify all nonchord tones: The harmonic rhythm is a chord per measure.

Example 19.16 M. Szymanowska, Nocturne in B♭M, mm. 27–31

2. Identify with RNs all the tonicizations and secondary functions in the following examples.

   a) Anthology, no. 31 (Paradis, *Sicilienne*), mm. 19–23.

   b) Example 19.16.

   c) Example 19.17.

      1) What happens to the mode after m. 32?

      2) Label the tonicizations in the following measures:

         Mm. 30–31:

         Mm. 34–35:

         Mm. 35–36 (Can this be a secondary key area? Why?):

         Mm. 38–39:

      3) What familiar progression can you identify in mm. 36–37? Comment on the voice leading required in this particular type of progression, and verify it in these measures.

Example 19.17 Carl Friedrich Zelter, "Abschied," mm. 28–39

EXERCISE 2 Write the following secondary diminished seventh chords in four voices.

FM: vii°$_7$/V Cm: vii°$_7$/III GM: vii°$_7$/IV Gm: vii°$_7$/ii Bm: vii°$^4_3$/iv A♭M: vii°$^4_2$/IV B♭M: vii°$^6_5$/V C♯m: vii°$^4_2$/V

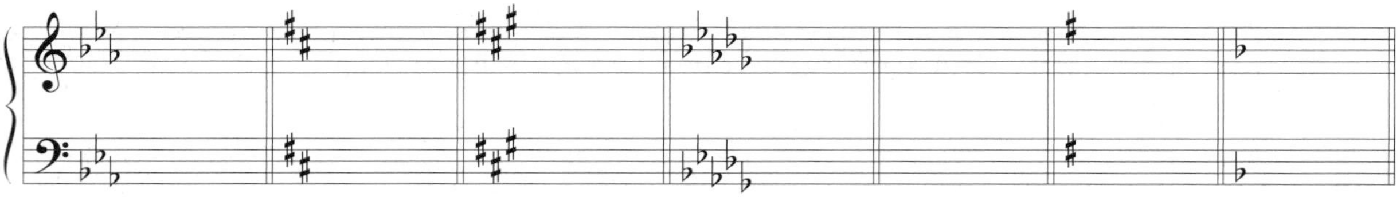

E♭M: vii°$^4_3$/vi DM: vii°$^6_5$/ii F♯m: vii°$^4_3$/III D♭M: vii°$^4_2$/vi Am: vii°$^6_5$/iv Em: vii°$^4_3$/III Dm: vii°$^4_2$/V

EXERCISE 3 Realize the following short progressions in four voices, and provide RNs where needed.

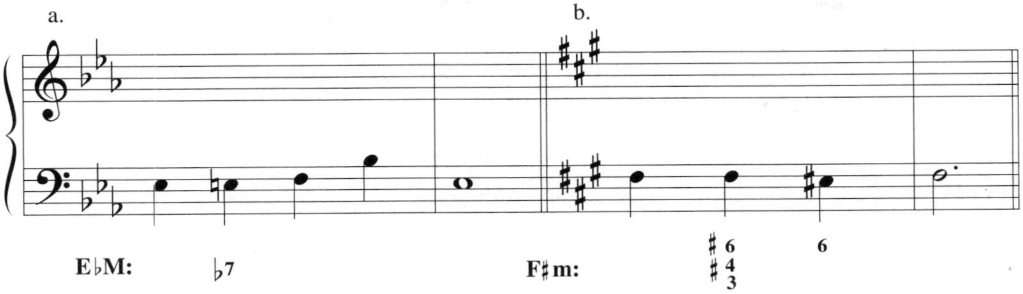

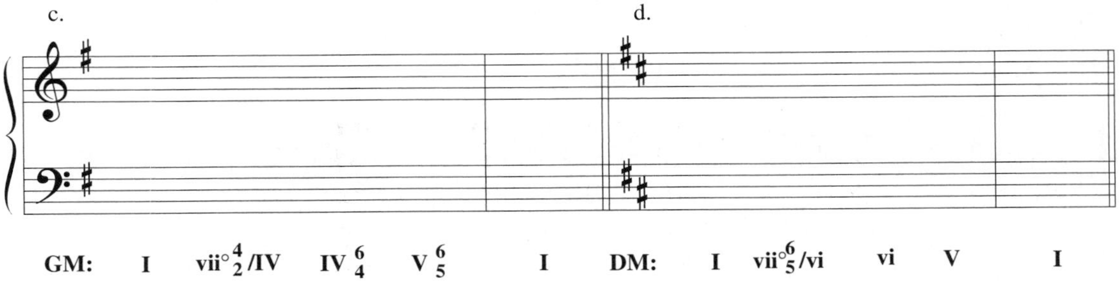

EXERCISE 4 Write the correct RNs for the following figured basses.

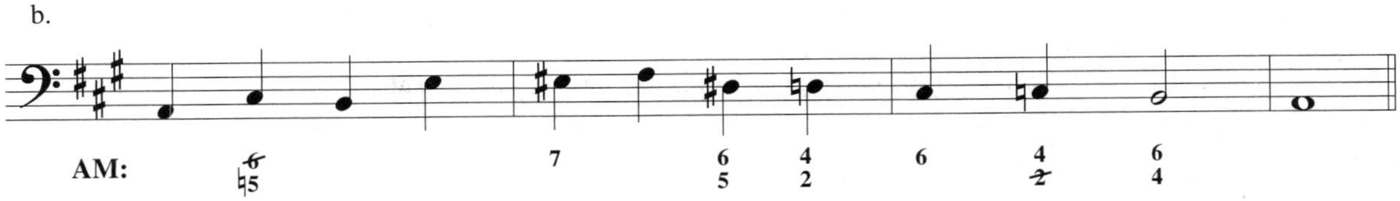

EXERCISE 5 Realize the following progression in four voices. Double-check your outer-voice frame for good counterpoint.

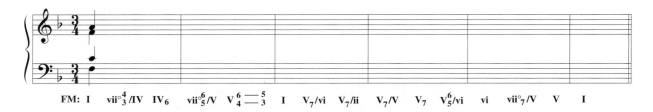

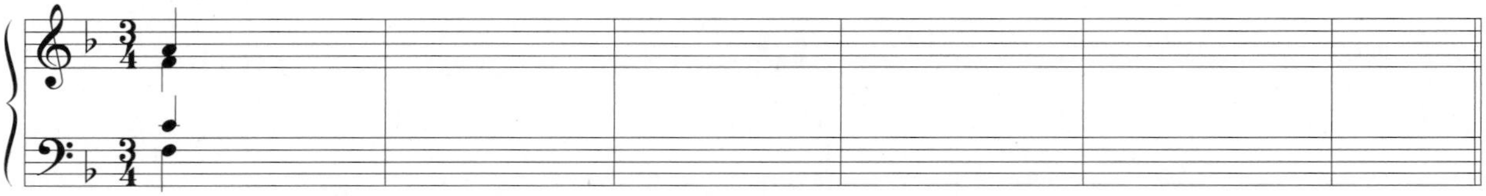

FM: I $vii^{\circ 4}_{3}$/IV IV_6 $vii^{\circ 6}_{5}$/V $V^{6\,—\,5}_{4\,—\,3}$ I V_7/vi V_7/ii V_7/V V_7 V^6_5/vi vi vii°_7/V V I

EXERCISE 6 Harmonize the following melody (based on Bach's Chorale "O grosser Gott von Macht") in four voices, in chorale style. The melody allows for various tonicizations, some of which are indicated under the staff. Use some kind of a secondary chord (a secondary dominant or, where possible, a secondary diminished seventh) to harmonize the indicated pitches.

Gm: /III /iv /VII

/IV /IV /iv /iv

Chapter 20

Modulation to Closely Related Keys

So far we have studied only music that stays in the same key. Because the change of key center for a tonicized chord or a secondary key area is only momentary, it does not really displace the main key center of the passage. Complete pieces, however, rarely remain in the same key. Changing the key center within a composition provides tonal variety to the music and often is a major element in long-range formal designs. The process of moving from one key center to another is known as **modulation.** In chapters 21 and 28 we will see that in formal types such as binary, sonata form, and rondo, large-scale tonal plans (achieved by means of modulation) are essential to the definition of form. And in chapter 22 we will see that in contrapuntal genres such as the invention and the fugue, modulation is a fundamental component in the processes of formal growth and development.

It should be stressed that modulation implies a change of key center. A **change of mode** between parallel keys, as between CM and Cm, is not considered a modulation, because the key center does not change (C in both cases). We should also note that the exact difference between a secondary key area and a modulation is not always clear. In general, a modulation will take place if the new key is clearly established by a complete pre-dominant/dominant/tonic progression, and preferably if it is confirmed unequivocally by means of an authentic cadence. These factors of tonal confirmation create a clear sense of a new key, as opposed to secondary key areas, where the presence of the main key is still felt. In this chapter we will study some of the most frequent techniques used by composers in modulations among *closely related keys.*

KEY RELATIONSHIPS: CLOSELY RELATED KEYS

Motion from one key to another is often accomplished in a smooth way, by means of a variety of techniques that make the key change as musically and perceptually logical as possible. A smooth modulation will be easier to accomplish if the scales of the keys involved are very similar in pitch content. The most similar scales occur between keys that either have the same key signature (such as CM and Am, the relative major/minor relationship), or the key signatures do not differ by more than one accidental (such as CM and GM/Em, a one-sharp difference, or CM and FM/Dm, a one-flat difference). Groups of keys whose signatures do not differ by more that one accidental are **closely related. Distantly related keys**, on the other hand, feature key signatures that differ by more than one accidental, such as CM and EM, A♭M, or C♯m.

The five keys that are closely related to any given key are its relative M/m key, those adjacent above and below this key in the circle of fifths, and their respective relative M/m keys, as illustrated in example 20.1. Thus, the keys closely related to DM are its relative minor Bm, AM (a fifth above D) and its relative minor F♯m, and GM (a fifth below D) and its relative minor Em. The same system applies to minor keys: The keys closely related to Dm are its relative major FM, Am (a fifth above D) and its relative major CM, and Gm (a fifth below D) and its relative major B♭M. Verify all these relationships in the circle of keys reproduced in example 20.1. From a different perspective, notice also that the closely related keys are those whose tonic triad is one of the diatonic major or minor triads within the original key. In CM, for instance, the closely related keys are Dm, Em, FM, GM, and Am, corresponding with all the major or minor triads that result from the CM scale.

Example 20.1

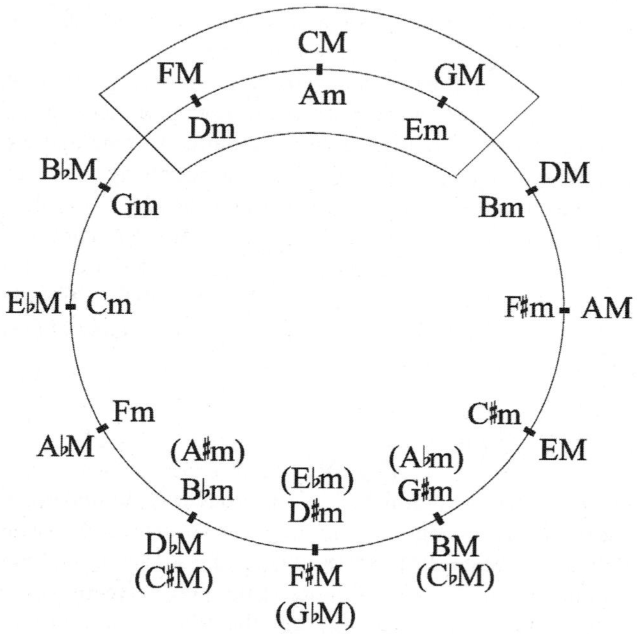

EXERCISE

To practice determining the set of closely related keys for a given key, refer to exercise 2 in worksheet 20 at the end of this chapter.

DIATONIC PIVOT CHORD MODULATION

Examine now example 20.2. Analyze the first four measures with Roman numerals (RNs), and you will see that the key of B♭M is clearly established by means of a standard diatonic progression that leads to the authentic cadence in mm. 3–4. The key is confirmed at the end of the initial period with a perfect authentic cadence (PAC) (mm. 9–10). The beginning of the new phrase in m. 11 is almost identical to m. 1. In mm. 12–13, however, we find an extended V_7 in FM, which indeed resolves to I in m. 14. The following measures confirm the new key, FM, by means of a series of V^4_2–I_6 progressions. The key center has thus changed from B♭ to F. The modulation from B♭M to FM, however, has been effected very smoothly and in a musically natural way. If you examine mm. 11–12, you will notice that we hear the first chord in m. 11 clearly as I in B♭M. In m. 12, however, we hear that a resolution to FM is coming, not only because of the clear V_7, but also because of the melodically striking E♮ (compare it with the equivalent E♭ in m. 2). How does the chord in between (m. 11, beats 1–2) function? In m. 1 we heard the same chord functioning as vi_6 in B♭, and this is also how it functions in m. 11. In retrospect, however, we also hear this same chord as ii_6, moving on to V_7, in FM. The chord then has a double function, serving as a **diatonic pivot chord** between the two keys, that is, *a chord that has a diatonic function in both of the keys for which it acts as a connection.*

The modulation that we have just studied is a diatonic pivot chord modulation, and it contains all the elements of a correct, smooth modulation:

1. *The first key* is established harmonically with a progression that includes a V–I and is preferably confirmed by an authentic cadence (notice that a key is not really established unless there is a V–I progression that defines it unequivocally).
2. *A diatonic pivot chord* connects the old key with the new key. A diatonic pivot chord is a chord that has a diatonic function in both keys. Modulations often involve more than one single pivot chord. In example 20.2, for instance, the initial B♭M I in m. 11 can also be interpreted as a IV in FM, thus providing us with the perfectly standard progression IV–ii_6–V_7 in FM. Measure 11 thus actually contains two diatonic pivot chords (I–vi_6 in B♭M become IV–ii_6 in FM).

   Any chord common to both keys can conceivably be a diatonic pivot chord. The best chords, however, are those that function as *pre-dominants in the new key,* because they can be naturally followed by the new dominant. The dominant of the old key, on the other hand, is a possible pivot chord, *but it is not normally a good one,* because it requires resolution to the tonic of the old key, and resolving it otherwise usually breaks the functional logic of the harmonic phrase.

Example 20.2 W. A. Mozart, Piano Sonata in B♭M, K. 333, I, mm. 1–16

Example 20.3

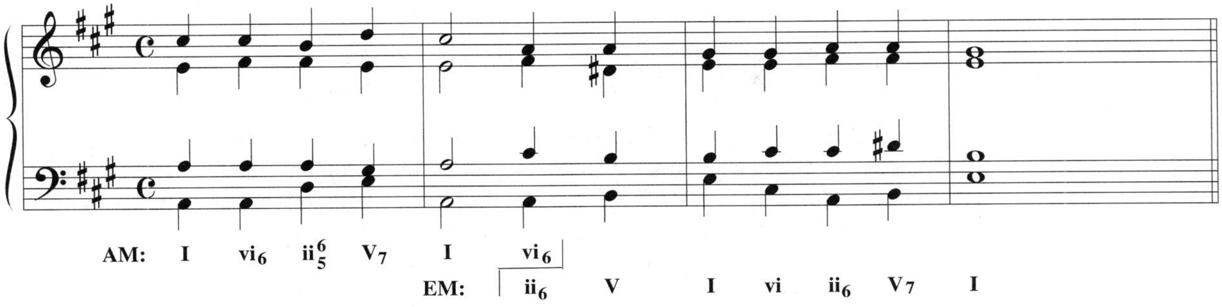

The double function of pivot chords will be indicated visually by means of a "bracket" (as indicated in both examples 20.2 and 20.3), which allows for the notation of both its old and its new functions.

3. *The new key* is itself established harmonically with a progression including V–I and is confirmed by further progressions or preferably by an authentic cadence.

All the preceding elements are clearly summarized in the modulating progression in example 20.3. (In our schematic examples of modulations in this and other chapters, keys will be minimally established by means of a simple progression.) Observe that in this example we could also label two diatonic pivot chords: I–vi$_6$ in AM become IV–ii$_6$ in EM.

EXERCISE

To practice determining the pivot function of a chord between two keys, refer to exercise 3 in worksheet 20 at the end of this chapter.

Determining the Diatonic Pivot Chord

The process we have followed to analyze the Mozart modulation shows you the way to determine a diatonic pivot chord:

1. Find the first chord that clearly indicates that we are moving to a new key (in the Mozart example, the V$_7$ in m.12). Typically (although not always), this "first chord" in the new key will contain an accidental.
2. Look at the chord immediately before this clear sign of a new key, and read it in both the old key and the new key. If you find more than one chord that can be read in both keys, you may interpret them as a pivot group.
3. In other words, the best way to determine the pivot chord is to analyze the passage from the beginning (in this case in B♭M) and from the end (in FM) at the same time,

and see where the two keys "meet" by means of a common element that acts as a diatonic pivot. In our discussion, the "meeting point" turned out to be clearly the second chord of m. 11, or also possibly all of m. 11. We will practice this process many times in the course of this chapter.

MODULATION TO V

We will refer to keys by the Roman numeral that represents their relationship to the original key. Thus the modulation to the key of the dominant (from CM or Cm to GM) will be "to V," or also I→V. A modulation from a major key to its relative minor (CM to Am) will be I→vi, and from a minor key to its relative major i→III. The supertonic key is ii, and a modulation to this key from a major key (CM to Dm) will be I to ii, or I→ii. And so on.

I to V

The most common modulation from a major key is to the key of the dominant, V. This is the modulation we discussed in example 20.2. Refer now to example 20.4. E♭M is established in mm. 6–9, and the fragment ends on a PAC in B♭M. In m. 9 we hear the E♭ chord as I in E♭M, but in mm. 10–11 two dominant-tonic progressions in B♭M leave little doubt we are modulating to V, as the cadence in mm. 12–13 confirms. What are the exact Roman numerals for the chords that establish B♭M in mm. 10–11? Notice that the resolution to I in m. 11 is preceded by a triple nonchord tone sonority in the right hand, beats 1 and 2, creating an "appoggiatura chord," a "chord of nonchord tones (NCTs)" that resolves in beat 3. Explain each of the three pitches as individual NCTs.

Because m. 9 is I in E♭M, and m. 10 already establishes B♭M, the only possible chord that may be interpreted as a diatonic pivot chord is precisely the E♭ chord in m. 9, which will be I in E♭M and IV in B♭M. This is a common pivot chord in the modulation from I to V, allowing for a very direct and quick switch of tonal center. Study this type of modulation as shown, in chorale style, in example 20.5.

To understand the possible diatonic pivot chords between two keys that hold a I–V relationship, you can imagine the triads in both CM and GM. By comparing their pitch content you can determine which triads are common to both keys.

Triad on	C	D	E	F(F♯)	G	A	B
CM	**I**	ii	**iii**	IV	**V**	**vi**	vii°
GM	**IV**	*V*	**vi**	*vii°*	**I**	**ii**	*iii*

The triads that include an F♯ in GM (V, vii°, and iii) are not found in CM, and they are indicated in italics in the preceding chart. These three triads are not possible pivot chords because they are not common to both keys. The remaining four triads (in bold face), on the other hand, are common to both keys. Because V in the original key is not usually the best pivot (it calls for a resolution to the original tonic), the preferable pivot chords are then I/IV, iii/vi, and vi/ii, all of which can function as pre-dominants in the new key.

Example 20.4 C. Schumann, "Ich stand in dunklen Träumen," mm. 6–13

I stood in dark dreams and gazed at her portrait,
And the beloved features mysteriously came to life.

EXERCISE

To practice analyzing a modulation to V from a given modulating bass line, refer to exercise 4a in worksheet 20 at the end of this chapter.

Modulating from V Back to I

After having modulated from I to V, say CM to GM, sooner or later the music is likely to return to the original "home key" by means of a V to I modulation, GM to CM, that is, up a P4. Refer to anthology, no. 28 (Mozart, Piano Sonata in B♭M, III). The movement is in B♭M. The section beginning in m. 24 and ending with a PAC in mm. 35–36, however,

Example 20.5

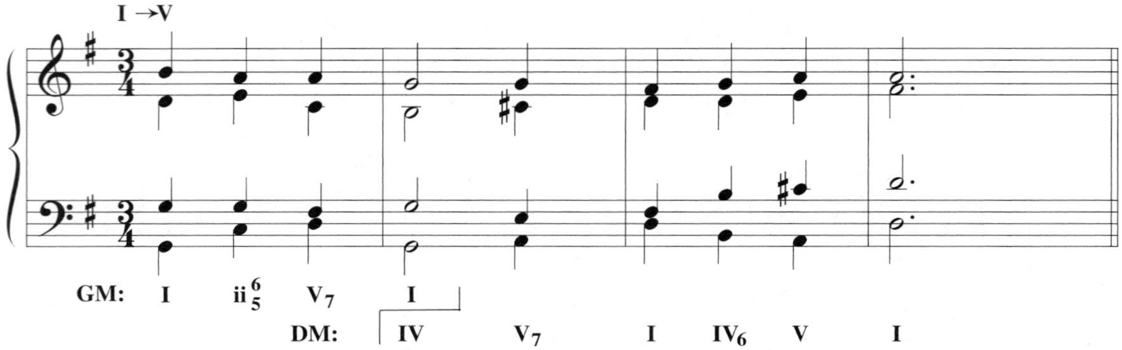

is in FM, the key of V. First, discuss in class the modulation from B♭M to FM, in mm. 20–21. Although you can explain it as a pivot chord modulation, you will notice that, in m. 20, the element that leads our ear toward FM is not so much a pivot chord process as a single, unaccompanied pitch. The *melodic introduction of the leading tone in the new key* is sometimes a sufficiently strong factor to support a modulation.

Beginning in m. 41 of this same example you will see that the original material returns, again in B♭M, although just a few measures earlier the previous section closed on a strong PAC in FM. How did we go back to the "home key"? If you disregard the series of ornamental chromatic passing tones in mm. 37–38, all that happens from m. 36 (I in FM) to m. 39 is that the pitch E♭ is added to the FM triad, turning it into V_7 of B♭M. Because in the modulation V→I the tonic in the original key is the same chord as the dominant in the new key, this is the most commonly (and effectively) used diatonic pivot chord for this modulation, as summarized in example 20.6.

Example 20.6

NOTE

It is interesting to observe that the modulation from the tonic directly to the subdominant key (I to IV) is quite unusual. If you think of it, however, as a modulation a P4 up, the relationship between keys is the same as in V back to I (a P4 up). In both cases (I to IV and V to I) the tonic in the first key is the same as the dominant in the second key. Practice writing or playing a modulation from GM (I) to CM (IV) using I in GM as the pivot chord.

MODULATION TO THE RELATIVE MAJOR AND MINOR KEYS

The most common modulation from a minor key is not to the key of the dominant, but rather to the relative major key, i to III. Because these two keys share the same scale, with the only exception of the raised $\hat{7}$ (the leading tone) in harmonic minor, the possible diatonic pivot chords are many, and the modulation is easily effected. The chart below illustrates the triad relationships in CM and Am, indicating the possible diatonic pivot chords in bold face.

Triad on	C	D	E	F	G(G♯)	A	B
CM	**I**	**ii**	iii	**IV**	V	**vi**	**vii°**
Am	**III**	**iv**	*V*	**VI**	*vii°*	**i**	**ii°**

The only triads in this chart that do not qualify as diatonic pivots are those in Am that include a G♯, that is, V and vii°. Otherwise, all the remaining triads can be used in the modulation between these keys. Example 20.7 illustrates several of these modulations schematically. Play or sing these modulations in class and hear the different double functions of the various pivot chords.

i to III

Example 20.8 shows how simple and direct the modulation from i to III can be. The first phrase establishes Bm and cadences in this key in m. 5. This same tonic chord is immediately reinterpreted as vi in the relative major, DM, and used as a pre-dominant moving to V_7 of DM in mm. 6–7. Refer to anthology, no. 11 (Bach, French Suite no. 3, Minuet), and study the modulation between these same two keys, Bm and DM, in mm. 1–16. Reading the music from the beginning, in Bm, you will find that the last clear sign of this key is the progression in mm. 12–13. Reading from the end, in DM, we see that the key is established in the last three measures of the passage, beginning with the V in m. 14. What is, then, the diatonic pivot chord, and how does it function in both keys?

EXERCISE

To practice writing a modulation from i to III from given Roman numerals, refer to exercises 4b and 6 in worksheet 20 at the end of this chapter.

Example 20.7

a. i → III

Dm: i iv V_7 i

FM: vi V^6_5 I ii^6_5 V_7 I

b. i → III

Dm: i iv $V^{6\,-\,7}_{4\,-\,\substack{5\\3}}$ i iv

FM: ii V_7 I IV $vii^\circ{}_7/V$ V_7 I

c. I → vi

FM: I V^4_2/IV IV_6 V_7 I IV

Dm: VI V_7 i IV $V^{6\,-\,7}_{4\,-\,\substack{5\\3}}$ i

d. I → vi

FM: I $vii^\circ{}_7/ii$ ii V_7 I $vii^\circ{}_6$

Dm: $ii^\circ{}6$ $V^{6\,-\,5}_{4\,-\,3}$ i V^6_5 i iv i

Example 20.8 J. Haydn, String Quartet op. 64, no. 2, Menuetto, mm. 1–14

Example 20.9 F. Schubert, "Am Feierabend," from *Die schöne Müllerin,* mm. 45–59

I to vi

The modulation from a major key to its relative minor, or I to vi, can use any of the same pivot chords we indicated in the preceding chart. The passage by Schubert reproduced in example 20.9 begins in FM and ends in Dm (the song as a whole is in Am). Measure 51 features the last FM tonic, whereas the cadence in Dm first appears in mm. 55–56. The two chords in between can be analyzed as diatonic pivot chords. What are the functions of these chords in each of the keys? Now look at the relationship between this modulation and the text. The boy speaking is a worker at a mill, sitting with his fellow workers in the quiet evening hour of leisure in the presence of the miller and the lovely millermaid. The translation of the text is as follows: "And the master speaks to all: your work has pleased me. And the maiden, my delight, wishes all a good night." How is the master represented tonally? What are the characteristics and register of the master's melody? Compare all of these with the music depicting the millermaid: How is the text reflected in the key, the harmonic progression, the melody, and the register?

WRITING PIVOT CHORD MODULATIONS

We will now practice writing modulating progressions using diatonic pivot chords. We will write these progressions in the usual form of a bass line with Roman numerals, following this procedure:

1. Write a progression in the original key, using any of the chords you have learned so far, including secondary dominant functions. The progression should establish the key by means of at least one pre-dominant/dominant/tonic chordal unit.
2. Think of a possible chord common to both keys that you may use as a diatonic pivot in the modulation. Write the chord and provide its double interpretation by means of the usual pivot symbol.
3. Write a progression in the new key. Establish the key immediately. Ideally, your pivot will act as pre-dominant in the new key and will lead to a dominant-tonic progression. After the key is thus established, continue the progression as you wish, and close with an authentic cadence (or perhaps a plagal cadence) that confirms the new key.

Study (and play if possible) the modulating progressions proposed in example 20.10. Then write a couple of modulating progressions in the spaces provided, using the keys indicated in each case.

Example 20.10

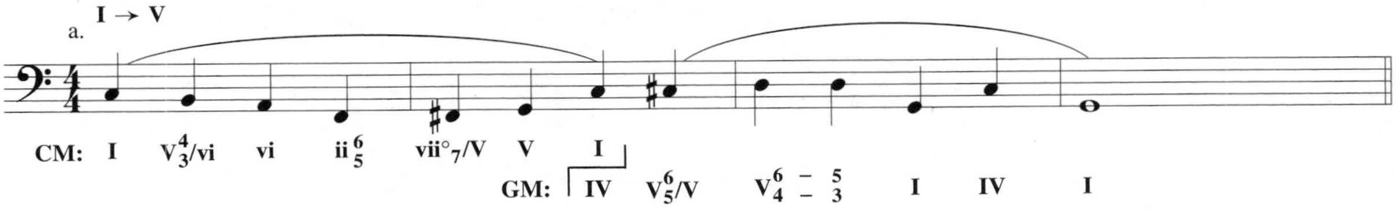

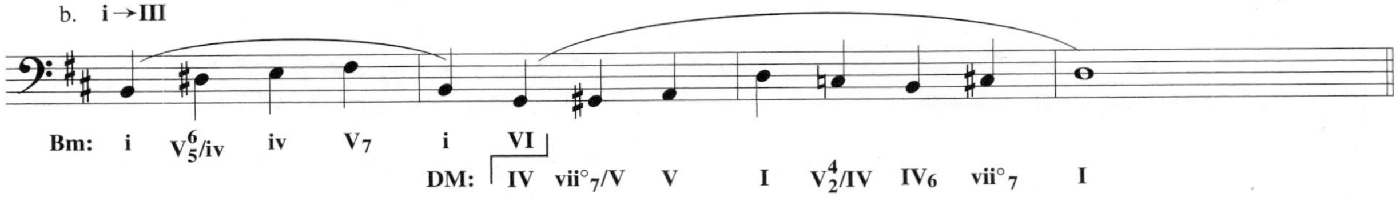

EXERCISE

To practice writing your own diatonic pivot-chord modulations, refer to exercises 7a and 7b in worksheet 20 at the end of this chapter.

CHROMATIC MODULATION: CHROMATIC PIVOT CHORDS

Modulations from a major key to the submediant and mediant keys are not quite as frequent as those we have studied so far, because they do not have the structural, form-defining role of modulations to V or to the relative major. They both can be effected by means of diatonic pivot chords. More often, however, modulations to ii or iii are of the type known as chromatic. Consider, for instance, the modulation from FM to Gm in example 20.11. Measure 17 begins on an FM tonic chord, which is not a possible diatonic pivot with Gm. The introduction of the pitch F♯, ♯$\hat{2}$, in the outer voices, and its subsequent resolution to the Gm tonic chord in the next measure announce the modulation to ii, confirmed by the

Example 20.11 J. S. Bach, Fugue 21 in B♭M, from *The Well-Tempered Clavier,* I, mm. 13–19

repetition of the cadence. From a voice-leading point of view, the modulation proceeds by melodic chromatic motion: the F in m. 17 becomes F♯, the leading tone in the new key, leading to G. From a harmonic point of view, there is no diatonic pivot chord in this modulation. We can speak, however, of a **chromatic pivot chord.** This is a chord that is chromatic (such as a secondary dominant) in one, or both, of the keys. In our example, the chord in beats 3–4 of m. 17, which includes the chromatic F♯, is chromatic in FM (V^6_5/ii) and diatonic in Gm (V^6_5). In other words, we first hear the dominant of the new key, Gm, as a secondary dominant, and only after that do we realize that it is actually a modulation. This modulation, then, is achieved by means of both chromatic voice leading (F to F♯) and a chromatic pivot chord.

A **chromatic modulation** to a closely related key is one in which one or both of the following conditions apply:

1. The main modulating procedure is ascending linear chromatic motion in at least one voice, which normally introduces the leading tone of the new key.
2. The pivot chord is not diatonic in both keys. It is frequently a secondary dominant or diminished seventh chord in the first key, while being the diatonic (primary) dominant or diminished seventh chord in the new key (the dominant of the new key is first introduced as if it were a secondary dominant in the original key, but then the new key is confirmed).

Three chromatic modulations are schematically illustrated in example 20.12.

Chromatic modulations are not exclusive to tonal motions to the keys of iii or ii. The modulation to V is often effected chromatically (can you figure out and explain a possible chromatic modulation from I to V?). Example 20.13, moreover, features a modulation from GM to its relative minor, Em, which includes not only chromatic voice leading, but also a chromatic pivot chord. GM is established in m. 4. What linear chromatic motion leads to Em in the next measure? The dominant in m. 5, beat 1, is diatonic in GM but not in Em. The second chord, on the other hand, is diatonic in Em, but not in GM. No diatonic pivot is present in this modulation. What is the chromatic function of this second chord (on the bass pitch B) in GM?

EXERCISE

To practice analyzing a chromatic modulation from a given modulating bass line, refer to exercise 5 in worksheet 20 at the end of this chapter.

WRITING CHROMATIC MODULATIONS

The following steps to write chromatic modulations to ii and iii are illustrated by the progressions in example 20.12. After you study these examples, practice writing your own chromatic modulations from a major key to the keys of ii and iii.

1. First establish the original key in the usual way.
2. Write a chromatic motion in the bass introducing the new leading tone. If you want to modulate to ii, the bass may move directly from $\hat{1}$ to $\sharp\hat{1}$, and on to $\hat{2}$

Example 20.12

(example 20.12a). If the modulation is to iii, the bass should not move, of course, from $\hat{1}$ to $\sharp\hat{2}$ (an augmented second). A bass motion $\hat{1}$–$\hat{4}$–$\hat{2}$–$\sharp\hat{2}$–$\hat{3}$, for instance, allows for a good harmonization that will also produce another chromatic motion ($\hat{4}$–$\sharp\hat{4}$) in an upper voice, besides the bass's $\hat{2}$–$\sharp\hat{2}$: I–IV–ii–V^6_5/iii–iii, and on to confirm the key of iii (example 20.12c).

Example 20.13 J. S. Bach, Chorale 167, "Du grosser Schmerzensmann," mm. 3–8

3. If you do not want to write the chromatic motion in the bass, introduce the dominant of the new key in root position first as a secondary dominant in the original key, and do not return to the original key, but move on to confirm the modulation (example 20.12b).
4. Finally, confirm the new key with a good progression and a cadence.

EXERCISE

To practice writing your own chromatic modulation, refer to exercise 7c in worksheet 20 at the end of this chapter.

MODULATION AND PHRASE STRUCTURE: SEQUENTIAL AND PHRASE MODULATION; MODULATING PERIODS

Modulations have a primary role in formal processes. Long-range tonal designs are realized by means of modulatory processes that provide tonal direction to complete movements. In the next chapter we will study some formal paradigms and see that they are closely associated with long-range tonal schemes. At a more local level, however, tonicization and modulation often have a structural role in generating phrase and period structures, as we will discuss in the following examples.

Sequential Modulation

In a **sequential modulation** or tonicization, the sequence is used as a means to change tonal center. This is often done by stating each sequence segment in a different key, as in the case of Bach's Minuet from French Suite no. 3 (anthology, no. 11). The key in mm. 23–24 is F♯m. In m. 25 an ascending sequence consisting of two segments first tonicizes Em (the key of iv with respect to the home key of the piece, Bm) in mm. 25–26, and then F♯M (the key of V) in mm. 27–28. This tonicized V leads to the return of the tonic key in m. 31. The long-range tonal plan outlined by this sequential passage is thus iv–V–i as key areas, or, in other words, a large authentic cadence at the phrase level, rather than the chord level.

Descending melodic sequences, normally accompanied by a circle-of-5ths harmonic sequence, are also a strong modulating procedure at the formal level. A circle of 5ths can be used to modulate virtually to any key, depending only on where the composer stops the circle. The circle can thus be used to go from one key to another, and moreover it may also tonicize each of the steps in the process. In example 20.14, a six-measure sequence is used to modulate from Fm to Cm (a modulation that Bach could have realized with only a couple of chords had he wanted to do so). Are any other degrees (that is, pitches) tonicized in the process?

Example 20.14 J. S. Bach, French Suite no. 2, Minuet, mm. 15–24

Example 20.15 E. Grieg, "The Death of Åse," from *Peer Gynt,* mm. 1–16

Phrase (or Direct) Modulation; Abrupt Modulation

Not all modulations proceed smoothly by means of a pivot chord. In the type of modulation known as **phrase modulation,** a phrase is in a key, and the next phrase is in a different key, which is presented more or less suddenly. In the passage by Grieg that appears in example 20.15, the first period (two phrases, mm. 1–8) is in Bm. The second period, mm. 9–16, is in F♯m, the key of the minor dominant. There is no transition between the keys, but rather the new key is presented suddenly as the new phrase begins in m. 9. This is a phrase modulation. Because in this type of modulation there is no transitional process between the two keys, it is also called **direct modulation.** Refer, for another example, to anthology, no. 32 (Beethoven, Sonata in Fm, op. 2 no. 1, III). The first phrase of the minuet, mm. 1–4, is in Fm. The second phrase (mm. 4–8) restates the same material as the first one, but now in A♭M. The new key is introduced by the new phrase, with no previous preparation.

Both of the preceding examples of direct modulation involve closely related keys and parallel phrases. Sometimes, however, the keys are not closely related and neither is the thematic material. Composers may want to introduce a new key in an abrupt way, for tonal surprise or to provide the music with a strong forward trust by means of tonal contrast. Example 20.16 illustrates this type of **abrupt modulation,** in this case from CM to E♭M, also introducing a new thematic idea along with the new key (m. 10).

Modulating Periods

A **modulating period** is a period that begins and ends in different keys. This type of period is most often found as the first section in binary forms, which we will study in

Example 20.16 J. Brahms, Symphony no. 4, III, mm. 1–14

the next chapter. The tonal function of a modulating period is to introduce and establish the tonic key, and then to move away from it, as part of a long-range formal tonal plan of departure from and return to the tonic key. The usual modulations are to the dominant key in major-mode compositions, and to the relative major in minor-mode pieces, although other modulations are also possible. Modulating periods are often parallel, and the modulation takes place in the second phrase. Such is the case in example 20.17, a period in the minor mode modulating to III. Where exactly does the modulation take place? What type of modulation is it? If it is a pivot chord modulation, identify a possible pivot chord and its double function. Beware that, because the texture is limited to two voices, you may have to imply the complete harmonies.

You will find several examples of modulating periods in the anthology, some of which we have already mentioned in this chapter, such as anthology, no. 32 (Beethoven, Sonata op. 2 no.1) and no. 11 (Bach, Minuet from French Suite no. 3). Anthology, no. 24 (Mozart, Sonata in DM, III, Tema) is a good example of a parallel period modulating to the dominant key. Analyze the modulation, finding and interpreting the pivot chord.

Modulation is one of the most essential harmonic processes in Western tonal music. It provides tonal variety necessary in complete compositions, it provides both a harmonic drive and tonal goals for long-range formal designs, and it contributes to creation of a tension between tonal definition and tonal instability, a basic element in formal generation of large movements. You have played many modulations in your life as a performer, and any of the compositions in your repertoire can illustrate modulating processes in one way or another. Find several of these modulations in pieces you perform, and bring them to class as examples. Specifically, try to find the following cases of modulation:

1. A modulation you especially like, perhaps because it leads from one key to another in an imperceptible, smooth way; or because it is very well crafted and perhaps you had always noticed how beautiful and effective the passage was; or because it is very surprising and you had always been struck by the boldness of harmonic motion in that passage; or for whatever other reason you may like it.
2. A modulating period. You may find these in the first section of a binary form (a minuet, a sarabande, or some other dance type).
3. A modulation from I to V or from i to III in the first movement of a sonata.

After you understand how modulations work, and what their formal function is, does this affect in any way your vision of music as a performer? How? Do modulations help you hear and transmit the principle of musical motion? Think of the tension that a modulatory process creates, and of the sense of arrival and the renewed musical impulse we feel when we reach the new tonic. Does the new tonic come along with new thematic material, further stressing the idea of renewal? How does the process of modulation contribute to the sense of instability and tonal motion in developmental sections? Does the developmental process lead to a return of the tonic key and of the original thematic material, and do we experience a release of tension when that happens?

Example 20.17 J. S. Bach, English Suite no. 3 in Gm, Gavotte I, mm. 1–8

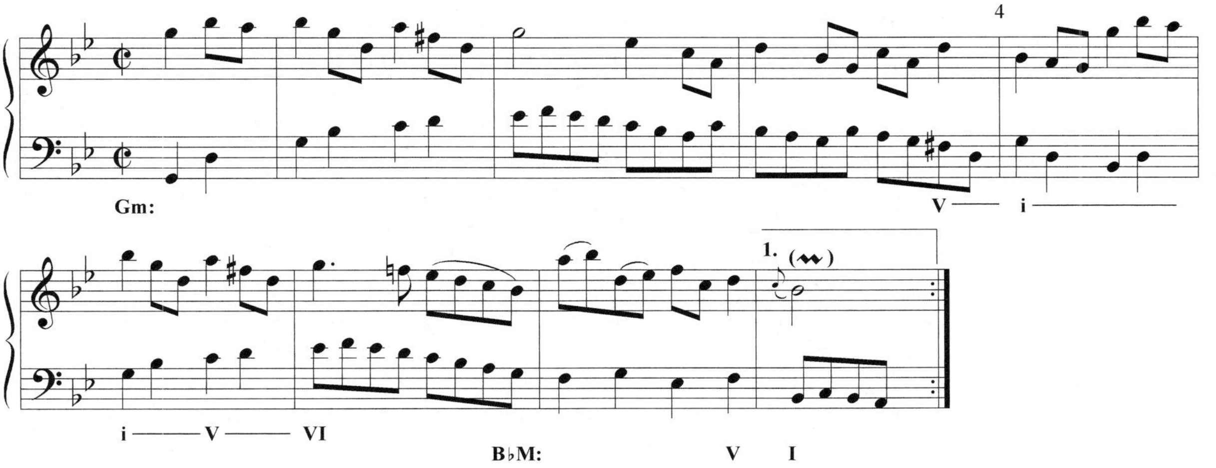

HARMONIZING MODULATING MELODIES

Modulating melodies often provide sufficient information for a clear harmonization of the modulating passage. Sing the Haydn melody in example 20.18a. You will immediately realize three things: It begins in Cm, it ends in Gm, and m. 6 displays clear signs of the modulation when F♯ and A♮, two pitches from the Gm scale, are introduced. (Note that in minor keys, modulations to the dominant are usually to the *minor* v, instead of V.) You will also notice that the melody appears to have two four-measure units, and that the end of the first unit can easily be harmonized with a V–i in Cm. In other words,

Example 20.18 J. Haydn, String Quartet op. 54, no. 2 in CM, II

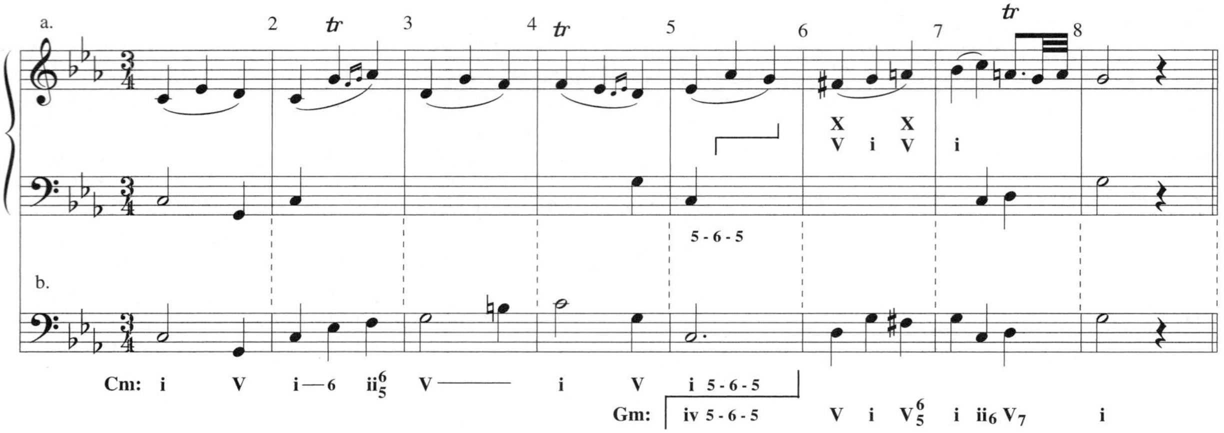

you have followed the first steps in the process to harmonize modulating melodies, which can be summarized as follows:

Procedure to harmonize a modulating melody:

1. Sing and play through the melody. Identify the opening and closing keys. If they are the same, identify any possible inner fragments in a different key.
2. Identification of a new key will ideally be facilitated by some melodic features such as accidentals (perhaps the new LT).
3. Identify possible points of articulation that may indicate cadential gestures (in the original or the new key). Write the bass for these cadences.
4. Identify the melodic area that clearly indicates the new key, and find a possible place for your pivot chord right before it.
5. Harmonize the rest of the melody according to the principles of good functional harmonization that you are familiar with.

In our example, after we have identified the opening and closing keys, the accidentals that indicate Gm, and the cadential points, we can write the bass for the cadences in mm. 4–5 (on C) and 7–8 (on G). Next, we will harmonize the modulation. In m. 6, already in Gm, the F♯–G–A can be harmonized with some kind of V–i–V progression, and in m. 5 before it, a C in the bass can support a 5–6–5 figure. In Cm, m. 5 would then be $i_{5\text{–}6\text{–}5.}$ Because the next measure is already in Gm, the pivot chord will need to be in m. 5. So the $i_{5\text{–}6\text{–}5}$ in Cm becomes $iv_{5\text{–}6\text{–}5.}$ in Gm. All of this process is illustrated by the notes in example 20.18a. All that is left is to complete the harmonization of the melody. A possible complete harmonization, using only bass line and Roman numerals, is shown in example 20.18b.

At times, *melodies do not indicate modulations clearly,* and then we need to use a bit more harmonic imagination to harmonize them. Sing or play the melody in example 20.19a. Our immediate reactions might be: It begins in BM, it cadences on B in m. 4, and the last

Example 20.19 J. Haydn, String Quartet op. 64, no. 2 in Bm, Trio

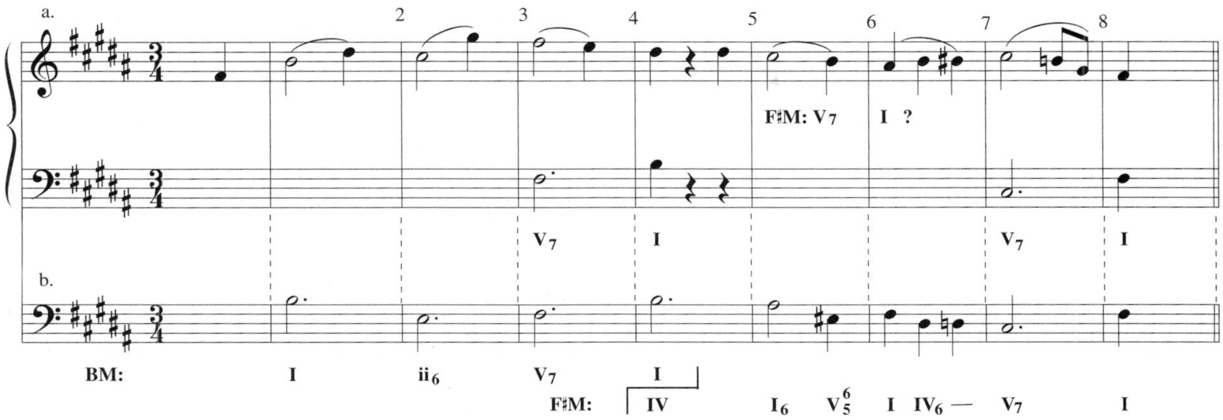

two measures indicate a cadence in F♯M, so we must have modulated to the dominant key. We write down all of this information, as in example 20.19b. Knowing that it modulates to F♯M, let's go back to mm. 5–6, which in principle could simply be harmonized in BM. Can they also be heard in F♯M? Try it: Harmonize m. 5, beat 3, as a V_7 in F♯, and resolve it to I in m. 6. It works. Then we need a pivot chord. You could use the first chord in m. 5, as V in BM and I in F♯. An even better pivot could be the BM chord in m. 4. A complete harmonization appears in example 20.19b. Notice that the B♯ in m. 6 is interpreted as a chromatic PT, accompanied by another chromatic PT in the opposite direction in the bass.

EXERCISES

To practice harmonizing a modulating chorale melody, refer to exercise 8 in worksheet 20 at the end of this chapter.

To practice harmonizing modulating periods, refer to exercise 10 in worksheet 20 at the end of this chapter.

To practice analysis of musical fragments including modulations, refer to exercise 1 in worksheet 20 at the end of this chapter.

FOR FURTHER STUDY

For additional chapter 20 materials, refer to the *Harmony in Context* Web page at www.mhhe.com/roigfrancoli2e.

ASSIGNMENT AND KEYBOARD EXERCISES

For analytical and written assignments and keyboard exercises based on the materials learned in this chapter, refer to chapter 20 in the workbook.

PITCH PATTERNS

Sing the melodic pitch patterns in example 20.20, and as you sing listen to the modulation in each of the patterns, paying special attention to the "pivot pitch" or pitches, or to the chromatic motion that effects the modulation. Practice improvising similar pitch patterns modulating to different keys.

Example 20.20

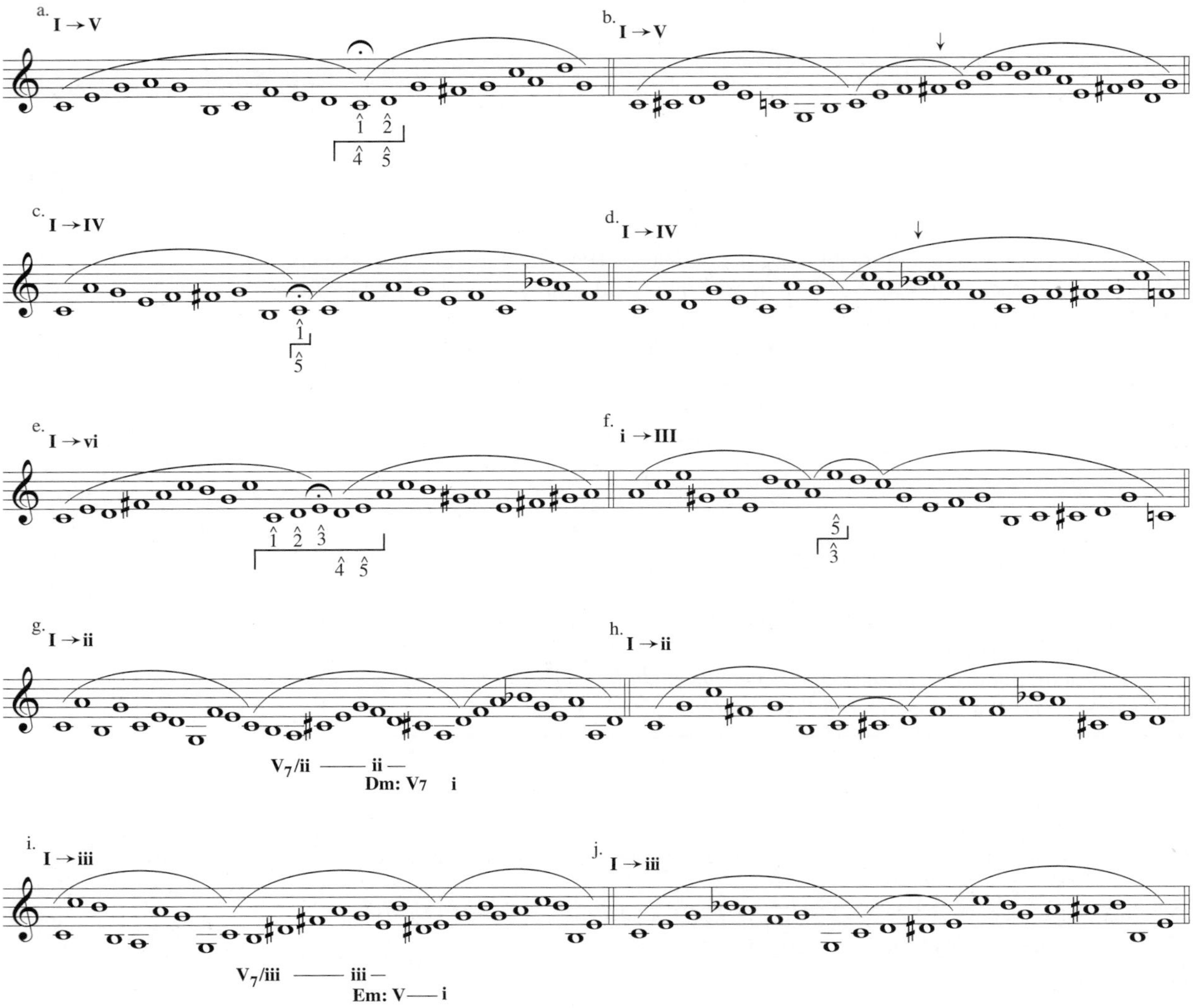

Terms for Review

Modulation
Change of mode
Closely related keys
Distantly related keys
Pivot chord modulation
Diatonic pivot chord
Diatonic pivot chord modulation
Chromatic pivot chord
Chromatic modulation
Sequential modulation
Phrase (direct) modulation
Abrupt modulation
Modulating periods

Worksheet 20

EXERCISE 1 Analysis. Study and analyze the modulations in exercises 1.1 to 10, and follow the steps listed below for each of them.

1. Identify (and write in the space provided for each exercise) the keys involved in the modulation.
2. Identify (and write in the space provided for each exercise) the modulation procedure from among the following:
   a) Diatonic pivot chord
   b) Chromatic pivot chord
   c) Chromatic modulation
   d) Phrase modulation
   e) Abrupt modulation
   f) Sequential modulation or tonicizations
3. If it is a pivot chord modulation, identify the exact pivot or pivots, and label it or them on the score with the pivot chord bracket notation, indicating the function of the chord in both keys.
4. For a chromatic modulation, circle the exact passage where chromatic voice leading is used to modulate.
5. For phrase, abrupt, or sequential modulations, mark the exact spot or spots where modulation occurs.

Examples for Analysis:

1. Example 20.21.

2. Anthology, no. 32, Beethoven, Sonata in Fm, op. 2, no. 1, Trio, mm. 41–50.

3. Anthology, no. 32, Beethoven, Sonata in Fm, op. 2, no. 1, Trio, mm. 51–66.

4. Example 20.22.

Example 20.21 J. Haydn, String Quartet op. 77, no. 1, Minuet, mm. 1–12

Example 20.22 C. Schumann, Trio in Gm, I, mm. 22–32

5. Anthology, no. 11, Bach, French Suite no. 3, Minuet, mm. 17–24.

6. Anthology, no. 34, Beethoven, Sonata in Cm, op. 13, III, mm. 16–25.

7. Anthology, no. 31, Paradis, *Sicilienne,* mm. 4–10.

8. Anthology, no. 20, Haydn, Piano Sonata in DM, II, mm. 1–12.

9. Example 20.23.

10. Anthology, no. 47, Schumann, "Ich grolle nicht," mm. 12–16.

Example 20.23 F. Schubert, Sonata in B♭M, D. 960, I, mm. 113–119

EXERCISE 2 Make a list of all five keys closely related to each of the following keys.

1. DM:
2. B♭M:
3. F♯m:
4. Fm:
5. C♯m:
6. D♭M:

EXERCISE 3 The following statements refer to diatonic pivot chord relationships. Fill in the blank in each statement.

1. I in DM becomes ________ in AM.
2. ________ in Gm becomes IV in B♭M.
3. I in ________ becomes V in A♭M.
4. iv in Em becomes ii in ________.

EXERCISE 4 The following two progressions represent modulations by diatonic pivot chord.

Progression a. Provide RNs for the given bass, accounting for the modulation and indicating the pivot chord with the usual bracket. Use secondary dominants or diminished seventh chords where possible.

a.

Progression b. Write a bass line for the given RNs. Be careful to modulate to the right key.

b.

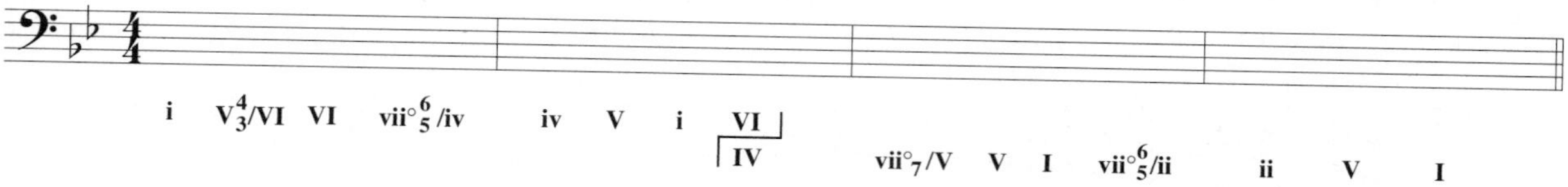

EXERCISE 5 The following progression represents a chromatic modulation. Provide RNs for the given bass, accounting for the modulation and indicating the pivot chord with the usual bracket. Use secondary dominants or diminished seventh chords where possible.

EXERCISE 6 After you are sure that your bass line for exercise 4b is correct, realize the progression in four voices on the staff below.

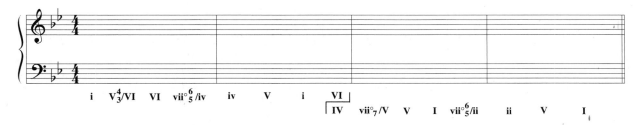

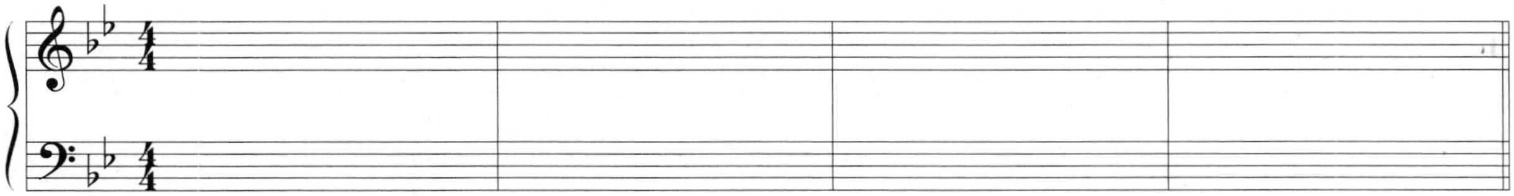

i V^4_3/VI VI vii°$^6_5$/iv iv V i VI

IV vii°$_7$/V V I vii°$^6_5$/ii ii V I

EXERCISE 7 Write the following modulations (bass and RNs). Choose an appropriate pivot chord for each of them and indicate it with the customary bracket.

a. A modulation from AM to EM. Use the following chords somewhere in your progression, along with any other chords you want: a series of successive secondary dominants, vii°$^6_5$/vi, and vii°$^4_2$/ii.

b. A modulation from Dm to FM. Use the following chords somewhere in your progression: vii°$^4_2$/V, vii°$^6_5$/IV, and an irregular resolution of V^6_5.

c. A chromatic modulation from B♭M to Dm, using secondary chords in various inversions in the process of establishing both keys.

a.

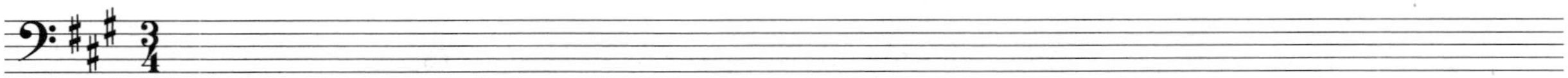

b.

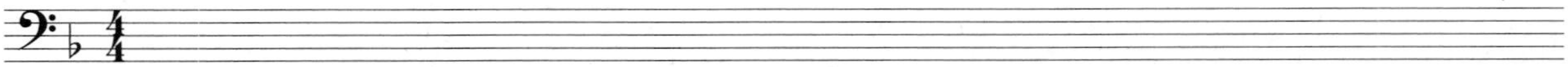

c.

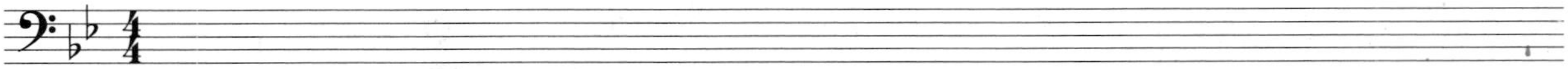

EXERCISE 8 Harmonize the following chorale ("Warum betrübst du dich, mein Herz") with a bass line and RNs, accounting for possible modulations. After you are sure that your harmonization works, add the two inner voices.

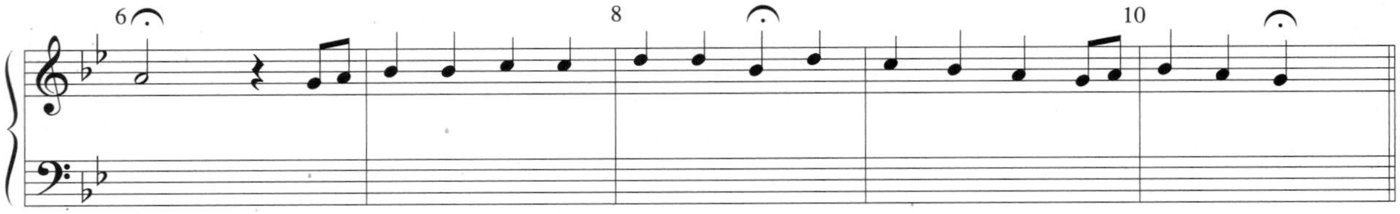

EXERCISE 9 Write simple keyboard accompaniments for the following modulating periods by Haydn. Provide RNs for your harmonizations and indicate your pivot chord in each case.

a. **Tempo di menuetto**

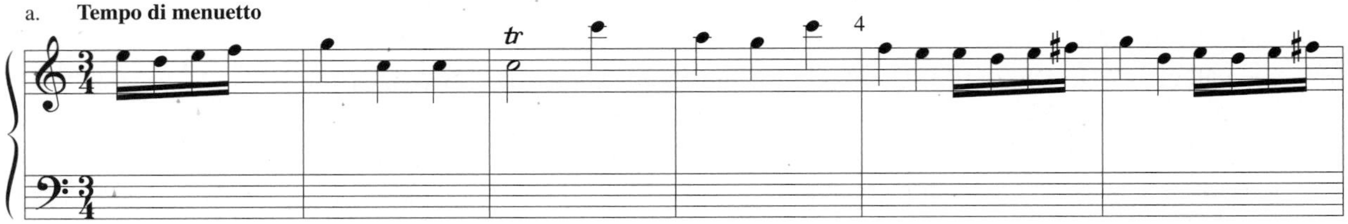

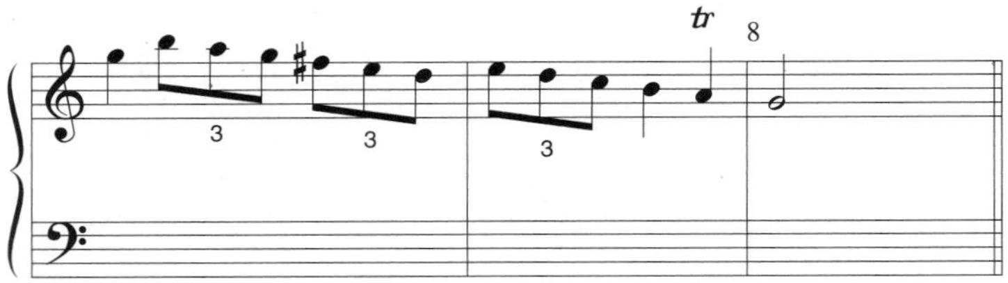

b. **Molto vivace**

Chapter 21

Small Forms: Binary and Ternary; Variation Forms

In chapters 2, 10, and 11, we studied the elements of form. We defined *form* as the tonal, rhythmic, and thematic relationships among musical units or sections, and we saw that *cadences* are a harmonic element of formal articulation. The basic formal units are the *motive, phrase segment, phrase,* and *period*. We learned to use *form diagrams,* which we called *bubble diagrams,* to express form graphically. Phrase segment relationships in these diagrams are indicated by lowercase letters with subscripts, whereas capital letters indicate thematic relationships between larger formal units.

In this chapter we will study how all of these formal elements come together to shape independent, complete formal units. We will first focus on the so-called small formal designs, binary and ternary, and we will then study variation forms.

We should emphasize that, because composers have used musical design and formal growth in free and creative ways, the study of form is fraught with difficulties. Even within more or less preestablished formal designs, the possibilities of variations, transformations, or exceptions are multiple. As William Rothstein states after defining ternary form, "however, as so often with matters of form, there are endless complications" (*Phrase Rhythm in Tonal Music,* p. 108). Form being indeed an ambiguous matter, in textbooks dealing with this topic there is no consistency or agreement on the exact terminology and definitions applied to formal types. Having clarified this, we will now attempt to provide as clear a discussion as possible.

THE BINARY PRINCIPLE

Binary pieces are structured in two parts, which we will call **reprises.** Binary is one of the most common formal designs in the baroque and Classical periods. In the baroque, the dance types that usually constitute a **suite** (such as **allemande, courante, minuet, bourrée, gavotte, sarabande, gigue,** etc.) were normally in binary form. In the Classical period, the most frequently found case of a piece in binary form is the minuet (and the trio) in sonatas or string quartets. You are quite likely to have performed numerous binary pieces in your musical life.

Example 21.1

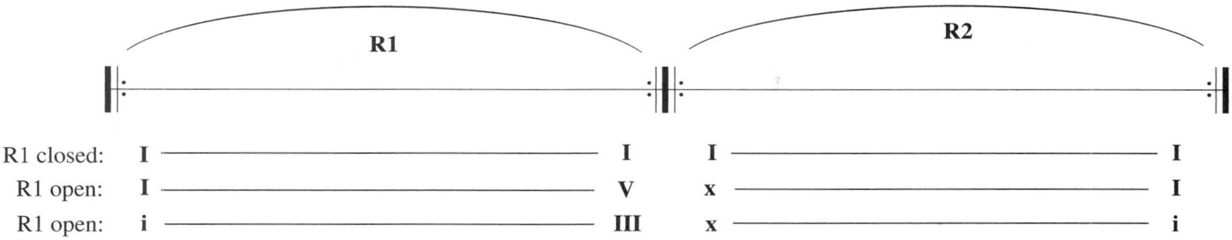

Each reprise in a binary design (which we will refer to as reprise 1 and reprise 2, abbreviated as R1 and R2) is usually, but not always, repeated. A reprise is **closed,** or harmonically complete, if it ends on the tonic of the main key, and it is **open,** or harmonically incomplete, if it does not. In binary, reprise 1 begins in the tonic key, and it may end on the tonic (closed), on a half cadence (HC) (open), or in a different key (open). Reprise 2 may begin and end in the tonic, or, more often, it begins on a key or harmony other than the tonic and ends on the tonic. Example 21.1 summarizes all these possibilities for the binary principle, with the "harmony other than the tonic" at the beginning of reprise 2 expressed by means of an "x."

BINARY TONAL TYPES

Because binary pieces, like most tonal pieces, begin and end on the tonic, tonal types are mostly determined by the harmony that closes reprise 1. We will now study the **binary tonal types,** which are represented graphically in example 21.2. The harmony that closes reprise 1 in each of these types is circled in this example.

1. *The Binary Tonic Type.* Refer to anthology, no. 6 (Minuet from *Notebook for Anna Magdalena Bach*). Reprise 1 closes with a perfect authentic cadence (PAC) in the tonic key. This is a binary piece of the **tonic type** (also called "sectional binary" by some authors). As in our minuet, the beginning of reprise 1 in this tonal type is usually a prolongation of the tonic, and the dominant is usually reached toward the middle of reprise 2, leading to a return of the tonic (see the cadence in m. 24 in the minuet, leading to the return of I in m. 25). This tonal type is shown in example 21.2a.
2. *The Binary Dominant Type.* The Haydn minuet in CM in anthology, no. 19 illustrates another binary tonal type, the **dominant type** (also called "continuous binary" in some texts). Reprise 1 ends on the dominant, in this case on a HC on V, without a modulation. A similar example of the same tonal type appears in anthology, no. 24 (Mozart, Sonata in DM, Tema), only in this case reprise 1 is a modulating period; that is, it ends with a PAC in the key of the dominant. The modulating

Example 21.2 Binary Tonal Types

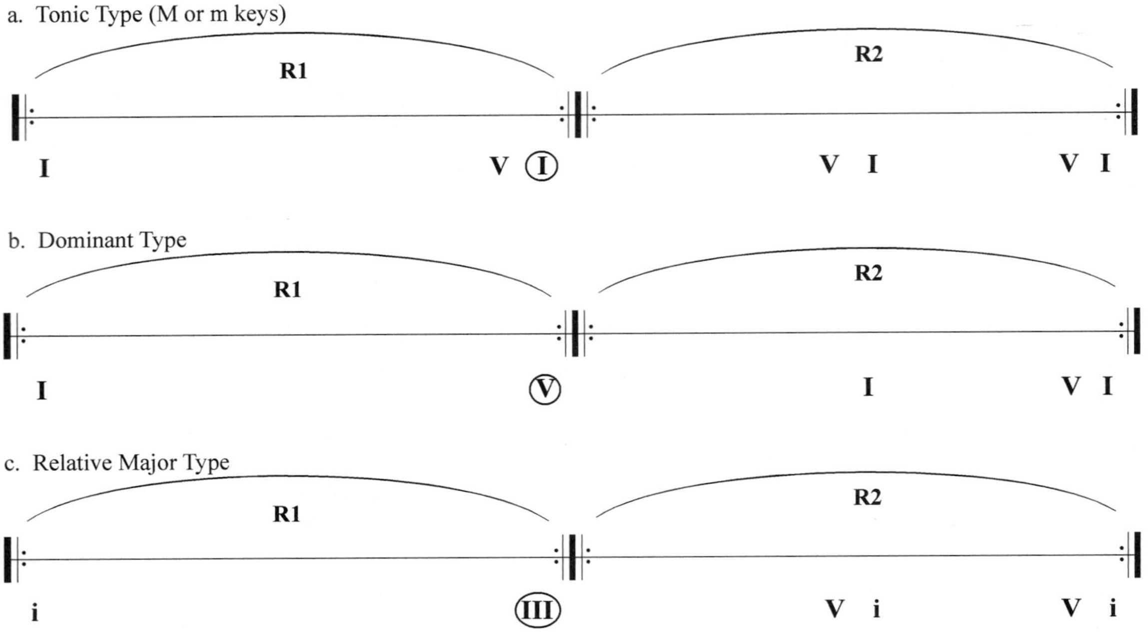

dominant type does not differ, essentially, from the nonmodulating type. In both cases, reprise 1 is open-ended, and in both cases the beginning of reprise 2 usually prolongs the V which closes reprise 1. This prolongation is extended all the way to the cadence on V toward the middle of reprise 2, before the tonic returns. This tonal type is represented in example 21.2b.

3. *The Binary Relative-Major Type.* In minor keys, the "dominant type" usually becomes the **relative major type,** that is, the modulation at the end of reprise 1 leads to III rather than V. An example of this type appears in example 21.10. At the end of reprise 1 we have reached the relative-major key, which is prolonged into reprise 2. The return of the tonic key in m. 19 (confirmed in m. 27) is preceded by an arrival on the dominant in m. 14, reiterated in m. 18. In other words, as in the dominant type, in the relative-major type we also reach V toward the middle of reprise 2, before moving back to the tonic. Both the V type and the III type are based on the familiar tonal paradigm, "tonic established/departure from tonic/return to tonic." See the formal diagram for the relative-major type in example 21.2c.

BINARY FORMAL DESIGNS

Different binary formal designs result from various possible thematic relationships between both reprises. In general, however, some formal traits are common to all binary designs:

1. Reprise 2 is often longer (sometimes as much as twice as long or more) than reprise 1.
2. Reprise 1 is usually divided into two phrases (constituting a period), and reprise 2 is itself divided into two sections, each of which can have several phrases. This sectional division is best expressed by the diagram in example 21.3a. We will use the abbreviations R1 and R2 to refer to reprise 1 and reprise 2, respectively, regardless of their thematic content. Lowercase letters will designate thematic relationship at the phrase level.

In our sample paradigms in example 21.3, we will assume that the two phrases in R1 are related thematically (a_1 and a_2), whereas the first phrase in R2 is contrasting (b),

Example 21.3 Binary Formal Designs

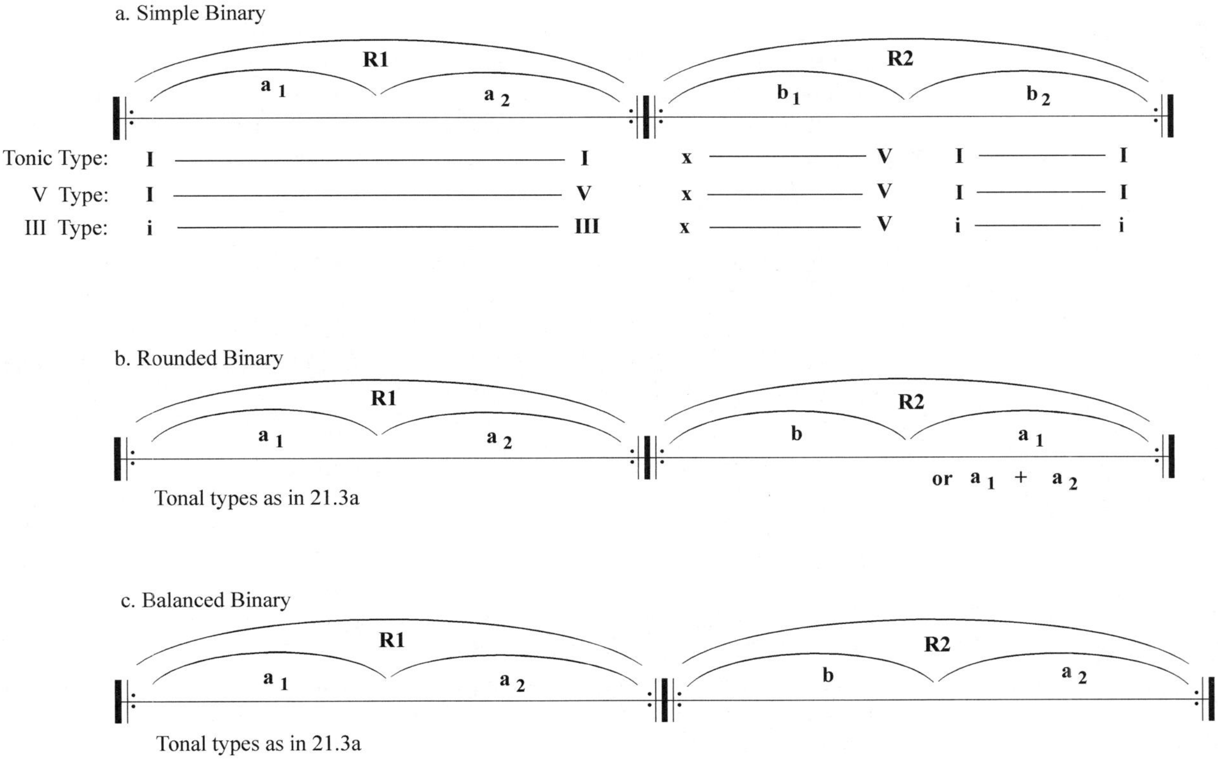

Example 21.4 J. Haydn, Piano Sonata in AM, Hob. XVI:5, II, Minuet

although various other thematic relationships are certainly possible. In general, the first phrase of R2 is the least stable harmonically, and it may have a developmental character both harmonically and thematically. The different binary formal designs are determined by the existence or nonexistence of a *return* of the main thematic material from reprise 1 in the tonic key toward the end of reprise 2, as we will discuss below.

Simple Binary

In the **simple binary** design, there is no return of the main thematic material from reprise 1, at the original tonic level, in the second section of reprise 2. Study example 21.4. This is a brief binary piece, with each reprise clearly delimited by repeat signs. The tonal and thematic structure of this minuet is summarized by the graph in example 21.5. Because there is no return of thematic material from reprise 1 in the second section of reprise 2 (in m. 13, where the tonic returns), this is a simple binary design. Otherwise,

Example 21.5

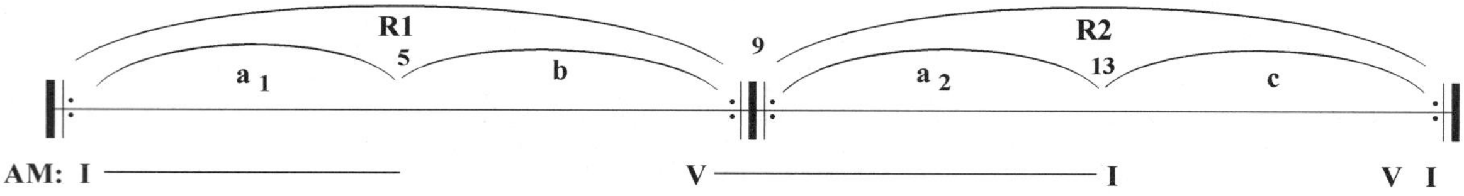

we can observe that the two phrases in R1 are contrasting (designated as a_1 and b). In R2, the first phrase is a varied statement of a_1, but now at the dominant level, hence the designation a_2, whereas the second phrase is based on new, contrasting material, labeled c in the diagram. From a tonal point of view, R1 moves from I to V. An extension of V in R2 leads to the return of I in m. 13. The piece is, then, in simple binary dominant-type form.

Analyze and discuss in class the minuet from the *Notebook for Anna Magdalena Bach* in anthology, no. 6. Review its tonal type (which we already mentioned), analyze the cadences and possible key areas, determine sections and their motivic relationships, and label them with appropriate letters. Then provide a complete formal graph following the model in example 21.5.

Rounded Binary

The formal design known as **rounded binary** features a return of the initial material from reprise 1 in the second section of reprise 2 (consult the formal diagram in example 21.3b).[1] The return, in the tonic key and at the same tonal level as the original statement, can be of two types. In the first type, the opening section of R1 (a_1 in our diagram) returns as the closing section of R2. In the second type, all of R1 ($a_1 + a_2$) returns as the final section of R2. Let us study two examples to clarify these two formal designs.

The binary piece in example 21.6a is of the dominant type. R1 is an eight-measure modulating period, divided into two phrases (mm. 1–4 and 5–8, featuring an a–b contrasting thematic relationship). R2 begins with a four-measure phrase (thematically contrasting or c) that prolongs the dominant key area established at the end of R1 and confirms it by means of a new cadence on the dominant in m. 12. After the cadence on V in m. 12, we can expect a return of the tonic key for the second section of R2. What we get is not only the return of DM, but also the return of the opening phrase, a. After three measures of "return" (mm. 13–15), the phrase is extended sequentially and finally closes with a PAC in DM. This piece is in rounded binary form because the opening section of R1 returns as the final section of R2. Study the formal diagram in example 21.6b: compare it with the piece and understand the relationship between both.

Refer now to example 21.7. This binary trio has a similar tonal structure to the one we have just discussed. It begins with an eight-measure reprise 1 modulating to the dominant and is also divided into two four-measure phrases with an a–b thematic structure. The first phrase of R2 prolongs the dominant key area for eight measures by means of a contrasting four-measure phrase repeated twice (mm. 9–12 and 13–16), leading to the expected return of the tonic key in the second section of R2. The return brings not only the tonic key (m. 17), but also the complete R1, including both the a and b phrases. The only difference between this return of R1 and the original R1 is that, in the original, the second phrase (mm. 5–8) modulated to V, whereas in the return the equivalent phrase (mm. 21–24) stays in the tonic key to allow for the final PAC on I.

---

[1] Some authors emphasize the ternary (that is, three-part) structure of this type of design, rather than its binary structure. From that point of view, the first reprise is an "exposition," the first section of R2 is a "contrasting middle," and the second section of R2 a "recapitulation." Although in this book we do not adopt this view, the interested student may find it articulated in detail in Caplin, *Classical Form,* pp. 71–86.

Example 21.6a J. Haydn, Piano Sonata in DM, Hob. XVI:4, Trio

Example 21.6b

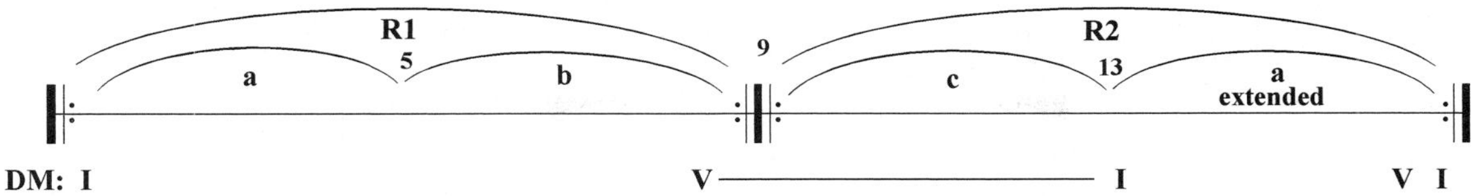

Example 21.7 L. v. Beethoven, String Quartet op. 18, no. 5, Trio

Example 21.7 (Continued)

To practice your understanding of rounded binary, analyze the following pieces from the anthology: no. 24 (Mozart, Sonata in DM, Tema) and no. 19 (Haydn, Minuet and Trio in CM). In the latter example, analyze both the Minuet and the Trio as separate examples of rounded binary. For each of these, discuss the tonal type (Is R1 a modulating period?), cadences and key areas, divisions into phrases, and relationships among phrases. What is the extent of the return? Does the complete R1 return, or only its first phrase? Finally, realize a complete formal diagram for each of these pieces.

Balanced Binary

In this formal design, what returns in the second section of R2 is neither the opening phrase from R1 nor the complete R1, but rather only *the final phrase of R1*, as expressed in the formal diagram in example 21.3c. A well-known example of the tonic-type balanced binary appears in example 21.8. R1 is an eight-measure parallel period, including a tonicized HC in m. 4, and a PAC on I in m. 8. These two cadences close the two phrases of R1, respectively, which form a parallel period (a_1–a_2). R2 opens with a contrasting b phrase that includes tonicizations of vi and V. (What chords are used to tonicize these degrees in mm. 9 and 11?) Finally, the closing phrase of R2 (mm. 13–16) turns out to be an almost literal return of a_2, the phrase that previously closed R1. The form is thus "balanced" by this ending phrase common to both R1 and R2, hence the name of this formal design. Notice that in a balanced binary of the dominant or relative major tonal types, in which the final phrase of R1 ends on V or III, the return of this second phrase of R1 at the end of R2 will lead to a cadence in the tonic key, rather than on V or III.

Example 21.8 W. A. Mozart, *Eine kleine Nachtmusik,* K. 525, III (Menuetto)

THE TERNARY PRINCIPLE

A piece in **ternary form** is any piece made up of three closed, independent parts. In principle, the formal and harmonic possibilities for this definition are many. The three parts may be related by a variety of formal designs, such as A–A–B, A–B–A, A–B–B, or A–B–C. We will focus here, however, on the most standard tonal and formal design

Example 21.9

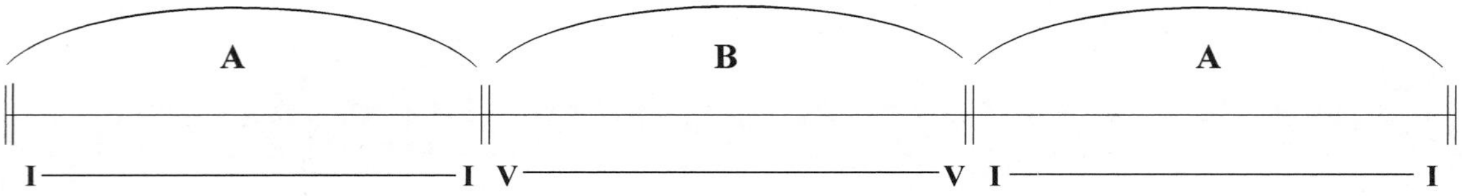

of ternary. In this design, summarized as A–B–A, the initial section, A, returns after a contrasting section, B. Moreover, the A sections are tonally closed, and the B section, which may be open or closed, is often (but not necessarily) in the dominant or relative major key. Example 21.9 shows a standard tonal and formal paradigm for this ternary principle.

Turn now to anthology, no. 46 (Schumann, Kinder Sonate no. 1), a splendid example of ternary composition. Because this piece contains many of the harmonic and formal concepts that you already know well by now, it is worth studying and discussing it in some detail. We will do so in the following guided analysis. First listen through it, and you will notice that the opening section, mm. 1–14, comes back at m. 35 in its entirety, with only a slight alteration toward the end to provide a brief cadential extension or *coda* (mm. 48–51). It is also immediately apparent that the first and last sections, the A sections, begin and end in GM, and that the middle B section begins and ends in Em. All three sections are then closed, and the middle section presents a contrasting tonal area, in the relative minor. We have thus identified our normative, standard ternary principle.

Next we can focus on each of the main sections separately. Identify all the phrases in the A section. Then continue reading. You will probably have identified a first four-measure phrase, with two clear phrase members. This initial phrase establishes the tonic key and presents the main thematic material of the section. Beginning at m. 5, we start moving away from the tonic. Where are we moving to tonally? What is the first indication of this modulation? Where are we sure that we have modulated? (Do not keep reading until you have answered these questions!) The move is to the dominant key, announced by the C♯ in m. 5, confirmed by the V–I progressions in DM in mm. 7–8, and further confirmed by the cadence in DM in m. 10. Now go back to m. 5. Here we are still in GM, but the next measure is in DM. Which chord is the pivot chord? And now go again to m. 10, where the cadence on DM takes place. In m. 11, the opening material comes back in GM. How did we modulate so fast from DM in m. 10 to GM in m. 11?

Now let's look at the B section (mm. 15–34). There is no question that it functions as a contrasting section, not only tonally, but also in several other ways. So let's ask the question: What changes between the A and the B sections? On the other hand, why do we feel that the unity of the piece is preserved? What is similar between the two sections? Answer these questions yourself. For contrast, discuss such elements as texture, rhythm, articulation, character, and type of melody. For unity and similarity, you may want to look at motivic content, and especially at the role of the perfect 4th as a motivic and melodic interval. Is the 4th an important interval in both the A and B sections? Moreover, look at the ascending eight-note motive in m. 2. Is it replicated in the B section?

The most interesting measures in the B section, from a harmonic point of view, are mm. 19–22. How are mm. 19–20 related to 21–22 melodically and harmonically? What are the secondary key areas in mm. 19–20 and 21–22, respectively? On the other hand, mm. 18–22 outline a circle-of-5ths progression. Identify each of the members of the circle (which is not complete).

Now that you have analyzed this interesting piece, listen to it again or play through it, and try to hear all the things you have discovered about it. Does your knowledge of form, tonal areas, tonal direction, and motivic and harmonic details make the listening or playing more enjoyable?

Compound Ternary

In the Classical period, one of the inner movements of sonatas and symphonies was often a *minuet* with its accompanying *trio,* after which you may have seen the familiar indication *Menuetto da capo.* The complete movement was, then, the minuet, the trio, and the complete minuet again. In this type of A–B–A design, which we call **compound ternary,** each of the three sections is a closed, independent piece in itself and, moreover, each of the sections is in one of the binary forms.

Refer to anthology, no. 19 (Haydn, Minuet from Divertimento in CM). The minuet is a V-type rounded binary in which all of reprise 1 returns in the second section of reprise 2, and the trio is a tonic-type rounded binary, also with the complete R1 returning as the second section of R2. Now listen to the complete movement, including the *Menuet da capo* as a single formal unit. You will, of course, recognize the A–B–A design of ternary, but because each of the sections is an independent binary piece, this is a compound ternary. Can you think of any compound ternary in your performance repertoire? If not, find (and listen to) an example of this formal design in some symphony by Haydn or Mozart.

The *Da Capo* Aria

The major three vocal genres of the baroque period were the opera, the cantata, and the oratorio. Although the function of each of these genres was very different, by the late seventeenth century all three were made up of the same kind of compositional types: *choruses, recitatives,* and *arias.*

Although several formal designs are found in baroque arias, perhaps the most frequent one is a ternary design known as ***da capo*** **aria.** This formal design fulfills the characteristics that we have studied for ternary designs: it is in three parts, the middle part is usually contrasting tonally and thematically, and the third part is a literal return of the first part. Because the return is literal, composers normally avoided copying it again and simply wrote the indication *da capo* at the end of the B section. At the end of the A section you are likely to find the indication *Fine,* telling the performer that this is the real end of the composition. *Da capo* arias often include passages, especially in the

A section, in which the orchestra plays alone. These passages are normally statements of the main thematic material and are called ***ritornellos.***

An example of a *da capo* aria is provided in anthology, no. 16 (Handel, "Lascia ch'io pianga," from *Rinaldo*). First discuss the A section. Is it closed? What is its formal and tonal design? Does it include an orchestral *ritornello?* Now look at the B section. It is shorter, accompanied only by the continuo, and, in spite of its shorter length, it is more chromatic than the A section. This B section also shows a typical characteristic of B sections in *da capo* arias: They usually begin and end in different keys, rather than featuring a closed tonal motion. After the major-mode A section in our example, the B section begins in the relative minor key, vi, and ends in the key of iii. This is a frequent tonal plan for *da capo* arias in major mode. In minor-mode arias, the B section often begins in the relative major and ends in the dominant key. These tonal designs are summarized in example 21.10.

It is interesting to note that, in a way, binary is more complex than ternary, mostly because of the various possibilities of tonal motion within the reprises and because of the several formal designs within the general binary paradigm. We should also point out that both binary and ternary generate larger, more complex forms, which we will study later in the book. Sonata form, an outgrowth of binary form, is a large binary design in which the first section of R2 becomes the development and the second section of R2 becomes a complete recapitulation of the complete R1, but now without the modulation away from the tonic key. The rondo form, on the other hand, is also an outgrowth of ternary. Ternary has three parts, A–B–A. If you continue the pattern of alternating a return (the refrain) with a contrasting section, you will come up with such typical rondo schemes as A–B–A–C–A or A–B–A–C–A–D–A. The formal principles we have learned in this chapter, then, set the stage for some of the major formal designs in the music literature.

Example 21.10

a.

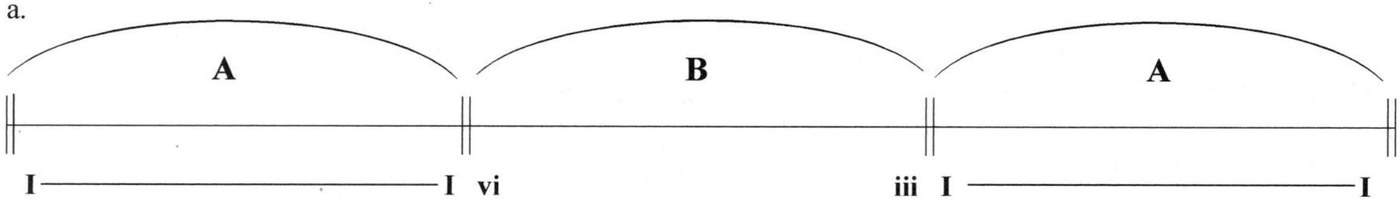

b.

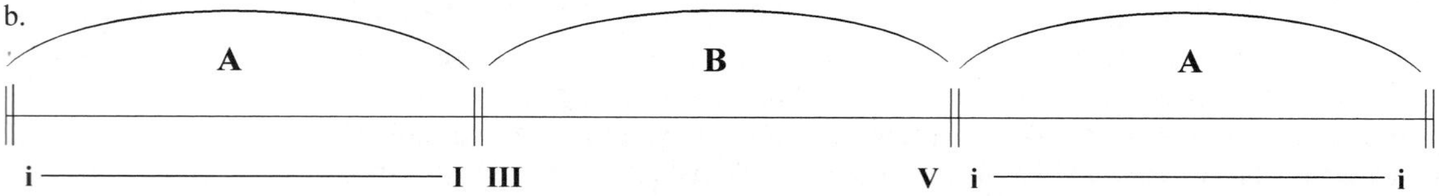

EXERCISES

To practice analyzing binary and ternary pieces, refer to exercise 1 in worksheet 21 at the end of this chapter.

For an assignment of an analytical paper on a binary or ternary piece, refer to chapter 21 in the workbook.

For melody harmonizations and composition exercises, refer to chapter 21 in the workbook.

VARIATION FORMS

The variation principle is a basic musical device often used in any type of composition. Composers frequently decide to repeat musical statements, and sometimes they do so literally (in what we call a **literal counterstatement**). At other times, however, the repetition is not literal, but varied (a **varied counterstatement**): The previous material may be altered or embellished in a number of ways, including addition of notes or figuration, simplification, rhythmic alteration, and so on. Examples of varied counterstatements appear, for instance, in anthology, no. 35 (Beethoven, Piano Sonata no. 21 in CM, *Waldstein*, I), in the context of the first movement of a sonata. Compare the initial theme (mm. 1–4) with its varied repetition in mm. 14–17. What did Beethoven change in the counterstatement? Now compare the statement of the new theme in EM that appears in mm. 35–42 with the immediate varied counterstatement in mm. 43–49. The difference here is quite considerable: What stays the same, and what is varied in the counterstatement?

We will now study the variation principle as a form-building process applied to complete movements or compositions. The types of compositions totally built on the variation principle are usually called "variations" or "theme and variations." The variations as a genre allow for great freedom on the composer's part. In their most usual compositional type, variations begin with the statement of a theme, a phrase, or a short piece (often in binary or ternary form) that is then restated in varied forms as many times as the composer wants.

Types of Variations

The first question we ask for each variation should be, as above: What stays the same, and what is varied? The following are some of the elements we can examine for this purpose: *key, mode, form, length, melody (both pitch and rhythm), tonal structure, precise harmonic sequence, bass, tempo, texture.* Some types of variations result from standard procedures that recur in variation sets by different composers. Some of these specific variation types are listed below.

1. **Ornamental variation:** The melody is elaborated (diminuted) by means of added notes.
2. **Simplifying variation:** The melody is simplified (reduced).
3. **Figural variation:** Built on a particular motive or figure (for instance, a triplet, a dotted figure, or some other repeated rhythmic motive).

4. **Contrapuntal variation:** Uses some kind of contrapuntal technique, such as imitation, canon, or free counterpoint.
5. **Characteristic variation:** In the style of some characteristic compositional type such as march, dance form, adagio, or finale.
6. **Double variation:** The first and second statements of each reprise in a binary form are written out, and each constitutes a different variation (instead of the more frequent repetition, by the repeat signs, of the same material).

Shape and Form of Complete Sets

Sets of variations constitute musical wholes, and composers design their musical shape and form thinking of the complete movement as a unit. For long-range design of shape, then, we must examine grouping, contrast, and tempi. Is there a rhythmic *crescendo* that groups several variations? Is there a pattern of increasing complexity? Is one of the central variations an *adagio,* functioning as a "slow movement" within the movement? Is the last variation a characteristic *finale,* in fast tempo and with brilliant figurations? Is there a long-range tonal design (such as, perhaps, M–m–M) that groups several variations? Does the grouping reveal any kind of long-range formal design (say, some kind of ternary)?

CONTINUOUS VARIATIONS

If we take into consideration the formal type of each variation and the connection between adjacent variations, there are two types of variation forms: continuous and sectional. In **continuous variations** the theme and each variation are usually short (one or two phrases) and there is no interruption between variations. In **sectional variations**, on the other hand, the theme and each variation are usually self-sufficient formal units (such as binary or rounded binary pieces), including a clear cadential pause at the end of the theme and each variation.

The most common type of continuous variation is built on a **bass ostinato** or **ground bass** (a melodic fragment repeated over and over again, and often associated with a harmonic progression). Study, for instance, Purcell's "Ah, Belinda," from *Dido and Aeneas* (anthology, no. 3). You will see that the complete aria is composed on a four-measure repeated bass phrase. Having identified this, you can ask yourself the following questions regarding this (or any other) bass-ostinato piece:

1. Is the bass phrase repeated unaltered every time, or is it ornamented?
2. Is it transposed in some section? To what tonal level or key area?
3. Is the bass phrase harmonized with the same progression every time it appears, or does the harmony change?
4. How is the melody phrasing related to the bass phrasing? Do they correspond? Or do they overlap? Overlap of phrases (which takes place when beginnings and endings of phrases in different voices do not correspond) is a frequent means to achieve continuity and a sense of continuous flow in this type of variation. Is this the case in our example?

5. What is the long-range form or shape of the complete piece? In Purcell's example, factors to consider are first, the repeat signs marking off a section at the beginning, then, the motivic character of the melody associated with the words "Peace and I. . . . " Do these words, and the motive that goes with them, return? Another factor to consider is the statements of the bass phrase in a secondary key area. How does this key area fit into the formal scheme created by the statement and return of the words "Peace and I . . . "?
6. What kind of contrapuntal device do you recognize, in the "Peace and I . . . " passages, between melody and bass? How does it contribute to the sense of phrase overlap? How does this overlap (the phrases "do not go together") depict what the words are expressing?
7. If you sing or play the vocal line, you will notice that, other than the "Peace and I . . . " fragments, the melody grows quite freely, with hardly any motivic references or repetitions (in contrast to the strict bass ostinato). This type of freely growing melody is characteristic of the baroque period and results from the technique known in German as ***Fortspinnung,*** or "spinning out."

Some Characteristic Ground-Bass Types

Continuous variations are often based on characteristic bass types such as the chaconne and folia. Characteristic bass formulas became popular in the Renaissance, both as grounds on which to improvise or as bass phrases on which to write variations. Two bass types widely used in the sixteenth century are the ***folia*** and the ***romanesca,*** shown in examples 21.11a and b. As with any ground bass, these bass formulas are usually associated with standard harmonic progression. Refer to example 14.11c, where you can review the progressions commonly used to harmonize the *romanesca* and *folia* basses, respectively.

The **chaconne** bass, on the other hand, is more typical of the baroque period, and it appears in various forms. The most common chaconne bass, however, is the **descending tetrachord** $\hat{1}$–$\hat{7}$–$\hat{6}$–$\hat{5}$ (or $\hat{1}$–$\flat\hat{7}$–$\flat\hat{6}$–$\hat{5}$ in minor), as shown in examples 21.11c and e (a *tetrachord* is a collection of four pitches, in this case outlining a descending P4). A chromatic elaboration of the descending tetrachord (of the type found, for instance, in "Dido's Lament," from Purcell's opera *Dido and Aeneas*) appears in example 21.11d. Because the descending tetrachord bass, in both its diatonic and chromatic forms, was often used in baroque operas as the basic structure for songs of sadness, loss, and mourning, it is often referred to as the **lament bass.** For examples of lament bass in popular music, listen to Percy Mayfield's song "Hit the Road, Jack" (as performed by Ray Charles) and Led Zeppelin's "Babe, I'm Gonna Leave You."

The term **passacaglia** also denotes a piece in continuous variation style on a ground bass, but composers have used this term to refer to a variety of basses. Sometimes passacaglia simply means the same as chaconne; that is, a piece titled *passacaglia* may be built on the descending tetrachord bass. At other times, a passacaglia is built on an original bass phrase, as in the case of the well-known Passacaglia in Cm by J. S. Bach (example 21.11e).

Example 21.11

To illustrate the type of ground-bass theme on which baroque composers built sets of *continuo* variations, three of the most famous among them appear in example 21.12. Corelli's Sonata "La Follia" is a set of variations on the popular folia bass (example 21.12a). Handel's Chaconne in GM (example 21.12b) is built on the major-mode, diatonic version of the chaconne bass. Bach's "Crucifixus," on the other hand, is built on the minor-mode chromatic version of the same bass. Why did Bach choose to use this bass for this particular section of his Mass? The example includes the first two statements of the bass phrase so that you can appreciate how Bach presents it with contrasting harmonizations from the very outset.

Ground basses are an important compositional technique in popular music. Besides the Ray Charles and Led Zeppelin songs mentioned previously, other popular songs that include ground basses are Del Shannon's "Runaway" (by Charles Westover and Max Crook), The Beatles's "I'll Be Back" (by Lennon and McCartney, from the album *A Hard Day's Night*), and The Lovin' Spoonful's "Summer in the City" (by John Sebastian, Mark Sebastian, and Steve Boone).

Example 21.12a Archangelo Corelli, Sonata *La Follia,* op. 5, no. 12, mm. 1–16

Example 21.12b G. F. Handel, Chaconne in GM

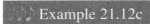

Example 21.12c J. S. Bach, "Crucifixus," from Mass in Bm, mm. 1–9 (vocal parts omitted)

SECTIONAL VARIATIONS

As we saw earlier, in **sectional variations** (the traditional type of "theme and variations"), the theme and each variation are independent formal units, separated by a conclusive cadence and a break in the musical flow. This is the most common type of variation in the Classical and Romantic periods. The first movement of Mozart's Sonata in AM, K. 331, in "theme and variations" form, is reproduced in anthology, no. 27. Listen to the *complete set,* and then discuss the following points in class.

1. We have already studied the form of the theme. Review what exact formal design it represents, and note that it is a totally self-contained, conclusive formal unit.
2. Is the formal design of the theme preserved intact in each of the variations?
3. Variations I–IV can be considered both *ornamental* and *figural* variations. Review the definitions of these terms, and explain how each of these four variations can be seen to represent both types. Can you trace the melodic structure of the original theme in each of the six variations?
4. In variations I and II, Mozart was not content with simply writing the complete first reprise using the same variation material (the same figuration, texture, etc.). Compare phrase 1 and phrase 2 in each of these two opening periods, and explain how Mozart varied the second phrase with respect to the first one.
5. The theme and variations I–IV can be heard as a formal group. Why? What is the character and function of variation III within this group? Of variation IV?

6. Considering their character within the complete set, variations V and VI are *characteristic variations*. What "genres" do they represent? Could variation V itself be an independent movement within a sonata? How about variation VI? What is the formal function of the added mm. 18–26 in this last variation?
7. Provide some kind of a diagram showing the overall grouping and formal design for the complete movement.

EXERCISES

To practice analysis of variations, refer to exercise 2 in worksheet 21 at the end of this chapter.

FOR FURTHER STUDY

For additional analysis using materials studied in this chapter, refer to the *Harmony in Context* Web page at www.mhhe.com/roigfrancoli2e.

ASSIGNMENT

For analytical and written assignments based on the materials learned in this and previous chapters, refer to chapter 21 in the workbook.

Terms for Review

Binary
Reprise
Suite: allemande, courante, sarabande, gigue, bourrée, gavotte, minuet-trio
Closed unit
Open unit
Binary tonal types: I type, V type, III type
Simple binary
Rounded binary
Balanced binary
Ternary
Compound ternary
Da capo aria
Ritornello
Variation forms
Literal or varied counterstatement
Ornamental variation
Simplifying variation
Figural variation
Contrapuntal variation
Characteristic variation
Double variation
Shape and form of complete sets
Continuous variations
Sectional variations
Bass ostinato
Ground bass
Fortspinnung
Folia
Romanesca
Chaconne
Descending tetrachord
Lament bass
Passacaglia

Worksheet 21

EXERCISE 1 Analysis. For each of the pieces to be analyzed, determine and discuss the formal and tonal types, the key areas in the complete piece, and construct a bubble diagram using the given line. The diagram should show sections (labeled with letters) and tonal motion.

In essence, the basic questions about this chapter's formal designs are as follows:

1. Binary or ternary?
2. If binary, does it feature a return in the tonic key?
   a) No return: Simple binary.
   b) Return:
      1) Of all of R1: rounded binary.
      2) Of the beginning of R1: rounded binary.
      3) Of the end of R1: balanced binary.

Examples for Analysis:

1. Anthology, no. 11, Bach, French Suite no. 3, Minuet.
   a) Form and formal design:

   b) Key areas:

   c) Bubble diagram:

2. Anthology, no. 32, Beethoven, Sonata in Fm, op. 2, no. 1.

   Menuetto

   a) Form and formal design:

   b) Key areas:

   c) Bubble diagram:

Trio

a) Form and formal design:

b) Key areas:

c) Bubble diagram:

3. Example 21.13.

a) Form and formal design:

b) Key areas:

c) Bubble diagram:

Example 21.13 J. Haydn, String Quartet no. 21, op. 9, no. 3, II

Example 21.13 (Continued)

4. Example 21.14.
   a) Form and formal design:

   b) Key areas:

c) Bubble diagram:

Example 21.14 R. Schumann, "An Important Event," from *Scenes from Childhood,* op. 15, no. 6

Example 21.14 (Continued)

5. Anthology, no. 32, Beethoven, Sonata op. 2, no. 1.

Menuetto and Trio (Complete Movement)

a) Form and formal design:

b) Key areas:

c) Bubble diagram:

6. Anthology, no. 17, Handel, "Amaz'd to Find the Foe so Near," from *Belshazzar*.
   a) Form and formal design:

   b) Key areas:

   c) Bubble diagram:

EXERCISE 2 Listen to Beethoven's Symphony no. 3 in E♭M (*Eroica*), op. 55, IV, and follow the score while you listen. Think of this movement as a set of variations and explain exactly what each of the following statements means.

a) These variations are on two elements: a bass (introduced in mm. 12–44) and a theme built on this bass.

b) Measures 76–107 constitute a double variation (variation 3).

c) The movement's first large section (part 1) is expository and ends in m. 107.

d) Measures 107–116 are transitional to the movement's second large section (part 2). Part 2 begins and ends with imitative sections.

e) Variation 4 is a contrapuntal variation.

f) Measures 175–210 constitute a double variation (var. 5).

g) A characteristic variation begins in m. 211 (var. 6).

h) The variation in mm. 258–277 (var. 7) contains an inversion of the theme, and it also features change of mode.

i) The variation beginning in m. 277 (var. 8) is a contrapuntal variation that closes part 2. One of its two subjects is related in some interesting way with the subject of the previous contrapuntal variation (var. 4).

j) Part 2 is a section of tonal and modal contrast within the overall tonal design of the movement.

k) The third large section of the movement (part 3) begins in m. 349.

l) Variation 9 is a double variation that features a tempo contrast.

m) Variation 10 presents a climactic "tempo augmentation" of the theme: Although it is written in the same values as usual, it sounds like an augmentation. Why, and where is it?

n) A long coda begins in m. 396. This coda has several distinct sections. What are they? What distinguishes each of them?

o) Provide a formal diagram of this movement, showing the long-range grouping of variations and the overall tonal design.

Chapter 22

Contrapuntal Genres

A variety of new genres and styles emerged and were developed during the Baroque period (approx. from 1600 to 1750). Two very different textural principles can be found in these genres. In the homophonic **thoroughbass texture,** on the one hand, a melodic line is supported by a harmonic bass (in which leaps are frequent) and the chordal realizations of the figures that accompany the bass. Polyphonic genres, on the other hand, receive an enormous impulse in this period, both in vocal and instrumental music. The polyphonic or contrapuntal style is often combined with the thoroughbass texture in what we know as **continuo polyphony,** found for instance in J. S. Bach's sacred music (such as his cantatas and Masses). In continuo polyphony a figured bass is added to an otherwise polyphonic texture. Baroque polyphony in general, whether or not the figured bass is present, is eminently *harmonic;* that is, it is a contrapuntal elaboration of underlying functional harmonic progressions. In this chapter we will study two contrapuntal genres of the baroque period: the *invention* and the *fugue.* Because J. S. Bach brought each of these genres to its highest level of development, we will focus especially on examples by this composer.

The importance of studying the genres that we will cover in this chapter goes much beyond their immediate historical significance. Contrapuntal techniques, as found in these genres, are essential to the compositional style of any historical period. Fugue and fugal techniques have been used by composers all the way to the present. Learning about these genres is learning about musical process in general, and although the literature we will study is centered on the keyboard, contrapuntal genres and the musical processes they embody can be found in the literature for any instrument, and hence should be a relevant component, at least from an analytical point of view, in the education of any musician.

THE TWO-VOICE INVENTION

In 1723, J. S. Bach published a pedagogical collection of fifteen two-voice and fifteen three-voice keyboard pieces, titled Inventions and Sinfonias, respectively. Although this is not a common genre in the Baroque period (there are hardly any precedents for it), Bach's inventions have become central pedagogical pieces both for the study of the keyboard and as compositional and contrapuntal models.

Although there is not a single standard type of tonal design and form in Bach's two-voice inventions, the following characteristics apply generally to the genre:

1. An **invention** is a *contrapuntal, imitative piece* in which the two voices are totally independent and equally important.
2. Inventions are characterized by *strict thematic unity*. They are usually built on a single theme, which is found pervasively throughout the composition.
3. Pieces begin with an *imitative* **exposition** (imitation is mostly at the octave, but in some cases it is at the fifth). The theme reappears in various keys within the invention.
4. Motion from one key area to another key area is effected by means of sequential passages, called **episodes,** often based on a descending or ascending circle of fifths.
5. Episodes are developmental areas in which the theme may be transformed in a variety of ways. In chapter 12 we studied some of the most frequent techniques of thematic development: Repetition and transposition, varied repetition (variation), sequence, change of mode, fragmentation, intervallic expansion and contraction, inversion, and rhythmic augmentation and diminution. All of these techniques may be found in developmental episodes in both inventions and fugues, and thus a review of chapter 12 might be useful at this point.
6. Secondary key areas normally involve *nearly related keys* such as the dominant, relative major or minor, and subdominant keys (sometimes also the supertonic key, the "dominant of the dominant").
7. The original key **returns** at the end of the invention, possibly along with a return of the initial point of imitation.

BACH: INVENTION NO. 3, IN DM

We will now analyze, as an example of the genre, Bach's Invention no. 3 in DM (anthology, no. 13).

1. *The Exposition.* This is the section in which the theme is presented by each voice in imitation. The exposition in our example comprises mm. 1–4 (to the downbeat of 5).
    a) Comment on the *theme:* what is its rhythmic characteristic? Notice the two halves (m. 1 and m. 2): how are they symmetrical (consider the grouping of notes)? How is the largest leap "strategically" placed? Comment on the progressive ascent from $\hat{1}$ to $\hat{5}$, and the subsequent descent from $\hat{5}$ to $\hat{1}$.
    b) What is the *interval of imitation*?
    c) Examine the *counterpoint to the theme* in mm. 3–4. As a general principle throughout the invention, when one voice is active (in sixteenth notes), the other

voice is less active (in eighth notes). Few measures in the whole invention feature sixteenth notes throughout the measure in both voices.

2. *Episode 1.* This episode (mm. 5–12) leads to the cadence on V (AM) in m. 12. It is remarkable in its simplicity: It is based on an A pedal (which establishes the new key) and on repetition rather than sequence. Notice the cadential formula in mm. 10–12: You will later see that Bach uses the same formula in each of the subsequent cadences. Comment on the motive in mm. 5–6. It is obviously derived from the theme, but with some variation. Explain exactly how it is derived.
3. *Episode 2.* A new episode (mm. 12–24) leads to the cadence in Bm (the relative minor) in m. 24. The first section, mm. 12–18, moves through an ascending fifth progression: A–E–B–F♯ (identify each of the steps in this circle of fifths on the score). The circle stops on F♯, V in the new key of Bm.

   Notice the imitative interplay ("give and take") between voices in mm. 12–18. Have notes been added to the original theme to come up with the version used in these measures? How does the motive proceed melodically in mm. 19–21? Do you recognize the cadential formula in mm. 22–24?
4. *Episode 3.* This episode (mm. 24–38) is also based on a "give and take" texture, and in this case voices are totally complementary: When one moves, the other is sustained. The episode leads to the cadence in AM (V) in m. 38.
   a) The imitative passage in mm. 24–32 is built on a very familiar progression. What is it?
   b) The passage in mm. 32–35, on the other hand, features an interesting free development on the theme, with active motion in both voices creating a drive toward the important cadence on V in m. 38.
   c) The cadential gesture in mm. 36–38 is slightly varied with respect to the previous ones, but do you still recognize our basic cadential formula?
5. *The return.* An extension of the AM cadence (mm. 38–42) leads to the return of DM and to the recapitulation of the initial point of imitation (mm. 43–46). How does the motive proceed melodically in mm. 39–41?
6. *The final episode and the codetta.* Compare the episode in mm. 47–54 with episode 1 (mm. 5–12). How do they differ texturally? And how do they differ tonally?
   a) Whereas the original episode has the function of leading away from the original key, this new, final episode stays within the key of DM and leads to what could be the closing cadence on D, in m. 54.
   b) Instead, Bach writes a deceptive cadence and a **codetta** (a brief coda), now taking us to the closing statement of the cadential formula and to the final cadence on D.

After discussing the complete invention in class, study the tonal/formal graph in example 22.1, and understand how it represents the design and structure of the piece. Comment on the long-range tonal plan provided by the key areas (circled in our graph).

Example 22.1

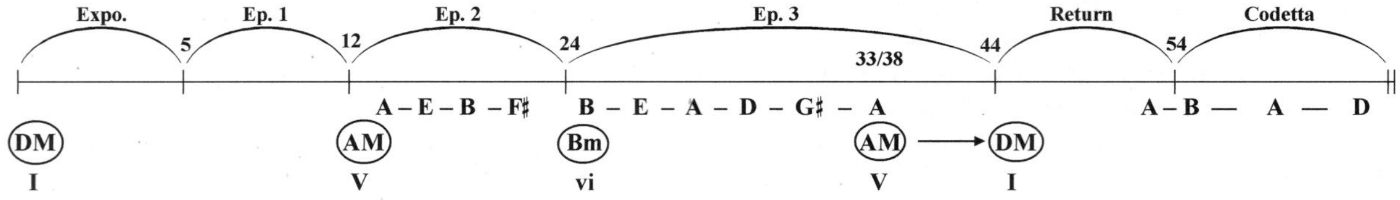

What familiar linear melodic figure is it based on? How is this plan replicated at a smaller scale in the return-codetta sections (mm. 44–59)?

The chart in example 22.2, on the other hand, is what we call a "distributional graph," a comparative study of melodic segments. By placing related motives one on top of the other we can see exactly how they are derived from the initial theme. Comment on this graph and how it shows the thematic transformations undergone by the original subject.

Example 22.2

EXERCISE

To practice analyzing an invention, refer to exercise 1 in worksheet 22 at the end of this chapter.

THE FUGUE

The contrapuntal genre *par excellence,* the **fugue,** developed throughout the sixteenth and seventeenth centuries to become one of the most elaborate and complex compositional types and a symbol of good contrapuntal and compositional craft. The genre reached its peak with J. S. Bach. As Robert Gauldin wrote in his counterpoint textbook, *A Practical Approach to Eighteenth-Century Counterpoint* (Englewood Cliffs, NJ: Prentice Hall, 1988), "despite the great accomplishments of the late Baroque masters, their efforts in the area of fugue pale against the achievements of J. S. Bach" (p. 210). Gauldin adds: "The fugal output of J. S. Bach is staggering. Aside from the collections (two volumes of the *WTC*, the seven Toccatas and Fugues for keyboard, and *Die Kunst der Fuge [The Art of Fugue]),* there are at least forty significant fugues for organ. These do not include the numerous choral movements cast in fugal style from cantatas or oratorios." The *WTC* is the *Well-Tempered Clavier,* a collection of forty-eight preludes and fugues in two volumes (24 + 24), each of which contains a prelude and a fugue in each of the twenty-four major and minor keys.

Just as with the invention, there is not a single formal or tonal type for the fugue. The fugue is a compositional procedure that can be adapted to numerous formal and tonal designs. In general, however, we can define the following characteristics for the genre:

1. A fugue begins with an imitative **exposition,** in which a **subject** presented by one voice is imitated by each of the other voices at the fifth (in the key of the dominant) or at the unison/octave (in the tonic key).
2. The remainder of the fugue is usually made up of alternating *middle entries,* statements of the *complete subject* in a variety of keys, and **episodes,** modulatory passages with a developmental character, usually sequential and based on the ascending or descending circle of fifths. After a modulating episode, the subject may be stated by a single voice (**middle entry,** ME), or by several voices in imitation (**middle entry group,** MEG).
3. Modulations are usually to closely related keys, although consecutive modulations may end up leading to keys distant from the original home key. At the end of the fugue there is a return to the tonic key, with or without a recapitulation of the subject in this key.
4. A variety of contrapuntal devices may be used throughout the fugue. Among these, the most common are the **stretto** (imitation of the subject at a closer metrical distance than the original imitation), augmentation or diminution, and inversion.
5. Fugues are often seamless formal entities, not clearly sectional, and we perceive them as a continuous flow of rhythmic and harmonic activity. They often create increasing and cumulating tension which may not be resolved until the final cadence.

The Exposition: Subject and Answer

Sing or play through the five subjects in example 22.3. In all of these examples you will notice some general traits of a good fugal subject: They all have definite, characteristic contours; they also have definite, characteristic rhythmic designs. Both traits together make these subjects clearly recognizable when they appear within the fugue. Moreover, a good subject usually has a strong rhythmic drive that propels it forward; it breaks easily into motives (thus allowing for fragmentation in developmental episodes), and it often has two contrasting halves (see subjects b, c, and d in example 22.3).

Now listen, following the score, to mm. 1–9 of Fugue no. 2 in Cm, from *The Well-Tempered Clavier,* I, anthology, no. 14). This fugue is in three voices, and this passage introduces all three, each beginning with a statement of the two-measure subject. In mm. 1–2, the alto states the *subject* in Cm, the tonic level. In mm. 3–4, the treble states the subject at the 5th, that is, at the dominant level. We will call this the **answer** (the subject transposed up a 5th). Finally, in mm. 7–8, the bass enters with the subject, again at the tonic level. Measures 1–9 are thus this fugue's *exposition.* The exposition ends as soon as the last voice completes its statement of the subject.

Real and Tonal Answers

You may have noticed that the answer of the Cm fugue (mm. 3–4) is not literally at the 5th: the initial interval C–G ($\hat{1}$–$\hat{5}$) in the subject is not answered with a G–D ($\hat{5}$–$\hat{2}$), but rather with a G–C ($\hat{5}$–$\hat{1}$). After this initial adjustment, however, the answer is not only a literal transposition of the subject at the upper 5th, but moreover it is in Gm, the key of the dominant. This type of answer, which includes a minor adjustment, usually at the beginning, is called **tonal answer.** Examine, on the other hand, the subject and answer in example 22.3a. Here the answer is literally at the 5th throughout. This is a **real answer.**

The following principles summarize the most frequent cases in which a subject will require a tonal answer:

1. If the subject begins on $\hat{5}$, the answer will usually begin on $\hat{1}$ and *not* on $\hat{2}$ (see example 22.3c).
2. If the subject begins with a motive based on $\hat{1}$–$\hat{5}$, the answer will respond with $\hat{5}$–$\hat{1}$ (and not $\hat{5}$–$\hat{2}$), as in example 22.3b. Similarly, a $\hat{5}$–$\hat{1}$ beginning will be imitated with $\hat{1}$–$\hat{5}$ (and not $\hat{2}$–$\hat{5}$), as in examples 22.3c and d.
3. A $\hat{1}$–$\hat{7}$ beginning will be imitated with a $\hat{5}$–$\hat{3}$ instead of $\hat{5}$–$\hat{4}$. See example 22.3e, where the initial $\hat{1}$–$\hat{7}$–$\hat{1}$ is answered with a $\hat{5}$–$\hat{3}$–$\hat{4}$, and not a literal $\hat{5}$–$\hat{4}$–$\hat{5}$.

The reason for each of these changes is that, although answers as a whole are in (or modulate to) the dominant key, it is customary that the opening motive (usually only two or three notes) is in the tonic key, in order to fit tonally with the end of the subject on the tonic. Minor adjustments like the ones we have just discussed are sufficient to solve the problem. Example 22.3f illustrates a connection between a subject and its tonal answer, followed by the tonally impossible connection with a real answer.

Example 22.3

a.
Real Answer
WCT I, no. 1
CM:
b.
Tonal Answer
Art of Fugue
Dm:
c.
Tonal Answer
WTC II, no. 1
etc.
CM:
d.
Tonal Answer
WTC I, no. 16
Gm:
e.
Tonal Answer
WTC I, no. 23
BM:
f.
Tonal Answer
(Gm)
Dm
Real!
Dm!
Gm:
(Gm)
Dm
(Gm)

EXERCISE

To practice writing fugal answers, refer to exercise 4 in worksheet 22 at the end of this chapter.

BACH: FUGUE NO. 2 IN Cm FROM *THE WELL-TEMPERED CLAVIER,* I

We will now study Bach's Cm fugue, reproduced in anthology, no. 14.

1. *The exposition.* We have already discussed the subject/answer entries in the exposition (mm. 1–9), and the tonal answer. When in a fugue the second voice comes in with the answer, the first voice provides a counterpoint to it (mm. 3–4). If the same counterpoint is repeated every time (or most of the time) the subject (S) appears in later entries, we call it a **countersubject** (CS). In this case, this is indeed a countersubject. Verify its appearance in mm. 7–8, 11–12, 15–16, 20–21, and 26–28, in all cases accompanying the subject. In mm. 7–8, the third voice comes in with S, the treble carries the CS, and the alto provides a further counterpoint, which, in this fugue, also appears every time S is stated subsequently. We will then call this second counterpoint CS2 (the previous CS then becomes CS1). Verify its appearance in all the statements of S listed above.

   The bridge. The answer, in m. 5, ends in Gm. But the new entry, the subject again, must begin in the tonic key. Before the subject comes in again, we need to modulate back to Cm. This modulation from the dominant to the tonic after the end of the answer is called the **bridge** (mm. 5–6). What techniques of melodic development do you recognize in this passage? Where are both voices derived from, and how? How do the motives proceed melodically?

   Double and triple counterpoint. Expositions are often written in **invertible counterpoint:** Voices may be texturally switched (top becomes bottom, and bottom becomes top) and the counterpoint still works. Invertible counterpoint in two voices is called **double counterpoint;** in three voices it is **triple counterpoint.** Compare mm. 17–18 with the bridge (mm. 5–6). Aside from the minimal addition of the treble in parallel 3rds with the bass motive, you will see that mm. 17–18 are basically built on the same two voices as mm. 5–6, only now they are inverted (and transposed). Measures 5–6 are thus written in invertible (double) counterpoint. Compare now mm. 20–21 with 7–8. The tonal level and pitch content are the same, but in mm. 20–21 all three voices have been switched around. Measures 7–8 are thus written in triple counterpoint.

2. *The middle entries (ME): tonal plan.* Middle entries are the complete statements of S throughout the fugue. Mark them on the score, and notice that they always appear in the form of S/CS1/CS2:

   a) ME1, E♭M (III), mm. 11–12.

   b) ME2, Gm (v), mm. 15–16 (the subject begins in Cm and modulates to Gm; it actually appears in the form of the answer, as in mm. 3–4).

   c) ME3, Cm (i), mm. 20–21.

   d) ME4, Cm (i), mm. 26–28.

The tonal plan for this fugue is straightforward: ME1 is in the relative major key, ME2 is in the minor dominant key, and ME3 is the return to i, and also a recapitulation, in Cm, of the complete three-voice statement of S/CS1/CS2 from mm. 7–8. ME4 is a final restatement of the three-voice complex, confirming the return to the tonic key, Cm.

The Pedal. Fugues often include a pedal point toward the end, on either the dominant or the tonic. The function of this **pedal** is to help release the accumulated harmonic and rhythmic tension created throughout the fugue. In our example, Bach wrote a pedal on $\hat{1}$ after the final perfect authentic cadence (PAC) in m. 29. Over the pedal, he wrote a final statement of S with a beautiful harmonization full of biting dissonances.

3. *The Episodes.* The above key areas and middle entries are connected by means of the following modulating episodes:

   a) *Episode 1, mm. 9–10.* Modulates from Cm to E♭M by means of a four-step circle of 5ths: C–F–B♭–E♭ (verify each step on the score). Where is the thematic material in each voice derived from? How are the two upper voices related texturally and contrapuntally?

   b) *Episode 2, mm. 13–14.* Moves from E♭M to Gm by means of an ascending circle of 5ths: E♭–B♭–F–C–G (identify each step on the score; several of these chords appear in first inversion). Comment on the melodic material: Is any of it derived from S?

   c) *Episode 3, mm. 17–19.* Modulates from Gm back to Cm in two sequences up by steps (identify both sequences, each of which has three segments). We have already seen that this episode is directly related with the bridge through invertible counterpoint.

   d) *Episode 4, mm. 22–26.* Does not modulate, but rather leads from Cm to Cm through a complete circle of 5ths. Identify each of the steps in the circle. Compare this episode with episode 1: They are both based on the same material, but whereas in episode 1 the circle stopped at E♭, here it continues until it reaches C again. Comment on the texture: How do the voices function contrapuntally? Are there any examples of continuous motion and of "give and take" counterpoint?

After you have studied this fugue, examine the tonal/formal graph in example 22.4, and understand how it summarizes the design and structure of this piece. Then listen to the fugue again and try to hear everything we have discussed.

Example 22.4

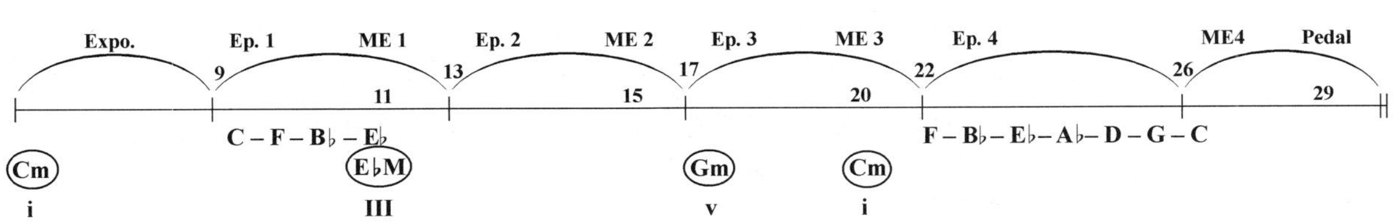

SOME ADDITIONAL FUGAL TECHNIQUES

Apply your knowledge of fugue to the analysis in class of Bach's Fugue no. 11 in FM, from *The Well-Tempered Clavier,* I (anthology, no. 15). Besides the usual concepts and sections that we have already studied, in this fugue you will find the following additional elements:

1. *Counterexposition.* After the exposition (mm. 1–13) and a brief nonmodulating episode (mm. 13–17), you will see that all three voices come in again with the same subject-answer-subject statements as before, still in the tonic key (mm. 18, 22, and 26, respectively). This "repetition" of the exposition is called a **counterexposition.** It may be in the tonic key, as in this case, or it may be in a related key.
2. *Stretto.* Examine the middle entry groups in mm. 37–44 and 47–54. In both MEGs all three voices state the subject. But if you compare the metric distance between statements here (two measures in each case) and in the exposition (four measures), you will see that in the MEGs entries are closer. Each of these MEGs is actually a *stretto,* a presentation of the subject in imitation at a closer distance than the original imitation.

Finally, study the exposition in example 22.5. This fugue is in three voices, but if you listen carefully you will hear "four" voices coming in in the exposition: alto (subject, m.1), treble (answer, m. 3), "tenor" (subject, m. 8), and "bass" (answer, m.12). That is, a full S–A–S–A cycle in four voices. The fourth entry is what we call an **extra entry,** and it allows the "faking" of a four-voice exposition in a three-voice fugue.

EXERCISE

To practice analyzing a fugue, refer to exercise 2 in worksheet 22 at the end of this chapter.

THE FUGATO

Composers sometimes use fugal techniques in the context of compositions other than fugues, such as variation forms. In such cases the fugal passages often take the form of a fugal exposition or perhaps the exposition and a developmental section (an episode), after which the texture changes back to a nonfugal, or even noncontrapuntal, style. Such a passage in the style of a fugal beginning in the context of larger formal types is called a **fugato.** You may listen to two fugatos in the last movement of Beethoven's Symphony no. 3, *Eroica.* The movement is a set of variations, and the large-scale middle section is both introduced and closed by fugatos. Listen to the opening fugato in mm. 117–175, and the closing fugato in mm. 277–348. To see where the subject of the first fugato comes from, listen to the opening of the movement. How is the subject of the second fugato related to the subject of the first fugato?

Example 22.5 J. S. Bach, Fugue no. 8 in D♯m, from *The Well-Tempered Clavier,* I, mm. 1–14

Notice also that in the second fugato, each entry of the subject in half notes is accompanied by a countersubject (or a second subject) in sixteenth notes. A fugue in which there are two subjects is called a **double fugue.** Beethoven's second fugato is, then, a double fugato. For an excellent example of double fugue, in which the main subject is always presented simultaneously with a countersubject, you may want to listen to the "Kyrie" from Mozart's *Requiem.*

PRACTICAL APPLICATION AND DISCUSSION

1. What have you learned in this chapter that you would consider valuable as a musician?
2. What do you know now that you did not know before about formal and tonal processes in the baroque period, and about musical processes in general? What have you learned about compositional craft?
3. How does this affect your understanding of the music you play and listen to? For instance, how does it affect your perception or performance of the Cm fugue?
4. Do you think you will be able to apply any of this knowledge in the future when you study an invention or a fugue?
5. Have you played any pieces in any of the genres we have studied in this chapter? Do you understand them better now? How? How does this understanding affect your performance? Can it give you a better sense of direction, of phrasing, of the role of sections as long-range formal and tonal units, of the piece as an organic whole made up of related parts?
6. Can you demonstrate any of the above by performing something in class?

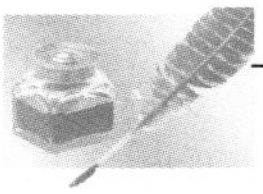

EXERCISE

For an assignment of an anlytical paper on a fugue, refer to exercise 3 in worksheet 22 at the end of this chapter.

FOR FURTHER STUDY

For additional chapter 22 materials, refer to the *Harmony in Context* Web page at www.mhhe.com/roigfrancoli2e.

ASSIGNMENT

For analytical and written assignments based on the materials learned in this chapter, refer to chapter 22 in the workbook.

Terms for Review

Thoroughbass texture
Continuo polyphony
Invention:
  Exposition, Episodes, Return, Codetta
Fugue:
  Exposition, Subject, Episodes, Middle entry, Middle entry group, Stretto, Answer, Real and tonal answers, Countersubject, Bridge, Invertible counterpoint, Double and triple counterpoint, Pedal, Counterexposition, Extra entry
Fugato
Double fugue

Worksheet 22

EXERCISE 1 Analyze Bach's Invention no. 6 in EM (the score and recording will be available at your music library). Turn in an annotated copy of the score, and answer the following questions.

1. Explain the characteristics of the exposition. How are the voices related in mm. 1–4 as compared to mm. 5–8? Provide the exact term for this type of counterpoint.

2. Measures 9–20. What is the harmonic function of this section? ________________
   What is the best term to describe its formal function? ________________________
   What thematic/harmonic techniques are used (be very specific, and circle pitches or fragments on the score as needed to illustrate what you mean).

3. Measures 21–28. Describe this section formally and tonally.

4. Measures 29–42. What is the formal function of this section within the whole piece?
   What techniques are used? ____
   What is the main key of this section? _______ What other secondary key areas are briefly touched on in mm. 33–36? ___________________________
5. What is the formal and harmonic function of the section beginning at m. 43?

6. Measures 51–60 are equivalent to a previous section in the piece. Which section (mm. nos.)? __________ How do the two sections differ tonally and texturally?

7. What is the overall form of the piece? Provide a simple bubble diagram (use the line provided below) with clear indication of sections and keys. Is there a standard term to designate this characteristic tonal and formal type?

EXERCISE 2 Analyze Bach's Fugue in B♭M, *WTC,* I, no. 21. The score and recording are available at your music library. On a copy of the score, provide a complete analysis of the fugue, indicating the usual, characteristic sections (including all appearances of the subject or answer) and contrapuntal or developmental techniques as they are found in this particular example. You may use some clear abbreviations such as S (subject), A (answer), ME (middle entry), Ep. (Episode). Be sure to mark on the score all appearances of such devices (if they are present in this fugue) as inversion, stretto, augmentation, and so on, and such techniques as fragmentation, sequence, circle of fifths, and so forth. Indicate also *all the main keys or key areas.*

Answer the following specific questions.

1. Is there a countersubject, or maybe more than one? If so, provide measure numbers and voice for its (their) first appearance.

2. Indicate two passages (provide two sets of measures) related by invertible counterpoint. Is it double or triple?

3. Is the answer real or tonal? Why is it as it is (real or tonal)?

4. Is there a bridge (provide mm. nos.)?
   What is the function of a bridge in a fugue?

5. Is there an extra entry (mm. nos.)?
6. Where does the exposition end?
7. Is there a counterexposition? What is a counterexposition?

8. Is there a stretto? What is a stretto?

9. Is there a return? Where?

10. Is there a pedal? Where?

EXERCISE 3 Write a brief analytical paper on Bach's Fugue in Gm, *WTC,* I, no. 16 (score and recording available at the library). You may use the discussion of the Cm fugue on pages 532–533 of the text as a model. The organization by sections used in that analysis is perfectly appropriate for your paper. Turn in an annotated score with clear indication of keys, tonal areas, cadences, sections, and compositional or contrapuntal techniques. Make sure you discuss (and mark on the score) the following specific points:

1. Subject.
2. Answer: tonal or real? Why?
3. Countersubject and invertible counterpoint.
4. Bridge.
5. Length of exposition.
6. Counterexposition? In what key?
7. All episodes and middle entries.
8. Stretto.
9. Return, pedal.
10. Any instances of inversion, augmentation, or diminution of the subject?

EXERCISE 4 Determine whether the answer to each of the following fugal subjects should be real or tonal. Then write the appropriate answer for each of them.

a. (Bach) **Answer:**

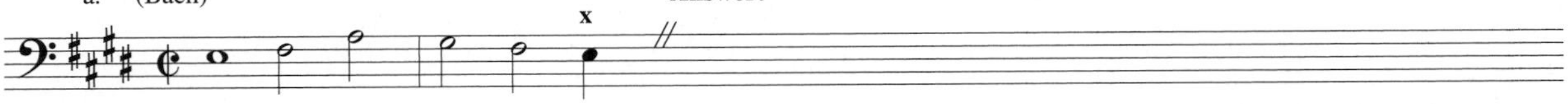

b. (Pachelbel) **Answer:**

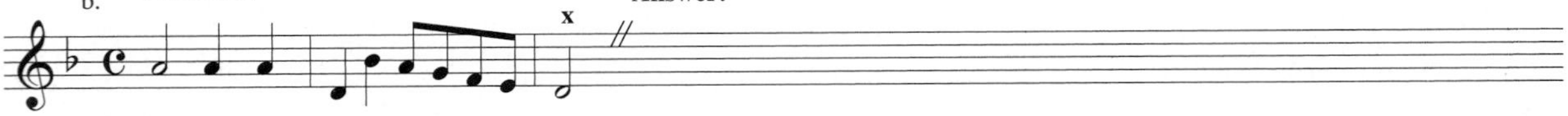

c. **Answer:**

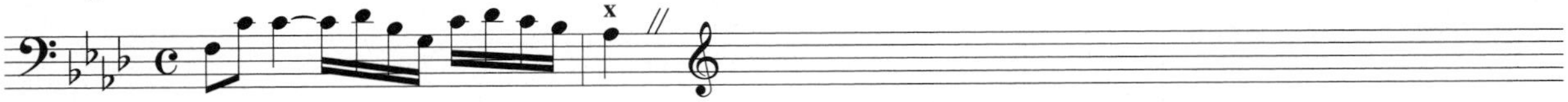

d. (Bach) **Answer:**

e. (Bach) **Answer:**

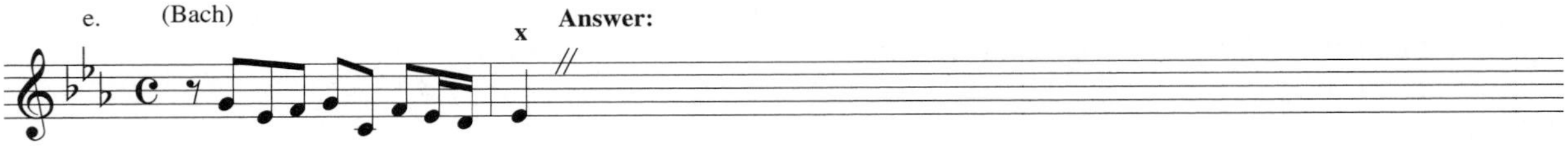

f. (Handel) **Answer:**

Chapter 23

Modal Mixture

The harmonic chromaticism we have studied so far results from tonicization or modulation. In the first part of this chapter we will study **modal mixture,** a type of chromaticism resulting from the mixture of scales and harmonies from the two different modes (major and minor) of the same key. Such mixture between the major and minor forms of the same key (that is, the parallel major/minor keys) can take the form of a change of mode for a fragment of music, or it can simply appear as a single chord from one mode used, or "borrowed," in the parallel mode. In all cases, the main scale in use, major or minor, is enriched chromatically by some pitches from the parallel scale. As a review of what these possible pitches are, look at example 23.1 for a comparison of scale degrees in each of the modes.

Although there are not so many different degrees between the modes, the chords that involve the different degrees are numerous. The main differences are the $\flat\hat{3}$, $\flat\hat{6}$, and $\flat\hat{7}$ in the minor mode. A number of chords that involve these degrees in the minor mode do not exist in the diatonic parallel major mode. There are also chords from the major mode that do not exist in minor. The term **borrowed chord** refers to a chord from one mode used in the other mode (that is, the borrowing takes place between parallel keys). As an exercise, make a list of chords from each mode that could be borrowed in the other mode. Although in principle borrowing chords from one mode into the other can go either way, *it is more common to borrow chords from the minor mode into the major mode,* and this will be the main focus of our discussion in this chapter.

Example 23.1

M:	1	2	3	4	5	6	7	1
m:	1	2	♭3	4	5	♭6 ♮6	♭7 ♮7	1

BORROWING CHORDS FROM THE MINOR MODE IN A MAJOR KEY

The triads from the (harmonic) minor mode that are foreign to major are i, ii°, III, iv, and VI. Three of these, ii°, iv, and VI, *involve the degree* $\hat{6}$. The same degree, moreover, is also present in $\text{ii}^{ø}_{7}$ and its inversions. All of these chords may be effectively borrowed in major modes, and among them the chords involving $\hat{6}$ (which in a major-mode context becomes $\flat\hat{6}$) are the most frequently borrowed. Another chord that properly belongs to the minor mode because of its inclusion of $\flat\hat{6}$, and which is often used in major keys, is vii°_{7}. Although this chord is indeed a borrowed chord when used in the major mode, we will not include it in this chapter because we already studied it in chapter 15.

iv and $\text{ii}^{ø}_{7}$ in the Major Mode

The minor subdominant ($\hat{4}$–$\flat\hat{6}$–$\hat{1}$) is used effectively in major keys as either a tonic prolongation (including plagal cadences) or as a pre-dominant chord (see the sample progressions in examples 23.2a and b). A iv prolonging a major tonic appears in example 23.3a. Notice how the simple use of $\flat\hat{6}$ instead of $\natural\hat{6}$ as an upper neighbor to $\hat{5}$ adds an element of chromatic and expressive interest to the passage. A similar plagal prolongation of I by means of iv can be observed in the plagal cadence that follows the perfect authentic cadence (PAC) in example 23.3b.

NOTE

The symbol $\text{iv}^{add\,6}$ in example 23.3b refers to an "added sixth chord," a common sonority in popular music and jazz. An added sixth chord consists of a triad plus a sixth as in our example, A♭–C♭–E♭–F. We would think of this chord in the last measure of our example as $\text{iv}^{add\,6}$ rather than ii^{6}_{5} (although the pitch content of these two chords is the same) because it is part of a clear plagal cadential gesture (I–iv–I).

Example 23.2

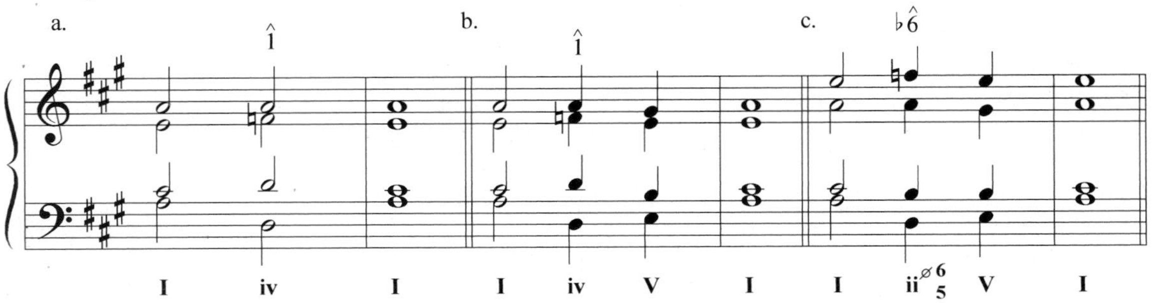

Example 23.3a Felix Mendelssohn, *Song without Words,* op. 102, no. 2, mm. 24–27

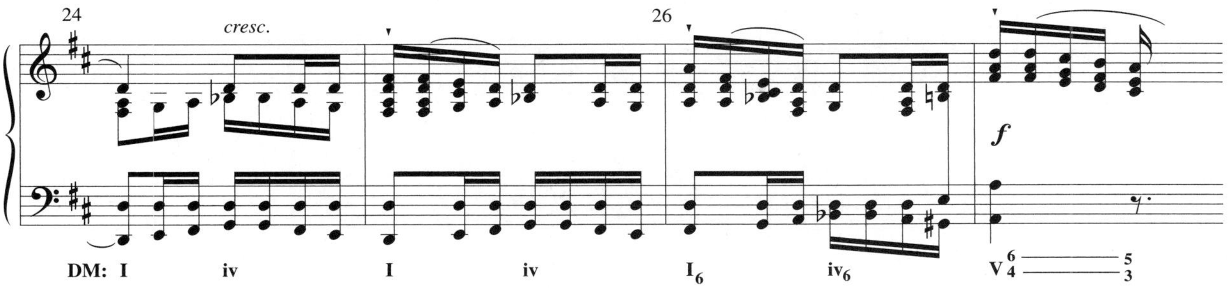

Example 23.3b D. Ellington, "I Let a Song Go Out of My Heart" (final cadence)

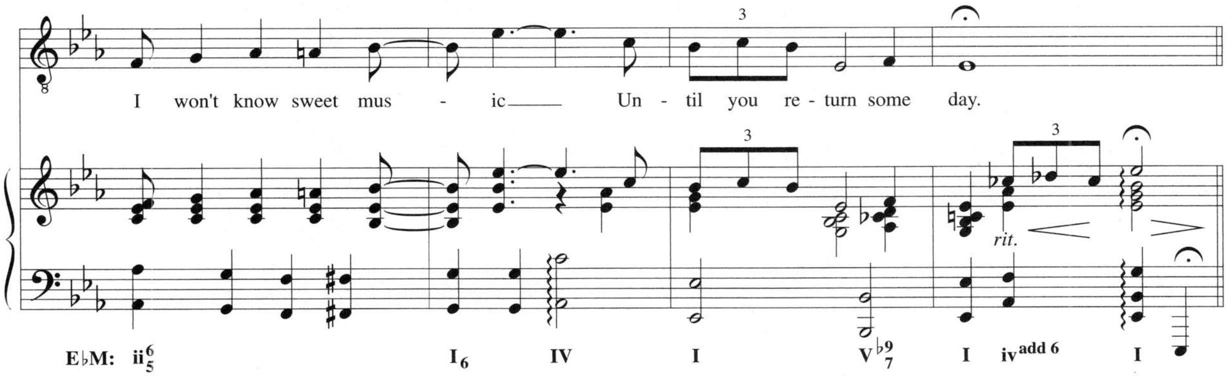

The minor-mode supertonic seventh chord, $\text{ii}^{\varnothing}_{7}$, is used as a pre-dominant chord in the major mode even more often than iv (see example 23.2c). In example 23.4, Bach approaches the cadential dominant in FM by means of a $\text{ii}^{\varnothing 6}_{5}$, the most frequent form of this chord. Notice that, here also, $\flat\hat{6}$ appears as an upper neighbor to $\hat{5}$. Other inversions of $\text{ii}^{\varnothing}_{7}$, however, are also found in the literature. In mm. 26–27 of example 23.5 we hear two occurrences of $\text{ii}^{\varnothing 4}_{3}$. Although in m. 27 it precedes a dominant that moves on to the tonic, both $\text{ii}^{\varnothing 4}_{3}$ chords in mm. 26 and 27 also have a linear function (see both the neighbor motion in the bass and the passing motion in the soprano). Examine also the rest of the example. Does it feature any tonicization?

In example 23.6, Beethoven takes advantage of the chromatic possibilities afforded by $\flat\hat{6}$ and $\natural\hat{6}$ by using both degrees in an interesting melodic interplay. The passage is in B♭M.

Example 23.4 J. S. Bach, Chorale 6, "Christus, der ist mein Leben," mm. 7–8

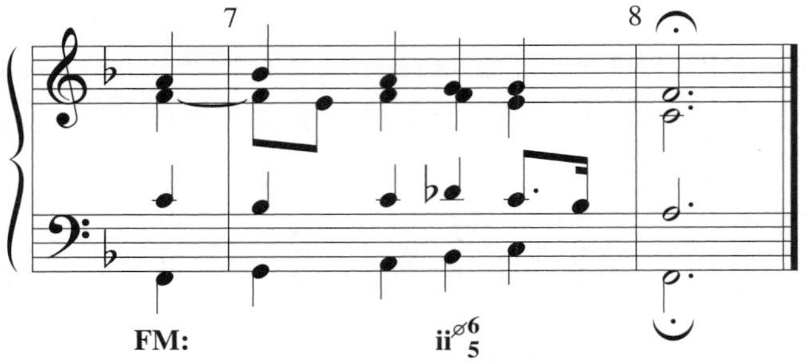

Example 23.5 Fanny Mendelssohn Hensel, "Du bist die Ruh," from *Six Songs,* op. 7, no. 4, mm. 26–32

Example 23.6 L. v. Beethoven, Piano Sonata in E♭M, op. 81a, I, mm. 35–42

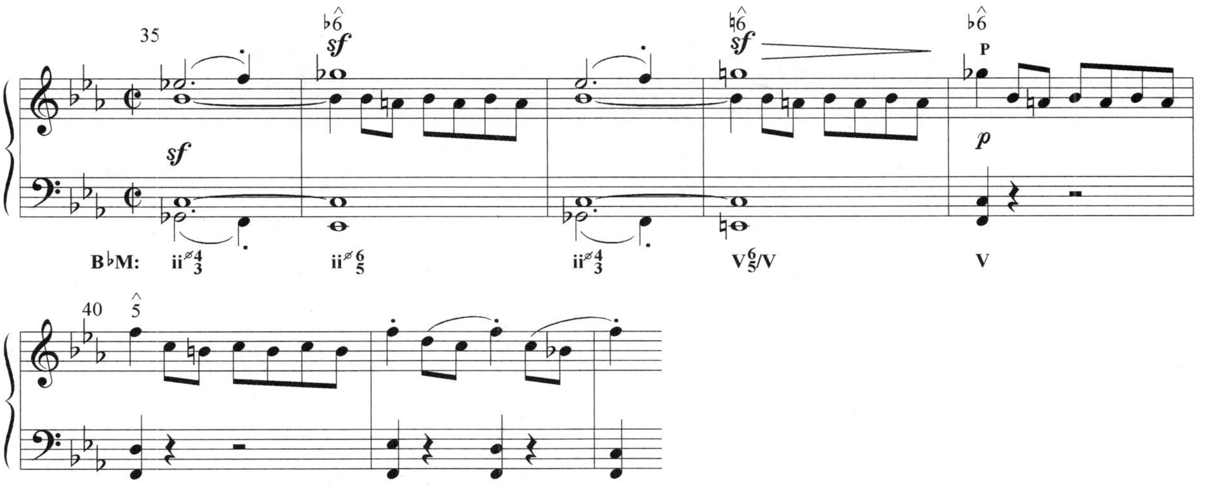

Mm. 35–36 feature two inversions of the ii$^{ø}_{7}$ chord, connected by a passing tone (note the voice exchange between outer voices in these measures). The melodic arrival on $\flat\hat{6}$ in m. 36 turns into an arrival on $\natural\hat{6}$ in m. 38, here harmonized with a V^6_5/V. The $\flat\hat{6}$ in m. 39, on the other hand, functions as a passing tone between $\natural\hat{6}$ (m. 38) and $\hat{5}$ (m. 40), over V.

♭VI and ♭III in the Major Mode

The notation "♭VI" and "♭III," that is, a Roman numeral preceded by a ♭ sign, refers to chords built on lowered scale degrees. Thus, the ♭ sign before the Roman numeral affects the root of the chord: ♭VI is a major chord built on $\flat\hat{6}$, and ♭III is a major chord built on $\flat\hat{3}$ (notice that the same two chords in the minor mode are diatonic, and hence labeled as VI and III).

♭VI is a beautiful chromatic chord, used with a variety of functions, all similar to the functions of the diatonic submediant, vi (see examples 23.7a to c). ♭VI includes two chromatic degrees, $\flat\hat{6}$ as the root, and $\flat\hat{3}$ as the fifth. Because of the strong half-step pull of $\flat\hat{6}$ toward $\hat{5}$, ♭VI can effectively function as a *pre-dominant chord.* This is exactly how it is used by Haydn in example 23.8.

On the other hand, V may also resolve to ♭VI in a striking, chromatic *deceptive progression.* In example 23.9, the dominant of EM in m. 102 resolves deceptively to a CM chord, a ♭VI in EM. Observe, however, that this ♭VI is then tonicized, creating a brief ♭VI secondary key area (mm. 103–105). The resolution of $\flat\hat{6}$ in the bass to $\hat{5}$ in mm. 106–107 takes us back to V in EM. (Notice the strong linear pull toward $\hat{5}$ created by the double half-step resolution of C *down* to B♮ and A♯ *up* to B♮; we will study the chord that results from this voice leading, an augmented sixth chord, in the next chapter.) The end of the passage is built on a pedal on $\hat{5}$. What chords does Beethoven write on this pedal?

Example 23.7

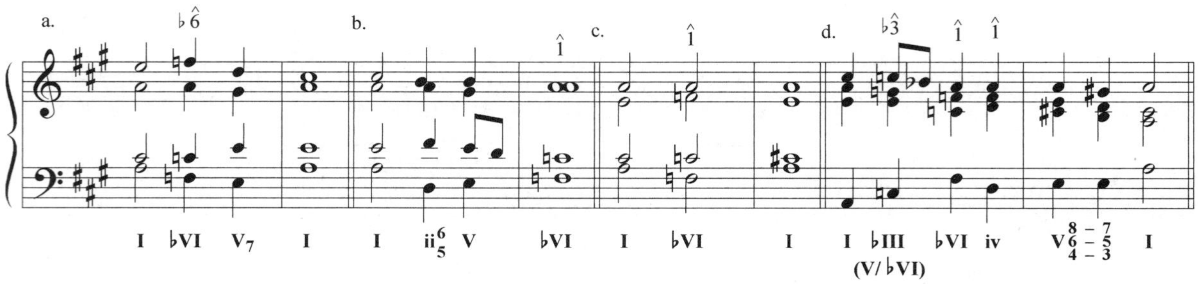

Example 23.8 J. Haydn, Symphony no. 101 in DM, IV, mm. 13–16

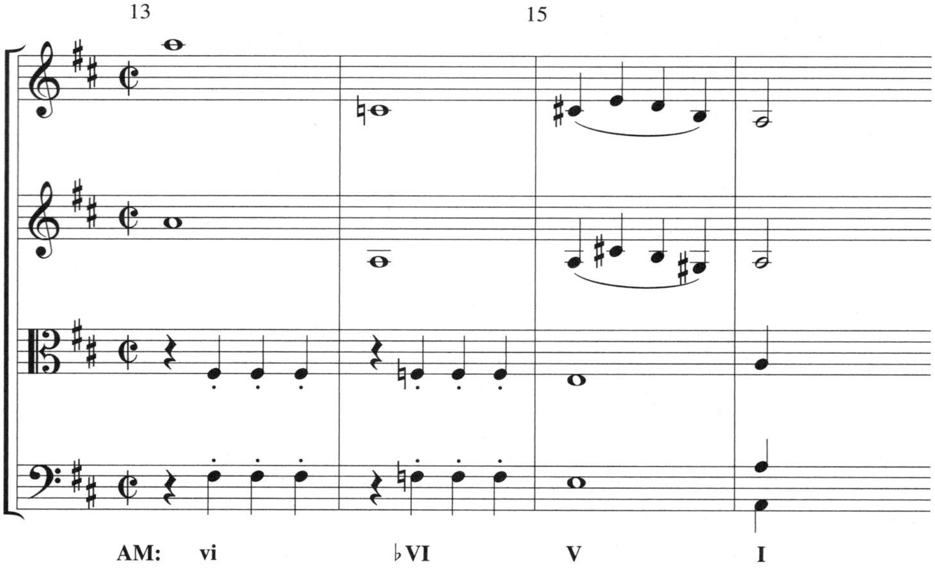

Typical Errors to Avoid

- Writing parallel 5ths and or 8ves in the ♭VI–V progression. The ♭VI–V_7 progression is easier to write from this point of view.
- Writing parallel 5ths in the V–♭VI deceptive progression. The standard voice-leading rules for the V–vi progression also apply to the "borrowed" deceptive progression.

Example 23.9 L. v. Beethoven, Piano Sonata in EM, op. 14, no. 1, I, mm. 101–109

♭VI may also function as a chord prolonging, or embellishing, the major tonic. Example 23.10 shows an instance of such a chromatic, prolonging progression, I–♭VI–I. The cadence also involves another borrowed chord. What is the chord, and what kind of cadence is this?

♭III is a relatively unusual chord. When it appears in the literature, it is often paired with ♭VI, and, in fact, it is often used as the secondary dominant of ♭VI (example 23.7d). In Modest Mussorgsky's phrase reproduced in example 23.11a, in E♭M, ♭III is indeed coupled with ♭VI in the progression ♭VI–♭III (or ♭VI–V/♭VI, although the secondary dominant progression never continues to its possible resolution, ♭VI). These chords here function as a surprising chromatic extension of the E♭M tonic triad that is prolonged in this passage. In example 23.11b, on the other hand, ♭III appears, in the context of a plagal cadential gesture, as part of a passing motion from IV to I (IV–♭III–P^6_4–I).

Example 23.10 J. Brahms, Symphony no. 3, II, cadence (mm. 128–134)

Example 23.11a Modest Mussorgsky, "The Great Gate of Kiev," from *Pictures at an Exhibition,* mm. 156–162

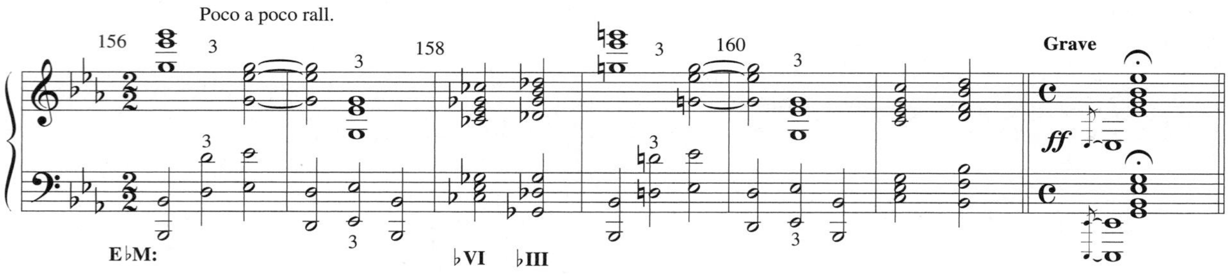

Example 23.11b George Harrison, "Something," from the album *Abbey Road* (The Beatles)

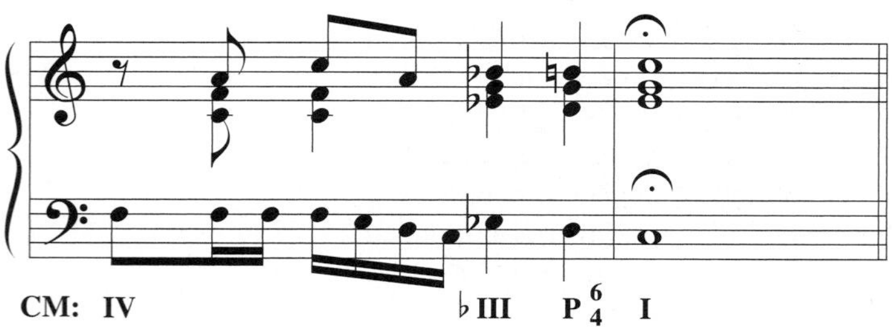

EXERCISE

To practice spelling borrowed chords, refer to exercise 2 in worksheet 23 at the end of this chapter.

To practice realizing progressions including modal mixture, refer to exercise 3 in worksheet 23 at the end of this chapter.

To practice harmonizing a melody including modal mixture, refer to exercise 4 in worksheet 23 at the end of this chapter.

BORROWING CHORDS FROM THE MAJOR MODE IN A MINOR KEY

Theoretically, the triads from major that are foreign to minor are I, ii, iii, IV, and vi (V and vii° are the same in both modes if we use the harmonic minor scale). Borrowing chords from the major mode in a minor key is less frequent than the other way around (borrowing from the minor mode in a major key). The only chords from major that are found in minor keys with some frequency are I, the major tonic chord, most often used in the context of a final tonic with Picardy third, and IV, used to harmonize $\sharp\hat{6}$ in the melodic-minor ascending segment $\hat{5}$–$\sharp\hat{6}$–$\sharp\hat{7}$–$\hat{1}$. Because we have already studied both of these cases (review examples 3.5g and h, and example 9.4e), we need not discuss them all over again, other than commenting on the short illustration that appears in example 23.12. The passage begins in FM and modulates to Am. The actual move toward Am is effected by the bass line in m. 10, with a strong $\hat{5}$–$\sharp\hat{6}$–$\sharp\hat{7}$–$\hat{1}$ melodic figure, where $\sharp\hat{6}$–$\sharp\hat{7}$–1 is harmonized with the progression IV_6–V^6_5–i. Does the passage actually end on an Am chord? Which of these chords are borrowed from the major mode? Now go back

Example 23.12 J. S. Bach, Chorale 96, "Jesu, meine Freude," mm. 9–11

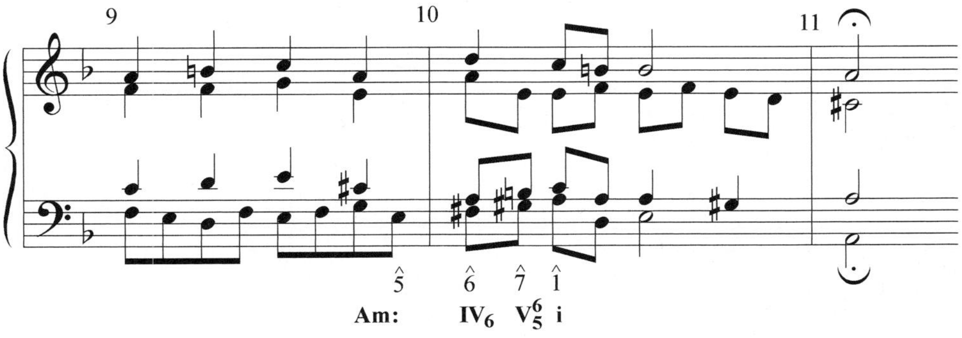

to m. 9. Are there any tonicizations in the short span leading from FM to Am? Bach truly could pack a lot of interesting harmony into only a couple of measures!

CHANGE OF MODE

Changes of mode from major to minor or from minor to major of the same key are frequently found in music. In purely instrumental music, modal change is normally used for tonal contrast and to introduce a factor of chromatic variety. Thus, a phrase that is first presented in a mode may be restated in the opposite mode rather than repeated in the same mode. Notice the element of surprise produced by the second phrase of Antonín Dvořák's period reproduced in example 23.13. The sense of forward motion that we feel because of the sudden change to GM could not have been matched by the simple repetition of the phrase in Gm.

In texted vocal music, modal change often has an expressive purpose, reflecting musically some aspect of the text, while also providing a factor of tonal variety. Listen to the fragment in example 23.14. The initial key is Am, while the mill worker explains how much more he could do if he had a thousand arms. (How is the constant turning of the millstone represented by the music?) Then, in mm. 16–19, we find out why he

Example 23.13 Antonín Dvořák, Slavonic Dance in Gm, op. 46, no. 8, mm. 1–8

Example 23.14 F. Schubert, "Am Feierabend," from *Die schöne Müllerin,* mm. 8–19

wishes he could perform such feats at the mill: to impress "die schöne Müllerin," the lovely millermaid. At the mention of the millermaid, the heart of the miller boy brightens up, and so does the music. How? As an unrelated question, can you explain the chromaticism in mm. 11–15?

CHARACTERISTIC SOPRANO-BASS PATTERNS AND ELABORATIONS OF THE I–V–I PROGRESSION

The most characteristic melodic degree that can be harmonized with iv, $\text{ii}^{\varnothing}_{7}$, $\text{ii}^{\varnothing 6}_{5}$, or $\flat$VI is $\flat\hat{6}$. Both iv and $\text{ii}^{\varnothing}_{7}$ work well to harmonize $\hat{1}$ and $\hat{4}$, and $\text{ii}^{\varnothing 6}_{5}$ can also harmonize $\hat{2}$. Besides $\flat\hat{6}$, $\flat$VI can also be used to harmonize $\hat{1}$ or $\flat\hat{3}$. Examples of progressions illustrating harmonizations of each or these degrees are shown in example 23.15, in the context of characteristic soprano-bass patterns using modal mixture.

Because the borrowed chords we have studied function either as extensions of the tonic (for instance, in the I–iv–I or I–$\flat$VI–I progressions) or as pre-dominants (as in I–iv–V–I or I–$\text{ii}^{\varnothing 6}_{5}$–V–I), their role in elaborating the I–V–I progression is the same as the role of the familiar diatonic (that is, not borrowed) versions of the same chords. For instance, the progression I–iv–V–I elaborates the I–V–I progression in the same way as the I–IV–V–I progression; I–$\text{ii}^{\varnothing 6}_{5}$–V–I is equivalent to I–$\text{ii}^{6}_{5}$–V–I; and I–$\flat$VI–iv–V–I functions as I–vi–IV–V–I does. These progressions with borrowed chords are chromatic versions of familiar diatonic progressions that elaborate the I–V–I progression.

Example 23.15

PRACTICAL APPLICATION AND DISCUSSION

For a summary of most of the borrowed chords we have just discussed, refer now to anthology, no. 53 (Verdi, *Il trovatore,* act 2, no 11). In the first place, what is the progression in mm. 5–6? Now examine the progression in mm. 7–8. In m. 7 we see an example of ♭III functioning as the dominant of ♭VI, in the progression V/♭VI–♭VI. The latter chord acts here as a pre-dominant, and the dominant prolongation in m. 8 seems to lead to a tonic in m. 9. Instead, the cadence is interrupted (or delayed) in m. 9 by a IV$^6_4$ which begins a new cadential process. What other pre-dominant chords are present in mm. 9–10? Which one is tonicized? Which one is a borrowed chord? Notice that this second cadential process finally finds resolution in m. 11.

EXERCISE

To practice analysis of musical fragments including modal mixture, refer to exercise 1 in worksheet 23 at the end of this chapter.

ASSIGNMENT AND KEYBOARD EXERCISES

For analytical and written assignments and keyboard exercises based on the materials learned in this chapter, refer to chapter 23 in the workbook.

PITCH PATTERNS

Sing the pitch patterns in example 23.16, and as you sing listen to the borrowed chord used in them. Then improvise similar pitch patterns using a variety of borrowed chords.

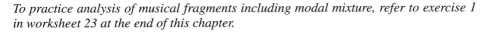

Example 23.16

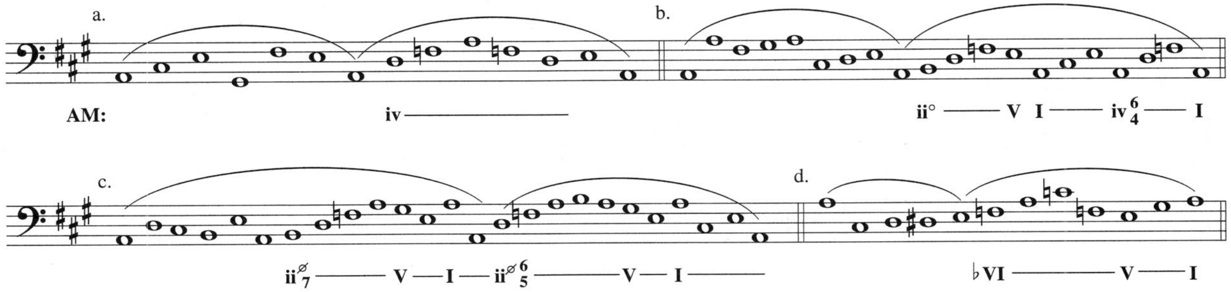

Terms for Review

Modal mixture
Borrowed chords
Borrowing from m into M
iv and $ii^{\varnothing}_7$ in the major mode
♭VI and ♭III in the major mode
Borrowing from M into m
Change of mode

Worksheet 23

EXERCISE 1 Analysis.

1. Analyze and explain the type of modal mixture in the following examples. If borrowed chords are involved, be specific as to what they are.

   a) Example 23.17.

Example 23.17 F. Schubert, *Wanderers Nachtlied,* op. 96, no. 3, mm. 4–6

   b) Example 23.18. In this example, some chromaticism results from tonicization, and some from borrowing. Explain all of it. Explain also the modulation.

   c) Anthology, no. 59, Beach, *Ecstasy,* mm. 27–31.

   d) Example 23.19.

Example 23.18 F. Chopin, Mazurka in GM, op. 67, no. 1, mm. 38–49

Example 23.19 J. S. Bach, Chorale 96, "Jesu, meine Freude," mm. 1–6

e) Example 23.20.

Example 23.20 W. A. Mozart, Piano Sonata in B♭M, K. 333, I, mm. 86–95

f) Anthology, no. 48, Schumann, "Widmung," mm. 3–6 and 10–13.

g) Anthology, no. 31, Paradis, *Sicilienne,* mm. 1–6.

EXERCISE 2 Spell the following borrowed chords in four voices in the given keys.

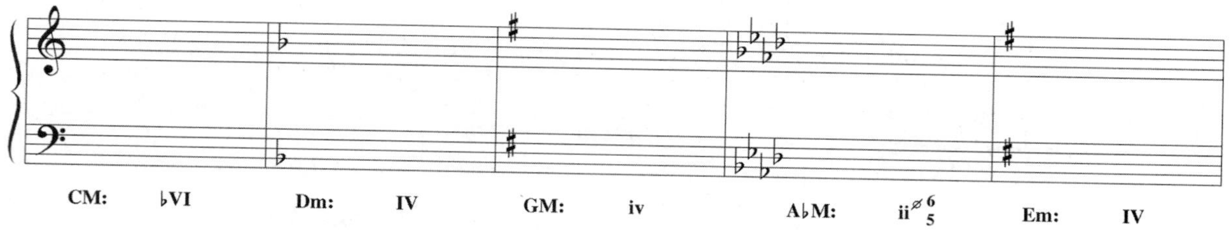

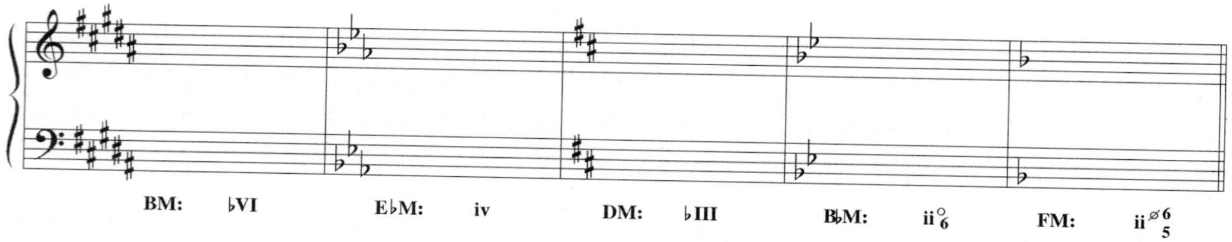

EXERCISE 3 Realize the following short progressions in four voices.

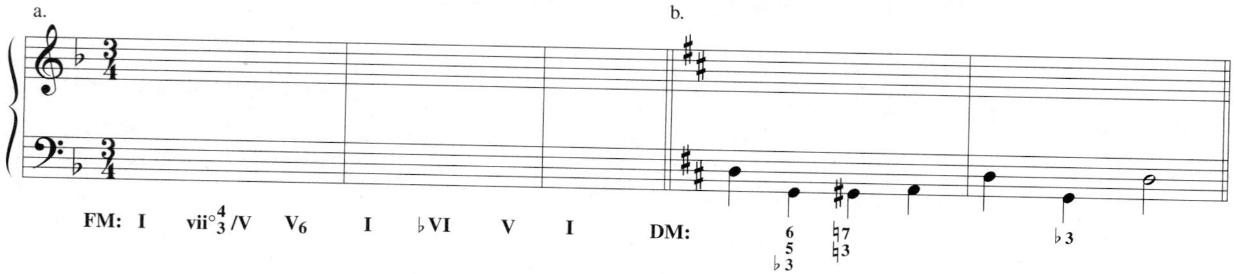

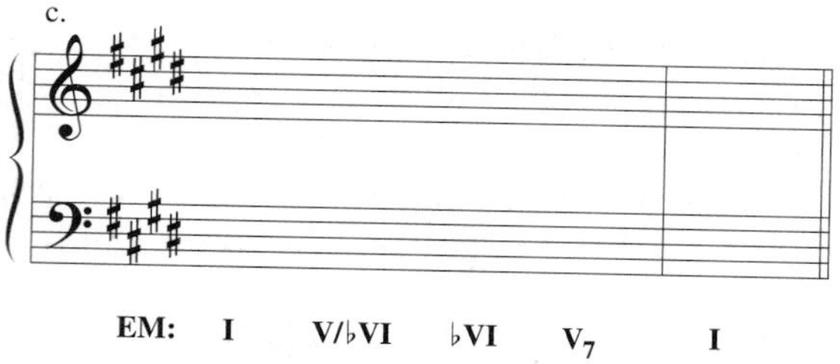

EXERCISE 4 Realize the following progressions in four-voice keyboard texture. Provide a RN analysis.

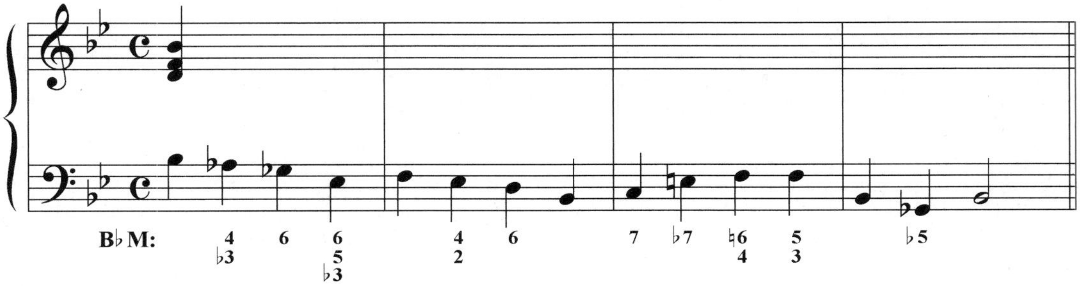

EXERCISE 5 Harmonize the following melody with a left-hand keyboard figuration, using borrowed chords where possible. Be sure to check your first-species outer-voice frame for correct voice leading.

EXERCISE 6 Write your own progressions (bass and RNs) in the keys and meters indicated below. Use the required chords, and any of the other chords we have already studied.

a) DM; include iv and a deceptive cadence to ♭VI.

b) E♭M; include $ii^{ø6}_{5}$, ♭III, and ♭VI.

a.

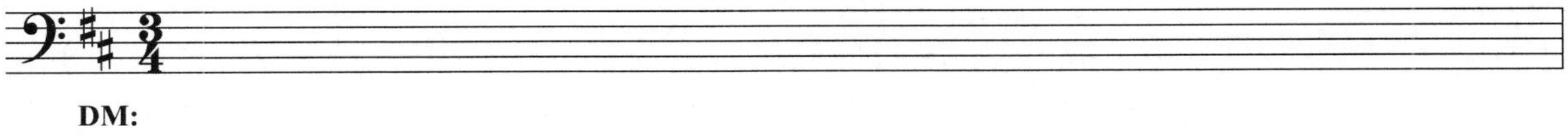

b.

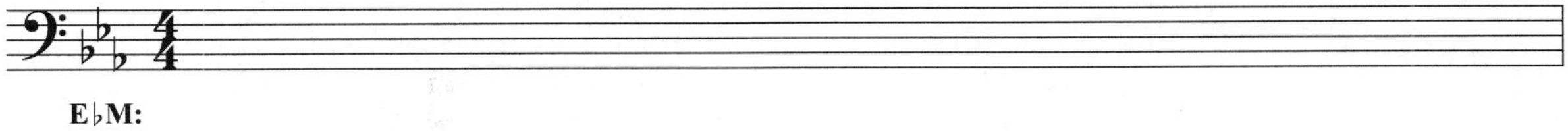

Chapter 24

The Neapolitan Chord

In chapters 24 and 25 we will study two types of chromatic chords that have a special expressive and dramatic power: the Neapolitan chord (♭II) and the augmented-sixth chords. Both types are based on the strong voice-leading tendency created by half-step relationships above and below such fundamental scale degrees as $\hat{1}$ and $\hat{5}$. Both appear in a variety of harmonic contexts, although their most common function is as pre-dominant chords.

THE NEAPOLITAN SIXTH

Study the passage by Paradis in example 24.1. The bass figure in the cadence is the familiar $\hat{4}$–$\hat{5}$–$\hat{1}$. The first chord in m. 9, however, on the bass $\hat{4}$, is not so familiar: It is an FM triad in the key of Em, that is, *a major triad on* ♭$\hat{2}$, here presented in first inversion. Because it was used widely (although not "invented") by seventeenth-century opera composers in the Italian city of Naples, it came to be known as the **Neapolitan chord.** More specifically, the chord appears most frequently in first inversion, with a pre-dominant function, as in example 24.1. Hence its usual name of **Neapolitan sixth,** and its frequent label, N_6. To avoid confusion with the N we have used to label "neighbor chords"; however, we will use the Roman numeral ♭II (♭II_6 in first inversion) to label the Neapolitan chord.

In the Paradis fragment we can observe some of the characteristics of this chord, which we can summarize as follows:

1. Because the Neapolitan chord contains scale degrees ♭$\hat{2}$–$\hat{4}$–♭$\hat{6}$ (♭$\hat{2}$–$\hat{4}$–$\hat{6}$ in minor), it is chromatic in both major and minor modes (technically, these degrees are diatonic in a Phrygian scale, and for this reason this chord is sometimes called the *Phrygian II*). Because of the presence of the minor-mode 6th degree, however, it belongs more properly to (and is more common in) the minor mode. It may certainly also be used in major, in which case it is a borrowed chord (example 24.2b).
2. The chord is most often used in first inversion, with a *pre-dominant function.* Compare the ♭II_6–V–i progression in example 24.2a with its very close relatives,

Example 24.1 Maria Theresia von Paradis, *Sicilienne,* mm. 7–10

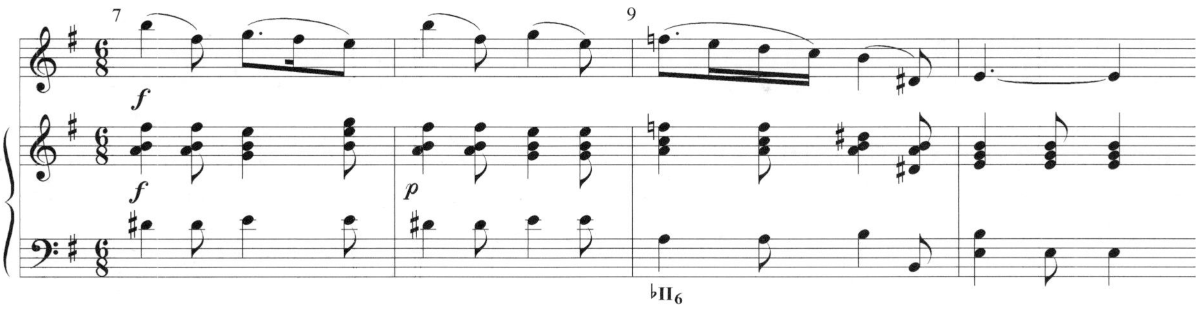

iv–V–i and ii°$_6$–V–i. Notice that all three progressions feature the bass motion $\hat{4}$–$\hat{5}$ supporting the pre-dominant/dominant harmonies. In four voices, it is best to *double the bass of* ♭*II*$_6$ (the third of the chord, $\hat{4}$).

3. ♭II$_6$ is most effective when its characteristic degree, ♭$\hat{2}$, is in the upper voice. *The normative voice leading for* ♭$\hat{2}$ *is to descend to* $\hat{7}$ (through the melodic interval of a diminished 3rd), which then resolves to $\hat{1}$. The melodic figure ♭$\hat{2}$–$\hat{7}$–$\hat{1}$ creates a most dramatic tension towards the resolution, $\hat{1}$, by means of the upper leading tone, ♭$\hat{2}$, and the lower leading tone, $\hat{7}$. This half-step voice leading toward $\hat{1}$ from both above and below is the characteristic trademark of this chord. In example 24.1, you can see the normative ♭$\hat{2}$–$\hat{7}$ in the piano's upper voice. Before resolving to $\hat{1}$, a change of voicing within the V$_7$ chord results in a move of $\hat{7}$ to an inner voice.
4. The V chord after a ♭II$_6$ may be ornamented, as is usual at cadences, with a cadential $^6_4$. The progression then becomes ♭II$_6$–V$^{6-5}_{4-3}$–I, as in example 24.2c. Notice that the $^6_4$ chord provides a passing step between ♭$\hat{2}$ and $\hat{7}$. The line now becomes ♭$\hat{2}$–$\hat{1}$–$\hat{7}$–$\hat{1}$.

NOTE

Beware that if ♭$\hat{2}$ *is in an inner voice, the* $^6_4$ *chord may very easily produce parallel 5ths, as illustrated by example 24.2e. With* ♭$\hat{2}$ *in the upper voice, the 5ths become correct parallel 4ths.*

Study the progressions in example 24.2 for instances of the voice leading we have just explained. As shown in this example, the most common outer-voice framework for the Neapolitan progression includes the double-neighbor motion ♭$\hat{2}$–$\hat{7}$–$\hat{1}$ (or ♭$\hat{2}$–$\hat{1}$–$\hat{7}$–$\hat{1}$ if a cadential $^6_4$ is used) over a $\hat{4}$–$\hat{5}$–$\hat{1}$ bass. Because the Neapolitan sixth functions most often as a pre-dominant chord, it has a clear role of elaborating the I–V–I progression, as shown in example 24.2. You may also see a "textbook" treatment of ♭II$_6$ in Beethoven's fragment reproduced in example 24.3.

Example 24.2

Typical Errors to Avoid

1. Resolving ♭$\hat{2}$ to ♮$\hat{2}$ instead of $\hat{7}$. Besides this being an unusual resolution, it also will easily produce parallel 8ves and a faulty +2 voice leading in the major mode (see example 24.2e).
2. Writing parallel 5ths if ♭$\hat{2}$ is in an inner voice and the resolution of ♭II_6 to V is done through a cadential $^6_4$ (see example 24.2e).

EXERCISE

To practice spelling Neapolitan sixth chords, refer to exercise 2 in worksheet 24 at the end of this chapter.

Example 24.3 L. v. Beethoven, Piano Sonata in C♯m, op. 27, no. 2, *Moonlight,* I, mm. 49–51

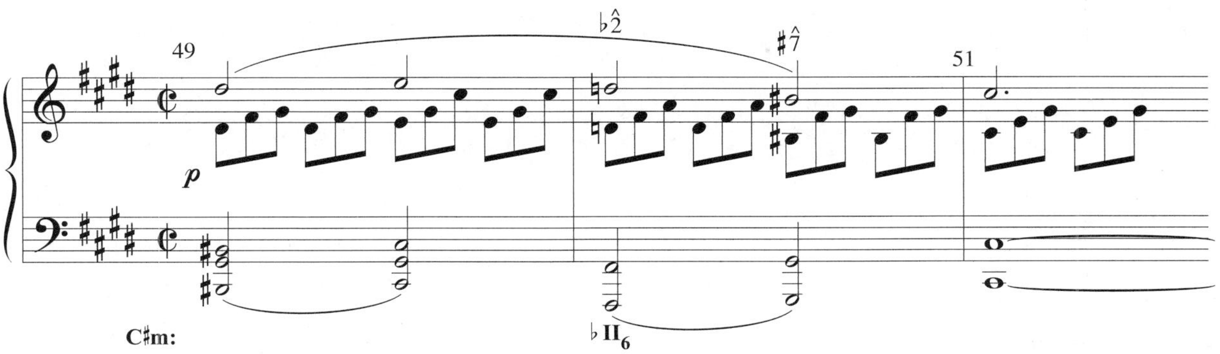

Other Harmonic Contexts for ♭II_6

Example 24.2d illustrates a frequent progression with ♭II_6, in which *vii°$_7$/V is inserted between the Neapolitan and its resolution to V.* This progression, as well as the possible cadential $^6_4$ elaboration of V, does not affect the basic voice-leading principles we discussed, as you can verify in example 24.2d. In these progressions, the vii°$_7$/V functions as a linear passing chord between the pre-dominant ♭II_6 chord and V.

Now study the phrase in example 24.4. You will see in it a standard use of ♭II_6, with a passing vii°$_7$/V leading towards the cadential V. This dominant, however, is elaborated by a cadential $^6_4$, which is itself further elaborated or prolonged contrapuntally (m. 172). Discuss this interesting cadential gesture and how it works linearly.

♭II_6 may also appear in the context of a succession of parallel $^6_3$ chords. Analyze anthology, no. 24 (Mozart, Sonata in DM, III, Variation 7), mm. 9–12, in Dm. First, notice the nice textural exchange between voices in mm. 9–10, and the compound melody which makes up one of the lines. Then, analyze the passage with Roman numerals (RNs). In m. 10 you will identify a short sequential fragment, made up of parallel $^6_3$ chords. Is there a ♭II_6 in the sequence?

Because in the major mode ♭II_6 is a borrowed chord, it sometimes appears along with other borrowed chords, usually for expressive purposes. The complete text for the passage of the song by Lang reproduced in Example 24.5 is: "It is a wondrous feeling that forever cripples the heart, When we experience our first disappointment—A feeling that we never get over." Our example begins with the words "the heart," in the key of CM. Beginning in m. 63, to the word "disappointment," and continuing from there ("a feeling that we never get over"), the mode of the music changes to minor.

Example 24.4 W. A. Mozart, Fantasia in Cm, K. 475, mm. 170–173

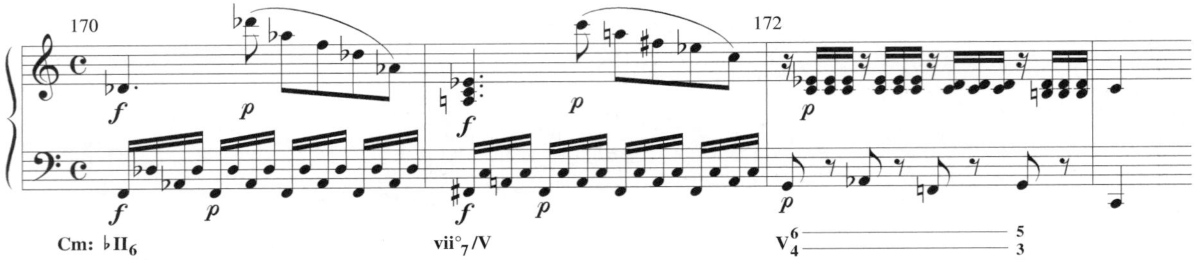

Example 24.5 J. Lang, "Ich gab dem Schicksal dich zurück," m. 59–68

The $\flat II_6$ in m. 66 is preceded by a prominent chord which, in the major-mode key of the complete passage, appears as a borrowed $\flat VI$. Both the change of mode and the Neapolitan help express the feeling of the heart crippled by disappointment. Examine the chords that follow $\flat II_6$. What chords are interpolated between the latter and its resolution to V?

EXERCISE

To practice realizing short progressions including Neapolitan chords, refer to exercise 3 in worksheet 24 at the end of this chapter.

TONICIZATION OF THE NEAPOLITAN

The Neapolitan chord, like any other consonant triad, may be tonicized. The dominant of the Neapolitan is, precisely, $\flat VI$ in major (or VI in minor). Because the resolution of this secondary dominant will usually be to a triad in first inversion ($\flat II_6$), the dominant appears often in $^4_2$ position. In example 24.6, in Gm, we hear $\flat II_6$ in m. 11, but before it moves to V in Gm, in m. 12 we hear its own dominant in third inversion, $V^4_2/\flat II$, followed again by $\flat II_6$. The Neapolitan is thus tonicized in m. 12. What are the remaining chords after m. 12? Here again, this passage with several $\flat II_6$ chords provides a musical setting to words of sadness and longing: "the sun moves in its course, like yours, my sorrows, deep in the heart, always to rise tomorrow." We see again how $\flat II_6$ is a chord suitable to add intensity to minor-mode expressivity.

THE NEAPOLITAN IN ROOT POSITION

Although the Neapolitan appears most frequently in first inversion, instances of the $\flat II$ chord in root position are also abundant in the literature. *Erlkönig* (anthology, no. 38) is one of Schubert's most famous songs, and perhaps his most touching one. It tells the story of a father riding late at night, holding his child in his arm. Throughout the ride, and the song, the somber king of the elves, the Erlking, is trying to take the boy with him, by lure or by force, to the realm of the spirits. After a long, tense ride in which the poor, scared boy keeps warning his father about the danger, the song ends climactically with the following words: "[The father] reaches home with effort and toil: In his arms the child lay dead!"

Musically, these measures (138–148) are among the most moving in the literature. What chord does Schubert choose to harmonize the arrival to the house, and the subsequent realization that the boy is dead (in mm. 143–146; the key is Gm)? In what position is the chord presented in mm. 143 and 145? What is the intervening chord in m. 144, and what is its function? Does the chord in m. 145 switch to a familiar position? How does it resolve? How does Schubert depict the horse's gallop, and what happens to this depiction after the rider arrives home? How does the texture express the extremely dramatic moment of the last sentence, when the child is found dead? (We will study this complete song in more detail in chapter 30.)

Example 24.6 F. Schubert, "An Mignon," op. 19, no. 2, mm. 9–16

TRITONE SUBSTITUTION: THE NEAPOLITAN AS A SUBSTITUTE FOR V_7

In jazz and popular music, the Neapolitan most often functions as a dominant substitute rather than a pre-dominant. This is indeed the case in example 24.7, where the final tonic chord ($I^{add\,6}$) is preceded by a Neapolitan (in this case a $\flat II^{\flat 9}_{7}$ which substitutes for a dominant seventh chord.

Notice that $\flat II_7$ (in CM, D♭–F–A♭–C♭) and V_7 (G–B–D–F) have two common tones (B/C♭ and F), whereas $\flat II^{\flat 9}_{7}$ (D♭–F–A♭–C♭–E♭♭) and V_7 have three common tones (B/C♭, D/E♭♭, and F). Because the roots of V_7 (G) and $\flat II_7$ or $\flat II^{\flat 9}_{7}$ (D♭) are a tritone apart, this type of substitution (in which we replace a chord with another chord whose root is a tritone away from the root of the chord being replaced) is known as **tritone substitution.**

EXERCISES

To practice realizing progressions including Neapolitan chords, refer to exercise 4 in worksheet 24 at the end of this chapter.

To practice harmonizing a melody including Neapolitan chords, refer to exercise 5 in worksheet 24 at the end of this chapter.

To practice analyzing musical fragments including Neapolitan chords, refer to exercise 1 in worksheet 24 at the end of this chapter.

Example 24.7 D. Ellington-J. Mercer-B. Strayhorn, "Satin Doll" (final cadence)

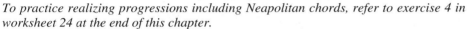

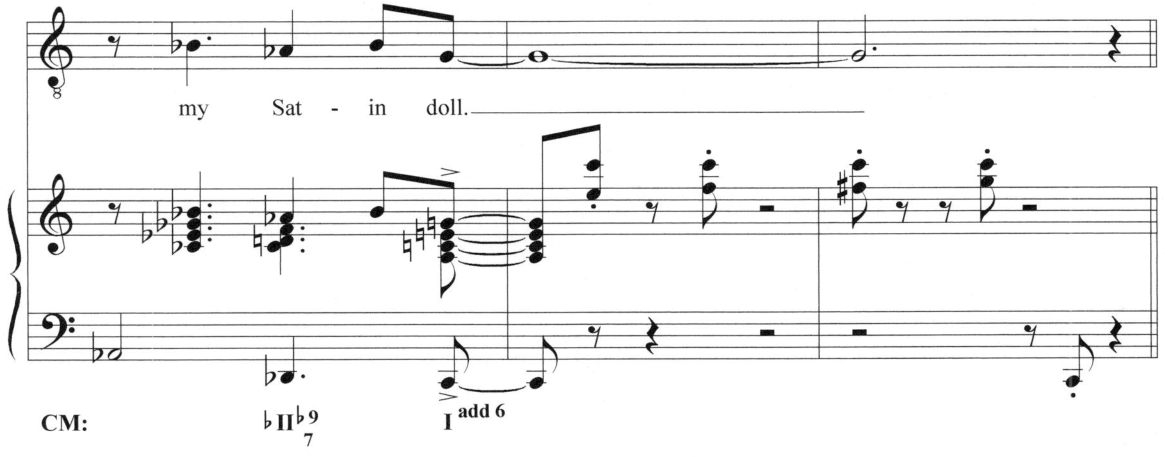

PRACTICAL APPLICATION AND DISCUSSION

A final example in this chapter on the Neapolitan will summarize a lot of what we have discussed. The passage in example 24.8 is in Dm. How is the Neapolitan used in m. 17? What chord does it move to? What is the progression in mm. 20–21? You will hear that mm. 20–22 create a strong directed forward motion toward the final resolution to the tonic in m. 23. Explain what the role of the half step is in creating such a powerful linear pull throughout these measures.

Example 24.8 W. A. Mozart, *Don Giovanni,* Overture, mm. 17–23

ASSIGNMENT AND KEYBOARD EXERCISES

For analytical and written assignments and keyboard exercises based on the materials learned in this chapter, refer to chapter 24 in the workbook.

PITCH PATTERNS

Sing the pitch patterns in example 24.9, and as you sing listen to the Neapolitan chord and its resolution. Then *improvise* similar pitch patterns using $\flat II_6$.

Example 24.9

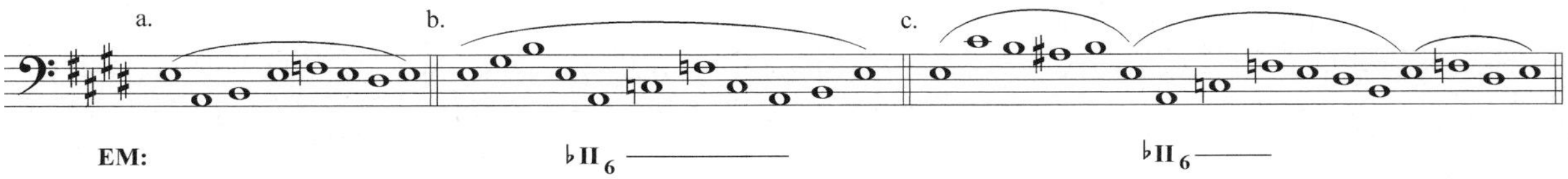

Terms for Review

Neapolitan chord
Neapolitan sixth ($\flat II_6$)
Tonicization of the $\flat$II chord
Tritone substitution

Worksheet 24

EXERCISE 1 Analysis. Identify the Neapolitan chords in each of the following examples:

1. Verify and mark the voice leading of the voice with ♭$\hat{2}$. Is the ♭II chord in first inversion or root position?
2. Provide RNs for the actual ♭II and also for the chords that precede and follow it.
3. What chord precedes ♭II? Is the ♭II chord tonicized?
4. Does ♭II resolve directly to V? Does it resolve to V through some other harmonies?

Examples for Analysis:

1. Example 24.10

Example 24.10 F. Chopin, Waltz in Am, op. 34, no. 2, mm. 145–152

2. Anthology, no. 35, Beethoven, *Waldstein* Sonata, mm. 132–136

3. Example 24.11

Example 24.11 F. Chopin, Prelude in Cm, op. 28, no. 20, mm. 11–13

4. Example 24.12

Example 24.12 F. Schubert, Symphony no. 9 in Cm, II, mm. 255–259

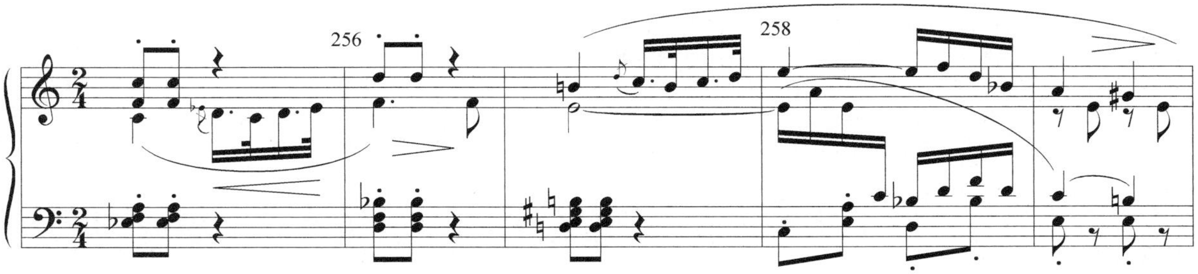

EXERCISE 2 Spell the following ♭II$_6$ chords in four voices, in the required keys.

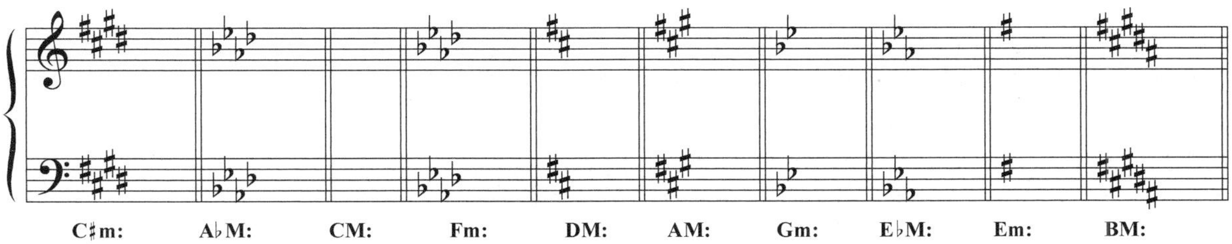

EXERCISE 3 Realize the following short progressions in four voices. Add RNs to the progressions with a figured bass. Be careful with your spelling and resolution of the Neapolitan chords in these progressions.

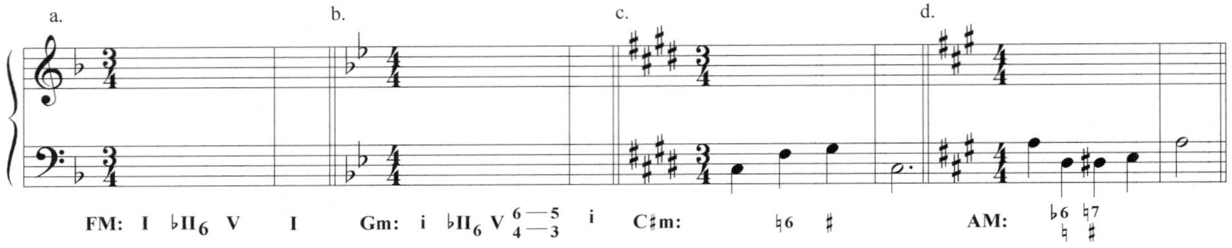

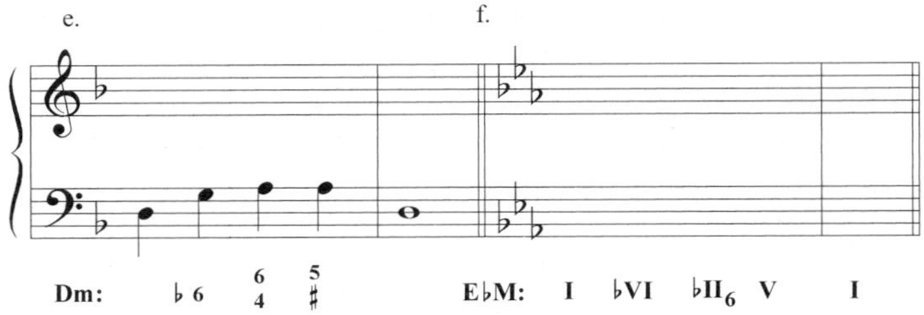

EXERCISE 4 Realize the following progressions in four voices. Provide a RN analysis for progression b.

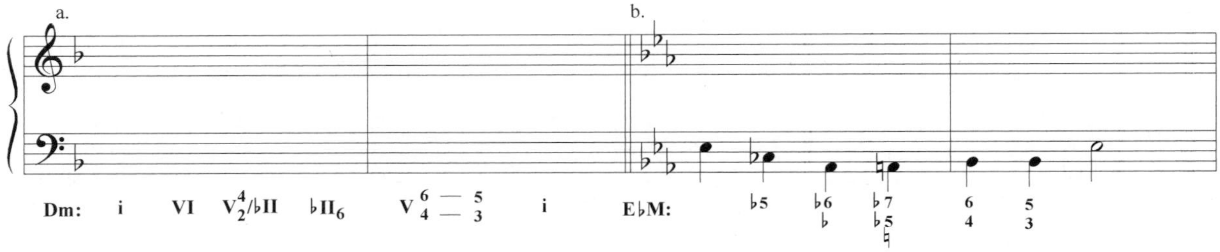

EXERCISE 5 Harmonize the following melody (adapted from Bach's Cantata BWV 21, no. 3) with a bass and RNs. In mm. 1–2, the harmonic rhythm is one chord per beat. In m. 3, you will have to adjust the harmonic rhythm to the needs of the melody.

The initial words of this aria's text are: "Seufzer, Tränen, Kummer, Not. Seufzer, Tränen, ängstlich's Sehnen." ("Sighing, tears, suffering, need. Sighing, tears, anguished yearning."). How do the melody and the harmony reflect the mood of the text? Would you say that Bach's use of dissonance in this phrase is also related with the character of the text? How? Can you comment on (and explain) the dissonance in m. 1, beats 1–2?

Chapter 25

Augmented Sixth Chords

In the $\flat II_6$ chord, the upper and lower leading tones to $\hat{1}$ are presented melodically. Examine now the short passage by Chevalier de Saint-Georges in example 25.1. The basic harmonic content of mm. 69–70 is a subdominant chord in Cm, which is first tonicized and then prolonged by means of a passing $^6_4$ (including the customary voice exchange). In m. 71, beat 4, the $\hat{4}$ from iv_6 moves chromatically to a passing $\sharp\hat{4}$, which continues, of course, to $\hat{5}$ (F–F♯–G). This is happening over a bass $\hat{6}$, which moves down to $\hat{5}$ (A♭–G). Notice that here we have the two leading tones (upper and lower) to $\hat{5}$, presented simultaneously, or harmonically. The interval between them, from $\flat\hat{6}$ up to $\sharp\hat{4}$, is an augmented sixth, +6. Although the process that we have described is linear, this augmented 6th between the two leading tones to $\hat{5}$ generates a very striking family of chords, the **augmented-sixth chords.**

In this chapter we focus on some types of +6 chords that display a *pre-dominant function.* These are the types most frequently found in eighteenth- and early nineteenth-century music. +6 chords with either a dominant function or functioning as linear embellishments to the tonic can also often be found in nineteenth-century music. We will study these +6 types in chapter 27, in the context of more advanced chromatic harmony.

Like the Neapolitan, the +6 chords with a pre-dominant function belong more properly to the minor mode, because they are constructed above a "minor" degree ($\hat{6}$ in minor, $\flat\hat{6}$ in major; in the following discussion we will refer to this degree as "$\flat\hat{6}$" regardless of the mode). But, also like the Neapolitan, the +6 chords are used both in minor and major keys. In example 25.2 you can see an example of an +6 chord in a major key, E♭M. Measure 38 begins with a IV_6. Two members of this chord then move chromatically toward $\hat{5}$: The bass, $\hat{6}$, moves to $\flat\hat{6}$, and on to $\hat{5}$. The middle voice, $\hat{4}$, moves up to $\sharp\hat{4}$ and on to $\hat{5}$. These are, again, our two leading tones to $\hat{5}$, both resolving by contrary motion to $\hat{5}$.

Example 25.1 Chevalier de Saint-Georges, Sonata no. 3 for Violin and Piano, mm. 69–72

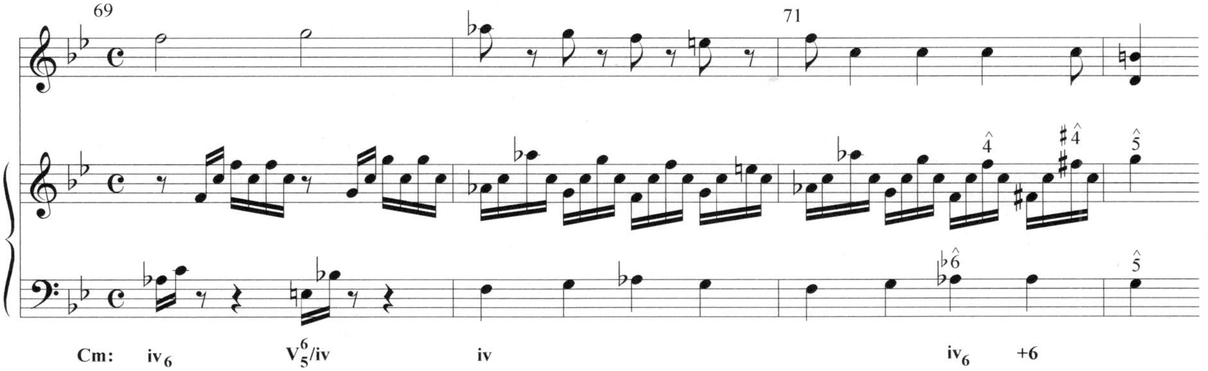

Example 25.2 Nicolò Paganini, Caprice op. 1, no. 14 for Solo Violin, mm. 35–39

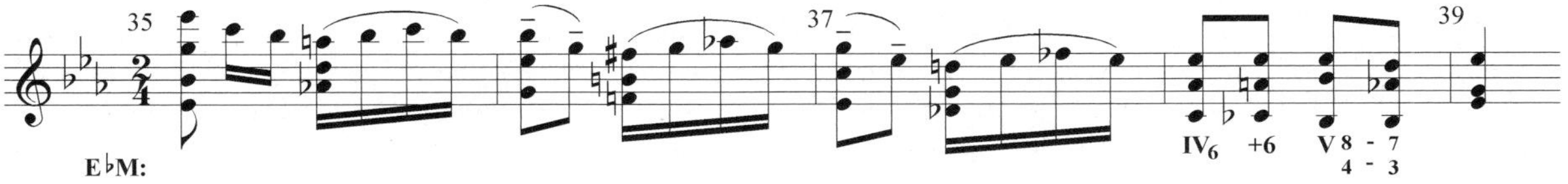

GENERAL FEATURES AND TYPES OF +6 CHORDS

In both examples 25.1 and 25.2 we can observe some common features of pre-dominant +6 chords:

1. +6 chords may appear both *in major or in minor* keys.
2. The basic framework for all pre-dominant +6 chords is the *+6 interval* between ♭$\hat{6}$ and ♯$\hat{4}$. ♭6 is normally in the bass.
3. The +6 chord includes at least one more pitch, and, as we can see in both of the preceding examples, this pitch is $\hat{1}$ (a M3 above the bass's ♭$\hat{6}$).
4. The +6 chord *resolves to V or V_7*. It may do so directly (as in example 25.1), or through the cadential $^6_4$ (as in example 25.2).
5. In either case, *both ♭$\hat{6}$ and ♯$\hat{4}$ resolve to $\hat{5}$* by contrary motion.
6. This simultaneous double leading-tone tendency toward $\hat{5}$ creates a strong tension in this chord, a directed motion toward V, which gives it its typical *pre-dominant function,* as well as a highly dramatic character.

Example 25.3

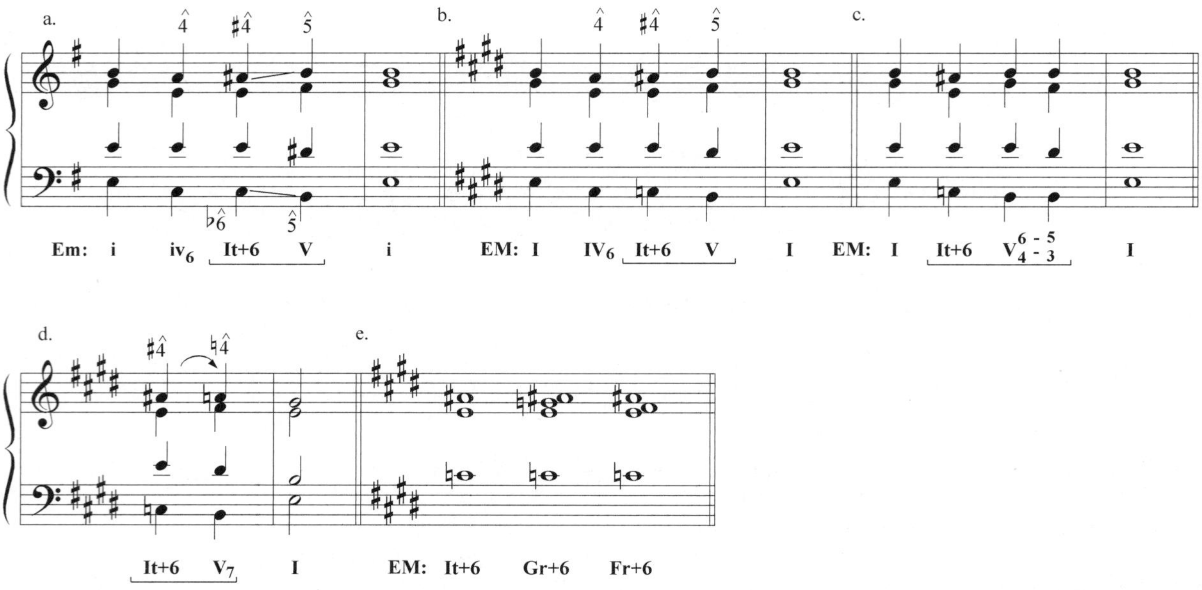

7. The +6 chord is often, although not always, approached from IV_6 (or iv_6). In major, it is sometimes preceded by a borrowed chord, such as iv_6 or ♭VI, both of which introduce $\flat\hat{6}$ in the bass.

Example 25.3 summarizes the standard voice leading and function for the type of +6 chord illustrated so far. The +6 chord made up of only three different pitches ($\flat\hat{6}$–$\hat{1}$–$\sharp\hat{4}$) is known as the *Italian +6* (It +6). In four voices, $\hat{1}$ should be doubled. Examples 25.3a to d show characteristic resolutions of the It +6 to V, V^{6-5}_{4-3}, and V_7. You will see that in the resolution of the +6 chord to V_7, $\sharp\hat{4}$ does not move up to $\hat{5}$, but rather down to the seventh of V_7, $\hat{4}$.

There are, however, two other common types of +6 chords, conveniently (if arbitrarily) labeled *German* (Gr +6) and *French* (Fr +6). Both chords add a fourth pitch to the basic $\flat\hat{6}$–$\hat{1}$–$\sharp\hat{4}$ framework of the It +6. In the case of the German +6, the added pitch is a P5 above the bass ($\hat{3}$ in minor, $\flat\hat{3}$ in major; we will refer to this degree as $\flat\hat{3}$ for clarity, regardless of the mode). The complete chord is then $\flat\hat{6}$–$\hat{1}$–$\flat\hat{3}$–$\sharp\hat{4}$. The added pitch in the French +6 is $\hat{2}$, resulting in a complete chord $\flat\hat{6}$–$\hat{1}$–$\hat{2}$–$\sharp\hat{4}$. Verify these degrees, and hear the sonority for each chord, in example 25.3e. We will now study examples of each of these three "national" varieties in some more detail, but before doing so, let us summarize the procedure to spell +6 chords.

Spelling +6 Chords

The following steps will guide you through the process of spelling +6 chords. You can use example 25.3e as a visual reference.

1. We will build all +6 chords on $\flat\hat{6}$, which we place in the bass. $\flat\hat{6}$ in the key of E (both EM and Em) is pitch C.
2. Notate $\sharp\hat{4}$ in one of the upper voices. $\sharp\hat{4}$ in E (M or m) is A♯. The $\flat\hat{6}$–$\sharp\hat{4}$ interval (C–A♯ in our example) constitutes the +6 interval common to all types of +6 chords.
3. The It +6 has only one more pitch besides $\flat\hat{6}$ and $\sharp\hat{4}$: $\hat{1}$, the pitch a M3 above $\flat\hat{6}$ (E in both EM and Em). This is the pitch we will double in four voices.
4. The Gr +6 has one more pitch besides the three pitches of the It +6: $\flat\hat{3}$, the pitch a P5 above $\flat\hat{6}$ (G♮ in our example).
5. The Fr +6 has one more pitch besides the three pitches of the It +6: $\hat{2}$, the pitch a +4 above $\flat\hat{6}$ (F♯ in our example).

THE ITALIAN +6

Example 25.3 summarizes the characteristics of the **It +6** (figured bass: +6 or ♯6): It contains three different pitches ($\flat\hat{6}$–$\hat{1}$–$\sharp\hat{4}$), and $\hat{1}$ is doubled in four voices. We referred to the dramatic power of the +6. The chord has indeed often been used for two purposes: to signal the arrival of an important structural cadential point or a point of formal articulation, and, in vocal music, to mark dramatically intense moments when the text so requires. An illustration of the latter appears in example 25.4, from Mozart's opera *Don Giovanni.* Donna Elvira is still in love with Don Giovanni, even after being betrayed by this libertine womanizer. In our example, she is begging him to change his life, over an embellished I chord in FM which turns out to be a pivot for a modulation to B♭M. Notice that the pivot and the "change" of tonal center come not only at the word "cangi" ("change"), but moreover introduce a sharp change of tone in the dialogue between the two characters: Don Giovanni now responds, with cold sarcasm, "Brava!" (meaning, "Yes, sure!"), and Donna Elvira's painful answer to his coldness is "Cor perfido!," "wicked heart!" How is her cry of suffering and heartbreak stressed musically, in mm. 10–11 of our example and twice again in the following measures? How is the harmonic and linear tension in m. 10 supported by such factors as texture and dynamics?

We find many examples of the +6 chord used as a *marker for formal articulation* in the music of Beethoven. Example 25.5 reproduces a fragment from a rondo by this composer. The form of a rondo is based on the alternation of a refrain, which always returns in the tonic key, and episodes that may present new material or develop the material from the refrain (in a formal scheme such as A–B–A–C–A–D–A). In example 25.5 we see the measures leading from the end of the C section, a developmental episode, into the return of the A material at m. 132. The dominant chord in this passage (reached in m. 129 and anticipated in m. 127) has a structural function within the overall form: to take us back to the return of the home key. What chord does Beethoven use to precede the arrival of the dominant in both of these measures?

Example 25.4 W. A. Mozart, *Don Giovanni,* Finale

Example 25.5 L. v. Beethoven, Piano Sonata in GM, op. 31 no. 1, III, mm. 126–34

EXERCISES

To practice spelling Italian +6 chords, refer to exercise 2.1 in worksheet 25 at the end of this chapter.

To practice realizing short progressions including Italian +6 chords, refer to exercises 3a to d in worksheet 25 at the end of this chapter.

THE GERMAN +6

As we saw in example 25.3e, the **German +6** chord (figured bass: $^{+6}_{5}$ or $^{\sharp 6}_{5}$) includes four different pitches, $\flat\hat{6}$–$\hat{1}$–$\flat\hat{3}$–$\sharp\hat{4}$. $\flat\hat{3}$ has thus been added to the basic core of the It +6. If you play or sing this chord, you will notice that its sonority is identical to a Mm_7 (that is, a V_7 type of sonority) on $\flat\hat{6}$, only that the seventh of the chord is spelled as an +6th. In example 25.6a we can see the Gr +6 in its conventional function as a pre-dominant chord, in this case preceded by ♭VI. Notice also that the Gr +6 (mm. 35–36) leads directly to V, and that Mozart's voice leading includes clear parallel 5ths. In fact, *the parallel 5ths between the Gr +6 and V are not only permissible, but frequently found in the literature.* There are several reasons why these parallel 5ths are permissible. In the first place, and as we can see in the Mozart example, the 5ths are not so evident if they appear, as they most often do, in the context of arpeggiated chords (that is, not presented as harmonic intervals) rather than in block chords or chorale textures. Moreover, we hear the +6 chord as a dissonant chord, and our attention is drawn to the linear resolution of the +6 interval (the dissonance) rather than to the parallel 5ths, especially if the +6 is placed in the outer voices and the 5ths involve an inner voice. In any case, these are the only parallel fifths in tonal harmonic theory in which you can indulge—and which you can enjoy without fear of being corrected!

Example 25.6a W. A. Mozart, Piano Sonata in FM, K. 332, I, mm. 31–40

Example 25.6b W. A. Mozart, *Don Giovanni,* Overture, mm. 10–13

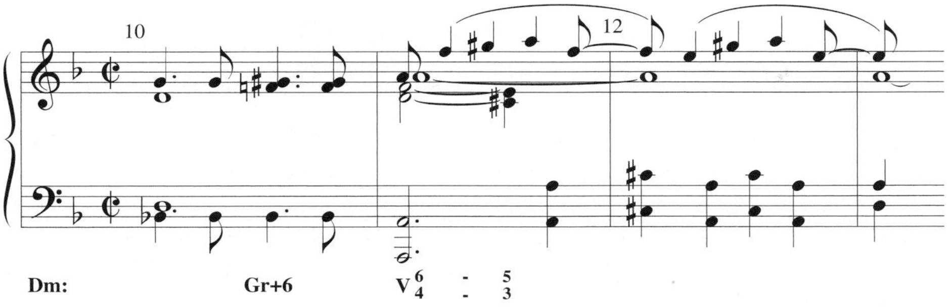

Very often, however, composers "hide" the parallel 5ths by means of an intervening cadential $^6_4$. This is the case in another Mozart example from *Don Giovanni* (example 25.6b). Can you find the parallel 5ths Mozart avoids by moving the Gr +6 to V (mm. 10–11) through a cadential $^6_4$? The conventional voice-leading possibilities for the Gr +6 are summarized in examples 25.15a and b.

Don Giovanni also affords good examples of the dramatic use of the Gr +6. Early in the opera, Don Giovanni kills the Commendatore in a fight, after having betrayed the latter's daughter, Donna Anna. Toward the end of the opera, in a defiant gesture, Don Giovanni invites the statue of the Commendatore to supper. As Donna Elvira, after her unsuccessful bid to change Don Giovanni's life, opens the door to leave, she runs into none other than . . . the statue coming for dinner! This passage in the opera, reproduced in example 25.7, illustrates the dramatic use of modulation, of the vii°$_7$ chord, and of the Gr +6 chord. The passage begins in B♭M, as Donna Elvira goes to the door. Her scream of terror ("Ah!") is marked by a secondary vii°$_7$ chord, vii°$_7$/ii. As it turns out, this vii°$_7$ chord actually functions as a chromatic pivot in a modulation up a step, to Cm, underscoring the heightening tension of Don Giovanni's words, "A scream, what can have happened?" Finally, the third statement of this questioning sentence is further stressed in m. 10 by a Gr +6 chord. Notice that in this case Mozart moves this chord directly to a V chord. How does he avoid the usual parallel 5ths?

Because the Gr +6 contains three common tones with ♭VI, it is often approached from that chord. The Haydn passage in example 25.8 is in GM. In m. 239 we hear a powerful deceptive cadence to a borrowed ♭VI, which is prolonged and tonicized for eight measures, until it becomes a Gr +6 by the simple addition of ♯$\hat{4}$ to the ♭VI triad. Here again, Haydn avoids the parallel 5ths in the same way Mozart did in example 25.7. How?

EXERCISES

To practice spelling German +6 chords, refer to exercise 2.2 in worksheet 25 at the end of this chapter.

To practice realizing short progressions including German +6 chords, refer to exercises 3e to h in worksheet 25 at the end of this chapter.

Example 25.7 W. A. Mozart, *Don Giovanni,* Finale

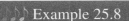

Example 25.8 J. Haydn, Symphony no. 100 in GM, *Military,* I, mm. 236–49

Alternative Spelling of the Gr +6: The Doubly Augmented Fourth Chord

Example 25.9 shows the beginning measures of a song by Schumann, in B♭M. You will notice two unusual things. First, the song begins with a Gr +6 chord, an unconventional chord to begin a piece with, to be sure. Second, this chord is spelled $\flat\hat{6}$–$\hat{1}$–$\sharp\hat{2}$–$\sharp\hat{4}$ instead of the more familiar $\flat\hat{6}$–$\hat{1}$–$\flat\hat{3}$–$\sharp\hat{4}$. In other words, $\flat\hat{3}$ has been replaced by its enharmonic spelling, $\sharp\hat{2}$. The reason is mostly of visual voice–leading logic: in major keys, when the Gr +6 moves to a cadential $^6_4$, one voice carries the voice leading $\flat\hat{3}$–$\natural\hat{3}$–$\hat{2}$. Sometimes composers use an alternative notation for this line, one that seems to reflect more logically the ascent from $\flat\hat{3}$ to $\natural\hat{3}$: $\sharp\hat{2}$–$\natural\hat{3}$; hence the enharmonic spelling of ♭3 in example 25.9. Verify this same alternative spelling in example 25.15c. Because of the doubly augmented 4th interval that this enharmonic spelling creates ($\flat\hat{6}$–$\sharp\hat{2}$), this chord is usually referred to as the **doubly augmented fourth chord.**

Example 25.9 R. Schumann, "Am leuchtenden Sommermorgen," from *Dichterliebe,* op. 48, mm. 1–4

EXERCISES

To practice spelling doubly +4th chords, refer to exercise 2.3 in worksheet 25 at the end of this chapter.

To practice realizing short progressions including doubly +4th chords, refer to exercises 3i and j in worksheet 25 at the end of this chapter.

THE FRENCH +6

The most peculiar and dissonant of the +6 chords is known as the **French +6** (figured bass: $\substack{+6\\4\\3}$ or $\substack{\sharp 6\\4\\3}$). The fourth pitch in this chord, added to the basic frame of the It +6, is $\hat{2}$. The total sonority, $\flat\hat{6}$–$\hat{1}$–$\hat{2}$–$\sharp\hat{4}$, includes two overlapping tritones and a major 2nd, besides the +6th. The function of this chord, as well as its resolution to V or to the cadential $\substack{6\\4}$, are the same as in the other two types of +6 chord. Example 25.10 illustrates Beethoven's use of this chord at a point of great formal significance—the beginning of the second theme (and the secondary key area, in the dominant key) in the first movement of the *Eroica* Symphony. The secondary key area begins in m. 45 on V of the dominant key, B♭M, approached from a Fr +6 in m. 44. Verify the pitches and spelling of this chord, as well as its voice-leading resolution to V in B♭M. Hear the powerful tension created by this dissonant sonority, so well used by Beethoven as a formal marker in this passage. The phrase by Celeste Heckscher in example 25.11, on the other hand, illustrates the resolution of a Fr +6 to a cadential $\substack{6\\4}$. Identify the chord, and double-check its spelling and voice leading.

Example 25.10 L. v. Beethoven, Symphony no. 3, op. 55, *Eroica,* mm. 37–49

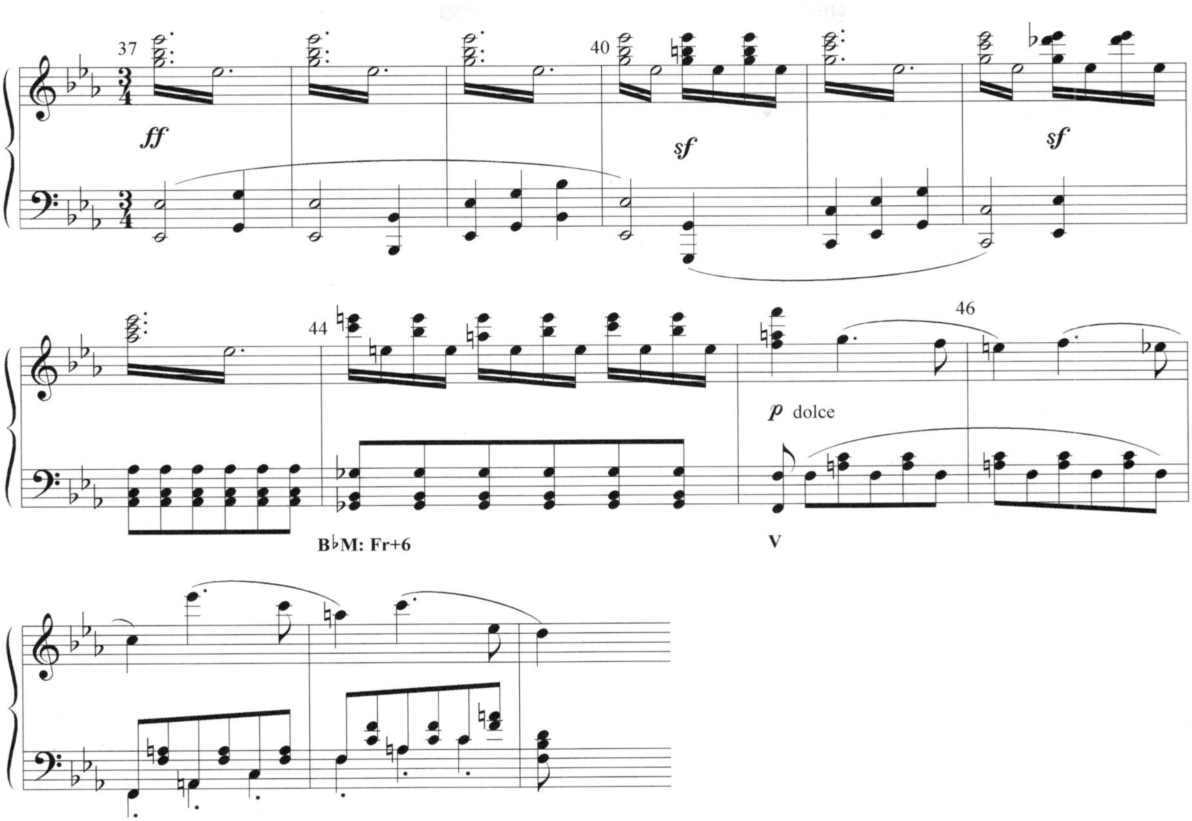

EXERCISES

To practice spelling French +6 chords, refer to exercise 2.4 in worksheet 25 at the end of this chapter.

To practice realizing short progressions including French +6 chords, refer to exercises 3k to n in worksheet 25 at the end of this chapter.

OTHER TYPES OF +6 CHORDS

Although the three characteristic types of +6 chords that we previously discussed usually appear individually, at times all three types are lumped into a **"moving" +6** chord, such as the one shown in example 25.12. The chord in m. 41, beat 3, begins as a Gr +6. But because of the moving viola line (the sixteenth-note figure), it immediately becomes

Example 25.11 Celeste Heckscher, *Valse Bohème,* mm. 77–84

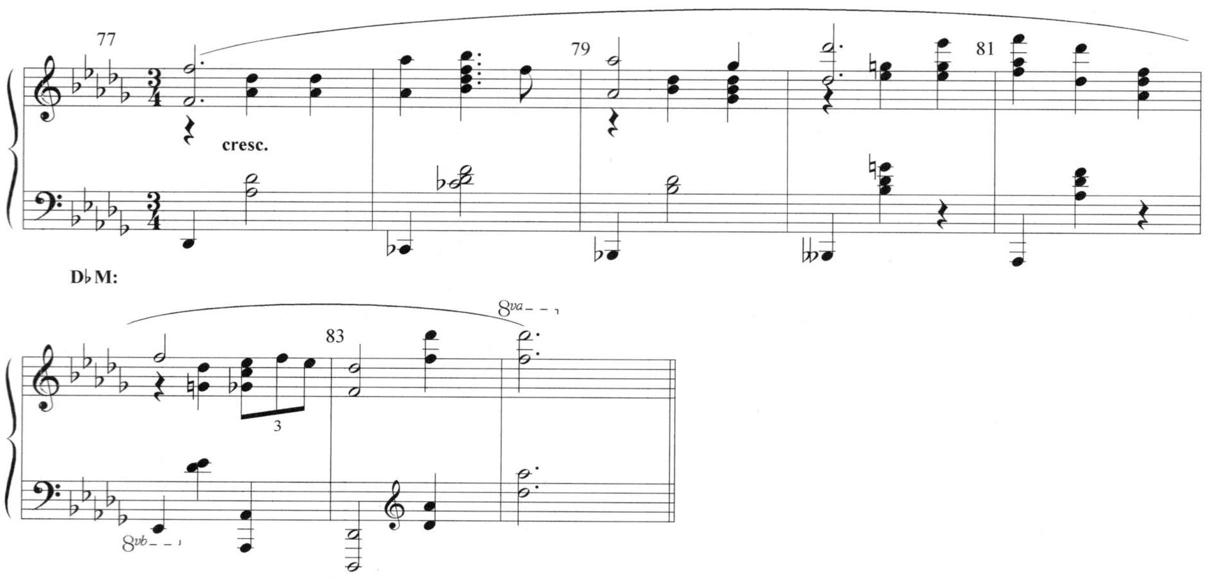

Example 25.12 J. Haydn, Quartet in B♭M, op. 64, no. 3, I, mm. 39–42

a Fr +6, and then an It +6, before it resolves to V in Fm. Because this type of moving +6 chord includes all three "nationalities," we could appropriately call it the "European Union +6 chord"!

The Diminished Third (°3) Chord

Inversions of the +6 chord are not frequent, because the chord is most effective when ♭$\hat{6}$ is in the bass (and, possibly, ♯$\hat{4}$ in the top voice). The inversion that places ♯$\hat{4}$ in the bass, however, also produces a chord strongly directed toward V. This inversion is found occasionally in music of the Romantic period. Because this chord includes the inversion of an +6, a diminished 3rd, counted from the bass upward, we call it the **°3 chord.** In the Verdi fragment reproduced in example 25.13, the music is coming from the key of AM. The Gr +6 chord in AM is F♮–A–C♮–D♯. In mm. 2–4 of our example you can see this chord with the D♯ in the bass (first spelled enharmonically as E♭) and the F♮ in the upper voice, thus spelling out a °3rd interval, and a °3 chord. The resolution in m. 5 is to V in AM, with all the conventional voice leading.

Example 25.13 G. Verdi, *Aida,* "Ritorna vincitor," mm. 1–6

Example 25.14 R. Schumann, *Papillons,* op. 2, no. 8, mm. 21–32

EXERCISES

To practice spelling diminished 3rd chords, refer to exercise 2.5 in worksheet 25 at the end of this chapter.

Secondary +6 Chords

All the +6 chords we have seen so far function as pre-dominant chords to the primary dominant, V. Secondary dominants, however, may also be preceded by their own **secondary +6 chord,** an event that is often part of a secondary key area. Example 25.14 is in D♭M, as indicated by the two initial chords, the cadence in m. 25, and the final cadence. In mm. 22–23 we hear a brief secondary key area of vi, closing with a V/vi in m. 24. The two chords that precede this V/vi (m. 23, beats 2–3) are examples of secondary +6 chords (of which type?). Complete the Roman numeral analysis of m. 22 to m. 24, beat 1, using the secondary-key area notation already started on the example.

SUMMARY

Example 25.15 provides a summary of spelling and voice leading for the Gr +6, Fr +6, and °3 chords. Study these carefully, and play these examples at the piano to learn the characteristic sound of these interesting chromatic chords.

Examples 25.3 and 25.15 show that the most effective outer-voice frame for the +6 progression includes the linear motions $\sharp\hat{4}$–$\hat{5}$ (or $\hat{4}$–$\sharp\hat{4}$–$\hat{5}$) in the soprano and $\flat\hat{6}$–$\hat{5}$

Example 25.15

in the bass. As in the case of the Neapolitan sixth, the +6 chord functions most often as a pre-dominant, and hence it has a clear role in the elaboration of the I–V–I progression, as shown in examples 25.3 and 25.15. In cases where another pre-dominant chord precedes it (usually iv_6 or IV_6, as in examples 25.3a and b or 25.15d), the +6 functions as a chromatic passing chord between the previous pre-dominant and the following dominant (that is, it functions as a chromatic elaboration of the pre-dominant).

TONAL RELATIONSHIP BETWEEN THE NEAPOLITAN AND THE +6 CHORDS

As we saw in chapter 24, the dominant of the Neapolitan chord is the ♭VI triad. We have also seen that the sonority of the Gr +6 chord is the same as a Mm_7 sonority on $\flat\hat{6}$. In other words, the dominant seventh of the Neapolitan, V_7/♭II, and the Gr +6 are the same sonority, although spelled differently. Example 25.16 shows the relationship between the two chords. As you can imagine, this opens up some interesting possibilities. If the Gr +6 and ♭II are connected by a dominant/tonic relationship, couldn't we use the Gr +6 respelled as V_7/♭II to modulate to such a distant key as the Neapolitan key (say, from Cm to C♯m or to C♯M)? This is indeed one of the distant modulations that we will study in the next chapter.

Example 25.16

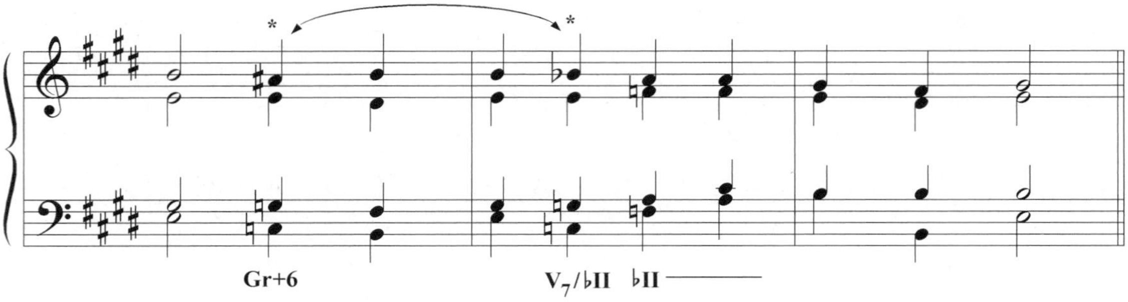

EXERCISES

To practice realizing progressions including +6 chords, refer to exercise 4 in worksheet 25 at the end of this chapter.

To practice harmonizing a melody including +6 chords, refer to exercise 5 in worksheet 25 at the end of this chapter.

To practice analyzing musical fragments including +6 chords, refer to exercise 1 in worksheet 25 at the end of this chapter.

FOR FURTHER STUDY

For additional analysis using materials studied in this chapter, refer to the *Harmony in Context* Web page at www.mhhe.com/roigfrancoli2e.

ASSIGNMENT AND KEYBOARD EXERCISES

For analytical and written assignments and keyboard exercises based on the materials learned in this chapter, refer to chapter 25 in the workbook.

PITCH PATTERNS

Sing the pitch patterns in example 25.17, and as you sing listen to the +6 chords and their resolution. Then, *improvise* similar pitch patterns using linearized +6 chords.

Example 25.17

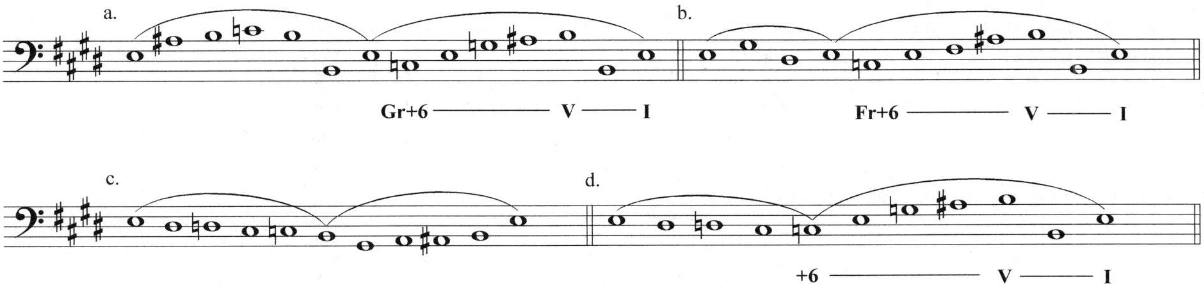

Terms for Review

Augmented sixth (+6) chords
It +6
Gr +6
Alternative spelling of the Gr +6 (the doubly augmented fourth chord)
Fr +6
"moving" +6
°3 chord
Secondary +6 chords

Worksheet 25

EXERCISE 1 Analysis. Identify the +6 chords in each of the following examples.

1. Identify the type of +6 chord ("nationality"). If it is a Gr +6, is it spelled with a $\flat\hat{3}$ or a $\sharp\hat{2}$?
2. Provide RNs for the actual +6 chord and also for the chords that precede and follow it.
3. Does the +6 chord resolve directly to V? Does it resolve to V through some other harmonies? Are parallel 5ths avoided?

Examples for Analysis:

1. Example 25.18

Example 25.18 W. A. Mozart, Sonata for Violin and Piano, K. 380, III, mm. 101–108

2. Example 25.19

Example 25.19 J. Brahms, Symphony no. 1 in Cm, II, mm. 1–4

3. Example 25.20

Example 25.20 W. A. Mozart, Piano Sonata in FM, K. 280, II, mm. 9–14

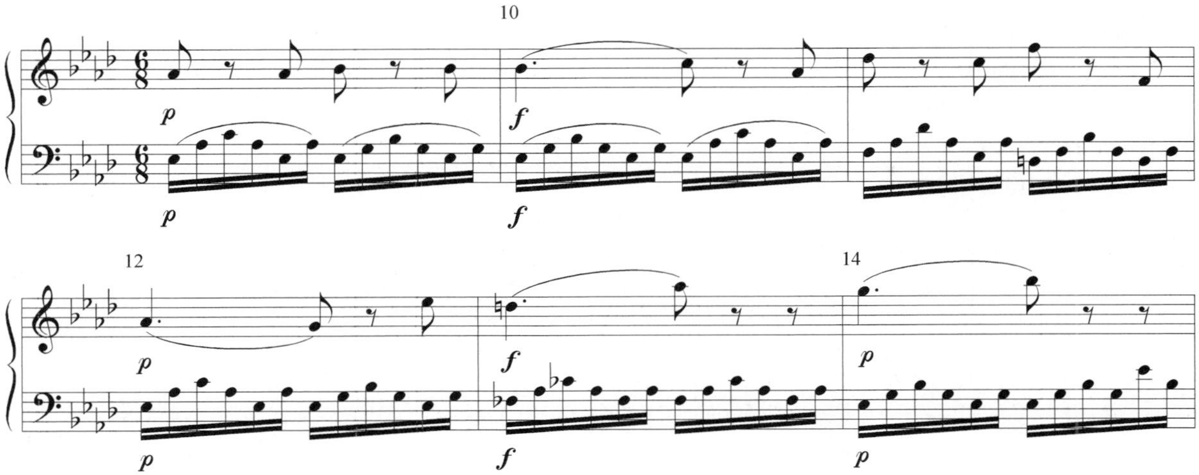

4. Anthology, no. 24, Mozart, Sonata in DM, III, Var. 7, mm. 3–4, 5–8, and 14–17

5. Anthology, no. 34, Beethoven, Sonata op. 13, *Pathétique,* III, mm. 6–7, 44–47, 131–135, and 182–186

6. Example 25.21

Example 25.21 F. Chopin, Prelude in Em, op. 28, no. 4, mm. 20–25

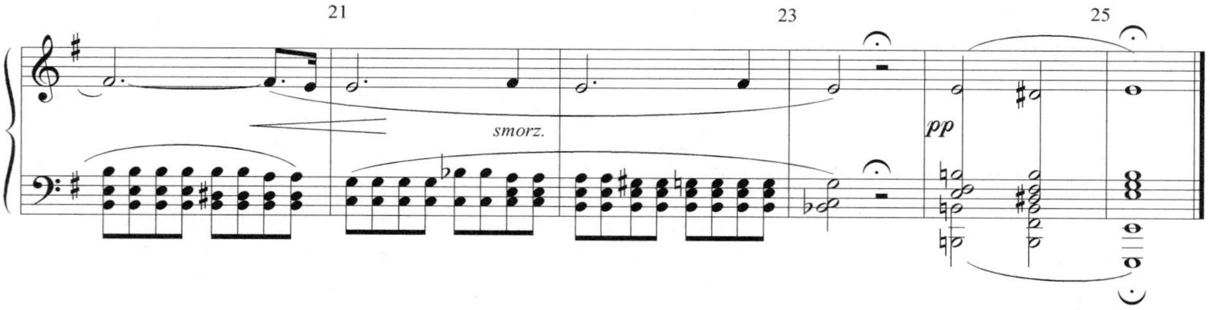

EXERCISE 2 Spell the following chords in four voices, in the required keys:

1. Italian +6 chords
2. German +6 chords
3. Doubly augmented 4th chords
4. French +6 chords
5. Diminished 3rd chords

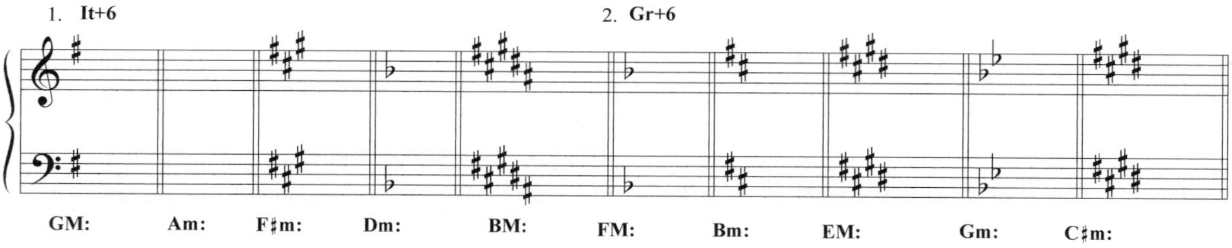

3. **Doubly +4** 4. **Fr+6**

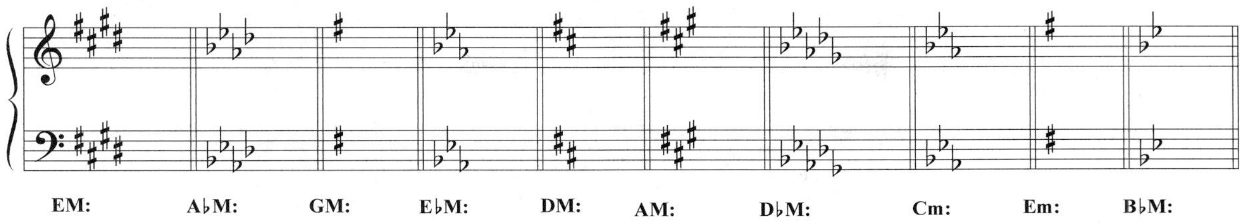

5. °3

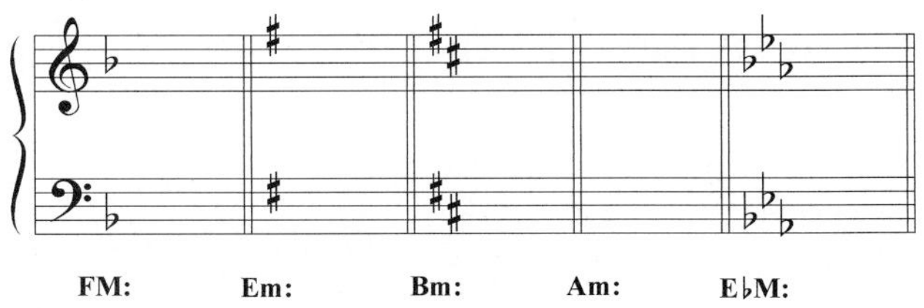

EXERCISE 3 Realize the following short progressions in four voices. Add RNs to the progressions with a figured bass. Be careful with your spelling and resolution of the +6 chords in these progressions.

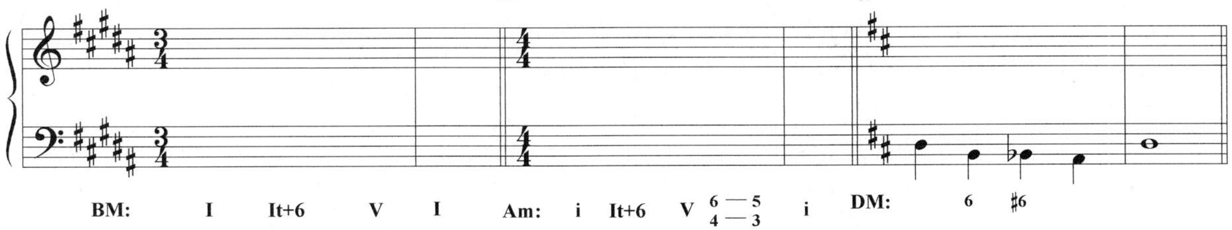

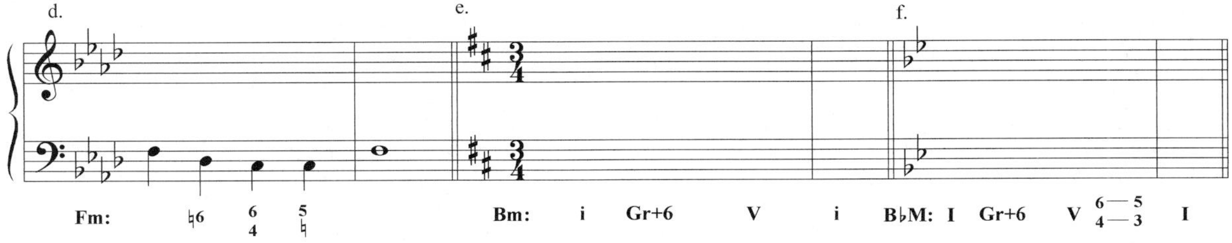

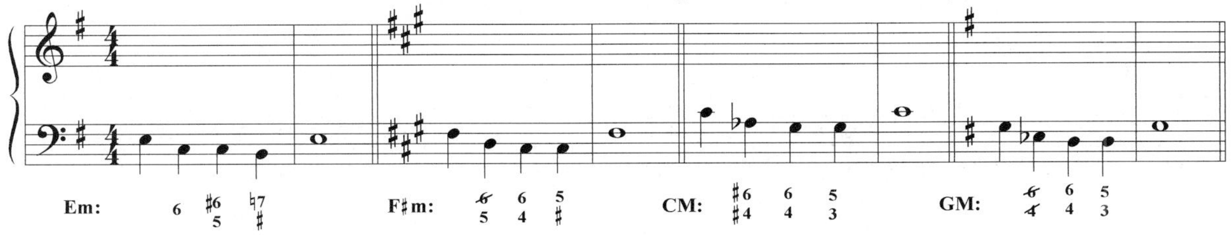

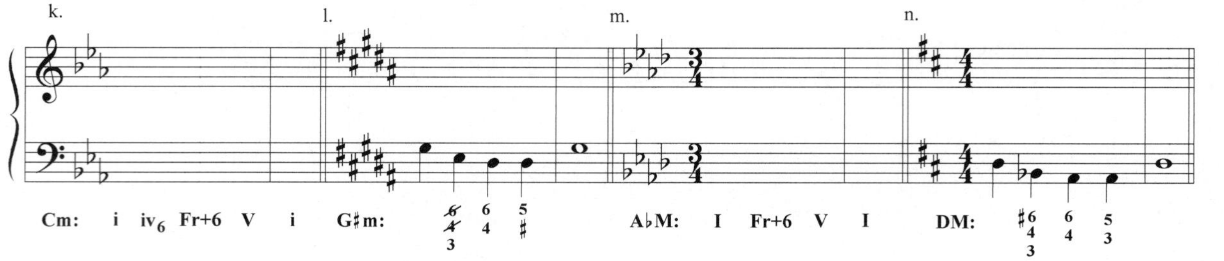

EXERCISE 4 Realize the following progressions in four voices. Provide a RN analysis for progression b.

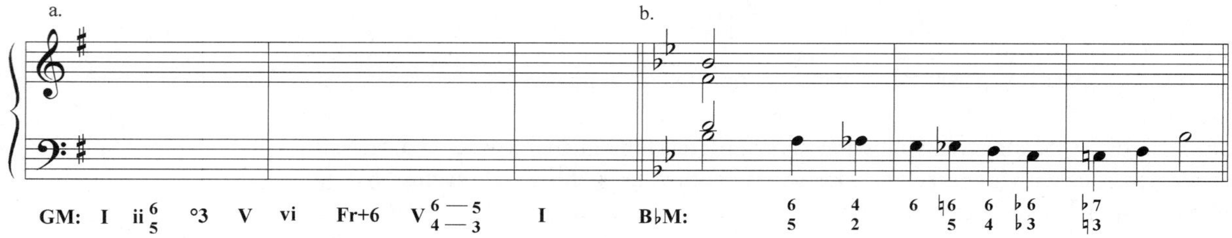

EXERCISE 5 Harmonize the following melody with a bass and RNs. Use an +6 chord where appropriate.

Chapter 26

Chromatic Modulatory Techniques: Modulation to Distantly Related Keys I

In this chapter we continue our study of modulation, focusing on techniques that allow tonal motion to distantly related keys. **Distantly related keys** are keys whose signatures differ in more than one accidental. Any two keys that are not closely related are distantly related, although the distance can be smaller or greater (for instance, CM and DM, with a difference of only two sharps, are not as distantly related as CM and C♯M, with a difference of seven sharps, or CM and F♯M, with a difference of six sharps). In this chapter we first study three types of modulation to distantly related keys: by *chromatic pivot chord,* by *enharmonic reinterpretation of the +6 chord,* and by *enharmonic reinterpretation of* vii°_7.

CHROMATIC PIVOT CHORDS

In chapter 20 we studied modulation by means of diatonic pivot chords, which we defined as chords that have a diatonic function in both of the keys for which they act as a connection. We also introduced **chromatic pivot chords,** chords that are not diatonic in at least one of the keys involved in the modulation. In this section we will further our study of chromatic pivot relationships, including those that allow modulations to distantly related keys.

Example 26.1 illustrates a few possible **chromatic pivot relationships** from CM to several other keys. Notice that the second key in this type of modulation may be closely or distantly related. Notice also that the pivot chord may be of three types, depending on whether it is chromatic in the first key, in the second key, or in both:

1. In the first type, **diatonic-chromatic,** the chord is diatonic in the first key and chromatic in the second. Both examples for this type (example 26.1a) involve borrowed chords in the second key, including a $\flat II_6$.
2. The second type, **chromatic-diatonic,** features chords that are chromatic in the first key and diatonic in the second. A frequent example for this type features a secondary dominant in the first key, which becomes the diatonic dominant of the second key (example 26.1b). In our second example, $\flat II_6$ (a chromatic chord) becomes a diatonic IV_6 in the new key.

Example 26.1

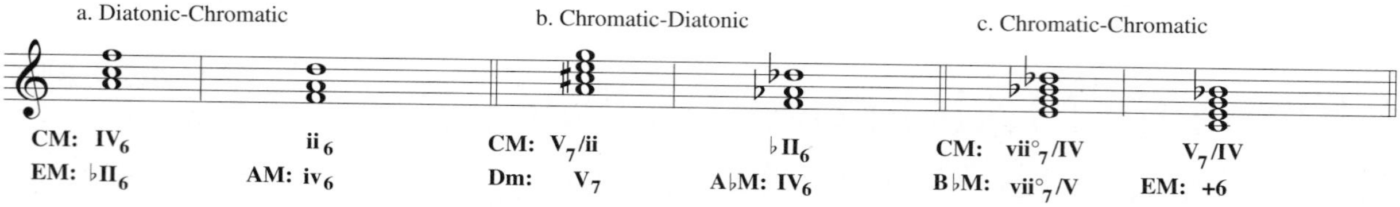

3. In the third type, **chromatic-chromatic,** the chord is chromatic in both keys. In example 26.1c, a secondary vii°$_7$ in the first key also becomes a secondary vii°$_7$ in the second key, and in the second example a secondary dominant in the first key becomes the Gr +6 chord in the second key. (This latter example takes advantage

Example 26.2 W. A. Mozart, *Die Entführung aus dem Serail,* act III, no. 18, mm. 11–17

of the fact that the Gr +6 sonority is the same as a Mm_7 sonority, but it involves an enharmonic respelling of the chord. Try it: How would you spell V_7/IV in CM, and how would you spell the same sonority but now functioning as the Gr +6 in EM? We will study enharmonic reinterpretation of the Gr +6 in more detail below.)

EXERCISE

To practice determining the chromatic pivot function of a chord between two keys, refer to exercise 2 in worksheet 26 at the end of this chapter.

The Diatonic-Chromatic Pivot Relationship

In example 26.2, taken from Mozart's *The Abduction from the Seraglio,* Pedrillo tells the story of the Spanish lady Kostanze, of whom he is a servant, and who has been the captive of a Moorish ruler. The beginning of our example, in which we learn that Kostanze has been sighing in despair day and night, is in GM. The second sentence refers to the lady's longing for freedom, and this allusion to the liberation that would allow her to return to her distant homeland comes with a modulation to the distantly related keys of F♯m/F♯M. Connecting both keys (G and F♯) is a chromatic pivot chord, the GM triad in first inversion, which is diatonic in GM (I_6) and chromatic in F♯ (♭II_6). Two progressions illustrating the *diatonic-chromatic* pivot relationship appear in example 26.3. Play these

Example 26.3

a.

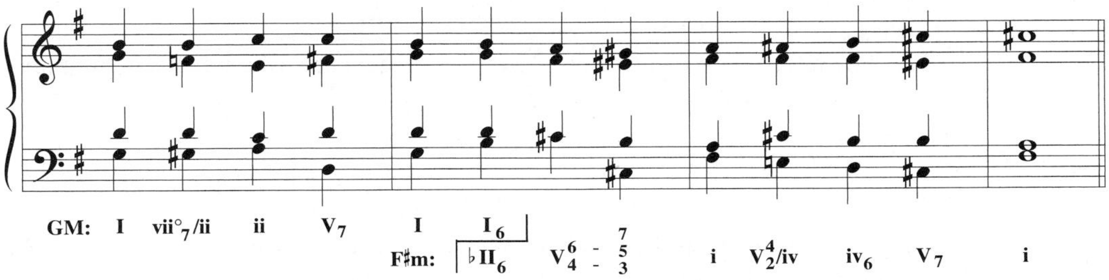

b.

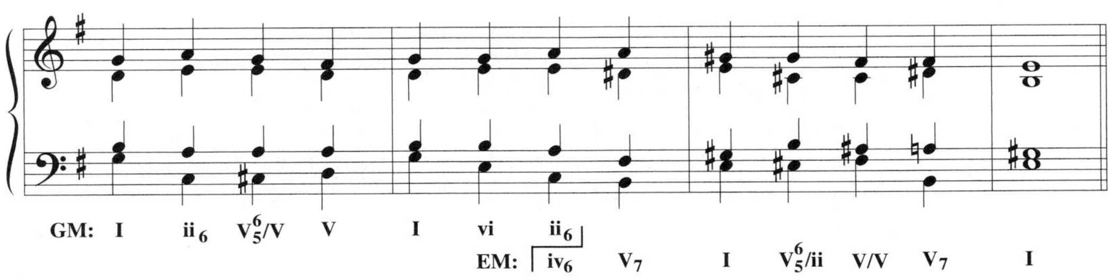

progressions, sing them in class, and hear the modulation and the pivot chord function in both keys.

The Chromatic-Diatonic Pivot Relationship

This chromatic pivot relationship between two keys is beautifully illustrated by the Brahms passage reproduced in example 26.4, although the keys involved here are not distantly related (Fm and D♭M, or i–VI). When you analyze the harmonies in mm. 25–32 you will see that the passage is based on a standard diatonic progression in Fm (i–VI–iv–V) which has been slightly elaborated: The V in m. 29 is extended by means of a deceptive resolution, and then it is tonicized before reaching the half cadence (HC) in m. 32. The pre-dominant iv in m. 27 is itself prolonged by means of the $\flat II_6$ chord in m. 28. In Fm, $\flat II_6$ is, of course, chromatic. Now refer to the progression after the HC (mm. 33–38). It begins with the same chord that we just heard in m. 28 ($\flat II_6$ in Fm), but now it moves on to the dominant of D♭M, which eventually resolves to the tonic of the new key (in first inversion, m. 38). In D♭M, the G♭M triad in m. 33 is a diatonic chord, IV_6. In other words, this is a *chromatic-diatonic* pivot that has taken us from Fm to D♭M.

Modulations are sometimes achieved by the introduction of the new dominant, which we first hear as a secondary dominant. The Beethoven passage in example 26.5 begins with a cadence in A♭M. In the context of this key, we hear mm. 29–30 as a tonicization of vi; that is, we hear the CM chord in m. 29 as a secondary dominant of vi (hence as a chromatic chord in A♭M). As the music goes on, we realize that we are modulating to Fm. The CM chord in m. 29 is, then, chromatic in A♭M and diatonic in Fm. This is a case of a chromatic-diatonic relationship in the form of the dominant of the new key first heard as a tonicizing secondary dominant in the old key.

The two progressions in example 26.6 summarize the two types of chromatic-diatonic pivot relationship we just studied.

The Chromatic-Chromatic Pivot Relationship

In this type of pivot relationship, the pivot chord is chromatic in both keys. A frequent type of chromatic-chromatic pivot features a chord with a secondary function in both keys. Refer to anthology, no. 32 (Beethoven, Sonata in Fm, op. 2 no. 1), mm 49–57. The passage begins in A♭M and ends in B♭m. The chord in m. 53 is a secondary $vii^{\circ 6}_{5}$/vi in A♭M, which leads not to vi (an Fm triad) but rather to V in B♭m (an FM triad) in m. 55. Our $vii^{\circ 6}_{5}$/vi in A♭M is thus also a $vii^{\circ 6}_{5}$/V in B♭m, hence it is a secondary chord in both keys, a *chromatic-chromatic* pivot chord. You may have remarked that the resolution from the $vii^{\circ 6}_{5}$/V in m. 53 to the V in m. 55 is effected through a passing chord in m. 54 (notice the chromatic linear motion in the bass, G–G♭–F). What is the chord in m. 54 that results from this chromatic passing motion? Study example 26.7a, a summary of the modulating progression we have just discussed. Play and sing the progression, and understand the chromatic-chromatic function of the pivot chord.

Example 26.4 J. Brahms, Sonata in Fm for Clarinet and Piano, op. 120, no. 1, I, mm. 25–38

Example 26.5 L. v. Beethoven, Piano Sonata op. 7 in E♭M, II, mm. 27–32

Example 26.7b illustrates the use of a chromatic-chromatic pivot chord to modulate between two closely related keys, CM and GM. Although one could argue that the dominant in this example's m. 4 could be interpreted as a diatonic pivot chord (I in GM), in this measure we do not hear this GM chord as a tonic at all, but only as V of CM. Then, we hear the following EM seventh chord as V_7/vi

Example 26.6

Example 26.7a

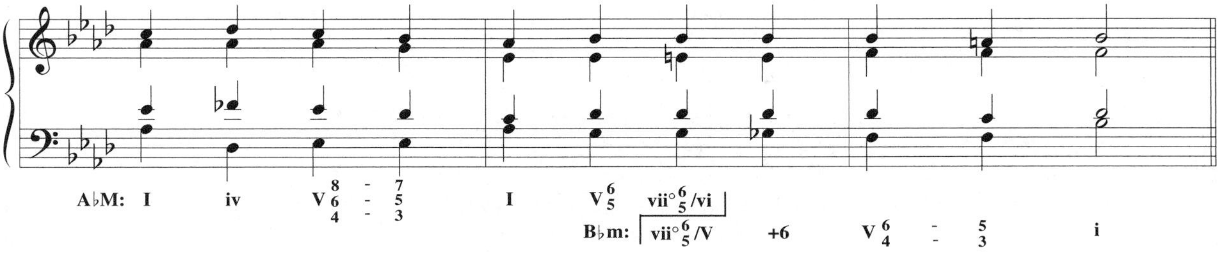

Example 26.7b Mike Love–Brian Wilson (The Beach Boys), "The Warmth of the Sun"

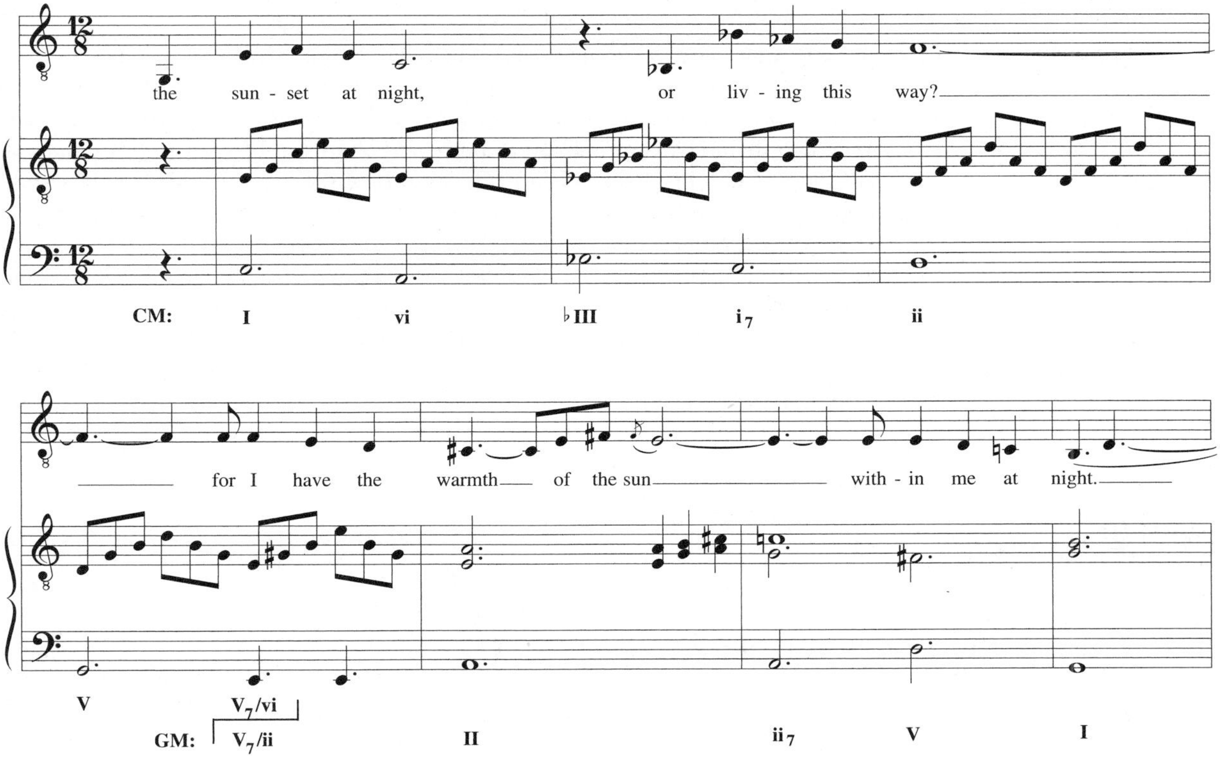

in CM. But by m. 6 we realize that we are moving to GM, and that the V_7/vi was actually a V_7/ii tonicizing a pre-dominant chord in GM. This secondary chord, chromatic in both keys, is then the actual pivot (a chromatic-chromatic pivot) between the two keys. Comment also on the use of borrowed chords in this passage. How many of them are there?

WRITING CHROMATIC PIVOT CHORD MODULATIONS

The process of writing a modulation involving a chromatic pivot chord is similar to the process we learned in chapter 20 of writing modulations using diatonic pivot chords.

1. You may first determine the keys you will use in your modulation, and then investigate possible chromatic pivot chords. For instance, if you want to modulate from FM to EM, you may take advantage of the fact that I in FM is the Neapolitan chord in EM, and thus you can use the diatonic-chromatic pivot FM: I_6/EM: $\flat II_6$.
2. Or you may want to use a specific pivot relationship (say, $\flat II_6$ in the first key) to modulate to some other key. Then you will investigate possible keys you can go to by means of that pivot. $\flat II_6$ in FM, for instance, can become IV_6 in D♭M, I_6 in G♭M, or V_6 in BM (try all these possibilities at the piano or on paper).
3. We will now write several progressions using some of these procedures. First, let us write a *diatonic-chromatic* pivot modulation from FM to EM. We would like our pivot chord to be a borrowed chord in the second key, EM. What diatonic chords in FM can function as borrowed chords in EM? iii in F becomes iv in E, and V in F becomes ♭VI in E. Because V of the old key is not the best possible pivot, we will choose iii/iv as a diatonic-chromatic pivot. Now we need to write a good progression in each of the keys, and connect the two progressions by means of our chosen pivot. Example 26.8 shows a possible realization of this modulation.

   Now try writing your own modulating progression using a diatonic-chromatic pivot. Choose your first key, and write a modulation in which some diatonic major triad in the first key becomes $\flat II_6$ in the second key.

Example 26.8

Example 26.9

4. Next, we will write some modulations using a chromatic-diatonic pivot. First, we want to write a modulation from DM using a borrowed chord in the first key, for instance, iv or iv_6, the Gm triad. The Gm triad can be found as a diatonic chord in quite a few keys (for instance, it is i in Gm, ii in FM, iii in E♭M, etc.). Because DM and FM are distantly related keys, and iv in DM is a pre-dominant chord in FM (ii, a good pivot), we choose FM as our second key. Then we try to write two interesting progressions in DM and FM, and connect them with the iv_6/ii_6 chromatic-diatonic pivot that we previously determined. Example 26.9 shows a possible solution for this modulation.

   Write now two modulations with chromatic-diatonic pivots. In the first modulation, begin in CM, and use as the pivot $♭II_6$ in CM, which will become V_6 in the new key. What key does this pivot take us to? Notice that this is an interesting distant modulation. What is the Roman numeral (RN) relationship between these two keys?

   For your second modulation, begin from a major key and modulate to the ♭VII key using the dominant of the new key first as a secondary dominant in the old key.

5. Finally, write your own modulation using a chromatic-chromatic pivot. As a suggestion, try beginning in A♭M and use $vii°_7/iii$ in the first key as your pivot. How can you go to FM using this chord as a chromatic-chromatic pivot?

EXERCISES

To practice writing your own chromatic pivot chord modulations, refer to exercises 3 and 11 in worksheet 26 at the end of this chapter.

MODULATION BY ENHARMONIC REINTERPRETATION OF THE GR +6

This interesting chromatic modulation takes advantage of the fact that the Gr +6 features the same sonority as a Mm_7 chord. Hence, a Gr +6 may be reinterpreted as a V_7 chord in a different key or, vice versa, a V_7 chord may be reinterpreted as a Gr +6. In both cases, the chord needs to be respelled enharmonically, even if it's only mentally (composers do not provide both spellings in actual music, although we will in most of our examples and exercises, to clarify the process as much as possible; the spelling in

Example 26.10

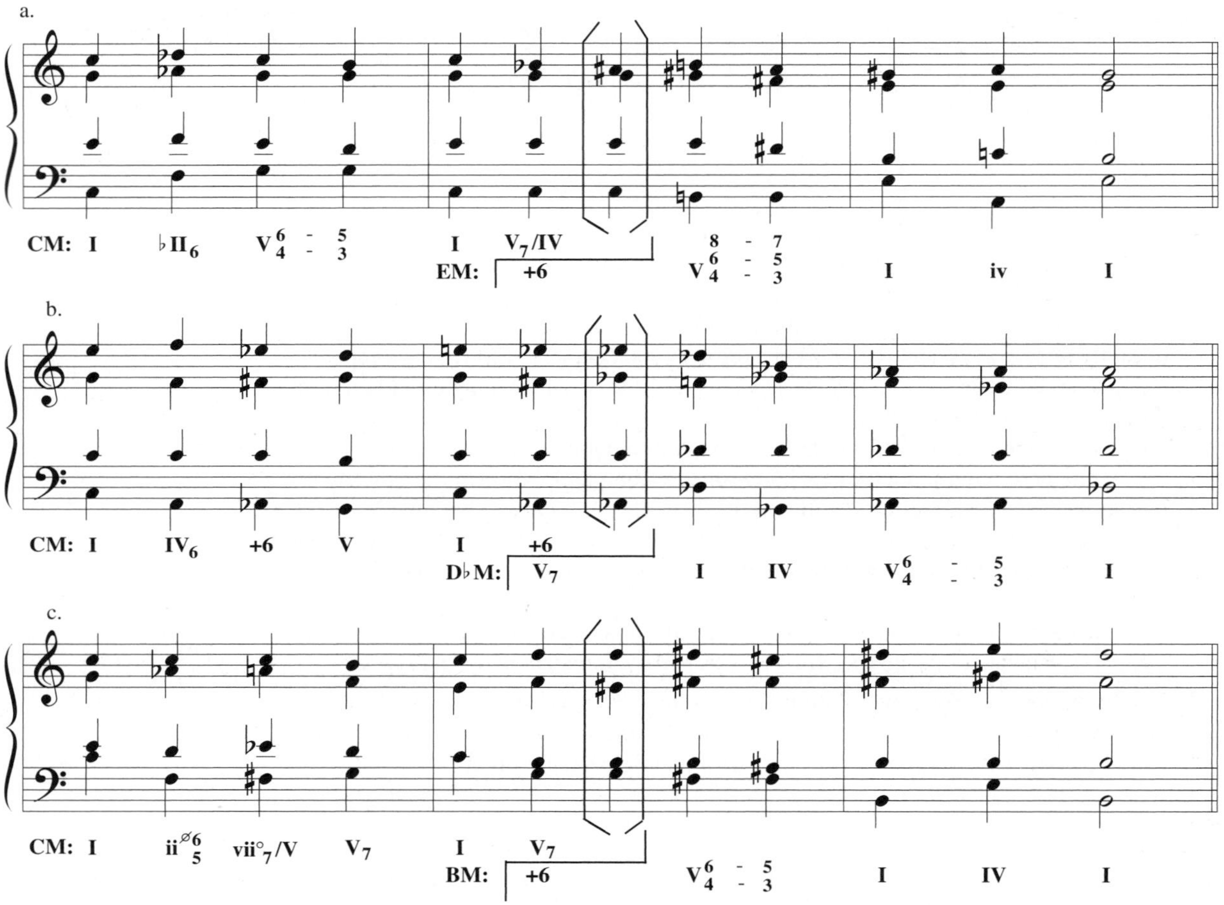

the second key will always be provided in brackets after the spelling in the first key). Example 26.10 shows you the most frequent pivot and key relationships using this type of reinterpretation. Essentially, they can be reduced to two types:

1. In example 26.10a, a V_7/IV in a major key is reinterpreted as a Gr +6 of a key a M3 above the original key (iii or III) by respelling B♭ as A♯.
2. In example 26.10b, the Gr +6 is reinterpreted as V_7 of a key a half step above the original tonic (the key of ♯i or ♯I; or also ♭ii or ♭II, the "Neapolitan" key) by respelling F♯ as G♭. In the reverse process (example 26.10c), V_7 in the original key becomes the Gr +6 of a key a half step below the original tonic by respelling F as E♯.

Modulation to iii or III Using the +6

Listen to example 26.11. Measures 23–26 are in A♭M. The chord in mm. 27–28, functions as vii°_{7}/ii in A♭M, although here it does not resolve as such. Instead, it moves to the chord in m. 29, which, coming from A♭M, sounds like V_7/IV. As such, it would be spelled as A♭–C–E♭–*G*♭. Instead, it is spelled as *A*♭–C–E♭–*F*♯, that is, as an +6 in C (M or m). Its resolution, indeed, confirms this function: It resolves to V^{6-5}_{4-3} in CM, which takes us to the next phrase in CM. We have modulated from a major key (I) to its mediant key (in this case the chromatic mediant, that is, major III, instead of the diatonic mediant, iii, or Cm) by enharmonically reinterpreting V_7/IV in the first key as an +6 chord in the second key.

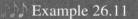

Example 26.11 L. v. Beethoven, Symphony no. 5 in Cm, II, mm. 23–33

Example 26.12

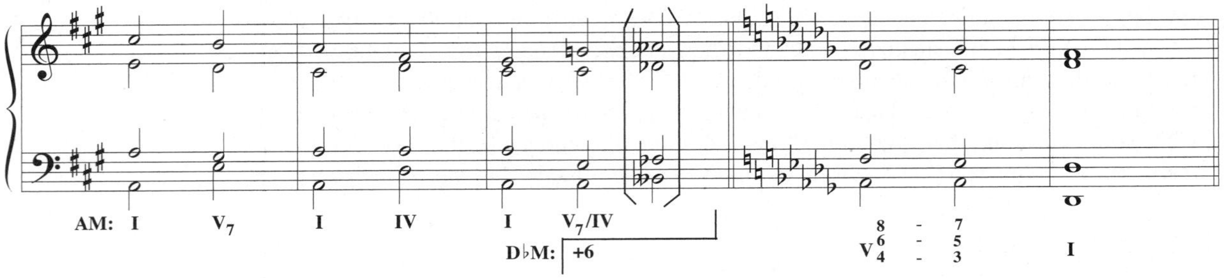

For another example of this modulation from I to the distantly related key of III, refer to anthology, no. 39 (Schubert, Waltz, op. 9, no. 14), mm. 17–24. The key of AM was established at the end of the previous section (mm. 15–16). Measures 17–20 continue in the same key, and at m. 21 we hear that, by the addition of the seventh, the AM tonic chord becomes V_7/IV. Although the chord in m. 21, however, is spelled as a V_7/IV in AM, it does not resolve as such, but is followed by a perfect authentic cadence (PAC) in D♭M. Play the progression in mm. 21–24, hearing the chord in m. 21 in D♭M. You will hear that it functions as a Gr +6 in this key, and in this way it provides a pivot in the modulation between the two distantly related keys. What is the correct spelling for the Gr +6 in D♭M? After you figure it out (and realize that it is a cumbersome spelling to be sure!), study the summary for this modulation as it appears in example 26.12.

Modulation Up or Down a Half Step Using the +6

Although a half step is the closest distance among pitches in the chromatic scale, it can also be the greatest tonal distance between two keys (for instance, CM and C♯M, with a difference of seven sharps). The modulation up or down a half step, however, can easily be effected with an enharmonic reinterpretation of the +6 chord. Consider, for instance, example 26.13. The key of AM is first established in the passage, and in m. 117 we hear a chord which, in AM, *sounds* like the Gr +6. The +6 interval (F–D♯), however, has been respelled enharmonically as a m7, F–E♭. Thus, the chord *looks* like a Mm_7, specifically like V_7 in B♭M. Its resolution to I in B♭M indeed confirms the modulation to the key a half step above AM, the "Neapolitan key," ♭II. The Gr +6 in AM has been reinterpreted as V_7/♭II.

An instance of the reverse process (down a half step) appears in example 26.14. This song is in Fm, and our example begins with a passage in the secondary key area of G♭M, the Neapolitan key (mm. 45–47, on a G♭M dominant pedal). V_7 in G♭, which appears several times in these measures spelled as D♭–F–A♭–*C*♭, is enharmonically respelled, in the last beat of m. 47, as D♭–F–A♭–*B*♮, that is, as the Gr +6 in Fm. The resolution of this chord in m. 48 confirms the modulation to Fm, a half step down.

Example 26.13 Louise Farrenc, Trio in Em, op. 45, I, mm. 113–121

Example 26.13 Continued

EXERCISE

To practice enharmonic spellings of V_7 and +6 chords, refer to exercise 4 in worksheet 26 at the end of this chapter.

WRITING MODULATIONS WITH +6 CHORDS

As an exercise, first write summaries in four voices of the modulations we have studied in examples 26.11, 26.13, and 26.14. The process of writing modulations similar to these is really quite simple (you can refer to example 26.10 for models):

1. To modulate from a major key to a key a M3 above its tonic (iii or III), after you write a complete progression establishing the first key, write a V_7/IV in this first key, and respell it as an +6 chord in the second key. Resolve this +6 to the dominant of the new key, and continue writing a complete progression in the new key.
2. To modulate from any M or m key to a key a half step above it, write the Gr +6 chord in the first key, and respell it as a V_7 in the new key. Then resolve this V_7 to the new tonic chord, a half step above the original tonic.
3. To modulate from any M or m key to a key a half step below it, write V_7 in the original key, and respell it as the Gr +6 chord in the new key. Then resolve this +6 to a dominant-tonic progression in the new key, a half step below the original key.

Try these three techniques with several keys of your choice.

Example 26.14 F. Schubert, "Gefror'ne Thränen," from *Winterreise,* no. 3, mm. 45–51

EXERCISES

To practice realizing modulations by enharmonic reinterpretation of +6 chords, refer to exercises 5 and 6 in worksheet 26 at the end of this chapter.

To practice writing your own modulation by enharmonic reinterpretation of +6, refer to exercises 10a and 11 in worksheet 26 at the end of this chapter.

MODULATION BY ENHARMONIC REINTERPRETATION OF vii°$_7$

As you will remember, there are only three different fully diminished seventh sonorities. All the vii°$_7$ chords in all keys, including all the secondary vii°$_7$s, are thus drawn

Example 26.15

from a very limited pool of only three sonorities! Obviously, this means that each of these sonorities has a great variety of possible spellings, functions, and resolutions. Take, for instance, the vii$^{\circ}_{7}$ on F♯, with F♯ as the leading tone. The same sonority can be built on A, C, or D♯, using each of these pitches as a leading tone. Each of these sonorities can be resolved to its tonic (G, B♭, D♭, or E, respectively). Example 26.15a shows each of these spellings in root position and its resolution to the corresponding tonic. Example 26.15b demonstrates how the same position can be reinterpreted to represent different inversions in different keys. Examples 26.15a and b assume only "primary" resolutions. Of course, the same sonority can also have numerous secondary functions in a great variety of keys. Example 26.15c shows just a few of these possibilities.

In other words, *by respelling and reinterpreting the function of vii$^{\circ}_{7}$, we could conceivably modulate from any key to any other possible key!* This is truly one of the most powerful techniques of chromatic modulation we have discussed so far. As an exercise, try to determine how you would modulate from CM (or Cm) to each of the other eleven M/m pairs of keys using vii$^{\circ}_{7}$ chords as pivots (identify the specific vii$^{\circ}_{7}$ you would use for each of the modulations).

Example 26.16 L. v. Beethoven, Piano Sonata in E♭M, op. 81a, I, mm. 91–98

Let us examine some examples from the literature using this procedure. In example 26.16 we find a modulation from G♭M to the distant key of Cm. After the V^6_5 in G♭M in m. 94, the chord in m. 95 first sounds like vii°$_7$ in this same key. Its spelling, however, is not F–A♭–C♭–E♭♭, as it would be if it were functioning in G♭M, but rather F–A♭–B♮–D, suggesting a vii°$^4_3$ in Cm. The resolution of the chord to i$_6$ in Cm, and the subsequent confirmation of this key, prove that the chord in m. 95 is indeed reinterpreted enharmonically as a means to effect this distant modulation.

The vii°$_7$ chord used as a pivot in the previous example functions as a "primary" chord in both keys. Look now at example 26.17. The modulation here is from CM to E♭M, also a distant modulation. How would you interpret the last chord in m. 15 in CM (think of the exact function and inversion)? Obviously, although it is spelled according to this function, it does not resolve to the expected chord in CM. Instead, we move to E♭M. Go back to the last chord in m. 15, and reinterpret it in this new key (providing its exact position). Does it need any enharmonic respelling? If you do this right, you will find that the chord functions as a secondary vii°$_7$/V in each of the keys (in first inversion for CM, in root position for E♭M). These two examples provide a brief but sufficient illustration of the manifold modulating possibilities afforded by the fully diminished seventh sonority.

Example 26.17 F. Schubert, Piano Sonata in Am, op. 164, I, mm. 10–17

EXERCISES

To practice enharmonic spellings of vii°$_7$ chords, refer to exercise 7 in worksheet 26 at the end of this chapter.

To practice realizing modulations by enharmonic reinterpretation of vii°$_7$ chords, refer to exercises 8 and 9 in worksheet 26 at the end of this chapter.

WRITING MODULATIONS WITH vii°$_7$ CHORDS

If you want to modulate from any key to any other key, you can certainly find some enharmonic reinterpretation of some vii°$_7$ that will take you there. Suppose that we want to go from E♭M to BM. The following procedure will help us find the right pivot to do so.

1. First, examine the "primary" vii°$_7$ chord in E♭M: D–F–A♭–C♭. (If you were not to find any good pivot relationship using this chord, you could follow the same process with any secondary vii°$_7$, until you found a pivot that suited you.)

Example 26.18

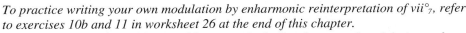

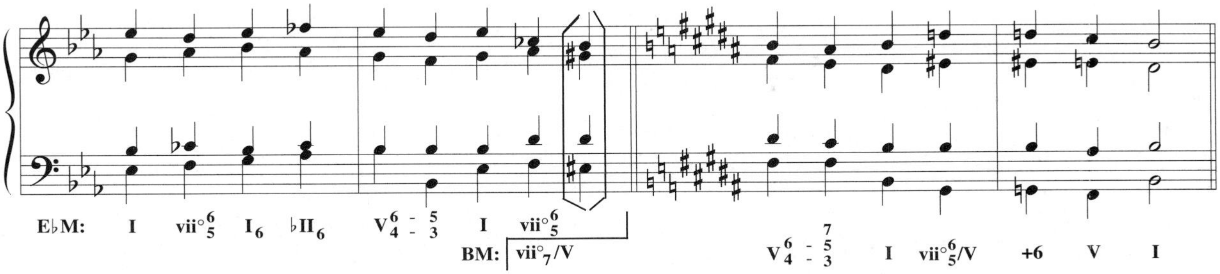

2. Can this chord be used as either the primary vii°$_7$ in BM, or perhaps as a secondary one? We see that although it cannot function as the primary chord, this is the same sonority as the one for vii°$_7$/V in BM (E♯–G♯–B–D). So we have a good pivot relationship on which to build our modulation.
3. Finally, it's all a matter of writing a good, musical realization of this modulation in the form of a modulating progression. Example 26.18 provides a sample realization of our modulation from E♭M to BM.

EXERCISES

To practice writing your own modulation by enharmonic reinterpretation of vii°$_7$, refer to exercises 10b and 11 in worksheet 26 at the end of this chapter.

To practice analysis of musical fragments including the types of modulation we have studied in this chapter, refer to exercise 1 in worksheet 26 at the end of this chapter.

FOR FURTHER STUDY

For additional analysis using materials studied in this chapter, refer to the *Harmony in Context* Web page at www.mhhe.com/roigfrancoli2e.

ASSIGNMENT AND KEYBOARD EXERCISES

For analytical and written assignments and keyboard exercises based on the materials learned in this chapter, refer to chapter 26 in the workbook.

PITCH PATTERNS

Sing the following melodic pitch patterns in example 26.19. As you sing, listen to the modulation in each of the patterns, paying special attention to the chromatic pivot or to the enharmonic reinterpretation that effects the modulation. Practice *improvising* similar pitch patterns modulating to different keys.

Example 26.19

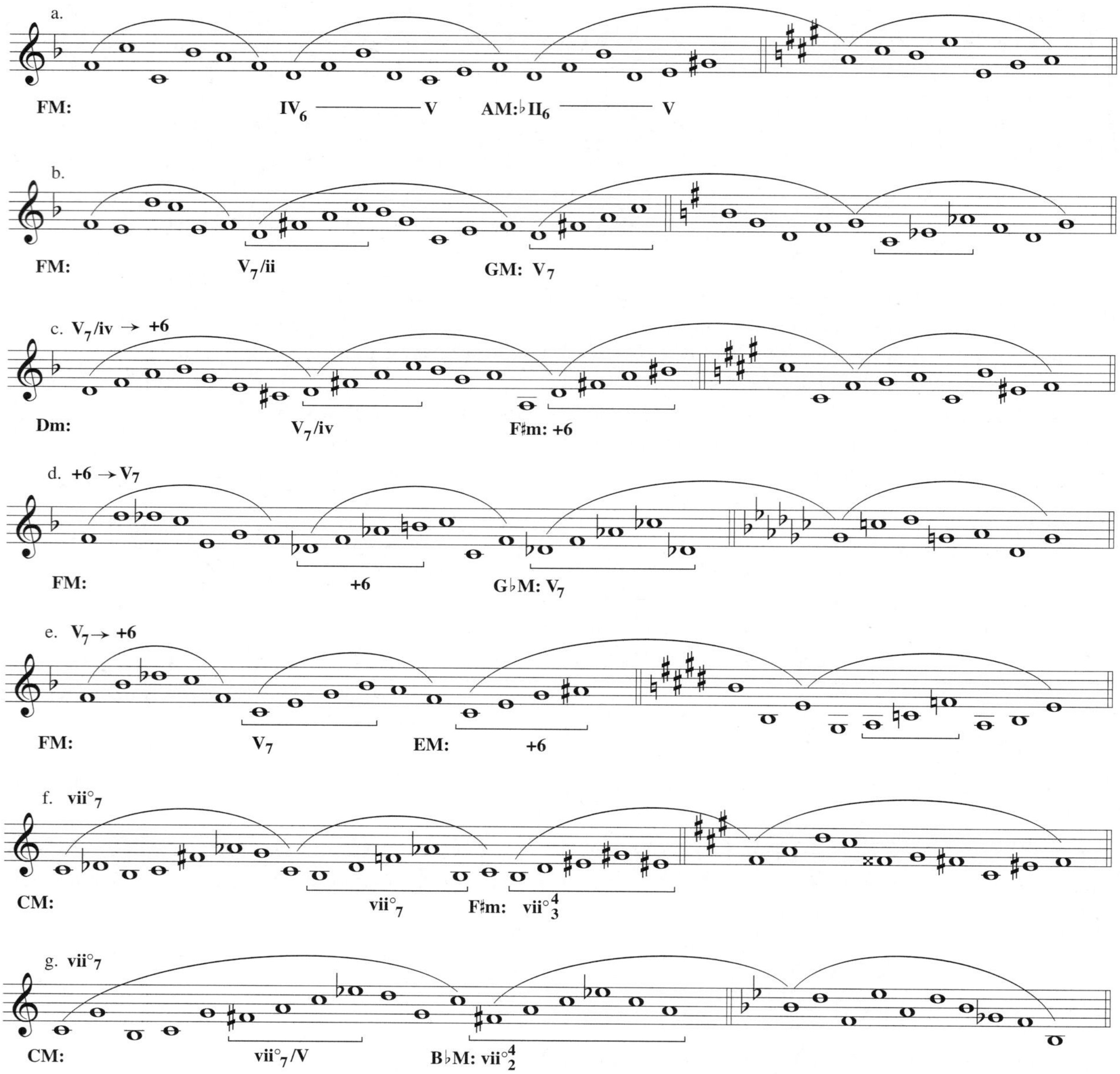

Terms for Review

Distantly related keys
Chromatic pivot chord
Chromatic pivot relationships:
 diatonic-chromatic, chromatic-diatonic, chromatic-chromatic
Modulation by enharmonic reinterpretation of the +6 chord
Modulation to iii or III using the +6
Modulation up or down a half step using the +6
Enharmonic reinterpretation of vii$^{\circ}_{7}$

Worksheet 26

EXERCISE 1 Analysis.

1. The modulation in example 26.20 features a chromatic pivot chord. Analyze the complete passage with RNs, and explain the modulation and the pivot chord.

Example 26.20 Chevalier de Saint–Georges, Aria "O Clemangis, lis dans mon âme," from *Ernestine*, mm. 90–101

2. The following examples feature the ♭II key area and/or modulations by enharmonic reinterpretation of +6. Analyze each of them, identify the modulations or the ♭II key area, the keys involved, and the exact function of the pivot chord in each of the keys.

   a) Example 26.21.

Example 26.21 F. Schubert, "Mein," from *Die schöne Müllerin,* mm. 58–65

Example 26.21 Continued

b) Anthology, no. 34, Beethoven, Sonata op. 13, *Pathétique,* III, mm. 193–210.

1) Explain the modulation from Cm to A♭M in mm. 197–203.

2) Then, explain the return to Cm in mm. 206–210.

c) Example 26.22.

d) Anthology, no. 38, Schubert, *Erlkönig.*

1) Explain the modulation in mm. 105–112.

2) Measures 116–123 are in Dm. What secondary key area of Dm is included in these measures?

3) Analyze mm. 131–148. What secondary key areas can you identify?

Example 26.22 J. Brahms, *Im Herbst,* mm. 1–5

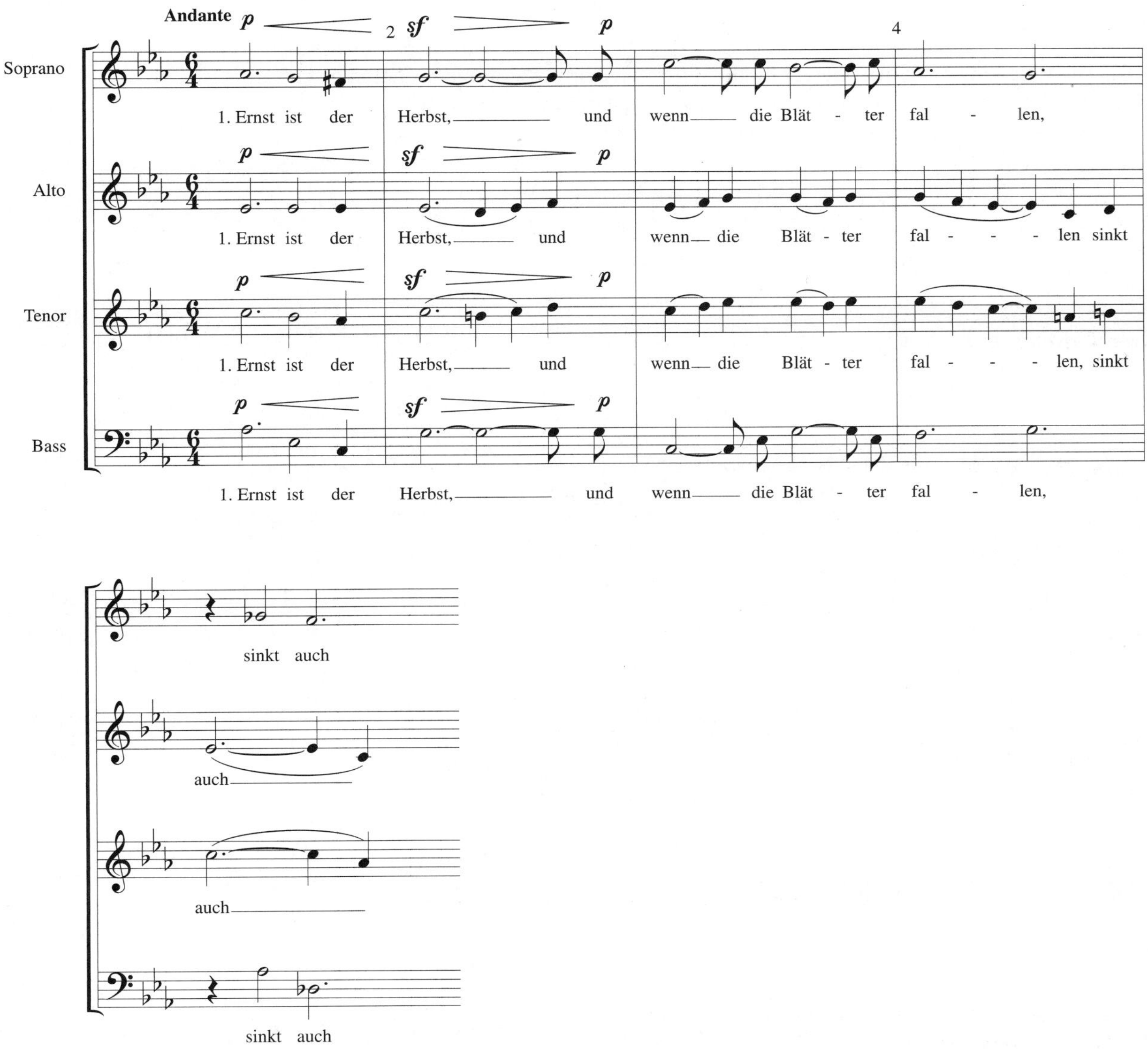

e) Anthology, no. 36, Beethoven, Sonata in E♭M, op. 7, II, mm. 33–51.

1) This movement is in CM. What is the key in m. 33?

2) Explain the modulation back to C, which actually takes place in mm. 36–37.

3. The following examples feature modulation by enharmonic reinterpretation of vii°_{7} chords. Analyze each of them, identify the modulations, the keys involved, and the exact function of the pivot chord in each of the keys.

a) Example 26.23.

b) Anthology, no. 51, Liszt, *Consolation* no. 4, mm. 23–25.

Example 26.23 F. Schubert, "Gefror'ne Thränen," from *Winterreise,* no. 3, mm. 30–37

EXERCISE 2 The following statements refer to chromatic pivot chord relationships. Fill in the blank in each statement.

Diatonic-Chromatic

1. IV_6 in ________ becomes $\flat II_6$ in C♯m.
2. VI in F♯m becomes V/V in ________.
3. ________ in Gm becomes $\flat II_6$ in AM.
4. iii in E♭m becomes ________ in DM.

Chromatic-Diatonic

1. $\flat II_6$ in Bm becomes V_6 in ________.
2. V_7/ii in ________ becomes V_7 in DM.
3. iv in EM becomes ________ in GM.
4. ________ in FM becomes IV_6 in D♭M.

Chromatic-Chromatic

1. V^4_3/vi in FM becomes V^4_3/V in ________.
2. vii°_7/iv in ________ becomes vii°_7/V in Gm.
3. ________ in C♯m becomes vii°_7/iv in Bm.
4. vii°_7/ii in B♭M becomes ________ in GM.

EXERCISE 3 Write the following chromatic pivot chord modulations (bass and RNs, with indication of the pivot chord).

a. From DM to C♯m using $\flat II_6$ of C♯m as a pivot.
b. From GM to E♭M using a borrowed chord in GM as pivot.
c. From CM to AM using a vii°_7 chord with a secondary function in both keys (for instance, vii°_7/ii in CM).

a.

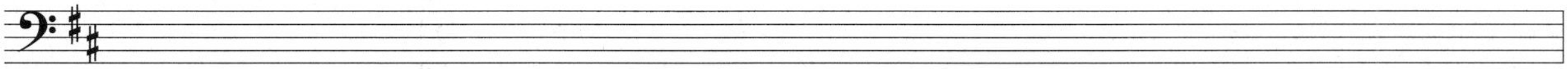

DM:

b.

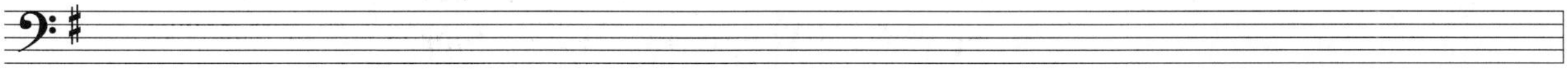

GM:

c.

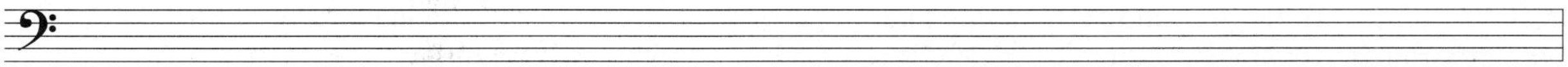

CM:

EXERCISE 4 In each of the spaces in this exercise, spell the first chord in the required key. Then respell the chord to function as required by the second Roman numeral, and indicate in which key it would have this second function. An example is provided for each of the three types of required respelling.

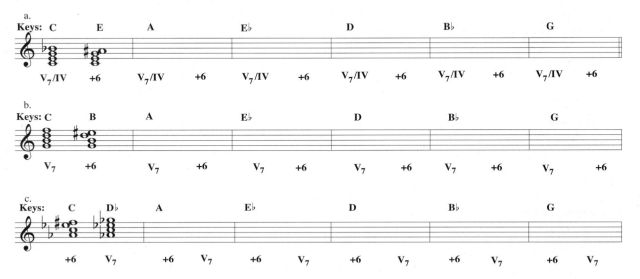

a.

Keys: C E A E♭ D B♭ G

V_7/IV +6 V_7/IV +6 V_7/IV +6 V_7/IV +6 V_7/IV +6 V_7/IV +6

b.

Keys: C B A E♭ D B♭ G

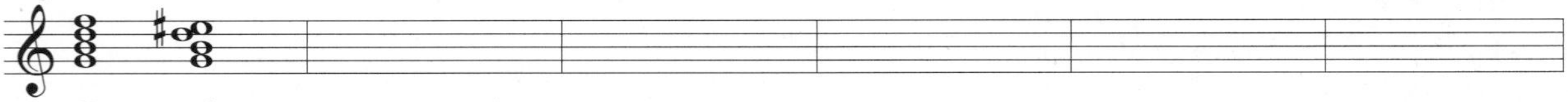

V_7 +6 V_7 +6 V_7 +6 V_7 +6 V_7 +6 V_7 +6

c.

Keys: C D♭ A E♭ D B♭ G

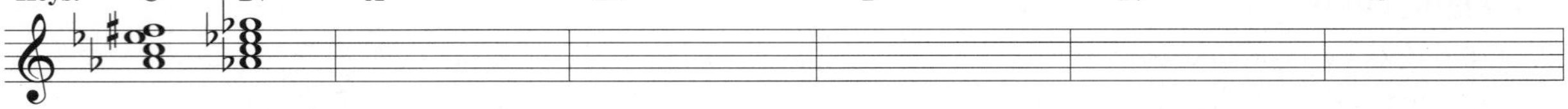

+6 V_7 +6 V_7 +6 V_7 +6 V_7 +6 V_7 +6 V_7

EXERCISE 5 The following RNs represent modulations by enharmonic reinterpretation of the Gr +6 chord. Write the bass line for each progression, and indicate what key we have modulated to in each case.

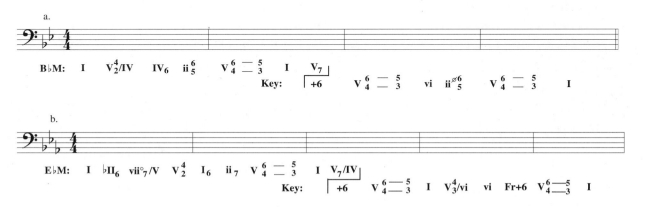

a.

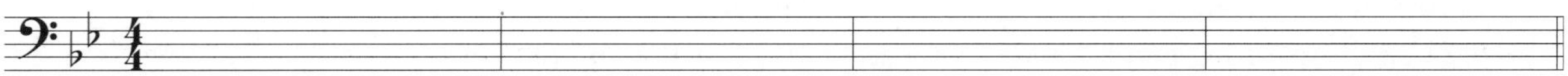

B♭M: I V^4_2/IV IV_6 ii^6_5 $V^{6\,-\,5}_{4\,-\,3}$ I V_7

Key: +6 $V^{6\,-\,5}_{4\,-\,3}$ vi $ii^{\varnothing 6}_{5}$ $V^{6\,-\,5}_{4\,-\,3}$ I

b.

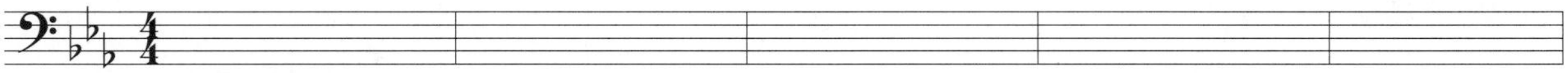

E♭M: I ♭II_6 vii°$_7$/V V^4_2 I_6 ii_7 $V^{6\,-\,5}_{4\,-\,3}$ I V_7/IV

Key: +6 $V^{6\,-\,5}_{4\,-\,3}$ I V^4_3/vi vi Fr+6 $V^{6\,-\,5}_{4\,-\,3}$ I

EXERCISE 6 Write the following modulating progression in four voices. Provide both enharmonic spellings for the pivot chord. Write the key signature for the new key after the double bar (in the space marked with an asterisk).

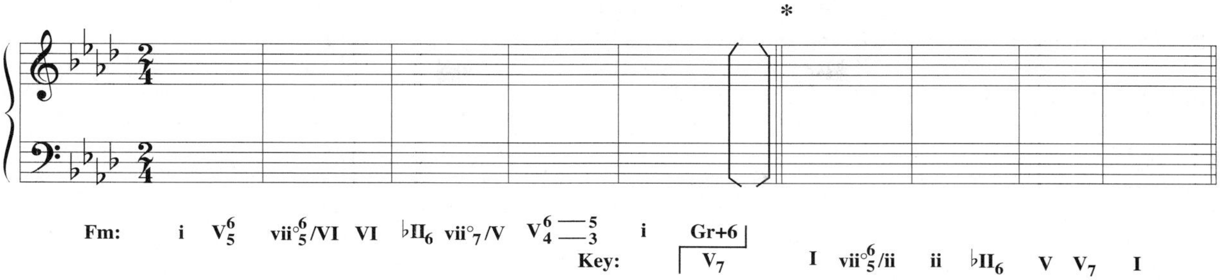

EXERCISE 7

a. Write and resolve vii°$_7$ in Fm. This chord may be used to modulate to three other minor keys by respelling it enharmonically. Indicate the keys and provide the spelling (leaving the chord in the same position), the correct RN, and the correct resolution to the corresponding tonic in each of the new keys. For a reference of what you are doing exactly, see example 26.15b in this chapter (although in that example the chords are not resolved).

b. Follow the same process as above, but now show how vii°$_7$ in B♭M functions in three other major keys.

c. The following statements refer to enharmonically respelled vii°$_7$ chords. Fill in the blank in each statement.

1. vii°$_7$ in B♭ becomes ________ in G.
2. ________ in G becomes vii°$^4_3$ in D♭.
3. vii°$^6_5$ in ________ becomes vii°$_7$ in E♭.
4. vii°$^4_2$ in F becomes vii°$^6_5$ in ________.

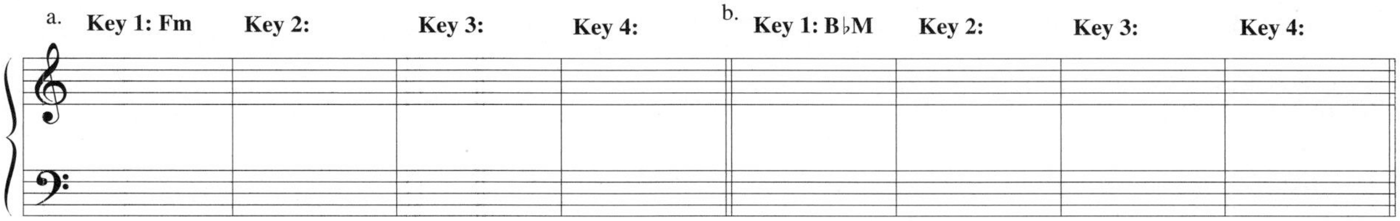

EXERCISE 8 The RNs in this exercise represent a modulation by enharmonic reinterpretation of vii°$_7$. Write the bass line and indicate what key we have modulated to.

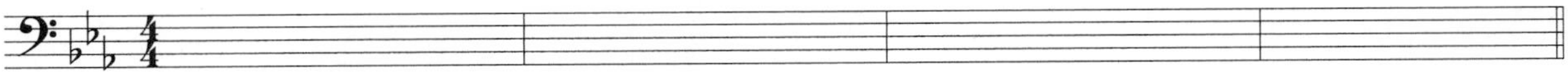

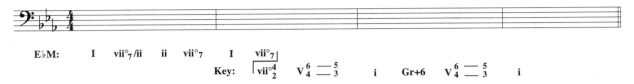

E♭M: I vii°$_7$/ii ii vii°$_7$ I vii°$_7$

Key: vii°$^4_2$ V$^{6}_{4}$—$^{5}_{3}$ i Gr+6 V$^{6}_{4}$—$^{5}_{3}$ i

EXERCISE 9 Write the following modulating progression in four voices. Provide both enharmonic spellings for the pivot chord. Write the key signature for the new key after the double bar (in the space marked with an asterisk).

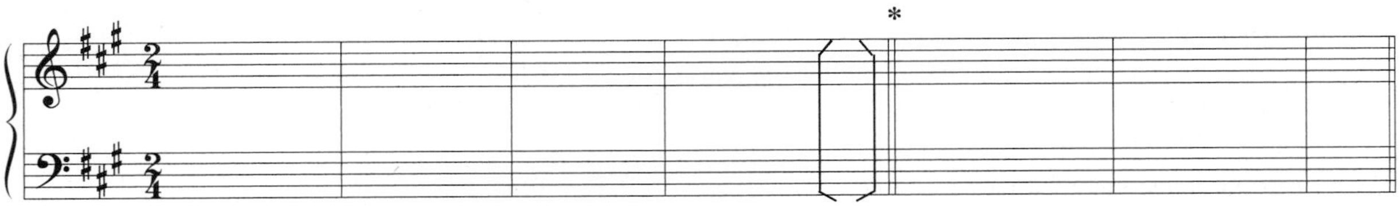

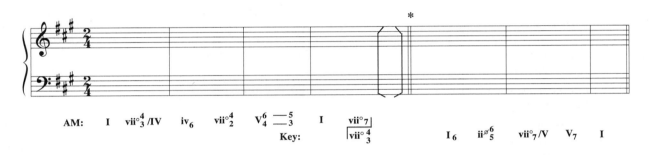

AM: I vii°$^4_3$/IV iv$_6$ vii°$^4_2$ V$^{6}_{4}$—$^{5}_{3}$ I vii°$_7$

Key: vii°$^4_3$ I$_6$ ii$^{ø6}_{5}$ vii°$_7$/V V$_7$ I

EXERCISE 10 Write your own modulating progressions (bass and RNs) using Gr +6 and vii°$_7$ chords as pivots.

a. A modulation from DM to its Neapolitan key using an enharmonic reinterpretation of the Gr +6.

b. A modulation from Gm to E♭M using an enharmonic reinterpretation of vii°$_7$ in Gm.

a.

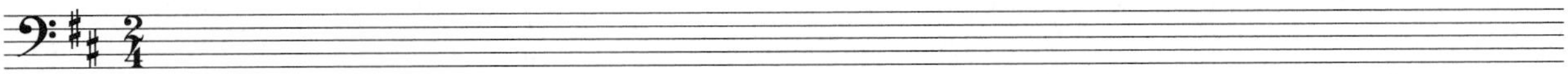

DM:

b.

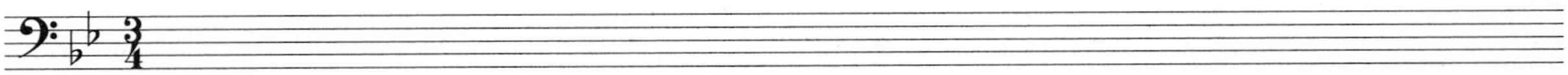

Gm:

EXERCISE 11 Choose one of the modulating progressions you have written in exercise 3 and one from exercise 10, and, using your own music paper, write two phrases based on your progressions for a melodic instrument with keyboard accompaniment.

Chapter 27

Modulation to Distantly Related Keys II; Linear Chromaticism I

In this chapter we will first continue our study of modulation to distantly related keys. We will focus specifically on chromatic third–related keys and on the technique of common-tone modulation. In the second part of the chapter we will study several types of chords usually generated by means of linear chromaticism.

CHROMATIC THIRD RELATIONSHIPS

Two triads are related by **chromatic third** if their *roots are a M or m 3rd apart,* and their members belong to *different diatonic scales* Example 27.1 presents a chart of all triads related by third with both a M and a m triad. The triads in parentheses (vi and iii in M, VI and III in m) have a *diatonic third* relationship with the tonic triad because their members belong to the *same diatonic scale* as the members of the tonic triad (vi: A–C–E and iii: E–G–B belong to the same diatonic scale as I: C–E–G, the CM "white-key" scale). The rest of the triads, on the other hand, display members belonging to different diatonic scales than the members of the tonic triad (both ♭VI: A♭–C–E♭ and III: E–G♯–B belong to different diatonic scales than I: C–E–G).

There are, then, six triads related by chromatic third to any M triad and six more related to any m triad. These triads are also called **chromatic mediants** because they are altered mediant and submediant chords. Four of the set of six chromatic third–related triads have a *common tone* with I or i, and two of the triads do not. The triads that do not have common tones with I or i are indicated in brackets in our example. Verify what the common tone with I is for each of the following triads: VI, ♭VI, III, and ♭III; and with i for triads vi, ♯vi, iii, and ♯iii.

EXERCISE

To practice determining the set of triads related to a given triad by chromatic third, refer to exercise 2 in worksheet 27 at the end of this chapter.

Example 27.1

(vi), VI — Am, AM
(iii), III — Em, EM
I — CM
♭VI, [♭vi] — A♭M, A♭m
♭III, [♭iii] — E♭M, E♭m

(VI), vi — A♭M, A♭m
(III), iii — E♭M, E♭m
i — Cm
♮vi, [♯VI] — Am, AM
♯iii, [♯III] — Em, EM

TRIADS RELATED BY CHROMATIC THIRD

Chromatic third relationships can exist between triads or between keys. We will first examine third–related triads. Consider, for instance, the beginning of Franz Liszt's "Il pensieroso" (example 27.2). The end of the phrase establishes the key of C♯m. The first two chords, on the other hand, are not related functionally within this key: The C♯m–Am triads do not belong to the same diatonic scale, and their relationship, i–vi, is not functional, but rather linear: The Am triad is a chromatic neighbor chord that prolongs i. The phrase, however, is strongly tied together tonally by the reiterated E in the right

Example 27.2 Franz Liszt, "Il pensieroso," from *Années de Pèlerinage,* mm. 1–4

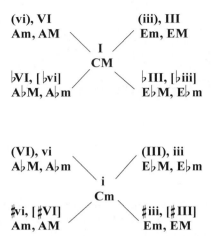

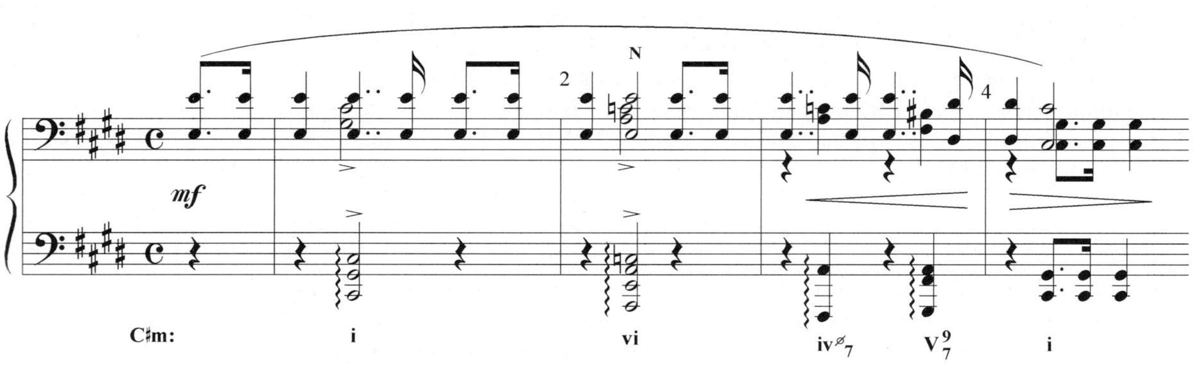

Example 27.3 Harmonic Reduction of Verdi's Recitative to "Celeste Aida," *Aida,* act I

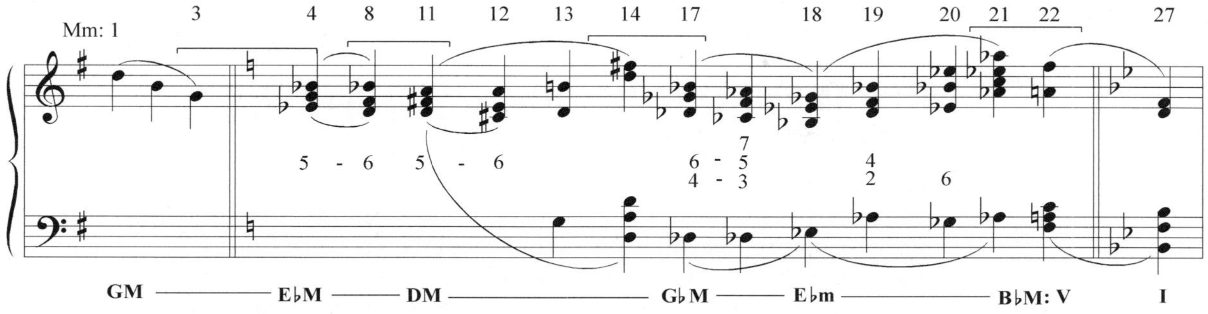

hand, the pitch that connects the C♯m and Am triads by common tone, and by the bass in descending 3rds (C♯–A–F♯) leading to the $\hat{5}$–$\hat{1}$ cadential motion. The third chord is an altered pre-dominant, a iv$_7$ with a lowered fifth (iv$^{ø}_7$). We will study altered chords (chords with a raised or lowered fifth) later in this chapter.

Because they do not belong to the same diatonic scale, and because, hence, they are not harmonically related according to the tenets of functional progression, chromatic third triads can suspend the sense of functional tonality momentarily. An interesting use of chromatic third–related triads can be found in the recitative introducing Verdi's famous aria, "Celeste Aida" (anthology, no. 55). Example 27.3 presents a harmonic reduction of the passage, in which all harmonies have been reduced to quarter notes, regardless of their duration in the music (slurs denote harmonic grouping). In this passage, the Egyptian general, Radames, expresses his ambition to be the leader in the upcoming war campaign against the Ethiopians, and to be able to dedicate his victory to his beloved Aida (a captive Ethiopian princess, none other than the daughter of the Ethiopian king Radames hopes to defeat!). The military trumpet calls reflect the mood of the occasion, and the seemingly erratic tonal content of the passage reflects the sense of brewing conflict. The path from the initial GM to the final B♭M (two keys related by chromatic third) takes us through the distant tonal areas of E♭M, DM, G♭M, and E♭m. Play through the reduction, and notice that some of the key areas are barely suggested (E♭M and G♭M, for instance).

The connection between several of the key areas is effected by direct motion between chromatic third–related triads (marked with brackets over the graph). In mm. 3–4, we move directly from a GM triad to an E♭M triad (I–♭VI in GM). In mm. 8–11, the motion is from a B♭M triad to a DM triad (♭VI–I in DM). In mm. 14–17, the motion is from a DM triad to a G♭M $^6_4$ sonority (I–III in DM, with III spelled enharmonically). And, finally, in mm. 21–22 we hear a nonfunctional connection between an A♭M triad (IV in E♭m, or ♭VII in B♭M) and an FM triad (V in B♭M). These nonfunctional triadic connections that are used to move from one key area to the next further weaken both the sense of functional tonality and the overall sense of tonal unity in this passage.

EXERCISE

To practice spelling triads related by chromatic third, refer to exercise 3 in worksheet 27 at the end of this chapter.

KEYS RELATED BY CHROMATIC THIRD: COMMON-TONE MODULATION

The chromatic third relationship among keys is a distant one (as illustrated by such key area relationships, in the Verdi example above, as GM–E♭M or DM–G♭M—an enharmonic spelling of the 3rd relationship DM–F♯M). The modulation between chromatic third–related keys, however, can be a very direct one because of the common tone some of them share. In the most direct type of **common-tone modulation,** the pitch common to the tonic chords of two keys is reinterpreted as the new degree in the second key and used as a **pivot pitch** to modulate. Common-tone (CT) modulation directly connecting tonic chords is possible only between tonics that do have a common tone (the keys in brackets in example 27.1 are thus excluded). That leaves four possible chromatic third–related keys from any M or m key. Example 27.4 shows the common-tone connection from both CM and Cm to each of these possible keys. (Common-tone modulation is also possible between diatonic third–related keys, and in these cases there are even two possible common tones between tonics.)

Third-related keys in general, and chromatic third–related keys in particular, were often favored by nineteenth-century composers, beginning with Beethoven and continuing with such composers as Schubert, Schumann, Brahms, Liszt, and Verdi. The fragment by Louise Farrenc in example 27.5 illustrates a direct modulation from BM to ♭VI, GM, using the common-tone B as the only connecting device. Notice how the BM tonic in m. 140 gives prominence to the pitch B in both hands, and how the GM tonic in m. 141 also begins with B in both piano lines.

The CT in common-tone modulations need not be only between tonic chords. In example 27.6 you can see a fragment of a song in FM by Beethoven. The fragment begins with a phrase on V_7 in FM and moves directly to I_6 in the new key, A♭M (♭III), taking advantage of the common tone C between V_7 in FM and I in A♭M, in both cases placed in the bass. Although this modulation uses a CT between V of the old key and I

Example 27.4

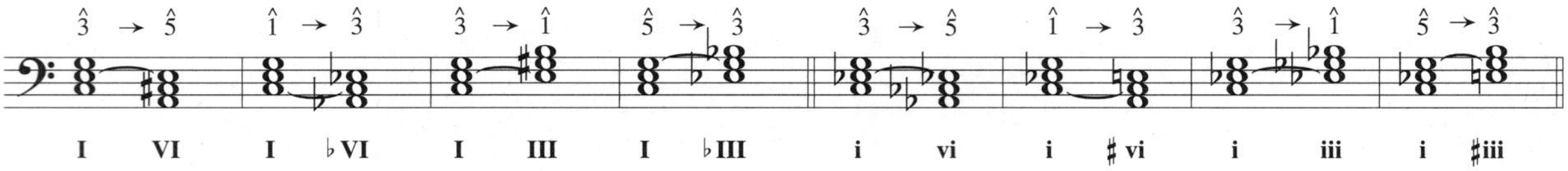

Example 27.5 L. Farrenc, Trio in Em. op. 45, I, mm. 133–148

of the new key, the tone, C, happens to be the same that would have been used to modulate directly from tonic to tonic of the same keys. A similar case appears in the excerpt reproduced in example 27.7. The passage begins in Bm, and moves to DM by CT. Does the CT connect the two tonics, or two chords other than the two tonics? Could the same CT have connected the two tonics? Are the two keys involved in this modulation related by chromatic third?

♭VI as a Key Area

Among the chromatic third–related keys displayed in example 27.1, ♭VI in M is the most frequently encountered in the repertoire. In long-range key schemes, the ♭VI key or secondary key area has a similar function as the ♭VI chord: It results from modal mixture, and it is really a key "borrowed" from minor. The modulation in example 27.8 illustrates that the pivot pitch in this motion from I to ♭VI is $\hat{1}$ in the original key. The tonic cadence in m. 24 stresses $\hat{1}$ as the bass and as the top pitch in both hands. The next measure, I in A♭M, includes the same pitch in the same register in both hands, now

Example 27.6 L. v. Beethoven, "Hoffnung," from *Four Ariettas and a Duet,* op. 82, no. 1, mm. 9–15

Example 27.7 W. A. Mozart, Fantasia in Cm, K. 475, mm. 24–27

with a $\hat{3}$ function. Consult this complete passage in anthology, no. 36, as an example of long-range mixture. The movement is in CM, and the key areas in mm. 22–51 are CM–A♭M–Fm–D♭M–Cm–CM, that is, I–♭VI–iv–♭II–i–I. In other words, the overall design is of descending thirds, and all the areas between the two C major tonic areas are borrowed from C minor.

An example from the anthology (anthology, no. 39, Schubert, Waltz, op. 9, no. 14) demonstrates the possible enharmonic spelling of ♭VI. The key scheme of this short waltz is D♭M–AM–D♭M. You will remember that in the previous chapter we discussed the second modulation, from AM back to D♭M by means of enharmonic reinterpretation of V_7/IV in AM, which becomes the +6 in D♭M. We can now look at the first modulation, in mm. 12–16, from D♭M to AM. This is really a modulation to ♭VI, which, however, has been respelled as AM to avoid the cumbersome key of B♭♭M. What is the common tone between these two keys? How is it spelled in each of the keys in our example?

EXERCISE

To practice writing a common-tone modulation, refer to exercise 4 in worksheet 27 at the end of this chapter.

Example 27.8 L. v. Beethoven, Piano Sonata op. 7 in E♭M, II, mm. 22–28

EXERCISE

To practice analyzing musical fragments including triads related by chromatic third or common-tone modulations, refer to exercises 1.1 and 1.2 in worksheet 27 at the end of this chapter.

LINEAR CHROMATICISM I: LINEAR CHROMATIC CHORDS

Throughout our study of harmony in previous chapters we have stressed that some chords are generated linearly—that is, they result from melodic processes rather than vertical chord generation. In the sections that follow we will continue our study of linear harmony, focusing on some chromatic chords that result from linear processes.

ALTERED TRIADS

Romantic composers (especially in the second half of the nineteenth century) often *altered the fifth of a major triad* chromatically. An **altered triad** is a major triad with an augmented or diminished fifth. Most commonly, triads are altered to become augmented,

Example 27.9 C. Schumann, "Notturno," from *Vier Stücke aus Soirées Musicales,* op. 2, no. 2, mm. 1–6

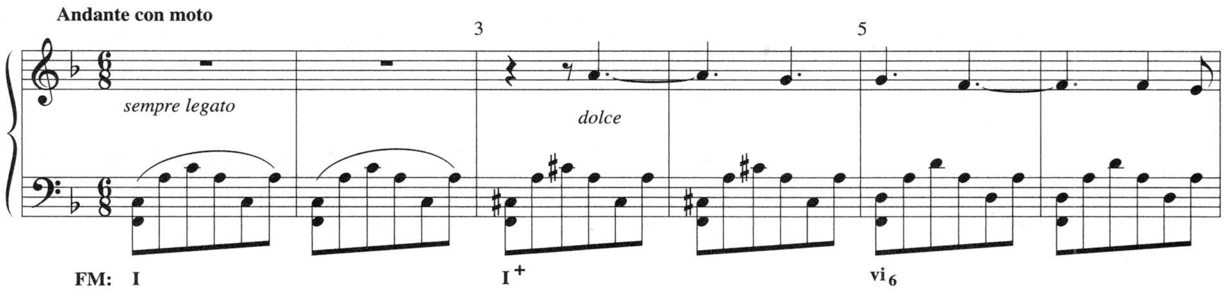

and among all the diatonic triads, V is the one most often presented with a sharpened fifth, to become V^+.

Altered triads are sometimes generated by chromatic linear motion. In example 27.9, a passing C♯, part of the linear gesture C–C♯–D in mm. 1–5, turns the initial I into an augmented triad, I^+.

Not all altered triads, however, result from such linear motions. Romantic composers also altered triads for dramatic, expressive, or simply coloristic purposes, to create a richer, more chromatic (and also less stable) harmonic vocabulary. In example 27.10, the dominant of FM appears both in its unaltered form (as V and V_7) and with a sharpened fifth, as V^+ and V^+_7. Identify each of the dominant chords in the passage and determine whether it is an altered chord.

Example 27.10 Alma Mahler, "Ekstase," from *Five Songs,* no. 2, mm. 15–23

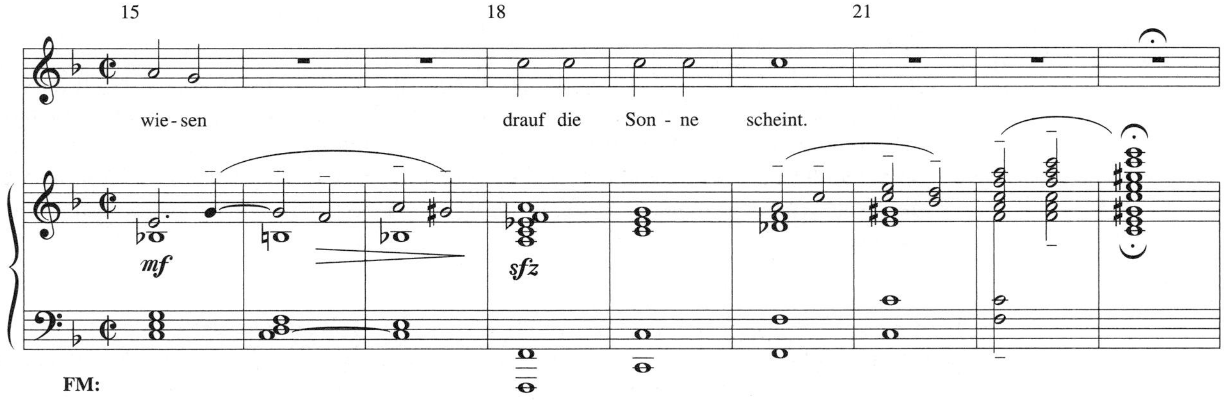

Example 27.11

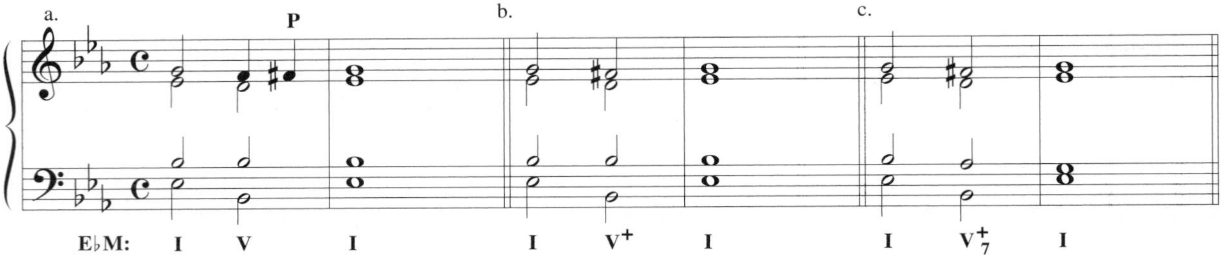

Examine the spelling and voice leading for the V^+ and V^+_7 chords in examples 27.11a to c. In four voices, the altered fifth should not be doubled and should moreover resolve upward to $\hat{3}$ (notice that resolving it down to $\hat{1}$ would create a melodic +2).

EXERCISE

To practice realizing short progressions including altered triads, refer to exercises 5a to c in worksheet 27 at the end of this chapter.

AUGMENTED SIXTH CHORDS WITH DOMINANT AND EMBELLISHING FUNCTIONS

In chapter 25 we studied that +6 chords with a pre-dominant function are based on the +6 interval between ♭$\hat{6}$ and ♯$\hat{4}$, and that their pre-dominant function results from the linear tendencies of both ♭$\hat{6}$ and ♯$\hat{4}$ to resolve to $\hat{5}$. In this section we will study two types of +6 chords that move directly to the tonic and that have a dominant and embellishing function, respectively.[1]

The +6 with a Dominant Function

Just as we build +6 chords using the pre-dominant ♭$\hat{6}$–♯$\hat{4}$ frame, it is possible to build +6 chords using the +6 frame provided by ♭$\hat{2}$ and $\hat{7}$ (♯$\hat{7}$ in minor), two degrees that have a linear tendency to resolve to $\hat{1}$. Because such +6 chords move indeed directly to the tonic, and because they include the leading tone, they have a dominant function. Most often, this type of +6 appears in the form of a Fr +6 on ♭$\hat{2}$ (♭$\hat{2}$–$\hat{4}$–$\hat{5}$–$\hat{7}$), as you can see in example 27.12.

[1] For a study of the different +6 functional types, with a detailed discussion of +6 chords that do not have a pre-dominant function, see Daniel Harrison, "Supplement to the Theory of Augmented-Sixth Chords," *Music Theory Spectrum* 17 (1995): 170–95.

Example 27.12

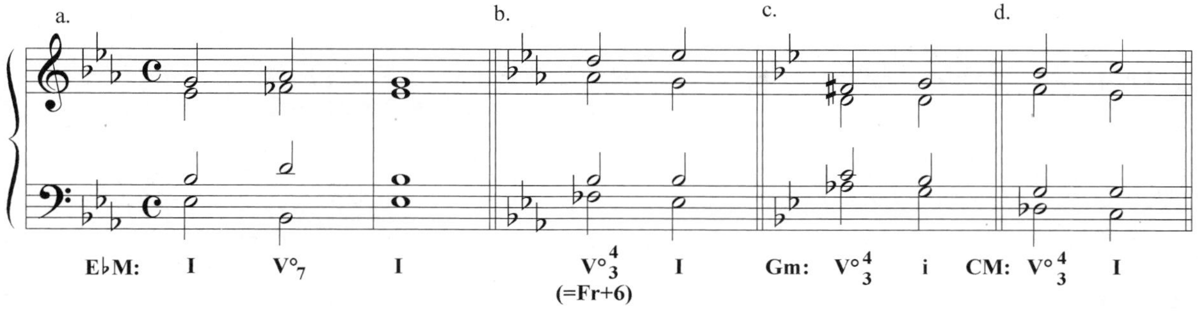

The dominant function of this type of Fr +6 becomes even more evident if we think of it as an altered V^4_3 chord. Example 27.12a illustrates a V_7 in E♭M with a diminished fifth, V°_7 (notice, in this example, that lowering the fifth of a major triad produces a sonority that is *not* a diminished triad, for instance, C–E–G♭, or B♭–D–F♭ in our example). This interesting sonority appears most often in second inversion, in the form of $V^{\circ 4}_3$. If you play example 27.12, you will recognize that this sonority is the same as the Fr +6 built on $\flat\hat{2}$. We can best think of this chord as a **Fr +6 on $\flat\hat{2}$, with a $V^{\circ 4}_3$ function,** and resolving directly to the tonic. To avoid confusion with the label for the pre-dominant Fr +6 on $\flat\hat{6}$, we will refer to the Fr +6 on $\flat\hat{2}$ as $V^{\circ 4}_3$. Examples 27.12c and d show the spelling and resolution of this chord in Gm and CM, respectively. In all cases, notice the linear motion to $\hat{1}$ of the upper and lower leading tones, $\hat{7}$ and $\flat\hat{2}$.

NOTE

To write a Fr +6 as an altered dominant, start from $\flat\hat{2}$. Build your Fr +6 sonority on this degree: $\flat\hat{2}$–$\hat{4}$–$\hat{5}$–$\hat{7}$. In other words, you have written a dominant seventh chord with a lowered fifth ($\hat{5}$–$\hat{7}$–$\flat\hat{2}$–$\hat{4}$), but in second inversion.

The expressive power of this chord is dramatically realized in the passage reproduced in example 27.13, taken from one of Schubert's most intense songs. In Heine's poem, a man goes back, after many years, to the house where his "dear one once dwelt." In front of the house, he finds a man "wringing his hands in overwhelming grief." The grief, "Schmerzensgewalt" in mm. 31–33, is musically depicted by our chord (m. 32). Does register play any role in this depiction? Explain the linear function of our $V^{\circ 4}_3$ as it connects III and i in these measures. Incidentally, the next appearance of the $V^{\circ 4}_3$ chord comes a few bars later, in m. 42, when the poet realizes that the man wringing his hands in pain is none other than . . . himself! (The title of the song is "Der Doppelgänger," "The Phantom Double"!)

Example 27.13 F. Schubert, "Der Doppelgänger," from *Schwanengesang,* no. 13, mm. 29–34

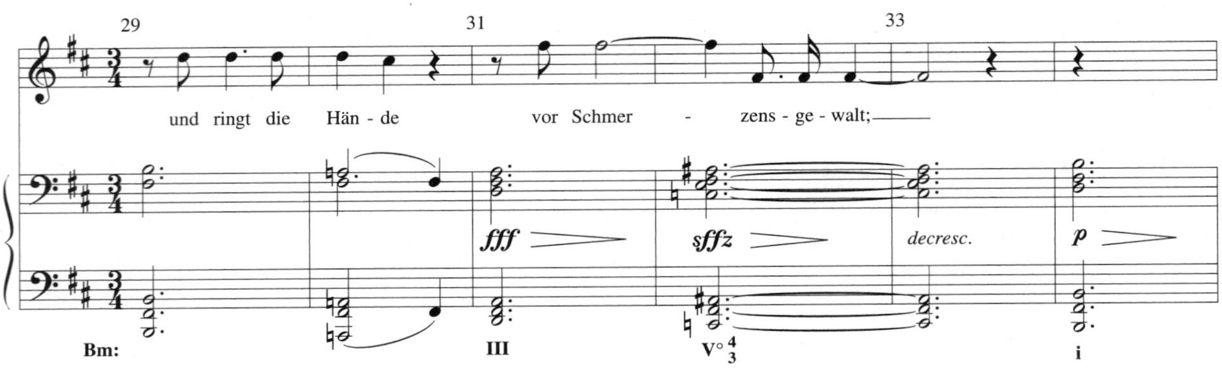

EXERCISE

To practice realizing short progressions including the Fr +6 as an altered dominant, refer to exercises 5d to f in worksheet 27 at the end of this chapter.

The Embellishing (or Common-Tone) Gr +6 Chord

Because the Gr +6 chord on ♭$\hat{6}$ has two common tones with the minor tonic chord ($\hat{1}$ and ♭$\hat{3}$) and one common tone with the major tonic ($\hat{1}$), it can be used as a chord prolonging the tonic, with a voice leading that takes advantage of the common tone or tones. Example 27.14a demonstrates the voice leading with both i and the +6 in root position

Example 27.14

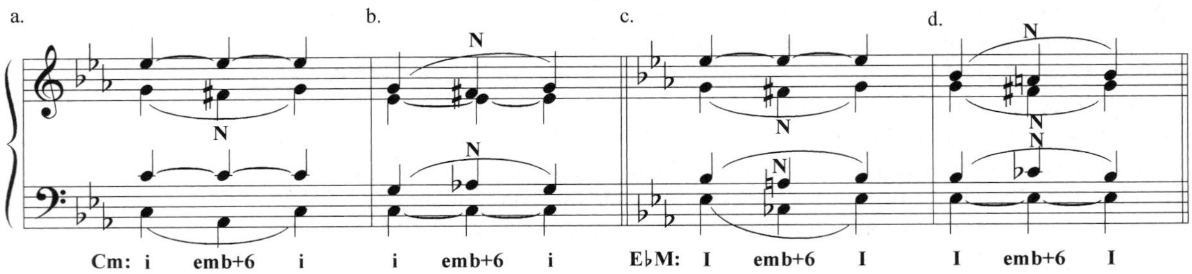

and with the root doubled in i: Two voices feature common tones, the bass moves by an arpeggiation of a third, and the third voice is a neighbor note. Example 27.14b shows the same chord, but with the prolonged (and common) $\hat{1}$ in the bass and the fifth doubled in i. The +6 chord is now in first inversion, and the voice leading features two neighbor notes (NNs).

Examples 27.14c and d present the same chords in a major key, with only one CT. The root-position example (with the root doubled in I) features two NNs, whereas the example with the +6 in first inversion and the fifth doubled in I features three NNs. (Notice, in the examples in the major mode, the enharmonic spelling of the fifth in the +6 chord, F♯ instead of G♭, to stress the NN function of this pitch.)

In other words, this is an +6 that functions linearly by means of CTs and NNs, and whose function is to prolong and embellish the tonic triad as a *neighbor chord.* We will then call it the *embellishing +6 (or common-tone +6).* Notice the similarities in both voice leading and function between this progression and the familiar embellishing N^6_4 progression (I–N^6_4–I).

NOTE

To write an embellishing +6 chord, think first of the spelling of the Gr +6 chord on $\flat\hat{6}$ *in the given key. Leave the CT or CTs in the same voice, and take each of the remaining pitches of the tonic triad to the closest pitch in the +6 chord.*

In the fragment by César Franck reproduced in example 27.15, the Gr +6 chord in AM is first introduced as a linear prolongation of the tonic chord, an embellishing +6, in m. 9. Compare this measure with example 27.14c, and verify the CT and NN functions. How could Franck have spelled this chord to clarify the NN role of the pitch C♮? When the chord appears again in m. 10, does it resolve as an emb. +6?

EXERCISE

To practice realizing short progressions including embellishing Gr +6 chords, refer to exercises 5g and h in worksheet 27 at the end of this chapter.

As we saw in example 27.14, the embellishing +6 can appear in any inversion. Play through, or listen to, example 27.16a. Then play through example 27.16b. This reduction represents the key areas in the Schubert example. Considering that Am is the main key of the passage, these areas are v–iv–vii–i. Each of these areas closes with a tonic embellished by an +6 chord, as indicated in the reduction. What type ("nationality") of +6 chord is it? In what inversion does it appear in the first three key areas? And in the last key area? Identify all the NN motions in this linear connection. Now examine the common tone between the +6 and the tonic in each key area. Where is it placed in each case? Is it stressed rhythmically or texturally in any way?

PRACTICAL APPLICATION AND DISCUSSION

1. Study and understand each of the modulations between the key areas in example 27.16a.
2. The text of this passage is as follows: "And as the cocks are crowing, I rise and look without; the day is cold and dreary, the ravens are screaming about." The title of the song is "Spring Dream," and the poem (by Wilhelm Müller) tells of a dream of spring, beauty, and love the poet just had. Upon awakening, he is confronted again by his reality: He is lonely, it is cold, gloomy, and the ravens are shrieking. How is this reflected by the music? The song is in AM. What is the mode of each of the key areas in this passage? Is this a tonally stable passage? How is the poet's dreary reality reflected by the tonality of this fragment? Are the crowings of cocks and the screams of ravens depicted musically in any way?
3. Discuss in class how your analyses of text and harmony would affect your performance of this passage. What moods and feelings would you try to transmit through your performance, and how?

Example 27.15 César Franck, Sonata for Violin and Piano, I, mm. 5–13

Example 27.16a F. Schubert, "Frühlingstraum," from *Die Winterreise,* no. 11, mm. 15–22

Example 27.16b

THE COMMON-TONE DIMINISHED SEVENTH CHORD

The **common-tone diminished seventh chord (CT °7)** is another linear chord which, like the emb. +6, is based on common tone and NN voice leading. This is a °7 chord that prolongs or embellishes any chord, provided that the root of the prolonged chord be a note of the °7 chord. Look at example 27.17 for clarification: The root of the E♭M chord

Example 27.17

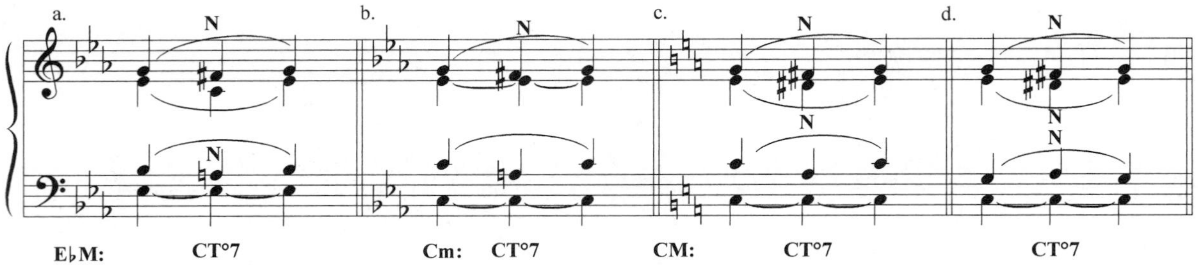

is a pitch also present in the following embellishing °7 chord, which spelled from its own root is F♯–A–C–E♭. This is a nonfunctional chromatic chord that prolongs the original triad by means of a CT, two NNs, and a leap of a third (or just a CT and three NNs if you doubled the fifth in the original chord, as in example 27.17d). If the prolonged chord is minor, then the °7 chord has two common tones (example 27.17b).

NOTE

To write a CT °7, find the °7 chord that contains the root of the given chord; leave this CT in the bass, and then take each of the pitches in the original chord to the closest possible pitch in the °7 chord. If you doubled the root in the original chord, your voice leading to the °7 chord will include two NN figures (only one for a minor chord) and a downward third arpeggiation in the upper voices. With a doubled fifth, you will have three NNs.

The CT °7 often appears at the beginning of a piece or phrase, providing an opening tonic prolongation in the form of a *neighbor chord.* This is exactly how it is used by Mendelssohn in example 27.18, where the chord returns to the tonic, completing the NN figures.

Refer back to Franck's excerpt in example 27.15. What is the chord that precedes the emb. +6? Notice the similarity of both chords, in pitch content and function. Example 27.19, on the other hand, presents a slightly different type of CT °7. It connects I with V^6_5, and, as it turns out, the root of I is not a CT with the °7 chord, but the root of V_7 (G) is. On the other hand, both the third and fifth of I (E and G) are common tones with the °7 chord. In other words, our °7 has two CTs with I and one CT with V_7. If you consider the basic melodic motion that these three chords harmonize (the C–C♯–D figure in the voice), what is the linear function of this CT °7?

Example 27.18 Felix Mendelssohn, *Rondo Capriccioso,* op. 14, mm. 4–8

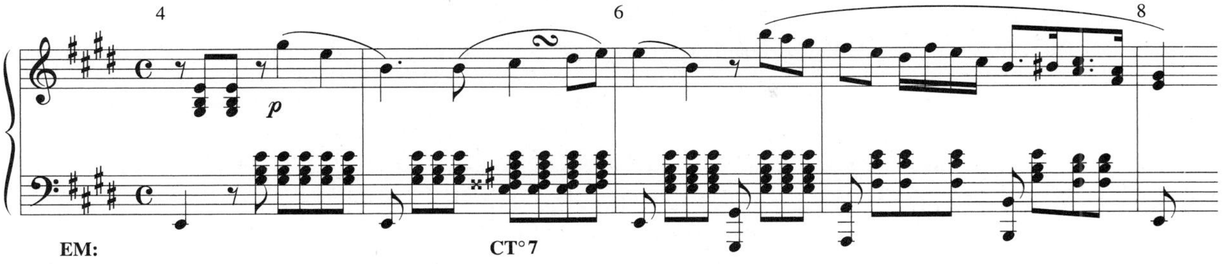

EXERCISES

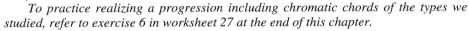

To practice realizing short progressions including CT°7 chords, refer to exercises 5i and j in worksheet 27 at the end of this chapter.

To practice realizing a progression including chromatic chords of the types we studied, refer to exercise 6 in worksheet 27 at the end of this chapter.

To practice analyzing musical fragments including chromatic chords of the types we studied, refer to exercise 1.3 in worksheet 27 at the end of this chapter.

Example 27.19 G. Donizetti, *Don Pasquale,* act III, no. 9

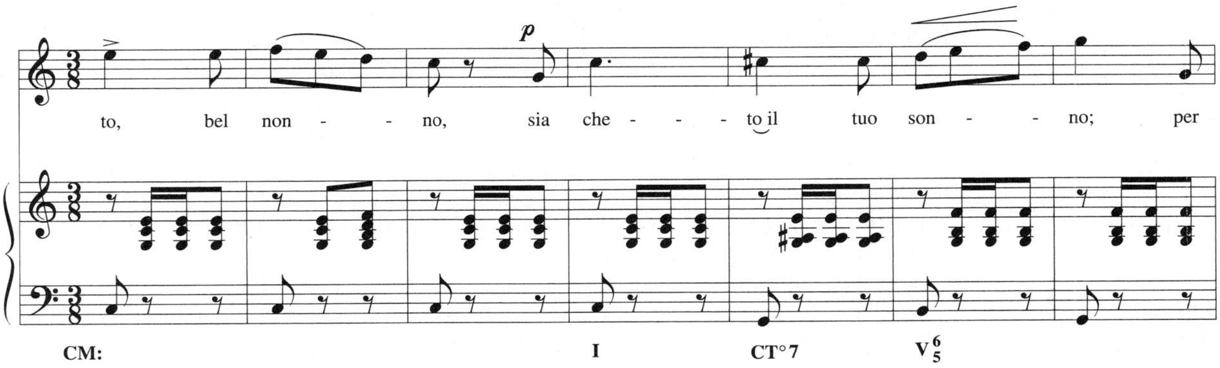

FOR FURTHER STUDY

For additional chapter 27 materials, refer to the *Harmony in Context* Web page at www.mhhe.com/roigfrancoli2e.

ASSIGNMENT AND KEYBOARD EXERCISES

For analytical and written assignments and keyboard exercises based on the materials learned in this chapter, refer to chapter 27 in the workbook.

PITCH PATTERNS

Sing the melodic pitch patterns in example 27.20, and as you sing, listen to the modulation to a chromatic third–related key in the patterns that include one. In the CT modulations, take time at the fermata to hear the new tonic as it relates to the common tone. Practice *improvising* similar pitch patterns modulating to different chromatic third–related keys. For the patterns that do not modulate, hear the linear chromatic chord featured in each of them.

Example 27.20

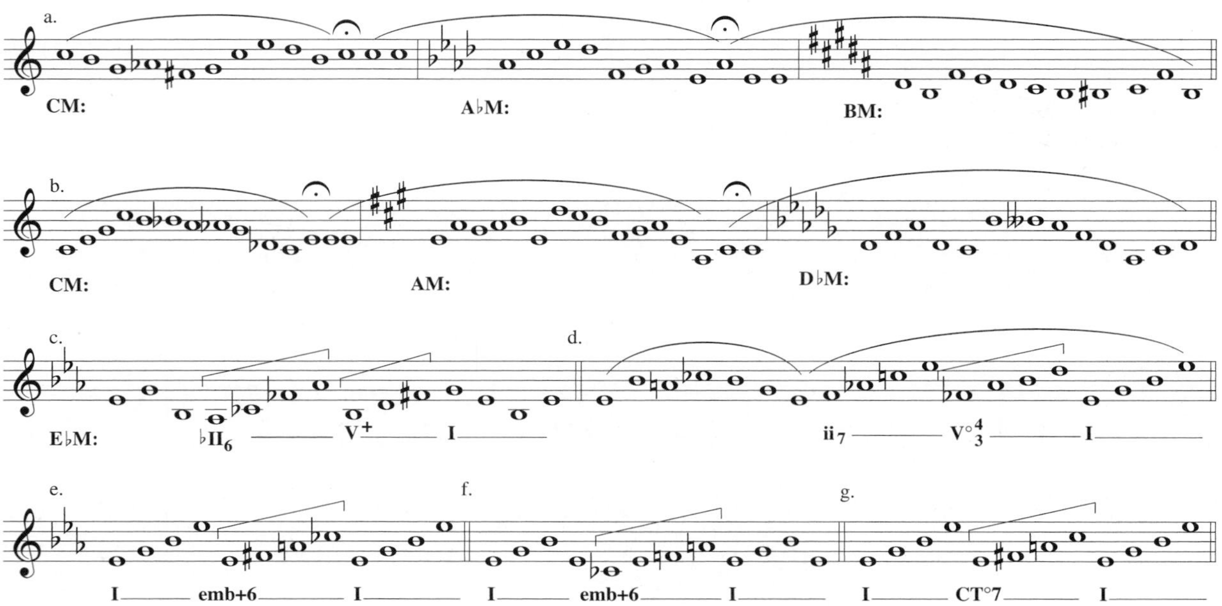

Terms for Review

- Chromatic third relationships
- Chromatic mediants
- Triads related by chromatic third
- Keys related by chromatic third with a given key
- Common-tone modulation
- Pivot pitch
- ♭VI as a key area
- Altered triads
- +6 with a dominant function
- Fr +6 on $\flat\hat{2}$ as $V^{\circ 4}_{\ 3}$
- Embellishing (common-tone) +6
- Common-tone °7 chord

Worksheet 27

EXERCISE 1 Analysis.

1. Study the chordal relationships in example 27.21. Provide Roman numerals (RNs), and explain with the correct term how the chords are related.

Example 27.21 Gabriel Fauré, "Les Roses d'Ispahan," op. 39, no. 4, mm. 47–51

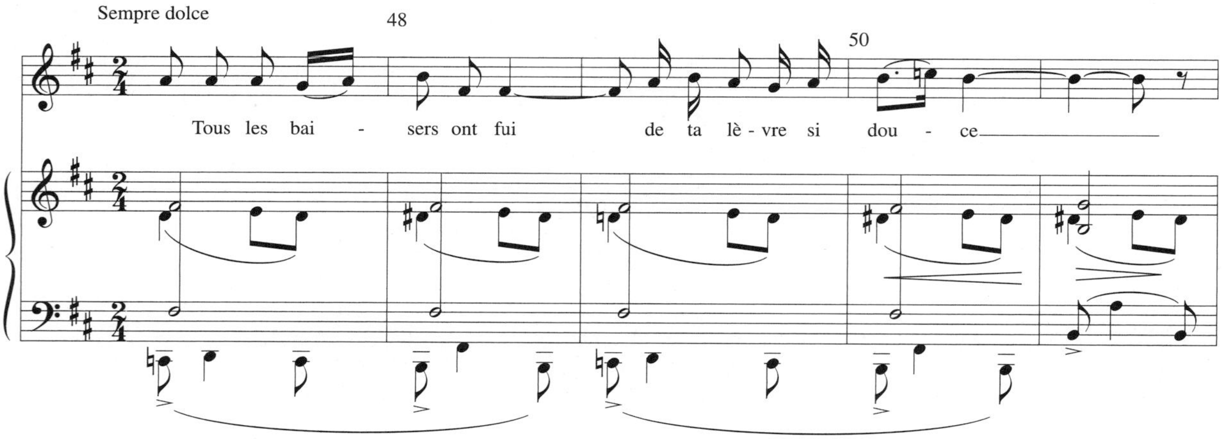

2. Study the modulations that follow. For each of them, determine these points:
    1. What keys are involved?
    2. How are the keys related (diatonic third, chromatic third, half step, etc.)
    3. What is the RN relationship between the keys? (Be aware of possible enharmonic spellings of keys.)
    4. What type of modulation is it?
    5. If it is a CT modulation, what is the CT? Or is there, perhaps, more than one CT?
    6. What are the functions of the triads used in the CT modulation?

Following are the modulations to be analyzed:

a) Example 27.22

Example 27.22 F. Chopin, Étude in A♭M, from *Trois Nouvelles Études,* mm. 14–18

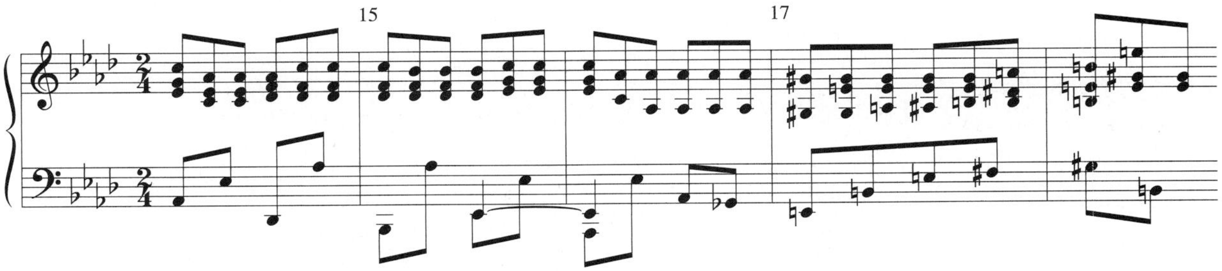

b) Anthology, no. 51, Liszt, *Consolation,* no. 4, mm. 15–18.

3. The following passages include examples of altered triads, Fr +6 as $V^{\circ 4}_{3}$, embellishing +6, or CT°7 chords. Identify and label the particular chord illustrated in each example, and determine its exact linear function (passing, neighbor/embellishing, etc.).

   a) Example 27.23

Example 27.23 J. Brahms, Piano Concerto no. 2, op. 83, III, mm. 16–18

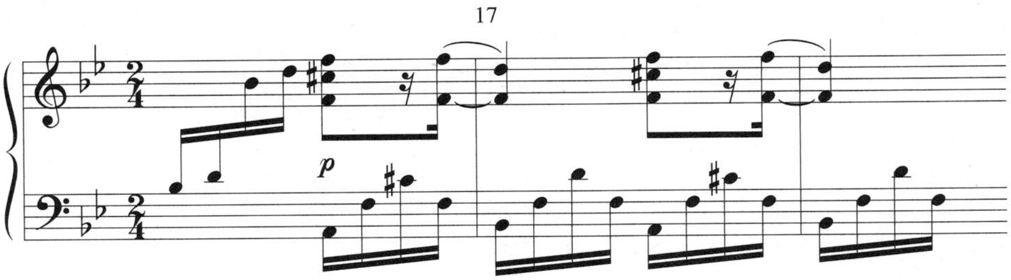

b) Anthology, no. 43, Fanny Mendelssohn, "Bitte," mm. 15–19

c) Example 27.24. This example features an embellishing +6 chord, which, however, is not in root position. What is the exact label for this chord?

Example 27.24 F. Chopin, Mazurka 45 in Am, op. posth. 67, no. 4, mm. 1–8

d) Example 27.25

Example 27.25 N. Dett, "Song of the Shrine," from *Enchantment,* II, mm. 1–4

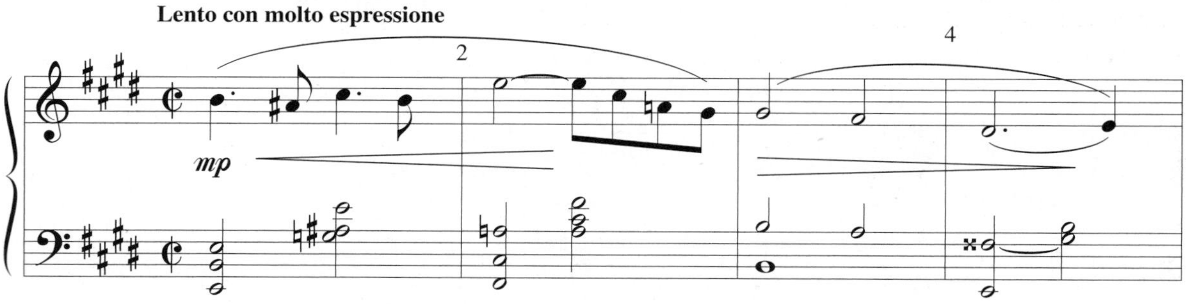

EXERCISE 2

1. List the six triads (or keys) related by chromatic third to each of the following triads (or keys). Write down both the triad name and the RN that indicates its relationship with the original triad.
2. Then circle the four triads that have a CT with the original triad.

EM:

B♭M:

F♯m:

Dm:

EXERCISE 3 Write each of the following triads (chromatic mediants) in the required keys.

EXERCISE 4 Write a CT modulation in four voices, from GM to a key of your choice, related to GM by chromatic third. In the first key area (GM), use a tonicized ♭VI and a secondary vii°$_7$. In the second key area, use a Gr +6.

EXERCISE 5 Realize the following short progressions in four voices. Pay attention to the RN quality (uppercase or lowercase), which may denote a chromatic-third relationship (for instance, I–III is not the same, of course, as I–iii).

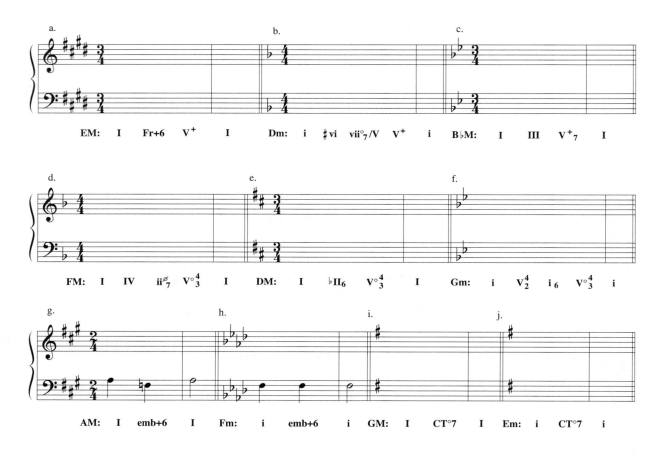

a. b. c.

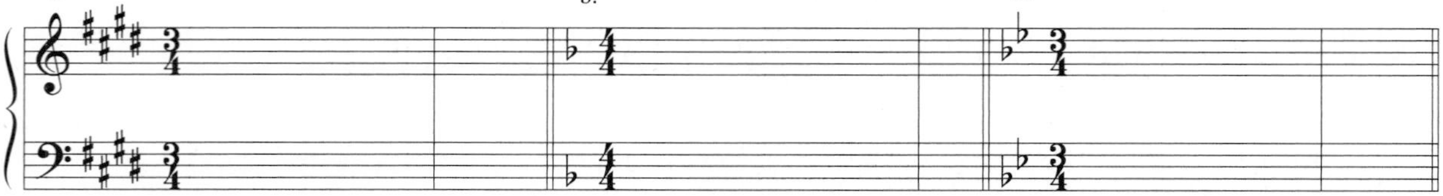

EM: I Fr+6 V$^+$ I Dm: i ♯vi vii°$_7$/V V$^+$ i B♭M: I III V$^+_7$ I

d. e. f.

FM: I IV ii$^ø_7$ V°$^4_3$ I DM: I ♭II$_6$ V°$^4_3$ I Gm: i V$^4_2$ i$_6$ V°$^4_3$ i

g. h. i. j.

AM: I emb+6 I Fm: i emb+6 i GM: I CT°7 I Em: i CT°7 i

EXERCISE 6 Realize the following progression in four voices.

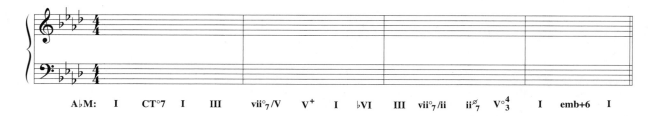

A♭M: I CT°7 I III vii°$_7$/V V$^+$ I ♭VI III vii°$_7$/ii ii$^ø_7$ V°$^4_3$ I emb+6 I

Chapter 28

Introduction to Large Forms

Large formal designs fall into several categories. Among these, the most standard types are sonata form and rondo, besides variation forms, which we already discussed in chapter 21. In this chapter we introduce the fundamental concepts involving sonata form and rondo, and we will study several examples of these formal types in some detail. Because of the wealth of possibilities they afford, however (and because different composers often treat them in different, idiosyncratic ways), a thorough discussion of these two large designs would require several chapters and is beyond the scope of this book. Students interested in furthering their study of large forms beyond the present introductory chapter should refer to any of the various available books devoted to the study of form.[1]

Sonata form and rondo as standard formal designs were particularly favored by composers in the Classical period, especially for the first and last movements of sonatas, symphonies, and concertos. Both of these formal designs are derived from smaller forms we have already studied (binary and ternary, respectively), and both merge in a formal type that we will see at the end of this chapter, the sonata-rondo.

SONATA FORM

This formal type is most frequently found in the opening *allegro* movement of Classical and Romantic sonatas and symphonies, and also sometimes in the slow movement and the closing fast movement of the same genres. **Sonata form** *is an outgrowth of the*

[1] I particularly recommend Douglass Green's *Form in Tonal Music* for a study of large forms in general. For studies that focus more specifically on formal designs in the Classical period, you may consult William Caplin's *Classical Form,* James Hepokoski and Warren Darcy's *Elements of Sonata Theory* (Oxford: Oxford University Press, 2006), Charles Rosen's *Sonata Forms* (New York: Norton, 1988), and Leonard Ratner's *Classic Music: Expression, Form, and Style* (New York: Schirmer, 1980).

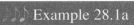

Example 28.1a A Rounded Binary Formal Design

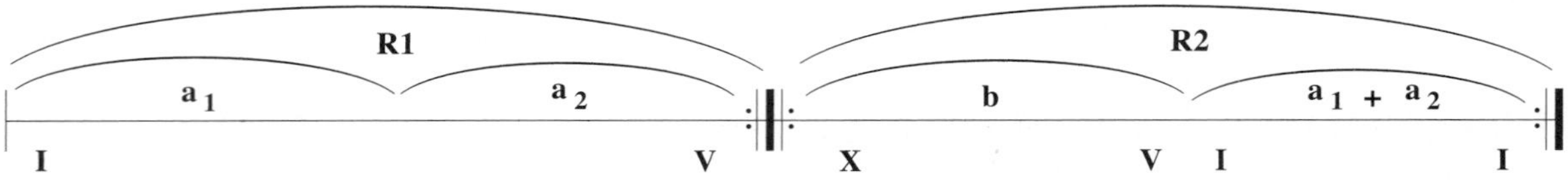

Example 28.1b A Sonata Form Design

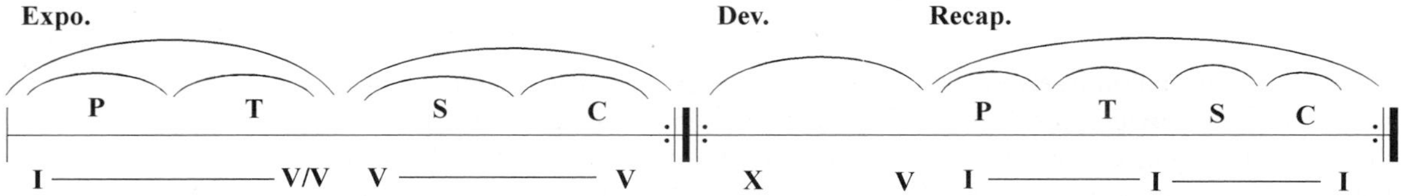

familiar rounded binary form, dominant type, as illustrated by example 28.1 (we are referring here to the type of rounded binary in which the complete first reprise comes back at the end of the second reprise). In both cases, the harmonic process consists of (1) establishment of the tonic key, (2) movement away from the tonic key and establishment of a secondary key area, (3) an area of harmonic instability that leads to (4) a return of the tonic key.

1. *The first reprise of binary* now becomes the **exposition.** As a general principle, the exposition contains *two key areas* (in the classical sonata form usually I and V, or i and III), which we will label **P** (for **primary**) and **S** (for **secondary**). P and S may each include a characteristic theme or a group of themes (which we will label P_1, P_2, etc., and S_1, S_2, etc.). Although the motion to a secondary key area is an essential element in the exposition, the existence of an independent S theme is not (although the S theme is most frequently independent from the P theme). In what we know as a *monothematic sonata form* (frequently favored by Haydn), the S key area is based on a transposition of the P theme.
2. Between P and S is usually a *modulating transition,* which we will label T. T may include its own theme **(independent transition),** or may use thematic material from P **(dependent transition).** T usually (although not always) ends with a half cadence (HC) in the secondary key. The frequently active rhythmic character of the transition as well as its modulating harmonic content create a drive toward this cadence around the middle of the exposition. The cadence itself has the double

function of marking the end of the first part of the exposition while opening the tonal space for the second part, the S area.[2]

3. The S area closes with a perfect authentic cadence (PAC) in the secondary key, V or III. This cadence may itself be followed by a **closing section** (possibly with its own theme) which confirms the secondary key area. Our label for the closing section will be C. A closing section comes after a clearly articulated cadence closing the last theme of the S area, and its function is to reinforce the important cadence at the end of the exposition, often by means of a chain of cadential gestures.
4. *The second reprise of binary* becomes, in sonata form, a large unit with two harmonic areas: (1) the **development** (corresponding with the first section of reprise 2 [R2] in rounded binary), a modulating, harmonically unstable area in which thematic material from the exposition may be developed (and new thematic material may be introduced); and (2) the **recapitulation,** usually (but not always!) a return of the complete exposition, only that now it is in the tonic key throughout (that is, T and S stay in the primary key, although here we must also say "usually but not always"!).
5. A great variety of developmental techniques may be found in developmental sections. Some of these may include fragmentation, sequence (on a circle of 5ths), thematic expansion or compression (either intervallically or rhythmically), variation, contrapuntal combination of different motives, textural changes, reharmonization, and so forth. You may want to review our study of developmental procedures in chapter 12. Before the recapitulation, and leading into it, there is usually a dominant prolongation, which we call **retransition.**
6. The motion to the secondary key area in the exposition and the harmonically unstable development create an extended area of dramatic tension that is resolved in the recapitulation. Although in the recapitulation there may be various tonicized areas (in particular, the subdominant is sometimes tonicized in the transition section of the recapitulation), this final large section in a sonata form is an area of tonal stability, which essentially stays in the tonic key. From a tonal point of view, the recapitulation provides a sense of balance and symmetrical proportions to the complete movement, following the familiar scheme "establishment of tonic (stability)-departure from tonic (instability)-return to tonic (stability)."
7. At the end of the recapitulation there may be a **coda,** which either extends the final cadence or, at times, becomes a **second development,** including modulations to new key areas, before finally reaching a closing cadence on the tonic.

We should emphasize that the criteria we have just provided are no more than generalizations. Exceptions to almost everything stated in these criteria do abound, as can be expected in a musical design as complex and rich in possibilities as sonata form. Any analysis of movements following this formal design thus requires some creative interpretation and a lot of flexibility, as we will soon realize. We will now study several specific sonata form movements in some detail.

---

[2] For a study of different types of midexposition cadences and their role within the complete exposition, see James Hepokoski and Warren Darcy, "The Medial Caesura and its Role in the Eighteenth-Century Sonata Exposition," *Music Theory Spectrum* 19 (Fall 1997): 155–83. See also their *Elements of Sonata Theory.*

MOZART, PIANO SONATA IN CM, K. 309, I (ANTHOLOGY, NO. 25)

1. *The Exposition (mm. 1–58).* First, listen to the complete movement. Then listen to the exposition again, marking the key areas as you listen. You will hear clearly that the secondary key area in GM (V) begins in m. 35, and that the section in mm. 21–32 is the modulating area, T.

   a) *Primary key area (P).* The tonic area extends from m. 1 to the cadence on C in m. 21. How many different themes can you identify? The opening theme, P_1 (mm. 1–8), clearly establishes the tonic key in the first two measures and is restated in mm. 8–14 (in a **counterstatement,** or repeated statement of a theme). Notice that m. 8 functions both as end of the first statement and beginning of the second (an *elision*). A second theme (still in CM, but now beginning on vi), P_2, starts in m. 15, and leads to the PAC in mm. 20–21. Discuss the phrase structure for the complete P area (mm. 1–21).

   b) *Transition (T).* A new theme, and a new accompaniment figure, mark the beginning of the modulating and independent transition, T (mm. 21–32). Where exactly does the modulation from CM to GM take place, and how? The transition closes on a HC in GM (that is, on V/V), which leads to the beginning of the secondary key area in GM. Notice the dramatic pause in m. 32, after the strong HC in G, which prepares and emphasizes the coming of the new theme. Hepokoski and Darcy have studied this type of transition (which results in what they call a **two-part exposition**) at length. They write: "The two-part exposition is characterized by a strong mid-expositional punctuation break, the *medial caesura*—most often articulating a half cadence—followed (almost invariably) by a rhetorical drop to *piano* marking the onset of a gentle, usually contrasting *secondary-theme zone* in the second key-area."[3] As you can easily verify, this narrative applies fully to the sonata we are analyzing.

   c) *Secondary key area (S).* Two measures extending V/V (mm. 33–34) introduce us to the S area, in m. 35. Two open statements of an initial GM theme (S_1) appear in mm. 35–42. As is often the case with S themes, S_1 is here contrasting with respect to P_1. Whereas the latter is characterized by a loud, energetic, and angular beginning gesture, S_1 is softer and more lyrical, as characterized in the definition of a two-part exposition we just quoted above. A new theme (S_2) is introduced in m. 43 and restated with variation in mm. 46–47. A cadential process that begins in m. 48 eventually leads to the extended cadential gesture of mm. 51–54.

   d) *Closing theme (C).* Following the cadence in m. 54 (which could certainly close the exposition) a final, closing theme (C) functions as a codetta or cadential extension. C also has a parallel structure, including a second statement (mm. 56–57) which varies the first statement. How exactly does it do so?

   e) *Thematic relationships.* If you look closely at the various themes in this exposition, you will notice a motive that recurs in most of them: a step in one direction

[3] Hepokoski and Darcy, "The Medial Caesura," p. 117.

Example 28.2

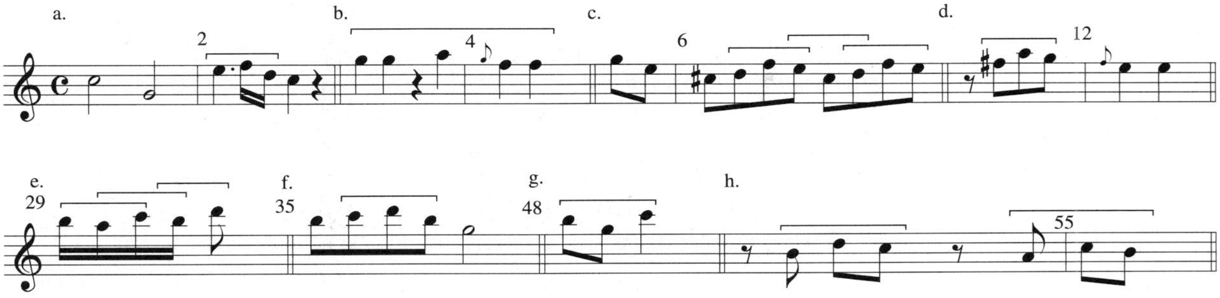

Example 28.3

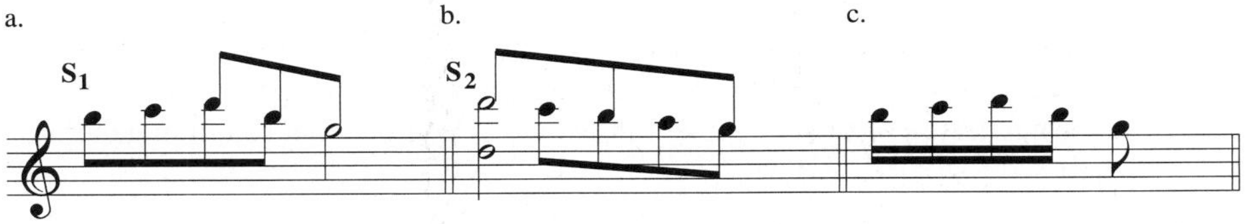

followed by a 3rd leap in the opposite direction or the other way around. Using a 2 or a 3 to designate a second or a third, and + or − signs for up or down, the possibilities are +2−3, −2+3, +3−2, or −3+2. The most prominent occurrences of this motive, including motives from the P, S, T, and C areas, are illustrated in example 28.2. The motive provides a connection among all of them. Notice also the connections between the S themes, illustrated in example 28.3. How is the motive in m. 45 (example 28.3c) related to m. 35 (example 28.3a)?

2. *The development (mm. 59–93).* Listen to the development section. Identify the key areas and the origin of the thematic material used in this section. What developmental techniques are used? When does the recapitulation really begin?
   a) Measures 59–62 are in Gm, and state P_1.
   b) Measures 63–66 move toward Dm. What is the origin of this theme? Is it a new theme? Or could it be derived from mm. 3–4?
   c) P_1 is stated in Dm in mm. 67–68, after which we move toward Am.
   d) A new section, beginning in m. 73, treats P_1 sequentially. What key areas are touched in mm. 73–82? Can you identify an example of thematic fragmentation in these measures?
   e) The C section (closing theme) is stated in complete form, but now in Am, in mm. 82–85, leading to an apparent recapitulation (return of the first theme) in

m. 86. This is, however, what is known as a **false recapitulation,** a return of the "right theme" but in the "wrong key," in this case Am.

f) Measures 90–93, a statement of P_1 outlining V_7 of CM, function as a *retransition* (RT), a dominant prolongation leading to the return of the tonic key.

g) The true recapitulation comes in m. 94, the return of P_1 in CM.

3. *The recapitulation (mm. 94–155).* Listen to the complete second reprise (development and recapitulation). Compare the recapitulation with the exposition, and determine what is the same and what is different. You will find the following discrepancies between these two sections:

a) Mozart varies the counterstatement of P_1 in the recapitulation (mm. 101–108). How? Analyze this passage harmonically if you have not done so yet.

b) Unlike many T sections in recapitulations, the T section here does modulate to the key of the dominant. The difference with the original T section, however, is that now it does not lead to a HC in GM, as it did in m. 32, but rather to a cadence on the tonicized G. How does this change in the cadential pitch at the end of T affect the S area in the recapitulation?

c) What is the key of the S area now? How does Mozart vary the S_1 theme?

As a conclusion of your analysis, study the formal diagram for the exposition and the development provided in example 28.4. Discuss how this diagram represents the tonal and formal design of this movement in particular and of sonata form in general.

Example 28.4 Formal Diagram for Mozart, K. 309, I

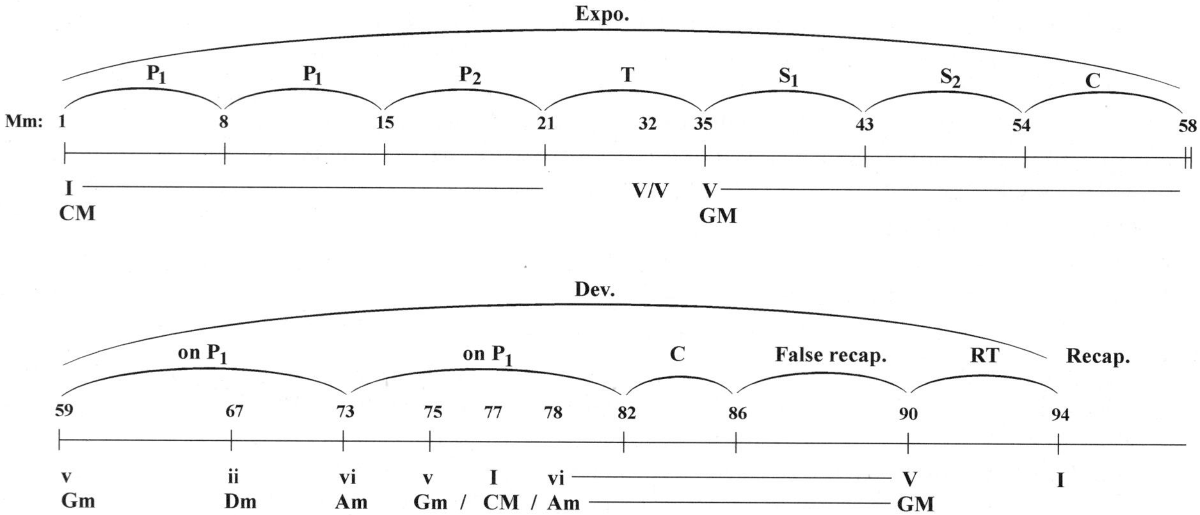

GUIDED STUDIES OF SONATA FORM

The following are guided analyses of two compositions in sonata form included in the anthology: Beethoven's Fm Sonata, op. 2, no. 1, I, and his celebrated *Waldstein* Sonata, I. Their most significant formal and tonal features are pointed out to help you work through these fascinating movements.

Beethoven, Piano Sonata No. 1 in Fm, op. 2, No. 1, I (anthology, no. 32)

1. Identify the modulating T area. Is it based on an independent theme? What sets apart the P area from T?
2. The S area begins in m. 20 with the S_1 theme. As usual in a classical sonata of the standard minor key type, S is in the key of III. What is unusual about the harmonization of S_1? When is the first time we hear III unequivocally in root position?
3. Compare the P theme with the S_1 theme. How are they similar, contrasting, or complementary? Think in terms of shape and contour.
4. We may call the theme in mm. 33–41 the S_2 theme, and the new theme after the PAC on III (m. 41) the C theme.
5. Study the development (mm. 49–101). What are its sections, and what themes are they based on? What are the various key areas? We have studied some of the tonal features of this development in previous chapters as examples of modulation. Review and discuss these features again, focusing especially on the following points:
   a) Explain the modulation from A♭M to Fm in mm. 52–55.
   b) What familiar modulating/developmental process takes place in mm. 63–74?
6. By m. 78 we are back in Fm, and in m. 81 we reach V in this key. For how long is this V prolonged? What is the function and name of this extended dominant prolongation? Where does it lead to?
7. How do you explain harmonically the interesting seconds in the bass, mm. 94–100?
8. Are there any discrepancies between the recapitulation and the exposition?
9. The final cadence could be in mm. 145–146. How is it delayed? What chords are tonicized in these final measures?

Beethoven, Piano Sonata No. 21 in CM, *Waldstein*, op. 53, I (anthology, no. 35)

The *Waldstein* Sonata is one of the masterpieces of Beethoven's middle period. The following comments will guide you through the analysis of its monumental first movement in sonata form.

1. *The exposition.*
   a) Analyze phrase 1 harmonically (mm. 1–4). What is unusual about this harmonic beginning? How is CM established? Does phrase 2 (mm. 5–8) confirm the tonic key? (What secondary key areas do phrase 1 and phrase 2 actually represent? What are the chords within each of these two areas?) Where is the first V–I progression in CM?
   b) In mm. 7–11 notice the fluctuation between the FM (as V of B♭) and Fm chords (and hence between A♮ and A♭, $\hat{6}$ and ♭$\hat{6}$). In mm. 12–14 you will also see the juxtaposition of Cm and CM. More of these M/m complexes will appear later in the movement.
   c) What is the formal function of mm. 14–21? What secondary key areas are represented here, and what are the chords within each area?
   d) Explain (or review) the modulation in mm. 21–23. Measures 23–34 function as the T section. What harmony is prolonged here?
   e) S_1 begins in m. 35. We have already seen that in his middle and late periods, Beethoven, like the Romantic composers after him, often preferred third-related keys over the functionally stronger fifth relationships favored in the Classical period. Explain how this applies to the S area in this sonata.
   f) Explain mm. 43–50 from a formal/thematic point of view.
   g) A new theme, S_2, appears in mm. 50–53. Brilliant keyboard figuration beginning in m. 58 leads to an extended cadential gesture in mm. 66–74.
   h) The brief section that follows functions as a codetta, C.
   i) Comment on the many counterstatements in this exposition. Are they literal or varied? What effect do they have on the length and scope of the exposition?
   j) Focus now on *thematic relationships.*
      1) The contour of P, in mm. 1–3, features two intervals: the 3rd, and the P5. How is it balanced by the motive in m. 4?
      2) The T area has two clear sections: mm. 23–30 and 31–34. How are they related thematically to P?

3) How is S_1 related to P, and how does it balance the contour of mm. 1–3?
4) The thematic relationship of S_2 with the previous themes is more obscure. Consider, however, the notes on beats 1 and 3 in mm. 50–51, along with the B in m. 52. How does the resulting line balance S_1?
5) Finally, comment on the C theme (mm. 74–77).

2. *The development.* The development can be broken up into several harmonic areas, as suggested by the following points:
   a) Explain the modulating process that leads from the closing C section in EM to FM in m. 90.
   b) FM/m is an important key complex throughout the development (Remember the $\hat{6}/\flat\hat{6}$, as well as CM/m juxtapositions in the opening measures!). You can think of mm. 90–104 as being in F and of the two other key areas in this section as secondary key areas of F. Which are these key areas, and how do they relate to F? Explain the thematic development in these measures. Where do the two motives in mm. 96–103 come from?
   c) A fast-moving harmonic and linear process takes place in mm. 104–112. Because it leads from i in Fm (m. 104) to V in FM (m. 112), this is also an extension of the F complex of keys. Review the linear process in mm. 105–109, and understand how it functions harmonically (a circle of 5ths) and linearly (a $^{4-6}_{2-3}$ sequence). What is the chord that precedes the arrival on V of F in m. 112?
   d) The modulating process in mm. 116–136 begins with a series of 5th-related key areas (FM–B♭M–E♭m) and continues with two common-tone (CT) modulations. The first of these, E♭m to Bm (i-vi spelled enharmonically), involves two keys related by chromatic 3rd (mm. 124–128). The second modulation, up a half step from Bm to Cm (mm. 128–132), uses two common tones between the tonic chord of the first key and the dominant of the second key. Verify each of these modulations and understand the CT procedure in each of them.
   e) What harmony is reached in m. 136? What is the formal/harmonic function of mm. 136–155? What happens in m. 156?

3. *The recapitulation.* In the first place, notice the length of what is left after this point: We are in m. 156, and we have 146 more measures to go! Comment on everything that is different between the recapitulation and the exposition.
   a) What is the function of the newly added mm. 169–173?
   b) We would now expect the S area to be in CM, and T to be nonmodulating. What do we find instead? How does the present key of S_1 provide a tonal balance to the key of S_1 in the exposition (with respect to the tonic key, CM)?
   c) Comment on the key of S_2 and C.
   d) A surprising series of events takes place after m. 245. After the C theme cadences in CM, we could expect some kind of conclusive gesture to end the movement. What we get is fifty-seven measures of coda!

4. *The coda as a second development*
   a) First, the C theme is extended through a modulation to Fm, as it did at the beginning of the development.
   b) In mm. 247–248, V_7 of Fm resolves deceptively to a statement of P in D♭M (the Neapolitan key used as a "coda key").
   c) We soon realize that Beethoven launched into an unexpected second development in the place of the coda. Notice, however, that this new development does not stray very far from CM, and that, as a matter of fact, it has a "cadential character" if we consider its long-range tonal motion. Let us examine some of its details:
      1) What key areas are touched upon in the first section of the development (mm. 249–259)? What familiar linear technique can you identify in the left hand of mm. 255–256? This first section, which started in the Neapolitan key (a "predominant function"), leads to the half cadence on V of CM in m. 259. (What chord does Beethoven use, in m. 258, to approach this important HC?)
      2) What part of P which was not used in the first development is developed now, in mm. 259 and following? The development in mm. 261–275 is largely based on sequences. Examine mm. 261–267, then 267–270, then 270–271, and finally 272–274, and explain the use of sequential techniques in these passages. From a harmonic point of view, this whole area (from m. 259 to 278) is a long motion from V in CM to, again, V in CM (mm. 278–283).
      3) A possible final cadence is set up again in mm. 282–283. The new surprise is a final statement of S_1, now in the tonic key which we were expecting in the recapitulation!
      4) We pointed out, in the opening measures and in the development section, the fluctuation between FM and Fm (resulting in a fluctuation between A♮ and A♭). How does this fluctuation between $\hat{6}$

and $\flat\hat{6}$ reappear in the extended half cadence in mm. 290–294?

5) A final statement of P, which recalls the very beginning of the exposition, finally closes this astonishing example of sonata form. Here, again, notice the final tonicization of the subdominant, and its appearance, once more, as an FM/m complex stressing the $\hat{6}/\flat\hat{6}$ fluctuation!

This discussion closes our study of sonata form. What is your impression of this movement? How does Beethoven achieve its monumental scope? How does it conform to, and how does it depart from, the standard sonata form design? What makes this movement so interesting and unpredictable? Do you understand the movement and its complexities better after this analysis?

EXERCISE

To practice analyzing a movement in sonata form, refer to exercise 1 in worksheet 28 at the end of this chapter.

THE RONDO

Listen to Haydn's Piano Sonata in DM, Hob. XVI:37, III (anthology, no. 21), an example of rondo form. You will recognize its character as typical of last movements in classical sonatas, concertos, and symphonies: It has a fast tempo, and its mood is light and playful. From a formal point of view, the **rondo** is usually simpler than the sonata form. The basic principle of a rondo is the recurrence of a **refrain,** which alternates with contrasting **episodes.** The contrast may be thematic, and also tonal: Whereas the refrain in a rondo *is always in the tonic key,* the episodes may be in different keys. Some authors prefer the term **couplets** for these contrasting areas, to avoid confusion with fugal episodes.

The simplest formal type that fits this definition is, of course, the familiar *ternary* form (or *aria* form), with an ABA design. Rondo form is indeed an outgrowth of ternary. Haydn's rondo is what we know as a five-part rondo, which, in its most frequent form, can be summarized as ABACA. Refrains in a rondo are closed harmonically and are often in *binary form.* The second episode (the C section), which tends to be larger, sometimes includes changes of tempo and meter and may have a developmental character. We may find a *modulating* **transition** (T) to connect the refrain with an episode, and a **retransition** (RT) to return to the refrain. Possible formal and tonal schemes for a five-part rondo appear in example 28.5.

Example 28.5 Five-Part Rondo Designs

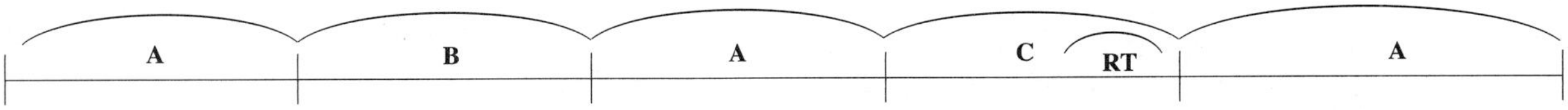

A	B	A	C	RT	A
I ——— I	V ——— V	I ——— I	i ——— i	V ———	I ——— I
I ——— I	i ——— i	I ——— I	IV ——— IV	V ———	I ——— I
i ——— i	III ——— III	i ——— i	iv ——— iv	V ———	i ——— i

A FIVE-PART RONDO: HAYDN, PIANO SONATA IN DM, HOB. XVI:37, III (ANTHOLOGY, NO. 21)

1. *The refrain.* When you listened to this piece you may have realized that mm. 1–20 constitute a closed formal unit, which returns later in a literal form (mm. 41–60) and in a slightly varied form (mm. 94–134). This is the recurring A section of this **five-part rondo,** its *refrain.* You may also have realized that this refrain is in rounded binary form, dominant type. Explain exactly what makes it so. Review, if necessary, the chapter on binary and ternary forms, and make sure you are familiar with all the types of binary before you continue the study of rondo. Explain exactly how the last return of A is varied (mm. 94–134).
2. *Episode 1.* The first contrasting episode, the B section (mm. 21–40), is in the parallel minor key, Dm. What is the form of this episode (be exact as to the specific formal design)? Explain how the thematic material in this section is contrasting with respect to the refrain. On the other hand, do the themes have anything in common (such as contour, important pitches, characteristic leaps, etc.)?
3. *Episode 2.* After the literal return of the refrain, the second episode (the C section, mm. 61–80), introduces the contrasting (but close) key of GM, the subdominant key. The form of this section is rounded binary, tonic type, in which the complete first reprise returns at the end of the second reprise. What is the harmonic and formal function of the section in mm. 81–93, and what term do we use for such a section?

A formal diagram showing formal relationships and key areas for this rondo appears in example 28.6. Study it and understand how it represents the form of the piece we have just analyzed.

Example 28.6 Formal Diagram for Haydn, Hob. XVI:37, III

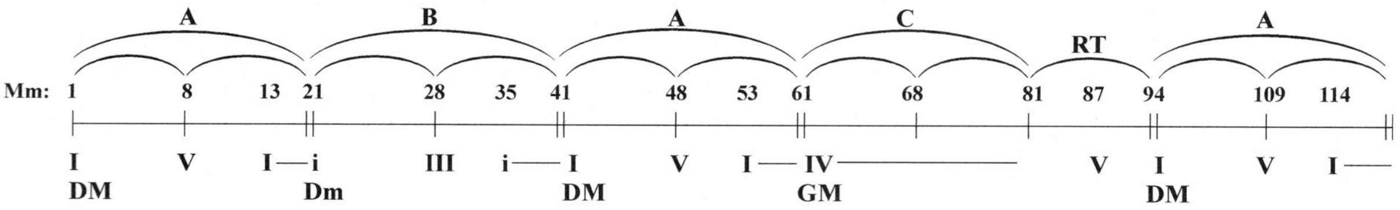

Haydn's five-part rondo is a simple example of this formal type. We will now study two more complex instances: a seven-part rondo by Beethoven and a sonata-rondo by Mozart. The format for these studies will be the same that we used in our "Guided Studies" of sonata form: These may be done as class discussions, following the analytical guidelines provided by the following comments and questions.

I. A Seven-Part Rondo: Beethoven, Piano Sonata in Cm, op. 13 ("Pathétique"), III (anthology, no. 34)

In a **seven-part rondo,** one more episode and refrain are added to the five parts we are already familiar with. A hypothetical formal design would be ABACADA. More often, however, the last three sections mirror the first three, in a design such as ABACAB′A, where the third episode is a return, perhaps varied, of the first episode. Example 28.7 shows some possible designs for this formal type.

In example 28.7 we see that the first three and last three parts are often grouped tonally, whereas the second episode (the middle part) is the one that is likely to feature the greatest tonal contrast, and the one that allows for the largest variety of choices. We will now see how this general formal type is represented by Beethoven's "Pathétique" rondo.

1. *The refrain (mm. 1–17).* Study and discuss the phrase structure for the opening section of this movement, the refrain (mm. 1–17). How many phrases are there in this section? How are they related thematically? We have already studied the subsequent modulating transition to E♭M, III, through the secondary key area of iv, and leading to the B section, the first episode in E♭M (review this discussion in chapter 18, in the section, "Secondary Key Areas").
2. *Episode 1 (mm. 25–61).* This is a rich episode from a thematic point of view. Where have we seen, earlier in this movement, the characteristic rhythm for its initial theme (mm. 25 and following)? The second theme of this episode, in m. 37, features the motive $\hat{1}$–$\hat{2}$–$\hat{3}$–$\hat{2}$–$\hat{1}$ (in triplets). Is this contour derived in any way from the opening theme (see mm. 1–2, including the initial anacrusic motive)? The third theme, on the other hand, presents a truly contrasting character (mm. 44–50). Comment on aspects of this theme. Notice also how many times Beethoven has already used a certain chord to approach an important dominant harmony: What are the chords in mm. 6 (beat 2), 32 (beat 1), and 46 (beat 2)?

   The theme in triplets returns in m. 51, now in a section with a transitional function (to modulate back to Cm), leading to the literal return of the refrain (mm. 62–78).
3. *Episode 2 (mm. 79–120).* In essence, this episode is a set of variations on a four-measure theme in two voices (mm. 79–82). Explain what these variations are exactly, and how many of them there are. Notice also the contrapuntal character of this C section, and the abrupt change of key from Cm to A♭M in mm. 78–79. What common element between these two keys allows for such a direct (and yet smooth) modulation? On the surface, the theme of this episode seems new and contrasting. How is it derived, however, from the opening theme? Refer specifically to mm. 5–6.

   The last variation (mm. 103–106) leads into a long prolongation of the Cm dominant (mm. 107–120). How do we call this type of prolongation, and where does it take us?
4. *Episode 3 (mm. 134–170).* The refrain that begins in m. 121 is not stated in its complete original form. How is its "third phrase" varied (mm. 129–133)? One might think that it functions as a modulating transition; actually, there is no "modulation," because the third episode is in the parallel major key, CM (beginning in m. 134). What is the chord leading to the new episode in m. 133 (beat 2)? Now compare episode 3 with episode 1. Other than the keys, is there any difference between them? Is episode 3 a D section, or rather a B′ section? Is there any reminiscence of the key from episode 1 (E♭M) in mm. 158–166?

Example 28.7 Seven-Part Rondo Designs

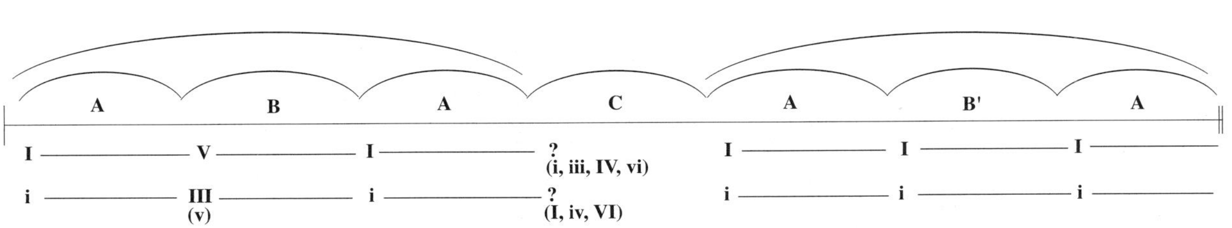

5. *The final refrain and the coda.* The final return of the refrain takes place in mm. 171–182. In what form does the third phrase of the refrain appear (mm. 179–182)? Are the original pitches there?

The cadence of this return is reached in m. 182. The additional section is a coda extending this Cm cadence. On what theme are mm. 182–193 based? And mm. 193–198 (notice the overlapping P4s, G–D/F–C)? The coda concludes with a surprising return of the initial theme in a last-minute recall of the key from episode 2, A♭M (VI). Review this interesting modulation which we already studied: What is the pivot chord function of the chord in m. 198? What kind of enharmonic reinterpretation takes place in m. 206, introducing the return of Cm only for the striking final cadence?

Study the formal/tonal diagram in example 28.8. How does it reflect the design of this movement? Does it conform to the standard designs of seven-part rondo that appear in example 28.7?

II. A Sonata-Rondo: Mozart, Piano Sonata in B♭M, K. 333, III (anthology, no. 28)

Listen to, and analyze, Mozart's B♭M rondo. It represents a formal type in which sonata form and seven-part rondo merge: **the sonata-rondo.** Go back to example 28.7, the diagram for the seven-part rondo formal types. The sonata-rondo is a logical consequence of this design: If the initial A and B sections are the primary and secondary key areas (P and S) in a sonata form exposition (with an added return of A in the tonic key), if the C section becomes a development, and if the final A–B′–A sections, all in the tonic key, function as the recapitulation, you will easily see how the two formal types (sonata and rondo) come together in this hybrid which we call sonata-rondo form (see example 28.9).

1. *The exposition.* In Mozart's B♭M rondo, the exposition comprises the sections from m. 1 to m. 64. The refrain (mm. 1–16) is followed by a modulating, transitional theme (T, mm. 16–24), leading to the secondary key area (the B section or first episode) in FM (V), mm. 24–36. A brief retransition (mm. 36–40) takes us to the return of the complete refrain in B♭M, mm. 41–56. The transitional theme now modulates to Gm (the relative minor) in mm. 56–64.
2. *The development.* The second episode, the C section, begins in m. 65, with its own new theme in Gm. After a new modulation to E♭M (IV), the section in mm. 76–105 has a clear developmental character. Why? What are the secondary key areas in this section? What previous themes are developed? What is the harmonic function of mm. 105–111? What do these measures lead to?
3. *The recapitulation.* The complete refrain returns, in B♭M, in mm. 112–127. The extended T section (mm. 127–148) now does not lead to FM, but rather to the prolonged B♭M dominant in mm. 144–148, which launches the return of the B section, now in the tonic key (mm. 148–171). After the brief cadenzalike passage in mm. 171–172 (a **lead-in** or ***Eingang,*** an improvisational passage used, especially in concertos, to introduce or lead into a solo passage or a return of an important theme), the refrain seems to return, for what should be the last appearance of the A section. Instead, we soon hear a new modulation to V (mm. 177–179), which begins an unexpected second development (the supposed return was, then, a **false return**)! What theme or motive is this development based on? Could you think of this second development as an extended prolongation of FM, the dominant of B♭M? If so, what is its tonal function in the long-range design of the movement?

   A new, longer lead-in on V finally takes us to the true return of the refrain in m. 200, followed by a cadential section (mm. 207–214) and by a closing coda (which briefly tonicizes the subdominant key) in mm. 215–225.

Provide a formal-tonal diagram for this movement, showing all the main and secondary key areas and how they correspond with major formal divisions.

Example 28.8 Formal Diagram for Beethoven, op. 13, III

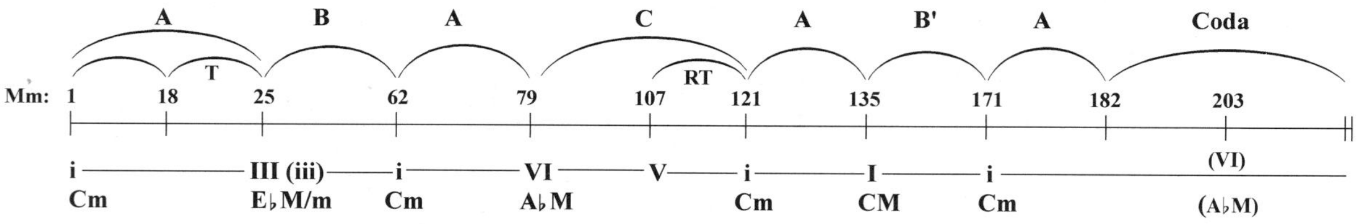

PRACTICAL APPLICATION AND DISCUSSION

Because the formal types we have studied in this chapter are essential in the Classical period, and to a certain extent also in the Romantic period, you will encounter them very often (and must certainly have come across them already) in your career as a performer, composer, or scholar.

What do you think is the significance of what you have learned in this chapter? How will it affect your understanding of complete movements? Do you think understanding the form, tonal plan, and thematic relationships of a large movement is important to you as a musician and performer? How? Will your knowledge of form affect the way you approach a large movement from now on, whether to listen to it or to perform it? The type of analysis we have demonstrated in this chapter tells us not only about sectional divisions and thematic connections, but also about long-range harmonic motion, directed harmonic tension, and tonal design. This allows you to hear large movements as single formal and tonal units, held together by underlying tonal structures that provide their coherence and forward drive. Are these concepts important to a performer? Discuss why and how (or why not and how not).

If anyone in the class is currently performing a movement in either sonata or rondo form, he or she may wish to perform it for the class and perhaps explain its formal and tonal characteristics. In any case, if you are a performer you can find a movement in either sonata or rondo form and play through it yourself. What has your new knowledge of form added to your understanding of this movement? How has it affected your performance of it or the way you hear it?

The following are some of the specific questions relating to sonata form which you may want to address in your discussion:

1. How can you enhance the transitional character of the T section to contribute to the urgency toward the S key area and theme?
2. How are the P and S themes different and contrasting in character, and how can you best emphasize the differences?
3. Can you contribute through your performance to the sense of instability and tonal motion of the development? What can you do to make sure that the tension and the sense of direction are kept throughout the development until they reach their goal (the return of the tonic key at the beginning of the recapitulation)?
4. How can you try to convince listeners that a "false recapitulation" is the real one, so that the effect of the real recapitulation is heightened?
5. The tension accumulated throughout the secondary key area and the development is resolved with the return of the tonic key and the opening theme at the beginning of the recapitulation. How can you enhance the structural significance of this important moment in a sonata form movement?
6. On the other hand, the rest of the recapitulation may be a long area of tonal stability. How can you make sure that you keep the level of musical motion and interest high now that you don't have the support of thematic development and unstable harmonic activity to create tension and excitement?

Example 28.9 Sonata-Rondo Designs

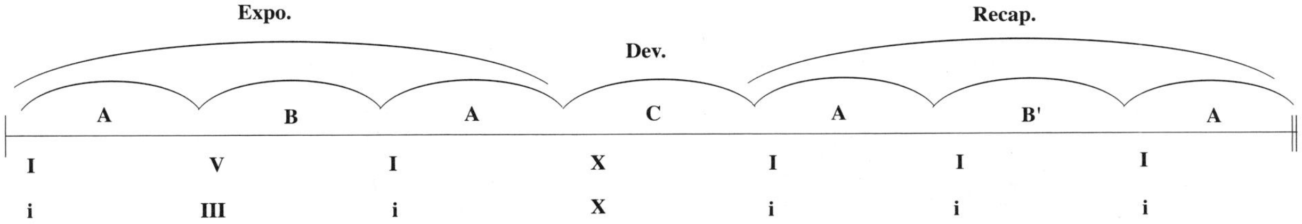

EXERCISE

For an assignment of an analytical paper on a movement in sonata-rondo form, refer to exercise 2 in worksheet 28 at the end of this chapter.

ASSIGNMENT

For analytical assignments based on the materials learned in this chapter, refer to chapter 28 in the workbook.

Terms for Review

Sonata form
Exposition
Primary key area
Secondary key area
P and S themes
Transition: dependent, independent
Closing section
Development
Recapitulation
Retransition
Coda
Second development
Counterstatement
Two-part exposition
False recapitulation
Rondo
Refrain
Episodes
Couplets
Transition
Retransition
Five-part rondo
Seven-part rondo
Sonata-rondo
Lead-in *(Eingang)*
False return

Worksheet 28

EXERCISE 1 Analyze Beethoven's Piano Sonata op. 10, no. 1, I, in sonata form. Turn in an annotated copy of the score (the score and the recording will be available at your music library). You should indicate the thematic/sectional content of the complete movement using the letter symbols we have learned in this chapter (P, T, S, C, etc.), and all keys and key areas for the complete movement.

Provide a formal diagram for the complete movement, and answer the following questions:

1. Exposition

   a) Measures 1–30, according to their formal and thematic function, are best described as:

   Explain the thematic content of these measures (which constitute a period) by phrases (how many phrases? how are they related?).

   b) Measures 32–56 are best described as:

   If we divide this section into five harmonic units, the key areas defined by the four first units are as follows: mm. 32–36, ________; mm. 37–40, ________; mm. 41–44, ________; mm. 45–48, ________. The harmonic function of mm. 48–55 is ________, leading into a new section in m. 56, in the key of ________.

   What is typical of Beethoven in the way the key areas in this section are related?

   c) Briefly explain the sectional/thematic/harmonic content of the rest of the exposition. Is it all one section, or does it break up into several subsections?

2. Development

   a) Explain the thematic content of the complete development (use the letter D to indicate any possible new theme in the development).

b) Indicate, with measure numbers, the five key areas clearly established in mm. 106–142, including m. 142. (Be careful: Dominants are not keys, they are only dominants! Keys are defined by the resolution of the dominant to the tonic.)

c) Indicate the key areas at mm. 142–156, and explain their relationship.

d) The harmonic/formal function of mm. 158–167 is (explain and provide the exact *term*):

3. Recapitulation. Compare the recapitulation with the exposition. What is the same in both sections? What are the differences?

EXERCISE 2 Write a short analytical paper on Beethoven's Piano Sonata in GM, op. 31, no. 1, III, in sonata-rondo form. The score and a recording will be available at your music library. The score can also be found in the Arlin anthology (*Music Sources*). You can use the guided analyses of Beethoven's and Mozart's rondos in this chapter as models for the organization of your paper. Turn in an annotated copy of the score.

The following are some specific questions about this particular movement by Beethoven which you should address in your paper.

1. What is interesting harmonically about the beginning?
2. Is there a T section between the tonic and dominant key areas in the exposition?
3. What contrapuntal technique is used in mm. 86–90? Where does this section lead?
4. What is the formal function of the C section (the second episode)? Discuss the harmonic processes in this section (mm. 98–129), with mention of all the specific key areas.
5. Is there a retransition after the C section? What chord does Beethoven use to approach this important point of formal articulation?
6. Is there a coda?
7. Beethoven uses variation techniques in several sections of this movement. Explain how this statement applies in mm. 1–32, 66–82, and 132–164. Compare also mm. 140–147 with 156–164.
8. Provide a formal diagram for the complete movement.

Chapter 29

Expanding Functional Tonality: Extended Tertian Chords; Linear Chromaticism II

Composers throughout the common practice period expanded the basic harmonic vocabulary in a variety of ways. In this chapter we examine two of the means used for this expansion of tonality. First, we will focus on extended tertian chords, which allow for both diatonic and chromatic expansions of functional sonorities and which introduce, in either case, strong elements of dissonance. In the second part of the chapter we will further our study of linear chromaticism, and we will see that diatonic frames can be expanded through both sequential and nonsequential chromaticism.

EXPANDING CHORDAL SONORITIES: EXTENDED TERTIAN CHORDS

The harmonic event illustrated in example 29.2a is familiar enough to you: The ninth of a 9–8 suspension over a V_7 chord resolves, as expected, before the bass has moved on to the next chord. In example 29.2b, on the other hand, the same ninth does not resolve before the bass moves, but rather resolves along with the bass into the next chord. In this latter case, we can say that the ninth is part of the chord, which thus becomes a **ninth chord** on V, or V^9_7. The origin of this chord is linear, as shown by example 29.2a. As an independent chordal sonority (example 29.2b) it still often functions as a linear chord. Occasionally, however, the ninth chord is used as an independent, nonlinear chord, which results from adding one more third on top of a seventh chord, as shown in example 29.1. If we add one more third on top of the ninth chord, we will have an **eleventh chord,** and yet one more third will produce a **thirteenth chord,** both shown in example 29.1. These chords as a family are normally called **extended tertian chords.**

All of these chords have several things in common:

1. They are highly dissonant and, most often, they are treated as such (the dissonance is resolved in some conventional manner, and sometimes, but not always, is also prepared).
2. They are most often used with a dominant function, although they can also appear, as we will see, on any degree of the scale besides $\hat{5}$.

Example 29.1

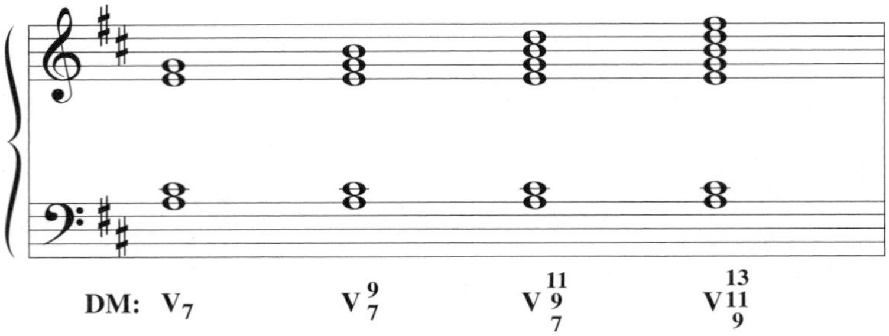

3. In musical practice we do not always find these chords in their complete form. Although they are often written in more than four voices (usually five, or at times more), in four-voice textures some pitches need to be left out. The seventh, however, is usually not left out in any of these chords.
4. Extended tertian chords usually appear in root position. Inversions of these chords are very rarely found in music.

We will now examine these characteristics as they apply to each of the specific extended tertian chords.

Ninth Chords

The dominant ninth is the most frequent of all extended tertian chords. The characteristics of the dominant ninth are as follows:

1. In a four-voice texture, the *fifth of the chord is omitted,* and the seventh is included.
2. The ninth (as well as the seventh) *resolves down by step.*
3. In the diatonic form of this chord, the ninth is major in major keys ($\hat{6}$) and minor in minor keys ($\flat\hat{6}$). The M9th chord V^9_7 is indeed normally found only in major keys. The m9th chord, on the other hand ($V^{\flat 9}_7$), can actually be used in both minor and major keys. In major keys, this is properly a "borrowed" chord, because of the use of $\flat\hat{6}$.
4. The ninth of the chord should at least be *at the distance of a 9th above the bass* (that is, it should not be a second above the bass).

Verify all the preceding points in example 29.2. Play or sing through these examples, and hear the dissonance of the 9th, its resolution, and whether the 9th is major or minor.

Franck began his sonata for violin and piano with a V^9_7 in AM, as illustrated in example 29.3. Identify all the members of this chord in the example. Is the chord complete? What actual pitch is the ninth? The chord is extended through m. 5. How? What kind of harmonic gesture takes place in mm. 6–8? Where is the V^9_7 actually resolved? Comment on the resolution of the ninth.

Example 29.2

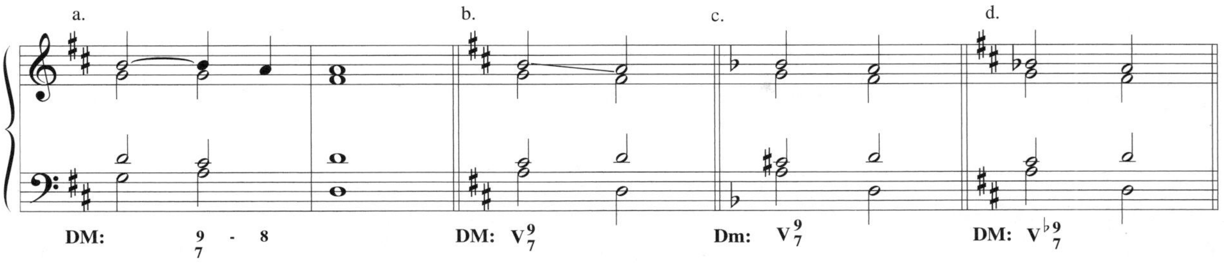

Example 29.3 C. Franck, Sonata for Violin and Piano, I, mm. 1–8

Example 29.4 Hugo Wolf, "Der Mond hat eine schwere Klag' erhoben," from *Italienisches Liederbuch,* mm. 15–18

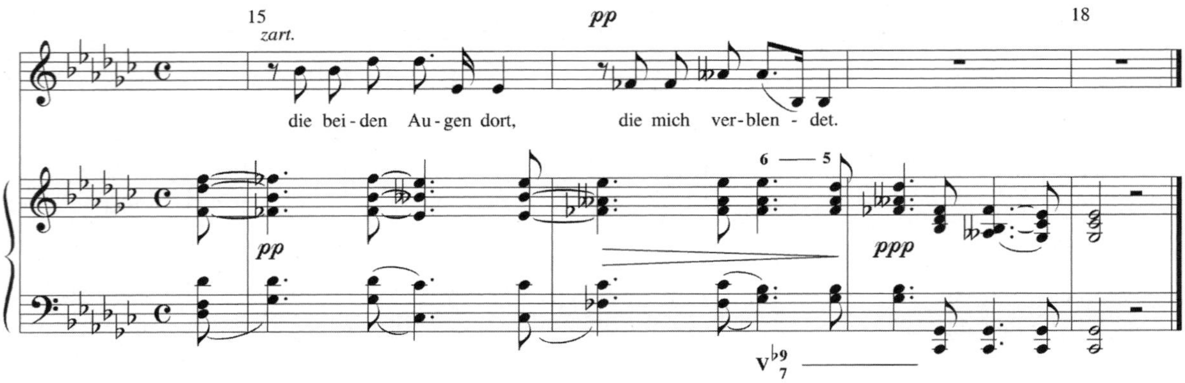

In the Franck example the ninth is major, which in a major key is a diatonic pitch. Now listen to the Hugo Wolf fragment in example 29.4, in C♭M. Focus first on the cadence, beginning with the G♭ chord in m. 16. The upper voice in the piano (E♭–D♭) is a simple 6–5 motion over the bass. You can see the actual dominant chord in the last eighth note of m. 16 and the first beat of m. 17. What kind of a ninth chord is this? What scale degree is A♭♭ in C♭M?

Now study the progression in mm. 15–16, leading to the $V^{\flat 9}_{7}$ which we just analyzed. You will recognize a circle-of-5ths bass (D♭–G♭–C♭–F♭) supporting a progression made up of three consecutive dominants leading to the pre-dominant on F♭. One of these chords is a secondary V^{9}_{7} chord. Which one, and what is the exact Roman numeral (RN) for it?

Eleventh and Thirteenth Chords

Listen now to example 29.5. The only two chords in this excerpt are a DM tonic chord and a linear chord that functions as a neighbor chord to the DM tonic. If you try to organize this chord in thirds over the bass note A ($\hat{5}$), you will find out that it can indeed be interpreted as a linear dominant chord. As a dominant harmony, the chord is missing the third (the C♯), and it includes instead a seventh, a ninth, and an eleventh (think of the interval of 11th as a compound 4th). By this functional interpretation, this is a $V^{11}_{\substack{9\\7}}$ chord.

Dominant eleventh chords are normally spelled according to the following conventions, especially in four voices:

1. The 11th in an eleventh chord should be an 11th (not a 4th) above the bass.
2. Because the pitch an 11th above $\hat{5}$ in V_{11} is actually $\hat{1}$, the third ($\hat{7}$) is usually omitted in this chord to avoid the harsh clash between the leading tone ($\hat{7}$) and $\hat{1}$.

Example 29.5 G. Fauré, *Les roses d'Ispahan,* op. 39, no. 4, mm. 6–10

3. In four voices, one more pitch must also be omitted. The two possibilities for the eleventh chord are root-fifth-seventh-eleventh (V^{11}_{7}, as in example 29.6a) or root-seventh-ninth-eleventh ($V^{11}_{\substack{9\\7}}$ chord, as in example 29.6b).
4. In the resolution of the V_{11} chord to the tonic chord, the eleventh stays in the same voice as a common tone with the tonic ($\hat{1}$).

In examples 29.6c and d we see yet another type of extended tertian chord, the *dominant thirteenth chord*. Examine the use of this chord by Chopin in example 29.7a. Then, read the following basic principles for writing the dominant thirteenth chord:

1. In this chord, neither the third nor the seventh is left out. Its most frequent form in four voices is, then, V^{13}_{7}.
2. The thirteenth (think of it as a compound sixth) may be major ($\hat{3}$) or minor ($\flat\hat{3}$), and it should always be a 13th (not a 6th) above the bass.

Example 29.6

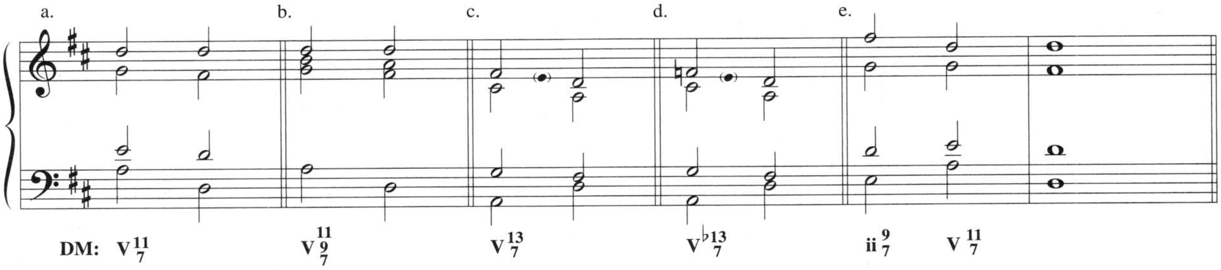

3. The thirteenth usually resolves by leaping down a third to $\hat{1}$. This leap is often bridged by a passing tone, as suggested in examples 29.6c and d. Occasionally, the thirteenth may also stay in the same voice as a common tone with the tonic, as you can see in example 29.7c.

Study the cadence in example 29.7b (mm. 127–129) by Alma Mahler. Identify the exact type of dominant chord (don't forget to take into account the voice part), and comment on its resolution. (We will study the first measure of this example later in this chapter.) The cadence in example 29.7c also includes a V_7^{13}, and in this case the thirteenth stays in the same voice as a common tone with the tonic. What other extended dominant chord can you find in this passage? This phrase also illustrates how, in jazz and popular music, extended tertian sonorities are an essential component of harmony. Notice how many dominant and nondominant extended chords (which we will study in

Example 29.7a F. Chopin, Prelude in F♯M, op. 28, no. 13, mm. 18–20

Example 29.7b A. Mahler, "In meines Vaters Garten," from *Five Songs,* no. 2, mm. 126–129

Example 29.7c Lorenz Hart–Richard Rodgers, "Bewitched," from *Pal Joey* (cadence in chorus)

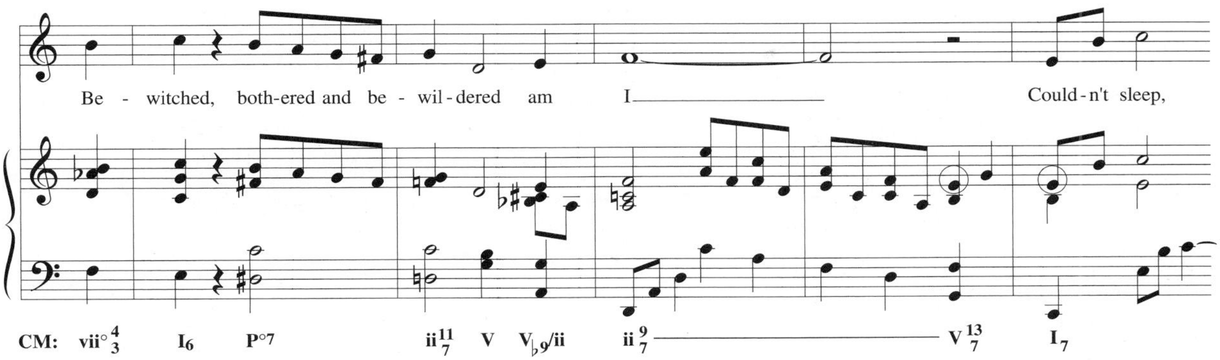

the next section) are featured in this example. As a final observation on this passage, comment on the passing °7 chord (P°7) in m. 1. In chapter 27 we studied another linear °7 chord, the CT °7 chord. Explain the linear nature of the P°7 in this example and specifically how it functions as a passing chord.

EXERCISE

To practice spelling and resolving dominant ninth, eleventh, and thirteenth chords, refer to exercise 2 in worksheet 29 at the end of this chapter.

Nondominant Extended Tertian Chords

As we previously mentioned, extended tertian chords can also have nondominant functions. In late nineteenth-century and twentieth-century music it is not rare to find ninth, eleventh, or thirteenth chords on any degree of the scale, including the tonic. Example 29.6e shows a progression using such chords. In general, the same spacing and voice-leading principles that apply to dominant ninths, elevenths, or thirteenths also apply to nondominant extended tertian chords. Verify spacing, voice leading, and treatment of dissonance in example 29.6e.

Two examples from the literature will illustrate these chords. The opening phrase from Kurt Weill's "Mack the Knife" does not contain a single unextended triad (example 29.8). As we just mentioned, seventh and extended tertian chords are the basic harmonic vocabulary of jazz and popular music, as this example well illustrates.

Notice that although the functional content of this phrase is quite simple (in essence, V–I–ii–V–I), the progression is greatly enriched by means of tertian dissonance applied to each of the three basic functions (tonic, pre-dominant, and dominant). Mary Lou Williams's fragment in example 29.9, on the other hand, includes an area of tonicization

Example 29.8 Marc Blitzstein–Bertolt Brecht–Kurt Weill, "Mack the Knife," from *The Threepenny Opera* (opening phrase)

Example 29.9 Mary Lou Williams, *Nite Life,* mm. 5–9

in which both the secondary dominant and the tonicized chord (V/VI and VI) are extended tertian sonorities. Identify both the secondary dominant and the tonicized chord and what kind of sonorities they constitute. Then examine example 29.7c again, and discuss the nondominant tertian chords in that phrase.

EXERCISES

To practice realizing progressions including a variety of extended tertian chords, refer to exercises 3 and 4 in worksheet 29 at the end of this chapter.

To practice analysis of musical fragments including extended tertian chords, refer to exercise 1.1 in worksheet 29 at the end of this chapter.

LINEAR CHROMATICISM II: LINEAR EXPANSIONS OF TONALITY

In chapter 27 we discussed a category of chromatic chords that result from linear motion (see section "Linear Chromaticism I: Linear Chromatic Chords"). We will now continue our study of linear chromaticism, focusing mainly on extended sequential and nonsequential processes that have the effect of expanding tonality.

APPOGGIATURA CHORDS

A factor that often contributes to the expansion of tonality in the late nineteenth century is the extensive use of nonchord tones (NCTs), especially appoggiaturas, which in turn create linear, nonfunctional sonorities. **Appoggiatura chords** are dissonant sonorities, often placed on downbeats, generated by melodic appoggiaturas. We can see illustrations of appoggiatura chords in some of the preceding examples in this chapter.

Look, for instance, at Alma Mahler's phrase in example 29.7b. The harmony in the first measure, m. 126, seems highly complex and chromatic. Now play the chordal reduction in example 29.10. In A♭M, it turns out to be a simple tonicization of ii

Example 29.10 Reduction of Example 27.7b

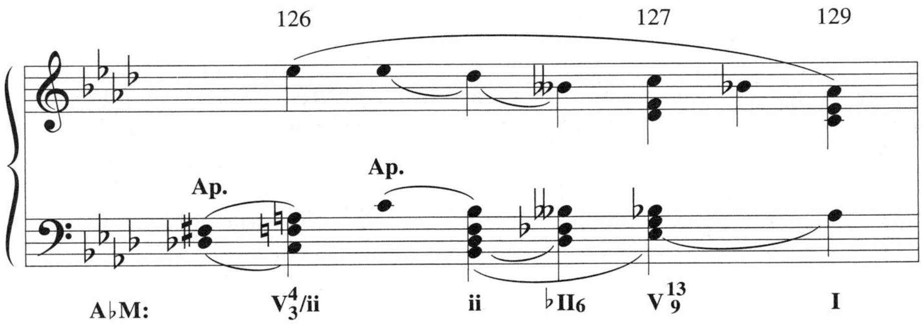

Example 29.11 N. Dett, Barcarolle, from *In the Bottoms,* mm. 1–8

followed by a ♭II$_6$ pre-dominant chord. What is it that makes this measure so chromatic and complex? Basically, all the appoggiaturas that create two appoggiatura chords (marked "Ap." on the graph, and notated without stems). Notice also the spelling of ♭II$_6$ on the score. How is it spelled? Now refer to the Wolf fragment in example 29.4. The last two measures contain only two functional chords: a dominant and a tonic. Can you explain the role of appoggiaturas and appoggiatura chords in this cadence?

Appoggiatura chords do not necessarily have to fall on the downbeats. The harmonization of the phrase by Dett reproduced in example 29.11 is strongly based on the principle of appoggiatura chords, and all of them are placed on a weak fraction of the beat (unaccented appoggiaturas). Play through the example, and notice how a simple functional progression is enriched by all the linear dissonance produced by the appoggiatura chords.

Now play through the short passage by Richard Wagner in example 29.12a. Think of it in EM. What is the role of nonchord tones, and specifically appoggiaturas, in this passage? Circle all of them on the score, and then try to reduce this texture to a functional chordal progression in block chords (a metric reduction). You will end up with a fairly simple progression, which you can verify in example 29.12b. You can see that most of the wonderful dissonant tension in this phrase is produced melodically by chromatic nonchord tones, one of the salient characteristics in the music of Richard Wagner. In m. 27 you can interpret the B♮ as a long 4–3 suspension resolving to the A♯. You can also think of it, however, as a chord tone creating an extended tertian dominant harmony. Which chord would this be exactly? Notice also that the G♯ in the top voice at the

Example 29.12a R. Wagner, *Tristan und Isolde,* Prelude to act I, mm. 25–28

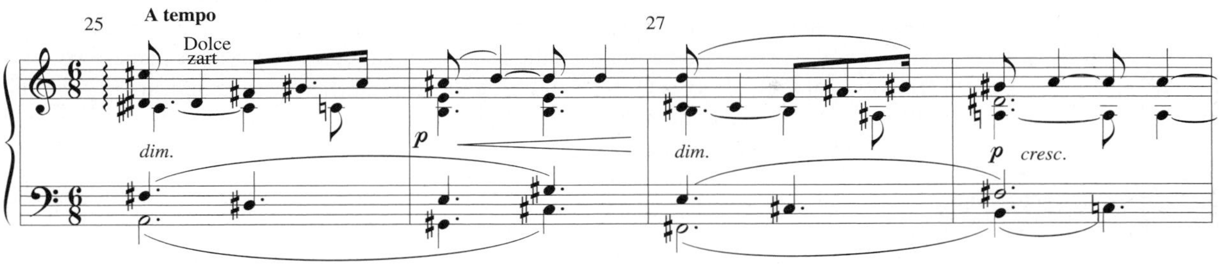

Example 29.12b Metric Reduction

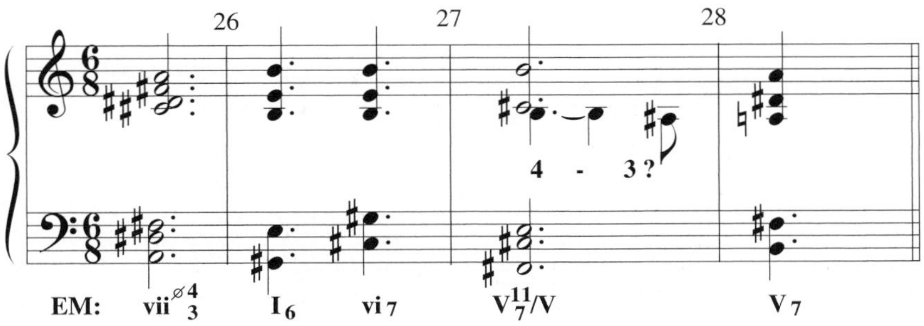

end of this measure is an anticipation, although it does not actually anticipate a chord tone in the next chord, but rather an appoggiatura.

CHROMATIC SEQUENCES REVISITED

In chapter 18 we studied the most usual types of **chromatic sequences.** Because chromatic sequences can suspend tonality momentarily, they are often used by Romantic and post-Romantic composers to enrich and expand their tonal structures. We will now review some of the most characteristic types of chromatic sequences in the context of linear expansions of tonality.

THE DESCENDING CIRCLE-OF-5THS SEQUENCE

As we know from chapter 18, if the successive chords in a descending circle of 5ths are all secondary dominants, the sequence is chromatic, and two of the voices feature descending chromatic lines. You can find this type of progression in examples 18.15b, d, e, and f. For a review of this sequence, refer to examples 29.13a and b. In example 29.13a, the succession of secondary dominants is in root position. Notice the two chromatic lines that result. If one of the two chromatic lines is placed in the bass, as in example 29.13b, the progression takes the form of alternating $\frac{4}{2}$ and $\frac{6}{5}$ chords.

Study mm. 32–37 from anthology, no. 45 (Chopin, Mazurka no. 49 in Fm). These measures are the continuation of a phrase in Cm which begins in m. 27. After the half cadence in m. 31, we hear a chromatic sequence that takes us through successive tonicizations of G, C, F, B♭, and E♭. A metric reduction of this passage appears in example 29.13c. Play through the reduction, and then discuss how the circle of 5ths is enriched by extensive use of chromatic nonchord tones.

Example 29.13

The Ascending 5–6 (or 6–5) Sequence

The chromatic sequence by ascending 2nds has already appeared in example 18.17. This pattern consists of an alternation of secondary dominants and their resolutions, with a resulting bass line that alternates a 4th up and a 3rd down (example 29.14a). If the secondary chords are in first inversion, then we have a chromatic line in the bass, above which $^6_3$ (or $^6_5$) and $^5_3$ chords alternate, as in example 29.14b. A simple case of this sequential pattern appears in example 29.14c, where the sequence involves only triads ($^6_3$–$^5_3$) rather than seventh chords. The same pattern (now in $^6_5$–$^5_3$ form) can also be

Examples 29.14a and b

a.

b.

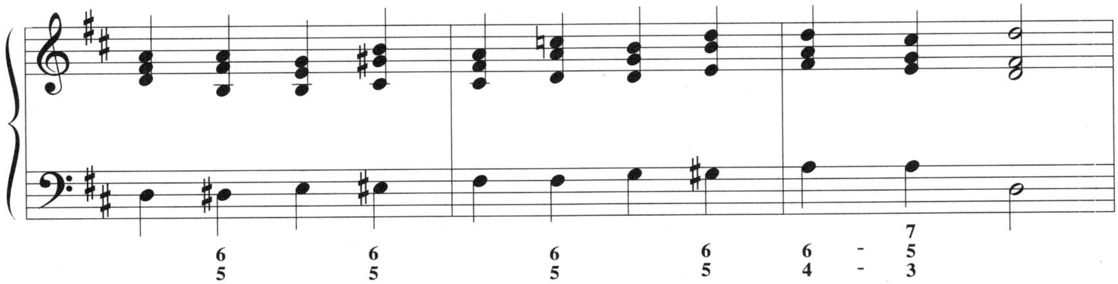

Example 29.14c Paul Vance–Lee Pockriss (The Cuff Links), "Tracy" (refrain)

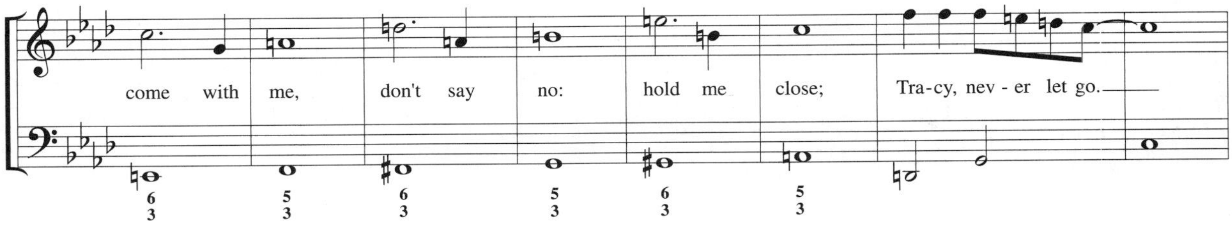

found underlying another fragment by Chopin reproduced in example 29.15a. First, verify in mm. 81–84 the basic ${}^{6}_{5}$–${}^{5}_{3}$ pattern in this sequence. Then notice how this linear pattern is embellished in a variety of ways. In the first place, the ${}^{5}_{3}$ chords (the resolutions of the secondary dominants) are themselves elaborated by means of 5–6 figures. Moreover, the complete texture is ornamented with chromatic nonchord tones. Study the reduction in example 29.15b, and identify all the NCTs in the actual music.

Example 29.15a F. Chopin, Mazurka no. 37 in A♭M, op. 59, no. 2, mm. 81–89

Example 29.15b

The Descending 5–6 Sequence

Whereas the basic voice leading in the 5–6 sequences we just discussed involves an ascending 5–6 or 6–5 sequential pattern, the equivalent descending 5–6 pattern over a chromatic bass is also very effective musically, as shown by the well-known excerpt in example 29.16a. As in the ascending 5–6 pattern, the sequence may involve only triads, and then the pattern results from alternating $^{5}_{3}$ and $^{6}_{5}$ chords over a chromatic bass (as in example 29.16b), or it may instead alternate $^{5}_{3}$ and $^{6}_{5}$ chords (as in both examples 29.16a and c).

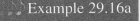

Example 29.16a Don Feldes–Don Henley–Glenn Frey (The Eagles), "Hotel California" (final verse)

Examples 29.16b and c

The $^{7}_{5}$–$^{6}_{3}$ Sequence

In example 29.17a you can recognize a standard 7–6 sequential pattern. While the 7th is sounding (the suspension), the only other pitch other than the bass is the third above it. In example 29.17b, you will see a slight change to this sequence: While the 7th is sounding, you also have a 3rd and a 5th above the bass; that is, you hear a complete $\substack{7\\5\\3}$ "suspension" chord. Now look at the resolution of the 7th to the 6th: To avoid the clash of the 6th with the 5th which was sounding before it, this 5th "gets out of the way," while the 3rd is sustained. The result is a $\substack{7\\5\\3}$–$\substack{6\\3}$ sequential pattern, which makes for an interesting and rich linear passage. Play through or listen to the Mozart passage in example 29.18a, and note that example 29.17b is simply a metric reduction of the Mozart example. Explain how the progression is elaborated in the music by means of NCTs.

Now play through example 29.17c. What in Mozart was a mostly diatonic sequential pattern, here becomes a highly chromatic linear phrase. But in essence the pattern is the same: a $\substack{7\\5\\3}$–$\substack{6\\3}$ sequence. The only real difference is that the bass moves chromatically at the same time as the 7th resolves to the 6th. Understand how this linear pattern works. Then, play through Wagner's phrase in example 29.18b, and verify that example 29.17c is its metric reduction. As you did with the Mozart example, explain the role of chromatic NCTs to enrich and elaborate this progression (in this case, quite extensively so!).

Finally, look at example 29.17d. The pattern here is essentially the same, but the 5th of the $\substack{7\\5\\3}$ sonority now moves to a 4th above the same bass. The result is a $\substack{7\\5\\3}$–$\substack{6\\4\\3}$ sequential pattern, in which both sonorities involved are seventh chords. Play this example, and then study how it represents a metric reduction of anthology, no. 45 (Chopin, Mazurka no. 49, in Fm), mm. 37–40. The Chopin phrase enriches this sequence in a variety of ways: It contains numerous chromatic NCTs, as well as voice exchanges in every measure, involving the soprano and tenor voices. Discuss these aspects of this example carefully. Observe also that the last "$\substack{7\\5\\3}$" is actually spelled, and functions, as an +6th chord in Fm. It is interesting to realize that all three passages we just studied (the Mozart, Wagner, and Chopin phrases) consist of linear passages leading to dominant harmonies.

Example 29.17

a.

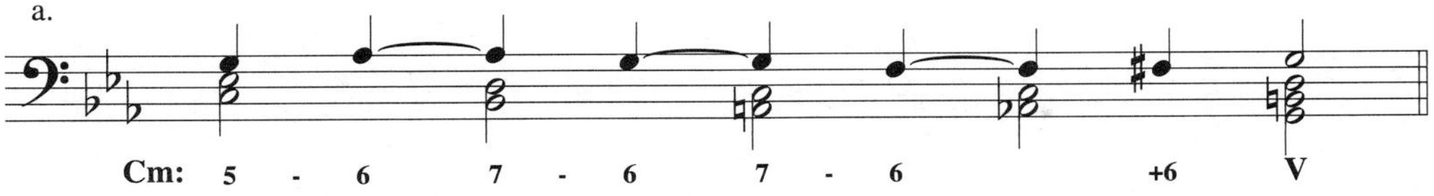

b. Mozart

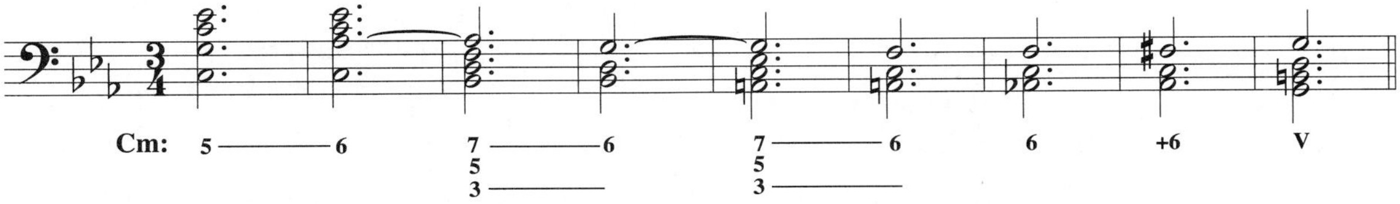

c. Wagner

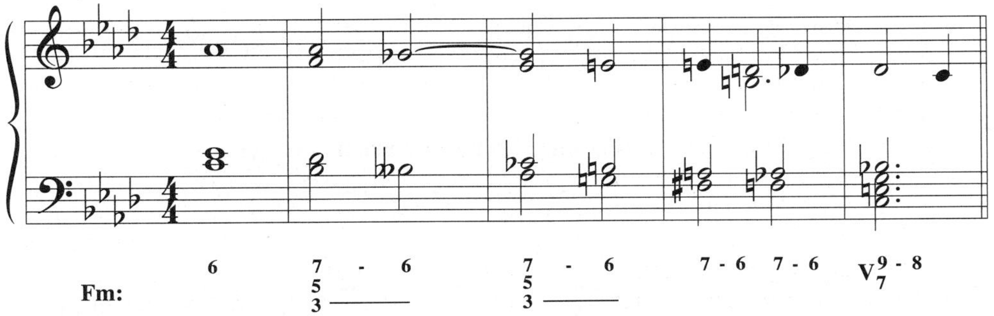

d. Chopin

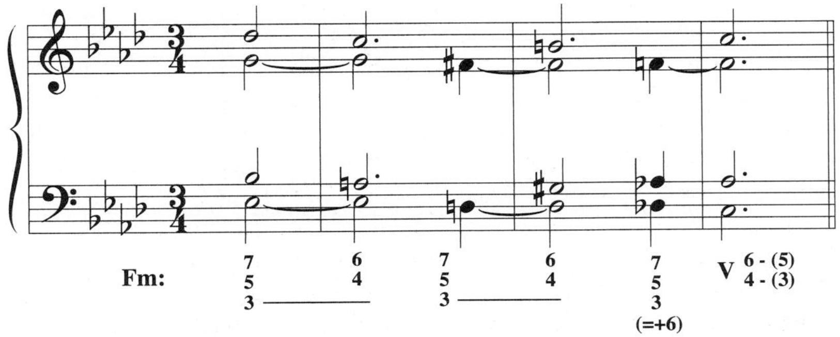

Example 29.18a W. A. Mozart, Symphony no. 39, I, mm. 160–168

Example 29.18b R. Wagner, *Tristan und Isolde,* Prelude to act III, mm. 11–15

EXERCISES

To practice realizing sequential progressions, refer to exercises 5 and 6 in worksheet 29 at the end of this chapter.

To practice analysis of musical fragments including chromatic sequences, refer to exercise 1.2 in worksheet 29 at the end of this chapter.

NONSEQUENTIAL LINEAR PROCESSES

We will now study a type of linear/harmonic process often used by Chopin and other composers in the second half of the nineteenth century. Listen to example 29.19, and pay attention to its harmonic content. Does it sound functional to you? How are chords connected? The piece is in Em, but what are the clear signs of an Em tonality? What is it that tells us clearly that we are in Em?

After you listen to the excerpt, play through example 29.20a. Does the piece begin with a clear Em chord? Is Em clearly defined by a dominant-tonic progression? The

Example 29.19 F. Chopin, Prelude in Em, op. 28, no. 4, mm. 1–13

following comments and concepts will help you understand the harmonic processes involved in this composition.

1. The basic frame for the phrase is provided by the outer voices. The melodic line is based on a NN motive, which outlines either a half step (B–C–B) or a whole step (A–B–A). In any case, and especially in its half-step form, this "sigh" motive gives the melody a character of mourning and grief. This character is confirmed by the bass line, which first outlines a chromatic descending tetrachord (G down to D), that is, a "lament bass," followed by several statements of the C–B half-step sigh.[1]
2. *Implied tonality.* The piece begins with a tonic chord in first inversion, a weak form of the tonic. There is no other Em triad in the complete passage, and there is not a clear dominant of Em until the half cadence in m.12. In other words, although we hear the phrase as being in Em, the key is **implied** rather than established.
3. *Tonal parenthesis.* Tonally, this phrase moves from the beginning i_6 to the ending V_7, and these two harmonies are connected through a succession of nonfunctional chords. This process illustrates the principle of **tonal parenthesis:** Although the beginning and end of the phrase tell us we are in Em, the harmonies within the phrase do not define the key in any clear way from a functional point of view. The tonal motion for this passage can thus be expressed as i_6–( )–V_7.
4. *Linear chromaticism.* What we find filling in the parenthesis, instead of a functional progression, is an area of *linear chromaticism* which actually provides tonal coherence to the passage by prolonging the initial tonic chord linearly. Looking at example 29.20a, how would you define the constructive principle of this type of linear chromaticism? In this example, the pitch or pitches that move from one chord to the next are represented as black note heads, and the pitches that remain are notated as white notes. The figures between the two staves refer to half-step voice leading: a 1 means motion by half step (1 semitone), a 2 means motion by step (2 semitones). We will think of the motivic neighbor figure in the melody (right hand, B–C–B) as a melodic NN, except where it is clearly part of the voice leading for a vertical sonority, as in m. 3.
5. *Voice leading as a constructive principle.* At a glance, we see that chord connections are based on *stepwise motion* in one or two voices at a time, and the remaining voices sustain *common tones.* Stepwise motion is mostly by descending half step, although in some cases also by whole step. *Chromatic voice leading* is thus the defining feature in this passage.
6. *Implied tonal regions.* As was mentioned above, a Roman numeral functional analysis of this passage does not yield any kind of logical result. Chords are not connected functionally, but linearly. We have an initial harmony (i_6), a final harmony (V_7), and we travel the space between them through linear, mostly chromatic voice leading. At some points, however, we can hear momentary tonal points of

[1] For an analysis of this piece which includes interesting discussions of its affective characteristics and of the linear design underlying its structure, see Carl Schachter, "The Triad as Place and Action," *Music Theory Spectrum* 17 (Fall 1995): 149–69.

Example 29.20

reference, especially when we fall on a Mm_7 sonority which seems to want to resolve to a tonicized degree. The first chord in m. 4, for instance, can be heard as a V_7/iv, and the chord in m. 7 similarly appears as a V_7/III. In both cases, however, the tonicizing tendency is not confirmed or resolved, and the chords proceed linearly. These would be cases of *implied tonal regions.* Tonal regions are implied or suggested *by means of their dominants,* but they are not confirmed by a resolution to the tonic.

7. *Underlying structure.* Example 29.20b shows a chordal reduction of this passage, charting a linear path through a possible underlying progression of implied tonal areas. In this graph, the opening and closing chords are shown as half notes, the significant chords within the phrase are shown as quarter notes, and the connecting linear elaborations (anticipations, neighbor notes, and passing tones) are shown without stems. The graph allows us to make several interesting observations. In the first place we notice that, after all, we do find an underlying linear sequential pattern in this passage, the series of 7–6 suspensions indicated by the figures under the graph. We see, moreover, that the root motion of the stemmed chords in mm. 2–7 (F♯–B–E–A–D) is the familiar circle of 5ths. The graph also shows how the underlying sequential structure is elaborated chromatically by means of anticipations, NNs, and PTs (passing tones), and that these linear elaborations (notated without stems in example 29.20b) are not sequential themselves. From a different perspective, if we group the $^6_{\substack{4\\3}}$–7 patterns in mm. 3–7, we see that each of these patterns can

be interpreted as implying a secondary key area (indicated as iv? and III? under the graph). Similarly, the final $^6_3$–7 pattern in mm. 9–10 represents the goal chords for the phrase, a pre-dominant-dominant progression in Em.

Example 29.21 shows an interesting case of harmonization that brings together the linear principles we have just discussed with elements of functional tonality. The chordal voice leading is strictly linear, and very much in the style of the Chopin example. The bass, however, provides a strong functional anchoring: It is based on a circle of 5ths. In Fauré we often find this type of extended linear procedure over a functional bass, as in this case. First, play through the passage or listen to it. Then, discuss the

Example 29.21 G. Fauré, "Après un rêve," mm. 1–9

voice leading in the piano's right hand. Then, analyze the passage functionally (with Roman numerals), with the understanding that each of the bass notes is the root of the chord above it. What key area is tonicized in mm. 3–4? What extended tertian sonorities can you identify in mm. 3–5? What is the triad on G in m. 6? How is the dominant chord in mm. 7–8 embellished linearly?

EXERCISES

To practice writing a passage using nonsequential linear chromaticism, refer to exercise 7 in worksheet 29 at the end of this chapter.

To practice analysis of a musical fragment based on nonsequential linear chromaticism, refer to exercise 1.3 in worksheet 29 at the end of this chapter.

FOR FURTHER STUDY

For additional chapter 29 materials, refer to the *Harmony in Context* Web page at www.mhhe.com/roigfrancoli2e.

ASSIGNMENT AND KEYBOARD EXERCISES

For analytical and written assignments and keyboard exercises based on the materials learned in this chapter, refer to chapter 29 in the workbook.

PITCH PATTERNS

Sing the pitch patterns in example 29.22, hearing their harmonic content. Pitch pattern a illustrates a variety of extended tertian sonorities. Pitch pattern c features a descending chromatic sequence and pattern d an ascending chromatic sequence. Finally, pattern e provides a summary of the nonsequential linear process found in Chopin's Em prelude.

Example 29.22

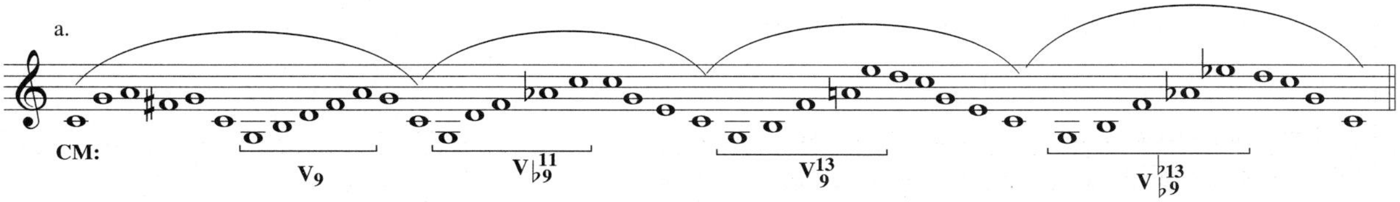

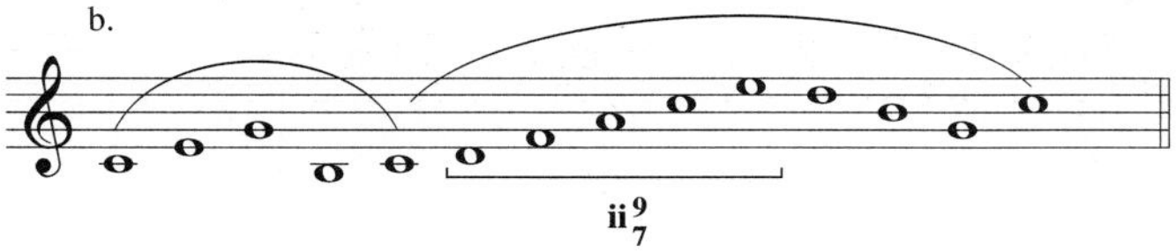

c.

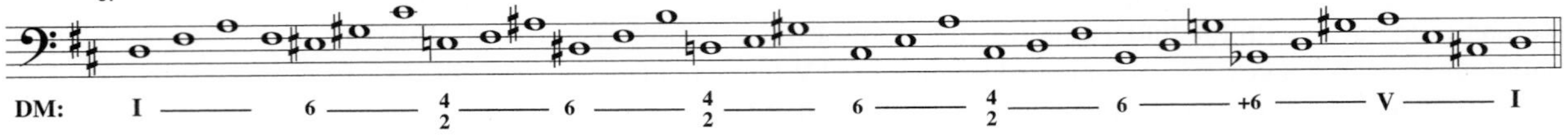

DM: I ——— 6 ——— $\begin{smallmatrix}4\\2\end{smallmatrix}$ ——— 6 ——— $\begin{smallmatrix}4\\2\end{smallmatrix}$ ——— 6 ——— $\begin{smallmatrix}4\\2\end{smallmatrix}$ ——— 6 ——— +6 ——— V ——— I

d.

I ——— $\begin{smallmatrix}6\\5\end{smallmatrix}$ ——— $\begin{smallmatrix}5\\3\end{smallmatrix}$ ——— $\begin{smallmatrix}6\\5\end{smallmatrix}$ ——— $\begin{smallmatrix}5\\3\end{smallmatrix}$ ——— $\begin{smallmatrix}6\\5\end{smallmatrix}$ ——— $\begin{smallmatrix}5\\3\end{smallmatrix}$ ——— $\begin{smallmatrix}6\\5\end{smallmatrix}$ ——— V ——— I

e. Chopin

Em:

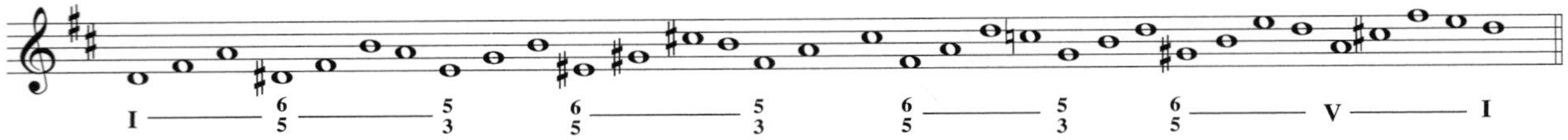

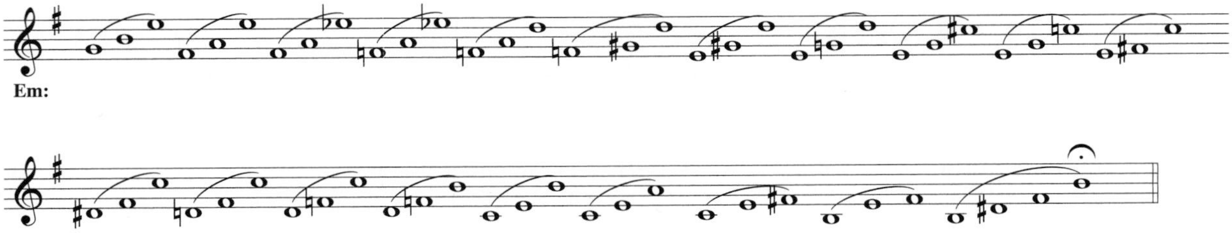

Terms for Review

Ninth chord
Eleventh chord
Thirteenth chord
Extended tertian chords
Nondominant extended tertian chords
Appoggiatura chords
Chromatic sequences

Circle-of-5ths sequence
Ascending 5–6 sequence
Descending 5–6 sequence
$\begin{smallmatrix}7\\5\\3\end{smallmatrix}$–$\begin{smallmatrix}6\\3\end{smallmatrix}$ sequence
Implied tonality
Tonal parenthesis

Worksheet 29

EXERCISE 1 Analysis.

1. The following passages include examples of extended tertian chords. Identify and label these chords, and verify the resolution of the dissonant chord members.
   a) Refer back to worksheet 23, example 23.18 (Chopin, Mazurka in GM, op. 67, no. 1). What extended tertian chord can you identify in m. 43?

   b) Example 29.23.

Example 29.23 L. v. Beethoven, Piano Sonata in Em, op. 90, I, mm. 67–71

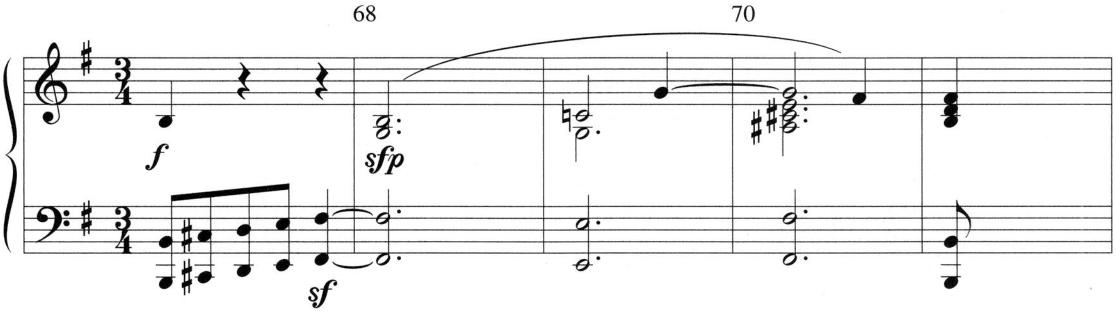

   c) Example 29.24. Comment on the use of melodic chromaticism and appoggiaturas in this passage. Discuss whether the passage is in CM or GM. What is the function of, and exact label for, the chord in m. 78?

Example 29.24 R. Wagner, *Tristan und Isolde,* act I, scene 5, mm. 76–82

d) Analyze each of the parallel phrase beginnings in example 29.25 and determine their harmonic differences.

e) Analyze mm. 13–21 of Amy Beach's *Ecstasy* (anthology, no. 59). The complete passage is in E♭M. You will find several interesting examples of tonicization, extended tertian chords, and appoggiatura chords in this fragment.

Example 29.25 R. Schumann, "Träumerei," from *Scenes from Childhood,* op. 15, no. 7

a.

b.

c.

d.

Example 29.25 Continued

e.

2. Analyze the following examples of chromatic sequences. Name the exact type of sequence, and provide the necessary figures to identify the sequential pattern.
   a) Anthology, no. 14, Bach, Fugue in Cm, *WTC,* I, mm. 17–20.

   b) Example 29.26
      1) Measures 11–16 can be analyzed as an extended $\begin{smallmatrix}7&6\\5&4\\3&3\end{smallmatrix}$ sequence. The beginning of the sequence is labeled for you on the example. Analyze the rest of it. The sequence is not always straightforward: In some cases the third is delayed by a 4–3 suspension, and in some other cases one or more linear chords are introduced between the $\begin{smallmatrix}7\\5\\3\end{smallmatrix}$ and its resolution to $\begin{smallmatrix}6\\4\\3\end{smallmatrix}$. But the resolution actually takes place in all cases.
      2) What extended tertian chords appear in m. 16, beats 3–4?
3. Study anthology, no. 45, Chopin, Mazurka 49 in Fm, mm. 1–15.
   a) On a separate sheet, explain the linear process in mm. 1–8 using the same concepts we applied to the analysis of Chopin's Prelude no. 4 in Em. Provide a diagram for these measures similar to the graph in example 29.20a.
   b) What is the main melodic difference between mm. 9–15 and mm. 1–8?

   c) Explain the modulation to AM. How are the two keys related?

Example 29.26 A. Beach, *Sous les étoiles,* op. 65, no. 4, mm. 11–18

EXERCISE 2 Write and resolve the following extended tertian chords in four voices.

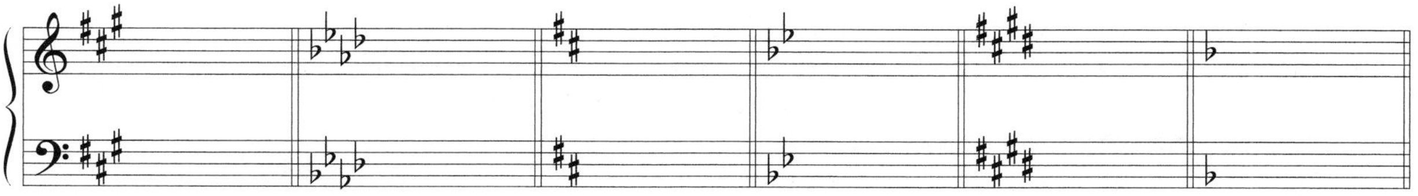

AM: V^9_7 I   Fm: V^9_7 i   Bm: V^{11}_7 i   Gm: $V^{11}_{9\,7}$ i   EM: V^{13}_7 I   FM: $V^{\flat 13}_7$ I

EXERCISE 3 Realize the short progressions in this exercise in four voices.

B♭M: I vi^{9}_{7} IV_{9} V^{9}_{7} I DM: I V^{9}_{7}/ii $\text{V}^{\flat 13}_{7}$/V V^{9}_{7} I

EXERCISE 4 Realize the following progression in four voices.

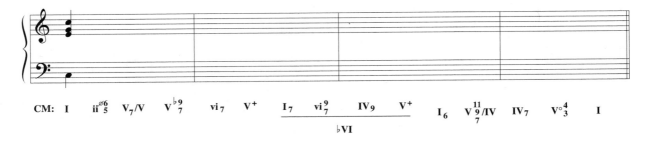

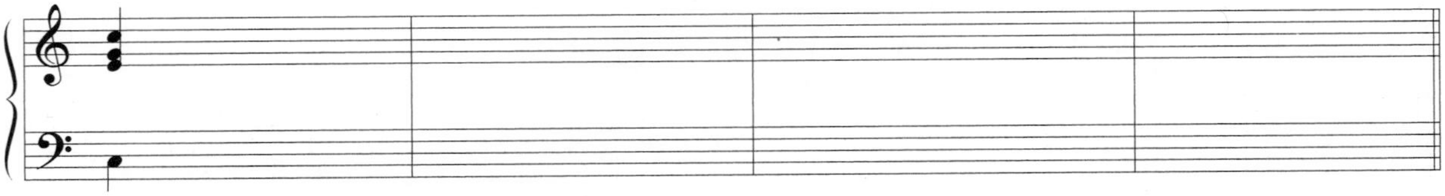

CM: I $\text{ii}^{\varnothing 6}_{5}$ V_{7}/V $\text{V}^{\flat 9}_{7}$ vi_{7} V^{+} I_{7} vi^{9}_{7} IV_{9} V^{+} I_{6} $\text{V}^{11}_{\substack{9\\7}}$/IV IV_{7} $\text{V}^{\circ 4}_{3}$ I

♭VI

EXERCISE 5

a) Realize the following sequential progression in four voices. Although accidentals have not been indicated in the figured bass, all chords should be inverted Mm_7 sonorities.

E♭M: $^{6}_{5}$ $^{4}_{2}$ $^{6}_{5}$ $^{4}_{2}$ $^{6}_{5}$ $^{4}_{2}$ $^{6}_{5}$ $^{4}_{2}$ $^{6}_{5}$ $^{4}_{2}$ $^{6}_{5}$ $^{4}_{2}$ $^{6}_{5}$

b) Realize the following sequential progression in four voices. All $^6_5$ chords should be inverted Mm_7 sonorities.

EXERCISE 6 Realize the following sequential progression in four voices. This is a diatonic sequence and all necessary accidentals are indicated in the figured bass.

EXERCISE 7 Write a progression in four voices using the same linear techniques we studied in Chopin's Prelude no. 4 in Em. Your progression will be in Gm, and although it will be similar to Chopin's, it should be different. Cover the path from i or i_6 to a final V or V_7 by means of stepwise voice leading (mostly by chromatic motion) and common tones. In this exercise you are illustrating the use of implied tonality, tonal parenthesis, linear chromaticism, and implied tonal regions. If possible, determine which underlying progression your linear chromaticism is elaborating (see example 29.20b for a model).

Chapter 30

The German Romantic *Lied*: Chromatic Harmony in Context

In this chapter we study representative examples of German ***Lieder*** (singular: ***Lied,*** "song"), the songs that constitute one of the most characteristic genres of the Romantic period. We will first focus in detail on two *Lieder* by Schubert and Schumann, and then we will analyze a song by Hugo Wolf to demonstrate modulation by enharmonic reinterpretation of the augmented triad. Many of the harmonic concepts we have learned in part 2 of this book, including various types of modulation to distantly related keys, will appear in the songs that we will study. For this reason, this chapter will also serve as a review of chromatic harmony in context.

THE GERMAN ROMANTIC *LIED*

Composers in the Classical period (such as Haydn, Mozart, and Beethoven) favored large formal structures driven by long-range tonal plans and extensive developmental processes, such as the ones we studied in chapter 28. Romantic composers, on the other hand, had an introspective interest in the soul, the passions, and the inner world of the individual. They often strove for *lyrical, intense poetic expression* through music. Some of the means they used for these expressive purposes were *lyrical melody, chromatic harmony,* and *harmonic color to depict mood.* The best vehicles for this intimate and subjective expression of emotions and moods were the "character piece" for piano (the typical Romantic short piano piece) and the song, the *Lied.*

The German *Lied* arose as a musical response and counterpart to the short lyrical poems by such major Romantic poets as Goethe and Schiller. Important composers of German Romantic *Lieder* are Franz Schubert (who composed over 600 songs), Fanny Mendelssohn, Robert and Clara Schumann, Josephine Lang, Pauline Viardot-García, Johannes Brahms, Hugo Wolf, Gustav and Alma Mahler, and Richard Strauss.

In principle, Romantic songs are a *musical expression of a poetic text.* This does not mean that the music necessarily follows the text in any particular way. A composer may choose, among other options, to depict the text musically in some detail (**text painting**), to depict or evoke only the general mood of the text, to give a personal interpretation of the text through music by means of distortion or exaggeration, or simply to ignore the text and its poetic meaning. In any case, because text and music are two essential components that come together in song, and because the music is usually built around the words in one way or another, the structure and content of the song's text should as a principle be considered carefully before examining the music. Some frequent themes one finds in Romantic poetry, and hence in Romantic songs, are death or loss, unrequited love, melancholy, yearning for the impossible, the irrational, contradictory, or complex aspects of the soul, and the psychic, mysterious aspects of nature.

Formally, *Lieder* can be of many types. **Formal types** are usually small and non-developmental. Among the most frequent types are the **strophic form** (each stanza of text is set to the same music), **ternary** (usually ABA), **binary** (AB, with a possible repetition of both sections, ABAB), and **through-composed** (which does not include any clear return or repetitions of material).

We recommend the following *general methodology* in the analysis of songs:

1. *The text.* What is the meaning of the poem? What moods, situations, or emotions does it depict? How many characters are there? Who is speaking, and in which tone? What is the form of the poem? How many verses are there, and how are they grouped into stanzas?
2. *The musical setting.* In general terms, what are the musical characteristics of the song? What are the textures, meter and rhythm, character, tempo, and dynamics of the setting? What are the melodic style and features (such as motives and phrase structure) of the vocal part? Do any of these musical traits seem to reflect any elements from the text? If there are different characters in the text, are they depicted musically in any particular way?
3. *The tonal and formal plan.* What is the formal design of the song? What is its long-range tonal plan? Do both the formal design and the tonal plan correspond in any way with the poem's structure and form?
4. *The harmonic detail.* Are there any modulations, fragments, or particular progressions we want to examine in detail because they seem to be especially interesting or because they seem to depict or reflect some specific elements of the text?[1]

We will first apply this methodology to a well-known song by Schubert, *Erlkönig*.

ANALYSIS 1: SCHUBERT, *ERLKÖNIG*

Listen carefully to this song, following the score (anthology, no. 38) and the translation of the text. *Erlkönig*, probably one of the most moving songs in the whole Romantic song literature, was written by Schubert on a text by Goethe in 1815, when he was only 18.

1. *The text and the story.* First, determine how many stanzas the poem has, how many characters are involved in it, and whether it has any recurring material (a refrain?).

---

[1] For an extensive introduction to all relevant aspects of *Lied* analysis, see Deborah Stein and Robert Spillman, *Poetry in Song: Performance and Analysis of Lieder* (New York: Oxford University Press, 1996).

Does the poem have a form determined by its dramatic content and its characters? How do you think this is a characteristically Romantic text?

The poem has eight stanzas, of which the first and the last are spoken by a narrator (N). Three more characters are involved in the story: the father (F), the son (S), and the Erlking (E) (in German folklore, a spirit who does mischief and evil, especially to children). Stanzas 2, 4, and 6 are dialogues between the son and the father, alternating with stanzas 3 and 5, where the Erlking speaks, and stanza 7, where both the Erlking and the son speak. The text is thus dramatic and narrative, including fast dialogue and a total of four characters.

This is the story of a father and child riding a horse late on a cold night. The evil Erlking constantly tries to seduce the poor, scared boy with charms and promises. In a three-way dialogue, the boy responds to the Erlking's approaches by desperate calls of fear to his father, who tries to reassure the son as well as he can, despite his own mounting tension. Song, dialogue, and tension keep spiraling until the riders reach home and the galloping rhythm stops. And then comes the chilling, final line: "In seinen Armen das Kind war todt" ("In his arms the child lay dead"). Characteristically Romantic features in this poem are its expression of powerful emotions (tension, fear), the proximity and presence of death, and the presence of a mysterious character from the psychic underworld (the Erlking).

2. *The musical setting*. The challenge of setting such a poem to music comes from having to characterize four different dramatic persons. Listen to the song again, and now focus on how Schubert deals with the challenge: How does the single singer differentiate between characters? How does Schubert achieve unity in a song with so much dialogue between so many characters? What is the general character (mood) of the song, and what musical elements contribute to it?

The action of the song takes place on a galloping horse. The first element that unifies the song is, of course, the galloping triplets in the piano, including the "galloping motive," in the piano's left hand, mm. 1–2. The song projects a mood of tension, which increases with the fear of the child. The ostinato triplet rhythm contributes to the increasing tension, and so does the quickening of the dialogue and the faster tempo, both toward the end. Most of all, tension and dramatic progression are determined by harmonic and tonal progression, as we will discuss below.

Register and harmony are the essential elements in the characterization of the four persons. The father, trying to be reassuring, sings in a low, deep register, but the chromaticism in his melodies suggests his underlying tension. The son, more and more scared, sings his chromatic melodies in a high register, becoming progressively higher. The sections of dialogue between father and son are tonally unstable, modulating sections. The Erlking tries to be charming and seducing (except toward the end, when he becomes threatening), and although he also sings in a high register, his melodies are diatonic, and his speeches are in the major mode, nonmodulating, and perfectly stable and closed tonally. Is the accompaniment for father and son different texturally than the accompaniment for the Erlking? Notice also the grouping of the persons in each of the stanzas. Stanzas 1, 4, and 6 are shared by father and son, while the Erlking sings his solo stanzas 3 and 5. By stanza 7, however, we have the Erlking and the son grouped together in the same stanza, representing the final victory of the Erlking in his attempt to take the child away from the father.

3. *The tonal and formal plan.* Examine the score again, and now identify the key areas in the complete song. Make a simple graph showing how these key areas correspond with the eight stanzas/musical sections. After you do this, study the tonal and formal graphs in examples 30.1 and 30.2, comparing them with both the score and your own graph.

The diagram in example 30.1 shows sections and their correspondence with text stanzas (in circled numbers), underlying tonal motion in the form of tonal areas and some other important tonal events, and speaking characters for each of the sections/stanzas (N, F, S, and E, above the staff). Example 30.2 presents a further reduction of the formal/tonal scheme, including stanzas, characters, and tonal motion. The grouping of the stanzas as represented in example 30.2 shows the initial and final sections spoken by the narrator and three large formal areas that group two stanzas each (2–3, 4–5, and 6–7). In each of these groups, the first stanza is a F–S dialogue, and the second stanza is an E monologue, except for stanza 7, which

Example 30.1

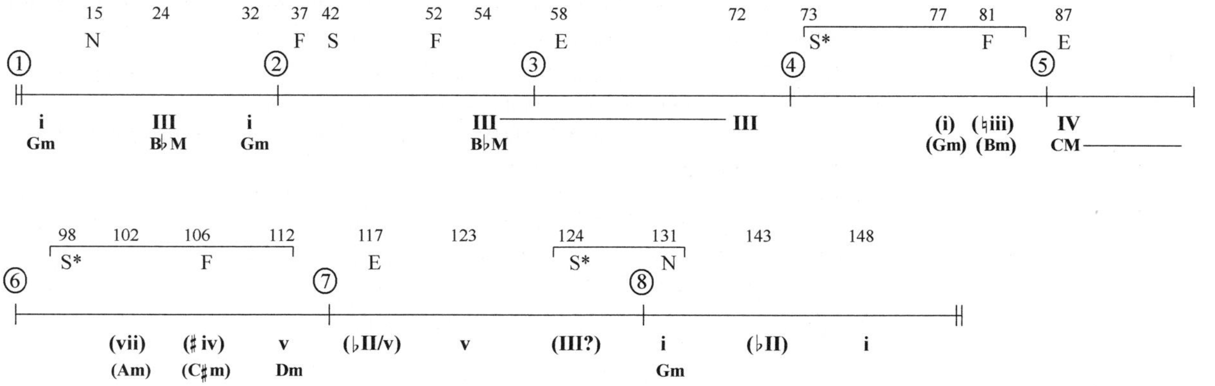

Example 30.2

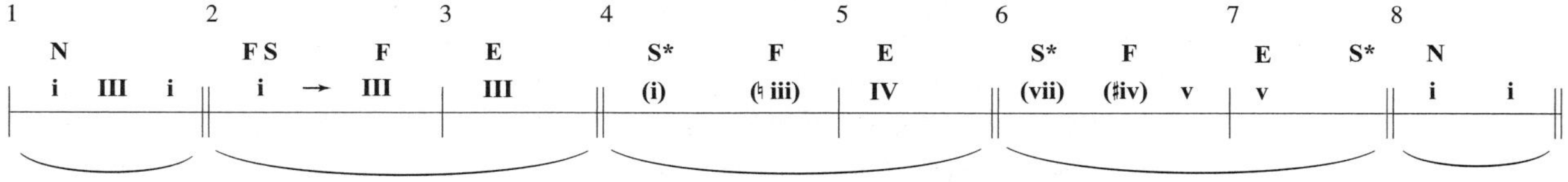

toward the end incorporates the last phrase by S. The three asterisked phrases by S (S*) are the recurring call of the child, "Mein Vater, mein Vater!" which functions as a refrain of sorts.

Several things become immediately apparent through these graphs:

a) Sections 1 and 8 frame the song, not only narratively, but also tonally. They are harmonically closed, in the tonic Gm, and section 1 prefigures the first large-scale tonal motion (to III, in sections 2–3) with a i–III–i motion.

b) E's monologues (3, 5, 7) are tonally closed and in major keys, except for the last one in the minor dominant key (the keys are III, IV, and v).

c) The F–S sections are modulating, and unstable tonally. In sections 4 and 6 key areas are touched on (the keys in parentheses on the graph), but only as stepping stones toward the following, stable sections. Sections 2, 4, and 6 are thus transitional.

d) The music rises by steps (see E monologues, in III, IV, and v), and we hear that especially in the son's calls of distress to his father (sections S*), which are one step higher each time, rising along with the tension.

e) The overall tonal plan, then, is i–III–IV–v–i. We can notice here two harmonic elaborations of this general tonal plan: the neighbor ♭II area in Dm, which ornaments v in mm. 117–119, and the implied III area in mm. 124–127. Taking these two secondary areas into consideration, we could think of the tonal plan as i–III–IV–v–(♭II/v)–v–(III)–i. We will comment more on this tonal design below.

4. *Harmonic detail*. Two aspects of this song deserve more detailed attention: first, the use of vii°$_7$ sonorities on pedals, and second, sections 4, 6, and the end of 7, all of which begin with the S* refrain (that is, the unstable sections, marked with brackets in example 30.1).

   a) Schubert uses the beautiful, but tense, sonority of a vii°$_7$ chord against a pedal in association with the son. First, in m. 25–27, vii°$_7$ of B♭ against the B♭ pedal accompanies the first mention of the child (see the reduction of these harmonies in example 30.3a). The next two appearances of this sonority take place during the child's first phrase, stressing the fear and tension of his words (mm. 42 and 47, against C and F pedals).

   b) All three beginnings of the S* sections also feature the same sonority. First, in mm. 73–76, the same chord which, in mm. 25–27 was functioning as vii°$_7$ of B♭ (A–C–E♭–G♭) now appears as F♯–A–C–E♭, vii°$_7$ of G, over a D pedal, and now leading to Gm (example 30.3b). In mm. 98–101, vii°$_7$ of A over an E pedal takes us to Am. Following the sequence up by steps of the "Mein Vater" cry (Gm–Am–B♭M), the next S* section begins in m. 124 with vii°$_7$ of B♭, spelled as if going to B♭. This is, again, the same chord which in mm. 25–27 took us to B♭, and in mm. 73–76 took us to Gm. The ambiguity is renewed here, where instead of the expected B♭, the chord takes us back to the home key, Gm (and hence B♭ is only implied). A chordal reduction of these measures is shown in example 30.3c.

Example 30.3

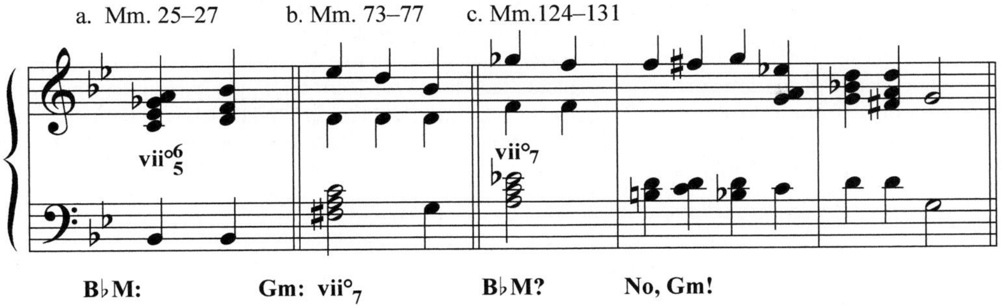

c) Now go back to the beginning of section 4, m. 73, and let us study the modulating process in the S* phrase. After the vii°$_7$ takes us to Gm, the music moves on immediately to Bm. How is this modulation realized? Gm to Bm is a chromatic third–related motion (i to ♯iii). There are two modulating techniques at work in these measures. One is the chromatic bass from G to B. The other one is the one you would expect in a chromatic third modulation. What is it? This modulation is shown in a reduced form in example 30.4a.

d) We do not stay in Bm for long, either (this is the unstable, modulating section). Instead, the music moves to CM by way of G. Bm to CM is a modulation from i to ♭II, the Neapolitan key. What is the role of G in both keys? You can see this even better in the next S* section, stanza 6, where the whole process is a step up from stanza 4. The vii°$_7$ took us to Am, and we move, by chromatic bass and common tone, to ♯iii, C♯m. In m. 106 we reach i in C♯m, and we move immediately to the minor Neapolitan key, Dm. How? What is the function of the modulating chord, the AM$_7$ chord in m. 108, in both keys? A chordal reduction of this modulation appears in example 30.4b.

Example 30.4

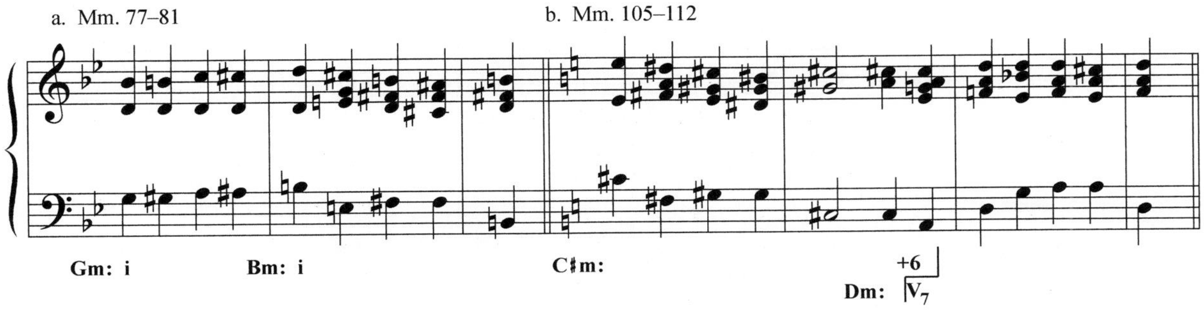

PRACTICAL APPLICATION AND DISCUSSION

Our study of *Erlkönig* serves as an introduction to the analysis of song. We have taken into account the text, its divisions and meaning, and its characters. We have seen how the music reflects the sections, meaning, and mood of the text. We have demonstrated that tonal motion, modulations, tonal stability and instability, rhythmic figuration, texture, and register, all serve the dramatic and textual purpose of the poem. After listening again to the song, discuss in class how the analysis and in-depth knowledge of the structure of the song can help you listen to it or perform it. Would you rather perform the song without having any of these insights on how it works and why? How could the insights affect and improve your performance?

For instance, how could you make sure that your performance contributed to the enhanced tension provided by the tonal plan as it rises by steps toward a higher register? How can you emphasize the sense of distress and instability in the S* sections? Stanza 8 features two important dramatic characteristics. First, the return of the narrator, instead of the expected response of the father to the last cry of his son, is a signal to the listener to expect the worst. Finally, when the riders reach home we learn the tragic outcome of the story, punctuated by the ♭II harmony and the closing recitative passage. What would you do to enhance the drama and horror of this section?

e) Finally, let us examine further the role of the Neapolitan in the song. Besides the modulations to Neapolitan areas we just discussed, a ♭II relationship appears prominently, as a brief key area, in mm. 117–119. This is the phrase where the Erlking goes from charm to threat: "Listen, I love you, but if you don't want to come, I'll take you by force!" We are in Dm, and we go directly to E♭M. We hear, again, the vii$^{\circ}_{7}$ on a pedal, this time vii$^{\circ}_{7}$/♭II in Dm (m. 118). The final, and most dramatic Neapolitan area, however, comes at m. 140, when the father reaches "home with effort and toil," only to find that his child is dead in his arms. Here again we hear, one last time, not only ♭II, but also the vii$^{\circ}_{7}$/♭II on the ♭$\hat{2}$ pedal.

As a conclusion of our analysis, examine example 30.5a. This example shows a reduction of the complete tonal structure of the song: beginning in Gm, motion through the areas of B♭M, CM, and Dm, the E♭ Neapolitan area as a neighbor note (NN) to D, then the implied B♭ area, and the return to Gm. As we saw above, this design can be summarized as i–III–IV–v–(♭II/v)–v–(III)–i. Now compare this sketch with example 30.5b, the "galloping motive" in the piano's left hand: $\hat{1}$–$\hat{2}$–$\hat{3}$–$\hat{4}$–$\hat{5}$–$\hat{6}$–$\hat{5}$–$\hat{3}$–$\hat{1}$. This is an instance

Example 30.5

of *replication of a melodic motive at the deeper level of tonal structure*. One can only admire Schubert's amazing compositional craft at age 18![2]

ANALYSIS 2: SCHUMANN, "WIDMUNG"

This song (anthology, no. 48), on a text by Friedrich Rückert, is from a collection titled *Myrthen*. It was composed in 1840, Schumann's "year of song," in which he composed a total of 127 songs. This was the same year in which he married Clara Wieck (to become Clara Schumann), after winning a court suit against her father to obtain his permission to get married. Fittingly enough, "Widmung," ("Dedication") is a love song. Listen to it following the score and words, and determine whether there is more than one character or mood represented by the text and music.

1. *The text and the song's meaning*. The poem has three sections: verses 1–6 display a clearly passionate character, verses 7–12 show the more contemplative, mystical aspect of love, and finally verses 13–17 are a return to the initial verses and passionate character. The tripartite form of the poem, of course, provides the structure for a song in ternary form, as the one Schumann wrote.

   One could see the text merely as a simple, if passionate, love poem. There is more to it, however. Schumann, who had a very active private world of inner fantasy, saw himself as divided into two personalities, represented by the imaginary characters *Florestan* and *Eusebius*. Florestan was the impetuous, passionate, and revolutionary Schumann. Eusebius, on the other hand, was the contemplative, introspective dreamer. (A third personality would join these two in later years, *Master Raro*, the wise and judicious moderator of the two contradictory personalities of Florestan and Eusebius.)

   "Widmung" thus has a self-referential quality: It contains expressions of love coming from both of Schumann's personalities. The A sections (first and third) represent the impetuous Florestan, whereas the calmer B section represents Eusebius. This is a good example of a Romantic "character piece," a piece that expresses one or more emotional or psychological "moods."

2. *The musical setting*. How are the two characters represented musically? First, examine the melody in both sections. How do the following melodic aspects help define Schumann's personalities: range, register, melodic contour (leaps or steps), and rhythmic values. Then look at the accompaniment. How does it represent the two different characters? Other factors that contribute to psychological depiction in the song are dynamics (how?) and tempo. You will have noticed that, even though there is no quantitative tempo change between sections (the beat remains the same), we perceive section B as being slower. Why?

---

[2] This motivic parallelism between the galloping motive and the song's tonal plan was first noted by Charles Burkhart in "Schenker's 'Motivic Parallelisms,'" *Journal of Music Theory* 22 (Fall 1978): 145–76. For a more extensive study of motivic parallelisms in this song, as well as an interesting discussion of textual and poetic images and their correspondence with musical structure, see Deborah Stein, "Schubert's *Erlkönig*: Motivic Parallelism and Motivic Transformation," *19th-Century Music* 13 (Fall 1989): 145–58.

3. *The tonal and formal plan.* We have already determined that both the text and the song are in ternary form. The key of the A section is A♭M. The key of the B section is EM. How are these two keys related? How are the modulations into and out of EM effected?

   The A♭M–EM relationship is an enharmonically spelled ♭VI relationship (as in A♭M–F♭M). This is, thus, a chromatic third relationship. The modulation in mm. 13–14 is a direct common-tone modulation between tonic chords, using the common A♭/G♯ as a connection (see example 30.6a). The return is a little more complex. In mm. 23–25, the secondary key area of AM (IV in EM) is established. The chord before the change of key signature (m. 25) is IV in EM (the AM triad), with several nonchord tones (NCTs) (identify and label them). From there we move directly to V_7 in A♭M, followed by a long pedal on $\hat{5}$ of A♭, leading to the return in m. 30.

   What made the motion between IV in EM (the AM triad) and V_7 in A♭ so effective? First, function: What is the AM triad in A♭M, and why does V_7 follow so naturally? Second, melodic connection: Is there a common tone between the two chords Schumann uses as a melodic pivot? A reduction of this modulation is shown in example 30.6b.

   What is significant about this long-range relationship? Romantic composers definitely preferred third relationships over fifth relationships in their structural plans, and both *Erlkönig* and "Widmung" are examples of this preference. (Examine, as a confirmation, how many adjacent keys are third-related in *Erlkönig*'s tonal plan.) Schumann, in particular, was especially fond of chromatic third relationships, as this song illustrates.

4. *Harmonic detail and text painting.* The harmony of "Widmung" is not especially venturesome. In the A section, the most notable harmonic event is the occasional presence of the pitch F♭, which not only introduces modal borrowing at the chordal level, but also prefigures the ♭VI modulation in section B. Does the F♭ have any textual significance? It first appears in m. 5 (What borrowed chord results from this F♭?), coloring the word *Schmerz* ("grief"). Its next appearance is in m. 10 (What is the borrowed chord here?), to the word *Grab* ("grave"). The association thus seems

Example 30.6

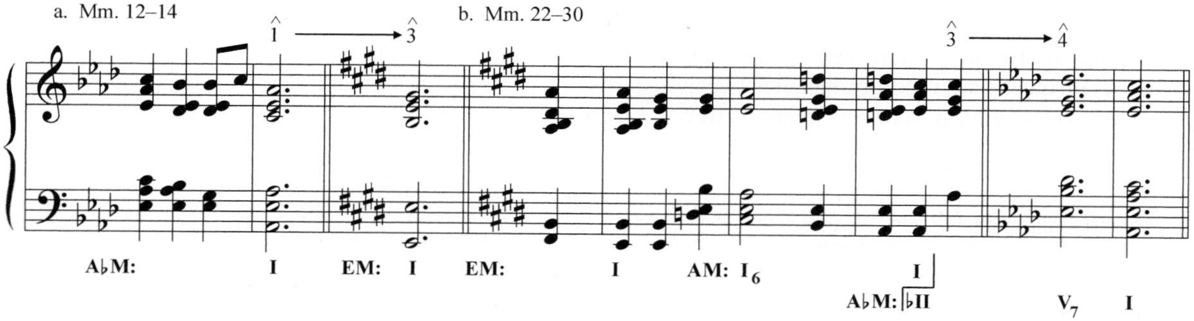

PRACTICAL APPLICATION AND DISCUSSION

How is this song Romantic? How does the above analysis help you as a listener or performer of the song? Is there anything in particular, in the above discussion, that you would want to project in a performance? How would you do so? Can you help depict, with your performance, the two different characters represented in the song? If you happen to have this song in your repertoire, you may want to perform it in class in light of this discussion.

to be quite obvious! Notice also another touch of text painting in the A section: What is the highest vocal pitch in the whole song? What textual concept is it associated with? The pitch is G♭ in mm. 8–9, and the words are "You my heaven, into which I soar"! Now, after soaring into heaven, the next phrase of text is "O you my grave." How does the melody move from heaven to the grave?

The harmony in the B section is also quite straightforward. What familiar linear chord appears in m. 15? What key area is tonicized in mm. 18–19? What is the NCT in m. 19, beat 1? And in m. 23, beat 1? How is the phrase "Du bist die Ruh' " depicted musically? (Think, for instance, of the bass!) How does texture depict the word *Frieden* ("peace")?

Notice now the interesting textual role of secondary key areas in the song. In both the A section (mm. 7–9) and the B section (mm. 18–19), the word *Himmel* ("Heaven"), is represented by secondary key areas: heaven and earth, of course, are not in the same "tonal levels"! The only other secondary key area is, in the B section, the AM key area in mm. 23–25. And here the words are "Your glance has transfigured me." Once the poet is transfigured, he is no more in the same "tonal level" either!

MODULATION BY ENHARMONIC REINTERPRETATION OF V$^+$

The augmented triad, like the °7 chord, is a symmetrical chord that divides the octave into equal segments. Whereas the °7 chord divides it into four segments (minor thirds), the augmented triad divides it into three major thirds. Just as there are only three different °7 chords, there are only four different augmented triads. If you begin from C, you will have different augmented triads on C, C♯, D, and D♯. The next triad, on E, contains the same pitches as the triad on C. This means that one sonority, with three different spellings, can function as V$^+$ in three different pairs of M/m keys. Example 30.7 demonstrates the three different spellings and resolutions of a single augmented triad, functioning as V$^+$ first in A♭M/m, then in CM/m, and finally in EM/m.

Example 30.7

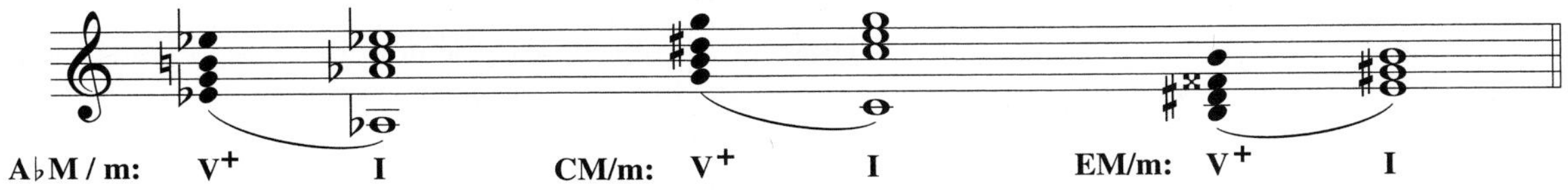

Example 30.8

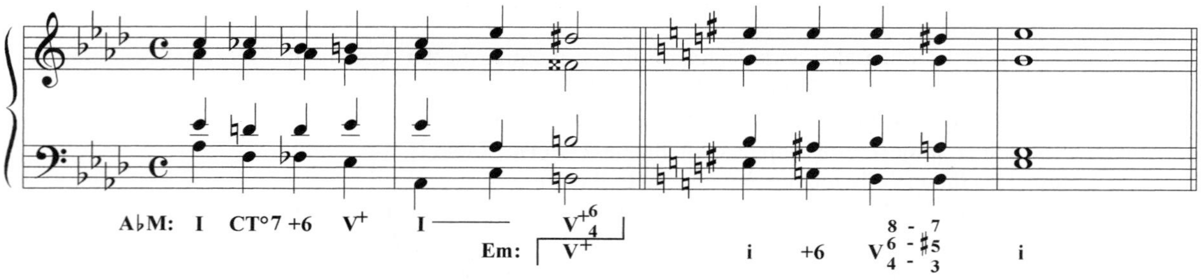

EXERCISE

To practice enharmonic spellings of V⁺ chords, refer to exercise 2 in worksheet 30 at the end of this chapter.

This capacity of the augmented triad to function as V⁺ in three different pairs of keys allows us to reinterpret it enharmonically in modulations to distantly related keys. Keys connected by this type of modulation are a M3rd apart. Example 30.8 illustrates one of the possible modulations using the triad from example 30.7. The modulation shown here, from A♭M to Em, is between two chromatic third–related keys whose tonics do not share a common tone (that is, one of the chromatic third modulations that cannot be effected by common tone). Play and study this modulation, and understand how it works, before moving on to the following analysis of the Wolf song.

EXERCISE

To practice writing your own modulation by enharmonic reinterpretation of V⁺, refer to exercise 3 in worksheet 30 at the end of this chapter.

ANALYSIS 3: WOLF, "DAS VERLASSENE MÄGDLEIN"

This song ("The Forlorn Maiden," from *Gedichte von Mörike*, anthology, no. 57), one of the best-known *Lieder* by Hugo Wolf, is based on a poem by Mörike, and it again contains many of the characteristic elements of Romantic poetry and song. Read the poem, and think about its structure, its character and moods, and its sections.

1. *The text and the story*. These are the reflections of a forlorn servant girl as she gets up in the early morning to start the fire and faces the prospect of one more sad and lonesome day. The setup is, thus, purely Romantic. In the first stanza we find out about the time of the day and the immediate circumstances (it is very early, cold,

and she has to get up to light the fire). There is also a moment of certain joy (second stanza), when the fire catches up and for a moment she gets carried away by the beauty of the flames and the sparks. Next, we find that she is in deep sorrow. The third stanza tells us about the reason for her sorrow: She has apparently been abandoned by the boy she loves, and she suddenly remembers that during the night she dreamed of him. The song ends with more tearful expressions of sorrow (fourth stanza).

The moods suggested by the poem are sadness, loneliness, and the sorrowful and painful state of someone who has been forsaken by a lover.

2. *The musical setting*. How does Wolf depict these moods musically? Try to determine the key of the song by examining its beginning and end. The beginning is very ambiguous: It is all dyads (not triads), and although we feel the presence of A as a tonal center, there is no A triad until m. 13. And then it is a major triad, although we were hearing Am as the implied tonality. The end does not clarify the problem completely: The last measures also feature dyads, this time open fifths on A, avoiding the major/minor definition. Both beginning and end transmit a sense of emptiness and ambiguity (the dyads, the undefined tonal center, the unclear mode of the song). Does this correspond with the young woman's state of mind? Could the missing root in the dyads, or the unclear tonal center and mode, reflect that something is missing from the maiden's life and her resulting feeling of emptiness?

   The melodic structure of the beginning also contributes to the sad mood. The melody is grouped into two-measure units, and each unit is made up of a descending fifth, E–A, D–G♯, C–F, and B–E. If you take the first pitch of each segment of the sequence, you also come up with a descending line, E–D–C–B. The melody drags our mood downward. Notice then what happens in mm. 13–18: For a brief moment, when the fire catches up, her mood lightens up. The key is clarified for the first time, and now it is in the major mode: AM. Moreover, look at the melody: It is ascending, like the flames, and the rhythms become more lively. Not for long, though. In mm. 19–22 we learn about her sorrow: The key goes down a half step (to A♭M), and the melody repeats the half step C–B. Of course, the half step is the traditional musical "sigh," the symbol of sorrow and lament. Here we have it both in the melody and in the keys! The melodic structure of these measures is summarized in example 30.9.

Example 30.9

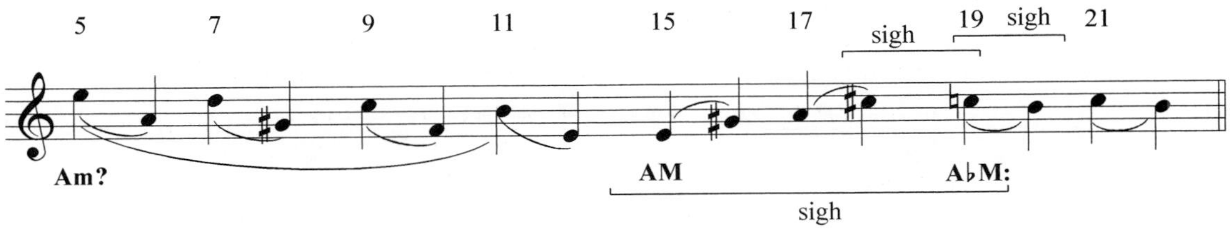

With the remembrance of her dream, the music becomes more agitated and tonally complex, and the melody reaches its highest pitches (mm. 27–34). Then we return to the original mood of sorrow, and to the initial, ambiguous musical materials (mm. 38–end).

The rhythm should also be mentioned as contributing to the character of the song: The obsessive, repeated rhythmic figure reflects the one thought she cannot get out of her mind and the one feeling she cannot ban from her heart.

3. *The tonal and formal plan*. How do you think the form of the song is determined by the poem? We have already seen that there is an initial section which returns, and that these sections correspond with stanzas 1 and 4. These two sections stay within what we could call the "ambiguous Am" key. The two middle sections, stanzas 2 and 3, can be grouped into one section. The main tonal characteristic of this middle section is its modulating character, and the tonal ambiguity provided by the use of the augmented triad, as we will see below. We have already seen that at m. 13 the mode changes to AM, and that the stanza ends with the A♭M section (mm. 19–22). In m. 23 we move to B♭M, until m. 31 where the "sigh" motive comes back, again in A♭M (compare mm. 31–34 with mm. 19–23). A modulating passage (mm. 33–37) takes us back to the return of the initial material in Am. The form can then be summarized as A–B–A. And the two secondary key areas in the B section (A♭M and B♭M) are chromatic neighbors to the two main keys, the Am/M pair. This formal/tonal plan is summarized graphically in example 30.10.

4. *Harmonic detail*. The most interesting harmonic feature of this song is the use of augmented triads, both to create tonal ambiguity and unrest within phrases and as a means to modulate. Before we look at this aspect of the song, however, notice the two chords in mm. 13–18. The chords alternated in these measures are the AM tonic, and a Mm_7 in third inversion, C♯–E♯–G♯–B, that is, the dominant seventh of F♯, V^4_2/vi in AM. Because it does not resolve to vi, however, this Mm_7 chord does not function as a secondary dominant. In other words, it is not a functional chord. What kind of chord relationship is this, between AM and C♯Mm_7? (As a hint, you studied this chord relationship in chapter 27.)

Example 30.10

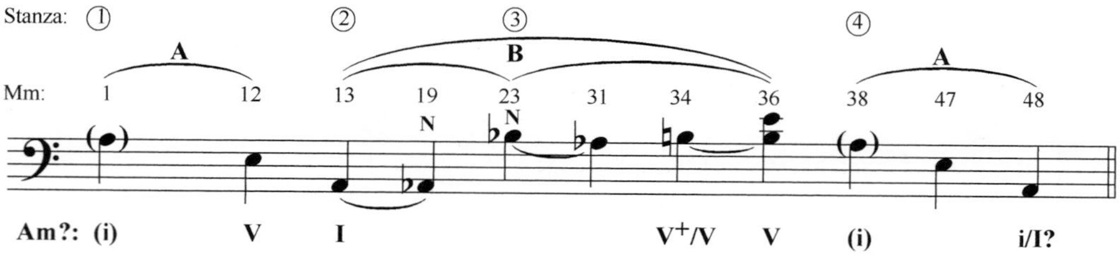

Let us examine the role of augmented triads in this song.

a) The augmented triad first appears in m. 20. What is its function here? Think of it as spelled from E♭ (E♭–G–B♮) and resolving to A♭M: V$^+$ of A♭.

b) Measures 23–26, the beginning of the B♭M area, is all based on augmented triads: I$^+$–V$^+$. Notice the connection between A♭M and B♭M (mm. 22–23): From V$^+$ in A♭M (E♭–G–B♮) to I$^+_6$ in B♭ (D–G♭–B♭, as Wolf spells it), all voices move down by half step. This motion from A♭M to B♭M again stresses the "sigh" motive.

c) In m. 31, we return to the A♭M area, with a I$^+$ on A♭. The chord in m. 32 is the same sonority as the V$^+$ in m. 20, but now its spelling is not E♭–G–B♮, but B–D♯–G. Think of it as B–D♯–F𝄪, and you will recognize V$^+$ in E. We realize its new function in mm. 34–36, when it goes first to Em, then to EM, the V of Am which takes us back to Am in m. 38. Look again at mm. 32–33. In A♭M, you would read these chords as V$^+$–I$^+$. In Am, you would read them as V$^+$/V–V$^+$. This second reading is confirmed in mm. 34–36.

d) What makes this modulation possible is the enharmonic reinterpretation of the augmented triads. Notice that the reinterpretation of V$^+$ in A♭M as V$^+$/V of A is the same as what you already studied in examples 30.7 and 30.8. Example 30.11 provides a summary of this modulation, showing how these chords are interpreted in both keys.

The passage in mm. 23–26, all based on augmented triads, represents an important juncture in the narrative. In the previous section the girl had been in an early morning dreamlike state, and suddenly reality dawns on her, with the remembrance, in the phrase beginning in m. 27, of her unfortunate state. Augmented triads are introduced precisely in the passage that takes us from the dreamy moments by the fire to the remembrance of reality and the anxiety that comes with it.

EXERCISE

To practice analyzing a Lied, *refer to exercise 1 in worksheet 30 at the end of this chapter.*

Example 30.11

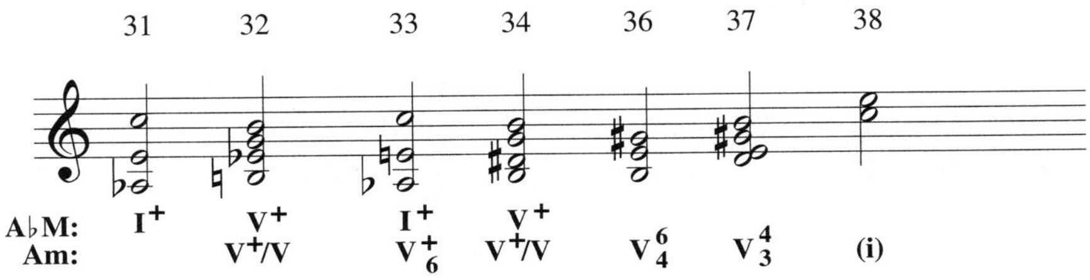

PRACTICAL APPLICATION AND DISCUSSION

To summarize, discuss in class how tonality, harmony, modulations, melody, rhythm, and texture contribute to the depiction of what our forlorn maiden felt that early morning when she got up to light the fire. Discuss also how this discussion of the song affects your hearing of it (listen to it again after finishing its analysis), and how it would affect your performance if you were to perform it.

From a more general point of view, what are your impressions of the expressive power of musical elements as displayed in these German *Lieder*? We are all aware that music in itself is expressive. In these songs, however, we can see in detail why it is expressive, what makes it so, and we see that it is not expressive by chance: Romantic composers knew very well how to use musical elements such as melody, harmony, rhythm, to express very specific feelings and moods or to depict situations. In these songs, composers achieved the artistic and expressive unity of poetry and music. These songs are truly "musical poems."

FOR FURTHER STUDY

For additional chapter 30 materials, refer to the *Harmony in Context* Web page at www.mhhe.com/roigfrancoli2e.

ASSIGNMENT AND KEYBOARD EXERCISES

For analytical and written assignments and keyboard exercises based on the materials learned in this chapter, refer to chapter 30 in the workbook.

PITCH PATTERNS

Sing the pitch patterns in example 30.12, and as you sing, listen to the modulation by enharmonic reinterpretation of an augmented triad.

Example 30.12

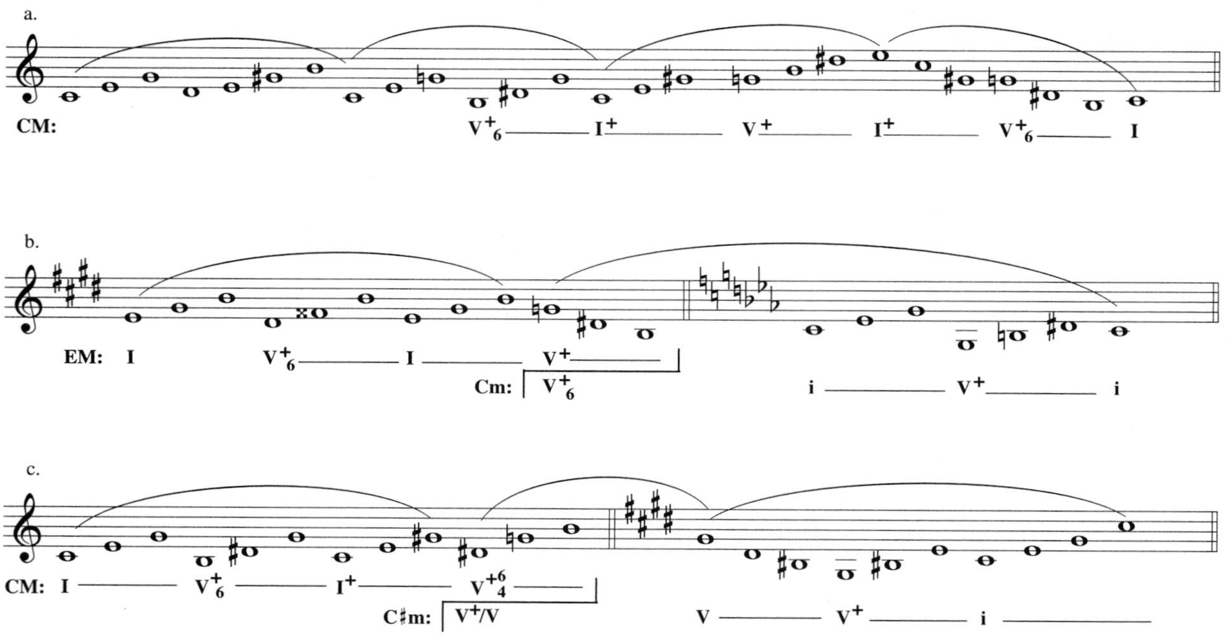

Terms for Review

Lied (Lieder)
Text painting
Formal types:
- strophic form, ternary, binary, through-composed

Schubert: *Erlkönig*
Schumann: "Widmung"
Modulation by enharmonic reinterpretation of V^{+}
Wolf: "Das verlassene Mägdlein"

Worksheet 30

EXERCISE 1 Analysis. Analyze anthology, no. 49, Schumann, "Am leuchtenden Sommermorgen," from *Dichterliebe*, op. 48. Answer the following questions with as much detail as possible.

1. Does the poem establish two contrasting moods? What moods?

2. What is the initial chord? Explain its spelling. What is unusual about this beginning?

3. Both in m. 1 and m. 6 this chord functions as ________ in the key of ________, and as such it resolves to ________.

4. How is the second chord in m. 8 related to the above chord? How does it function here, and in what key?

5. Focus now on mm. 8–13. The first chord in m. 9 is a linear chord leading to the second chord. Explain how the first chord works linearly, and what the function of the second chord is. What key area is suggested in mm. 8–9? How is this key area related (by RN) to the original key?

6. Thinking of the key area suggested in mm. 8–9, how does the second chord in m. 9 resolve? What is the exact RN and function of the first chord in m. 10 with respect to the key area of m. 9?

7. On the other hand, the first chord in m. 10 is also part of a harmonic pattern that follows (mm. 10–11), and which leads back to the original key. Explain clearly, and using all the correct harmonic terms, how mm. 8–13 function harmonically, and what pivot chords are used between key areas.

8. Now look at the text for these measures (mm. 8–12). Does the tonal ambiguity reflect the mood of the text? Could we also say, now, that the opening chord itself also reflects and announces the ambiguous moods of the text?

9. Who is speaking beginning in m. 17? What is the secondary key area in mm. 17–19? How is the secondary tonic in m. 17 related to the main key? What words of the text does this relationship emphasize?

10. Explain the linear chord in m. 16, beat 2. Can you also explain this chord functionally with respect to the key of m. 17? What kind of an altered chord is it from a functional point of view?

11. Write a concluding paragraph explaining how this song reflects the content of the poem it is based on.

EXERCISE 2 Write V^+, and resolve it to I, in EM. This chord may be used to modulate to two other major keys by respelling it enharmonically. Indicate the keys, and provide the spelling (leaving the chord in the same position) and the correct resolution to the tonic in each of the new keys.

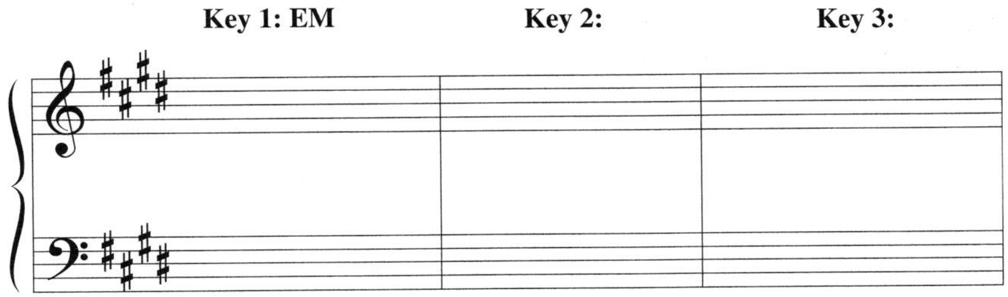

EXERCISE 3 Write a modulation in four voices by enharmonic reinterpretation of V$^+$, from C♯m to a key of your choice.

C♯m:

Chapter 31

Toward (and Beyond) the Limits of Functional Tonality

In the last chapter of this book we will study a variety of harmonic techniques and musical processes used by composers in the latter part of the nineteenth century and the beginning of the twentieth century. Some of the procedures we will see have the effect of weakening functional tonality; others suspend tonality, create a sense of tonal ambiguity, or provide the means to organize triadic sonorities in alternative ways to functional tonality. The weakening and eventual dissolution of tonality in the late Romantic harmonic language which we will study in the present chapter is one of the determinant factors that eventually led to the search, on the part of composers in the early twentieth century, for alternative systems to organize their pitch structures.

TONAL AMBIGUITY AND IMPLIED TONALITY

In our study of Chopin's Prelude no. 4 in chapter 29, we introduced the concept of implied tonality. Because tonal ambiguity and implied tonality are harmonic concepts essential to our understanding of much music from the late-Romantic period, we will devote some time to them now, focusing on a piece that demonstrates these ideas extensively: the Prelude to Wagner's *Tristan und Isolde*. The opera, one of Wagner's great masterpieces, is based on a medieval story of Celtic origin, which at the same time contains all the ingredients for a fervently Romantic drama. Tristan, a knight, has been sent to fetch the bride who has been chosen for his king in a mostly political arrangement. The mother of the bride prepares a love potion to help her win the love of the king but, by a fateful mistake, Tristan and Isolde end up drinking the love potion themselves. The rest of the story is best summarized by Wagner himself in his program notes to the performance of the Prelude, in the following sentences, which amount to a Romantic manifesto on life, love, and death:

> Fired by [the love potion's] draught, their love leaps suddenly to vivid flame, and they have to acknowledge that they belong only to each other. Henceforth no end to the yearning, longing, rapture, and misery of love: world, power, fame, honor, chivalry, loyalty,

and friendship scattered like an insubstantial dream; one thing alone left living: longing, longing unquenchable, desire forever renewing itself, craving and languishing; one sole redemption: death, surcease of being, the sleep that knows no waking!

The *Tristan* Prelude

Example 31.1 is an annotated piano reduction of mm. 1–46 of the ***Tristan* prelude,** slightly less than half its complete length. This limited fragment will suffice to illustrate the characteristics of Wagner's harmonic and formal style in his later works (best represented by *Tristan und Isolde* and *Parsifal*). Listen to the example, or if possible to the whole prelude, and play through it if you have sufficient keyboard skills. How do you think this music grows formally? What are the fundamental compositional blocks and elements? Is it periodic? Are there clear cadences? How is tonality defined? What "key" is the prelude in? How are keys defined? Are chords clearly identifiable? If not, why not? What is the dramatic and expressive result of all these musical traits? After you have tried to answer at least some of these questions, read the following comments.

1. You will have heard that this music moves in a *continuous flow.* It is *nonperiodic,* and phrases are open-ended. Cadences are systematically avoided or resolved deceptively, so that clear arrivals on any kind of tonic chord or tonicized degree are avoided.
2. The music is *highly motivic.* The prelude contains a number of characteristic motives which will become prominent throughout the opera. These are called ***Leitmotifs,*** musical ideas that are associated with a particular person, idea, or situation in the drama. Several of these motives are labeled in our example according to generally accepted designations.
3. Formal growth results from the *spinning out of motives.* This music is based on *continuous development* and on an unending flow of melody. *Sequences* are often used as a developmental technique.
4. *Tonality is obscured* by the avoidance of cadences and of arrivals on a tonic. Moreover, there is not a single clear tonal center (***tonal ambiguity***), and tonal centers are not clearly defined. Key areas are more often defined by unresolved dominants than by arrivals on a tonic (***implied tonality***). The resulting effect is of *constant* ***tonal fluctuation.***
5. Chords and harmony are further obscured by the extensive use of *chromatic nonchord tones* (NCTs) (especially suspensions, appoggiaturas, and passing tones).
6. Each of the above elements contributes to the dramatic purpose of this music. Wagner achieves an unparalleled constant buildup of tension, unresolved and continuous tension, which provides a suitable musical setting for the "longing, longing unquenchable, desire forever renewing itself, craving and languishing." The tension does not really find resolution until the very end of the opera, when Tristan and Isolde find the fulfillment of their tragic love only in death, and the music finally reaches a resting point on a long BM tonic chord.

Example 31.1 R. Wagner, Prelude to *Tristan und Isolde*, mm. 1–46

Example 31.1 Continued

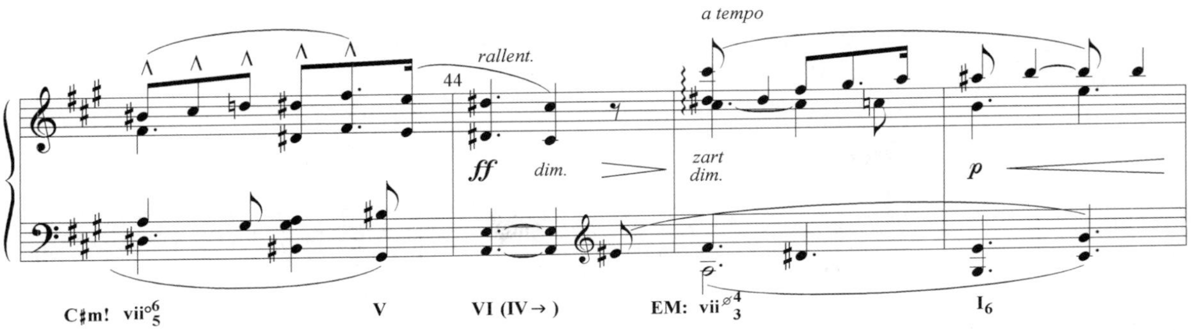

We will now study some of these particular musical characteristics as they appear in our excerpt.[1]

The opening unit (mm. 1–17). *The "Tristan chord."* The principles of tonal ambiguity and implied tonality are present from the very outset of the prelude. The initial idea (mm. 1–3) includes two motivic units: the "love" motive (mm. 1–2), with its descending chromatic gesture, and the desire motive (mm. 2–3), chromatically ascending. The key signature indicates Am or CM. This opening gesture ends on a chord that appears to be V_7 of A, so we'll think of this opening as being in Am. The prelude opens with one of the most mysterious, and certainly one of the most famous, chords in tonal literature, widely known as the **Tristan chord.** The sonority sounds like a half-diminished seventh chord on F (in ascending thirds, F–A♭–C♭–E♭, spelled as F–G♯–B–D♯). In itself, this is an extremely ambiguous chord which, as is very often the case with late-Romantic harmony, allows for several possible interpretations. Let us see some of these possible interpretations:

1. Because in Am this chord seems to be totally nonfunctional, some authors have interpreted the G♯ as being an appoggiatura, and then the A in m. 2 becomes the real chord tone. This has allowed for two interpretations: as B–D♯–F♮–A, it is an altered form of V_7/V in Am (with a lowered fifth). As F–A–B–D♯ it is the Fr +6 chord in Am. A possible criticism to either interpretation is that the G♯ takes most of the measure and is five times as long as the brief A. Shouldn't one perhaps think of the G♯ as the "real tone," and the A as a passing tone?

---

[1] An interesting collection of historical and analytical studies on the prelude, along with the orchestral score, can be found in the Norton Critical Score, Richard Wagner, *Prelude and Transfiguration from Tristan and Isolde*, ed. Robert Bailey (New York: Norton, 1985). Especially interesting from an analytical point of view are the contributions to the collection by Robert Bailey ("An Analytical Study of the Sketches and Drafts," pp. 113–46), and William Mitchell ("The *Tristan* Prelude: Techniques and Structure," pp. 242–67). Some of the ideas in the following discussion of the Prelude are borrowed from these two sources. Piano reductions of the complete Prelude can be found in the music anthologies by Charles Burkhart (*Anthology for Musical Analysis*, Fort Worth: Harcourt Brace, 1994) and Mary Wennerstrom (*Anthology of Musical Structure and Style*, Englewood Cliffs, NJ: Prentice Hall, 1982).

Example 31.2 Wagner, *Tristan,* Prelude, m. 82; Prelude to act III, mm. 1–2; and the "Tristan chord" (Prelude, mm. 2–3)

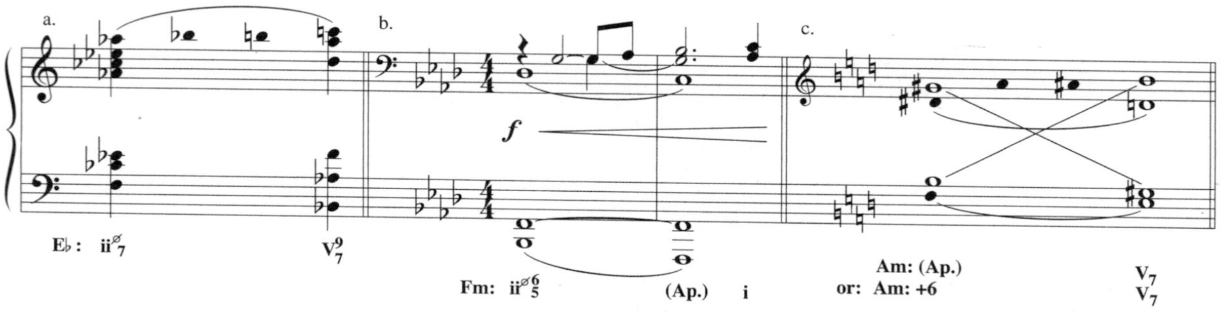

2. The chord appears numerous times later in the opera, in a variety of other tonal contexts which stress the ambiguous quality of this sonority, but which also show its use by Wagner as a more functional ∅7 chord. Examples 31.2a and b, for instance, show appearances of this same sonority as $ii^{\varnothing}_7$ in E♭ and (transposed up a step and inverted) as $ii^{\varnothing 6}_{5}$ in Fm.
3. If we consider, then, the G♯ in the first chord of the prelude as the "real" chord tone, a linear interpretation of this chord, as presented in example 31.2c, seems to be plausible. *The chord has two common tones with* V_7*, the B and the G♯, which undergo a voice exchange, whereas the other two tones are appogiaturas that move by chromatic voice leading to tones in* V_7. According to this interpretation, we can think of the Tristan chord as an *appoggiatura chord* of the same type we studied in chapter 30.
4. Considering the G♯ as the chord tone, however, also allows for yet another interpretation that is not contradictory with the one we have just discussed. If you organize the sonority F–B–D♯–G♯ as F–G♯–B–D♯, you can verify that it is actually a type of +6 chord, framed by the +6 interval F–D♯. Although the standard "nationalities" for +6 chords are indeed the most commonly found types, we should not just dismiss the possibility of other intervallic arrangements for the two inner pitches that fill in the +6 framework in an +6 chord. The Tristan chord, from this perspective, is then an +6 chord in Am that resolves, as expected, to V_7, as shown in the alternative interpretation under example 31.2c.[2]

[2] The linear interpretation of the Tristan chord was proposed by Mitchell in the article cited in footnote 1. The interpretation as an F–G♯–B–D♯ +6 chord, on the other hand, is proposed by Daniel Harrison in his article "Supplement to the Theory of Augmented-Sixth Chords," cited in chapter 27. Harrison calls this type of +6 chord the "dual German-sixth chord."

The double-tonic complex. In mm. 5–7 a second statement of the initial idea leads to a Mm_7 chord on G, V_7 of CM. And yet a third statement leads to V_7 of EM (or V_7/V in Am). Within the first twelve measures of the piece, Wagner has already established the tonal conflict that will prevail for the rest of the prelude. The music fluctuates between Am and CM (along with some other key areas), and EM is stressed throughout, both as a chord and as a key area, as the dominant of A. The prelude concludes on a dominant of C, leading to the beginning of act I in Cm. Moreover, modal definition is far from clear in *Tristan*, and thus both Am/AM and CM/Cm are present in the music. This fluctuating aspect of the prelude's tonal center (between Am/M and CM/m) is well expressed by the term **double-tonic complex.**

The opening unit concludes with a deceptive resolution of V_7 in Am (to the F chord in m. 17). Notice that this resolution completes the full-octave chromatic ascent that started in m. 2 in the top voice (from G♯ to the G♯–A, an octave above it).

The second unit (mm. 18–24). The theme that begins in m. 17, beat 2, is known as the "glance" motive. The FM chord in m. 17, which functioned as a deceptive resolution of V_7 in Am, is immediately reinterpreted as IV in CM, and in mm. 18–20 we are back in the CM key area. Not for long, though: In mm. 21–22 Dm is implied (What is the chord in m. 21, beat 2, in Dm?), and in m. 24 we hear again V of EM (that is, V/V in Am). If we think of this section in Am throughout, the key areas are then III–iv–V (or CM–Dm–EM), all in fast succession. In m. 24 we reach some kind of a cadence on A (bass E–A), embellished by an appoggiatura chord. Could it be our first arrival on A as a tonic? As a matter of fact, it is the clearest arrival on A in the whole prelude, only it is AM, not Am; and as the music continues into mm. 25–26, clearly in EM, we hear the AM chord, retrospectively, as IV in E!

The third unit (mm. 25–36). In mm. 25–29 we hear the "love potion" motive, in a sequential passage in which EM is again implied. The bass motive in mm. 28–29 is known as the "death" motive (B–C–D♯). In the measures that follow, several key areas are implied in fast succession: CM in mm. 32–33 (the glance motive again), and then FM and Dm (both briefly tonicized in mm. 35–36).

The fourth unit (mm. 36–44). Notice the harmonization of the theme that begins in m. 36, beat 2 (the "magic casket" motive). We hear the two chords (on D♭ and C) as +6–V_7 in FM, then repeated an octave higher. What comes after is a sequence on this same motive, up by steps: we hear +6–V_7 in GM, and then what would have been another sequence segment in A (mm. 40–41) turns into a return of the glance motive and of the EM key area. You will have observed that in all these "key areas" (F, G, E) we have not encountered a tonic chord. All three have been "established" (or implied) by their respective dominants.

Look at the second chord in m. 42 (F♯ in the bass). It sounds like vii^{o6}_{5} of E, that is, vii^{o6}_{5}/V in A. And the new key signature, three sharps, seems indeed to announce AM. Now listen to m. 43. The first chord is the same sonority we just heard as vii^{o6}_{5}/V in A, now reinterpreted as vii^{o6}_{5} in C♯m! And by the time we get to the AM chord in m. 44, it comes as a deceptive resolution of V_7 in C♯m, that is, as VI in C♯. Or does it? Our excerpt really ends in m. 44, but we have included two more measures to show that actually the music goes on to EM, so we can also hear the AM in m. 44 as IV in EM! In other words, in spite of the "AM" key signature, we hear our AM chord in m. 45 in either C♯m or EM, but certainly not in AM!

So why this long discussion of a fragment from the *Tristan* prelude? Because it illustrates, perhaps better than any other work of the period, a stage in the history of tonality. In this stage, tonal ambiguity and instability become the norm, rather than tonal definition and stability. The music is in a state of constant tonal fluctuation, key areas are implied rather than established, chords often allow for several possible interpretations, and key areas are defined more by dominant than by tonic chords. Formally, the music is highly motivic, and melodic, motivic cells become the essential building blocks.

Tristan und Isolde has often been seen as a turning point in music history. Because of the enormous impact it had on composers, it represents an important step in the process toward the breakup of tonality. Composers who were directly influenced by Wagner's harmonic and melodic idioms in this opera include, among many others, Anton Bruckner, Max Reger, Hugo Wolf, Gustav Mahler, Richard Strauss, and Arnold Schoenberg in Germany and Austria, and César Franck, Gabriel Fauré, and Claude Debussy in France.

EXERCISE

To practice analysis of musical fragments featuring tonal ambiguity, implied tonality, or the double-tonic complex, refer to exercises 1.1 and 1.2 in worksheet 31 at the end of this chapter.

EQUAL DIVISIONS OF THE OCTAVE

The diatonic scale divides the octave unequally into some combination of tones and semitones. Functional harmonic root motions are based on unequal divisions of the octave that result from the diatonic scale, such as major and minor thirds and perfect fifths and fourths. There are, however, five possible divisions of the octave into equal segments. Each of these divisions requires the use of tones foreign to the diatonic scale. These *symmetrical divisions* are as follows:

1. The **chromatic scale** divides the octave into twelve semitones. There is only one chromatic scale.
2. The **whole-tone scale** divides the octave into six whole tones (example 31.3a). There are only two possible whole-tone scales using different pitches.
3. A **cycle of minor thirds** (the fully diminished seventh chord) divides the octave into four minor-third segments (example 31.3b). There are only three possible different °7 chords.
4. A **cycle of major thirds** (the augmented triad) divides the octave into three major-third segments (example 31.3c). There are only four possible different augmented triad chords.
5. The **tritone** divides the octave into two tritone segments (example 31.3d). There are six possible different tritones.

Example 31.3

Because all of these equal divisions of the octave produce nondiatonic pitch relationships, using them as roots on which chords are built or as key areas will produce chromatic, nonfunctional tonal relationships. This feature of equally divided octaves was used by composers in the late-Romantic period (and certainly also in the twentieth century) to expand (or to suspend) functional tonality. The examples we will now study illustrate some of these harmonic relationships.

First, examine example 31.4, which begins in E♭M. The passage moves sequentially up by whole steps: FM is tonicized in m. 151, GM in m. 152, and then AM and

Example 31.4 F. Chopin, Ballade no. 1 in Gm, op. 23, mm. 150–154

BM in m. 153, leading to a $^6_4$ chord on C♯ in m. 154. This progression by whole steps has obviously taken us away from E♭M very quickly! Although the music returns to E♭M shortly after this passage, the whole-tone scale allowed Chopin to create a moment of "tonal parenthesis."

The keys tonicized in the Wagner fragment in example 31.5 also quickly take us away from the initial CM. As the Knights of the Grail assemble for a banquet, this solemn processional music moves through the distant keys of CM, E♭M, G♭M, and AM. Verify each of these keys on the score. How has the octave been divided by these key areas?

The Brahms phrase in example 31.6, on the other hand, takes us through the key areas of Cm, G♯m, Em, back to Cm, and again to G♯m, all in the space of five measures. Identify each of the tonicized chords in these key areas. How are they related intervallically? The chords on the downbeats of mm. 24 and 26 are particularly dissonant against the bass, and obviously do not resolve until beat 2. What kind of chords are they?

The following example by Maurice Ravel will illustrate the close relationship between two of the symmetrical divisions of the octave: the tritone and the whole-tone scale. The roots of the chord pairs in mm. 45–48 of example 31.7 are related by tritone: F–B, E♭–A. Now look at mm. 49–50, where you will see a bass motion in which ascending tritones alternate with descending major 3rds. Put all the pitches of this bass together as a scale, and you will come up with a whole-tone scale. Notice that this scale contains two symmetrical halves of three notes each, and that the two halves are

Example 31.5 R. Wagner, *Parsifal*, act I, scene 2, mm. 30–41

Example 31.5 Continued

Example 31.6 J. Brahms, "Treue Liebe dauert lange," from *Romanzen aus Magelone*, op. 33, mm. 23–27

at the distance of a tritone (F–G–A//B–C♯–D♯). Ravel is here taking advantage not only of the symmetrical division of the octave, but also of the symmetrical division of the whole-tone scale!

EXERCISES

To practice writing progressions using equal divisions of the octave, refer to exercise 2 in worksheet 31 at the end of this chapter.

To practice analysis of musical fragments featuring equal divisions of the octave, refer to exercise 1.3 in worksheet 31 at the end of this chapter.

Example 31.7 Maurice Ravel, Waltz no. 1, from *Valses nobles et sentimentales*, mm. 45–51

PARSIMONIOUS VOICE LEADING: THE PLR MODEL

Although the music of late nineteenth-century composers such as Liszt, Wagner, Franck, Richard Strauss, and others is triadic, we have already seen that their triadic progressions often do not follow the functional model based on the circle of 5ths and on tonic/pre-dominant/dominant relationships. We have already studied several alternative techniques of chordal organization (sequential and nonsequential linear progressions, symmetrical divisions of the octave, etc.). Now we will study another alternative model that accounts for many of the triadic relationships in the music by composers in the Romantic period, and which we will refer to as the **PLR model,** or also as **parsimonious voice leading.**[3]

[3] This section is a pedagogical adaptation of recent work by David Lewin, Brian Hyer, and Richard Cohn. I am especially indebted to the following articles by Cohn: "Maximally-Smooth Cycles, Hexatonic Systems, and the Analysis of Late-Romantic Triadic Progressions," *Music Analysis* 15 (1996): 9–40, and "Neo-Riemannian Operations, Parsimonious Trichords, and Their *Tonnetz* Representations," *Journal of Music Theory* 41 (1997): 1–66.

Example 31.8

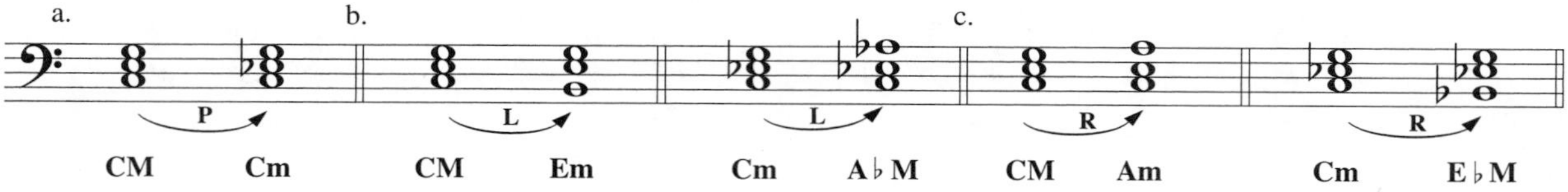

Examine example 31.8. In example 31.8a, the two triads form a parallel major-minor pair, defining a P (parallel) relationship. In example 31.8b, the fifth of one triad is the same pitch as the leading tone for the other triad (for instance, the fifth of the Em triad, B, is the same pitch as the leading tone for the C triad; and the fifth of the Cm triad, G, is the same pitch as the leading tone for the A♭M triad), hence the label L (for "leading-tone exchange"). In example 31.8c, the triads form a relative major-minor pair, and they define the R (relative) relationship. In all three cases, note that:

1. Each of the pairs includes a major and a minor triad. PLR transformations are always between a M and a m triad.
2. In all cases, the voice leading includes two common tones, while a single tone moves by half step (in P and L) or whole step (in R). Hence the term *parsimonious voice leading* (*parsimonious* means "frugal, stingy").
3. In L and R transformations, triad roots are third-related, although root relationships are not the main issue in this type of linear transformation, essentially based on common-tone and stepwise voice leading.
4. It is interesting to note that, although these transformations are usually associated with nonfunctional, highly chromatic music, the only chromatic triadic relationship in example 31.8 results from the P transformation (CM and Cm are chromatically related). You can verify that both L and R transformations, on the other hand, are effected between diatonically related triads. In other words, whereas P involves chromatic voice leading, the voice leading in both L and R simply involves a diatonic step.

The *Tonnetz*

A useful graphic tool to understand these three types of triadic transformations, their interaction, and the type of progressions they can generate, is a two-dimensional matrix of tones, or harmonic network, usually known by the German term ***Tonnetz.*** Although several types of *Tonnetze* can be designed, each showing different tonal relationships, the type which we will introduce here, the *parsimonious Tonnetz,* is best represented

Example 31.9

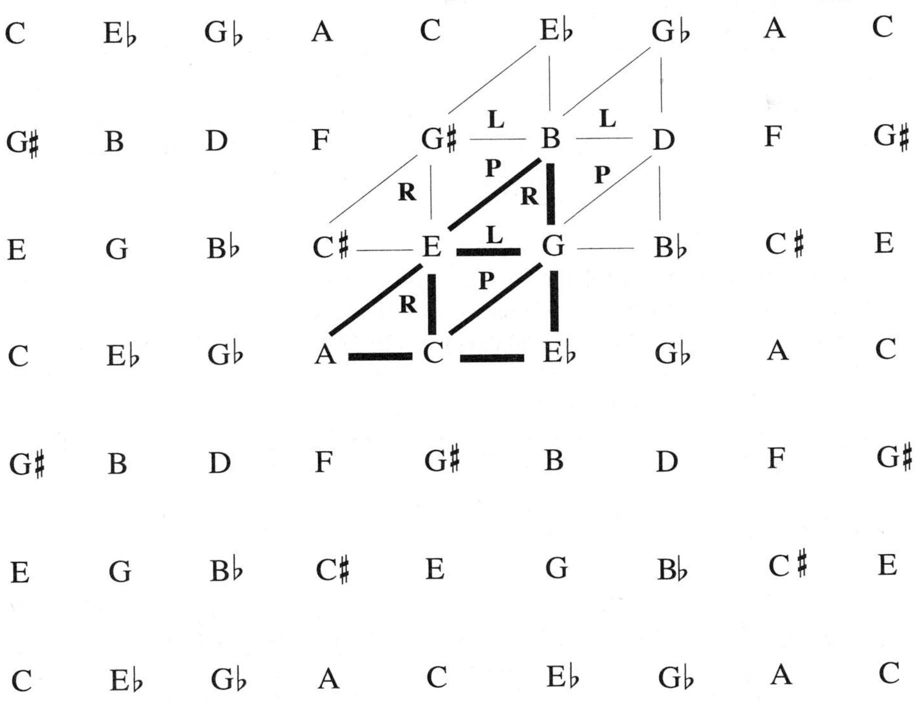

by a matrix in which tones are related by minor thirds in horizontal lines and by major thirds in vertical lines. Examine the *Tonnetz* in example 31.9, and understand how it works. Begin, for instance, from the center pitch, C, and see the intervallic increments of m3 to its right and left, and of M3 above and below. Now let us see how PLR transformations work within this *Tonnetz*.

1. A triad is represented by a triangle of adjacent pitches. Find, for instance, the CM triad, C–E–G.
2. Pairs of triads represented by adjacent triangles are related by PLR operations, and hence feature parsimonious voice leading. The three triads that share an edge with the CM triad, for instance, form the collection of triads related to CM by PLR (these triads are indicated by boldface lines in example 31.9).
3. In all cases, P-related triads share a hypotenuse; L-related triads share a horizontal edge; and R-related triads share a vertical edge. Identify these relationships on the *Tonnetz,* first from the CM triad, then from other triads.

4. As it is obvious from the *Tonnetz,* it is not possible to have two of the same operations in a row (PP, RR, or LL), unless you want to go back to the same triad you started with (as in CM–Cm–CM). Thus, after P you must have L or R; and after L you must have P or R. Before we go on, try to experiment playing several progressions using the *Tonnetz* as a guide (in other words, try "navigating the *Tonnetz*").

You will have found out that because after each move you can go in two possible directions, the number of possible different progressions is quite limitless. Composers, however, have often favored progressions that feature consistent motions within the *Tonnetz*. And this brings us back to the equal divisions of the octave.

Roots by M3: The PL Progression

Study the progression underlying the passage by Brahms in example 31.10. If we think of it in terms of root progression, we come up with the triads A♭M–G♯m–EM–Em–CM–Cm–A♭M–G♯m–EM. Find this progression in the *Tonnetz*. You will observe several things:

1. Roots in the Brahms progression move by major 3rds; hence, they divide the octave symmetrically, and that is why after three pairs of M/m triads, we are back to the original pair.
2. The *binary operation* (a pair of operations) that produces this equal division by M3 is PL (or its retrograde, LP).
3. The PL binary operation is represented in the *Tonnetz* by a vertical line of transformations. Example 31.11a shows a reduction of the Brahms progression, in which the single pitch that moves from one chord to the next is represented with a black notehead. Example 31.11b shows the vertical path for this binary cycle as abstracted from the *Tonnetz*.

Roots by m3: The PR Progression

Refer to anthology, no. 51 (Liszt, *Consolation*, no. 4), mm. 18–26. Play through the passage and identify the key areas that are tonicized. You will see that beginning in m. 18, beat 3, we are in D♭M, followed by D♭m in m. 21, EM and Em in m. 22, Gm in 23, and back in D♭M in m. 26. Find the beginning of this progression, D♭M–D♭m–EM–Em–Gm in the *Tonnetz*. You will see that:

1. Roots in this progression move by minor thirds, producing another equal division of the octave.
2. The *binary operation* that produces this equal division by m3 is PR (or its retrograde, RP).
3. The PR binary operation is represented in the *Tonnetz* by a horizontal line of transformations.
4. Liszt skips one step in the parsimonious progression by moving directly from Em to Gm, instead of Em–GM–Gm. Then he leaps a tritone by going directly from Gm back to D♭M. He nevertheless stays within the same horizontal path of transformations. How many steps in the process does he skip to leap from Gm to D♭M?

Example 31.10 J. Brahms, Concerto for Violin and Cello, I, mm. 270–278

5. Example 31.12a is a chordal reduction of Liszt's progression (where the tonicized key areas are shown as half notes), followed in example 31.12b by a PLR reduction of the complete parsimonious progression on which it is based (with the steps skipped by Liszt indicated in parenthesis). Example 31.12c shows the horizontal path for this binary cycle as abstracted from the *Tonnetz*.

Example 31.11a

Example 31.11b

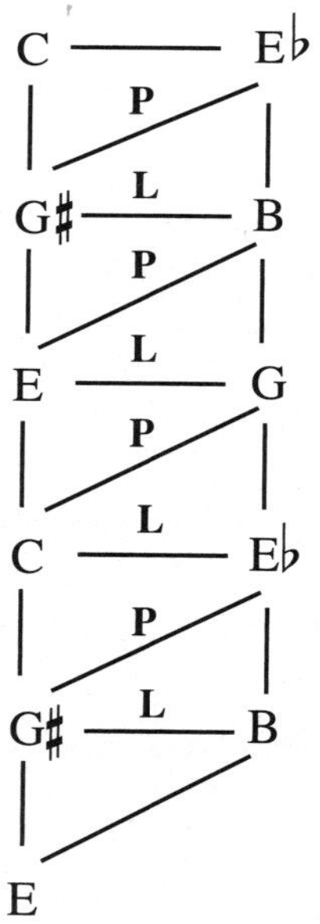

Roots Alternating M3 and m3: The LR Progression

We will now look at what is perhaps one of the most spectacular examples of parsimonious voice leading in the whole music literature: Beethoven's 9th Symphony, II, mm. 143–167, reproduced in piano reduction in example 31.13. Beginning in CM, the passage travels through the following triads: CM–Am–FM–Dm–B♭M–Gm–E♭M–Cm–A♭M–Fm–D♭M–B♭m–G♭M–E♭m–BM–G♯m–EM–C♯m–AM. That is, nineteen different

Example 31.12

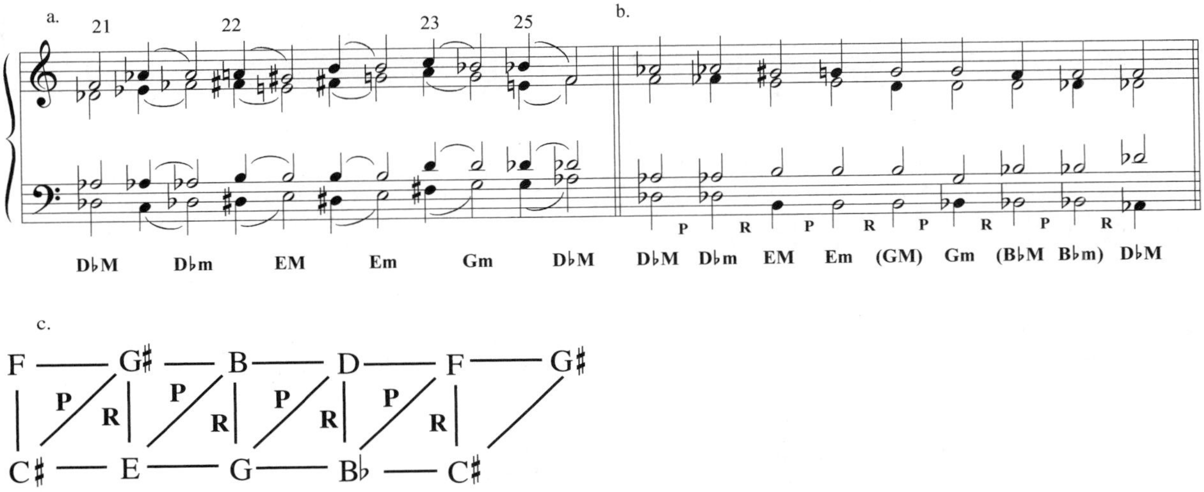

triads in fast succession. Considering that there is a combined total of twenty-four major and minor triads, Beethoven gets close to (but falls short of) going through all of them! Of course, we would need to extend our *Tonnetz* from example 31.9 in order to see it represented in its totality. You can easily find, however, at least fragments of this progression in the *Tonnetz,* and you can verify the following observations:

1. Roots in this progression move by alternating major and minor thirds. This is not, then, a case of equal division of the octave.
2. The *binary operation* that produces the alternating M3s and m3s is LR (or its retrograde, RL).
3. The LR binary operation is represented in the *Tonnetz* by a diagonal line of transformations.
4. Example 31.14a is a reduction of a portion of Beethoven's LR progression, and example 31.14b shows the diagonal path for this binary cycle as abstracted from the *Tonnetz*.

EXERCISES

To practice writing parsimonious progressions, refer to exercises 3 and 4 in worksheet 30 at the end of this chapter.

To practice analysis of PLR progressions, refer to exercise 1.4 in worksheet 31 at the end of this chapter.

Example 31.13 L. v. Beethoven, Symphony no. 9 in Dm, op. 125, II, mm. 142–175

Example 31.14a

Example 31.14b

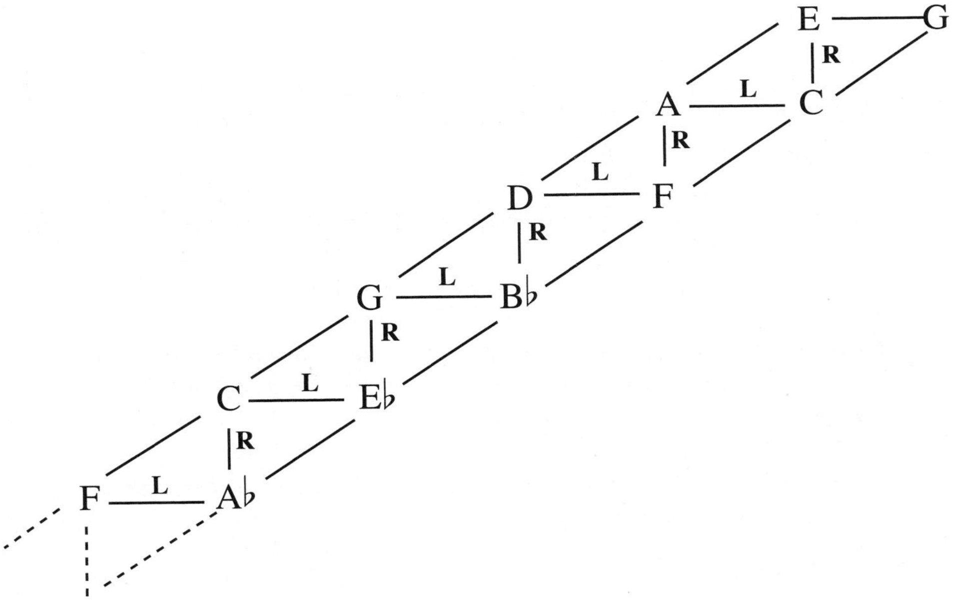

BEYOND THE CONFINES OF FUNCTIONAL TONALITY

The types of harmonic processes we studied previously (implied tonality, double-tonic complex, equal division of the octave, parsimonious voice leading, etc.) obviously resulted in a weakening of functional tonality. In some cases, however, similar processes lead not only to the weakening of tonality but, beyond that, to passages or pieces in which tonality is altogether absent. This is illustrated by the Franz Liszt example we will now examine.

An Example by Franz Liszt

The opening section of Liszt's *Faust* Symphony (example 31.15) is an excellent illustration of avoidance of tonal definition through the use of augmented triads and of long-range equal division of the octave. Some of the salient aspects of pitch organization in this passage can be outlined as follows:[4]

1. The lack of tonal definition becomes clear at the very outset of the movement. After the initial fortissimo A♭, mm. 1–2 feature a series of four arpeggiated augmented triads with roots descending by half steps, which not only do not create any sense of functional tonality, but moreover introduce the twelve pitches of the chromatic scale within two measures. The thematic material for the rest of the passage is also based to a great extent on augmented triads. Notice the descending scalar passage in mm. 9–10, based on two overlapping augmented triads (the two descending triads D♭–A–F and C–A♭–E).
2. Looking at the long-range design for this passage, we see that the bass in mm. 1–2 unfolds a chromatic scale from A♭ to E, and that E is again reached in m. 11 after the descending scalar passage in mm. 9–10. After the fermata, the initial thematic material is repeated beginning on E, now unfolding a chromatic motion from E to C. C is also the high point we reach in m. 15, and an octave lower in m. 17. The descending scalar passage in mm. 20–21 now leads to A♭, providing a sense of circularity to the complete section (which, of course, also started on an A♭).
3. In summary, we notice that no particular key is defined or established throughout this opening section. The pitches that stand out as points of formal articulation are A♭–E–C–A♭. Here again, the long-range design of the passage outlines an augmented triad, which divides the tonal space into equal segments.
4. Moreover, these same pitches constitute the main tonalities for the complete composition. The first movement is in Cm (with an important section in EM). The second movement is in A♭M, with a final passage that oscillates between A♭ and E. The third and final movement oscillates between the tonal centers C and E, and includes a final section that begins in A♭M and ends in CM. The equal division of the octave is here applied to the tonal design of a complete symphony.
5. We should remember that this opening is a musical evocation of the opening of Goethe's *Faust*, a monologue in which Faust expresses his disenchantment with life, philosophy, and religion, his desire to extend the limits of his knowledge, and his willingness to turn to magic to attain his goals. Liszt uses the augmented triad in a nontonal context, both as a chord and as a long-range framework, for his musical depiction of Faust's psychology and state of mind. Because of its ambiguous character and tonal implications, the augmented triad was indeed used in association with magic and mystery by composers before and after Liszt.

---

[4] An analysis of this passage, on which the present discussion is based, can be found in R. Larry Todd, "Franz Liszt, Carl Friedrich Weitzmann, and the Augmented Triad," in *The Second Practice of Nineteenth-Century Tonality,* ed. by William Kinderman and Harald Krebs (Lincoln: University of Nebraska Press, 1996), pp. 153–77.

Example 31.15 F. Liszt, *Faust* Symphony, I, mm. 1–22

PRACTICAL AND CLASS DISCUSSION

In this chapter we have studied various harmonic techniques that contribute to the weakening of functional tonality. In some cases, functional tonality disappears altogether. How is tonal and harmonic coherence achieved in this type of composition in which functional relationships are missing? From our discussions, you will have noticed that linear relationships and stepwise voice leading are frequent elements of coherence in this type of nonfunctional harmonic language. Another possible factor of coherence is the symmetrical division of the octave into equal segments.

Discuss how melody and harmony are intertwined in the *Tristan* prelude. What has priority in Wagner's example, melody or harmony? The sense of forward motion (quite overwhelming!) in Wagner is created by numerous elements that constantly pile up tension. What are these elements? Although the music moves by itself, performances of the prelude vary enormously. Whereas some of them stress and play up the tension, others fall short of communicating and expressing the emotional and dramatic conflicts this music contains. If you were a conductor, how would you try to convey the dramatic power of this music? What elements would you use to your advantage to keep the music alive and moving forward? Would our above discussion of the piece help you in any way for this purpose?

PITCH PATTERNS

Sing the pitch patterns in example 31.16, which feature equal divisions of the octave.

Example 31.16

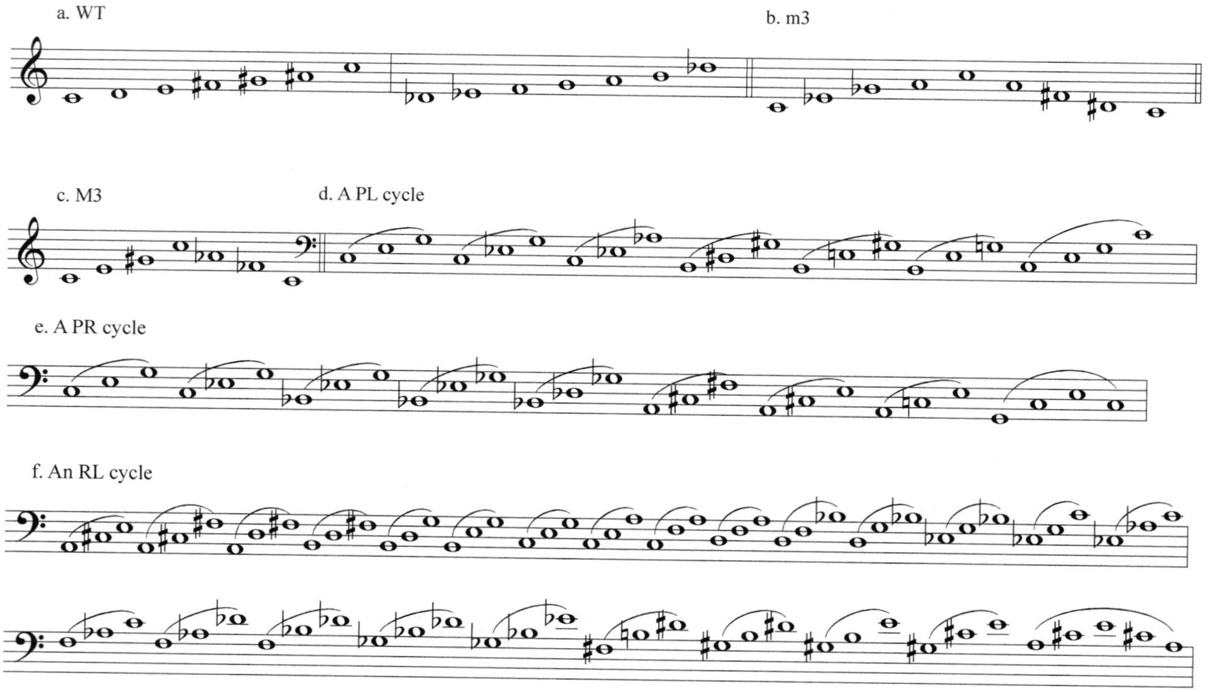

FOR FURTHER STUDY

For additional chapter 31 materials, refer to the *Harmony in Context* Web page at www.mhhe.com/roigfrancoli2e.

ASSIGNMENT AND KEYBOARD EXERCISES

For analytical and written assignments and keyboard exercises based on the materials learned in this chapter, refer to chapter 31 in the workbook.

Terms for Review

Tristan prelude
Leitmotif
Tonal ambiguity
Implied tonality
Tonal fluctuation
"Tristan chord"
Double-tonic complex
Equal divisions of the octave: chromatic scale, whole-tone scale, cycle of minor thirds, cycle of major thirds, tritone
PLR model
Parsimonious voice leading
Tonnetz
PLR binary operations: PL, PR, and LR

Worksheet 31

EXERCISE 1 Analysis.

1. Example 31.17. On a separate sheet, write a brief essay explaining the tonal ambiguity of this passage (which reflects the tonal ambiguity of the complete song). Does the term *double tonic complex* apply to this phrase? A translation of Goethe's poem on which the song is based is provided. How do the tonal characteristics of this phrase (and of the song) reflect the meaning of the poem?

Example 31.17 F. Schubert, "Erster Verlust," mm. 17–22

First Loss

Oh, who will bring back the fair days,
Those days of first love,
Oh, who will bring back but one hour
Of that sweet time!

Lonely I feed my wound,
And with ever-renewed lament
I mourn the lost happiness.

Oh, who will bring back the fair days,
That sweet time!

2. Example 31.18. On a separate sheet, write a brief essay on this example, discussing the following:
   a) Explain the tonality of this excerpt. What are the keys? How are they established? What are the elements of tonal ambiguity?
   b) How does melody obscure harmony in this example?
   c) Explain the following specific passages from a harmonic point of view: mm. 1–4, 5–8, 10–12 (What key is implied in these measures?), and 13–15.
   d) This collection of songs dates from 1901–1904. What specific influences from Wagner and *Tristan* can you identify in this fragment?

Example 31.18 Gustav Mahler, "Nun seh' ich wohl, warum so dunkle Flammen," from *Kindertotenlieder*, mm. 1–15

3. Comment on root and triad relationships in the following examples.
   a) Example 31.19.

Example 31.19 C. Franck, "Choral no. 1 Pour Grand Orgue," mm. 19–23

   b) Example 31.20. In this example, focus on the relationship among tonicized triads.

Example 31.20 F. Chopin, Nocturne in GM, op. 37, no. 2, mm. 129–132

4. Refer to anthology, no. 51, Liszt, *Consolation*, no. 4. Determine the key areas in mm. 6–9 and 10–17. Explain exactly how these keys are related by PLR transformations. For this purpose, it will be useful to consider the modulation in m. 14 as passing through AM before moving on to F♯m.

EXERCISE 2 On your own music paper, write four different progressions using equal divisions of the octave, in the following keys, respectively: EM, D♭M, Am, and Fm.

EXERCISE 3 Write the following parsimonious progressions in four voices: (1) a PL progression, (2) a PR progression, and (3) an LR progression. Begin each of the progressions on a B♭m triad. (Use your own music paper for this and the following exercise.)

EXERCISE 4 Write a phrase for piano (melody and accompaniment) based on a PR parsimonious progression, beginning on an Fm triad.

Appendix

Transposing Instruments

If you play a scale notated as CM on a flute, an oboe, a bassoon, a trombone, a violin, or a variety of other instruments, what you will hear will actually be a CM scale. This statement would be trivially obvious if it were not that you do *not* hear a CM scale in many other instruments when you play what is notated like one. A scale notated as CM will sound a M2 lower (sounding like a B♭M scale) when played on a clarinet in B♭. Or it will sound a P5 lower (sounding like an FM scale) when played on a horn in F. These are what we call **transposing instruments.** In all these instruments, the actual sounding pitches are not the same as those notated. Example 1 shows how some common transposing instruments would sound if they all read the same opening of our familiar "The First Noël" notated in CM. As you will see, if they all played together from the same score in C, the resulting sound would be quite interesting indeed! The following comments refer to this example:

1. When we say that an instrument is "in B♭" we mean that if that instrument plays a notated C the actual sound (or "concert pitch") will be B♭. A clarinet in B♭ sounds a M2 lower than notated. We hear both the pitches and, therefore, the key, transposed down a M2.
2. When we say that an instrument is "in F" we mean that if that instrument plays a notated C the actual sound will be F. A horn in F sounds a P5 lower than notated. We hear both the pitches and, therefore, the key, transposed down a P5.
3. Based on these two examples, explain what we mean when we say that an instrument is in E♭ or in A, and what we hear exactly when an alto saxophone (in E♭) or a clarinet in A plays our tune notated in CM.

Example 1 shows how you should read transposing instruments when you find them notated on a score. Writing for these instruments, however, presents the opposite problem. Example 2 shows how we should notate a melodic fragment from

Example 1

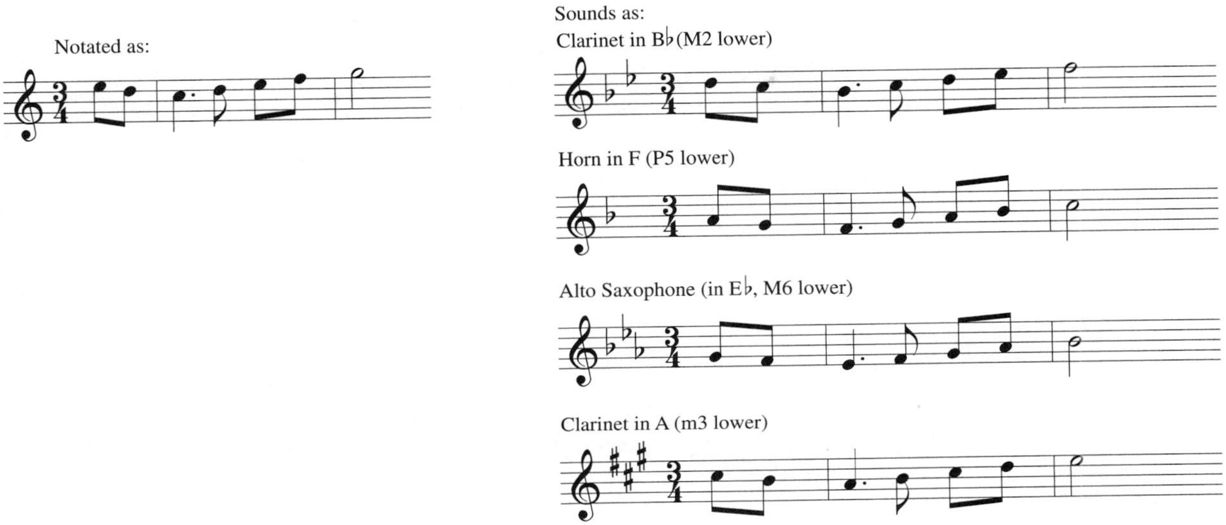

Maurice Ravel's *Bolero* if we want it to sound "in C" on the same transposing instruments we discussed previously. If these instruments now played this fragment as notated for each of them, the resulting sound would be a unison line in CM. The following comments refer to this example 1:

1. If you want a clarinet in B♭ to sound a B♭, you need to write a C. To notate a line for clarinet in B♭, you should then transpose it a M2 higher. The same applies to the key signature: if the resulting key is CM, you should notate the clarinet's key signature transposed a M2 higher, in DM.
2. If you want a horn in F to sound an F, you need to write a C. To notate a line for horn in F, you should then transpose it a P5 higher. Of course, the key will also be transposed a P5 higher, but, by an old notational convention, we do not write a key signature in French horn parts. Instead we write the accidentals before each note. In example 2, you will see that the horn has been indeed transposed to GM, but we write the necessary sharp signs before each F, rather than in the key signature. This convention applies only to the French horn and does not affect any other transposing instrument.

Example 2

Concert pitch (flute)

Clarinet in B♭: notated a M2 higher

Horn in F: notated a P5 higher

Alto Saxophone (in E♭): notated a M6 higher

Clarinet in A: notated a m3 higher

3. Now comment on how (and why) we should notate the same line for an alto saxophone in E♭ and a clarinet in A, based on example 2.

The following table provides a summary of transpositions in the transposing instruments most commonly found in orchestras and bands (other transpositions are possible for instruments such as the horn and the trumpet). The following instruments are in C, and hence are written in concert pitch: flute and piccolo (notated an octave lower than it sounds), oboe, bassoon, contrabassoon (notated an octave higher than it sounds), trumpet in C, trombone, tuba, and all string instruments (the double bass is notated an octave higher than it sounds).

Transposing Instruments

Instrument	Sound with Respect to Notation	Transposition Needed to Notate
English horn (in F)	P5 lower	P5 up
Clarinet in B♭	M2 lower	M2 up
in A	m3 lower	m3 up
in E♭	m3 higher	m3 down
Bass clarinet in B♭	M9 lower (M2 + 8ve)	M2 + 8ve up
Soprano saxophone in B♭	M2 lower	M2 up
Alto saxophone in E♭	M6 lower	M6 up
Tenor saxophone in B♭	M9 lower (M2 + 8ve)	M2 + 8ve up
Baritone saxophone in E♭	M13 lower (M6 + 8ve)	M6 + 8ve up
Horn in F	P5 lower	P5 up
in E♭	M6 lower	M6 up
in E	m6 lower	m6 up
in D	m7 lower	m7 up
Trumpet in B♭	M2 lower	M2 up
in D	M2 higher	M2 down

EXERCISE 1

1. Suppose that the melody in exercise 1a, from Felix Mendelssohn's Violin Concerto, II, is to be performed as notated by a clarinet in B♭, an English horn, and an alto saxophone. Write, in the spaces provided, what the melody would sound like as played by each of these instruments.
2. Suppose that you need to write the Polish folk tune in exercise 1b to be performed in unison by a soprano saxophone, a horn in F, and a clarinet in A. In the spaces provided, write the correct part for each of these instruments as they would have to perform it in order for the melody to sound in FM as notated in the given version. Notice the accidentals in this melody, and make sure you transpose them correctly.

a.
Andante
5
Clarinet in B♭
English Horn
Alto Saxophone

b.
Allegro
Poland
Soprano Saxophone
Horn in F
Clarinet in A

Musical Example Index

A

Abbey Road (Harrison), "Something," 548
"Abschied" (Zelter), 462
"Ach Gott, wie manches Herzeleid" (Chorale 217) (Bach, J. S.), 80
"Ach Gott und Herr," (Chorale 40) (Bach, J. S.), 402
"Ach Gott vom Himmel, sieh darein" (Chorale 3) (Bach, J. S.), 249
Adagio in Fm, for Piano (Saint-Georges), 256
Aida (Verdi)
  "Celeste Aida," 629
  "Ritorna vincitor," 587
Album for the Young, op. 68 (Schumann)
  "Armes Waisenkind," 351
  "Ein Choral," 229
  "War Song," 147
"Alle Menschen müssen sterben" (Chorale 153) (Bach, J. S.), 326
"All My Loving," from *With the Beatles* (Lennon-McCartney), 109
"Alma del core" from *La costanza in amor vince l'inganno* (Caldara), 257
"Almost Like Being in Love" from *Brigadoon* (Lerner-Loewe), 369
"Als der gütige Gott" (Chorale 159) (Bach, J. S.), 324
"Am Feierabend" from *Die schöne Müllerin,* no. 5 (Schubert), 346, 476, 551
"Am leuchtenden Sommermorgen," from *Dichterliebe,* op. 48 (Schumann)
"An Mignon," op. 19, no. 2 (Schubert), 566
Années de Pèlerinage (Liszt), "Il pensieroso," 628
"An Wasserflüssen Babylon," (Chorale 5) (Bach, J. S.), 367
"Après un rêve" (Fauré), 688
"Aria di Govannini" from the *Notebook for Anna Magdalena Bach,* 186
Arlen, Harold: "If I Only Had a Brain," from *The Wizard of Oz,* 391
"Armes Waisenkind," *Album for the Young,* op. 68 (Schumann), 351
The Art of Fugue (Bach, J. S.), 304
"Aufenthalt," from *Schwanengesang,* no. 5 (Schubert), 345
"Aus meines Herzens Grunde," (Chorale 1) (Bach, J. S.), 327

B

Bach, Carl Philipp Emanuel: Piano Sonata no. 4, from *Sonaten für Kenner und Liebhaber,* 387
Bach, Johann Sebastian
  The Art of Fugue, 304, 529
  Brandenburg Concerto no. 2, 291
  Brandenburg Concerto no. 3, 275
  "Chaconne" from Partita no. 2 in Dm for Violin Solo, 317
  Chorale 1, "Aus meines Herzens Grunde," 327
  Chorale 3, "Ach Gott vom Himmel, sieh darein," 249
  Chorale 5, "An Wasserflüssen Babylon," 367
  Chorale 6, "Christus, der ist mein Leben," 544
  Chorale 8, "Freuet euch, ihrChristen," 416
  Chorale 14, "O Herre Gott, dein göttlich Wort," 138, 335
  Chorale 19, "Ich hab' mein' Sach' Gott heimgestellt," 445
  Chorale 20, "Ein feste Burg is unser Gott," 364
  Chorale 21, "Herzlich thut mich verlangen," 56, 456
  Chorale 25, "Wo soll ich fliehen hin," 364
  Chorale 29, "Freu' dich sehr, o meine Seele," 206
  Chorale 32, "Nun danket alle Gott," 200
  Chorale 34, "Erbarm dich mein, O Herre Gott," 202
  Chorale 40, "Ach Gott und Herr," 402
  Chorale 42, "Du Friede fürst, Herr Jesu Christ," 251–252
  Chorale 45, "Kommt her zu mir," 325
  Chorale 54, "Lobt Gott, ihr Christen allzugleich," 171
  Chorale 67, "Freu'dich sehr, o meine Seele," 139
  Chorale 69, "Komm, Heilliger Geist, Herre Gott," 351
  Chorale 76, "Freu' dich sehr, o meine Seele," 206
  Chorale 80, "O Haupt voll Blut and Wunden," 122, 401
  Chorale 94, "Warum betrübst du dich, mein Herz," 448
  Chorale 96, "Jesu, meine Freude," 549, 556
  Chorale 111, "Herzliebster Jesu, was hast du verbrochen," 161
  Chorale 117, "O Welt, ich muss dich lassen," 367
  Chorale 135, "Gott der Vater, wohn uns bei," 334
  Chorale 138, "Jesu, meine Freude," 331
  Chorale 143, "In dulci jubilo," 270, 350
  Chorale 153, "Alle Menschen müssen sterben," 326
  Chorale 159, "Als der gütige Gott," 324
  Chorale 160, "Gelobet seist du," 122
  Chorale 167, "Du grosser Schmerzensmann," 401, 481
  Chorale 181, "Gott hat das Evangelium," 122
  Chorale 193, "Was bist du doch, O Seele, so betrübet," 325
  Chorale 196, "Da der Herr Christ zu Tische sass," 163
  Chorale 197, "Christ ist erstanden," 271

Bach, Johann Sebastian (*Cont.*)
Chorale 217, "Ach Gott, wie manches Herzeleid," 80
Chorale 298, "Weg, mein Herz, mit den Gedanken," 67
Concerto for Two Violins, BWV 1043, 384
"Crucifixus," from Mass in Bm, 516
English Suite no. 3 in Gm, Gavotte I, 485
French Suite no. 3, "Minuet," 482
French Suite no. 5 in GM, "Gavotte," 316
Invention no. 1 in CM, 291
Invention no. 3 in DM, 298, 385
Invention no. 4 in DM, 396
Mass in Bm, "Kyrie," 18
A Musical Offering (Retrograde canon), 296–297
Partita no. 1 in B♭M, for Harpsichord, Menuet I, 278
Partita no. 2 in Cm, for Harpsichord, 74
Partita no. 2 in Dm for Violin Solo ("Chaconne"), 30, 31
Sonata no. 1 for Flute and Keyboard, BWV 1030, IV, 373
The Well-Tempered Clavier
Fugue no. 21 in B♭M, 478
Fugue no. 24 in Bm, 18
Fugue no. 2 in Cm, 204, 303, 381
Fugue no. 3 in C♯M, 303, 319
Fugue no. 8 in D♯m, 295, 296
Fugue no. 16 in Gm, 397
Prelude 22 in B♭m, 454
Prelude no. 6 in Dm, 9
Ballade in BM, op. 10, no. 4 (Brahms), 358
Ballade no. 1 in Gm, op. 23 (Chopin), 726
Il barbiere di Siviglia, act V, no. 3 (Rossini), 224
"Barcarolle," from *Three Pieces,* op. 28, no. 1 (Beach), 355
Bartók, Béla, *Music for String Instruments, Percussion, and Celesta,* I, 18
Beach, Amy
"Barcarolle," from *Three Pieces,* op. 28, no. 1, 355
Sous les étoiles, op. 65, no. 4, 695
The Beach Boys: "The Warmth of the Sun," 603
The Beatles (White Album) (The Beatles): "I Will" (Lennon-McCartney), 299
Beethoven, Ludwig van
Four Ariettas and a Duet, "Hoffnung," 632
Für Elise, 142
Piano Concerto no. 4, op. 58, 440
Piano Sonata in Cm, op. 10, no. 1, 361–362
Piano Sonata in C♯m, op. 27, no. 2, *Moonlight,* 563
Piano Sonata in EM, op. 14, no. 1, 343, 547
Piano Sonata in EM, op. 90, I, 691
Piano Sonata in E♭M, op. 81a, I, 545, 613
Piano Sonata in GM, op. 31, no. 1, 579
Piano Sonata in GM, op. 49, no. 2, 194
Piano Sonata op. 7 in E♭M, II, 602, 634
Rondo op. 51, no. 1, 344
Seven Peasant Dances, WoO 168, no. 4, 130
Seven Variations on "God Save the King," 332
Sonatina in GM, 416
String Quartet op. 18, no. 5, Trio, 505–506
Symphony no. 3 in E♭M, op. 55 *(Eroica),* 211, 585
Symphony no. 5 in Cm, 300, 301, 607
Symphony no. 7, 294
Symphony no. 9 in DM, 736–737
Trio op. 1, no. 1, 408
"Begin the Beguine" from *Jubilee* (Porter), 442
"Benedictus" from *Missa pro defunctis* (Lassus), 74–75
"Die Beschwörung" (Viardot-García), 211
"Bewitched" from *Pal Joey* (Rodgers-Hart), 673
Blitzstein, Marc: *The Threepenny Opera,* "Mack the Knife," 674
Brahms, Johannes
Ballade in BM, op. 10, no. 4, 358, 359
Concerto for Violin and Cello, 733
Im Herbst, 621
Intermezzo in CM, op. 119, no. 3, 31
Piano Concerto no. 2, op. 83, 647
Romance, op. 118, no. 5, 264
Romanzen aus Magelone, "Treue Liebe dauert lange," 728
Sonata in Fm for Clarinet and Piano, op. 120, no. 1, 601
Symphony no. 3, 548
Symphony no. 4, 484
Symphony no. 4, op. 98, 331
Symphony no. 1 in Cm, 593
Brandenburg Concerto no. 2 (Bach, J. S.), 291
Brandenburg Concerto no. 3 (Bach, J. S.), 275
Brecht, Bertolt: *The Threepenny Opera,* "Mack the Knife," 674
Brigadoon (Lerner-Loewe), "Almost Like Being in Love," 369

C

Caldara, Antonio: "Alma del core" from *La costanza in amor vince l'inganno,* 257
"Candle in the Wind" from *Live in Australia* (John), 212–213
"Can't Buy Me Love," from *A Hard Day's Night* (Lennon-McCartney), 369
Cantional (Schein), "Wirf Christenleut," 339
Caprice op. 1, no. 14 for Solo Violin (Paganini), 575
"Celeste Aida," from *Aida* (Verdi), 629
"Chaconne" from Partita no. 2 in Dm for Violin Solo (Bach, J. S.), 317
"Chaconne," from *Trois Leçons* (Handel), 202
Chaconne in GM (Handel), 515
Chopin, Frédéric
Ballade no. 1 in Gm, op. 23, 726
Étude in A♭M, from *Trois Nouvelles Études,* 647

Étude in CM, op. 10, no. 7, 10
Étude in E♭m, op. 10, no. 6, 304
Mazurka in Am, op. 7, no. 2, 192
Mazurka in A♭M, op. 59, no. 2, 680
Mazurka in Am, op. posth. 67, no. 4, 291, 648
Mazurka in B♭M, op. 7, no. 1, 148
Mazurka in GM, op. 67, no. 1, 556
Mazurka in Gm, op. posth. 67, no. 2, 427
Nocturne in GM, op. 37, no. 2, 744
Prelude in Cm, op. 28, no. 20, 571
Prelude in Em, op. 28, no. 4, 594, 685
Waltz in Am, op. 34, no. 2, 570
Chorales by J. S. Bach
Chorale 1, "Aus meines Herzens Grunde," 327
Chorale 3, "Ach Gott vom Himmel, sieh darein," 249
Chorale 5, "An Wasserflüssen Babylon," 367
Chorale 6, "Christus, der ist mein Leben," 544
Chorale 8, "Freuet euch, ihr Christen," 416
Chorale 14, "O Herre Gott, dein göttlich Wort," 138
Chorale 19, "Ich hab' mein' Sach' Gott heimgestellt," 445
Chorale 20, "Ein feste Burg is unserGott," 364
Chorale 21, "Herzlich thut mich verlangen," 56
Chorale 25, "Wo soll ich fliehen hin," 364
Chorale 32, "Nun danket alle Gott," 200
Chorale 34, "Erbarm dich mein, O Herre Gott," 202
Chorale 40, "Ach Gott und Herr," 402
Chorale 42, "Du Friede fürst, Herr Jesu Christ," 251–252
Chorale 45, "Kommt her zu mir," 325
Chorale 54, "Lobt Gott, ihr Christen allzugleich," 171
Chorale 67, "Freu'dich sehr, o meine Seele," 139
Chorale 69, "Komm, Heilliger Geist, Herre Gott," 351
Chorale 80, "O Haupt voll Blut and Wunden," 122
Chorale 94, "Warum betrübst du dich, mein Herz," 448
Chorale 96, "Jesu, meine Freude," 549, 556
Chorale 111, "Herzliebster Jesu, was hast du verbrochen," 161
Chorale 117, "O Welt, ich muss dich lassen," 367
Chorale 135, "Gott der Vater, wohn uns bei," 334
Chorale 138, "Jesu, meine Freude," 331
Chorale 143, "In dulci jubilo," 270
Chorale 153, "Alle Menschen müssen sterben," 326
Chorale 159, "Als der gütige Gott," 324
Chorale 160, "Gelobet seist du," 122
Chorale 167, "Du grosser Schmerzensmann," 401
Chorale 181, "Gott hat das Evangelium," 122
Chorale 193, "Was bist du doch, O Seele, so betrübet," 325
Chorale 196, "Da der Herr Christ zu Tische sass," 163
Chorale 197, "Christ ist erstanden," 271
Chorale 217, "Ach Gott, wie manches Herzeleid," 80
Chorale 298, "Weg, mein Herz, mit den Gedanken," 67
"Choral no. 1 Pour Grand Orgue" (Franck), 744
"Christ ist erstanden" (Chorale 197) (Bach, J. S.), 271
Christmas Oratorio, no. 8 (Saint-Saëns), 335
"Christus, der ist mein Leben" (Chorale) (Bach, J. S.), 544
Concerto for Two Violins, BWV 1043 (Bach, J. S.), 384
Concerto for Violin, op. 64 (Mendelssohn), 363
Concerto for Violin and Cello (Brahms), 733
Concerto in E♭M for Horn and Orchestra, K. 447 (Mozart), 233
Corelli, Archangelo: Sonata *La Follia,* op. 5, no. 12, 515
"Crucifixus," from Mass in Bm (Bach, J. S.), 516

D

"Da der Herr Christ zu Tische sass" (Chorale 196) (Bach, J. S.), 163
"The Death of Åse" from *Peer Gynt* (Grieg), 483
"Der Doppelgänger," from *Schwanengesang* (Schubert), 638
Dett, Nathaniel
from *In the Bottoms,* 676
Enchantment, "Song of the Shrine," 648
Don Giovanni (Mozart)
Finale, 578, 582
Overture, 568, 581
Donizetti, Gaetano
Don Pasquale
act II, scene IV, 218
act III, "Introductory Chorus," 148, 149
act III, no. 9, 643
Lucia di Lammermoor
act I, no. 3, "Regnava nel silenzio," 217
act III, "Tu che a Dio spiegasti l'ali," 215–216
"Don't Cry for Me Argentina" from *Evita* (Rice-Webber), 406
"Du bist die Ruh," *Six Songs,* op. 7, no. 4 (Hensel), 544
"Du Friede fürst, Herr Jesu Christ" (Chorale 42) (Bach, J. S.), 251–252
"Du grosser Schmerzensmann" (Chorale 167) (Bach, J. S.), 401
Dvorák, Antonín: Slavonic Dance in Gm, op. 46, no. 8, 550

E

Ecossaise D. 158 (Schubert), 147, 158
"Ein Choral," *Album for the Young,* op. 68 (Schumann), 229

"Ekstase," from *Five Songs,* no. 2 (Mahler), 635
Ellington, Duke
"I Let a Song Go Out of My Heart," 543
"Satin Doll," 567
Enchantment (Dett), "Song of the Shrine," 648
English Suite no. 3 in Gm, Gavotte I (Bach, J. S.), 485
Die Entführung aus dem Serail, act III, no. 18 (Mozart), 598
"Erbarm dich mein, O Herre Gott" (Chorale 34) (Bach, J. S.), 202
Ernestine (Saint-Georges) "O Clemangis, lis dans mon âme," 618
"Erster Verlust" (Schubert), 742
Étude in A♭M, from *Trois Nouvelles Études* (Chopin), 647
Étude in CM, op. 10, no. 7 (Chopin), 10
Étude in E♭m, op. 10, no. 6 (Chopin), 304
Étude-Mazurka, "La Favorite" (Sloman), 423
"Everybody's Talkin'" (Neil), 136, 137
Evita (Rice-Webber), "Don't Cry for Me Argentina," 406

F

Falla, Manuel de: *The Three-Cornered Hat*, "The Neighbor's Dance," 287
Fantasia in Cm, K. 475 (Mozart), 265, 564, 633
Fantasie Negre (Price), 223
Farrenc, Louise: Trio in Em, op. 45, I, 609, 631
Fauré, Gabriel
"Après un rêve," 688
"Les Roses d'Ispahan," op. 39, no. 4, 646, 671
Faust Symphony (Liszt), 738–739
Feldes, Don: "Hotel California," 681
"Ein feste Burg is unser Gott" (Chorale 20) (Bach, J. S.), 364
Five Songs (Mahler, A.)
"Ekstase," 635
"In meines Vaters Garten," 672
"Fly Me to the Moon (In Other Words)" (Howard), 385
Foster, Stephen
"Gentle Annie," 279
"Jeanie with the Light Brown Hair," 283
"Oh! Susanna," 27
Four Ariettas and a Duet, op. 82, no. 1 (Beethoven), "Hoffnung" 632
The Four Seasons (Vivaldi)
"Spring," 106
"Winter," 107
Franck, César
"Choral no. 1 Pour Grand Orgue," 744
Sonata for Violin and Piano, 640, 669
French Suite no. 3, "Minuet" (Bach, J. S.), 482
French Suite no. 5 in GM, "Gavotte" (Bach, J. S.), 316
"Freu' dich sehr, o meine Seele" (Bach, J. S.)
Chorale 29, 206
Chorale 76, 206
"Freuet euch, ihr Christen," (Chorale 8) (Bach, J. S.), 416
Frey, Glenn: "Hotel California," 681
From Ariel's Revelation (Reichardt) "Frühlingsblumen," 276, 277, 375
"Frülingstraum," from *Winterreise* (Schubert), 641
Fugue no. 2 in Cm, from *The Well-Tempered Clavier* (Bach, J. S.), 204, 303, 381
Fugue no. 3 in C♯M from *The Well-Tempered Clavier* (Bach, J. S.), 303, 319
Fugue no. 8 in D♯m, from *The Well-Tempered Clavier* (Bach, J. S.), 295, 296
Fugue no. 16 in Gm, from *The Well-Tempered Clavier* (Bach, J. S.), 397
Fugue no. 24 in Bm, from *The Well-Tempered Clavier* (Bach), 18
Für Elise (Beethoven), 142

G

"Gefror'ne Thränen" from *Winterreise,* no. 3 (Schubert), 611, 622
"Gelobet seist du" (Chorale 160) (Bach, J. S.), 122
"Gentle Annie" (Foster), 279
Gershwin, Ira and George: "Someone to Watch Over Me," from *Oh Kay!,* 292, 293
"Gloria" from *Messa di Gloria* (Puccini), 441
Gloria (Vivaldi) "Laudamus Te," 433
"God Save the King," Seven Variations on (Beethoven), 332
"Goodnight My Someone" from *The Music Man* (Willson), 214
"Gott der Vater, wohn uns bei" (Chorale 135) (Bach, J. S.), 334
"Gott hat das Evangelium" (Chorale 181) (Bach, J. S.), 122
"Got to Get You Into My Life" from *Revolver* (Lennon-McCartney), 271
"Gott sei mir Sünder gnädig" (Lang), 310
Granados, Enrique: *Escenas Románticas,* no. 5, 239, 449
"The Great Gate of Kiev" from *Pictures at an Exhibition* (Mussorgsky), 548
Grieg, Edvard: *Peer Gynt*
"The Death of Åse," 483
"The Rape of the Bride (Ingrid's Lament)", 244–245

H

Hammerstein, Oscar II: "Oh, What a Beautiful Mornin' ," from *Oklahoma,* 262
Handel, George Frederic
Chaconne in GM, 515
Messiah, "Surely He Hath Borne Our Griefs," 368
Minuet in F, 434
Sonata for Flute and Continuo, op. 1, no. 7, 71–*72*

Suite de Pièces, Passacaglia, 395
Trois Leçons, "Chaconne," 202
Harburg, E. Y.: *The Wizard of Oz,* "If I Only Had a Brain," 391
A Hard Day's Night (The Beatles)
"Can't Buy Me Love" (Lennon-McCartney), 369
"A Hard Day's Night" (Lennon-McCartney), 191
Harrison, George: "Something" from *Abbey Road,* 548
Hart, Lorenz: *Pal Joey,* "Bewitched," 673
Haydn, Joseph
Piano Concerto in DM, Hob. XVII:37, III, 452
Piano Concerto in DM, Hob. XVIII: 44, II, 76
Piano Sonata in AM, Hob. XVI:5, 502
Piano Sonata in CM, Hob. XVI:3, II, 195
Piano Sonata in CM, Hob. XVI:20, 239
Piano Sonata in C♯m, Hob. XVI:36, 261
Piano Sonata in DM, Hob. XVI:4, 504
Quartet in B♭M, op. 64, no. 3, 586
String Quartet op. 9, no. 21, 519–520
String Quartet op. 54, no. 2, 486
String Quartet op. 64, no. 2, 475, 487
String Quartet op. 76, no. 3, 285
String Quartet op. 76, no. 5, 404
String Quartet op. 77, no. 1, 430, 491
Symphony no. 101 in DM, IV, 546
Symphony no. 100 in GM, *(Military),* 583
Trio in FM, Hob. XV:6, 218
Trio in GM, Hob. XV:5, 234, 235
Heckscher, Celeste: *Valse Bohème,* 586
Henley, Don: "Hotel California," 681
Hensel, Fanny Mendelssohn: *Six Songs,* op. 7, no. 4, "Du bist die Ruh," 544
"Herzlich thut mich verlangen" (Chorale 21) (Bach, J. S.), 56
"Herzliebster Jesu, was hast du verbrochen" (Chorale 111) (Bach), 161
"Hexenlied," *Zwölf Gesänge,* op. 8, no. 8 (Mendelssohn), 364
Hindemith, Paul, Interlude from *Ludus Tonalis,* 6
"Hoffnung," from *Four Ariettas and a Duet,* op. 82, no. 1 (Beethoven), 632
"Hosanna in excelsis" from *Missa Gabriel Archangelus* (Palestrina), 266
"Hotel California" (Feldes-Henley-Frey), 681
Howard, Bart: "Fly Me to the Moon (In Other Words)", 385

I

"I Ain't Down Yet" from *The Unsinkable Molly Brown* (Willson), 228
"Ich gab dem Schicksal dich zurück" (Lang), 564
"Ich hab' mein' Sach' Gott heimgestellt" (Chorale 19) (Bach, J. S.), 445
"Ich stand in dunklen Träumen" (Schumann, C.), 471
"If I Only Had a Brain" from *The Wizard of Oz* (Harburg-Arlen), 391
"I Let a Song Go Out of My Heart" (Ellington), 543
Im Herbst (Brahms), 621
"An Important Event," no. 6 from *Scenes from Childhood,* op. 15 (Schumann, R.), 451
"In dulci jubilo" (Chorale 143) (Bach, J. S.), 270, 350
"In meines Vaters Garten," from *Five Songs,* no. 2 (Mahler), 672
Interlude from *Ludus Tonalis* (Hindemith), 6
Intermezzo in CM, op. 119, no. 3 (Brahms), 31
In the Bottoms (Dett), 676
Invention no. 1 in CM (Bach, J. S.), 291
Invention no. 3 in DM (Bach, J. S.), 298, 385
Italienisches Liederbuch (Wolf), "Der Mond hat eine schwere Klag' erhoben," 670

J

Jacquet de la Guerre, Elizabeth: Suite in Am, Sarabande, 257
Jarre, Maurice: "Somewhere, My Love" from *Doctor Zhivago,* 453
"Jeanie with the Light Brown Hair" (Foster), 283
"Jesu, meine Freude" (Chorale 138) (Bach, J. S.), 331, 556
"Jesu, nun sei gepreiset," (Chorale) (Bach, J. S.),
John, Elton: "Candle in the Wind" from *Live in Australia,* 212–213
Jubilee (Porter) "Begin the Beguine," 442
Jupiter Symphony (Mozart), 311–314

K

Kern, Jerome, "Smoke Gets in Your Eyes" from *Roberta,* 136, 137
Kindertotenlieder (Mahler), "Nun seh' ich wohl, warum so dunkle Flammen," 743
Eine kleine Nachtmusik, K. 525, III (Menuetto) (Mozart), 507
"Kommt her zu mir" (Chorale 45) (Bach, J. S.), 325
Kreisler, Fritz
Liebesleid, 453
"Praeludium and Allegro," for Violin and Piano, 8
"Kyrie" from Mass in Bm (Bach, J. S.), 18

L

"Là ci darem la mano" from *Don Giovanni* (Mozart), 415
"La Favorite," Étude-Mazurka (Sloman), 423

Lang, Josephine
Frühzeitiger Frühling, 450
"Gott sei mir Sünder gnädig," 310
"Ich gab dem Schicksal dich zurück," 564
Lassus, Orlando de: "Benedictus" from *Missa pro defunctis,* 74–75
"Laudamus Te" from *Gloria* (Vivaldi), 433
Lennon, John
"All My Loving" from *With the Beatles,* 109
"Can't Buy Me Love" from *A Hard Day's Night,* 369
"Got to Get You Into My Life" from *Revolver,* 271
"A Hard Day's Night" from *A Hard Day's Night,* 191
"I Will" from *The Beatles* ("White Album"), 299
"Lucy in the Sky with Diamonds" from *Sgt. Pepper's Lonely Hearts Club Band,* 190
Lerner, Alan Jay: "Almost Like Being in Love" from *Brigadoon,* 369
"Les Roses d'Ispahan," op. 39, no. 4 (Fauré), 646, 671
"Libiamo ne'lieti calici," *La Traviata* (Verdi), 129, 232, 308
Liebesleid (Kreisler), 453
Liszt, Franz
Années de Pèlerinage, "Il pensieroso," 628
Faust Symphony, 738–739
Lloyd Webber, Andrew: *Evita,* "Don't Cry for Me Argentina," 406
"Lobt Gott, ihr Christen allzugleich," (Chorale no. 54) (Bach, J. S.), 171
Loewe, Frederick: "Almost Like Being in Love," from *Brigadoon,* 369
Love, Mike: "The Warmth of the Sun," 603
Lucia di Lammermoor (Donizetti)
"Regnava nel silenzio," 217
"Tu che a Dio spiegasti l'ali," 215–216
"Lucy in the Sky with Diamonds" from *Sgt. Pepper's Lonely Hearts Club Band* (Lennon-McCartney), 190
Ludus Tonalis (Hindemith), 6

M

"Mack the Knife" from *The Threepenny Opera* (Weill-Blitzstein-Brecht), 674
Mahler, Alma: *Five Songs*
"Ekstase," 635
"In meines Vaters Garten," 672
Mahler, Gustav: *Kindertotenlieder,* "Nun seh' ich wohl, warum so dunkle Flammen," 743
Martínez, Marianne: Sonata in AM, 250, 295
Mass in Bm (Bach, J. S.)
"Crucifixus," 516
"Kyrie," 18
Mazurka in A♭M, op. 59, no. 2 (Chopin), 680
Mazurka in Am, op. posth. 67, no. 4 (Chopin), 291
Mazurka in B♭M, op. 7, no. 1 (Chopin), 148
Mazurka in GM, op. 67, no. 1 (Chopin), 556
Mazurka in Gm, op. posth. 67, no. 2 (Chopin), 427
McCartney, Paul
"All My Loving," from *With the Beatles,* 109
"Can't Buy Me Love," from *A Hard Day's Night,* 369
"Got to Get You Into My Life" from *Revolver,* 271
"A Hard Day's Night," from *A Hard Day's Night,* 191
"I Will" from *The Beatles* ("White Album"), 299
"Lucy in the Sky with Diamonds," from *Sgt. Pepper's Lonely Hearts Club Band,* 190
"Mein" from *Die schöne Müllerin* (Schubert), 619
Mendelssohn, Felix
Rondo Capriccioso, op. 14, 643
Song without Words, op. 102, no. 2, 543
Violin Concerto op. 64, 363
Zwölf Gesänge, op. 8, "Hexenlied," 364
Menuet I, from Partita no. 1 in B♭M, for Harpsichord (Bach), 278
Mercer, Johnny: "Satin Doll," 567
Messa di Gloria (Puccini), "Gloria," 441
Military Symphony (Symphony no.100) (Haydn), 583
Minuet from *Notebook for Anna Magdalena Bach,* 499
Minuet in F (Handel), 434
Missa Gabriel Archangelus, "Hosanna in excelsis" (Palestrina), 266
Missa pro defunctis, "Benedictus" (Lassus), 74–75
Missa Quam pulchra es, "Sanctus" (Palestrina), 253
"Der Mond hat eine schwere Klag' erhoben" from *Italienisches* (Wolf), 670
Moonlight Sonata (Piano Sonata C♯m, op. 27, no. 2) (Beethoven), 563
Mozart, Wolfgang Amadeus
Concerto in E♭M for Horn and Orchestra, K. 447, 233
Don Giovanni
Finale, 578, 582
Overture, 568, 581
Die Entführung aus dem Serail, act III, no. 18, 598
Fantasia in Cm, K. 475, 265, 564, 633
Eine kleine Nachtmusik, K. 525, III (Menuetto), 507
"Là ci darem la mano," *Don Giovanni,* 415
Piano Concerto in CM, K. 467, 56
Piano Sonata in AM, K. 331, 191, 193
Piano Sonata in B♭M, K. 333, 190, 468, 557
Piano Sonata in B♭M, K. 570, 160
Piano Sonata in CM, K. 309, 195
Piano Sonata in CM, K. 330, 185, 344
Piano Sonata in Cm, K. 457, 344, 360
Piano Sonata in DM, K. 279, 300
Piano Sonata in DM, K. 284, 81, 315, 356
Piano Sonata in FM, K. 280, 250, 593
Piano Sonata in FM, K. 332, 281, 580

Piano Sonata in GM, K. 283, 389
Sonata for Violin and Piano, K. 372, 379
Sonata for Violin and Piano, K. 377, 243–244
Sonata for Violin and Piano, K. 380, 592
Sonata for Violin and Piano, K. 481, 424
String Quartet K. 173, 424
String Quartet K. 421, 441
Symphony no. 39, K. 543, in E♭M, 396, 684
Symphony no. 40 in Gm, I, 305, 366, 405
Symphony no. 41, K. 551, *Jupiter,* 311–314
A Musical Offering (Retrograde canon) (Bach, J. S.), 296–297
Music for String Instruments, Percussion, and Celestal (Bartók), 18
The Music Man (Willson), "Goodnight My Someone," 214
Mussorgsky, Modest: *Pictures at an Exhibition,* "The Great Gate of Kiev," 548

N

"The Neighbor's Dance" from *The Three-Cornered Hat* (Falla), 287
Neil, Fred: "Everybody's Talkin'", 136, 137
Nite Life (Williams), 674
Nocturne in B♭M (Szymanowska), 170
Nocturne in GM, op. 37, no. 2 (Chopin), 744
Notebook for Anna Magdalena Bach
"Aria di Govannini," 186
Minuet, 499
"Notturno," from *Vier Stücke aus Soirées Musicales,* op. 2, no. 2 (Schumann, C.), 635
"Nun danket alle Gott," (Chorale 32) (Bach, J. S.), 200
"Nun lob,' mein' Seel,' den Herren," (Chorale) (Bach, J. S.),
"Nun seh' ich wohl, warum so dunkle Flammen" from *Kindertotenlieder* (Mahler), 743

O

"O Clemangis, lis dans mon âme" from *Ernestine* (Saint-Georges), 618
"Oh, What a Beautiful Mornin'," from *Oklahoma* (Rodgers-Hammerstein), 262
"O Haupt voll Blut and Wunden" (Chorale 80) (Bach), 122, 401
"O Herre Gott, dein göttlich Wort," (Chorale 14) (Bach, J. S.), 138, 335
Oh Kay! (Gershwin-Gershwin), "Someone to Watch Over Me," 292, 293
"Oh! Susanna" (Foster), 27
"Oh Were My Love Yon Lilac Fair!" from *Twenty-three Songs,* op. 43, no. 3 (Beach)
Oklahoma (Rodgers-Hammerstein)
"Oh, What a Beautiful Mornin'", 262
Originaltänze, op. 9 (Schubert)
no. 3, 175
no. 16, 439
no. 26, 135
Overture from *Don Giovanni* (Mozart), 568, 581
"O Welt, ich muss dich lassen" (Chorale 117) (Bach), 367

P

Paganini, Nicolò: Caprice op. 1, no. 14 for Solo Violin, 575
Palestrina, Giovanni
Missa Gabriel Archangelus, "Hosanna in excelsis," 266
Missa Quam pulchra es, "Sanctus," 253
Pal Joey (Rodgers-Hart)
"Bewitched," 673
Papillons, op. 2, no. 8 (Schumann), 588
Paradis, Maria Theresia von: *Sicilienne,* 561
Partita no. 2 in Cm, for Harpsichord (Bach), 74
Partita no. 2 in Cm, for Harpsichord (Bach, J. S.), 74
Partita no. 2 in Dm for Violin Solo (Chaconne) (Bach, J. S.), 30–31
Passacaglia, from *Suite de Pièces* (Handel), 395
Peer Gynt (Grieg)
"The Death of Åse," 483
"The Rape of the Bride (Ingrid's Lament)", 244–245
"Il pensieroso," from *Années de Pèlerinage* (Liszt), 628
Phidile (Schubert), 76
Piano Concertos
Beethoven
no. 4, op. 58, 440
Brahms
no. 2, op. 83, III, 647
Haydn
in DM, Hob. XVII:37, III, 452
in DM, Hob. XVIII: 44, II, 76
Mozart
in CM, K. 467, II, 56
Piano Sonatas (Bach, C. P. E.)
Sonaten für Kenner und Liebhaber, 387
Piano Sonatas (Beethoven)
in Cm, op. 10, no. 1, 361–362
in C♯m, op. 27, no. 2, *Moonlight,* 563
in E♭M, op. 7, 602, 634
in EM, op. 14, no. 1, 343
in EM, op. 90, I, 691
in E♭M, op. 81a, I, 545
in GM, op. 31, no. 1, 579
in GM, op. 49, no. 2, 194
Piano Sonatas (Haydn)
in AM, Hob. XVI:5, 502
in CM, Hob. XVI:3, 195
in CM, Hob. XVI:20, 239
in C♯m, Hob. XVI:36, 261
in DM, Hob. XVI:4, 504
Piano Sonatas (Mozart)
in AM, K. 331, 191
in B♭M, K. 333, 190, 557
in B♭M, K. 570, 160
in CM, K. 309, 195
in CM, K. 330, 185
in Cm, K. 457, 344, 360
in DM, K. 279, 300
in DM, K. 284, 81, 315, 356
in FM, K. 280, 250, 593
in FM, K. 332, 281, 580
in GM, K. 283, 389

Piano Sonatas (Schubert)
in AM, op. 164, 614
in B♭M, D. 960, 493
Pictures at an Exhibition (Mussorgsky), "The Great Gate of Kiev," 548
Pockriss, Lee: "Tracy," 679
"Pop Goes the Weasel," 27
Porter, Cole: "Begin the Beguine," from *Jubilee,* 442
"Praeludium and Allegro" for Violin and Piano (Kreisler), 8
Prelude in Cm, op. 28, no. 20 (Chopin), 571
Prelude in Em, op. 28, no. 4 (Chopin), 594, 685
Prelude no. 22 in B♭m, from *The Well-Tempered Clavier* (Bach, J. S.), 454
Prelude no. 6 in Dm from *The Well-Tempered Clavier,* I (Bach), 9
Prelude to *Tristan und Isolde* (Wagner), 719–721
Price, Florence: *Fantasie Negre,* 223
Puccini, G.: Gloria" from *Messa di Gloria,* 441

Q

Quartet in B♭M, op. 64, no. 3 (Haydn), 586

R

Rachmaninoff, Sergei: *Rhapsody on a Theme of Paganini,* op. 43, 304, 380
"The Rape of the Bride (Ingrid's Lament)," from *Peer Gynt* (Grieg), 244–245
Ravel, Maurice: Waltz no. 1 from *Valses nobles et sentimentales,* 729
"Regnava nel silenzio" from Lucia di Lammermoor (Donizetti)
Reichardt, Louise: *From Ariel's Revelation,* "Frühlingsblumen," 276, 277, 375
Rhapsody on a Theme of Paganini, op. 43 (Rachmaninoff), 304, 380
Rice, Tim: *Evita,* "Don't Cry for Me Argentina," 406
Rigoletto, act I, no. 9, "Caro nome" (Verdi), 176
Rimsky-Korsakov, Nikolay: *Scheherazade,* III, 291
"Ritorna vincitor" from *Aida* (Verdi), 587
Roberta (Harbach-Kern), "Smoke Gets in Your Eyes," 136, 137
Rodgers, Richard
Oklahoma, "Oh, What a Beautiful Mornin'," 262
Pal Joey, "Bewitched," 673
Romance, op. 118, no. 5 (Brahms), 264
Romanzen aus Magelone (Brahms)
"Treue Liebe dauert lange," 728
Rondo, op. 51, no. 1 (Beethoven), 344
Rondo Capriccioso, op. 14 (Mendelssohn), 643
Rossini, Gioachino: *Il barbiere di Siviglia,* act V, no. 3, 224

S

Saint-Georges, Chevalier
Adagio, 256
Ernestine, "O Clemangis, lis dans mon âme," 618
Sonata II for Violin and Piano, 240, 421
Sonata III for Violin and Piano, 575
Symphonie Concertante in AM, op. 10, no. 2, 288
Saint-Saëns, Camille: *Christmas Oratorio,* no. 8, 335
"Sanctus" from *Missa Quam pulchra es* (Palestrina), 253
Sarabande from Suite in Am (Jacquet de la Guerre), 257
"Satin Doll" (Ellington-Mercer-Strayhorn), 567
Scenes from Childhood (Schumann, R.)
"An Important Event," 451
"Träumerei," 693–694
Scheherazade, III (Rimsky-Korsakov), 291
Schein, Johann Hermann: "Wirf Christenleut," from *Cantional,* 339
Scherzo-Tarantella, op. 16 (Wieniawski), 328
Die schöne Müllerin (Schubert)
"Am Feierabend," 346
"Mein," 619
"Ungeduld," 345
Schubert, Franz
"An Mignon," op. 19, no. 2, 566
Die schöne Müllerin
"Am Feierabend," 346, 476, 551
"Mein," 619
"Ungeduld," 345
"Erster Verlust," 742
"Originaltänze," op. 9
no. 3, 175
no. 16, 439
no. 26, 135
Phidile, 76
Piano Sonata in AM, op. 164, I, 614
Piano Sonata in B♭M, D. 960, 493
Schwanengesang
"Aufenthalt," no. 5, 345
"Der Doppelgänger," 638
"Ständchen," 346, 350
Symphony in Bm, "Unfinished," 426
Symphony no. 9 in Cm, 571
Valse Nobles, op. 77, no. 6, 224
Valse Sentimentales, op. 50, no. 3, 213, 319
Waltz op. 9, no. 13, 343
Walzer, Ländler und Ecossaisen, op. 18
Ecossaise no. 2, 146
Ländler, no. 3, 125
Wanderers Nachtlied, op. 96, no. 3, 555
Winterreise
"Frülingstraum," 641
"Gefror'ne Thränen," 611, 622
Zwanzig Walzer, op. 127, no. 13, 156
Schumann, Clara
"Ich stand in dunklen Träumen," 471
Trio in Gm, op. 17, 360, 409, 492
Vier Stücke aus Soirées Musicales, op. 2, "Notturno," 635
Schumann, Robert
Album for the Young, op. 68
"Armes Waisenkind," 351

"Ein Choral," 229
"War Song," 147
Dichterliebe, op. 48
"Am leuchtenden Sommermorgen," 584
"Wenn ich in deinen Augen seh," 270
Papillons, op. 2, no. 8, 588
Scenes from Childhood
"An Important Event," 451, 521–522
"Träumerei," 693–694
Symphony no. 3 in E♭M, I, 30, 31
Schwanengesang (Schubert)
"Aufenthalt,", 345
"Der Doppelgänger," 638
"Ständchen," 346, 350
Scott, Clara: *Twilight Fancies*, 421
"Sempre libera" from *La Traviata* (Verdi), 308, 309
Seven Variations on "God Save the King" (Beethoven), 332
Sgt. Pepper's Lonely Hearts Club Band (Lennon-McCartney), "Lucy in the Sky with Diamonds," 190
Sicilienne (Paradis), 561
Six Songs, op. 7, no. 4, "Du bist die Ruh" (Hensel), 544
Slavonic Dance in Gm, op. 46, no. 8 (Dvorák), 550
Sloman, Jane: "La Favorite," Étude-Mazurka, 423
"Smoke Gets in Your Eyes" from *Roberta* (Harbach-Kern), 136, 137
"Someone to Watch Over Me," from *Oh Kay!* (Gershwin-Gershwin), 292, 293
"Something" from *Abbey Road* (Harrison), 548
"Somewhere, My Love" from *Doctor Zhivago* (Webster-Jarre), 453
Sonata for Flute and Continuo, op. 1, no. 7 (Handel), 71–*72*
Sonata for Violin and Piano, K. 377 (Mozart), 243–244
Sonata for Violin and Piano, K. 380 (Mozart), 592
Sonata for Violin and Piano, K. 481 (Mozart), 424
Sonata for Violin and Piano (Franck), 640, 669
Sonata II, for Violin and Piano (Saint-Georges), 240, 421
Sonata III, for Violin and Piano (Saint-Georges), 575
Sonata in Fm for Clarinet and Piano, op. 120, no. 1, I (Brahms), 601
Sonata *La Follia,* op. 5, no. 12 (Corelli), 515
Sonata no. 1 for Flute and Keyboard, BWV 1030, IV (Bach), 373
Sonatina in GM (Beethoven), 416
"Song of the Shrine," from *Enchantment* (Dett), 648
Song without Words, op. 102, no. 2 (Mendelssohn), 543
Sous les étoiles, op. 65, no. 4 (Beach), 695
"Spring" from The Four Seasons (Vivaldi), 106
"Ständchen," from *Schwanengesang,* no. 5 (Schubert), 346
Strayhorn, Billy: "Satin Doll," 567
String Quartets (Beethoven)
op. 18, no. 5, Trio, 505
String Quartets (Haydn)
op. 54, no. 2, 486
op. 64, no. 2, 475, 487
op. 76, no. 3, 285
op. 76, no. 5, 404
op. 77, no. 1, 430
String Quartets (Mozart)
K. 173, 424
K. 421, 441
Suite de Pièces (Handel) Passacaglia, 395
"Surely He Hath Borne Our Griefs," from *Messiah* (Handel), 368
Symphonie Concertante in AM, op. 10, no. 2 (Saint-Georges), 288
Symphonies (Beethoven)
no. 3 in E♭M, op. 55 *(Eroica),* 211, 585
no. 5 in Cm, 300, 301, 607
no. 6, I, 293–294
no. 7, I, 294
no. 9 in DM, 736–737
Symphonies (Brahms)
no. 4, op. 98, 331
no. 1 in Cm, II, 593
Symphonies (Haydn)
no. 100 in GM, *(Military),* 583
no. 101 in DM, IV, 546
Symphonies (Mozart)
no. 40 in Gm, I, 305
no. 41, K. 551, *Jupiter,* 311–314
Symphonies (Schubert)
in Bm, "Unfinished," 426
no. 9 in Cm, 571
Symphonies (Schumann)
no. 3 in E♭M, I, 30, 31
Szymanowska, Maria: Nocturne in B♭M, 171, 364, 460

T

Taylor, James: "Your Smiling Face," 388
The Three-Cornered Hat (Falla), "The Neighbor's Dance," 287
The Threepenny Opera (Weill-Blitzstein-Brecht), "Mack the Knife," 674
"Tracy" (Vance-Pockriss), 679
"Träumerei," from *Scenes from Childhood* (Schumann, R.), 693–694
La Traviata (Verdi)
"Libiamo ne'lieti calici," 129, 232, 308
"Sempre libera," 308, 309
"Treue Liebe dauert lange," from *Romanzen aus Magelone* (Brahms), 728
Trio in Em, op. 45, I (Farrenc), 609, 631
Trio in FM, Hob. XV:6 (Haydn), 218
Trio in GM, Hob. XV:5 (Haydn), 234, 235
Trio in Gm, op. (Schumann, C.), 360
Trio in Gm, op. 17 (Schumann, C.), 360, 409
Trio op. 1, no. 1 (Beethoven), 408
Tristan und Isolde (Wagner)
act I, scene 5, 692
Prelude, 719–721
Prelude to act I, 677
Prelude to act III, 684
Trois Leçons (Handel) "Chaconne," 202
Il Trovatore, act II, no. 15, "E deggio e posso crederlo?" (Verdi), 185

"Tu che a Dio spiegasti l'ali" from Lucia di Lammermoor (Donizetti),
Twilight Fancies (Scott), 421

U

"Unfinished" Symphony in Bm (Schubert), 426
"Ungeduld," from *Die schöne Müllerin,* no. 7 (Schubert), 345, 350
The Unsinkable Molly Brown (Willson), "I Ain't Down Yet," 228

V

Valse Bohème (Heckscher), 586
Valse Nobles, op. 77, no. 6 (Schubert), 224
Valses nobles et sentimentales (Ravel), Waltz no. 1, 729
Valses Sentimentales, op. 50, no. 3 (Schubert), 213, 319
Vance, Paul: "Tracy," 679
Verdi, Giuseppe
Aida
"Celesta Aida," 629
"Ritorna vincitor," 587
Il trovatore
act II, no. 14, 436
"E deggio e posso crederlo?", 185
La Traviata
"Libiamo ne'lieti calici," 129, 232, 308
"Sempre libera," 308, 309
Rigoletto
"Caro nome," 176
Viardot-García, Pauline: "Die Beschwörung," 211
Vier Stücke aus Soirées Musicales, op. 2, no. 2 (Schumann, C.) "Notturno," 635
Vivaldi, Antonio
The Four Seasons, "Spring," 106, 293
The Four Seasons, "Winter," I, *Ritornello,* 107
Gloria, "Laudamus Te," 433

W

Wagner, Richard: *Tristan und Isolde*
act I, scene 2, 726–727
act I, scene 5, 692
Prelude, 719–721
Prelude to act I, 677
Prelude to act III, 684, 722
Waltz in Am, op. 34, no. 2 (Chopin), 570
Waltz no. 1 from *Valses nobles et sentimentales* (Ravel), 729
Waltz op. 9, no. 13 (Schubert), 343
Walzer, Ländler und Ecossaisen, op. 18 (Schubert, Franz)
Ecossaise, no. 2, 146
Ländler, no. 3, 125, 146, 147, 155, 158
Wanderers Nachtlied, op. 96, no. 3 (Schubert), 555
"The Warmth of the Sun" (Love-Wilson), 603
"War Song," *Album for the Young* op. 68 (Schumann), 147
"Warum betrübst du dich, mein Herz" (Chorale 94)(Bach, J. S.), 448
"Was bist du doch, O Seele, so betrübet" (Chorale 193) (Bach, J. S.), 325
Webber, Andrew Lloyd: *Evita,* "Don't Cry for Me Argentina," 406
Webster, Paul Francis: "Somewhere, My Love" from *Doctor Zhivago,* 453
"Weg, mein Herz, mit den Gedanken" (Chorale 298) (Bach, J. S.), 67
Weill, Kurt: *The Threepenny Opera,* "Mack the Knife," 674
The Well-Tempered Clavier (Bach, J. S.)
Fugue no. 2 in Cm, 204, 303, 381, 530
Fugue no. 3 in C♯M, 303, 319
Fugue no. 8 in D♯m, 295, 296
Fugue no. 21 in B♭M, 478
Fugue no. 24 in Bm, 18
Prelude no. 22 in B♭m, 454
Prelude no. 6 in Dm, 9
Wieniawski, Henryk: Scherzo-Tarantella, op. 16, 328
Williams, Mary Lou: *Nite Life,* 674
Willson, Meredith
"Goodnight My Someone" from *The Music Man,* 214
"I Ain't Down Yet" from *The Unsinkable Molly Brown,* 228
Wilson, Brian: "The Warmth of the Sun," 603
"Winter" from The Four Seasons (Vivaldi), 107
Winterreise (Schubert)
"Frülingstraum," 641
"Gefror'ne Thränen," 611, 622
"Wir Christenleut" from *Cantional* (Schein), 339
The Wizard of Oz (Harburg-Arlen), "If I Only Had a Brain," 391
Wolf, Hugo: *Italienisches Liederbuch,* "Der Mond hat eine schwere Klag' erhoben," 670
"Wo soll ich fliehen hin," (Chorale 25) (Bach, J. S.), 364

Y

"Your Smiling Face" (Taylor), 388

Z

Zelter, Carl Friedrich: "Abschied," 462
Zwanzig Walzer, op. 127, no. 13 (Schubert), 156
Zwölf Gesänge, op. 8 (Mendelssohn), "Hexenlied," 364

Subject Index

A

Abrupt modulation, 483. *See also* modulation
Accents
  agogic, 31, 38
  dynamic, 31
  harmonic, 321
  metric, 25–26, 320
  neighbor notes, 192
  passing tones, 189 (*See also* Passing chords)
  rhythmic, 30
Accidentals, 4–6, 43, 79
  in figured bass parts, 71, 72
Accompaniment
  Alberti bass, 130, 343, 348
  arpeggiated chords, 133, 161 (*See also* arpeggiated chords)
  keyboard harmonizations, 348–349
Adagio, 22
Added sixth chords, 542
Additive meter, 27–28
Aeolian mode, 46, 47. *See also* Minor modes
Agogic accents, 30, 38
Aida (Verdi), "Celeste Aida," 629
Alberti bass, 130, 343, 348
Album for the Young (Schumann, R.)
  "Ein Choral," 229, 234
  "Folk Song," 277, 278, 311, 336, 337
  "War Song," 147
Allegretto, 22
Allegro, 22
Allemande, 498
Altered chords, 400
Altered triads, 634–636
Alternate doublings, 390
Alto, 110, *111*
Alto clef (C clef), 3, *4*
Anacrusis, 26
Andante, 22
Années de PèlerinageI (Liszt) "Il pensieroso," 628
Answer of a fugue, 530
Antecedent-consequent structure, 278
Anticipation, 193
"Apparent mediant," dominant as, 336–337, 340
Applied dominant chords. *See* Secondary dominant chords
Appoggiatura chords, 195, 675–676
Arias, 509
Arpeggiated chords
  bass, 133, 161
  keyboard harmonizations, 129–130, 343
  $^6_4$ chords, 210–211
Ascending 5-6 (or 6-5), 679–680
Asymmetrical (additive) meter, 27–28
Asymmetrical periods, 281
Augmentation, 297
Augmented chords
  doubly augmented fourth, 583–584
  in *Faust* Symphony (Liszt), 738
  sixth chords (+6)
    dominant and embellishing functions, 636–641
    French (Fr +6), 576, 584–585, 637
    general features and types of, 575–577
    German (Gr +6), 576, 579–581
    Italian (It +6), 577–579
    moving +6, 585, 587
    relationship to Neapolitan sixth chords, 589–590
    secondary, 588
    spelling, 577, 589
    Augmented intervals, 10–11, 114
Augmented triads, 57, 707–708, 710–711, 725, 738
Authentic cadences, 136, 260–262
  imperfect authentic, 136, 160, 261–262 (*See also* Imperfect authentic cadences)
  perfect authentic cadences, 260–261, 299 (*See also* Perfect authentic cadences)

B

Bach, Carl Philipp Emanuel: Piano Sonata no. 4, from *Sonaten für Kenner und Liebhaber,* 386, 387
Bach, Johann Sebastian
  "Chaconne" from Partita no. 2 in Dm for Violin Solo, 317
  Chorale 3, "Ach Gott vom Himmel, sieh darein," 249
  Chorale 14, "O Herre Gott, dein göttlich Wort," 138, 335
  Chorale 19, "Ich hab' mein' Sach' Gott heimgestellt," 445–446
  Chorale 20, "Ein feste Burg is unserGott," 364
  Chorale 21, "Herzlich thut mich verlangen," 56, 456
  Chorale 25, "Wo soll ich fliehen hin," 364
  Chorale 34, "Erbarm dich mein, O Herre Gott," 201, 202
  Chorale 42, "Du Friede fürst, Herr Jesu Christ," 251–252
  Chorale 94, "Warum betrübst du dich, mein Herz," 447–448
  Chorale 135, "Gott der Vater, wohn uns bei," 334
  Chorale 138, "Jesu, meine Freude," 331
  Chorale 196, "Da der Herr Christ zu Tische sass," 163
  Chorale 298, "Weg, mein Herz, mit den Gedanken," 67
  chorales, voice overlap and voice crossing in, 117
  contrapuntal art, 84
  counterpoint in chorales, 121–123
  "Crucifixus," from Mass in Bm, 514, 516
  French Suite no. 3, "Minuet," 473, 482
  French Suite no. 5, "Gavotte," 283, 316, 317
  fugues, 529
  harmonic syncopation in chorales, 322

Bach, Johann Sebastian (*Cont.*)
Invention no. 1 in CM, 291
Invention no. 3 in DM, 298, 385, 526–528
Invention no. 3 in DM, Theme, 298
A Musical Offering (Retrograde canon), 296–297
Partita no. 2 in Cm, for Harpsichord, 74
"Was Gott tut," 159, 188, 189, 194
The Well-Tempered Clavier, 529
Fugue no. 2 in Cm, 204, 532–533
Fugue no. 3 in C♯M, 303, 319
Fugue no. 8 in D♯m, 295, 296, 535
Fugue no. 11 in FM, 534
Fugue no. 24 in Bm, 18
Prelude 22 in B♭m, 454–455
Bailey, Robert, 721n
Balanced binary form, 501, 506. *See also* Binary form
Bar lines, 23
Baroque period
binary forms, 498
chorale texture, 76
contrapuntal art, 84
dance forms, 498
Picardy third, 151
polyphonic textures, 525
system of numerical symbols, 70
tempos, 22
vocal genres, 509
Bartók, Béla, *Music for String Instruments, Percussion, and Celesta,* I, 18
Bass afterbeat figuration, 129, 343
Bass arpeggiation, 133, 161
Bass clarinets, transposition for, 747
Bass clef (F clef), 3, *4*
Bass note of chords, 59. *See also* Inversions of chords; Root position
Bass ostinato, 512
Bass reductions: Haydn's Piano Sonata in DM, Hob. XVII:37, III, 451, 452
Bass voice, 110, *111*
Beams, 33
Beats, 21
division, 23, 26
irregular, 28–29
and meter, 19
strong and weak, 25–26
value of, 23
Beethoven, Ludwig van
Für Elise, 142
Italian +6 chord, 577
Piano Sonata in Fm, op. 2, no. 1, 277
Seven Peasant Dances, WoO 168, no. 4, 130, 277
Sonata in GM, op. 49, no. 2, 193, 194
Sonata op. 2, no. 1, III, Trio, 388
Sonata op. 10, no. 1, 195, 240, 311, 665
String Quartet op. 18, no. 5, Trio, 505–506
studies of species counterpoint, 84–85
Symphony no. 5, III, 300, 301
Symphony no. 6, I, 293–294
Symphony no. 7, I, 294
Symphony no. 9 in DM, op. 125, II, 734–735, 736–737
Symphony no. 3 in E♭M, op. 55 *(Eroica),* 211, 297, 523–524, 534, 584, 585
Trio op. 1, no. 1, 408
Bernstein, Leonard, *West Side Story,* "America," 29
Binary forms
balanced, 501, 506
compared to ternary forms, 510
dominant type, 499
formal designs, 501–506
German *Lieder,* 699
reprises, 498, 499, 500
rounded, 503–506, 652
simple, 501, 502–503
tonal types, 499–500
Binary operation, 732, 735
Block chords, 147, 343
Blues progression, 368
Boone, Steve, "Summer in the City," 514
Borrowed chords
defined, 541
from major mode in a minor key, 549–550
minor mode in major key, 541, 542–548
soprano-bass patterns and I-V-I progression, 552
Bourrée, 498
Brahms, Johannes
Ballade in BM, op. 10, no. 4, 358, 359
Concerto for Violin and Cello, 733
Romance, op. 118, no. 5, 264
Symphony no. 4, op. 98, 331
Bridges, in fugues, 532
Broken chords, 55
Bubble diagrams, 279, 498
Burkhart, Charles, 705n, 721n

C

C clef (Alto clef), 3, *4*
Cadences, 86, 260–273, 498
authentic, 136, 260–262
clausula vera, 98
deceptive, 265–266, 337
extensions, 299–300
formulas, *94–95*
half, 136, 263–264
identifying, 139–140
imperfect authentic, 136, 160, 261–262
involving I and V, 136–137
leading-tone, 252, 262
melodic patterns, 275
perfect authentic (V-I), 260–261
phrygian, 98, 264
pitch pattern exercises, 267–269
plagal, 264–265
$^6_4$ chords, 215–218, 219, 221
summary and voice leading, 267
in voice leading, 148, 150
"Camptown Races," 22
"Candle in the Wind" from *Live in Australia* (John), 212–213
Canons, 296
Cantatas, 509
Cantus firmus, 85, 88, 91
Capital-letter Roman numerals, 68
"Celeste Aida," from *Aida* (Verdi), 629
Chaconne bass, 318, 513
Chains of suspensions, 201–203
Characteristic variation, 512, 517. *See also* Variation forms

Chopin, Frédéric
Mazurka in Am, op. 7, no. 2, 192
Mazurka 43 in Gm, op. posth. 67, no. 2, 433
Chorales by J. S. Bach
Chorale 3, "Ach Gott vom Himmel, sieh darein," 249
Chorale 14, "O Herre Gott, dein göttlich Wort," 138, 335
Chorale 19, "Ich hab' mein' Sach' Gott heimgestellt," 445–446
Chorale 20, "Ein feste Burg is unserGott," 364
Chorale 21, "Herzlich thut mich verlangen," 56
Chorale 25, "Wo soll ich fliehen hin," 364
Chorale 34, "Erbarm dich mein, O Herre Gott," 201, 202
Chorale 42, "Du Friede fürst, Herr Jesu Christ," 251–252
Chorale 94, "Warum betrübst du dich, mein Herz," 447–448
Chorale 135, "Gott der Vater, wohn uns bei," 334
Chorale 138, "Jesu, meine Freude," 331
Chorale 196, "Da der Herr Christ zu Tische sass," 163
Chorale 298, "Weg, mein Herz, mit den Gedanken," 67
Chorale-style harmonizations, 112–118. *See also* Part writing of chorales; Voice leading
Chorale texture, 76
Chord progressions, 41
writing, 320–324
Chords
altered, 400
appoggiatura, 195, 675–676
block, 147, 343
broken, 55
connecting tonic and dominant, 133–134
consonant, 56
diatonic pivot, 467–470
dissonant, 56
dominant seventh (V_7), 129, 227–242 (*See also* Dominant function, seventh chords)
extended tertian, 667–675 (*See also* Extended tertian chords)
identifying, 66
labeling with Roman numerals, 68–70
linear, 72, 133 (*See also* Linear chords)
Neapolitan sixth, 560–569 (*See also* Neapolitan sixth chords)
notating, voicing, and spacing, 110–112
position, 59–60
root of, 59
structural, 129, 152
subdominant, 152–153 (*See also* Subdominant chords)
tertian, 55
triads, 57–60 (*See also* Triads)
Choruses, 509
Chromatic/Chromaticism. *See also under individual topics*
ascending bass, 433
chords, 400
chromatic harmony, 400–401
consecutive secondary dominant chords, 431
descending bass, 432, 433
half step, 6
linear, 667–697 (*See also* Linear chromaticism)
mediants, 627
passing tones, 189
pivot chords, 477–479, 597–604
chromatic-chromatic, 598
chromatic-diatonic, 597
diatonic-chromatic, 597, 599–600
scales, 4
as an equal division of the octave, 724–729
secondary leading-tone chords, 456–458
sequences, 677–684 (*See also* Sequences)
ascending 5-6 (or 6-5), 679–680
descending 5-6, 681–682
descending circle of fifths, 380–385, 430–433, 677–678
third relationships, 627–633
common-tone modulation, 630–633
triads, 628–639
Chromatic scale, 4, 49
pitches, 5
Chromatic tones, 400
Church modes, 46–47
Circle of fifths, 43, *44*. *See also* Circle-of-fifths sequences
key relationships, 466
Circle-of-fifths sequences, 107–108
ascending, 385–386
diatonic-seventh chords, 383–385
with inversions, 381–383
with inverted secondary dominants, 432
for minor keys, 46
voice-leading variants for, 381–382
Clarinets, transposition for, 747
Classical period
binary forms in, 498
sectional variations, 516
sonata form in, 651
tempos, 22
Clausula vera, 98
Clefs, 3–*4*
Closed reprise, 499
Closed spacing of chord notes, 112
Closely related keys, 465–467
Closing sections in sonata forms, 653
Codas, 299, 653, 658, 662
Codetta, 299, 527
Cohn, Richard, 730n
Common practice period, 39
Common time, 23
Common-tone relationships
diminished seventh chord, 641–643
modulation, 630–633
in *Tristan und Isolde* (Prelude) (Wagner), 722
Complete-complete/incomplete voice leading, 230
Compound duple, 23
Compound intervals, 12
Compound melody, 318–324
Compound meter, 23, *25*
Compound ternary, 509
Compound triple, 23
Concerto for Violin, op. 64 (Mendelssohn), 362, 363

Concerto for Violin and Cello (Brahms), 733
Concerto in E♭M for Horn and Orchestra, K. 447 (Mozart), 233, 234
Consequent-antecedent structure, 278
Consequent structure, 278
Consonant intervals, 14
  consonant chords, 56, 60
  species counterpoint, 84–85
Consonant neighbor note (NN), 92
Consonant $^6_4$, 211
Continuo, 71, 525
Continuous binary, 499
Continuous variations, 512–515. *See also* Variation forms
Contours of melody, 120. *See also* Melodic/Melody
Contrapuntal genres, 84, 378. *See also* Counterpoint
Contrapuntal motion, 114
Contrapuntal textures, 73
Contrapuntal variation, 512
Contrary motion, 88, 89, 114–115
Contrasting periods, 280
Corelli, Archangelo: Sonata *La Follia,* op. 5, no. 12, 514, 515
Counterexpositions, 534
Counterpoint
  in Bach chorales, 121–123
  in Baroque style, 84
  double, 532
  free, 73
  imitative, 73
  invertible, 532
  in musical style, 73
  part writing in chorales, 114–115
  species, 84–100 (*See also* Species counterpoint)
  triple, 532
Counterstatements, 654
Countersubjects, 532
Courante, 498
Crook, Max, "Runaway," 514
Cut time, 23
Cycle of major/minor thirds, 725

D

Da capo arias, 509–510
Darcy, Warren, 653n, 654
Deceptive cadences, 265–266, 337
  secondary dominant chords resolving to, 337
  secondary dominant of submediant in, 340
Dependent transitions, 652
Descending 5-6 sequence, 681
Descending tetrachords, 513
Dett, Nathaniel: from *In the Bottoms,* 676
Development in musical forms. *See also* Form modulation
  and modulation, 465
  sonata form, 653, 655–656, 658
  in *Tristan und Isolde* (Prelude) (Wagner), 719–721, 722
Development techniques, 290–298
  augmentation, 297
  changing modes, 293, 465, 550–552
  diminution, 297
  fragmentation, 293–295
  interpolation, 301
  inversions, 295–296
  melodic retrograde, 296–297
  melodic sequence, 108, 292–293
  phrase extensions, 298–301
  repetition and transposition, 290–292
Diagrams. *See also* Reductions
  bubble, 279, 498
  form, 279–280, 282, 498
  line, 279
Diatonic half-step, 6
Diatonicism, 411–412
Diatonic pivot chords, 467–470, 477–478
Diatonic scale, 4, 5, 40
Dido and Aeneas (Purcell) "Dido's Lament," 513
Diminished chords
  common-tone diminished seventh chord, 641–643
  third chord (°3), 587
  triads, 57
Diminished intervals, 10–11, 114, 134
Diminution, 297
Direct (hidden) unison, 89, 116
Direct modulation, 483
Dissonant intervals, 14
  dissonant chords, 56, 60 (*See also* Extended tertian chords)
  species counterpoint, 87, 89, 91–92, 93, 95
  suspensions, 96, 97
Dissonant neighbor note, 92
Distantly related keys, 466
Distributional graphs, 528
Divertimento in CM, Hob. XVI:, Minuet and Trio (Haydn), 232
Divisive meter, 23
Dominant function, 40, 145
  augmented sixth chords (+6), 636–641
  binary form, 499–500
  eleventh chords, 670–671
  establishing key in *Tristan und Isolde* (Wagner), 718
  mediant chords (iii or III), 336
  modulation from (V→I), 471–472
  modulation to (I→V), 470–471, 485
  ninth chords, 668–673
  secondary dominant chords, 402–419 (*See also* Secondary dominant chords)
  seventh chords, 227–242
    complete and incomplete voice-leading, 230
    inversions of, 232–238 (*See also* First inversion of chords; Second inversion of chords; Third inversion of seventh chords)
    I-V-I progression, 237–238
    Neapolitan sixth chords substituting for, 567
    root position, 227–228
    soprano-bass patterns, 236–237
    voice-leading guidelines, 229–232
  thirteenth chords, 671–672
  triads, 131
    in deceptive cadences, 265
    first inversion used as a neighbor chord, 232–233
    functioning as diatonic pivot chords, 470
Dominant type binary, 499
Don Giovanni (Mozart), 577, 581

Donizetti, Gaetano
Lucia di Lammermoor
"Regnava nel silenzio," 217
"Tu che a Dio spiegasti l'ali," 215–216
Dorian mode, 46, *47*
Dots, 21
Dotted notes, 33
Dotted quarter, 23, 26
Double counterpoint, 532
Double dots, 21
Double flat symbols, 5
Double fugue, 535
Double passing tones, 189
Double periods, 282
Double sharp symbols, 5
Double-tonic complex, 723
Double variations, 512
Doubling voices, 110–112
alternate, 390
dominant seventh chords, 227–228
first inversion triads, 164
leading-tone chords, 248–249
seventh chords, 354–355
$^6_4$ chords, 219
supertonic chords, 175, 176
Doubly augmented fourth chords, 583–584
Downbeats, 26
Duple meter, 23, *24, 25,* 26
Durational symbols, 19–21, *20*
Dyads, 5
Dynamic accents, 31

E

Eighth notes, *20*
Eleventh chords, 667, 670–671
Elisions, 277
Embellished suspensions, 199–200
Embellishing German augmented sixth chords, 638–639. *See also* German augmented sixth chords
Embellishing $^6_4$ chords, 212. *See also* $^6_4$ chords
English horns, transposition for, 749, 750
Enharmonic spellings, 5, 6, 11, 43
in "Das Verlassene Mägdlein" (Wolf) *Gedichte von Mörike,* 274
German augmented sixth chords, 579–580
of V+, 707–708
in "Widmung" from *Myrthen* (Schumann, R.), 706
Episodes
Fugue no. 2 in Cm from *The Well-Tempered Clavier* (Bach), 533
fugues, 529
rondos, 526, 659–662
Equal temperament, 4
Erlkönig (Schubert), 699–705
Eroica Symphony (Beethoven), 211, 297, 523–524, 534, 584, 585
Escape tones, 194
Expositions
in fugues, 529, 530
imitative, 526
in inventions, 526–527
sonata form, 652, 654, 657
Extended tertian chords, 667–675
eleventh chords, 667, 670–671
ninth chords, 668–673
with nondominant functions, 673–675
thirteenth chords, 667, 671–672

F

F clef (Bass clef), 3, *4*
False recapitulation, 656
Farrenc, Louise: Trio in Em, op. 45, 630, 631
Fauré, Gabriel: "Après un rêve," 688
Faust Symphony (Liszt), 738–739
Fifth note of chord, 39
Fifth progressions, 106–107
circle of fifths, 381–386 (*See also* Circle of fifths)
submediant and mediant chords in, 334–335
voice leading in, 115–116
Figural variations, 511, 516
Figured bass (thoroughbass), 70, 80, 525
accidentals in, 71, 72
checklist, 72
for diatronic seventh chords, 70
for diatronic triads, 70
procedure for realizing, 172
symbols for, 61
First inversion of chords, *59,* 60, *61.* *See also* Inversions of chords
doubling voices in, 164
Neapolitan sixth chords, 560
passing leading-tone chords, 249–250
seventh chords, 354
dominant, 232–238
secondary dominant of submediant in, 423
secondary dominant of the subdominant, 409
secondary dominant of the supertonic, 420
secondary leading-tone chords, 451–454
supertonic chords, 176–178
triads
I-V-I progression, 166–167
neighbor first-inversion dominant chord, 232–233
pitch patterns, 168
prolongation of tonic, 160–162
soprano-bass patterns, 165–166
uses and functions, 159–160
voice leading, 164
"The First Noël," 38, 40, 41, 746
First-species counterpoint, 88–90, 96
Five-part rondo form, 659, 660–661
Five Songs (Mahler, A.), "In meines Vaters Garten,"
5-6 technique, 390–391, 433
ascending, 679–680
descending, 681
melodic motion, 176
Flags (beams), 20
Flat symbols, 5, 6
Folia bass, 338, 339, 341, 513
"Folk Song" from *Album for the Young* (Schumann), 277, 278, 311, 336, 337
Form, 260, 274, 498
antecedent-consequent structure, 278
binary, 498–506 (*See also* Binary form)
in Classical period, 498
diagrams, 279–280, 282, 498
German Lieder, 699
in Romantic period, 651
rondo, 510, 659–662

Form (*Cont.*)
sonata, 651–659
ternary, 507–510
tonic-dominant tonic relationship, 135–139
variation, 511–515 (*See also* Variation forms)
Form diagrams, 279–280, 498
for Beethoven, Sonata op. 10/1, 282
for Kuhlau, Sonatina in FM for piano, 280
for Mozart, "Die Zufriedenheit," 282
4-3 suspensions, 96, 98, 198
Fourth-species counterpoint, 95–100
Fragmentation, 293–295
Franck, César: *Sonata for Violin and Piano,* 639, 640, 669, 670
Free counterpoint, 73
French augmented sixth chords, 576, 584–585, 637
French horns, transposition for, 747
French Suite no. 3 (Bach, J. S.) "Minuet," 473, 482
French Suite no. 5 (Bach, J. S.) "Gavotte," 283, 316, 317
"Frühlingsblumen" (Reichardt), 276, 277, 278
"Frülingstraum," from *Winterreise* (Schubert), 639, 640, 641
Fugato, 534–535
Fugues, 529–534
additional techniques, 534
answer of, 530
bridges, 532
codetta, 299, 527
counterexposition, 534
countersubject, 532
double, 535
episodes, 529
expositions, 529, 530, 532
extra entry, 534
invertible counterpoint, 532
middle entries, 529, 532–533
middle entry group, 529
pedal points, 533
real answer, 530
returns, 526
strettos, 529, 534
subject of, 529
triple counterpoint, 532
Fugues (Bach, J. S.), *The Well-Tempered Clavier*
no. 2 in Cm, 532–533
no. 3 in C♯M, 303, 319
no. 8 in D♯m, 295, 296, 535
no. 11 in FM, 534
no. 24 in Bm, 18
Fully diminished seventh chords, 61, 357–359
Functional tonality, 39
Fundamental progression, 131–134. *See also* Tonic-dominant-tonic relationship
Fundamental (root), 57
Fux, Johann Joseph, 84, 85–*86*

G

G clef (Treble clef), 3, *4*
Gauldin, Robert: *A Practical Approach to Eighteenth-Century Counterpoint,* 529
Gavotte, 498
Gedichte von Mörike (Wolf) "Das Verlassene Mägdlein," 274
German augmented sixth chords, 576, 579–581
functioning as neighbor chords, 639
used as embellishing chords, 638–639
German Lieder, 698–716
enharmonic spellings of V+, 707–708
Erlkönig (Schubert), 699–705
formal types, 699
"Das Verlassene Mägdlein" from *Gedichte von Mörike* (Wolf), 708–711
"Widmung" from *Myrthen* (Schumann, R.), 705–708
Gershwin, Ira and George: "Someone to Watch Over Me," from *Oh Kay!,* 292, 293
Gigue, 498
Gradus ad Parnassum (Fux), 84
Granados, Enrique: *Escenas Románticas,* no. 5, 239
Grand staff, *3,* 4
Grave, 22
"Greensleeves," 22
Grieg, Edvard: "The Death of Åse," from *Peer Gynt,* 483
Ground bass, 338, 512–515

H

Half cadences, 136, 263–264
Half diminished seventh chords, 61, 355, 356–357
inversions of, 357
supertonic, 362
Tristan chord used as, 721–722
voice-leading, 356–357
Half notes, 91
Half steps, 5, 41
Handel, George Frederic
"Chaconne," from *Trois Leçons,* 202
Chaconne in GM, 514, 515
"Surely He Hath Borne Our Griefs," from Messiah, 368
A Hard Day's Night (The Beatles) "I'll Be Back" (Lennon-McCartney), 514
Harmonic accent, 321
Harmonic/Harmony
chords, 55–56
figured bass, 70–73
function, 68–70, 145–146
implied, 275
intervals, 6
labeling chords with Roman numerals, 68–70
rhythm, 179, 308–314
irregular, 311
keyboard figurations, 342–348
levels of, 311–314
metric-harmonic congruence, 321
syncopation, 321–322
tempo, 311
tonal and metric accents, 25–26, 320
writing chord progressions, 320–324
sequences, *107,* 108, 318, 378–398 (*See also* Sequences, harmonic)

syncopation, 182
triads (*See also* Triads), 57–60
Harmonic progression, 106–110, 134
Harrison, Daniel, 723n
Haydn, Joseph
Divertimento in CM, Hob. XVI:, Minuet and Trio, 232
Minuet in CM, 258
Piano Concerto in DM, Hob. XVII:37, III, 451–452
Piano Sonata in CM, Hob. XVI:3, II, 195
Piano Sonata in CM, Hob. XVI:20, 239
String Quartet op. 54, no. 2, 485–486
String Quartet op. 76, no. 5, 404
Trio in FM, Hob. XV:6, 218
Trio in GM, Hob. XV:5, 234, 235
Heckscher, Celeste: *Valse Bohème,* 586
Hemiola, 29
Hepokoski, James, 653n, 654
"Herzlich thut mich verlangen" (Chorale 21) (Bach), 56, 456
Hindemith, Paul: Interlude from *Ludas Tonalis,* 6
Homophonic music, 75–76
Homorhythm, 76
Horn fifths, 89, 116
Horns, transposition for, 747
Hyer, Brian, 730n

I

"I'll Be Back" (Lennon-McCartney) from *A Hard Day's Night,* 514
Imitation, 73
Imitative counterpoint, 73
Imperfect authentic cadences, 136, 160, 261–262
Imperfect consonances, 14, 98
Implied harmonies, 275
Implied tonality, 686. *See also* Tonal/Tonality
tonal ambiguity, 717–724
in *Tristan und Isolde* (Prelude) (Wagner), 717, 718, 721
"An Important Event," no. 6 from *Scenes from Childhood,* op. 15 (Schumann, R.), 451
Incomplete-complete voice leading, 230
Incomplete neighbor tones, 133, 134, 193–194, 371
Independent transitions, 652
India, rāga system, 39, 49
Initial extensions, 298–299
"In meines Vaters Garten," from *Five Songs* (Mahler), 672, 675
Inner voices, 116
Instruments, transposition for, 746–750
Interpolation, 301
Intervals
ascending, 6
augmented and diminished, 10–11
compound, 12
consonant and dissonant, 14
descending, 6
expansion or contraction of, 295
inversions, 13
major and minor, 8, 11
perfect, 7–*8,* 11
quality of, 6
simple, 12
size of, 6
types of, 6
whole and half steps and accidentals, 4–6
In the Bottoms (Dett), 676
Inventions, 526
Inventions (Bach)
no. 1 in CM, 291
no. 3 in DM, 298, 385, 526–528
no. 3 in DM, Theme, 298
Inversions of chords
circle of fifths progressions, 382–383 (*See also* Circle of fifths sequences)
dominant sevenths, 232–238
first inversion, 59, 60 (*See also* First inversion of chords)
half-diminished sevenths, 357
inverted dominant triads used as neighbor chords, 232–233
Neapolitan sixth chords, 560, 587
prolongation in chord progressions, 160–162
secondary dominant chords, 423
secondary dominant of dominant chords, 403–406
secondary dominant of the subdominant, 409
secondary dominant of the supertonic, 420–421
secondary leading-tone chords, 451–454
second inversion, 59, 60 (*See also* Second inversion of chords)
supertonic triads, 176–178
and thematic growth/development, 295–296
third inversion of sevenths, 234–235, 354 (*See also* Third inversion of seventh chords)
Invertible counterpoint, 532
Ionian mode, 46, 47
Irregular beat division, 28–29
Irregular harmonic rhythm, 311
Italian augmented sixth chords, 576
I-V-I relationship. *See* Tonic-dominant tonic relationship
"I Will" from *The Beatles* ("White Album") (Lennon-McCartney), 299

J

Jazz music
added sixth chords, 542
Church modes, 46
compound intervals, 12
extended tertian chords, 673
Neapolitan sixth chords in, 567
subdominant sevenths, 368
John, Elton: "Candle in the Wind" from *Live in Australia,* 212–213
"Joy to the World," 41
Jupiter Symphony (Mozart), 311–313

K

Karnatic (South Indian) music, 49
Kern, Jerome, "Smoke Gets in Your Eyes" from *Roberta,* 136, 137
Key, defined, 43
Keyboard figurations, 342–348
Key relationships
distantly related keys, 466 (*See also* Modulation)

Key relationships (*Cont.*)
in inventions, 526
Neapolitan key area, 589
simple binary form, 503
sonata form, 652, 653, 654–656
Key signatures, 42–46
Kinderman, William, 738n
Krebs, Harald, 738n
Kreisler, Fritz: *Liebesleid,* 453
Kuhlau, Friedrich: Sonatina in FM for piano, 240
form diagram for, 280
Kyrie, from *O magnum mysterium* (Victoria), 84

L

Lament bass, 513
Lang, Josephine: "Gott sei mir Sünder gnädig," 310
Largo, 22
Lassus, Orlando de, 84
Leading-tone cadences, 262
Leading-tone chords, 40, 112, 248–259
in cadences, 252
as dominant substitute, 251–252
doubling and voice leading, 248–249
I-V-I progression, 254–255
passing, 249–250
resolving, 116
sevenths, 359–362
soprano-bass patterns, 254
Leading-tone notes
in dominant of the dominant chords, 403
in first inversion dominant chords, 232–238
indicating a modulation, 472
irregular resolution of, 431
in part writing, 116
Ledger lines, *3*
Led Zeppelin: "Babe, I'm Gonna Leave You," 513
Leitmotifs, 718
Lennon, John
"All My Loving," from *With the Beatles,* 109
"I'll Be Back" from *A Hard Day's Night,* 514
Lento, 22
Lewin, David, 730n
"Libiamo ne'lieti calici" from *La Traviata* (Verdi), 129, 232, 308, 311
Lieder, 698–716. *See also* German Lieder
Linear chords, 72, 133
chromaticism, 667–697
dominant seventh inversions, 232 (*See also* Dominant function, seventh chords)
eleventh, 667, 670–671
ninth, 668–673
prolongation use, 238–239
Linear chromaticism, 667–697
altered triads, 634–636
appoggiatura chords, 675–676
augmented sixth chords (+6) with dominant functions, 636–638
augmented sixth chords (+6) with embellishing functions, 638–641
common-tone diminished seventh chord, 641–643
nonsequential, 685–689
sequences, 677–684 (*See also* Sequences)
descending 5-6, 681–682
Line diagrams, 279
Lines, *3*
Liszt, Franz
Années de Pèlerinage, "Il pensieroso," 628
Faust Symphony, 738–739
Literal counterstatement, 511
Locrian mode, 47
Lovin' Spoonful, "Summer in the City," 514
Lower-neighbor figure, 132, 133
LR progressions, 734–735
Lydian mode, 46, *47,* 85

M

"Mack the Knife," from *The Threepenny Opera* (Weill-Blitzstein-Brecht), 674, 673, 674
"Maelzel's metronome," 22
Mahler, Alma: "In meines Vaters Garten," from *Five Songs,* no. 2, 672, 675
Major intervals, 8, 11
Major-major/minor seventh chords. *See also* Seventh chords
Major-minor tonality, 39
Major modes, 41
augmented sixth chords in, 574, 575
borrowing chords from, 549–550
dominant ninth chords in, 668
key relationships, 43–45
Neapolitan sixth chords, 560
secondary dominant of mediant, 425
secondary dominant of submediant, 422
secondary dominant of supertonic, 420
tonic to dominant (I±V) modulation, 470
Major scale, 40
Major triads, 57. *See also* Triads
Mann, Alfred, *The Great Composer as Teacher and Student,* 85
"Mary Had a Little Lamb," 22
Mayfield, Percy, "Hit the Road, Jack," 513
Mazurka in Am, op. 7, no. 2 (Chopin), 192
Mazurka 43 in Gm, op. posth. 67, no. 2 (Chopin), 427
McCartney, Paul
"All My Loving," from *With the Beatles,* 109
"I'll Be Back" from *A Hard Day's Night,* 514
Measures, 23
Medial caesura, 654
Mediant note, 38, 40
Mediant triads (III or iii), 330–331
dominant as "apparent mediant," 336–337
I-V-I progression, 342
soprano-bass patterns, 340
as 5th-related chord, 334–335
Medieval Church modal system, 46–47
Melodic development techniques, 290–298. *See also* Development techniques
Melodic/Melody, 120–121
cadential patterns, 275
compound, 318–324
development techniques, 292–293

harmonizing, 179–183, 342–348, 485–487
intervals, 6
leading-tone note indicating modulation, 472
metric reduction, 314
in part writing, 120–121
and phrase structure, 274–289 (*See also* Phrase structure)
sequences, 108, 292–293
sequential modulation, 482
seventh chords, 61
with $^6_4$ chords, 210
and species counterpoint, 85–88
with supertonic chords, 179–183
tendencies of scale degrees, 40–41
Melodic minor scale, 41
Melodic retrograde, 296–297
Mendelssohn, Felix: Concerto for Violin, op. 64, 362, 363
Meter, 19, 21. *See also* Rhythm
accents, 25–26, 320
additive, 27–28
asymmetrical (additive), 27–28
choosing, 26–27
compound, 23, *25*
irregular relationships, 29–31
metric-harmonic "rhyme," 320–321
notation, 23, 26–33
simple, 23, *24*
symmetrical (divisive), 26
Meter signatures (time signatures), 23, 33
in compound meters, 23–24
in simple meters, 23
Metric-harmonic relationships, 320–321
conflict, 321
congruence, 321
Metric reductions, 314–318
Metronome markings, 22
Middle entries, 529, 532–533
Minor intervals, 8, 11
Minor key signatures, 45–46
Minor-minor seventh chords, 61
Minor modes, 41–42
augmented sixth chords in, 574, 575
borrowing chords from, 542–548
dominant ninth chords in, 668
Neapolitan sixth chords, 560
secondary dominant of mediant, 425
secondary dominant of submediant, 422
secondary dominant of supertonic, 420
Minor triads, 57
Minuets, 498, 499
Mitchell, William, 721n, 723n
Mixolydian mode, 46, *47,* 49, 85, 86
Modal scales, spelling, 48–49
Moderato, 22
Modes, 39–42. *See also* Scales
borrowing chords from, 541, 542–548 (*See also* Borrowed chords)
changing of, 293, 465, 550–552
church, 46–47
identifying, 47–48
major, 39–41, 41 (*See also* Major modes)
minor, 41–42 (*See also* Minor modes)
modal mixture, 541–559
transposed, 48
Modified sequences, 292
Modulation, 400, 465
chromatic pivot chords (*See also* Chromatic/Chromaticism, pivot chords), 477–479
chromatic to ii and iii, 479–481
closely related keys, 465–467
diatonic pivot chord, 467–470
dominant to tonic (V±I), 471–472
to mediant (iii or III), 473
periods, 282–283
phrase structure, 282–283
relative major or minor keys, 473–476
to submediant (vi or VI), 476
tonic to dominant (I→V), 470–471, 485
distantly related keys, 466, 597
chromatic pivot chords (*See also* Chromatic/ Chromaticism, pivot chords), 597–604
common tone, 630–633
by enharmonic spelling of leading tone seventh chords, 611–615
by enharmonic spellings of augmented sixth chords, 605–611
linear chromaticism (*See also* Linear chromaticism), 627–650
harmonizing modulating melody, 485–487
modulating period, 483–484, 485
phrase structure, 481–484
sequential, 482 (*See also* Sequences)
Monophonic music, 73
Monteverdi, Claudio, *Orfeo,* 106
Motion
contrary, 88, 89, 114–115
intervallic, *89–90*
in part writing, 113, 114–116
seventh chords, 61 (*See also* Seventh chords)
species counterpoint, 85, 87
tonic-dominant-tonic relationship, 132, 133, 134
types of, 88, 114
Motives, 274
as basic formal unit, 498
in inventions, 527
rhythmic, 274
in *Tristan und Isolde* (Wagner), 718
Moving augmented sixth chords, 585, 587
Mozart, Wolfgang Amadeus
The Abduction from the Seraglio, 599
Concerto in E♭M for Horn and Orchestra, K. 447, 233, 234
"Die Zufriedenheit," 281
Don Giovanni, 577, 581
Fantasia in Cm, K. 475, 265
harmonic sequences, 378
inversions of V_7, 232
Piano Sonata in AM, K. 331, 138, 191, 193, 224, 225, 277, 278, 516
Piano Sonata in B♭M, K. 333, 190, 224, 225, 260–261, 278, 468–469
Piano Sonata in B♭M, K. 570, I, 160
Piano Sonata in CM, K. 309, 195, 224, 225, 277
Piano Sonata in DM, K. 284, III, 81, 283, 315, 316

Mozart, Wolfgang Amadeus (*Cont.*)
Piano Sonata in FM, K. 332, 281, 580
horn 5ths in, 116
Piano Sonata in GM, K. 283, 389–390
Sonata for Violin and Piano, K. 481, 423, 424, 432
Sonata in AM, 232, 278
Sonata in DM, 232
String Quartet K. 173, 423, 424, 435
Symphony no. 41, K. 551, *Jupiter,* 311–313
Symphony no. 40 in Gm, K. 550, 313, 366, 404–405
Musical style
Baroque, 84 (*See also* Baroque period)
counterpoint in, 73
and part writing, 120–121
Renaissance, 84, 123 (*See also* Renaissance period)
"My Country 'Tis of Thee," 41

N

Nadir of melody, 87
Natural minor scale, 41
Natural symbols, 5
Neapolitan sixth chords, 560–569
harmonic contexts for, 704
relationship to augmented sixth chords, 589–590
in root position, 565
substitute for dominant seventh chords, 567
tonicization of, 565
Neighbor chords, 150
common-tone diminished seventh chord used as, 642
first inversion dominant, 132–134
German augmented sixth chords (Gr +6) functioning as, 639
$^6_4$ chords, 212–214, 219, 221
V_6 as, 162
Neighbor group, 193
Neighbor notes, 93, 94, 132, 400
accented, 192
consonant and dissonant, 92
incomplete, 193–194
nonchord tones, 192–193
Neil, Fred, "Everybody's Talkin'", 137
Ninth chords, 668–673
Nonchord tones, 81, 188
anticipation, 193
appoggiaturas, 195
chromatic, 189, 718
escape, 194
figured-bass parts, 71
incomplete neighbors, 193–194
neighbor notes, 71, 192–193
passing tones (*See also* Passing tones), 130, 189–192
pedal points, 203–204
summary of, 204
suspensions (*See also* Suspensions), 197–203
voice leading guidelines, 196–197
Notation, 2–4
cadential $^6_4$ chords, 217
durational symbols, 19–21, *20*
meter, 26–33
rhythm, 19, 32–33
Note heads, 19
Numerical suffixes, 2

O

Oblique motion, 88, 114
Octaves, equal division of, 724–729
"Oh! Susanna," 26, 41
Open reprise, 499
Open spacing of chord notes, 112. *See also* Chords
Opera, Baroque period, 509
Oratorios, 509
Ornamental pitches, 55, 71
Ornamental variations, 511, 516
Ostinatos, 512
Outer voices, 116

P

Pachelbel, Johann: Canon in D, 387
Palestrina, Giovanni Pierluigi da, 84
"Hosanna in excelsis," from *Missa Gabriel Archangelus,* 266
Paradis, Maria Theresia von: *Sicilienne,* 232
Parallel $^6_3$ chords, 388–390
Parallel keys, 45–46
Parallel motion, 88, 114. *See also* Motion
Parallel octaves/fifths
German augmented sixth chords (Gr +6), 580–581
Neapolitan sixth chords, 562
suspensions, 202
in voice leading, 115
Parallel periods, 278–279
Parallel unisons, 117
Parsimonious voice leading, 729–737
LR progression, 734–735
PL progression, 732
PR progression, 732–733
Tonnetz, 730–732, 735
Part writing of chorales, 112–118. *See also* Voice leading
changes of voicing or position, 118
melodic style, 120–121
three types of progressions, 118–120
voice independence, 121–123
voice leading conventions, 113–118
Passacaglia, 513
Passing chords, 215. *See also* chords
Passing leading-tone chords, 249–250
Passing motion, 132, 133, 134. *See also* Motion
Passing $^6_4$ chords, 214–215, 219. *See also* $^6_4$ chords
Passing tones, 73, 91, 93, 130, 132, 189–192, 400. *See also* Nonchord tones
accented, 189
in Beethoven's *Seven Peasant Dances,* WoO 168, no. 4, 130
chromatic, 189
Pathétique Sonata (Piano Sonata in Cm, op. 13 (Beethoven), 661
Pedal points, 203–204, 454–455, 533
Pedal $^6_4$ chords, 212. *See also* $^6_4$ chords
"Il pensieroso" from *Années de Pèlerinage* (Liszt), 628
Pentatonic scale, 49
Perfect authentic cadences, 260–261, 299
in sonata forms, 653
in voice leading, 136
Perfect fifths, 7, 9, 89

Perfect fourths, 7, 14, 89
Perfect intervals, 7–*8,* 11
  motions into, *89–90*
Perfect unison, 7, 89
Perfect 8ve (P8), 7, 9, 88
Performance practice
  Erlkönig (Schubert), 699–705
Period, 138, 277, 498
Period structure, 277–283
  contrasting period, 280
  double period, 282
  modulating period, 282–283, 483–484, 485
  symmetrical and asymmetrical periods, 281
  three-phrase period, 281
Phrase, 138, 498
  defined, 275
  identifying, 139–140
Phrase extensions, 298–301
  cadential extension, 299–300
  initial extension, 298–299
  interpolation, 301
Phrase Rhythm in Tonal Music (Rothstein), 498
Phrase structure
  antecedent-consequent structure, 278
  elisions, 277
  modulation, 481–484
  parallel period, 278–279
  period structure, 277–283
  phrase groups, 283
  phrase segments, 276–277, 498
  sentence structure, 277
Phrygian cadences, 98, 264
  as a half cadence, 263–264
Phrygian mode, 46, *47,* 49, 85, 86
  Neapolitan sixth chords, 560
  species counterpoint, 98
Piano, keyboard figurations, 342–348. *See also* Accompaniment
Piano Concerto in DM, Hob. XVII:37, III (Haydn), 451–452
Piano Sonatas (Beethoven)
  in Cm, op. 13 ("Pathétique"), 661
  in Fm, op. 2, no. 1, 277
  No. 21 in CM, *Waldstein,* op. 53, 657–658
  No. 1 in Fm, op. 2, 657
Piano Sonatas (Haydn)
  in CM, Hob. XVI:20, 239
  in DM, Hob. XVI:37, 660
Piano Sonatas (Mozart)
  in AM, K. 331, 138, 191, 193, 224, 225, 277, 278, 516
  in B♭M, K. 333, 190, 224, 225, 260–261, 278, 468–469, 662
  in B♭M, K. 570, I, 160
  in CM, K. 309, 654–656
  in DM, K. 284, III, 81, 283, 315, 316
  in FM, K. 332, 116, 281, 580
  in GM, K. 283, 389–390
Picardy third, 151, 549
Pitch
  intervals, 6–12
  notation, 2–4
Pitch pattern exercises
  augmented sixth chords, 590–591
  borrowed chords, 553
  cadences, 267–269
  chromatic third relationships, 644
  dominant seventh chords, 241
  enharmonic spellings of augmented triads, 712
  equal divisions of the octave, 740
  extended tertian chords, 689–690
  first inversion triads, 168
  harmonic sequences, 393
  keyboard harmonizations, 348–349
  leading-tone triads, 255
  modulations, 488, 615–616
  Neapolitan sixth chords, 568–569
  secondary dominant chords, 412–413, 437
  secondary leading-tone chords, 458
  supertonic chords, 183–184
  $^6_4$ chords, 222
  tonic and dominant triads, 141
Pivot chords
  chromatic, 478–479
  diatonic, 477–478
Pivot pitches, 488, 630
Plagal cadences, 264–265
  added sixth chord, 542
  in voice leading, 148, 150
Plainchant, 85
PL progressions, 732–734
PLR model, 730
Polyphonic music, 73, 84
  thoroughbass texture, 525
Popular music
  added sixth chords, 542
  Neapolitan sixth chords, 567
Pre-dominant chords
  augmented sixth chords, 574, 589 (*See also* Augmented chords, sixth chords)
  as diatonic pivot chords, 467, 470
  Neapolitan sixth chords, 589
  seventh chords, 370, 371
  submediant chords, 334
  supertonic chords, 174
Preparation, 96, 197
Presto, 22
Primary key area in sonata form, 652, 654. *See also* Sonata form
Primary triads, 146. *See also* Triads
Progression by fifths. *See* Circle of fifths; Fifth progressions
Progression by seconds, 108
Progression by thirds, 108, *109*
  PL and PR progressions, 732–734
  sequences on descending, 332
  using mediant and submediant chords, 340
Prolongation in chord progressions, 133, 145, 152, 212
  by combination of several linear chords, 238–239
  first inversions used for, 160–162
  leading-tone triads, 248, 249
  $^6_4$ chords in, 233
  submediant triads, 332
  tonic-dominant-tonic relationship, 133
PR progressions, 732–733
Pulses, 19, 21
Purcell, Henry: *Dido and Aeneas,* "Dido's Lament," 513

Q

Quadruple meter, 23, *24, 25,* 26
Quarter notes, *20*

R

Rachmaninoff, Sergei: *Rhapsody on a Theme of Paganini,* op. 43, 304, 380

Rāgas, 39, 49
Range, 38
Ravel, Maurice
Bolero, 747
Waltz no. 1 from *Valses nobles et sentimentales,* 728–729
Real sequences, 292
Recapitulations (conclusions)
false, 656
sonata form, 653, 656, 658
Recitatives, 509
Reductions. *See also* Diagrams
bass, 451, 452
metric, 314–318
Refrains, 659, 660, 661
Regular harmonic rhythm, 311
Reichardt, Louise, "Frühlingsblumen," 276, 277, 278
Relative keys, 46
Relative major type binary, 500
Renaissance Church modes. *See* Church modes
Renaissance period
bass types, 513
contrapuntal art, 84
counterpoint, 84, 123
leading-tone cadences, 252
modal system, 85
Picardy third, 151
polyphony, 85
Repeated block chords, 343
Repeated broken chords, 343
Reprises, in binary forms, 498, 499, 500
Resolution, 96, 197, 198
irregular, 431
of the tritone, 248
Rest, notation of, 20
Retardation, 203
Retransitions, 653
Retrograde canons, 296
Returns, 526
Rhapsody on a Theme of Paganini, op. 43 (Rachmaninoff), 304, 380
Rhythm
accents, 30
defined, 19
durational symbols, 19–21
harmonic, 179, 308–313
meter, 25–28 (*See also* Meter)
motives, 274
tonal accents, 320
Rhythmic notation, 19, 32–33
elements of, *20*
Ritornellos, 106, 510
Romanesca bass, 338, 339, 341, 513
Roman numerals, 68
Romantic period
altered triads, 635
German Lieder, 698
sectional variations, 516
sonata form in, 651
tempos, 22
tonal ambiguity in, 717–724
Rondo form, 510, 659–662
Root note of chord, 39, 59
Root position, 57
circle of fifths progression, 381, 384 (*See also* Circle of fifths)
dominant seventh chords, 227–228
Neapolitan chords, 565
supertonic chords, 174–175
Rothstein, William, 138n, 275, 498
Rounded binary form, 503–506, 652. *See also* Binary form
Rounds, 296
"Row, Row, Row Your Boat," 22
Rückert, Friedrich, 705

S

Saint-Georges, Chevalier de: Sonata II, for Violin and Piano, 420, 421
Sarabande, 498
Saxophones, transposition for, 749, 750
Scales, 38. *See also* Modes
chromatic, 4, 724–729
degree name, 40, 58
diatonic, 2, *3,* 4, 5, 40
major, 40
melodic tendencies of degrees, 40–41
pentatonic, 49
whole-tone, 49, 725, 728
Scenes from Childhood, op. 15 (Schumann, R.), "An Important Event," no. 6 from, 451
Schachter, Carl, 686n
Schubert, Franz
"Der Doppelgänger," from *Schwanengesang,* 637, 638
Erlkönig, 699–705
Symphony in Bm, "Unfinished," 426
Valse Sentimentales, op. 50, no. 3, 213, 319
Walzer, Ländler und Ecossaisen, op. 18
Ecossaise no. 2, 146, 147
Ländler, no. 3, 125
Schumann, Clara Williams: Trio in Gm, op. 17, 360, 409, 455
Schumann, Robert
Album for the Young
"Ein Choral," 229, 234
"Folk Song," 277, 278, 311, 336, 337
"War Song," 147
Scenes from Childhood, op. 15
"An Important Event," 451
Symphony no. 3 in E♭M, I, 30, 31
Scott, Clara: *Twilight Fancies*, 420, 421
Sebastian, John and Mark: "Summer in the City," 514
Secondary dominant chords
as chromatic pivot chords, 479
consecutive, 431
deceptive resolutions of, 429
of the dominant, 403–406
I-V-I progression, 410–412, 428–429
of the mediant (V/iii), 425–426
sequences with, 429–435
soprano-bass patterns, 410, 428
spelling, 402, 417
of the subdominant, 407–410
of the submediant, 422–425
of the subtonic, 426–427
of the supertonic, 420–421
tonicization, 402
Secondary key areas, 435–436
in sonata form, 652, 654
Secondary leading-tone chords, 403, 446–451
analysis of Mozart songs, 457–458
chromatic harmonization, 456–458
examples from the literature, 448–451
inversions of, 451–454

over pedal points, 454–455
spelling, 446
tonic-dominant-tonic relationship, 455
voice leading, 446–448
Second development, 653
Second inversion of chords, 59
sevenths, 354
dominant, 233–234
French augmented sixth functioning as, 637
leading-tone chords, 359–361
secondary dominant of the dominant chords, 404
secondary dominant of the submediant in, 423
secondary leading-tone chords, 451–452
supertonic chords, 366
$^6_4$ chords, 210
Second-species counterpoint, 91–93
Sectional binary form, 499. *See also* Binary form
Sectional variations, 512, 516–517
Semitones, 5, 8, 49
Sentence structure, 277
Sequences
chains of suspensions, 201–203
harmonic, *107,* 108, 318, 378–398
ascending 5-6 (or 6-5), 679–680
ascending seconds, 433–434
chromatic, 677–684 (*See also* Chromatic/ Chromaticism, sequences)
circle-of-fifths sequences, 380–386, 430–432 (*See also* Circle of fifths)
descending 5-6, 681–682
by descending and ascending steps, 388–391
descending thirds, 386–388, 434–435
5-6 technique, 390–391
7-6 technique, 390
summary of, 392–393
writing, 398
in *Tristan und Isolde* (Wagner), 718
Seven-part rondo form, 661–662
7-6 suspensions, 96, 97, 98, 199, 390
Seventh chords, 60–62
circle of fifths, 383–385
common-tone diminished seventh chord, 641–643
diatonic, 61–62
diatonic, Roman numerals for, 69–70
dominant, 129, 227–242 (*See also* Dominant function, seventh chords)
dominant of the dominant, 403–406
doubling and voice-leading guidelines, 354–355
fully diminished, 61, 355, 356–357, 357–359, 725
half diminished, 61, 355, 356–357
I-V-I progression, 370–371
leading-tone, 355
preparation of, 231, 354
secondary leading-tone chords, 446–451 (*See also* Secondary leading-tone chords)
soprano-bass patterns, 370
subdominant chords, 367–370, 407–410
supertonic, 362–366
Sforzando mark *(sf),* 31
Shannon, Del, "Runaway," 514
Sharps and flats, order of in key signatures, *44*
Sharp symbols, 5, 6
Similar motion, 88, 114
Simple binary form, 501, 502–503. *See also* Binary form
Simple intervals, 12
Simple meters, 23, *24*
Simplifying variation, 511
6-5 suspensions, 96, 97, 199
$^6_4$ chords
arpeggiated, 210–211
cadential, 215–218, 219, 221
consonant, 211
dissonant, 212
doubling, 219
I-V-I progression, 221
Neapolitan sixth chords, 563
neighbor, 212–214, 219, 221
passing, 214–215, 219, 221
pedal, 212
soprano-bass patterns, 220–221
voice leading guidelines, 219
Sixteenth notes, *20*
Sixty-fourth notes, *20*
Sloman, Jane: "La Favorite," Étude-Mazurka, 423
Solfège syllables, 141
Sonata form, 651–659
Sonata for Violin and Piano, K. 481 (Mozart), 423, 424, 432
Sonata for Violin and Piano (Franck), 639, 640, 669, 670
Sonata *La Follia,* op. 5, no. 12 (Corelli), 514, 515
Sonata-rondo: Mozart, Piano Sonata in B♭M, K. 333, III, 662
Sonatas for piano. *See* Piano Sonatas
Soprano, 110, *111,* 120
Soprano-bass patterns, 134–135
characteristic, 149, 151
Spaces, *3*
Spacing of chord notes, 112. *See also* Chords
Species counterpoint, 84–85. *See also* Counterpoint, first species; Counterpoint, fourth species
first-species, 88–90, 96
fourth-species, 95–100
melodic line, 85–88
second-species, 91–93
syncopated, 97–98
third-species, 93–95
two-part, 88
and voice leading (*See also* Voice leading), 123, 134
Staff, 3
Stein, Deborah, 705n
Stems, 19, 32
Stepwise motion, 120
Strettos, 529, 534
String Quartet K. 173 (Mozart), 423, 424, 435
String Quartet op. 18, no. 5, Trio (Beethoven), 505–506
String Quartets (Haydn)
op. 54, no. 2, 485–486
op. 76, no. 5, 404
Strophic form, 699
Structural chords, 129, 152. *See also* Chords

Subdominant chords (IV or iv), 146–148
  elaborating the I-V-I progression, 152–153
  plagal cadences, 264–265
  secondary dominant chords, 407–410
  sevenths, 367–370
  triads, 146–149
Subject of a fugue, 529
Submediant notes, 40
Submediant triads, 330, 332–334
  I-V-I progression, 342
  as pre-dominant, 334
  as prolongation of the tonic, 332
  soprano-bass patterns, 340–341
  as 5th-related chord, 334–335
Subphrases, 277
Substitutes, 145
Subtonic notes, 41
Subtonic triads, 341
Supertonic chords
  first inversion, 176–178
  harmonizing melody, 179–183
  I-V-I progression, 179
  root position, 174–175
  secondary dominant of, 420–421
  sevenths, 362–366, 543
  soprano-bass patterns, 178
Supertonic notes, 40
Supporting parallel melody, 75
Suspensions, 96, 97, 98, 197–203
  chains of, 201–203
  changes of bass note, 200–201
  embellished, 199–200
  retardation, 203
  2-1 suspensions, 96, 98
  2-3 suspensions, 96, 199
  4-3 suspensions, 96, 98, 198
  6-5 suspensions, 96, 97, 199
  7-6 suspensions, 96, 97, 98, 199
  9-8 suspensions, 96, 97, 98, 199
  9-10 suspensions, 96
  types of, 198–199
Symmetrical (divisive) meter, 26
Symmetrical periods, 281
Symphonies (Beethoven)
  no. 5, III, 300, 301
  no. 6, I, 293–294
  no. 7, I, 294
  no. 9 in DM, op. 125, II, 734–735, 736–737
  no. 3 in E♭M, op. 55 *(Eroica),* 211, 297, 523–524, 534, 584, 585
Symphonies (Brahms)
  no. 4, op. 98, 331
Symphonies (Mozart)
  no. 41, K. 551, *Jupiter,* 311–313
  no. 40 in Gm, K. 550, 314, 366, 404–405
Symphonies (Schubert)
  "Unfinished," 426
Symphonies (Schumann)
  no. 3 in E♭M, I, 30, 31
Syncopated voice, 95
Syncopation, 29
  harmonic, 321–322
  species counterpoint, 97–98

T

Tempo, 22
Tempo markings, 22
Tendency tones, 131
Tenor, 110, *111*
Tenor clef (C clef), 3, *4*
Ternary forms, 507–510
  compound ternary, 509
  da capo aria, 509–510
  German *Lieder,* 699
Tertian chords, 55
Text painting, 698, 706
Texture, 73–76, 373
  in Baroque style, 76, 525
  chorale, 76
  contrapuntal, 73
  defined, 73
Thematic growth/development, 290–298
  augmentation, 297
  change of mode, 293
  diminution, 297
  fragmentation, 293–295
  intervallic expansion or contraction, 295
  inversion, 295–296
  melodic retrograde, 296–297
  melodic sequence, 292–293
  repetition, 290–292
  transposition, 291–292
  variation, 292
Third inversion of seventh chords, 234–235, 354
  secondary dominant of the dominant, 404
  secondary dominant of the subdominant, 409
Third progressions. *See* Progression by thirds
Third relationships, chromatic, 627–633. *See also* Chromatic/Chromaticism, third relationships
Third-species counterpoint, 93–95
Thirteenth chords, 671–672
Thirty-second notes, *20*
Thoroughbass, 61, 70, 71, 72, 80, 172, 525
Three-phrase periods, 281
Through-composed form, 699
Ties, 21
Todd, R. Larry, 738n
Tonal/Tonality, 68
  accents, 320
  ambiguity, 717–724
    equal divisions of the octave, 724–729
    Faust Symphony (Liszt), 738
    in Romantic period, 717–724
    Tristan und Isolde (Prelude) (Wagner), 717–724, 718
  answers, 530
  center, 38, 42, 43, 135
  establishment-departure-return, 457
  fluctuation, 718
  implied, 717–724 (*See also* Implied tonality)
  parenthesis, 686
  secondary key areas, 435–436
  sequences, 292
  system, 39
  transposition, 42–43
Tonic-dominant-tonic relationship, 131–134
  cadences involving, 135–137
  dominant seventh, 237–238
  as form-generating structure, 135–139
  incomplete neighbor motion in, 133
  leading-tone chords, 254–255
  mediant triads, 342
  model to elaborate, 152–153

neighbor figures, 132, 133, 134
neighbor motion in, 132
passing motion in, 132, 133, 134
secondary dominant chords, 410–412, 428–429
seventh chords, 370–371
$^6_4$ chords, 221
soprano-bass patterns, 134–135
subdominant chords, 152–153
with subdominant harmonies, 152–153
submediant triads, 342
supertonic chords, 179
voice leading, 133–134
Tonic function, 145
to dominant (I→V), modulation, 470–471, 485
key
balanced binary form, 501, 506
rounded binary form, 503
notes, 38, 40, 68
tonicization, 402
of Neapolitan sixth chords, 565
sequential modulation, 482
triads, 68, 131
Tonicization. *See* Tonic function
Tonnetz, 730–732, 735
Transitions, in sonata form, 652–653, 654, 656
Transposition
church modes, 48
for instruments, 746–750
key signatures, 42–43
La Traviata (Verdi)
"Libiamo ne'lieti calici," 129, 232, 308, 311
"Sempre libera," 308, 309
Treble clef (G clef), 3, *4*
Triads, 38, 55, 57–60, 112
altered, 634–636
augmented, 57
diatonic, 58
diminished, 57
dominant (*See also* Dominant function), 131
figured bass symbols for, 70
inversion, 59–60, 72
leading-tone, 131 (*See also* Leading-tone chords)
major (M), 57
mediant, 330–331 (*See also* Mediant triads)
minor (m), 57
root position, 59, 60, 79
subdominant, 146–149 (*See also* Subdominant chords)
submediant, 330, 332–334 (*See also* Submediant triads)
supertonic (*See* Supertonic chords)
tonic, 68, 131
Tonnetz, 730–732, 735
Trio in Em, op. 45 (Farrenc), 630, 631
Trio in FM, Hob. XV:6 (Haydn), 218
Trio in GM, Hob. XV:5 (Haydn), 234, 235
Trio in Gm, op. 17 (Schumann), 360, 409, 455
Triple counterpoint, 532
Triple meter, 23, *24, 25,* 26
Tristan chord, 721–723
Tritones, 11, 725
equal division of the octave, 724–729
Tritone substitution, 567
in Waltz no. 1 from *Valses nobles et sentimentales* (Ravel), 728
Tritones, in "Diminished Fifth" from Mikrokosmos (Bartók), equal division of the octave,
Il trovatore (Verdi), 185
Trumpets, transposition for, 749, 750
"Twinkle, Twinkle," 41
Two-part counterpoint, general guidelines for, 88
Two-part expositions, 654
Two-voiced inventions, 525–526

U

Unison, 117
Upbeats, 26
Upper-neighbor figure, 132, 133

V

Valse Bohème (Heckscher), 586
Valses nobles et sentimentales (Ravel)
Waltz no. 1, 728–729
Value of the beat, 23
Variation forms
continuous, 512–515
sectional, 512
shape and form of complete sets, 512
types of, 511–512
Varied counterstatement, 511
Verdi, Giuseppe
Aida, "Celeste Aida," 629
Il trovatore, act II, no. 15, "E deggio e posso crederlo?", 185
La Traviata
"Libiamo ne'lieti calici," 129, 232, 308, 311
"Sempre libera," 308, 309
Viardot-García, Pauline, "Die Beschwörung," 211
Victoria, Tomás Luis de: *Kyrie,* from *O magnum mysterium,* 84
Vivace, 22
Vivaldi, Antonio
The Four Seasons
"Spring," 293
"Winter," 106–107
Voice crossing, 90, 117
Voice exchange, 161
Voice independence, 121–123
Voice leading. *See also* Part writing of chorales
basic conventions, 113–118, 134
cadential chords, 267
cadential $^6_4$ chords, 217
changing voicings in part writing, 118
+6 chords, 576, 589
circle of fifths progressions, 381–382 (*See also* Circle of fifths)
as a constructive principle, 686
deceptive progression, 337
descending circle of fifths progressions, 380 (*See also* Circle of fifths)
dominant seventh chords, 229–230
forbidden parallels, 115
fully diminished seventh chords, 358
guidelines, 150–151
half-diminished sevenths, 356–357
Italian +6, 576
I-V-I progression, 133–134

Voice leading (*Cont.*)
leading-tone chords, 248–249
mediant chords (iii or III), 330, 333, 338
nonchord tones, 196–197
parsimonious, 729–737
perfect authentic cadences, 261
secondary leading-tone chords, 446–448
seventh chords (V), 354–355
$^6_4$ chords, 219
and species counterpoint, 123
supertonic chords, 175, 176
supertonic seventh chords, 365–366
tonic-dominant-tonic progression, 133–134
triads (*See also* Triads), 164
types of progression, 118–120
Voice overlap, 89
in part writing, 89, 117
Voicing a triad in four voices, 110–112

W

Wagner, Richard
Tristan und Isolde
act I, scene 2, 725, 726–727
Prelude, 719–721, 722
Prelude to act I, 10, 676, 677
Prelude to act III, 722
Waltz no. 1 from *Valses nobles et sentimentales* (Ravel), 728–729
"Was Gott tut" (Bach, J. S.), 159, 188, 189, 194
The Well-Tempered Clavier (Bach), 529
Fugue no. 2 in Cm, 204, 532–533
Fugue no. 3 in C♯M, 303, 319
Fugue no. 8 in D♯m, 295, 296, 535
Fugue no. 11 in FM, 534
Fugue no. 24 in Bm, 18
Prelude 22 in B♭m, 454–455
Wennerstrom, Mary, 721n
Westover, Charles, "Runaway," 514
Whole-note rest, 33
Whole steps/tones, 5, 8
Whole-tone scales, 49
as equal division of the octave, 725
in Waltz no. 1 from *Valses nobles et sentimentales* (Ravel), 728
"Widmung" from *Myrthen* (Schumann, R.), 705–708
Wieck, Clara. *See* Schumann, Clara Williams, Mary Lou
Winterreise (Schubert), "Frülingstraum," 639, 640, 641
Wolf, Hugo, *Gedichte von Mörike,* "Das Verlassene Mägdlein," 274, 283

Z

Zenith of melody, 87, 92
"Die Zufriedenheit" (Mozart), 281